BIBLICAL APOCALYPTICS

A Study of
the Most Notable
Revelations of God
and of Christ

Milton S. Terry

BAKER BOOK HOUSE
Grand Rapids, Michigan 49516

Reprinted 1988 by
Baker Book House

ISBN: 0-8010-8888-7

Reprinted from the edition published by
Eaton & Mains (New York) and
Curts & Jennings (Cincinnati)
in 1898

PREFACE

THAT God has at many times and in many ways revealed himself to men is a doctrine fundamental to the Christian faith, and the canonical writings of the Old and New Testaments are believed to be a truthful presentation of such divine revelations. These scriptures comprise a great variety of literature. In them we find ancient ballads, national songs, sacred lyrics, family records, theocratic history, lively narrative, charming romance, poetical dramas, visions and dreams of signal import, impassioned oracles of prophecy, and epistles and memoirs of the early Christian Church. Nearly every form of literary composition known to men is represented in the unique volume. Fables, riddles, enigmas, allegories, parables, types, symbols, and idealistic pictures worthy of the most transcendent genius appear in great number and variety. It would seem that infinite Wisdom intended to appropriate every form and class of human writing in order to make each in some way contribute its portion to the preparation of an authoritative textbook for instruction in righteousness.

This great variety of composition and modes of thought among the sacred writers has been too often overlooked. The Bible as a whole has been extolled for its supernatural contents to such an extent that not a few seem to have concluded there can be nothing really human about it. Such presumptions of absolute perfection in a book act as barriers against a thorough scientific investigation of its contents and are prejudicial to the interests of truth. All ideas of a normal progress in the revelation are excluded, and apologists, assuming that the morality of the patriarchs and judges of Israel must needs be consistent with Christian ethics, have become entangled in inextricable difficulties. The result has been a one-sided and misleading trend of thought, which has furnished occasion for all manner of vagaries in biblical interpretation. The opening chapters of Genesis have been supposed to be an infallibly correct deliverance of the Creator himself on cosmology, geology, astronomy, and natural science, and many have taken in hand to reconcile the record and the facts. In a similar way it has been presumed that the Book of Revelation contains detailed predictions of the Roman papacy, the wars of modern Europe, and the fortunes of Napoleon.

Criticism, on the other hand, has too often gone to the extreme of ignoring the divine element in the Scriptures, and has in recent years so persistently looked after the original sources whence the biblical writers derived their material that the higher purpose of the sacred penman has been lost from sight. Gunkel, for example, in his *Schöpfung und Chaos* (Göttingen, 1895), takes great pains to show that the first chapter of Genesis is inconsistent with the lofty concept of all creation by one God which appears in Isa. xl, 22; xlii, 5; xliv, 24; xlv, 7, 12. He finds there, on the contrary, numerous ideas and expressions which he considers so many echoes of most ancient times and fragments of cosmogonic myths. The chaos of darkness and the brooding of the Spirit over the waters are a reminiscence of the world-egg among the Indians, Egyptians, and Phœnicians. He concludes that Gen. i is mainly of Babylonian origin, and Gen. ii a fragment of old Canaanitish thought. In the various Old Testament allusions to the monsters of the waters, leviathan, Rahab, and the serpent, he finds traces of primeval myths which the biblical writers have worked into their compositions. Also in the symbols of Rev. xii he seems concerned only to prove a mythical origin for the ideas of the woman, the man child, the red dragon, the war in heaven, the great eagle, and the flight into the wilderness. That the analogies are often striking is apparent to every observer, and such investigation into the origin and subsequent history of mythical ideas is of much archæological interest. How far the biblical writers, first and last, appropriated material from mythical and legendary sources is simply a question of fact and presents a legitimate field of scientific inquiry. But the real meaning and purpose of the Scriptures may be quite independent of that question. It matters not whence the material of Gen. i and ii has been derived as to its possible primitive sources, nor how much the authors of Job and Isaiah knew about the myths of Rahab and the dragon in the sea; nor whether John, in Rev. xii, associated with the great red dragon and the war in heaven any well-defined ideas of the mythology of the ancient world. The one paramount question with the true interpreter of these Scriptures is, What ideas did the biblical writer intend to impart to his readers? It is not necessary to know all about a particular metaphor or the history of a familiar emblem in order to understand the purpose for which an author may employ it. All human speech is to a great extent a dictionary of forgotten figures of thought. There is a traditional element in a thousand familiar concepts which have passed from age to age, from race to race, and even from one religion to another. When, therefore, biblical criticism busies itself almost solely with questions of the origin of documents, and the more or less probable sources of particular figures of thought and of speech, it is apt to become one-sided and to miss the real object of the sacred writers. Our continuous inquiry in the present volume is not, Whence did the biblical writers derive their literary material? nor, How far did they modify older compositions to suit their plan? nor, What ancient myths and legends have they embodied in their books? but rather, What use have they made of their material, such as it is, for the higher purposes of divine revelation and instruction? We shall have no controversy with the methods or results of scientific criticism. We gratefully accept the facts and side-lights which archæological research has brought forth to the help of biblical study; but our work is constructive rather than analytical. Our chief aim is to show that the great religious lessons of these Scriptures do not depend for their value on questions of sources, and authorship, and dates of composition. The imperishable treasure of the Word remains, and may even be enhanced in its manifold capabilities by being thus enshrined in vessels noticeably human. Thus indeed may one see that "the highest human is divine."

In accordance with this general view I have chosen for exposition those portions of the Holy Scriptures which are remarkable for symbolical presentations of the works and ways of God. Happily it is no longer claimed among intelligent divines that all portions of the Bible are of equal value. A considerable number of the books are of a composite character, and some parts of single books as well as some entire books are better adapted than others to inculcate religious doctrine and morals. The relative importance of the different parts may be differently estimated, but it will scarcely be disputed that those scriptures which purport to contain particular revelations of the works and purposes of God are entitled to special consideration. The apocalyptic element in the Old Testament occupies a larger place than is commonly supposed. The Pentateuch and the Psalms, as well as the Prophets, contain a large amount of pictorial symbolism, and the Book of Genesis exhibits a symmetry of structure comparable to that of the Apocalypse of John. These apocalyptic portions of the Old Testament are essential to a proper understanding of the contents and structure of the New Testament Book of Revelation.

A careful study of these scriptures as a distinctive class of writings will show that the New Testament Apocalypse is the normal conclusion of a series of biblical revelations, which from beginning to end make known, reiterate, and emphasize the fundamental truth that God is the Creator and Ruler of the heavens and the earth.

He is the first and the last, and his holy purposes contemplate all the ages and conditions of the world. Clouds and darkness are round about him, his ways are in many places past finding out, but truth and righteousness are the basis of his throne, and he will surely punish the wicked and glorify the pure and good.

The exposition of John's Apocalypse naturally occupies the largest as well as the concluding portion of the present volume. A rational interpretation of this remarkable production of inspired genius is one of the great needs of our time. The vagaries of literalist and "world-historical" expositors on the one hand have been offset by the conflicting theories of analytical criticism on the other, and the general confusion has thereby become worse confounded. Our work will naturally be looked upon with disfavor by both these classes of writers. One will be scandalized by the fact that our exegesis finds nowhere in the prophecies of this book a prediction of Turkish armies, or papal bulls, or the German Reformation of the sixteenth century. The other class will find fault with the relatively small space given to the discussion of recent critical hypotheses of the composite structure of the book. In respect to all these criticisms we must let our interpretation speak for itself. If it is in the main sound and tenable all conflicting theories are thereby seen to be at fault, and it would be a bootless task to fill our pages with polemics which could be of no practical use to the common reader. If we are fairly successful in showing that the Apocalypse of John is a fitting conclusion to the biblical apocalypses and dependent mainly for its imagery on what is clearly traceable in the Hebrew Scriptures, and that it is in substance and scope only a symbolico-prophetic amplification of our Lord's eschatological discourse as preserved in the synoptic gospels, we are thereby sufficiently vindicated against the charge of not paying detailed attention to other expositions.

The Old Testament apocalypses are a necessary introduction to the interpretation of Jesus's eschatological sermon on the Mount of Olives and to that of the Apocalypse of John. If the reader will take pains to examine our references he will find ample proof that the principal sources of the New Testament prophetic language and imagery are the Hebrew Scriptures. Little help for valid exposition is to be found in the apocryphal apocalypses.[1] They are

---

[1] A brief account of apocryphal apocalypses is given in the Appendix to this volume. However valuable for other purposes, none of them are capable of shedding any considerable light on the canonical Scriptures. Their secondary and inferior character serves rather by its obvious contrast to enhance the real dignity and originality of the biblical apocalypses.

all at best but weak imitations, and move in a lower realm of thought. There is no evidence that the biblical revelations were in any considerable degree dependent upon that class of literature. Much less are we to search in heathen mythology for an immediate source of the imagery employed in the revelations of Daniel and John. That the war of nature's elements, and the concepts of dragons and monsters of the abyss have their varying mythological analogies in the traditions of ancient peoples, is simple matter of fact; but it is quite a different proposition to affirm that a New Testament writer appropriated such myths as a direct source of his symbolism. Whatever may have been their remote origin in the prehistoric times, and however the Israelitish people first or gradually came into contact with them, generations of Hebrew psalmists and prophets had so far consecrated them to the uses of a lofty theistic conception of the world that in the time of our Lord they had lost, for the devout Jew, their polytheistic connotation. John's Revelation is no loose compilation of documents, no incongruous structure of fragments. The author was a sublime genius, easily comparable with Dante and Milton, who found the suggestions of his imagery in the Hebrew Scriptures, but had the native ability and the divine inspiration to adapt his material to the scope and plan of his apocalypse. His originality is seen, not in the invention of all his symbols, but in the unique structure and the sublimity of his completed work.

It is not the purpose of the present volume to furnish a textual commentary on the portions of Scripture here brought into discussion. The nearest approach to a full exposition is made in the treatment of the Apocalypse of John. No other method seemed so suitable for presenting in detail the import of that most notable revelation of " things about to come to pass." Being the consummation and crown of all the biblical apocalypses, it properly called for fuller treatment, and for the convenience of the reader the text (in the main that of the Anglo-American Revised Version) has been inserted in immediate connection with the exegesis. It was part of my original plan to incorporate a new translation, accompanied with critical and exegetical footnotes, of all the Old Testament apocalypses, but this was soon found to be impracticable within the limits of a single volume. My purpose is rather to write a comprehensive and readable book, adapted to serve as a suggestive help toward the proper understanding of those scriptures which are regarded as peculiarly obscure. In carrying out this purpose I have also kept in view the hope of showing every candid and thoughtful reader that the divine purpose and the abiding lessons of these holy writings are not endamaged by the results of scientific criticism.

For the sake of any who may feel regret that I concede so much to the findings of modern higher criticism I take this opportunity to say that I have in some instances allowed the claims of a radical criticism, which I am personally far from accepting as established, for the very purpose of showing that the great religious lessons of the scripture in question are not affected by critical opinions of the possible "sources," and date, and authorship, and redaction. To me and to many it is a pitiable spectacle to behold devout and learned men wasting their energy in the maintenance of a traditional theory of the origin of such books as Genesis and Isaiah and Daniel, as if the divine purpose and sole value of these scriptures must needs rest upon a questionable hypothesis of their human authorship. We cannot believe that the God and Father of our Lord Jesus Christ has any respect for a tradition of the elders that cannot commend itself by open, manly, convincing argument, but presumes rather to hold its ground by dogmatic assertion and ecclesiastical oppression. For the Church's sake, for the sake of an untrammeled Gospel, for Christ's sake, let devout and conscientious criticism be at liberty to perform its legitimate work. God will smite that whited wall of a Protestantism which boasts its encouragement of a free and fearless searching of the Scriptures, and yet dishonors its throne of judgment by imposing stripes on the truth-loving disciple of Jesus, who studies with all diligence to present himself approved unto God and to handle aright the word of truth.

It has long been my purpose to write three volumes on biblical interpretation and doctrine. The first of these, entitled *Biblical Hermeneutics*, appeared fourteen years ago (1883), and forms one of the volumes of the "Library of Biblical and Theological Literature," edited by Crooks and Hurst. The present treatise is the second in my plan, and, in nature and scope, is supplementary to the *Hermeneutics*, being an extended application and illustration of the principles of interpretation set forth therein. The remaining volume, on *Biblical Dogmatics*, will be an essay toward a luminous, simple, and systematic statement of the principal doctrines of the Old and New Testaments.

TABLE OF CONTENTS

9

BIBLICAL APOCALYPTICS

CHAPTER I

INTRODUCTION TO BIBLICAL APOCALYPTICS

1. IDEA AND SCOPE OF APOCALYPTICS.

THE Greek word Apocalypse (ἀποκάλυψις) means an uncovering, or laying open to view ; a disclosure. This idea has been, through Latin ecclesiastical literature, transferred into our language by the word Revelation. Both these words have become common in theological literature, but in English usage the term revelation has acquired a wider meaning, and is employed to denote the entire body of religious truth as set forth in the Holy Scriptures, while the word Apocalypse is confined more particularly to the last book of the New Testament canon, and to a number of pseudepigraphical works of a similar literary character. In the language of the New Testament, however, the word apocalypse denotes a divine revelation of something that was before unknown to men. The salvation introduced by the coming of Jesus Christ is spoken of as a light destined to serve as an apocalypse to the nations of the earth (Luke ii, 32). The Gospel itself is said (in Rom. xvi, 25, 26) to be an apocalypse of the mystery of redemption through Christ, which was kept in silence from eternity until preached by Jesus and his apostles. Paul declared that he received his gospel, not from man, but through an apocalypse of Jesus Christ (Gal. i, 12) ; and many years later, acting in conformity with an apocalypse, he went up to Jerusalem and laid before the brethren a statement of the Gospel which he preached among the Gentiles (Gal. ii, 2). He claimed also to have been favored with visions and a superabundance of apocalypses (2 Cor. xii, 1, 7). But in a manner to be more particularly observed is the heavenly manifestation of Jesus Christ himself, in his execution of judgment on the wicked and awarding glory to the righteous, called " the apocalypse of the Lord Jesus " (1 Cor. i, 7; 2 Thess. i, 7 ; 1 Peter i, 7, 13 ; iv, 13). It is called in Rom. ii, 5, an "apocalypse of the righteous judgment of God." In special harmony with this idea the one prophetic book of the New Testament is entitled the "Apocalypse of Jesus Christ."

An apocalypse is in its nature associated with prophecy ; for no genuine prophet of God goes forth with an authoritative word

11

except he first receive some manner of heavenly apocalypse. But we must distinguish between apocalypse and prophecy. Paul recognizes this distinction in 1 Cor. xiv, 6. Apocalypse is to be understood especially of the heavenly disclosure, in the reception of which the man is comparatively passive ; prophecy denotes rather the inspired human activity, the uttering forth of the truth revealed within. He who receives an apocalypse sees, hears, feels, realizes in some way that the "hand of God" is upon him, making known within his soul what was not thus known before ; but he who prophesies proclaims the word of revelation, and may accompany it with exhortation, warning, and rebuke. The apocalypse is generally concerned with impending or future events ; the prophesying may deal alike with things past, present, or future. Where the subject-matter of a prophetical book consists mainly of instruction, expostulation, threatening, or rebuke, we call it prophecy, and think especially of the personal human activity that gives utterance to the word ; when, however, it consists mainly of visions of the unseen world, symbolical descriptions, and a forecasting of future judgments and mercies, we call it apocalypse, and think of extra human and supernatural disclosures.

The biblical apocalypses, therefore, are those sacred books and portions of books which contain revelations or disclosures of God's view of things. They unfold a concept of the world and of man which may be thought of as the superior gift of one who has been exalted above the world, and has looked upon the movements of "many peoples and nations and languages and kings" as they appear before the throne of God. Such revelations magnify the idea of God's interposition in all the affairs of men and nations. They emphasize with mighty assurance the doctrine that the wickedness of the wicked must sooner or later meet righteous retribution, and that the obedient children of God shall be crowned with glory. They accordingly admonish us that the world had a beginning, has its cycles and ages and dispensations, and moves steadily onward to a divinely foreseen goal. Many of the questions of biblical eschatology fall properly within the domain of apocalyptics, and should be studied in the light of the fully developed organism of the biblical revelations.

Biblical apocalyptics has for its province that entire body of canonical literature which represents the idea of special divine revelation as above defined. Its scope is therefore very extensive. It aims by means of pictorial communications to disclose what is important for man to know about the creation and government of the world by the ever-living God. The most ancient traditions of Israel embody truths which appear, in some cases, to be cast in apocalyptic form, but the more notable apocalypses are devoted to the disclosure of God's purposes of judgment and salvation. Especially do they reveal the kingdom of God in its age-enduring conflict with the powers of evil. Many of these revelations were given in times of trouble and discouragement, when the people of God were suffering bitter wrongs. The inspired seer was enabled to look beyond the evils of his own times and behold the great day of the Lord approaching. Beyond the great and terrible day of divine judgment on the evildoers he saw a blessed golden age in which all wrongs were to be recompensed, and eternal dominion and power and glory were to become the portion of the true servants of God.

2. IDEA AND METHODS OF REVELATION.

The first clear perception of any truth as it dawns upon the human understanding may be properly called a revelation. It may come in a moment, in the twinkling of an eye, or it may come gradually, and after long and laborious search. It is as truly a revelation in the one case as in the other. It may come as an intuition of the soul ; it may be suggested by the word or action of another ; it may be given in a dream, and so vividly as to impress one with an ideal never to be forgotten. It may be communicated by the direct and formal impartation of a thought from one intelligent person to another. But whenever a new idea gets possession of a man, no matter when, where, or in what manner he acquires it, it is of the nature of an apocalypse. How many have said, upon perceiving some new truth, "That was a revelation to me ! "

God revealed himself to the Hebrew prophets in many separate communications and in many different modes (Heb. i, 1). As modes of revelation visions and dreams are mentioned in Num. xii, 6. When Abraham was about to receive a momentous disclosure of the woes and triumphs of his posterity it is said that a deep sleep and a horror of great darkness fell upon him (Gen. xv, 12). Probably all men have at some period of their lives been deeply impressed by images conveyed to them in dreams. When the eyes are closed in sleep, and the conscious operations of sense are suspended, there often come upon the soul vivid reminiscences of recent cares, or pictures of impending trouble, and sometimes startling premonitions of events to come. These may or may not be revelations, but it is easy to see that they may be the method by which a revelation can be conveyed to the mind. Jacob's dream at Bethel was a real apocalypse of the great future of his posterity in the history of redemption. The dreams of Joseph and of Pharaoh were symbolic revelations of things that were to come. In Judg. vii, 13, 14, we read of the presageful dream of a Midianite, which inspired one party with dismay and another with triumphant hope. Nebuchadnezzar's dream and Daniel's night vision (Dan. ii and vii) are conspicuous elements of the most formally apocalyptic book of the Old Testament. Such premonitory dreams are wont to leave a spell of trouble on the soul (comp. Dan. ii, 1, 3, 4, 5, 7, 15, 28 ; Gen. xli, 8), and the impression may remain for years.

The vision of an apocalyptist is spoken of as if it were of the nature of a dream (comp. Dan. ii, 19 ; vii, 1 ; Acts xvi, 9 ; xviii, 9). Nathan's revelation touching David's house and kingdom was given in a vision of the night (2 Sam. vii, 4, 17). The psychological condition adapted to the reception of an apocalypse may be regarded as a part of God's own preparation of the prophet for his word. Peter's symbolic vision on the housetop was seen at the hour of midday. It is called an ecstasy (Acts x, 10), and by its uplifting power his inner sense became possessed of a new and to him startling revelation. The ecstasy, however, may have been part of a dream which came to him during a moment of sleep. At such an hour and place it would have been very natural for him to have fallen into a sleep. Balaam is represented in Num. xxiv, 3, 4, as the man whose eye was closed, while yet by means of an unveiled inner sense he beheld the vision of the Almighty. In all such experiences the soul becomes a mirror which reflects the images cast upon it by the supernatural Revealer.

The passage in Num. xii, 6–8, which speaks of visions and dreams as modes of prophetic revelation, informs us further that Jehovah was pleased to communicate with Moses in a more intimate way : " With my servant Moses will I speak mouth to mouth, even manifestly, and not in riddles; and the form of Jehovah shall he behold." Whatever be the precise meaning of this, the tradition prevailed in Israel that no prophet had been honored like Moses, " whom Jehovah knew face to face " (Deut. xxxiv, 10). It may not *now* be said, however, that no prophet has since arisen who knew God as intimately as Moses, but it would be profitless for us to speculate upon the possibilities of the higher forms of communion between God and man. We can only make appeal to such facts as have manifest relation to this general subject. Paul speaks of having visions and revelations of God while in such a state of ecstasy that he knew not whether he were in the body or apart from the body (2 Cor. xii, 1–4). He was " caught up even to the third heaven," " caught up into paradise, and heard unspeakable words, which it is not lawful for a man to utter;" but his own statements show that the revelations and the manner of receiving them were not of a nature to be capable of outward demonstration. They were matters of inward consciousness, not of objective reality. The vision, however, had for him a reality as certain as his vision of Christ when on his way to Damascus (Acts ix, 3–7), or that of the man of Macedonia at Troas (Acts xvi, 9).

It is an error, too prevalent in modern times, to say that "visions and revelations of God" are things of the past. The apocalypses of the Scriptures have, indeed, such originality and comprehensiveness that we may safely affirm that nothing of the kind has since been given to any man which contains additional revelation of an important character. But, according to Jesus, John the Baptist was not surpassed by any before his day, and yet "the one who is an inferior in the kingdom of heaven is greater than he" (Matt. xi, 11). We disparage the abiding presence and operation of the Holy Spirit when we imply that God no longer reveals himself to man. It is as true to-day as when it was first written that "there are diversities of workings, but the same God, who worketh all things in all, and to each one is given the manifestation of the Spirit for that which is profitable" (1 Cor. xii, 6, 7). This "manifestation of the Spirit" must first be revealed within before it can be made known without. If it be true that there have come no new or additional revelations of God since the apostolic age, such fact magnifies the completeness of "the revelation of Jesus Christ," but does not signify that the same eternal truths have not been revealed by the same Spirit to thousands of thousands since that day. The revelations have come in dreams and visions, in the reading of the Scriptures, in the songs of the Church, in the testimonies of devout hearts, in the facts of Christian history, and in secret meditation and prayer. It is no less a divine revelation because it comes to us in other forms than visions and dreams. Perhaps the superior character of Moses's intimacy with God was due to the fact of his long life of study, meditation, and service no less than to occasional visions of a burning bush or a smoking mountain. Elijah learned by his apocalypse in Mount Horeb that "a voice of gentle stillness" is of greater spiritual significance than miraculous wind and earthquake and fire (1 Kings xix, 12). The revelation that comes to the Christian believer now, after long struggles, doubts, and fears, may be even more trustworthy than the one he receives in a dream or a vision of the night. We do not take away from the greatness and excellency of the ancient revelations by magnifying the modern gifts and works of the Spirit. The ancient apocalypses were given, time and again, that we, "upon whom the ends of the ages are come " (1 Cor. x, 11), might be blessed with the superior light and admonitions of accumulated revelations.

3. FORMS OF APOCALYPTIC COMPOSITION.

When one has received within his soul a revelation, or a series of revelations, and proceeds to embody them in the form of a writing, his composition, like all other books produced by human brains and hands, may be supposed to bear the characteristics of his human personality. We have no ground for the assumption that the sacred writers were mechanical or passive instruments in the hand of God. They were men of like passions with us, and the literary productions they have left us bear all the marks of variety of genius and individuality. The differences between Genesis and Job and Jeremiah and John's Apocalypse are notably conspicuous. We should not, therefore, assume that the tropes and parables and allegories and symbols of the biblical writers were supernaturally supplied by the Spirit of God. Nor should the apocalyptic narratives be supposed to be matters of actual history. We do not make such a claim for the narrative of Nathan's parable in 2 Sam. xii, 1–4; why should we make it for the symbolic apocalypse of Micaiah in 1 Kings xxii, 19–23? When Zechariah records his visions of angelic horsemen among the myrtle trees (Zech. i, 8), or Joshua standing before the angel of Jehovah confronted with Satan as his accuser (iii, 1), or the flying roll and the ephah (v, 1, 6), we are not to suppose that his records are in every case a prosaic statement of real objective facts actually witnessed by himself. They are rather symbolic pictures, designed to convey an impressive object lesson to all who read the book of his prophecy. In like manner we hold that the symbols employed in the visions of Daniel the prophet are evidences of the genius and art of the author of that book, as well as profound revelations of the mystery of God in the history of the world. We need not ignore or deny the human elements in order to magnify the value of the revelation. So, too, Isaiah's vision of the throne of God (Isa. vi, 1–4), and Ezekiel's portraiture of the cherubim and the wonderful wheels (Ezek. i, 1–18), and John's description of the New Jerusalem, are the creative elaborations of human genius as truly as they are heavenly revelations. The visional symbols of the prophets, like the parables and allegories of our Lord, were employed as choice vehicles for instruction in the things of God, and, like the metaphors and similes of all literature, are to be regarded as creations of human thought. A metaphor or a symbol is no more supernatural because found in Isaiah than if found in the books of Zoroaster or the Vedic songs.

It seems best, on the whole, to regard also a number of the most ancient biblical traditions as embodied in the form of symbolism. We shrink from the hazardous presumption of making their value, as a part of the biblical revelation, dependent on the belief that they are actual history. The pictures of the creation, the expulsion from the garden of Eden, and the earliest migrations and inventions of men are explained in the following pages as having more the nature of apocalyptic symbolism than of literal history. Such prophetic songs as those of Jacob (Gen. xlix) and of Moses (Deut. xxxii and xxxiii) may also be the product of a much later time than the assumed occasion which they represent. We narrow the scope and possibilities of divine inspiration when we dogmatically assume that, among all the divers portions and modes of God's speaking in and through the prophets, we are not to believe that he ever moved a Hebrew writer to compose a poem adapted in its ideal to enhance the thoughts of the divine purpose in the past history of the tribes of Israel.

We recognize in the biblical apocalypses a series of divine revelations touching the kingdom, the power, and the glory of God. A revelation of world-wide importance may be designedly given in ideal form. It ought not to shake our confidence in God's word to discover that he has given it so largely in imaginary pictures, in magnificent framework of embellished traditions, ravishing poetry, delightful allegory, suggestive parables, memorable dreams, and symbols of imperishable significance. The fullness and completeness, as well as the transcendent excellence, of the revelations contained in this long series of divine communications are a convincing witness that the holy men of old wrote as they were moved by the Spirit of God.[1]

4. APOCALYPTIC SYMBOLISM.

Inasmuch as one of the more conspicuous features of apocalyptics is the use of symbols we should give some special attention to the facts and principles which affect the interpretation of these peculiar signs. A revelation given in dreams and visions may most naturally appropriate a visional image for its embodiment. The figure employed is, in every such case, a sign of something apart from itself. The rainbow, for example, is not a symbol of itself, or of another rainbow, but of a gracious covenant between God and the

---

[1] In *The Expositor* of January, 1889, p. 11, Farrar makes the following statements, which some would do well to ponder: "God knows no orthodoxy but the truth; and the attempt to identify orthodoxy, without examination, with preconceived and purely traditional opinions, is rooted in cowardice, and has been prolific of casuistry and disaster."

earth. The significance of the sign must be inferred from some well-known fact associated with its use, or some quality which it naturally suggests.

Apocalyptic symbols are many and various, and may be classified as figures, acts, names, numbers, and colors. A symbolical act is one which conveys to the beholder a lesson of peculiar significance. A symbolical name is significant because of some well-known historic facts with which it is associated. When Isaiah calls the chiefs of Jerusalem "rulers of Sodom" (Isa. i, 10) he employs the word Sodom in a metaphorical sense, as containing a symbol in a name. Sometimes names, acts, and colors are mentioned merely as attributes of symbols otherwise significant, and in many cases the apocalyptic symbol is a composite picture in which a number of formal elements are combined. In every kind and class of symbols, however, it will be seen that the sign is only an emblem or formal representation of the thing signified.[1]

(1) Symbolical Figures.

The great beasts which appear in Daniel's visions are explained as symbols of great kingdoms. The heads, horns, wings, teeth, and feet are described as all together making up the figure of a monstrous animal, and all these parts were doubtless intended to have some measure of significance. The great sea, lashed by the winds of heaven (Dan. vii, 2), was itself suggestive, and, like the waters on which John saw the accursed harlot, was an appropriate symbol of multitudinous peoples (Rev. xvii, 15), out of whose commotions and revolutions great empires have arisen. The horn of an animal is taken to represent a king, and is an obvious symbol of organized military power. The invasion of a mighty army is portrayed as the overflowing of a tremendous stream, which breaks over its banks and inundates an entire land (Isa. viii, 7, 8). Horses of different colors appear in the visions of Zechariah and of John, and denote dispensations and modes of executing divine judgment. The Levitical tabernacle, or tent of meeting, is conceived and constructed after a divinely revealed pattern, and serves the purpose of a composite symbol in pointing out the holy and blessed ideal of Jehovah dwelling with his people. It is virtually an anticipation of John's picture of the heavenly Jerusalem conceived as the tabernacle of God with men.

---

[1] In his somewhat elaborate Essay on the Characteristics and Laws of Prophetic Symbols (2d ed., New York, 1854, pp. 16–19), Winthrop seems at times to overlook this important principle, and makes God and Christ and angels symbols of themselves.

(2) *Symbolical Acts.*

Many of the figures mentioned above are represented as at times in motion, and the movements are not without significance. The going forth of the horses and chariots in Zech. vi, 1, is no less suggestive than the standing still of the horses and their riders in the vision of Zech. i, 8. The measuring of Jerusalem and the temple (Zech. ii, 2 ; Rev. xi, 1), the flying of an eagle or an angel in midheaven (Rev. viii, 13; xiv, 6), the waving of a sharp sword, or its issuing from one's mouth and going forth to smite nations (Gen. iii, 24 ; Rev. i, 16; xix, 15)—these and all similar images are of symbolic import. The lifting up of the brazen serpent by Moses was a symbolico-typical act (John iii, 14), as were also Isaiah's walking naked and barefoot for three years (Isa. xx, 2–4), Jeremiah's hiding his girdle by the Euphrates (Jer. xiii, 1–11), his breaking the potter's bottle in the valley of Hinnom (xix, 1), his putting a yoke on his neck, and hiding stones in the brick kiln (xxvii, 1–14; xliii, 8–13), Ezekiel's portraiture of the siege of Jerusalem upon a brick, and his lying on his side for many days (Ezek. iv), his cutting off his hair and destroying it in different parcels (v). To the same class belong also Hosea's marrying an adulterous woman, and Zechariah's making crowns for the head of Joshua (Zech. vi, 9–15). Ezekiel's vision of the resurrection of dry bones (Ezek. xxxvii, 1–14) is a composite picture, and is represented as passing before the prophet's eye in a series of successive scenes. Such a picture must be studied as a whole rather than in its separate details, and so, in general, we may say of all symbolical acts.

(3) *Symbolical Names.*

A great many proper names are employed in the Scriptures as typical or representative of characters conspicuously associated with them in history. Thus the names Balaam, Jezebel, Sodom, Egypt, and Babylon are used in the Apocalypse of John. The name David is a synonym for a king of Davidic character in such texts as Jer. xxx, 9; Ezek. xxxiv, 23; xxxvii, 24; Hosea iii, 5. Elijah the prophet is a symbolical name in Mal. iv, 5. Similarly, in Isa. xix, 23, Egypt and Assyria are named as synonymous with any and all great nations that shall in the Messianic age unite with God's people in the worship of Jehovah. On the other hand, Edom, Moab, and Ammon are symbols of ancient and hereditary enemies (Isa. xi, 14; Dan. xi, 41). In other instances names of suggestive significance are invented for a symbolic purpose, as Lo-ruhamah and Lo-ammi, in Hosea i, 6, 9; Aholah and Aholibah, in Ezek. xxiii, 4; Nicolaitans,

Antipas, Abaddon, and Apollyon, in the New Testament Apocalypse.

(4) Symbolical Numbers.

That certain numbers are symbolically used in the prophetical books is conceded by all interpreters. Three, four, seven, ten, twelve, forty, and seventy appear to have special significance, but that significance can be ascertained only by a careful study of the usage of the sacred writers. The number three is employed in such relations as to suggest that, so far as it may ever convey any mystical meaning, it is the number of God, expressive of divine fullness in unity. The thrice repeated benediction of Num. vi, 24–26; the trisagion of Isa. vi, 3, and Rev. iv, 8; and the threefold name in Matt. xxviii, 19; 2 Cor. xiii, 14, seem to favor this idea. The number four, on the other hand, is noticeably associated with the agencies of divine judgment upon the world and upon man. Thus we observe the four successive plagues of locusts in Joel i, 4; the four riders on as many different colored horses, and the four horns, the four smiths, and the four chariots in Zech. i, 8, 18, 20; vi, 1–8; the four horses in Rev. vi, 1–8; and the wars, "famines, pestilences, and earthquakes" in Matt. xxiv, 7, and Luke xxi, 10, 11. It appears to be a constant habit of apocalyptics to represent punitive judgments in a fourfold manner. In like manner "the four winds of heaven" and "the four corners of the earth" comprehend, in Hebrew thought, the compass of the living world of man.

The number seven is of more frequent occurrence, and, being the sum of three and four, suggests the idea of some mystical relation between God and man, the number of a sacred covenant. In some places it seems to have a kind of proverbial significance (Matt. xviii, 22; Luke xvii, 4). Ten is commonly regarded as suggestive of completeness, so that ten horns may not specifically denote ten kings so much as a full dynasty or succession of kings. Twelve is the number of the tribes of Israel and of the disciples of Jesus, and its double in Rev. iv, 4, appears to have some allusion to this fact. Multiplied by itself a thousand times it stands for the number of the elect Israel of God (Rev. vii, 4; xiv, 1). The numbers forty and seventy are associated with periods of judgment, calamity, and exile (Gen. vii, 4; Num. xiv, 34; Ezek. xxix, 11, 12; Jer. xxv, 11, 12).

There are other numbers of symbolical import, as the "time, times, and half a time," the forty-two months, and the thousand years of the books of Daniel and the Revelation of John. These can be treated properly only in connection with the whole prophecy in which they occur. No formal or mechanical laws are available in the interpretation of such symbolic numbers, or in determining

the import of prophetic designations of time. The passages in
Num. xiv, 33, 34, and Ezek. iv, 5, 6, are specific, and can be legitimately applied only to the cases there referred to. They are no
sufficient warrant for the absurd conclusion that in other passages
the word day stands also for a year. So, too, the "seventy weeks"
of Dan. ix, 24, are elements of an exceptional prophecy, and furnish
no general law or rule for the interpretation of other prophecies.

(5) *Symbolical Colors.*

After the rainbow had become the symbol of a blessed covenant
of God with man its more prominent colors would naturally become
associated with ideas of heavenly grace and beauty. The blending
of blue, purple, and scarlet in the construction of the tabernacle
(Exod. xxv, 4) served both for beautiful ornamentation and for
suggestions of divine excellence and glory. White garments
became symbolic of the righteous acts and holy character of the
saints of God. But red and black are suggestive of bloodshed and
pestilence (Rev. vi, 4–6). Colors are mentioned in the biblical
apocalypses as symbolic attributes of the figures on which they
appear, not as independent symbols.

5. Apocalyptic Repetition.

The habit of repeating the same matter under different symbols,
and so of presenting it from different points of view, is a very
noticeable formality of biblical apocalyptics, and yet it has been
strangely ignored by many expositors. A most conspicuous illustration is given in the prophetic dreams of Joseph and Pharaoh.
The first dream of Joseph was of sheaves in the harvest field, his
second of the sun and moon and eleven stars (Gen. xxxvii, 5–11);
but they were both symbolic of the same thing, not of two different
events. They both alike indicated his subsequent elevation and
honor. The two dreams of Pharaoh, one with the picture of the
kine and the other of ears of corn, were explained as one, and it is
written that the dream was repeated unto Pharaoh twice "because
the thing is established of God, and God will shortly bring it to
pass" (Gen. xli, 25, 32). The dream of Nebuchadnezzar was interpreted as an apocalypse of four great kingdoms which were destined
to be destroyed and superseded by a kingdom not of this world.
The same great truth was afterward revealed to Daniel in a dream
and visions of the night (Dan. ii, 19, 31–44), under an entirely different set of symbols. The king of Babylon might naturally think
and dream of worldly empire under the figure of a colossal image,
of which he himself was the head of gold; but the Jewish prophet's

vision discerned the grasping, ravenous, cruel, and beastly character of the oriental despotisms, and depicted them accordingly. To the mind of the heathen despot the kingdom of heaven was a rude stone, strangely cleft from the mountain; but to the prophet's mind it was truly a heavenly dominion, possessed by holy myriads both human and divine. The third and fourth beasts appeared to the prophet very dreadful and powerful, especially the fourth ; and so in a further vision (chap. viii) he beholds another picture of the same two world-powers under the figures of a ram and a he-goat. The fourth beast, which is described in vii, 7, as a nameless monster, appears again in the revelation of chap. xi, where the ten kings appear as the kings of the south and of the north, by whose continual wars the land of Israel was trodden down, and the contemptible and blasphemous king described in xi, 21–45, is a fuller revelation of the " little horn " of previous visions. So, too, in Zechariah, the four chariots drawn by different colored horses (chap. vi) are an obvious counterpart of the horses and riders seen among the myrtles in chap. i, 8. The seven bowls of plagues in Rev. xvi are an impressive repetition of the woes symbolized by the seven trumpets in chaps. viii–xi. All such apocalyptic repetitions serve the twofold purpose of intensifying the divine revelation and showing that "the thing is established by God, and that he will shortly bring it to pass."

6. OTHER PECULIARITIES OF APOCALYPTICS.

Among the noticeable features of apocalyptic writing is the double picture of judgment and salvation. One persistent and fundamental doctrine of all the biblical revelations is that penal retribution shall surely overtake the wicked, but the righteous shall inherit riches of grace and glory. These ideas are set in signal form in the two symbols which were placed at the east of the garden of Eden (Gen. iii, 24). The sword of flame suggests the thought of divine justice which demands the punishment of sin ; while the cherubim, symbols of endless Edenic life, convey to fallen man the blessed hope of a restored paradise, to be secured through the redeeming righteousness of God. All the other apocalypses repeat in some corresponding outline this double lesson of the Edenic symbols. Abraham has "a horror of great darkness," and the judgment of nations impressed upon him in connection with the promise of a glorious future for his posterity. Balaam sees that Israel's final triumphs will not be attained without conflict with foes and the overthrow of Jehovah's enemies. In the great apocalyptic books we find full delineations of the fury to be poured out upon the hostile nations, and the glory that will come to the faithful people of God. The first part of Ezekiel's prophecies (chaps. i–xxxii) consists mainly of announcements of judgment upon rebellious Israel and the nations; while the second part (chaps. xxxiii–xlviii) is correspondingly full of consolation for the obedient people of God. The first part of John's Apocalypse (chaps. i–xi) portrays the terrible vengeance of the Lamb upon his enemies, offset in every judgment stroke by some bright vision of heavenly glory for such as are redeemed by his blood; and the second part (chaps. xii–xxii) shows how the struggling Church, the wife of the Lamb, must needs pass through most bitter persecutions before the seed of the woman shall bruise the old serpent's head. But the old serpent, the devil, and all his hosts, are ultimately cast into the lake of fire, while the people of God appear in heavenly glory "as a bride adorned for her husband."

In view of such continuous presentation of both judgment and mercy it is not strange that the apocalyptic scriptures also abound with incidental rebukes, warnings, and counsels for those to whom the writing was first addressed. Thus Joel's vivid portraiture of the day of Jehovah is accompanied with impassioned commands and exhortations. Zechariah's vision of the restoration of Jerusalem (chap. ii, 1–5) is immediately followed by a call to the people of Zion, who yet dwell in Babylon, to escape from the land of exile.

It should be noticed also that the later apocalyptists appropriate very freely both the symbols and language of their predecessors, and modify them to suit their own particular purpose. Ezekiel makes use of the vision of Isaiah. Zechariah and Daniel have much in common; and there is scarcely a symbol or figure of note in the Apocalypse of John which has not been appropriated from the writers of the Old Testament.

As one who remembers an impressive dream and hastens to write it down, so the writers of divine revelations sought to commit their God-given thoughts to writing (Dan. vii, 1), and John says he was commanded to write in a book the things which he saw (Rev. i, 11). Compositions thus prompted may be expected to have peculiarities, nor need we be surprised to find that they often take on the spirit and forms of poetry. Besides the visions and symbols employed for conveying the divine revelation, these writings naturally make use of bold metaphors, sudden exclamations of emotion, and various similes and other figures of speech which are characteristic of impassioned writing. So important is it for us to study these facts that we devote a separate chapter to the apocalyptic elements conspicuous in the best Hebrew poetry.

CHAPTER II

APOCALYPTIC ELEMENTS IN HEBREW SONG

THERE has been no little misapprehension, both of single compositions and of entire books of the Bible, by reason of a failure to recognize the pictorial element which is conspicuous therein. The Hebrew tongue is itself the language of metaphor and passion. The frequent occurrence of the word "behold" is a mark of the animated and pictorial character of the composition. The heart smitten with deep emotion is wont to express its thoughts in glowing style, and often, where the form of composition is not that of poetry, the sentiment and language are elevated quite above the manner of prose.

It is worthy of note that nearly two fifths of the Old Testament are in the style and spirit of Hebrew poetry. This fact demands consideration when we study these ancient writings as the embodiment of divine revelation. A rigid adherence to the letter of a highly wrought composition may blind one's eyes to the rich spiritual significance of the grand total impression it was designed to make. In many cases it involves the absurdity of reducing purely imaginative concepts to crass mechanical notions which could have no external reality in the world of sense. This may be illustrated by the following passage from the eighteenth psalm (verses 6–15):

In my distress I call Jehovah,
And unto my God I cry out ;
He hears from his temple my voice,
And my cry before him comes into his ears.
Thereupon the earth shakes and trembles,
And the foundations of the mountains move,
And shake to and fro because of his anger.
There went up a smoke in his nostrils,
And a fire out of his mouth devours ;
Coals were kindled from it.
He bowed the heavens also and descended,
And thick darkness was under his feet ;
And he rode upon a cherub and flew,
And sped swiftly on the wings of the wind.
He makes darkness his hiding place,
His surroundings, his booth, are a gathering of waters, dark clouds of the skies.
From the darkness before him his dark clouds passed,
Hail and coals of fire.

Jehovah also thundered in the heavens,
And Elyon gave his voice,
Hail and coals of fire.
And he sent out his arrows and scattered them,
And many lightnings, and discomfited them.
Then were the channels of the waters seen,
And exposed were the foundations of the world,—
At thy rebuke, O Jehovah,
At the blast of the wind of thy nostrils.

The simplest reader of this psalm observes that, in answer to the prayer of the one in distress, Jehovah reveals himself in marvelous power and glory. He disturbs for his sake all the elements of the earth and the heavens. He descends from the lofty sky as if bending down the visible clouds and making a pathway of massive darkness under his feet. He seems to ride upon a chariot, borne along by cherubim, and moving swiftly as the winds. At this point the imagery is remarkably parallel with that of Ezekiel's apocalyptic vision (Ezek. i, 4, 5, 22–26). In the psalmist's thought winds, fire, hail, smoke, clouds, waters, lightnings, and earthquake are conceived as immediately subservient to Jehovah, who interposes for the rescue of his devout servant.

But who would presume to put a literal interpretation upon compositions like this? The cultivated and appreciative reader feels at once that he is in touch with highly wrought imaginative poetry. A dissecting literalism, which would presume to construct a dictionary of metaphors and apply its own special definitions uniformly and mechanically to the exposition of such a scripture, must needs lead into confusion and error. It borders on folly to ask, in the study of such a psalm, when and where God actually bent down the visible heaven and made a pathway of clouds on which David or anyone else saw him descend.[1] But we do see, in all such emotional word-pictures, how vividly the Hebrew poets apprehended the presence of God in human experience, and also in the phenomena of the natural world. The concepts and expressions are in keeping with the anthropomorphism peculiar to Hebrew modes of thought.

The ninety-seventh psalm is of similar apocalyptic character. Jehovah is celebrated as sovereign of the world, and all the forces

---

[1] Perowne's comment on the passage is as follows: " David's deliverance was, of course, not really accompanied by such convulsions of nature, by earthquake, and fire, and tempest ; but his deliverance, or rather his manifold deliverances, gathered into one, as he thinks of them, appear to him as marvelous a proof of the divine power, as verily effected by the immediate presence and finger of God, as if he had come down in visible form to accomplish them."—*The Book of Psalms*, new translation, with notes, etc., vol. i, p. 186. American ed., Andover, 1876.

of earth and heaven are the ministers of his will.　Perowne translates the first part of the psalm as follows :

> Jehovah is king: let the earth be glad,
> Let the multitude of the isles rejoice.
> Cloud and darkness are round about him,
> Righteousness and judgment are the foundation of his throne.
> A fire goeth before him,
> And devoureth his adversaries round about him.
> His lightnings gave shine unto the world,
> The earth saw and trembled.
> The mountains melted like wax at the presence of Jehovah,
> At the presence of the Lord of the whole earth.
> The heavens have declared his righteousness,
> And all the peoples have seen his glory.

It may here be pointed out that the religious purpose and real
value of these apocalyptic songs are not affected by the critical
question of their literary origin.　The authorship of the ninety-
seventh psalm is confessedly unknown.　The Hebrew text is without a title.　The Septuagint ascribes it "to David, when his land is
established ;" but this heading has no real worth in criticism.
Delitzsch regards the psalm as a product of postexilic times and in
its subject-matter a compilation out of the earlier literature.　The
eighteenth psalm, however, claims in its title to be a triumphal
hymn of David, "who spoke unto Jehovah the words of this song
in the day of Jehovah's delivering him out of the hand of all his
enemies and out of the hand of Saul."　It is also inserted, with the
same superscription, in the narrative of David's history as written
in the Second Book of Samuel (chap. xxii).　"The author of the
Books of Samuel," says Delitzsch, "found the song already existing
as Davidic; the difference between his text and that of the Psalter
shows that, even when he wrote, the song had been handed down
by tradition for a considerable length of time."[1]　But others have
questioned the Davidic authorship, and in quite recent times it has
been suggested that it is an ideal hymn of the Israelitish people,
"who, as a reward for their irreproachableness and piety, expect
the erection of the Messianic kingdom through a theophany, and
along with it Israel's dominion of the world."[2]

One may naturally feel that the setting aside of the explicit statements placed at the head of such a song is a serious disparagement
of the Hebrew writers.　But a thorough study of the biblical literature, and the manner of its transmission and use by the Jewish

---

[1] Commentary on the Psalms, *in loco*.
[2] Cornill, *Einleitung in das A. T.*, p. 119.　Freiburg, 1891.

people, will show that little value is to be given to the titles and superscriptions of these ancient songs. The habit of poetical embellishment led the Hebrew annalists to introduce fragments of song, and sometimes entire poems, into their narratives of the great events of the nation. If tradition report that a song was sung, or a prayer offered, or a speech made on some great historic occasion, there will not be wanting men of literary genius in subsequent times to write a composition presumably appropriate for such occasion. Songs celebrating great and notable events are not usually written on the day of their occurrence. On the contrary, they are as a rule the products of a much later time, and may be composed centuries afterward. Even poets of our own day compose psalms, lays, and ballads which they assume to put into the lips of holy men of old, and which may well be believed to represent the real life and spirit of an ancient hero. The Greek historians do not hesitate to formulate the very orations spoken by chieftains of a former age. The reader who will take pains to compare the correspondence between Solomon and Hiram, as given in 1 Kings v, 2 Chron. ii, and Josephus (*Ant.*, viii, 2, 6), will observe the freedom with which Jewish writers made record of such things. David's words, as recorded in 1 Chron. xxix, are probably a very free report, and therefore very largely the composition of another than David. In 1 Chron. xvi, 7-36, David is represented as putting into the hand of Asaph and his brethren a psalm of thanksgiving which, upon examination, is found to be compiled out of three probably post-exilic hymns (namely, Psalms xcvi, cv, 1-15, cvi, 1, 47, 48). Delitzsch holds, in reference to this composite ode, that the chronicler "strings together familiar reminiscences from the Psalms after the manner of a mosaic, in order to express approximately the festive mood and festive strains of that day."

Such being the habit of the Hebrew writers, no serious weight should be given to the mere critical question of dates and authorship in poems which the historical writers, for purposes of embellishment, incorporate in the body of their narratives. A given poem may or may not have been composed at the time of the event it celebrates, or by the person to whom it is attributed. Such a question must be determined by internal evidence rather than external testimony. If the two agree, no question need be raised ; if they do not agree, no serious consequences need be feared by allowing a rational criticism to do its legitimate work.

The fragments of poetry interwoven with the narrative of Numbers xxi are obviously designed in that connection to serve the purpose of pictorial embellishment. Verses 14 and 15 are cited from "the Book of the Wars of Jehovah." Verses 17 and 18 and 27–30 are evidently the productions of ballad singers of the nation; but whether they were composed in the same generation as that of the events celebrated or in a later age may be an open question. In the account of Joshua's great battle at Gibeon (Josh. x) the unknown writer quotes a fragment from "the Book of Jasher" (verses 12 and 13), and incorporates it in his narrative so naïvely that the majority of his readers have understood the poetical citation as well as its entire context to be a plain prosaic statement of fact. By calling attention to the constituent elements of these ancient writings modern biblical criticism has led most recent expositors to distinguish the poetry from the prose. The writer of the Book of Joshua quoted this fragment from the national anthology just as the compiler of the Books of Samuel quoted David's lamentation over Saul and Jonathan from the same source,[1] and also introduced the eighteenth psalm to adorn his narrative of David's life.

As parallel with these facts of the Hebrew literature, and as a further illustration in point, we may turn to the famous "Song of Moses," as recorded in Exod. xv, 1–18. This splendid poem celebrates the triumph of Jehovah and his people at the Red Sea. The God of Israel is here depicted as "a man of war," who hurls the chariots and hosts of Pharaoh into the sea. By the blast of his nostrils the waters were heaped up.

> Thou didst blow with thy wind, the sea covered them;
> They sank as lead in the mighty waters.
> Thou didst stretch out thy right hand,
> The earth swallowed them.

There can be no reasonable doubt that this poem celebrates a momentous event in the history of Israel. One of the later psalmists also broke out in rapture over the thought of his nation's rescue from Egypt, and declared that Jehovah "rebuked the Red Sea," led Israel "in the depths as in the wilderness," and covered their enemies with waters so that "there was not one of them left." Then he adds, "They believed his words; they sang his praise" (Psalm cvi, 9–12). But while the psalmist thus referred to the

---

[1] The Book of Jasher, which contained the elegy preserved to us in 2 Sam. i, 17–27, must have been compiled after the time of David. The obvious inference is that the Book of Joshua, which also makes use of it, was also written after the reign of David, and therefore some centuries after the time of Joshua. But such a book of national songs may have contained many a ballad as old as the time of Joshua. The questions of date and authorship must rest mainly on internal evidence; but a scientific and devout exegesis may well protest against a persistent construing of the language of such poetical citations as unquestionable statements of fact.

wonderful interposition of God in behalf of his people and declared in general terms that "they sang his praise," the compiler of the Book of Exodus incorporates in his narrative the song which Moses and Israel sang on the occasion of their deliverance. But must we now believe that the song of Exod. xv, 1-18, is a composition of Moses and the identical language employed on the occasion referred to? A question of this kind cannot be permanently settled by dogmatic presumptions or assertions. Scientific criticism avers that songs of this character are not usually written on the day of victory or the next day thereafter. It makes appeal to the facts of literary usage and to the license freely taken by annalists in adorning their narratives with illustrative and appropriate pieces of poetry. It maintains that such expressions as "thy holy habitation" (Exod. xv, 13), and "the mountain of thine inheritance; the place which thou hast made for thy dwelling, O Jehovah; the sanctuary which thy hands have established" (verse 17), are less natural and appropriate for Moses and Israel at the Red Sea than for Israel after they were established in Canaan. But the "Song of Moses" as it now stands in Exod. xv, 1-18, may be a later revision of what was sung by Moses and Israel.[1] A popular national ode would be likely to undergo many verbal changes and receive much supplement in the course of centuries, and such a poem may preserve the spirit of the occasion for which it was first written after having undergone modifications of a radical character. Later poets would naturally have celebrated such a triumph as that of Israel at the Red Sea, and numerous ballads of like cast may have become current among the people. An historian accustomed to adorn and enliven his description of great events by the insertion of such spirited songs would thus employ a current "Song of Moses" without ever entertaining the question of its authorship and date. No critic questions the historical purpose or occasion for which this song was written. Nor need we for one moment doubt that God could have inspired

---

[1] Jephthah's daughter and her companions came out to meet her father "with timbrels and with dances" on his return from the victory over the Ammonites (Judg. xi, 34). In like manner the women of Israel celebrated the triumphs of Saul and David, and sang (1 Sam. xviii, 7):

> Saul hath slain his thousands,
> And David his ten thousands.

So the great victory at the Red Sea would elicit spontaneous outbursts of exultation from Moses and the children of Israel, and Miriam and the women would respond to it "with timbrels and with dances." But that the song of Exod. xv, 1-18, was composed and committed to memory by the people of Israel before any celebration of their victory may reasonably be questioned.

Moses with ability to write the song within one hour after he
"shook out the Egyptians in the midst of the sea" (Exod.
xiv, 27), and to have prophesied of the sanctuary that was to be established
five hundred years thereafter in Jerusalem, the mountain of his
inheritance. But the question is not one of *possibilities*, but of
facts and probabilities. Devout criticism, in the handling of these
questions of authorship and date, is in no conflict with the *supernatural*, but it does cry out against the *unnatural*. It insists that
the true supernatural, which lies back of all divine revelation, is
conserved more surely by a rational than by an irrational and unnatural exegesis.

Keeping in mind, then, the habit of the old Hebrew annalists in
their free use of current songs to embellish and enliven narrative,
we are not to be disturbed at finding poetry and prose singularly
blended in the historical books of the Old Testament. Not infrequently one hesitates to say whether a description is to be understood literally or as a metaphorical embellishment of facts. For
example, we read in Exod. xiii, 21, 22, as follows :

Jehovah went before them by day in a pillar of cloud to lead them the way;
And by night in a pillar of fire to give them light;
That they might go by day and by night :—
And there departed not the pillar of cloud by day,
And the pillar of fire by night from before the people.

These statements and their numerous parallels in other parts of
the Scriptures [1] may be understood either as a record of outward,
visible, historic fact, or as a poetical picture of the wonderful
providence which was conspicuous in Israel's deliverance from their
numerous dangers at the period of the exodus. But who is to
determine absolutely for all readers which of these two interpretations is the more correct? Some will insist that we must believe
these words as plain literal statements or sacrifice the trustworthy
character of the entire biblical record of the exodus. They refuse
to allow any opinion outside of these alternatives. But others,
equally learned and devout, see no more necessity for insisting on
a literal interpretation of the pillar of cloud and of fire in these
passages than of the cherub and the pavilion in Psalm xviii, 10, 11.
They insist that in all such descriptions of divine interposition we
have so many illustrative examples of the genius of the Hebrew
writers for highly wrought word-painting. Where opinions differ
on such a matter of literary judgment each reader must be allowed
the liberty of deciding for himself and not for another.

[1] Comp. Exod. xiv, 19, 24; xl, 38; Num. ix, 15; x, 34; xiv, 14; Deut. i, 33; Neh.
ix, 12, 19; Psalm lxxviii, 14; xcix, 7; cv, 39; Isa. iv, 5; 1 Cor. x, 1.

As a further illustration of the apocalyptic elements in Hebrew song we cite the following passage from the song of Deborah (Judg. v, 4, 5):

> O Jehovah, when thou didst go forth out of Seir,
> When thou didst march out of the field of Edom,
> The land trembled, also the heavens dropped;
> Also the clouds dropped water.
> The mountains quaked before Jehovah,
> Yon Sinai before Jehovah, the God of Israel.

Let us observe next how the same idea is expressed in Psalm lxviii, 8, 9:

> O God, when thou didst go forth before the people,
> When thou didst march in the wilderness,
> The land trembled and the heavens dropped before God,
> Yon Sinai before God, the God of Israel.

What is most conspicuous in these verses is their vivid concept of the immediate presence of God with his people. He marches like a great hero at the head of the thousands of Israel, and clouds and storms, earthquake and flood are recognized as outward symbols of his majesty. The obvious allusion is to the march of the Israelites through the wilderness of Sinai. The signal interpositions of the Almighty in behalf of his people, from the time of their leaving Egypt until their entrance into the land of promise, were thus celebrated in the national songs.[1]

The Song of Moses, in Deut. xxxii, is as fundamental and suggestive in the apocalyptic character of much of its language as it is exquisite in its literary form. It celebrates the principles of the divine government of the world, extols the righteousness and goodness of Jehovah as contrasted with the perverseness of Israel. It reveals God as the judge and avenger of his people, who will come quickly and pour out his fury upon the wicked, redeem his own people, and cause them to exult with him in everlasting triumph. Witness the conclusion of the song (verses 39–43), which may be suitably rendered as follows:

> Behold ye now that I, even I, am he,
> And there are no gods with me.
> I put to death, and make alive again;
> I dashed in pieces, and I will restore;
> And there is no deliverer from my hand.
> For I lift up unto the heavens my hand,
> And say, I live forever!

---

[1] "The journey through the desert—of which Sinai was the central point—by the giving of the law and the impartation of doctrine, by the wonderful provision of food and the gift of victory, and by the infliction of awful judgments, became one continuous act of divine revelation."—Cassel, in Lange's Commentary, on Judg. v, 4.

If I make sharp the lightning of my sword,
And take fast hold of judgment with my hand,
I will turn vengeance on my enemies,
And them that hate me I will recompense.
I will make drunk my arrows with blood,
And my sword shall feed on flesh,—
From the blood of spoil and of captivity,
From the head of the waving locks of the foe.
O nations, sound aloud his people's praise,
For he the blood of his servants will avenge,
And vengeance turn upon his enemies,
And make his land and people free from guilt.

"The prayer of Habakkuk the prophet" (Hab. iii) is remarkable for its apocalyptic concepts of the divine government of the world. God is portrayed as coming from Teman and Mount Paran, covering the heavens with his glory. Beams of light stream from his radiant form while he stands and measures the earth, makes the nations tremble, and scatters the eternal mountains. Note especially verses 10 and 11:

The mountains saw thee and were in pain,
The tempest of waters passed by;
The deep uttered his voice,
On high his hands he lifted.
Sun and moon stood in their lofty abode,
At the light of thine arrows as they went,
At the brightness of the lightning of thy spear.

There are incorporated in the Pentateuch two apocalyptic songs of such exceptional significance as to justify a more extended comment. They are the oracular blessings attributed to Jacob and Moses, and recorded in Gen. xlix and Deut. xxxiii. These superior products of ancient Hebrew literature were in their nature adapted to become very popular and to be repeated familiarly among the tribes of Israel. They are both in substance poetic apocalypses of various struggles and triumphs of the twelve tribes as supposed to be foreseen by the patriarch and the lawgiver. It was a prevalent opinion of antiquity that highly gifted souls, at the moment of their departure from the world, were wont to prophesy. Socrates is represented in Plato's *Apology* as saying to his judges: "Now, O men who have condemned me, I would fain prophesy to you; for I am about to die, and that is the hour in which men are gifted with prophetic power."

That Socrates uttered something of this kind to his judges is altogether probable; that he spoke these very sentiments is certainly not impossible. But the well-trained student of history and literature knows that it is equally possible, and no less probable, that these words, as well as all the rest of the *Apology*, are the language and thought of Plato. In the introduction to his translation of this dialogue Jowett observes : "In what relation the *Apology* of Plato stands to the real defense of Socrates there are no means of determining." The same thing may be said of the oracular blessings ascribed to Jacob and Moses. Their genuineness must be subjected to the same tests. Did these ancient worthies of the Hebrew people compose and utter the poems in question before their death? He would be bold indeed who would assume the affirmative of this question, and insist withal that the credibility and value of these scriptures depend upon our maintenance of that affirmative.

The fundamental question, first of all to be determined, is one of fact touching the usage and methods of literary art. All the studied compositions of human genius belong essentially to a department of the fine arts, and there is no good reason for excluding Hebrew poems and apocalypses from the same category. Is it, then, or is it not the habit of poets to transfer themselves in imaginative thought to bygone times, and compose sentiments appropriate for great heroes on particular occasions? This question answers itself with everyone who is familiar with the literature of any cultivated people. What we have already shown in our observations on the Song of Moses in Exod. xv is therefore applicable also to the great poems of Gen. xlix and Deut. xxxiii. The authorship and date of such productions are legitimate questions of criticism. It is usually the case that an author, writing long after the event to which his composition refers, betrays by incidental words and allusions the real period when he lived. The prevailing verdict of modern criticism is that both these oracular poems belong to a period long after the days of Moses. But the approximate date of each is a more difficult question, and they have been assigned by different critics to almost every period between the time of David and the Babylonian exile. This diversity of opinion, however, need not be considered strange, when even greater diversity exists respecting the time and place of the composition of the Book of Job. Our sole object in these pages is neither to maintain nor deny the genuineness of these prophetic songs, but to show that their value for doctrine and instruction in righteousness is not dependent on that question of criticism. We see no antecedent improbability, much less an impossibility, in such men as Jacob and Moses uttering these prophetic blessings on the tribes of Israel. But we are bound in all honor and truthfulness to affirm that it was just as possible, and much more in accord with what we know of the literature of other peoples, for inspired poets of the times of David, or later, to have written them. The author in each case transfers himself in imagination to the position of the great hero to whom the song is attributed. The prophecy of Jacob purports to be a survey of the future of the twelve tribes as seen by the patriarch in Egypt when he was about to die. The blessing of Moses assumes to be the words with which "the man of God blessed the children of Israel before his death." Both of these poems move in the same general line of thought, but with such numerous variations as two different writers, at the times supposed, would naturally have conceived. Jacob's oracle has a more secular cast, and contains curses as well as blessings; Moses's blessing has a more spiritual and theocratic tone, and contains no word of censure for any of the tribes. In Jacob's prophecy Simeon and Levi are associated, and are both condemned because of their wanton cruelty in the slaughter of the Shechemites (comp. Gen. xlix, 5–7, and xxxiv, 25–31). But in Moses's blessing Simeon is not mentioned, and Levi is extolled as the well-tried priest and teacher of the chosen people. In Gen. xlix, 8–12, Judah is praised among his brethren as preeminent for leadership, conquest, royalty, and wealth; but in Deut. xxxiii, 7, he is passed over with a few words of doubtful import. From Moses's point of view the ultimate glories of the tribe of Judah seem to be hidden by reason of the nearer vision of the priesthood of Levi and the prosperity of Joseph. In both poems Joseph receives notable distinction, for Jacob's passionate fondness for his favorite son was ever memorable, and Moses could not be supposed to ignore "the myriads of Ephraim and the thousands of Manasseh."

These prophetic compositions are obviously the products of different periods, but in their contents and general form they are noticeably analogous. There are also verbal correspondencies which show that they are not altogether independent of each other. The patriarch, in telling his children what shall befall them in the after time, is portrayed as a prophet of the future; but Moses's blessing contemplates the conquest of Canaan as already accomplished, and Israel dwelling safely in a land of corn and wine. The opening words in Moses's blessing, however, are more apocalyptic in style than anything to be found in the prophecy of Jacob. The Hebrew text of Deut. xxxiii, 2, is probably corrupt; but with slight emendation we may read it thus:

> Jehovah forth from Sinai came,
> And he beamed out of Seir for them;
> He shone forth from Mount Paran,
> And came unto Meribah-Kadesh:
> At his right hand springs (gushed) for them.

This is a poetic concept of God's wonderful kindness toward his people during all their journeys in the desert, and should be compared with Judg. v, 4, 5, and Psalm lxviii, 8, 9. But it would seem very unnatural for Moses to say what is written in verse 4 :

> Moses commanded us a law,
> An inheritance for the assembly of Jacob.

The probability is that both these songs received modifications in the course of years. The entire exordium of Moses's blessing (verses 2–5) may have been the addition of a later hand. But whatever their origin and history, they occupy their appropriate places in the volume of divine inspiration, and their apocalyptic elements are obvious. They constitute together a twofold poetic picture of the struggles and triumphs of the tribes of Israel.

The oracles of Balaam, as written in Num. xxiii and xxiv, are also deserving of our notice on account of their apocalyptic style and setting. They are more general in their scope than the blessings of Jacob and Moses, but they are of the nature of prophetic blessings on the tribes of Israel. The famous soothsayer is summoned from the mountains of the East to "curse Jacob and utter wrath against Israel," but Jehovah puts words of blessing in his mouth, and he declares that he "cannot go beyond the word of Jehovah, to do either good or evil of his own mind."

What is very conspicuous in Balaam's oracles is their fourfold repetition of blessings. First he speaks from a position whence he can behold the extreme portion of the camp of Israel, and where Balak had prepared for him seven altars, seven bullocks, and seven rams. There "he took up his parable and said" (Num. xxiii, 7–10):

> From Aram Balak leads me,
> The king of Moab from the mountains of the East:
> Come, curse for me Jacob,
> And come, be wroth against Israel.
> How shall I curse whom God has not cursed?
> And how shall I be wroth (when) Jehovah is not wroth?
> For from the summit of the rocks I see him,
> And from the hills I behold him:
> Lo, it is a people that dwells in separation,
> And among the nations reckons not himself.
> Who has counted the dust of Jacob,
> Or, by number, the fourth of Israel?
> Let me die the death of the righteous,
> And let my last end be like his.

The king of Moab is chagrined and offended by such words, and takes Balaam to another part of the mountain whence he may not see the whole camp ; but the second oracle (Num. xxiii, 18–24) is

a fuller blessing than the first, and declares that no enchantment or
divination can prevail against the people of God. Thereafter, in
varied form, a third and a fourth oracle of blessing follow, each
predictive of the future glory of Israel (see Num. xxiv, 3–9, and
15–34). In his God-given strength

> He shall devour the nations, his enemies,
> And shall break their bones in pieces,
> And with his arrows smite them through.
>
> .   .   .   .   .   .
>
> There shall come forth a Star out of Jacob,
> And a scepter shall rise out of Israel,
> And he shall smite through the corners of Moab,
> And break down all sons of tumult.
> And Edom shall become a possession,
> Even Seir shall become a possession—his enemies.

Besides Moab and Edom (which is in the poetic parallelism not
different from Seir) five other nations are referred to, namely,
Amalek, the Kenite, Asshur, Kittim, and Eber, seven in all, which
are to come in contact with the people of Jacob. In all this we
may see the outline of an apocalypse of Israel's future struggles
and triumphs among the nations. The fourth oracle is worthy to
be compared with the fuller prophecies of Isaiah (chaps. xiii–xxiii),
Jeremiah (xlvi–li), Ezekiel (xxv–xxxii), Amos (i, ii), and Zephaniah
(ii). All these are but amplified delineations of the concept of
divine judgment on the nations, and of God's overruling wars and
revolutions so as to secure in the end the peace and glory of his
people—the righteous nation. In Joel iii, 2, we have it all summed
up in a single picture thus: "I will gather all nations and bring
them into a valley of Jehoshaphat, and will plead with them there
for my people." This idea of bringing all the nations into judgment, and out of them all redeeming those who fear God and
work righteousness, is a fundamental concept of the biblical
revelations.

   The conclusion we reach from this brief study of apocalyptic
songs is that in a faithful and thorough interpretation of them their
subjective ideal elements must be duly recognized. Whether they
stand apart as independent psalms or are incorporated in the historical narratives, their essential contents as revelations of the righteousness and mercy of God are in either case the same. When
they are assigned by their headings to a particular author or occasion such assignment is not in itself sufficient always to determine
the authorship or the date of the poem. For the highest literature
abounds with compositions which gifted poets have written as

appropriate for persons and events of a distant past.[1] And it requires but a slight examination of the habit of the Hebrew historians to see how freely they made use of such poetic compositions to embellish their lifelike annals.

In view of what has now been shown and of what follows in the next chapter, we may here appropriately cite the words of Herder. "Poetry," he observes, "is a divine language, yet not in the sense that we understand by it what the divine Being in himself feels and utters; whatever was given to the most godlike men, even through a higher influence, to feel and experience in themselves, was still human. . . . The spirit of poetry was first exhibited in significant names and expressions full of imagery and of feeling, and I know of no poetry in the world in which this origin is exhibited in greater purity than in (that of the Hebrews). The first specimen which presents itself in it (Gen. i) is a series of pictures exhibiting a view of the universe, and arranged in accordance with the dictates of human feeling. Light is the first uttered word of the Creator, and the instrument of divine efficiency in the sensitive human soul. By means of this the creation is unfolded and expanded. The heavens and the earth, night and day, the diurnal and nocturnal luminaries, creatures in the sea and on the land, are measured and estimated with reference to the human eye, to the wants and the powers of feeling and of arrangement peculiar to man. The wheel of creation revolves upon a circumference embracing all that the eye can reach, and stands still in himself as the center of the circle. In giving names to all, and ordering all from the impulse of his own inward feeling, and with reference to himself, he becomes an imitator of the Divinity, a second Creator, a true ποιητής, a creative poet." [2]

---

[1] It is an interesting fact, worthy of notice here for its suggestive analogy, that the beautiful poem entitled "Milton's Prayer of Patience," written by Miss Elizabeth Lloyd, of Philadelphia (afterward Mrs. Howell), passed in England as Milton's own composition, and was even included in an Oxford edition of Milton's works as a newly discovered poem. The first stanza is:

> I am old and blind!
> Men point at me as smitten by God's frown;
> Afflicted and deserted of my kind;
> Yet am I not cast down.

See the entire poem and introductory note in Schaff and Gilman's *Library of Religious Poetry*, p. 10. New York, 1881.

[2] *The Spirit of Hebrew Poetry*, translated from the German by James Marsh, vol. ii, pp. 6, 7. Burlington, 1833.

CHAPTER III

APOCALYPSE OF CREATION

The Book of Genesis, as we now possess it, is a composition without real parallel or counterpart in the literature of the world. And it is, moreover, noteworthy that, in the canonical arrangement of the books of the Old and New Testaments, the first and last books of our Bible treat respectively of what was first and what shall be last. The early chapters of Genesis and the entire Book of Revelation have been most variously interpreted, and there is little probability of general, much less of universal, agreement for generations to come. A peculiar haze of uncertainty has accordingly settled over the first and last books of the Bible, suggestive of the impenetrable mystery which, to finite minds, must ever hang over the beginning and the end of all things.

Criticism has very thoroughly established the composite character of the Book of Genesis. And even the ordinary reader can hardly fail to observe that ancient poems, genealogical tables, primeval traditions, and various religious ideas have been appropriated by the writer and incorporated in one continuous narrative. This composite character of the book is not to be considered a disparagement of its value. In fact, the real value of such an ancient production may be in several ways enhanced by reason of its use of the testimony of various witnesses. Scientific criticism may legitimately busy itself with minute study of the constituent documents, and determine if possible their probable origin and date.[1] It may discover in the original sources matters of great archæological importance quite independent of the purpose for which the compiler of Genesis put the book in its present form. How far he appropriated poems or genealogies without abridgment or change, and to what extent subsequent editorial revision may have modified

---

[1] In current critical analysis it is common to designate the three principal literary sources of Genesis by the letters J, E, and P. J is believed to be a prophetic writer who generally employs the name Jehovah (or *Yahweh*) when speaking of God; E as uniformly employs the name *Elohim ;* but these documents became early united, and the combined work is often designated by J E. P represents a later (priestly) narrative, distinguished by various peculiarities of thought and style. The combination of all these into one readable narrative was the subsequent work of the author of our Pentateuch (or, rather, the Hexateuch). There is substantial agreement among the critics that Gen. i, 1–ii, 3, belongs to P, and ii, 4–iv, 26, to J.

the composition as a whole, are open questions which may never be finally settled. Our present contention is that the religious value of the Book of Genesis, as an inspired scripture, is independent of all such questions of scientific research. Whatever the authorship and purpose of its original constituent elements, the book as it now lies before us exhibits a well-defined plan and purpose. It opens with a sublime sevenfold picture of creation by the word of God (chaps. i, 1–ii, 3), and thence proceeds with a more or less detailed series of "generations," descriptive of the beginnings of nations and of "the twelve tribes of Israel."

Any satisfactory interpretation of Genesis must be preceded by a DETERMINATION OF THE CLASS OF LITERATURE TO WHICH IT BELONGS. It has been quite generally assumed that the book is a plain prosaic narrative, and that it should be read and understood as any other historical record of facts. The lives of the great patriarchs Abraham, Isaac, and Jacob are described in a manner so simple and lifelike, and touch incidentally so many facts related to well-known cities and nations of antiquity, that there appears at first sight no reason to question their genuine historical character. But when we examine the earlier chapters of the book (i–xi) we observe a number of things which at once suggest doubts as to the real character of the composition. The story of the serpent conversing with the woman ; the cherubim and flaming sword at the east of the garden of Eden ; the punishment of Cain and his marriage and city building ; the astonishing longevity of the descendants of Seth, and the carnal intercourse of the sons of God with the daughters of men, are not of a character that naturally commands confidence in their historicalness. In no other literature of the world would such compositions as these be accepted to-day as genuine history. We may and do hold our entire Bible to be unique in comparison with all other books—and the Book of Genesis is exceptionally unique among the various portions of the Bible ; but do these facts justify the conclusion that all the contents must be historical ?

If, however, the Book of Genesis is a compilation of various documents, it is very presumable that some of the documents may and others may not have historical value. Sound sense and scientific criticism may unite in saying that each part or distinguishable section of such a book is entitled to be judged by its own peculiar nature and style. The dogmatic assertion, sometimes made, that if one part is historical all is historical, and if one part is unhistorical all is unhistorical, cannot possibly determine a matter of this kind. Who would allow such a principle of judgment to control him in the study of the Book of Ezekiel or one of the historical dramas of Shakespeare ?

It has from ancient times been felt by the most devout and thoughtful interpreters that much in the earlier chapters of Genesis must be understood in some other than a literal sense. St. Augustine spoke of the "ineffable days" of creation, and all the common readers since his time have wondered that light should have been separately created three days before the sun. But the discoveries of science have effectually exploded the old notion of the creation of earth and heavens in six ordinary days, and for more than a hundred years expositors have been striving to adjust the statements of the first chapter of Genesis to the well-ascertained facts of geology and astronomy.

But while men were striving to "reconcile Genesis and geology" a great side-light was thrown upon the whole subject of the biblical cosmogony by the discoveries of Assyriology. The creation tablets procured from the ruins of Nineveh give us the Assyrian account of the beginning of all things, and we are impressed with what seems a very remarkable correspondence, in general outline, with the sevenfold picture of the first of Genesis. The first tablet opens thus :

> At that time the heaven above had not yet announced,
> Or the earth beneath recorded a name ;
> The unopened deep was their generator,
> Mummu-Tiamat was the mother of them all.
> Their waters were embosomed as one, and
> The cornfield was unharvested, the pasture was ungrown.[1]

The second tablet has not been found, but from some fragments it appears to have described some preparations for insuring the triumph of light over darkness. The third and fourth tablets describe the victory of light, and the formation of the heavens and the sea out of the Chaos Tiamat. The fifth tells of the establishing of the sun, moon, and stars in the heavens to determine the measure of the days, months, and years. No portion of the sixth tablet has yet been found, but a mutilated part of the seventh speaks of the creation of living creatures, such as the cattle of the field and creeping things.

In addition to this Assyrian record there has also been discovered a Cuthæan or Babylonian legend. It appears on the fragments of two tablets from Cutha in Babylonia, and differs from the Assyrian account as much as the second chapter of Genesis differs from the first. It names Tiamat as the great mother, and speaks of seven kings who were brothers, and appeared as begetters, and their

---

[1] See "The Assyrian Story of the Creation," translated and annotated by A. H. Sayce, in *Records of the Past*, new series, vol. i, pp. 122–146.

armies were six thousand in number. These tablets portray no successive acts of creation, but seem to have been designed to record some of the primordial struggles of nature to emerge from the original chaos.[1]

These discoveries of Assyriology have given additional interest to the traditions of other ancient peoples concerning the origin of things. The Greek and Latin poets, the old Norse mythology, and the Persian legends have their analogies. The Vedic Song of Creation probably embodies the earliest speculations of the kind among the Indo-European races. The following lines are especially worthy of note :

> Then there was neither being nor not-being.
> The atmosphere was not, nor sky above it.
> Of day and night there was yet no distinction.
> Alone that One breathed calmly, self-supported.
> Other than It was none, nor aught above It.
>
> Darkness there was at first in darkness hidden;
> This universe was undistinguished water.
> That which in void and emptiness lay hidden
> Alone by power of fervor was developed.
>
> The source from which this universe has risen,
> And whether it were made, or uncreated,
> He only knows, who from the highest heaven
> Rules,—the all-seeing Lord,—or does not he know ?[2]

In view of these corresponding ideals of creation among the great nations of antiquity, brought into conspicuous notice by specialists in comparative philology, the modern expositor of Genesis is called upon to show what relations, if any, these different cosmogonies hold to each other. The superiority of the Hebrew narrative is conceded. "We are accustomed," says Wellhausen, "to regard this first leaf of the Bible as surrounded with all the charm that can be derived from the combination of high antiquity and childlike form. It would be vain to deny the exalted ease and the uniform greatness that gives the narrative its character. The beginning especially (verses 2 and 3) is incomparable."[3] But it is not so easy to determine the relative date of this Hebrew narrative and to say whether its author made use of, or was independent of, the cosmological traditions of other nations than his own.

---

[1] See "The Babylonian Story of the Creation according to the Tradition of Cutha," translated and annotated by A. H. Sayce in *Records of the Past*, new series, vol. i, pp. 147–153.

[2] From the 129th hymn of the tenth book of the Rigveda, as translated in *The Rigveda*, by Adolf Kaegi, English version by R. Arrowsmith, p. 90. Boston, 1886.

[3] *Prolegomena to the History of Israel*, p. 298. Edinburgh, 1885.

There are those who insist that the biblical cosmogony is a divine revelation, given miraculously to some one of the earliest fathers of our race, and thence transmitted without error until it received through Moses its present setting at the beginning of the Pentateuch. But is it not evident, upon sober reflection, that this hypothesis is in its very nature an assumption which no man is competent to prove? Where is there a shred of evidence to show that any such piece of composition was ever transmitted through generations existing thousands of years before the dawn of well-attested history? Who is he who presumes to know so much about the uncorrupted traditions of the twenty centuries and more before Moses? The same old statement of the Jewish Talmud which tells us that "Moses wrote his own book, and the section about Balaam and Job," says also in the same paragraph that " David wrote the Book of Psalms by the aid of the ten ancients, Adam, Melchizedek, Abraham, Moses, Heman, Jeduthun, Asaph, and the three sons of Korah !" What value can the intelligent student of history put upon such rabbinical conjectures? The hypothesis in question rests upon a priori presumptions of what a divine revelation ought to be, and can adduce no other sort of evidence in its favor.

Another hypothesis is that the biblical story of creation holds a relation to corresponding conceptions among other nations analogous to the relation which the Israelitish religion holds to other ancient religions. Of its literary origin and history we have no positive knowledge. Whether it were carried as an ancestral tradition by Abraham when he migrated out of Ur of the Chaldees, and whether it were developed or modified during the subsequent history of the Hebrews in Palestine; or whether it first took definite form at the time of Israel's later contact with Assyria and Babylon, and was put in writing as we now have it by some contemporary of Ezekiel—on any one of these suppositions it may still be regarded as a portion of the divine revelation with which the Hebrew people were intrusted. In whatever sense it is accepted as a revelation or apocalypse of God's creative relation to the world, the date of its composition is one question and its character as a revelation is another. It was just as competent for the God of Israel to communicate the revelations of Genesis to a contemporary of Ezra as to a contemporary of Moses.

But to what extent and in what way may we believe the first chapters of Genesis to be a revelation of God? In no other way, we may answer in general terms, than the Book of Joshua, and Judges, and Samuel, and Kings, and Chronicles, and Ecclesiastes, and Proverbs, and Job are revelations of God. None of these books make any claim to be supernatural compositions, but we accept them all as written embodiments of various religious doctrines, and to that extent as revelations of truths which it is important for man to know. We do not believe that Genesis, more than these other books, was given to instruct men in astronomy, or geology, or chemistry, or any other department of natural science. The numerous attempts that have been made to harmonize science and the Bible by showing that the "days" of Genesis accord with the periods of geology, or with æonic phases of cosmological development, have been proven fallacious, and have reacted damagingly upon the mistaken apologists of the Bible. We gain nothing for the honor of the Scriptures by attempting to force upon them a meaning they were never intended to convey.[1]

But if these opening chapters of the Bible are a revelation of God's creative relation to the world, may they not be apocalyptical in character? Is it not fitting that the canon of Scripture should open as well as close with an apocalypse? The ideal character of Gen. i, 1–ii, 3, may be quite naturally inferred as much from its artificial symmetry of structure as from the peculiar style of its contents. The six days are set over against each other in two sets of triads, the first day corresponding noticeably with the fourth, the second with the fifth, and the third with the sixth. The sevenfold structure may be thus outlined:

1. LIGHT (verses 2–5).
2. HEAVEN (6–8).
3. LAND AND VEGETATION (9–13).

4. LUMINARIES (14–19).
5. CREATURES OF THE HEAVEN AND THE WATERS (20–23).
6. LAND ANIMALS AND MAN (24–31).

7. THE SABBATH REST (ii, 1–3).

Not a few eminent scholars have called this first section of Genesis a poem. Rorison, in his essay on "The Creative Week," calls it "the inspired Psalm of Creation."[2] It has indeed its monoto-

---

[1] When a man like the late Professor C. H. Hitchcock claims with an air of dogmatic assurance that "the creative chapter was designed at the outset [after remaining misunderstood for fifty-nine centuries] to confirm the truth of the sacred narrative in a remote skeptical age" (*Bibliotheca Sacra*, 1867, p. 436), one is at a loss to conjecture its real value for the many generations who perused it during the intervening millenniums, and may marvel still more to observe that after this long waiting it has so slight an influence on the average skeptic! The radical fallacy of all these pompous claims is the tacit assumption that the Scriptures were designed to anticipate the discoveries of science.

[2] In "Replies to Essays and Reviews," p. 285. New York, 1862. Delitzsch observes that "the Scripture, according to which God creates the world in twice three days by ten words of power, and completes it in seven days, teaches that God is the principle of all numbers."—*Com. on Isaiah*, at chap. vi, 3.

nous repetitions of statement, its artificial periods, and its sevenfold structure; but these qualities are hardly sufficient to entitle the composition to the rank of poetry. They belong rather to the formality of apocalyptics, where the narrative may be of the most simple and prosaic style, and yet present an ideal picture.[1] The same observation holds true of the narratives of allegory and parable.

We prefer, accordingly, to call this first section of the Hebrew Scriptures an apocalypse of creation. It is as truly a sevenfold revelation of a beginning as the Apocalypse of John is a mystic revelation of an end. Both of these writings inculcate in emphatic form that the Lord God of Israel is the first and the last, the beginning and the end. The seven days of the cosmogony are no more to be interpreted literally than are the seven trumpets of the Apocalypse. Indeed, the repetitions of "God said" in Genesis suggest some analogies to be found in the sounding of the seven trumpets. At the sounding of the first trumpet the earth was smitten; at the second, the sea; at the third, the rivers and fountains; at the fourth, the sun; at the fifth, the abyss; at the sixth, the armies of Euphrates were set loose, and, at the seventh, "great voices in heaven" announced the advent and reign of the Lord and his Anointed. The days of Genesis are as symbolical as the trumpets of the Apocalypse, and can no more successfully be identified (or shown to correspond) with ascertained æons of geology and cosmical evolution than can the trumpets with successive historical events.

In the correspondency of the two sets of triads, as shown above, we observe the method of apocalyptic repetition. Such correspondency presents an idealism of conception rather than a record of physical facts, and suggests by its varied repetitions an order of progress in the work of God. The repetition points to the organic as following the inorganic, and the higher forms of life come last.

Our interpretation of this remarkable composition cannot therefore proceed on any method of literal correspondencies. The narrative is no more a treatise on natural science than it is an almanac. It is rather a pictorial object lesson, as profitable for the present age as for any period in the past. It is conceded that, as an ideal cosmogony, this record surpasses immeasurably all the analogous

---

[1] "It has never seemed to us," says Matheson, "that the dignity of this narrative lay in its being an almanac. We have always held that, apart altogether from questions of authorship, it ought to be interpreted as the visions of the prophets are interpreted; in other words, to be classed with those portions of Jewish literature whose mission was to teach in symbols."—*Can the Old Faith Live with the New?* p. 117. Edinb., 1889.

compositions of the nations. Whatever words, phrases, or allusions in it may have sprung from ancient ethnic mythologies the Hebrew writer has so far eliminated the polytheistic elements as to give its fundamental ideas a most definite theistic setting. The poets and prophets of the Hebrew nation are full of expressions which in doctrinal import are identical with the main lessons which all classes of readers may readily find in this ideal picture of creation.

Among the great truths which this apocalyptic picture is adapted to inculcate, and which the first readers as well as the last, the unlearned as well as the learned, have ever recognized, we emphasize the following :

1. God is at the beginning of all things, and is himself without beginning. He is the source of light, and has brought forth by the word of his power the things which are seen out of that which was not seen ; for he is light, and in him is no darkness at all. Comp. Heb. xi, 3; 2 Cor. iv, 6; 1 John i, 5.

2. God is a Being of infinite wisdom, power, and goodness. He is revealed in his creation as the supreme Personality, the intelligent ground or reason of the order of nature, comprehending, dividing, disposing the elements of the universe according to his will. Comp. Psalm xxxiii, 9; cxlviii, 5, 6; Job xxxviii, 4–11; Rom. i, 20.

3. All the growths of nature are products of his wisdom and energy, and their countless kinds and classes are perfectly known to him. And all the swarms of living things, in the waters or in the air, as truly as the higher orders of creation, subserve in some way the purposes of his will. Comp. Psalm civ, 14; cxlvii, 8; cxlviii, 10; Matt. x, 29.

4. This infinite Intelligence not only brought the heavens and the earth and all their hosts into organic forms, but he also rules them by established laws and determines their movements and periods. Comp. Isa. xlvi, 9, 10; Psalm civ, 19.

5. The creation exhibits an ordered progress from the lower to the higher, and the animal series culminates in man, who is made in the image of God, and who stands forth as God's highest representative in the visible world. Comp. Psalm viii, 4–8.

6. The Creator is depicted as a Being of benevolence. His good will toward all creatures possessed of sentient life is manifest in that he blessed them and willed their increase so as to fill the earth and possess it. Comp. Psalm civ, 14, 27; cxxxvi, 25; cxlv, 15, 16; cxlvii, 9.

7. God is also revealed as having an æsthetic nature. He is conceived as having delight in the things which he brings into visible form. And it is indicated at the close of the word-picture that no

good work of heaven and earth is truly *finished* without the blessed consummation of repose after action. Into such blessedness of the æsthetic contemplative rest of God, man and his divine Creator may come very close to each other. Comp. Heb. iv, 10; Isa. lvi, 2; lviii, 13.

All these and other similar lessons of religious value have been apparent in this record from the time of its origin. Why should we be anxious to make it mean more, or something different?

Passing now to the second chapter of Genesis (verses 4–25), we observe, in the first place, that it differs from the preceding in scope and outline very much as the Babylonian record of creation differs from the Assyrian. The point of view is different, the sub-ject-matter is special, and the style of concept and composition is all that one could expect of two different writers. A most reason-able hypothesis is that the author of the Book of Genesis appro-priated this document of unknown origin, modified it, perhaps, in some places, and added it as a supplementary picture of the crea-tion of man. It is not, strictly speaking, a duplicate account of the creation, for it is not a cosmogony, but an ideal picture of the intro-duction of the first human pair into the world. With the exception of a few incidental allusions to natural growths the narrative is concerned solely with the first man, and is in substance an amplifi-cation of what has been already depicted in apocalyptic style in chap. i, 26–28. It accords with the habit of biblical apocalyptics to enhance the leading features of an ideal picture by artificial repe-tition, and so our author deemed it important to take up again that part of the work of the sixth day which referred to man, and show more fully how "he created them male and female."

1. In exhibiting this correspondence we observe the apocalyptic form and style of Gen. i, 26 : "Let us make man in our image." Here God speaks as in the presence of a heavenly council, and the plural form of utterance is best explained as part and parcel of a vivid word-picture. Compare the similar style in Gen. iii, 22; xi, 7, and Isa. vi, 8. The Almighty is conceived as taking counsel with the holy ones who stand about his throne (comp. 1 Kings xxii, 19), and announcing to them the purpose of a higher order of created life on earth. That purpose was accomplished by creating man in the image of God. But the first picture furnished no details, and the scope of the second and supplementary narrative is, after the manner of apocalyptic repetition,[1] to enlarge the concept already given, and also to exalt and emphasize the relative importance of man in God's creation. The supplemental scenes of this second and

---

[1] See above, in the Introduction, pp. 21, 22.

more anthropomorphic picture are no more inconsistent with the statements of Gen. i, 26–31, than the eighth chapter of Daniel is inconsistent with the seventh.

2. Understanding the passage as an apocalyptic repetition and enlargement of Gen. i, 26–28, we should next attend to the correct translation of Gen. ii, 4–6. The first part of verse 4 is the author's heading of the section which ends with chap. iv, 26. Like all the other similar headings of the subsequent sections, it refers to what follows, not to what precedes.[1] As a title it should stand by itself, and the passage introductory to the account of the formation of man (verses 4–6) should be read thus :

These are the generations of the heavens and the earth when they were created.

> In the day of Jehovah God's making of earth and heavens,
> No plant of the field was yet in the earth,
> And no herb of the field was yet sprouting,
> For Jehovah God had not caused it to rain upon the earth;
> And there was no man to work the ground.
> And a mist was going up from the earth,
> And it watered the whole face of the ground.

In this poetic passage we evidently have a purely ideal conception. The imaginative element is even more conspicuous than in the previous chapter, and the successive statements fall quite naturally into the form of Hebrew parallelisms. The poetical author presents a peculiar ideal of the desolateness of the earth before the appearance of man. His waste and empty land is a prehuman chaos as compared with the precosmogonic chaos of chap. i, 2. He conceives all growths of nature and all lower orders of living things as somehow subordinate to man, and subservient to his needs. No plant or herb seems to have existence or significance for him except as it exists for man's sake. We do not understand the writer as intending to show that the creation of man preceded all growths of nature. Nor are we to suppose, from the order of state-

---

[1] Comp. v, 1; vi, 9; x, 1; xi, 10, 27; xxv, 12, 19; xxxvi, 1, 9; xxxvii, 2. This uniformity of usage sufficiently refutes the idea of some expositors that the heading of ii, 4, refers to what precedes rather than what follows. Some critics, however, think this heading has become displaced, having originally stood at the beginning of the first chapter; but this is a pure conjecture. If originally there we can see no conceivable reason for any one transferring it to its present position. The author's plan seems rather to have been, first, to portray creation as a sevenfold manifestation of God in the heavens and the earth, and thereafter to describe successive generations or evolutions of things thus organized. Hence the import of the phrase בְּהִבָּרְאָם, *when they were created;* that is, upon their being created. The cosmogony is presupposed, and the writer's next object is to depict the formation of man out of the dust of the earth and the breath of God.

ments in verses 7 and 8, that the preparation of the garden of Eden was subsequent to the formation of man. The chronological order of the events described should have no prominence in such a series of poetic pictures, but the different parts of the one great picture may best be seen when arranged in apocalyptic correspondency, as follows:

1. THE PRIMEVAL NATURAL CONDI-
TIONS (verses 4-6).

2. FORMATION OF MAN FROM DUST OF
THE GROUND AND THE BREATH
OF GOD, AND HIS LOCATION IN
THE GARDEN (7-15).

3. THE PRIMEVAL MORAL LAW (16, 17).

4. FORMATION OF WOMAN FROM THE
MAN AS HIS COUNTERPART AND
COMPANION (18-22).

5. THE TRUE PRIMEVAL MARRIAGE RE-
LATION (23-25).

These are the five great features of the picture, and their rela_tions are ideal rather than chronological. The planting and water-ing of the Edenic garden is as truly symbolical as the formation of the woman from the man's rib. The divine origin of man, created male and female, is no less a truth of revelation because symbol-ically portrayed; and the enlarged and varied picture of this second chapter adds very greatly to that of chap. i, 26–31. As the crowning feature of the six days' work was the concluding Sabbath rest, so the concluding feature of this second and supplemental revelation is the hallowed marriage covenant. The creation of man as male and female has its physical and moral conditions, its outer and inner aspects, suggestive of holy mysteries. Its consummation, in God's plan, is the uniting of the twain in one flesh, one heart, one blended life. This hallowed union is beautifully conceived in Ruth i, 9, and iii, 1, as a state of rest (מְנוּחָה and מָנוֹחַ). And the rabbins have a saying that the man is restless while he misses the rib that was taken out of his side; and the woman is also restless until she gets under the man's arm, whence she was taken. Man is thus seen to be incomplete without woman, and the marriage relation is the normal condition of human life. Monogamy is the true primeval law, written in the deepest intuitions of the heart (Mark x, 5–9), and the moral basis of hallowed family life. The woman appears in the picture as having been originally formed from the man, and so impliedly dependent upon him. He accordingly holds the nor-mal headship in the marriage covenant (1 Cor. xi, 3; 1 Tim. ii, 11, 12; 1 Peter iii, 1). But there is an ancient interpretation of the symbolism of the rib, which speaks on this wise : " The part of man of which the woman was formed was not taken from his head, as if she were to be a lord over him; nor from his feet, as if he might tread upon her; but from his side, to show that she was to be his companion and equal."

Both these chapters, therefore, and both sets of delineations are of the nature of an apocalypse. Their value is to be seen in their religious and ethical suggestions, not in supposed statements of historic or scientific facts. The highest and purest conception of the marriage relation is revealed in a symbolical picture. It is enhanced in our thought as an Edenic state of rest and happy companionship, confirmed by a moral law of monogamy, and typical of the mystic but real union that exists between Christ and his Church (Eph. v, 23–32 ; comp. Matt. xix, 4–8). Furthermore, as God's ideal *hexaemeron* of work is consummated in divine repose, so all earthly life and labor look to a like blessed issue. The whole creation yearns and travails for "the liberty of the glory of the children of God" (Rom. viii, 20–22), and "there remaineth a Sabbath rest for the people of God" (Heb. iv, 9). That will be the ultimate union of Christ and his bride—the Lamb's wife.

The statements about the trees of the garden, the tree of life, and the tree of the knowledge of good and evil are an important part of the symbolic picture. They serve in the most simple way to show that man was created with clear intimations of immortality and in the most positive conditions of moral responsibility. The great truth enunciated is that man was made a moral being, subject to the restraints and tests of moral law. We look in none of the details of the composite picture for mystic or recondite meanings. The rivers and gold and onyx of the garden are merely incidental drapery of an ideal scene, having no more separate significance in themselves than the minor details of the New Jerusalem in John's Apocalypse.

Perhaps the most remarkable statement in the whole chapter is that of verse 7 : "Jehovah God formed the man of the dust of the ground, and breathed into his nostrils the breath of life ; and the man became a living soul." Here the man is represented as a product of the heavens and the earth by the breath of God. But *how* the earth and the heavens united in the forming of the first man is left in mystery. The language is as well adapted to the concept of a long period of evolution as to that of an instantaneous creation.

The result of our study thus far is the conviction that in these opening chapters of Genesis we are not to look for historic narrative, nor contributions to natural science, but to recognize a symbolic apocalypse of God's relation to the world and to man. The great fundamental truths herein set forth have been apprehended by all bygone generations of readers, and are as apparent to the common reader as to the learned philosopher.

CHAPTER IV

EDENIC APOCALYPSE OF SIN AND JUDGMENT

THE third chapter of Genesis is closely connected with the second, so that in the plan of the compiler its contents are brought under the heading of the "generations of the heavens and the earth." It is the influence of dogmatic prepossessions that leads some to persist in treating this scripture as a prosaic history. "There is no other Eastern book in the world," says Farrar, "which we should have dreamed of understanding literally if it introduced speaking serpents and magic trees. Even the rabbis, stupidly literal as were their frequent methods, were perfectly aware that the story of the fall was a philosopheme—a vivid pictorial representation of the origin and growth of sin in the human heart. The inspired character of the narrative is to me evinced by the fact that all the literature of the world has failed to set forth for human warning any sketch of the course of temptation which is comparable in insight to this most ancient allegory. The effect of a prohibition in producing in man's free will a tendency to disobedience; the peril of tampering with temptation and lingering curiously in its vicinity ; the promptings of concupiscence, reinforced by the whisperings of doubt ; the genesis of sin, from the thought to the wish, from the wish to the purpose, from the purpose to the act, from the act to the repetition, to the habit, to the character, to the necessity, to the temptation of others ; the thrilling intensity of reaction in the sense of fear, shame, and of an innocence lost forever ; the certain and natural incidence of retribution; the beginning of a new life of sorrow and humiliation; the working of deathful consequence with all the inevitable certainty of a natural law—all this, and the awful truth that death is the wages of sin, and the fruit of sin, and that death *is* sin, has been set forth since then by all the loftiest literature of the world. Yet all the literature of the world, even when it speaks through the genius of a Dante and a Milton, has added and can add nothing essential to the primeval story of Genesis, which it can but illustrate and expand." [1]

1. The apocalyptic elements of the chapter appear most noticeably in the latter portion (verses 14–24), but the remarkable picture

---

[1] *The Bible: Its Meaning and Supremacy*, pp. 242, 243. New York, 1897.

of temptation and sin is presented in verses 1–8. It shows how sin entered into the world through disobedience of moral law, and is the result of a misuse of personal freedom. We behold in symbolic outline the development of the sense of guilt in human consciousness. The opened eye of the soul perceives the nakedness of the flesh, and there follows a speedy effort to conceal the shame. The threefold form of the temptation is profoundly comprehensive, and symbolizes all possible methods of Satanic assault. "The woman saw that the tree was good for food, and that it was a delight to the eyes, and to be desired to make one wise." These three appeals of temptation are addressed to what John calls "the lust of the flesh, and the lust of the eyes, and the pride of life" (1 John ii, 16), and it is notable that when our Lord, "the second Adam," was tempted of the devil his adversary employed the same threefold manner of assault.

2. The anthropomorphic concept of "Jehovah God walking in the garden in the cool of the day," and calling unto the man with the inquiry, "Where art thou?" suggests an idea of judgment common to all revelations of the coming of the Lord. He comes to bring to light the works of darkness, and we note how the searching words of the Judge reveal the sin and guilt of the transgressors, and contain the several sentences of divine judgment. Then, says the Targum of the Pseudo-Jonathan, "the Lord God brought the three of them into judgment." Verses 14–19 embody three prophetic oracles of condemnation, namely, (1) on the serpent (14, 15), (2) on the woman (16), and (3) the man (17–19). We should observe that the divine judgment bases itself on the evil desert of sin. The penal visitation must take place, not for the cause of expediency, nor for the good of the criminal, but because moral beings have transgressed and deserve retribution. And so, in all subsequent revelations, punishment comes because of evildoing. The secrets of all hearts must be revealed, and retribution is in proportion to moral desert.

3. The tempter is presented under the symbol of the serpent.[1]

---

[1] In this picture the serpent appears as one of the creatures of God, but "more subtile than any beast of the field which Jehovah God had made." In Amos ix, 3, allusion is made to the serpent that is in the bottom of the sea, and Psalm lxxiv, 13, speaks of breaking the heads of the dragons or monsters of the waters. As the serpent became the symbol of the evil one, so the mythological monsters of the sea and sky would naturally in time be conceived as archenemies of God and man. In Rev. xii, 3, 9, the "great red dragon" is identified with "that old serpent called the Devil and Satan, who deceives the whole world." Whence the apocalyptic writers derived these symbols, how far they appropriated them from current traditions, and how far they modified them to suit their own purposes, are questions which do not now admit of certain solution.

He appears as the father of lies (comp. John viii, 44), and is the first
of the three to receive the sentence of judgment. His accursed
future is to be connected with a terrible conflict in which he himself
is destined to be the greatest sufferer. Two lines of posterity are
referred to, the seed of the serpent and the seed of the woman. His
offspring are the ungodly of every generation. "He that doeth sin
is of the devil" (1 John iii, 8), and all such evildoers are characterized by Jesus as serpents and offspring of vipers (Matt. xxiii, 33).
The seed of the woman, on the other hand, are the long line of
godly souls that keep the commandments of God and struggle to
maintain the truth. Its fullest ideal, as brought out in later revelations, is the great company of whom Christ is head and chief.
They suffer with him, and with him also shall be glorified (Rom.
viii, 17). The final triumph of the woman's seed will not be won
without the bruise and pain of many a wound. The old serpent is
ever striking at the heel. His modes of attack are always stealthy
and despicable; but the godly seed are wont to strike boldly at the
head of the enemy, for they know the conflict to be a life-and-death
struggle. The end will not be finally consummated until the conquering seed shall have put all his enemies under his feet and abolished death (1 Cor. xv, 25, 26).

4. The sentence upon the woman foretells the pains and anxieties
of motherhood, and also woman's instinctive devotion and subjection to her husband. That upon the man announces for him a life
of toil, the sorrow of eating the herb of the field instead of the
fruits of paradise, and the doom of returning to the dust of the
ground. Thus "through one man sin entered into the world and
death through sin ; and so death passed unto all men, for that all
sinned" (Rom. v, 12). And thus we have another prophetic
phase of the woes that must attend the long conflict already
referred to.

5. It is worthy of notice that in each of the oracles of judgment
there is a fourfold curse. The serpent is (1) cursed above all cattle
and beasts; (2) he is to move prostrate and eat dust; (3) he is to
suffer the continual enmity of the woman's seed, and (4) ultimately
be crushed beneath his conquering heel. The woman is destined to
suffer (1) the pains of conception, (2) the labor of childbirth, (3) the
yearning for a husband, and (4) subjection to the man's authority.
The curse of the man is (1) sorrowful eating of herbs, (2) the plague
of thorns and thistles, (3) the sweat and toil for food, and (4) returning to the dust. So in other analogous scriptures it will be seen
that apocalyptic judgments move in fourfold strokes, or phases.
Witness the four plagues of locusts in Joel (i, 4), the four horns,

the four smiths, and four chariots of Zechariah's visions (Zech. i, 18, 20; vi, 1).

6. The naming of the woman (verse 20) has a logical connection with the promise touching her seed (verse 15). While the name *woman*, already given (Gen. ii, 23), was significant of her origin from man, the name *Eve* (Hebrew *Hawwah*) means life, life-spring, or quickener of life, and may be regarded as a symbolical name, suggestive of the hopeful destiny of the race as then foreshadowed. This giving of a new name immediately after the sentences of sorrow and death suggests a living world to come. It need not be regarded as farfetched or fanciful to adduce here the analogy of the sealing of God's servants on their foreheads in the apocalypse of John (Rev. vii, 3). The name there written was the name of God and of the Lamb (Rev. xiv, 1; xxii, 4): "my new name" (Rev. iii, 12). And as, in the visions of John, the sealing of a new name on the foreheads of the elect Israel was followed by the sight of "a great multitude, clothed with white robes," so this naming of Eve is followed by the clothing of "Adam and his wife" with garments made by God. But without laying stress on the analogy with the vision of John we may see a symbolical significance in the clothing divinely prepared for these prisoners of hope. As an impressive object lesson it is adapted to illustrate the divine provision of redemption to cover human guilt and shame. Certainly the whole picture, as here presented to our thought, is to be understood as the symbolism of apocalyptics rather than the record of actual history.

7. Verses 22–24 are a vivid representation of the purpose and execution of divine judgment. First, there is a council in heaven, as if between Jehovah and his holy ones (comp. Gen. i, 26). No events occur on earth which have not been previously the subject of divine counsel. Similarly, in the Book of Job, we have first the scene in the presence of Jehovah and the sons of God, where Jehovah's pleasure and purposes touching his servant Job are determined before any assault of Satan is permitted to take place (Job i, 6–12; ii, 1–6). The judgment in respect to the first transgressors is that they must not continue at the tree of life. The broken law had said, "Thou shalt surely die," but the woman has already received the new name Eve, and her seed is destined to bruise Satan under his feet (Rom. xvi, 20). The great conflict between the serpent's and the woman's seed cannot be fought out in the garden of Eden, nor in conditions of immediate command of the tree of life. The rapidity with which the judgment is executed is intensified in our thought by the striking *aposiopesis* at the close of verse 22. The sentence is left unfinished, and the act of expulsion from the

garden is immediately recorded. This speedy execution of divine judgment is in keeping with all subsequent apocalypses of impending woes. When a prophet declares, as a divine revelation, that the day of Jehovah is near, or that he cometh quickly, we may be sure that his word is no delusion. The language of such oracles is treated with violence when expounded as consistent with centuries of delay. Such perversion of most explicit declarations of immediate judgment partakes too much of the serpent's comment, "Ye shall not surely die."

8. This Edenic apocalypse concludes with the placing at the east of the garden, toward the sunrise, two symbolic figures, cherubim and flaming sword (verse 24). As Moses lifted up the brazen serpent in the sight of the penitent Israelites, so were these signs "caused to dwell" (הִשְׁכִּין) in the vision of fallen man, and to "guard the way of the tree of life." How much such a vision may have signified when first seen or recorded we cannot tell, but with the fullness of New Testament revelation it has rich suggestions. A flame of fire in the shape of a sword is an appropriate symbol of divine justice, such justice and judgment as demanded the expulsion from the garden of Eden. At the gate of paradise it proclaims that he who promises a future triumph over Satan must himself be just. The redemption of man must be accomplished in perfect harmony with the righteousness of God. The cherubim, on the other hand, would seem most naturally to symbolize another thought. Here they are simply mentioned, as if well known. They are described in the visions of Ezekiel (chap. i) as living creatures, combining in complex form the four highest types of animal life, namely, man, lion, ox, and eagle. Over their heads the prophet saw enthroned "the appearance of the likeness of the glory of Jehovah" (Ezek. i, 26, 28). In Rev. iv, 6–8, they also appear as living creatures at the throne of God. In the Mosaic tabernacle two cherubim of gold were placed in the holy of holies, one at each end of the mercy seat, with their faces toward each other (Exod. xxv, 18, 20). Hence Jehovah is often spoken of as dwelling with cherubim (1 Sam. iv, 4; 2 Sam. vi, 2; Psalm lxxx, 1; xcix, 1; Isa. xxxvii, 16). In a vision of Isaiah the seraphim appear as holding in the heavenly temple the same relation to the divine glory which the cherubim held in the Mosaic tabernacle (Isa. vi, 1–3). In all these scriptures they are to be understood as symbols, not as real creatures or personal beings. They always appear in most intimate relation to God, and filled with intensity of life.

As now the fiery sword represents the righteous judgment of God, the cherubim may best be regarded as symbols of the love which secures eternal life and heavenly glory through the mystery of redemption in Christ. They image forth an incarnation of divine life in creature form, by means of which all that was lost in Eden might be restored to heavenly places. Fallen man, redeemed and filled with the Holy Spirit, shall again have power to come to the tree of life which is in the paradise of God (Rev. ii, 7; xxii, 14). It is significant that these impressive symbols were set to guard the passage to the tree of life.[1] That "way" was not to be closed up forever (comp. John xiv, 4, 6). It was and is guarded both by justice and love, and shall be during all the conflict between the serpent's and the woman's seed, and until "there shall be no more curse" (Rev. xxii, 3). Then the redeemed of Adam's race, having washed their robes, shall obtain "authority over the tree of life," and shall "enter through the gates into the city" (Rev. xxii, 14). Thus the New Testament vision of new heavens, new earth, and new Jerusalem is but a fuller apocalypse of what was foreshadowed by this ancient revelation. The whole earth is to become a blessed Eden (comp. Micah iv, 1-5), and the holy city out of heaven is, like the Edenic garden, to be a holy of holies, into which all who have "washed their robes and made them white in the blood of the Lamb" (Rev. vii, 14) shall freely enter. Then, in highest reality, God's tabernacle shall be with men, and he will dwell with them, and wipe away every tear, and death shall be no more (Rev. xxi, 3, 4).

It is to be observed that, in the apocalypse of the heavenly Jerusalem, no cherubim appear about the throne of God and of the Lamb. In their places, beholding the face of God and having his name on their foreheads, are the multitude in white robes (Rev. xxii, 3, 4; comp. Rev. vii, 9-17). From them the curse of sin has been removed, and, radiant in eternal life, they are the reality of what the Edenic cherubim are but symbols.

---

[1] The reader may be interested in the following note of Dillmann on the cherubim : "The cherubim cannot be used as a proof that the Paradise legend was borrowed from the Babylonians. It is still very doubtful whether the winged bulls with men's heads, which, among the Babylonians and Assyrians, like the sphinxes of the Egyptians, guard the approaches to the temples and palaces, bore the name *Kirubi*, in addition to their usual names. But the old Hebrew conception of the cherubim, as it expresses itself in Psalm xviii, 10, cannot have been taken from these colossal bulls, or else in the old Babylonian time bulls must have been capable of flying. The cherubim, considered only as keepers of Paradise, by their connection with the sword of flame, clearly betray their origin as a representation of the clouds of the thunderstorm. . . . The cherubim, elsewhere the bearers and attendants of descending Deity, have here the function of being guardians of the unapproachable dwelling of God, and of the divine blessings and treasures ; and the garden is characterized as a real dwelling-place of God just by the fact that the cherubim guard it."—Commentary on Genesis, *in loco*, English translation by Stevenson. Edinb., 1897.

We have ventured thus to anticipate the light of New Testament revelations in order to enhance the significance of the apocalyptic elements in the early chapters of Genesis. It is true that we thus read into the ancient records ideas of a later age, but it is like all other cases where the light of the Gospel revelation enables us to see a profound suggestiveness in the events, the types, and the symbols of the Hebrew Scriptures. So, too, the coming of Christ, and that alone, has made manifest the deep, full import of many Messianic prophecies. The Edenic apocalypse is clearly seen to set forth an age-long conflict in the moral world, and to foreshadow what the end shall be. Other and later revelations show many details and crises of this wonderful conflict, but this ancient oracle contains the germ and substance of them all. It is a most remarkable revelation to stand at the beginning of the Holy Scriptures, and it is well for us, at this early stage of our apocalyptic studies, to point out the fact that the last prophetic book of the canon makes conspicuous use of the symbols and suggestions of the first three chapters of Genesis, and seems divinely adapted to stand as its final counterpart.

CHAPTER V

APOCALYPSE OF THE ANTEDILUVIAN WORLD

THE fourth and fifth chapters of Genesis offset and supplement each other as a twofold revelation of the earliest developments of human society. We have here, as I conceive, not a realistic history, but a pictorial representation of human society in prehistoric times. The double picture seen in the two parallel genealogies accords with the habit of duplicate symbolism so common in apocalyptic revelations. The two lists of names serve to connect Adam and Noah, and show the two types of human life which developed in varying degrees: the pious worshiper on the one side, and the sensual and grasping worldling on the other. These two chapters, following directly after the announcements of chap. iii, 15, 16, set forth the fulfillment of those oracles in the earliest exhibitions of the conflict between the seed of the serpent and that of the woman. "Cain was of the evil one, and slew his brother" (1 John iii, 12). In his punishment we have a signal illustration of penal retribution working itself out by divine law in the guilty soul and in his posterity. Cain propagates a type of human life which runs altogether to violence, worldliness, and lust. But in the line of Seth, conceived as divinely appointed to take the place of Abel, whom Cain slew (iv, 25), we see men calling on the name of Jehovah, and then the generations of Adam are outlined through long rounds of years, until they, too, become so mixed with the prevailing wickedness of the world that the sacred writer sees in the universal depravity the sons of God prostituting themselves to all extremes of lust and violence. The contents of chap. iv, 1–vi, 8, may be set forth under the following heads:

1. The story of Cain and Abel, iv, 1–8.
2. The punishment of Cain, iv, 9–15.
3. Cainite development and power, iv, 16–24.
4. Seth in place of Abel, iv, 25, 26.
5. Generations of Adam through Seth, v, 1–32.
6. Prostitution and wickedness of the sons of God, vi, 1–8.

In these several parts of the chapters we observe among many lessons the following:

1. *The story of Cain and Abel* (iv, 1–8), while notably true to well-known facts of human experience, and so faithful a picture

that it may well be taken as a literal narrative of fact, is nevertheless best explained as allegorical, and as designed to unfold a faithful picture of the manifold workings of human hearts in relation to one another and toward God. For we observe :

(1) The names are symbolically suggestive of two different ideals of human life. The first glad mother is represented as going into a rapture of pride over her firstborn son. She gives him a name significant of *acquirement of power*, as if he were indeed a son of Jehovah. But when she bears his brother she gives him a name that seems to be synonymous with *vanity*. This human tendency to magnify and extol what is external and worldly, or what ministers to human pride, appeared in Israel when they gloried in Saul, and, not sufficiently estimating noble qualities of heart, saw in him an ideal king. Cain seems to have been the strong as compared with Abel the weak.

(2) Here we note two of the earliest forms of human employment, husbandry and keeping of small cattle. Cain, the firstborn, derives his sustenance from the fruit of the ground, the most primitive form of natural self-support. The first families of men were not savages, nor, from the nature of things, could they be what we now understand as civilized. Rustic simplicity would soon be supplemented by such appropriation of the lower animals as would meet new wants and enlarged experience. But the incidents of diverse employments and tastes furnish many occasions of jealous rivalry.

(3) The offerings which Cain and Abel make to Jehovah are a most interesting illustration of the religious element in all men. Whatever their pursuits or tastes, they recognize a power above them, and seek to obtain his favor. Thus in these acts of the first sons of Adam we see an apocalypse of the origin of religion. The religious instinct is an intuition of God, and is an essential element of the rational and moral constitution. It manifests itself in a feeling after God by offerings, by sacrifices, by pilgrimages to supposed holy places, and by prayer.

(4) The approval or disapproval of God depends on the disposition of the worshiper's heart. This early revelation embodies this one essential and fundamental truth of all religion : "If thou doest well, thou shalt be accepted; if thou doest not well, sin coucheth at the door." It also embodies in a most vivid picture the truth of Prov. xv, 8 : "The sacrifice of the wicked is an abomination to the Lord: but the prayer of the upright is his delight."

(5) This last named fact is also an illustration of the manner in which God speaks to every man, and shows "the work of the law written in their hearts, their conscience bearing witness therewith,

and their thoughts one with another accusing or else excusing" (Rom. ii, 15).

(6) It is also worthy of note that, in this earliest revelation of the development of sin in a perverse heart, we are shown so clearly its damning elements. The obvious disparity of two lives, the one evil and the other good, begets a feeling of jealousy, which readily grows into envy and hatred. Then no appeals of God or conscience restrain. The perverse will breaks down the power of all good motives, deliberately chooses evil, and proceeds to darkest crimes. In this picture the apostle saw how "the children of God are manifest, and the children of the devil. . . . Cain was of the evil one, and slew his brother. And wherefore slew he him? Because his works were evil, and his brother's righteous" (1 John iii, 10, 12).

(7) The fratricide itself was but the natural outcome of such hatred in the heart. "Every one that hateth his brother is a murderer" (1 John iii, 15). One of the most impressive lessons of this scripture is the revelation of the human heart in its fearful possibilities of evil. It shows how a child of man can make himself a child of the devil (John viii, 44).

(8) The piety of Abel, on the other hand, is passed over with few words. The one great fact of his glory was that Jehovah had respect unto him and his offering. He did well, and sin did not couch at his door. And so it is written, as one of the imperishable lessons: "By faith Abel offered unto God a more excellent sacrifice than Cain, through which he had witness borne to him that he was righteous, God bearing witness in respect of his gifts; and through it he being dead yet speaketh" (Heb. xi, 4).

2. *The punishment of Cain,* as depicted in Gen. iv, 9–15, is a graphic delineation of the sure consequences of personal wickedness and guilt. God's judgment of him, as with Adam, begins with the searching question, WHERE? (comp. iv, 9, and iii, 9.) Cain's denial, "I know not," shows how easily the murderer plays the liar, and how naturally these two sins go together (comp. John viii, 44). To this is added the question of bold and impudent defiance, "Am I my brother's keeper?" But vain are lies and boldness of heart before the all-seeing God. Jehovah hears the drops of Abel's blood[1] crying out like so many imploring tongues for vengeance on the heartless murderer, and he pronounces on him the twofold curse, (1) that he shall no longer prosper in cultivating the ground that has received his brother's blood, and (2) that he shall become a fugitive and a wanderer in the earth.

---

[1] The Hebrew word for *blood* in Gen. iv, 10, is in the plural, suggestive of streams or drops of blood, each one of which has an imploring voice.

In his own heart and conscience the murderer feels the burden of a fourfold penalty: (1) An unbearable sense of guilt and shame; (2) separation from God; (3) exclusion from the confidence and fellowship of men; (4) a horrible fear of retribution from his fellow-men, all of whom may justly feel themselves avengers of the blood of Abel. The mark or sign which Jehovah appointed for Cain, while saving him from the violence of men, was nevertheless a most suggestive declaration that the way of the criminal is hard. The brand of God's wrath is on him. And so this apocalypse of crime proclaims that vengeance belongeth unto Jehovah, and he will recompense (Deut. xxxii, 35; Psalm xciv, 1; Rom. xii, 19; Heb. x, 30). The guilty soul forever bears its penal mark of self-condemnation—"a certain fearful expectation of judgment."

3. *The Cainite development*, symbolized in Gen. iv, 16–24, is a brief but suggestive scripture. Cain " goes out from the presence of Jehovah," like a bold adventurer, determined if necessary to work his way without God in the world. He dwells in the land of *Nod*, a symbolic name, meaning *wandering*, and having obvious allusion to the language used in verse 12. He goes out to abide in the land of the exile to which the judgment of heaven has appointed him. This new residence is "on the east of Eden," or rather in front of Eden; that is, over against that original abode of innocence and love. We should compare the picture of Ishmael, who was destined to be "a wild ass among men, his hand against every man, and every man's hand against him," and his dwelling *over against*, or *in front of*, all his brethren (Gen. xvi, 12).

In this land, the opposite of Eden, he becomes the father of a mighty race. Six names are given, including his own, ending with Lamech, who has two wives and begets three sons, who in turn become the *fathers* or founders of new arts and enterprises. The land no longer yielding her strength unto him, as decreed in verse 12, he builds a city and names it after one of his sons. The names of Jabal, Jubal, and Tubal-cain (representatives respectively of nomad life, inventions of musical instruments, and the forging of implements of brass and iron), point to the gradual development of the arts and improvements of civilization. The bigamy of Lamech suggests the sensual demoralization that usually keeps pace with the luxuries of worldliness, and his song to Adah and Zillah (verses 23 and 24) is probably best understood as an impious exultation over feats of strength which became possible after the invention of weapons of iron. He boasts that he can now avenge his own wrongs ten times more completely than Jehovah purposed to avenge the slaying of Cain.

In all this we have a picture of the earliest outgrowth of human ambition and pride. The city life as opposed to that which is more simple and primitive has its accompanying temptations and refinements of fleshly luxury and vice; and arts and inventions may be made to serve the purposes of worldly lusts, of cruel vengeance, and of savage brutality.

4. Gen. iv, 25, 26, is no part of the Cainite genealogy, but a new departure from iv, 1, 2, 8, and is designed to show the divine appointment of *Seth in place of Abel,* whom Cain slew. These two verses serve also to conclude the writer's ideal of the generations of the heavens and the earth (chap. ii, 4), and to make a transition to the series of generations of Adam, which follows in the next chapter. This first series of generations furnishes impressive revelations of the genesis and development of sin in the race of Adam, but also shows, by this conclusion, that in the midst of prevailing wickedness an elect and righteous seed was raised up to propagate religious worship, and begin, as it were, a new departure in the progress of humanity.

5. *The generations of Adam through Seth* are rapidly outlined in chap. v, and serve to connect Adam and Noah. Ten names appear in the genealogy, a stereotyped form of statement is maintained throughout, and the numbers are so extravagant when understood of the years of individual life that one may readily suppose them to be symbolical and indicative of the lifetime of clans or families rather than of individuals. Taking the entire chapter as an apocalyptic picture of the continuous but passing and disappearing generations of mankind, we find that each name has four things affirmed, in constant repetition, like so many lines of a monotonous rhythm. Thus, for example:

> Seth lived 105 years, and begat Enosh;
> And Seth lived after he begat Enosh 807 years, and begat sons and daughters;
> And all the days of Seth were 912 years;
> —And he died.

This is an impressive method of declaring the great fact, enunciated in simple form in Eccles. i, 4:

> Generation goeth, and generation cometh,
> And the earth forever standeth.

Both these forms of statement set forth the same great fact of human history, but the one is apocalyptic and pictorial, making use of symbolical names and numbers, while the other is more general and epigrammatic. In the long prehistoric ages of human development the same continuous repetition of births, family growths, and the invariable sequence of death terminating the variable experiences of life, were as certain as the rising of the sun and the going down of the same.

The exceptional statement concerning Enoch, "the seventh from Adam" (Jude 14), that he "walked with God, and was not, for God took him" (verse 24), arrests attention. The Septuagint translators, followed by the writer of Heb. xi, 5, say: "He was not found, because God translated him." This the New Testament writer and all subsequent readers have understood to mean that he "was translated so as not to see death." The passage thus portrays the hallowed godly life which issues in immortality, and is but another way of expressing the lofty thought of John xi, 36: "Every one who lives and believes in me shall never die." Such lives of exalted fellowship with God were lived, according to this scripture, in the ancient prehistoric times. The number of "all the days of Enoch," three hundred and sixty-five, is symbolic of an ideal cycle of perfect human life, a full year of years; and men who attained such perfection of fellowship with the Elohim are apocalyptically styled sons of the Elohim (comp. Gen. vi, 2).

In comparing the names of the two genealogies as given in Gen. iv, 16–18, and v, 12–31, we observe the close similarity between Cain and Kenan, Irad and Jared, Mehujael and Mahalalel, Methushael and Methuselah, while the names Enoch and Lamech are identical in the two lists. The names in the Sethite line, so far as they differ from the corresponding ones in Cain's line, have been thought to be varied on purpose to convey some loftier or better ideal. Thus Mehujael means "smitten of God," while Mahalalel means "praise of God." But this view does not seem to hold good with all the varying names. It is worthy of note, however, that Cain means the "begotten" or acquired one, and Seth the "appointed" one. Thus the head of the one line is conceived as of the flesh and earthy, while the other is chosen and appointed of God (comp. Gal. iv, 23). Cain's son Enoch is associated with the building of a city, but Seth's son Enosh, the seventh from Adam, walks with God. The Lamech of Cain's line is synonymous with polygamy and violence; the Lamech of Seth's line begets the famous child of consolation and comfort (v, 29):

> From our work and from the toil of our hands,
> From the ground which Jehovah cursed.

6. *The prostitution of the sons of God*, and consequent increased wickedness of man on the earth, completes the picture of "the book of generations of Adam." For Gen. vi, 1–8, is the conclusion of

this second series of generations (namely, Gen. v, 1–vi, 8) as the birth and appointment of Seth in chap. iv, 25, 26, is the conclusion of the section headed, "These are the generations of the heavens and the earth" (ii, 4). The passage also serves as a preparation for the story of the flood and a transition to the "generations of Noah" (vi, 9). It is not a realistic history, but a poetical picture. The compiler of Genesis seems to have appropriated a current legend of the early world, and converted it into a symbol of enormous depravity. Man, created in the image of God, and having attained in examples like Enoch the fellowship and fruition of God, prostitutes his godlike powers and capabilities to the lusts of the flesh. How enormous the wickedness when such "sons of the Elohim" (vi, 2; comp. v, 22, 24), capable of walking with God and having God *take* them, sought no more to please God, but looked with groveling lust on the fair daughters of men, and "took them wives of all that they chose." Thus it came to pass that "every imagination of the thoughts of man's heart was only evil continually" (vi, 5).

This picture of excessive wickedness calls for an expression of divine judgment, and such a declaration of judgment is given in the style of apocalyptic portraiture. Jehovah is conceived as looking down on the corrupted world of men, and grieved at heart to see that all their thoughts and projects are continually evil. He utters his purpose of wrath, in verses 3 and 7, in a manner that suggests the presence of a heavenly council, as in chaps. i, 26, and iii, 22. His fury is such that he decrees to wipe out man and beast and creeping thing and fowl from off the face of the ground. All this belongs, obviously, to the bold imagery of apocalyptics and poetry, not to the literature of prosaic history. The entire passage is a highly wrought picture of the intensity of divine indignation against a world sunken into gross wickedness. Its doctrine of divine justice is no different from that revealed in the expulsion of man from the garden of Eden, but it is set forth in a style peculiarly its own.

CHAPTER VI

APOCALYPSE OF NOAH AND THE FLOOD

THE deluge which occurred in the days of Noah is presented in Genesis as the first great world-judgment upon mankind. Throughout the biblical narrative Noah appears as the great central figure to whom God reveals his purpose to punish the wickedness of men, and to rescue from the overwhelming flood the righteous man who alone found favor in his sight. Traditions of a similar terrible catastrophe are found among all the ancient historic nations, and may well be regarded as originating in an actual event, which occurred in the very early history of the race, before the wide dispersion of families and tribes, and which made an indelible impression in the imagination and memory of men. The various traditions have many things in common, and also many and great differences. The biblical narrative of Gen. vi, 9–ix, 29, appears to have been compiled from two different sources, with, perhaps, some additions (for example, ix, 20–27) from a third distinct tradition. The purpose of the compiler is not to preserve and perpetuate a history of the flood, but to set forth its conspicuous religious lessons of terrible judgment on the wicked, and marvelous grace and salvation for the righteous. Viewed in this light it discloses numerous elements of an apocalyptic character. Its repetitions of statement serve the purpose of all apocalyptic duplication, namely, to show that "the thing is established of God, and God will speedily bring it to pass" (Gen. xli, 32). The writer is not careful to harmonize or reconcile his different sources, but weaves them together so as to produce a composite picture suitable for his purpose. His detailed numbers, dates, and minor incidents are in some parts as prosaic as those of the last nine chapters of Ezekiel, but, taken all together as one piece, they are as truly apocalyptical as are the tedious details of Ezekiel's ideal temple and land.

The apocalyptic elements in Gen. vi, 9–ix, 29, and the truths therein set forth for our instruction in righteousness and in God's purposes, both of judgment and of grace, are mainly the following:

1. The first four verses of the section (Gen. vi, 9–12) are in substance a repetition of what has gone before, and may be read in the preceding section. This prepares the way for God's revelation of his purpose of grace to Noah and his family, and for the description

of the ark of his salvation from the coming flood. This righteous man and his household represent a small "remnant according to the election of grace," which is to be rescued from a perishing world. The ark itself thus becomes a symbol of the salvation of God. Comp. 1 Peter iii, 20 ; Heb. xi, 7.

2. Jehovah's word to Noah in vii, 1–4, varies in some points from that of vi, 18–21. He is commanded in the one place to take of the clean beasts by sevens, and beasts that are not clean by twos ; but the order of vi, 20, is to take "two of every sort." From the apocalyptic point of view, however, there is no need of supposing discrepancy or contradiction or an oversight of the writer of Genesis. However discrepant the original documents may have appeared in their independence and separateness, the compiler of our book presents the one as a later revelation than the other, and coming to Noah only seven days before his entrance into the ark. Whether consciously or unconsciously, he has incorporated both statements after the manner of apocalyptic repetition. So Daniel sees in one vision a beast with ten horns, out of which comes a little horn (Dan. vii, 7, 8). A later vision reveals the little horn as coming out of four horns (viii, 8, 9). There is no essential inconsistency. The later vision supplies additional features as seen from another point of view. So our author evidently designed to present the oracle of vii, 1–4, as a later word to Noah, given after the ark had been completed, and shortly before the terrible catastrophe of judgment was about to break upon the earth.

3. The judgment of the flood marked the end or consummation of an age, and is a notable type of every similar crisis in human affairs which the prophets are wont to call "the great and terrible day of the Lord." Such crises break in sudden horror on a perverse and unbelieving generation (comp. Matt. xxiv, 38, 39). "The world that then was, being overflowed with water, perished ; but the heavens that now are, and the earth, by the same word have been stored up for fire, being reserved against the day of judgment and destruction of ungodly men" (2 Peter iii, 6, 7).

4. That great world-judgment was not only the signal end of an old world, but it also ushered in a new era in the history of man. The family of Noah, the eight elect souls, who were delivered by the gracious interposition of God (comp. 1 Peter iii, 20 ; 2 Peter ii, 5; Heb. xi, 7), were a chosen remnant destined to open a new age, receive new commandments, and enter into covenant relations with God. In all these facts we recognize a type of the consummation of another and more historic age, when a wicked and adulterous generation were visited with overwhelming judgment, and

their city and sanctuary were destroyed as with a flood (Matt. xxiv, 15-22; comp. Dan. ix, 26, 27). That unparalleled catastrophe of woe also marked the end of one age and the beginning of another, in which the "remnant according to the election of grace," who recognized in Jesus Christ their Prince and Saviour, went forth in all the world to establish his kingdom of righteousness.

5. When Noah and his family went forth out of the ark he publicly recognized the divine mercy, builded an altar unto Jehovah, and offered appropriate sacrifices thereon. Jehovah was delighted with this new beginning (viii, 21, 22), and declared that he would no more curse the ground because of man. He gave assurance of the perpetuity of "seedtime and harvest, and the cold and heat, and summer and winter, and day and night." All this suggests the dawn of a new creation, and the new commandment, which is written in Gen. ix, 1-7, reminds us of that which was given in the apocalypse of the first creation (Gen. i, 28-31). Man is again to "multiply and fill the earth;" all things are put in subjection under him, and flesh as well as the green herb is given him for food. But he is solemnly charged to abstain from eating blood, which is the symbol of life, and is admonished that man was made in God's image, and whoso sheds human blood forfeits his own life. All these things present ideals of a new era in the world's history, a higher civilization, a more sacred regard for human life, and a fuller recognition of God's image in man.

6. Immediately after the new commandment there follows (Gen. ix, 8-17) the oracle of a new covenant, the sign and seal of which is the "bow in the cloud." The Edenic apocalypse had for its signs the cherubim and the flaming sword; the Noachic covenant has the significant symbol of the rainbow. This latter appears again and again in subsequent revelations, and is always suggestive of the gracious covenant made with all living things that survived the deluge. Noah and his family, in blessed covenant with God, with their eyes turned to that symbolic sign of grace, going forth hopefully to replenish the earth and fill it with a better people than before, prefigure the hopeful beginning of every new era in the developing history of humanity. And so, after the overthrow of many barbaric systems of world-power, and when the old covenant of Sinai was waxing aged and ready to vanish away (Heb. viii, 13), the seer of Patmos saw heaven opened, and a rainbow round about the throne of God (Rev. iv, 1, 3).

7. The cheerful token of the rainbow inspires hope, but does not insure against the perverse tendencies of human nature, nor save all saints from falling into shame. Even the coming of Christ, the

glad proclamation of salvation for men, and the glorious visions of the enthroned Lamb and the New Jerusalem have been followed by lamentable wickedness. We are not to wonder, therefore, that many evils appeared after the flood, even in the family of Noah. The drunkenness of the patriarch and the sensual levity of his sons are plainly pictured before us, and have their lessons of admonition for all time. Whatever amount of historic fact Gen. ix, 20–27, contains, the passage as it comes to us is a poetic oracle. After Noah recovered from the effect of his wine, and knew the acts of his sons, he was seized with the spirit of prophecy, and said :

> Cursed be Canaan !
> A slave of slaves shall he be to his brothers.
> Blessed be Jehovah, God of Shem,
> And unto him let Canaan be a slave.
> Let God spread Japheth far abroad,
> But let him dwell within the tents of Shem,
> And unto him let Canaan be a slave.

We recognize in this blessing of Shem a Messianic oracle. It is God who is to dwell in the tents of Shem, and the word is fulfilled in the fellowship and communion of Jehovah with the posterity of this son of Noah, from whom sprang Abraham, and Israel, and Judah, and David, and the Christ.

CHAPTER VII

APOCALYPSE OF THE DISPERSION OF NATIONS

THE genealogies and statements of Gen. x, 1–xi, 26, stand in noticeable correlation with those of Gen. iv, 16–v, 32, and serve both to show how the nations were divided and scattered abroad in the earth after the flood, and to connect Noah through Shem with Abraham. The compiler of Genesis seems in this section to cross the border line between historic and prehistoric ages. But whatever the accuracy or inaccuracy of the several ethnographical statements, the great purpose of this scripture is not to give instruction in details of history or science, but to convey a vivid picture of the formation, development, and dispersion of the families and races of mankind. In this respect the picture can be shown to be faithful and true.

It is not essential for instruction in righteousness that every detail of these ancient records be proven to be accurate. A great picture, viewed in its entirety and in the light of its purpose, might be inexact in some of its minor parts, but impressively truthful as a whole. So important truths may be conveyed by means of the symbolism of archaic genealogies as well as by the symbolism of dreams and visions of the night.

The section headed " generations of the sons of Noah " (x, 1–xi, 9) is composed of two distinct documents. The first is a genealogy or table of nations and countries (x, 1–32); the second is an account of the dispersion of men and its causes (xi, 1–9).

1. The first is a comprehensive and valuable outline of a threefold multiplication of mankind after the flood. It has reference to their *families*, their *languages*, their *lands*, and their *nations*, and accordingly names of tribes, tribe-fathers, cities, provinces, and nations are mixed together, so that in some cases it is impossible to say whether the given name be that of an individual, a land, or a nation. Some critics find traces of at least three different sources in this list of nations and countries. The apocalyptic and religious purpose of the table of nations is not affected by such questions of minute criticism. The compiler doubtless made up this table as he did other portions of his work, from a variety of material at his command. His one great purpose is to write a telling word-picture of the origin and multiplication of families, languages, and nations

as they spread themselves abroad over the face of the earth, and took possession of the various lands they occupied and to which they gave their several names. Whatever inaccuracies of detail or of minor statement the table may contain (we know not that any have been proven), it furnishes a faithful picture of the origin and spread of nations in the earth. It is a curious fact that almost everyone who attempts to tell us a tradition of his ancestral history is wont to carry his story back to three brothers.

2. The second part of this section (xi, 1–9) is another picture of the same great facts, drawn from another point of view, and having the nature and purpose of apocalyptic repetition. The fact, alluded to in the previous chapter, that the different families and nations of men made use of different *tongues* or languages (x, 5, 20, 31) as well as occupied different lands, calls for additional notice, and is here conceived both as a judgment and a means of scattering the children of men abroad upon the face of all the earth. The diversity of human tongues is accordingly to be thought of both as a cause and as a result of the dispersion of mankind into widely separated families and countries. In itself it may well be regarded as a misfortune, and in the conception of biblical writers it is much more than a misfortune (comp. Deut. xxviii, 49 ; Psalm cxiv, 1 ; Isa. xxxiii, 19; Jer. v, 15; Ezek. iii, 5).

(1) That we have In Gen. xi, 1–9, an imaginative picture, not a record of historic fact, is apparent (1) in the dramatic style of description, (2) in the remarkable anthropomorphism of its conception of Jehovah, and (3) in the apocalyptic council implied in the language of verse 7 (comp. Gen. i, 26 ; iii, 22).

(2) The judgment depicted is a formal condemnation of the use of human speech (which is the outward expression of " every imagination of the thoughts of the heart; " comp. chap. vi, 5), as a means of carrying on projects of worldly ambition and pride. The building of the city and the tower " whose top may reach unto heaven " is a picture of the same defiant spirit which appears in the words of the " day star, son of the morning," who says in his heart, " I will ascend into heaven ; I will exalt my throne above the stars of God; I will ascend above the heights of the clouds; I will be like the Most High " (Isa. xiv, 12–14). Whatever the origin and real facts about the story of the tower of Babel, the biblical writer appropriated it as the symbol of heaven-aspiring ambition in the form of great combinations to further worldly schemes of power. All the great world empires, which had their basis " in the land of Shinar " (Assyria, Babylon, Persia) are to some extent figured in this city and tower which were to have reached unto heaven. The

universal monarchy of a human chieftain was the vain dream of all
the great oriental world-rulers, and what better was it than the fancy
that all families and nations of men can be fashioned into one form
of thought and expression by political plans which human language
can propound?

(3) As a result of the diversity of language men are scattered
abroad over all the world, and kept apart in their various lands and
nationalities. The language of a people is a mighty factor of their
civilization and culture and an index of their national character.
Schlegel has called language "the general, all-embracing art of
man." When this is employed to build up vain schemes of human
ambition it will be made to defeat itself and scatter what it would
fain unite. But when it is made to serve the purpose of glorifying
God, and, in Messianic idealism, all peoples, nations, and languages
unite to serve the Christ of God (comp. Dan. vii, 14), then the
curse of Babel shall be changed into the blessing of Pentecost
(comp. Acts ii, 6). And so the great purpose and real lessons of
Gen. xi, 1–9, are religious, not historical or scientific.

The short section entitled "the generations of Shem" (Gen. xi,
10–26), stands in the same relation to the preceding section as does
"the book of the generations of Adam," in Gen. v, 1–32, to that
which preceded it, and ended with the story of Cain, and his city
building and other enterprises over against the garden of Eden.
Thus we are shown how human plans of worldliness and pride
repeat themselves again and again in the course of ages. But
God's purpose of election and redemption also shows itself again
and again in the same ages. While the worldly spirit seeks to
make itself a *name* (שם, xi, 4), and is defeated by the judgment
of heaven, God plans to make for himself and those who love and
serve him a name that will outlast the cities and empires of the
world. He chooses Shem, whose name (שם) in this connection
seems peculiarly significant and suggestive, and we are shown how
he purposes to dwell in the tents of this son of Noah (comp. Gen.
ix, 27), and secure a righteous seed upon the earth in whom all the
families and nations shall be blessed. So Shem's line is traced to
Terah, the father of Abram, Nahor, and Haran. And then, in the
next section, which bears the title of "the generations of Terah"
(verse 27), we read the manifold revelations of Jehovah to Abram,
the great father, and to Abraham, the father of a great multitude,
to whom he binds himself by promise and oath to make him a great
nation, and make his name (שם) great, and through his seed bless
all the nations.

CHAPTER VIII

APOCALYPSE OF ABRAHAM

A STUDY of the life of Abraham, as set forth in the Book of Genesis, will discover a series of revelations and promises similar to those seen in the life of Noah. We venture to exhibit them as a sevenfold apocalypse. They constitute a designed variety in the midst of a great organic unity, and show a very obvious relation to the Messianic hope of the Hebrew nation. The compiler, here as in other parts of Genesis, has appropriated material from various sources, but he so connects the varying traditions as to make them serve the purpose of reiterated assurances of the loftiest hopes of his nation. It was fitting that the Messianic hope, as revealed to the great "father of the faithful" and the "friend of God," should be repeated in many portions and forms, and thus show, like the duplicated dreams of Joseph and of Pharaoh, that all was established in the purpose of God, and would certainly come to pass (Gen. xli, 32). For of all the patriarchs of antiquity Abraham stands out as the most honored, a prophet, priest, and king, who sees by repeated favors of heaven the day of the Messiah, and is glad (John viii, 56). To him, therefore, more appropriately than to any other in that ancient time, came a sevenfold apocalypse of the promised Seed through whom all nations were destined to be blessed.

1. The first passage contains the divine call of Abraham, and combines revelation, commandment, and promise (Gen. xii, 1-3):

> Now said Jehovah unto Abraham,
> Go get thee from thy land and from thy kin and from thy father's house,
> Unto the land which I will show thee.
> And I will make of thee a great nation,
> And I will bless thee and make thy name great,
> And be thou a blessing.
> And I will bless them that bless thee,
> And him that treats thee lightly I will curse,
> And blessed in thee shall be all the families of the earth.

2. The second revelation was the promise of the land of Canaan. As he first passed through the land and halted at Shechem, Jehovah appeared unto him and assured him that he would give that land unto his posterity, and he built an altar there and also one at

Bethel (xii, 6–9). But after he had passed through the length of the land, gone down into Egypt, returned and separated from Lot, Jehovah thus addressed him (xiii, 14–17):

> Lift now thy eyes and look from the place where thou art,
> Northward and southward and eastward and westward;
> For all the land thou seest, to thee I give it,
> And to thy seed forever.
> And I will make thy seed as the dust of the earth,
> So that if a man can number the dust of the earth,
> Then also may thy seed be numbered.
> Rise, walk in the land to its length and to its breadth,
> For unto thee I give it.

3. Another revelation and promise, attributed by most critics to a different writer, is recorded in Gen. xv. It is interwoven with a narrative which seems to distribute it into portions given on two successive nights. We may fancy the patriarch lying down to sleep under the open sky, heavy and despondent over the uncertain prospect of posterity of his own. In his dreams Jehovah utters a new word of assurance, and impresses the same by a soul-stirring vision. Upon his asking how he can expect a great future when " Dammesek Eliezer " appears to be his only possible heir, he receives the following oracle (Gen. xv, 1, 4, 5).

> Fear not, Abraham, I am a shield for thee,
> And great exceedingly is thy reward.
> This man shall not become thy heir,
> But one that shall go forth from thy own loins,
> He shall become thy heir.
> Look now unto the heavens and count the stars,
> If indeed thou art able to count them,
> Thus shall thy seed be.

4. In connection with the foregoing oracle there came also a prophecy of bondage and triumph (verses 9–21). From this record as it now stands one might infer that all the rest of that night the patriarch meditated and communed with God, and with the break of morning asked some further token (verse 8). He is ordered to prepare five representative offerings, and all that day he busies himself in preparing the victims and keeping off the birds of prey. " But when the sun was going down, a deep sleep fell upon Abram, and behold a horror of great darkness fell upon him." Then the vision of " a smoking furnace and a flaming torch," symbols of God's presence, passed between the pieces of the victims, thereby sealing the covenant and assuring Abram of his great inheritance. And a word of Jehovah accompanied the vision (verses 18–21), naming ten Canaanitish nations as destined to yield up their possessions to

the promised seed of Abram. These heathen tribes are fitting types of all the kingdoms of this world which must at last become the kingdom of Jehovah and his Anointed.

5. The seventeenth chapter of Genesis contains what may be appropriately termed the oracles of the Abrahamic covenant. Herein the Holy One reveals himself under the name EL SHADDAY, ordains the covenant of circumcision, and gives to the patriarch and his wife new names of prophetic significance:

> And thy name shall no more be called Abram,
> But thy name shall be Abraham,
> For the father of a multitude of nations have I made thee.
> And I will make thee exceeding fruitful,
> And I will make thee into nations,
> And kings shall come forth from thee.
> And I will establish my covenant between me and thee,
> And with thy seed after thee for their generations for an everlasting covenant,
> To be a God unto thee and to thy seed after thee (Gen. xvii, 5–7).

The name of Sarai is changed to Sarah, and she is destined to be a mother of nations. "Kings of peoples shall be from her."

> Sarah thy wife shall bear unto thee a son
> And thou shalt call his name Isaac,
> And I will establish my covenant with him,
> For an everlasting covenant for his seed after him (Gen. xvii, 19).

6. The sixth revelation to Abraham was an angelophany (Gen. xviii). Celestial messengers appeared to him in the form and habits of ordinary men. The promise of a son was repeated, Sarah's unbelief rebuked, and the impending doom of Sodom and Gomorrah declared. In the revelation of the overthrow of Sodom, and in the intercession of Abraham, we learn how the righteous are the salt of the earth, how wonderful are the long-suffering and the righteousness of God, and with what blended humility and boldness man may intercede with God in prayer.

7. The seventh and last revelation of God to Abraham came in connection with the severest trial of his faith, the command to offer up his only son (Gen. xxii). It represents the patriarch's sublimest act of devotion, and the perfection of his faith in God. The oracle is confirmed by two immutable things, God's oath and promise:

> By myself have I sworn, saith Jehovah,
> That inasmuch as thou hast done this thing,
> And didst not spare thy son, thy only one,
> That in blessing I will bless thee
> And in multiplying I will multiply thy seed as the stars of heaven,

And as the sand which is on the shore of the sea,
And thy seed shall possess the gate of his enemies.
And in thy seed shall all the nations of the earth be blessed (Gen. xxii, 16–18).

Thus the last of the series of revelations and promises to the chief patriarch of the Hebrew race closes with the same prediction of a blessed seed as that with which the first was distinguished; but this last was confirmed by Jehovah's oath.[1]

---

[1] Stanley's observation on the sacrifice of Abraham is worthy of note: " The doctrine of the *types* of the ancient dispensation has often been pushed to excess, but there is a sense in which the connection indicated thereby admits of no dispute, and which may be illustrated even by other history than that with which we are now concerned. . . . Abraham and Abraham's son in obedience, in resignation, in the sacrifice of whatever could be sacrificed short of sin, form an anticipation which cannot be mistaken of that last and greatest event which closes the history of the chosen people. We leap as by a natural instinct from the sacrifice in the land of Moriah to the sacrifice of Calvary. There are many differences; there is a danger of exaggerating the resemblance, or of confounding in either case what is subordinate with what is essential. But the general feeling of Christendom has in this respect not gone far astray. Each event, if we look at it well and understand it rightly, will serve to explain the other. In the very point of view in which I have just been speaking of it the likeness is most remarkable. Human sacrifice, which was in outward form nearest to the offering of Isaac, was in fact and in spirit most entirely condemned and repudiated by it. The union of parental love with the total denial of self is held up in both cases as the highest model of human, and therefore as the shadow of divine, love. ' Sacrifice ' is rejected, but ' to do thy will, O God,' is accepted (Heb. x, 5, 7)."—*History of the Jewish Church*, First Series, pp. 55, 56. New York, 1869.

CHAPTER IX

APOCALYPTIC DREAMS

THE unfolding revelation of God may be traced onward, as it is continued in different parts and various forms to the descendants of Abraham. To the mother of Ishmael it is revealed twice over that her child by Abraham should be the father of a great and powerful nation (Gen. xvi, 11, 12; xxi, 17, 18). To the mother of Esau and Jacob, when "she went to inquire of Jehovah," there came this oracle (Gen. xxv, 23):

> Two nations are in thy womb,
> And two peoples shall be separated from thy bowels;
> And the one people shall be stronger than the other people,
> And the elder shall serve the younger.

The promise made to Abraham is twice repeated unto Isaac, first at Gerar (Gen. xxvi, 2–5) and again at Beersheba (xxvi, 24). Under the spell of inspiration Isaac himself pronounced prophetic blessings upon Jacob and Esau (xxvii, 27–29 and 39–40). These blessings are essentially apocalyptic in character, and foreshadow the future of great peoples. They are to be interpreted as broad and general in their scope, not descriptive of particular events in history, but depicting metaphorically far-reaching purposes of divine Providence. But more notable for our purpose than these fragmentary oracles are the prophetic dreams recorded in the Book of Genesis. The first in prophetic significance of all these is Jacob's dream at Bethel. Having fled from the wrath of his brother Esau, he came to the spot where Abraham long before had viewed the land of promise northward and southward and eastward and westward (Gen. xiii, 14). He, too, looked abroad over the goodly landscape, and may be thought of as beholding the hills and clouds afar towering up like a sublime stairway into heaven as he "lay down in that place to sleep." For in his dream that night he "saw a ladder set up on the earth, and the top of it reached to heaven; and behold the angels of God ascending and descending on it." The vision seems to have been that of a gigantic stairway, composed of mountains and clouds piled one above another and stretching far aloft into the upper heavens. Far above stood the visional semblance of the person of Jehovah, who spoke and reiterated to Jacob the promise made before to Abraham (comp. Gen. xxviii, 13–15, with xiii, 15–17). This apocalyptic dream embraces the ideals of a theophany and an angelophany, and in its complex symbolism is profoundly suggestive. Jacob and his seed were destined to be the chosen people through whom God was pleased to vouchsafe his highest revelations to mankind and bring the true salvation to the world (John iv, 22). That salvation is ministered by innumerable hosts of angels (Heb. i, 14; xii, 22). In the light of John i, 52; xiv, 4, 6; Heb. ix, 8, we may see in the ladder a symbol of the mediation of the Son of man, in connection with whom the angels of God are continually ascending and descending to minister to such as shall be heirs of salvation. In that mystery of grace we may think of God as bending down from his heavenly throne, laying hold on the true seed of Abraham (Heb. ii, 16), and lifting them up to the heavenly places.

In connection with this vision Jacob received the promise of Jehovah's presence in all his journey and of a safe return to that land (Gen. xxviii, 15); and the writer of Genesis is careful to note that "God appeared unto Jacob again when he came back from Paddan-aram, and blessed him," and called his name Israel, and repeated the promise of Abraham (Gen. xxxv, 9–13). So Jacob received a new name, as had Abram and Sarai in the former time. The divine oracle recorded in Gen. xxxv, 10–12, is twofold, as seen by the twice-repeated "God said unto him." The first is a repetition of the blessing received with his new name at Penuel (xxxii, 28); the second a repetition of the promise made so often before to Abraham and Isaac. The whole is presented as a visional apocalypse, for it is not only said that God "appeared" unto him, but also, after the revelation, he "went up from him in the place where he spake with him" (verse 13; comp. Gen. xvii, 22).

The dreams of Joseph, as recorded in Gen. xxxvii, 5–10, should be studied in connection with each other, and their points of likeness and unlikeness compared. Both are prophetic of a future relation between himself and his brethren, and the repetition under different symbols has doubtless the same import as that of the doubling of Pharaoh's dream given in Gen. xli, 32. The first dream is that of a scene on earth, and contemplates only Joseph and his brethren; the second scene is laid in heaven, and contemplates his father and mother as well as his brethren. Thus the repetitions of apocalyptic symbolism seek for variety of form where there is no material difference of signification.

The same observations apply to the dreams of the two officers of Pharaoh (Gen. xl, 8–19), so far as the two dreams correspond in their formal elements. It was natural that the butler should dream of the vine with its buds, and blossoms, and clusters of grapes; and that the baker should dream of baskets of bread. The three days for fulfillment were alike in both. But for "each man according to the interpretation of his dream" there was impending a different destiny: the one was unto life, the other unto death. The two dreams of Pharaoh (Gen. xli, 1–7) are more closely parallel than those of Joseph. The only noticeable difference is in the imagery of their symbolism: seven heifers or cows in the first, and seven ears of grain in the second. In the interpretation it is said that "the dream was doubled unto Pharaoh twice because the thing is established by God, and God will shortly bring it to pass" (xli, 32). In this statement we have a most important principle of hermeneutics for understanding the formal repetition of apocalyptic scenes.

CHAPTER X

APOCALYPSE OF THE EXODUS

THE narrative of the Exodus as recorded in Exod. i–xv contains so many impressive pictures both of the goodness and severity of God that we do well to call attention to some of the more remarkable passages. Criticism finds in these chapters, as in Genesis, a combination of various ancient documents, but no analysis of them need concern our present purpose or materially affect the great religious lessons which they are adapted to inculcate. In searching in them for whatever has an apocalyptic aspect we may conceive the entire picture, from the call of Moses to his song of triumph, as a magnificent drama.

1. The first act is the vision of the burning bush, and is accompanied with the divine call of Moses to deliver Israel out of the cruel bondage of Egypt (Exod. iii). The symbolism of the bush, burning with fire but not consumed, was significant of the fact that the burning judgments of God never destroy anything that is pure and good. The oppressions of Egypt could not consume Israel ; the wrath of Pharaoh cannot harm Moses. God's people are imperishable. This idea may be traced in many subsequent revelations. God Almighty is a consuming fire. He burns up what is worthless and perishable; but " the remnant according to the election of grace " shall never be destroyed. God's fires of trial only purify and make them more conspicuous and wonderful. In connection with this symbol we read the verbal revelation to Moses of the God of Abraham, of Isaac, and of Jacob, the God who calls himself I AM WHO AM, and who assures Moses and the elders of Israel that he will smite the land of Egypt and lead his people forth with a mighty hand.

2. In Exod. vi, 1–8, we have what purports in the connection to be another and later call of Moses, coming to him in Egypt after he had asked permission of Pharaoh for Israel to go forth out of Egypt. He again receives assurance that Israel shall be redeemed from their bondage, led in triumph out of Egypt, and given possession of the land promised to their fathers. Furthermore, the Holy One now reveals himself by a new name, the profound significance of which was unknown to the fathers: "I am Jehovah. And I appeared to Abraham, to Isaac, and to Jacob as El-Shadday, but by my name Jehovah I was not known to them."

3. In Exod. vii, 1-13, we have a third oracle, assuring Moses and Aaron of Jehovah's presence and help in leading out the children of Israel. The oracle was followed by the miracle of the rod of Aaron becoming a serpent and swallowing the rods of the magicians, who imitated the wonderful sign by their secret arts. This sign was significant and suggestive. It was a kind of prelude to the ten plagues, symbolizing Jehovah's triumph in the realm of Egyptian superstition, and disclosing the helplessness of all the gods of Egypt.

4. The ten plagues may be regarded as so many scenes in the fourth act of this sublime drama. They increased in power and horror as one followed rapidly after another, and the last plague was followed by "a great cry throughout all the land of Egypt, such as there hath been none like it, nor shall be like it any more" (xi, 6). Nowhere in all literature is there to be found a sublimer exhibition of Jehovah's power over the forces of nature and the superstitions of men. The imagery of these plagues is largely appropriated in the New Testament Apocalypse of John to portray the "terrors and great signs from heaven," which there figure as trumpets of woe and bowls of wrath—visitations of judgment on the enemies of God.

5. The passover was instituted (Exod. xii, xiii) to symbolize and commemorate the redemption of Israel from Egypt, and the salvation of their firstborn at the awful hour when all the firstborn of the land of Egypt died. How this sacred feast became a type and symbol of "the marriage supper of the Lamb," as well as "the communion of the body of Christ," is well known.

6. Then followed the march of Israel out of the land of bitter oppression, and their complete deliverance at the Red Sea. The obdurate king of Egypt is portrayed as fiercely pursuing the people of Jehovah, and as overwhelmed with his army in the midst of the sea. How like the vision of the dragon in John's Apocalypse (xii, 13-16), who poured out of his mouth a river of water after the woman that fled into the wilderness, "and the earth opened her mouth and swallowed up the river!"

7. The final act in this drama of the Exodus is the picture of redeemed Israel, standing in triumph on the further shore of the sea, and singing "the song of Moses." This entire picture was evidently in the mind of John when he wrote of the glassy sea mingled with fire and of the victorious multitude standing by it with the harps of God, singing the song of Moses and of the Lamb (Rev. xv, 2, 3).

These plagues of Egypt are called Jehovah's "great judgments"

(Exod. vi, 6; vii, 4; Num. xxxiii, 4). They stand out in Holy Writ as signal examples and illustrations of the manner in which God executes judgment (Exod. xii, 12) on wicked men and nations. Compare the use of the word *judgments* in Ezek. xvi, 41; xxv, 11; xxviii, 22; xxx, 19, and Isa. xxxiv, 5. The prophetic way of speaking of such visitations of judgment is to call them a "great and terrible day of Jehovah" (comp. Isa. xiii, 6, 9; Joel i, 15; ii, 1, 2, 11, 31; Amos v, 18; Zeph. i, 14–16). These awful judgments on Egypt were a great and terrible day of the Lord. It is common to conceive the day of judgment as a formal assize, in which God sits as Ruler and Judge to hear testimony and pronounce decisions of merit and demerit, according to the works of men. Under a like figure we might speak of Jehovah as sitting in judgment upon the cruelties and idolatries of the Egyptians. Pharaoh and all his guilty associates in the oppression of Israel were brought to the bar of God. They stood before the judgment seat of Jehovah, and received just recompense for their deeds. But we should not forget that the imagery of throne, and bar, and judgment seat, and trial, and sentence is but the drapery of human conceptions of judgment. The great essential truth in all this imagery is that God condemns and punishes his enemies and causes them that obey him to triumph. And whether the visitation of wrath come in the form of a flood of waters to drown the world, or in fire and brimstone to destroy the wicked cities of the plain, or in the plagues of Egypt, it is in every case a coming of God to judgment; or, if one adopt the other form of statement, a bringing of both the just and the unjust before the tribunal of the Supreme Judge of the heavens and the earth.

CHAPTER XI

APOCALYPTIC SYMBOLISM OF THE TABERNACLE

A COMPREHENSIVE study of biblical apocalyptics requires at least a brief notice of the mystic symbolism of the sacred tent, which figures so conspicuously in the narrative of the Levitical worship.[1] The structure is called the "tent of meeting," the "tent of the testimony," and the "dwelling of the testimony." Its symbolism is essentially the same as that of the temple of Solomon, and the allusions in John's Apocalypse to the "temple of God opened in heaven," and "the tabernacle of God with men" (Rev. xi, 19 ; xxi, 3), cannot be explained without reference to the significance of this symbolism.

The tabernacle and the temple, as described in the Old Testament books, were comparatively small structures, inadequate for the accommodation of a large congregation, and not designed for such a purpose. A great assembly might draw near and stand "at the door," so to speak, and witness what was visible from without, but only consecrated priests and Levites were permitted to enter and perform the sacred rites of worship. So all Israel worshiped by proxy, and the officiating priest was their minister before God. The holy places were, (1) the court, where the altar of burnt offerings and the laver stood ; (2) the holy place, where were the table of showbread, the golden candlestick, and the golden altar of incense ; and (3) the holy of holies, in which was "the ark of the covenant."

What, now, was the symbolical import of this sacred tent? It would lead only to confusion and error to seek for mystical significance in the minor details of the structure. The boards, the curtains, the loops, the taches, the rods and the rings, and such like may all be passed over as mere incidentals necessary to the different parts of the tent. The main structure had two apartments,

---

[1] We open no controversy here with the criticism which assigns the Levitical law and ritual to the post-Mosaic time. Whether instituted by Moses and Aaron, or by prophets of a later time, or in exilic or postexilic time, its symbolism is obviously identical with that of the Solomonic temple, and is recognized in Heb. ix, 2–9, as a figure of the holiest Christian mysteries. As it is now embodied in our sacred books the various pictures of tent and ritual are rich in suggestions of "heavenly things," and very profitable for instruction in righteousness.

and these, with their chief articles of furniture, may reasonably be supposed to represent the principal ideas intended. The words employed in describing these parts suggest the fundamental thought of their significance. The principal names are the *dwelling* (מִשְׁכָּן) and *tent* (אֹהֶל), and the passage which, above all others, points out the one great idea embodied in the tabernacle is Exod. xxix, 42–46 : "It shall be a continual burnt offering throughout your generations, at the door of the *tent of meeting* before Jehovah, where *I will meet* with you, and speak unto thee there. And there *I will meet* with the sons of Israel, and he (that is, Israel) shall be sanctified in my glory. . . . And *I will dwell* in the midst of the sons of Israel, and I will be their God, and they shall know that I am Jehovah their God, who brought them out of the land of Egypt that *I might dwell among* them." Here obviously the one great thought is that of JEHOVAH MEETING AND DWELLING WITH HIS PEOPLE, and sanctifying them in his glory. It is difficult not to think that the Saviour had this divine thought in mind when he prayed for his followers "that they may be one, even as we are one ; I in them and thou in me, that they may be perfected into one," and, furthermore, that "where I am they also may be with me, that they may behold my glory, which thou hast given me : for thou lovedst me before the foundation of the world" (John xvii, 23, 24).

With this clew to the meaning we think of the tabernacle as a material symbol of the dwelling of God with his people. The two apartments, known as the holy place and the holy of holies, represent the true relations of Israel and Jehovah. It is the twofold fellowship of the human and the divine. God condescends to dwell with man that man may dwell with God in eternal life. By virtue of this blood-bought relationship the true Israel of God become sanctified in the divine glory (Exod. xxix, 43). The "many mansions" (μοναί, *dwellings, abiding places*, John xiv, 2) of the Father's house in the heavens are but the fuller realization and perfection of the believer's fellowship with God on earth. In the mystery of this blessed symbolism we see a type as well as a symbol of the New Testament Church and kingdom of God, a spiritual house (1 Peter ii, 5), a habitation of God in the Spirit (Eph. ii, 22). The two holy places, separated by the veil, suggest how closely God and man may come together in holy communion, and the chief symbols of the two apartments show the terms, or conditions, of the fellowship.

In accordance with this main thought we may easily infer the significance of the principal objects belonging to the sacred tent.

The holy of holies was the secret presence chamber of Jehovah, and the ark, containing the tables of the law covered by the mercy seat, was a symbol of the deepest mystery of the kingdom of grace. It was a picture of "mercy covering wrath." The ark was a small chest, made of most durable wood, and overlaid within and without with gold. Within this were deposited "the two tables of testimony," so called because the Ten Commandments were a monumental witness of Jehovah against sin. The mercy seat, or *capporeth* (כַּפֹּרֶת), was a golden cover for the ark, and it was made exactly of the same dimensions as the length and breadth of the ark itself, and sprinkled with blood on the great day of atonement. Thus it became a symbol of "the redemption which is in Christ Jesus, whom God set forth to be an expiatory covering (ἱλαστήριον=capporeth) through faith in his blood" (Rom. iii, 25). The cherubim at the ends of the mercy seat, with their faces toward each other, and spreading out their wings on high (Exod. xxv, 20), seem there as at the gate of Eden to guard the way of life, and suggest the ultimate glory of the redeemed who shall have power over the tree of life which is in the paradise of God (comp. Rev. ii, 7 ; xxii, 14).

As the most holy place and its furniture symbolized Jehovah's relations to his people, and showed how and on what terms God condescends to dwell with men, so, on the other hand, the holy place and its furniture and ministering priest represented the true relation of Israel to God. As the officiating priest stood in the holy place, facing the holy of holies, he had at his right hand the table of showbread, at his left the candlestick, and immediately before him the golden altar of incense. The twelve cakes of showbread on the table represented the twelve tribes of Israel continually presented as a living sacrifice before God, and the candlestick with its seven lamps was another symbol of Israel standing as the light of the world. But the more direct worship of God on the part of his people was symbolized by the offering of incense on the golden altar, which stood immediately before the veil and in front of the mercy seat (Exod. xxx, 6). This offering of incense was an expressive symbol of the prayers of the saints (Psalm cxli, 2 ; Rev. v, 8 ; viii, 3, 4), and, accordingly, the people were wont to pray without at the time when the priest offered incense within (Luke i, 10).

The altar of burnt offering and the laver which were in the court had also their significance. There could be no approach unto God on the part of sinful man, no possible meeting and dwelling with him, except by reason of the offerings made at the great altar in front of the holy tent. No priest might pass into the holy places of the tabernacle until sprinkled with blood from that altar (Exod.

xxix, 21), and the live coals used for the burning of incense before Jehovah were taken from the same place (Lev. xvi, 12). Nor might any priest minister at the altar or enter the tabernacle without first washing at the laver (Exod. xxx, 20, 21). So the great altar continually proclaimed that without the shedding of blood there is no remission, and the priests' ablutions suggest the fundamental truth that without the "washing of regeneration" no man may enter the kingdom of God.

The symbolism of the tabernacle is recognized in Heb. ix, 1–12, and Christ's entrance "into heaven itself, now to appear in the presence of God for us," is illustrated by analogies in the worship of the Levitical tabernacle. It may also be observed that as the most holy place in the temple was a perfect cube (1 Kings vi, 20), the same was probably the case in the tabernacle, and this fact may have suggested the figure of the new Jerusalem in John's Apocalypse, the length and breadth and height of which were equal (Rev. xxi, 16). This ideal of perfection is to be realized when that holy city shall have so come down out of heaven from God that a great voice from the throne may say, "Behold, the tabernacle of God is with men, and he shall dwell with them" (Rev. xxi, 3).

CHAPTER XII

APOCALYPTIC PASSAGES IN THE HISTORICAL BOOKS

WRITINGS which we call historical the Jews classed among the prophets. The books of Joshua, Judges, Samuel, and Kings stand in the Jewish canon as the "Earlier Prophets." They all contain passages which bear the clear marks of pictorial description, and some of these are so obviously conceived in the apocalyptic style as to demand our attention before passing on to the prophetic books of more formal apocalyptic character.

I. FALL OF JERICHO.

The fall of Jericho as described in Josh. v, 13–vi, 27, is a mixture of history, vision, and prophecy. Jericho was the first great city of the Canaanites which stood in the way of Israel when they entered upon the conquest of the land of promise. It was a representative of the entire Canaanitish power and hostility with which the chosen people were called to contend, and its signal overthrow was prophetic of the ultimate ruin of every enemy that stands in the way of the progress of the kingdom of God. It was fitting, therefore, that the fall of this great city should be set forth in a manner corresponding to its importance as an obstacle in Israel's way. The angel of Jehovah appeared to Joshua in a human form, with a drawn sword in his hand (Josh. v, 13), and announced himself as "Prince of the host of Jehovah." Joshua at once "fell on his face to the earth, and worshiped" (comp. Ezek. i, 28; iii, 23; Dan. viii, 17; Rev. i, 17). He was, like Moses at the bush (Exod. iii, 5), commanded to put off his sandal from his foot, and thereupon he received a revelation of the manner in which the city of Jericho was to be given into his hand. The men of war were to march round the city once each day for six successive days, and the angel said : "Seven priests shall bear seven trumpets of rams' horns before the ark: and the seventh day ye shall compass the city seven times, and the priests shall blow with the trumpets. And it shall be, that when they make a long blast with the ram's horn, and when ye hear the sound of the trumpet, all the people shall shout with a great shout ; [1] and the wall of the city shall

---

[1] Is not this blast of trumpets and great shout the source of Paul's imagery in 1 Thess. iv, 16 ? The signal shout (κέλευσμα) and the trump of God (comp. "the last trumpet" in 1 Cor. xv, 52) seem to have been employed by the apostle in metaphorical allusion to

fall down under it, and the people shall go up every man straight before him" (Josh. vi, 4, 5). The remainder of the chapter records the speedy fulfillment of this revelation to Joshua. The conquest of Canaan, as well as the exodus from Egypt and the march through the wilderness, has supplied the imagery of later apocalypses and figured largely in Christian allegory and song. The deliverance from the oppression and idolatries of Egypt has been regarded as a symbol of redemption from the power of sin; the march through the desert a figure of man's probationary life, and the crossing into Canaan a type of the Christian's transit to the heavenly country. So later scriptures also speak of the fathers who "were all baptized unto Moses in the cloud and in the sea; and did all eat the same spiritual meat, and did all drink the same spiritual drink" (1 Cor. x, 2–4). At the beginning and at the end of the journey through the wilderness they "were saved through water" (comp. 1 Peter iii, 20–22).

Notable analogies are also traceable between the fall of Jericho and the fall of that "great city which (in John's Apocalypse xi, 8) spiritually is called Sodom and Egypt." The trumpet-signaled fall of Jericho furnished John the imagery of the seven trumpets which sounded the overthrow of the apostate city which killed the prophets, and stoned the messengers, and crucified the Son of God (Rev. viii, 6–xi, 19), and "Babylon the great" is represented as falling before the fierceness of God's wrath when the seventh angel poured out the seventh bowl of wrath upon the air (Rev. xvi, 17–19).

It should be observed, further, that according to Josh. v, 2–12, the overthrow of Jericho was preceded by Israel's renewal of their divine covenant relations in the rites of circumcision and the passover. The old Israel that came out of Egypt died in the wilderness, and "all the nation was consumed because they hearkened not unto the voice of Jehovah" (verse 6). But a new generation was called and consecrated to possess and eat the fruit of the land of Canaan. All this is strikingly typical of that later period when a new Israel was chosen by the Prince of life, who became "the mediator of a better covenant, enacted upon better promises" (Heb. viii, 6). He instituted the two sacraments of a new dispensation, and firmly established his Church in the world, before he sent forth his armies to destroy the faithless city and scatter the apostate nation that had become drunken with the blood of saints. As Jericho must needs be destroyed before the new generation of Israel could go forward to the conquest of the land of promise, so also

the shouting and trumpeting at the fall of Jericho. Israel's great shout was like the voice of an archangel, and the blast of the seven trumpets was God's own trumpet-signal of the fall of the city and the triumph of his people.

must Jerusalem perish before the new spiritual Israel, the "remnant according to the election of grace" (Rom. xi, 5), could move forward to subject the world to the Messiah's reign.

II. THE HOUSE AND THRONE OF DAVID.

When David became established as king of Israel, and had builded for himself a royal palace, he conceived the purpose of building a temple of God, more suitable, as he thought, than the tent of curtains which inclosed the ark of the covenant (2 Sam. vii, 1, 2). But that night there came a word of Jehovah to Nathan the prophet which opposed this project, but opened a vision of future glory to the house and kingdom of David. "Wilt thou build me a house in which to dwell?" so in substance ran the oracle; "nay, rather, I, Jehovah, will make a house for thee : I will set up thy seed after thee, and establish the throne of his kingdom, and thy house and kingdom shall be made sure before thee forever" (2 Sam. vii, 5–16).

This revelation opened to David and his people a new ideal of Messianic hopes. He understood that it pointed onward into far future times. It was the germ of many a Messianic psalm, a pledge of "the sure mercies of David." The main thought is that David is to be succeeded by a royal seed, to whom Jehovah also will be a Father, and whom he will chastise with many "stripes of the children of men." This seed is not to be understood of Solomon only, or of any other one individual ; not even of the Messiah only. The seed of the woman, the seed of Abraham, and the seed of David are generic and comprehensive terms, but not exclusive of the Messiah in whom the ultimate and stainless glory is to culminate. "The holy seed" (Isa. vi, 13), which "shall come forth a shoot out of the stock of Jesse" (Isa. xi, 1), are not exempt from human trial and chastisement, for thereby they are proven to be true sons of God and become "partakers of his holiness" (comp. Heb. xii, 2–10).

And so the revelation of what was to befall David's house "for a great while to come" (verse 19) deserves some recognition among the apocalypses of sacred history. It bears upon its face the two great sentiments of judgment and love, symbolized by the Edenic sword and cherubim, and repeated in manifold forms as the word of divine revelation opens more and more the mysteries of the kingdom of heaven.

III. APOCALYPTIC DREAMS OF SOLOMON.

When Solomon became established on the throne of his father David, and went to Gibeon to offer sacrifice, "Jehovah appeared to him in a dream by night" and asked him the great desire of his heart (1 Kings iii, 4, 5). His request for "an understanding heart" was so pleasing to God that he at once received the gracious response recorded in 1 Kings iii, 11-14. But years after this, when Solomon had completed the building of the temple, "Jehovah appeared to him a second time" and repeated to him the promises made to David his father (see 1 Kings ix, 2-9). Nor does this second revelation complete all the word of Jehovah to Solomon. A fragment of similar content appears in 1 Kings vi, 11-13; and another oracle, spoken after Solomon's heart had been turned after other gods, is recorded in 1 Kings xi, 9-13. It declares that because of his sins divine judgment will surely follow, and his kingdom shall be rent in twain.

But all the kingdom I'll not rend away;
One tribe will I deliver to thy son,
For David's sake, my servant,
And for the sake of Jerusalem, which I have chosen.

IV. Jehovah's Word to Jeroboam.

The two oracles spoken by the prophet Ahijah, and recorded in 1 Kings xi, 29-39, and xiv, 5-16, contain apocalyptic elements. The first was accompanied by the rending of Ahijah's new garment into twelve pieces, a symbol of the rending of Solomon's kingdom and the giving of the ten tribes to Jeroboam. The word of the prophecy promises blessing and prosperity on condition of obedience, but implies failure and ruin in case of evildoing. The second oracle was a revelation of judgment upon the house of Jeroboam and upon the kingdom of Israel, which was destined to be rooted up and scattered beyond the river Euphrates. That day of judgment came on swiftly. The death of the child, as Jeroboam's wife came to the threshold of the house (1 Kings xiv, 17), was a beginning of sorrows. The assassination of Nadab, Jeroboam's son and successor, and the slaughter of "all the house of Jeroboam" followed quickly (xv, 25-30). Finally, the kingdom of the ten tribes perished, and "Jehovah removed Israel out of his sight, as he spake by the hand of all his servants the prophets" (2 Kings xvii, 23).

V. Other Apocalyptic Fragments.

In 1 Kings xvi, 2-4, we find a prophecy of Jehu, the son of Hanani, which is in substance a repetition of what Ahijah uttered against Jeroboam in chap. xiv, 7-11. It is an impressive illustration of the Nemesis of history that Baasha, who received the kingdom by violence, should be doomed by the same form of prophetic utterance as that which announced the fall of Jeroboam. It was during the reign of Baasha that Hanani, the seer, uttered the prophecy recorded in 2 Chron. xvi, 7-9. The fearful oracle of judgment, spoken by Elijah against Ahab and Jezebel (1 Kings xxi, 19-24) is also worthy of comparison with the foregoing, and should be studied in connection with its repetition in 2 Kings ix, 6-10. Micaiah's vision, in 1 Kings xxii, 19-23, is in the form of an apocalypse. The prophet may have appropriated his imagery from the very scene before him. The kings and their surrounding hosts, assembled at the gate of Samaria, were suggestive of the King of kings on his heavenly throne, surrounded by his hosts of angels. He "strikes through kings in the day of his wrath" and "judges among the nations" (comp. Psalm cx).

CHAPTER XIII

APOCALYPSES IN THE BOOK OF ISAIAH

THE Book of Isaiah, as it has come down to us, is a compilation. The last twenty-seven chapters have no natural connection with the preceding portions of the book, and their historical standpoint is not the time of Isaiah the son of Amoz. They are preceded by four chapters of historical matter (Isa. xxxvi–xxxix), which appear much more appropriately in 2 Kings xviii, 13–xx, with which they are in substance identical. Whatever the authorship of these historical chapters, the poetical "writing of Hezekiah" in chap. xxxviii, 9–20, is not a composition of Isaiah. Other chapters also, as we shall see, contain evidences of a date later than the days of Isaiah. Aside from smaller subdivisions there are five easily distinguished sections[1] of the book, and these might have been originally put together as a pentateuch in order to form a collection of prophecies coordinate with the five books of law and five books of psalms. In the absence of any certain data it is at least a plausible hypothesis that the first *threefold collection* of holy writings among the Jews consisted of three pentateuchs, each bearing the name of the most representative man in the laws, the psalms, and the prophecies of the chosen nation. This might have taken place in the days of Ezra, whose proficiency as "a ready scribe in the law of Moses " (Ezra vii, 6), determined the form and limits of the books of the law; while the pentateuchs of David and Isaiah were afterward supplemented by many other books which were felt to be "profitable for instruction in righteousness " (2 Tim. iii, 16). In this manner the original pentateuchal character of the prophets and the psalms may have been ignored and forgotten.

I. ISAIAH VI.

The sixth chapter of Isaiah contains the prophet's own account of his divine call. His vision of Jehovah of hosts, seated upon his throne in the midst of winged seraphim, is a word-picture of remarkable sublimity. It is dated in the year that King Uzziah died. That old monarch, after a prosperous reign of two and fifty years, was dying of leprosy in his separate house (2 Kings xv, 5). The

---

[1] Namely, chaps. i–xii, xiii–xxiii, xxiv–xxxv, xxxvi–xxxix, and xl–lxvi.

princes and chief men of Judah had grown proud and voluptuous, and had introduced strange customs from foreign lands. The daughters of Zion gloried in excessive displays of jewelry, and walked abroad with outstretched throat and ogling eyes. Divine judgments were beginning to fall upon the proud kingdom of Samaria, and the colossal world-power of Assyria was beginning to show its ominous form like a dark storm-cloud on the distant horizon. In the midst of such external conditions the prophetic call of Isaiah took the form of an apocalyptic vision. We are scarcely competent, with Delitzsch, to say that God enabled Isaiah when awake, and not when sleeping and dreaming, to look into the invisible world and behold as a supersensible reality what he describes. It may have been a dream or vision of the night. But whether waking or sleeping the prophet seems to have been standing in the court of the temple, where he had probably often stood and gazed upon the great folding doors, on which were carved the figures of "cherubim and palm trees and open flowers" (1 Kings vi, 35). Suddenly in his vision the doors were opened, and the intervening veils were parted, and he beheld with open face the interior of the holy of holies. But the objects seen were not the material symbols which occupied that inner sanctuary. The prophetic rapture carried the vision of the prophet to the throne of God in heaven, and revealed a theophany of overwhelming grandeur and sublimity. The vision holds so high a rank among apocalyptic scenes that we transcribe and annotate the entire chapter:

In the year that King Uzziah died I saw the Lord sitting upon a throne, high and lifted up, and his train [1] filling the temple. Seraphim were standing above him,[2] six wings to every one; with twain he was covering his face, and with twain he was covering his feet, and with twain he was flying.[3] And one called to another and said,

Holy, holy, holy,[4] Jehovah of hosts,
The fullness of all the earth is his glory.

And the foundations of the thresholds moved to and fro by reason of the voice of him that called, and the house was full of smoke.

Then said I, Woe is me! for I am undone ; for a man unclean of lips am I, and in the midst of a people unclean of lips I dwell : for mine eyes have seen the King,

---

[1] *Train.* The flowing skirts of his royal robes, which seemed to the seer to fill the heavenly temple.

[2] The seraphs appear to have been in a hovering attitude, as if poised on their outstretched wings above and around the throne.

[3] These verbs in the imperfect tense here indicate the apparently continuous action of the wings.

[4] The entire scene, but especially this *trisagion*, was adapted to impress the prophet with a deep sense of the holiness of God. It is to be noted that "the Holy One of Israel " is a phrase that occurs often in Isaiah, and seems like the echo of this *trisagion*.

Jehovah of hosts. And there flew unto me one of the seraphim, and in his hand a live coal, which he had taken from the altar; and he touched my mouth, and said, Lo, this hath touched thy lips, and thy iniquity is taken away and thy sin is covered.

Then I heard the voice of the Lord, saying, Whom shall I send, and who will go for us?[1] And I said, Lo, here am I; send me. And he said, Go, and thou shalt say unto this people,

> Hear ye continually but do not understand;
> And keep on seeing but do not perceive.
> Make the heart of this people fat,[2]
> And their ears make heavy and their eyes besmear,
> Lest they see with their eyes, and hear with their ears,
> And their heart understand, and turn, and be healed.

Then said I, How long, O Lord? And he said, Until cities are laid waste without inhabitant, and houses without man, and the land shall become an utter desolation, and Jehovah shall remove men far away,[3] and great shall be the deserted space in the midst of the land.

And yet in it (shall be) a tenth, and it in turn shall be again for burning: as a terebinth, and as an oak, in which, when they are felled, a stump (remains); (so) is a holy seed its stump.[4]

This apocalyptic vision is to be compared with that of Micaiah in 1 Kings xxii, 19–22, that of Ezekiel (chap. i), and that of John (Rev. i, 12–20, and iv). The comparison will show the originality and superior qualities of Isaiah. The reader cannot fail to admire the magnificent conception and execution of this scripture as a piece of literature. But we regard it as something more than a mere creation of poetic genius. Its inspiration was from heaven. It records an experience that was profoundly real to Isaiah. His divine call took vivid form as a revelation from the very throne of God. But like all the great and gifted souls, who have been called of God and sent forth on epoch-making ministries, Isaiah has clothed his divine concepts in his own human style. So did Jeremiah, and Ezekiel, and all the rest. Isaiah was probably a young man when he received his call. Ezekiel was in his thirtieth year when "the heavens were opened unto him, and he saw visions of God" (Ezek. i, 1). Moses was an old man of eighty years when he beheld the vision of the burning bush, and was called to deliver

---

[1] *For us.* Here we note again the implication of a heavenly council as in Gen. i, 26; iii, 22; 1 Kings xxii, 19.

[2] The word of prophecy, if unheeded, becomes a means of dulling the moral sense, and is thus a savor from death unto death (2 Cor. ii, 16).

[3] That is, into foreign exile.

[4] This last clause is thought by Cheyne to be a postexilic addition. But such a view is purely conjectural, and seems less probable than that it is a fragmentary sentence of the author himself, left incomplete, at the time of the first writing, and never afterward revised.

Israel. But Samuel was a little child when he first heard the word of Jehovah, announcing, "Behold I am about to do a thing in Israel at which both the ears of every one that heareth it shall tingle" (1 Sam. iii, 11). Jeremiah also was but a child when "Jehovah put forth his hand, and touched his mouth, and said, Behold, I have put my words in thy mouth: see, I have this day set thee over the nations and over the kingdoms, to pluck up and to break down, and to destroy and to overthrow; to build and to plant" (Jer. i, 9, 10). We may not enter into the psychological details of the method of receiving such epoch-making calls, nor is it competent for us to say just how far the writer's own human genius has embellished the form of the heavenly vision that accompanied his call.

It is important to observe the immediate effect of this vision upon the prophet. It wrought an overpowering conviction of the holiness of God. That look within the veil, that awful vision of the heavenly King upon his throne, the splendor and the voices of the seraphim, crying, "Holy, holy, holy," and the trembling of "the foundations of the thresholds," all together so overwhelmed the youthful seer that he cried out, "Woe is me!" No sinful man can face such majesty and live (comp. Gen. xxxii, 30; Exod. xxxiii, 20; Judg. vi, 22; xiii, 22), and the cry of the prophet was therefore but the natural exclamation of a feeling heart enrapt with such a vision of the Holy One. A personal conviction of the enormity of sin, as it appears in the light of infinite holiness, is indispensable to the highest style of prophet, and it is interesting to note that "the Holy One of Israel" is a frequent expression in Isaiah. "The whole Book of Isaiah," says Delitzsch, "bears traces of the impression of this ecstasy." We note further that when the burning coal from the heavenly altar touches the lips of the prophet, and removes the sin so deeply felt, he at once becomes obedient to the divine call.[1]

The word of the Lord to Isaiah was like an oracle of doom to the sinful nation. It was to prove "a savor from death unto death." At this dark forecast the prophet cried, "How long, O Lord?" and

---

[1] "It is in perfect harmony with the analogy of faith to suppose that the dark speech or enigma of Isaiah's early vision lay in his mind and fructified, till at length he attained that full insight into its meaning which is expressed in verses 9–13. The immediate object of the vision was to set before Isaiah the ideal of prophecy as a lifework, as opposed to the primitive view connecting it too closely with isolated ecstatic moments. Isaiah stands, in consequence of this revelation, between two schools of prophecy. To his predecessors the source of inspiration was more or less external and intermittent; to him it was internal and perennial."—Cheyne, *The Prophecies of Isaiah*, introduction to chap. vi.

he is told that the judgments will come, one after another, until the cities of the land become a spectacle of desolation, and the people go into some far-off region of exile. But the concluding statement (verse 13) contains a germ of hope. After the land of Israel has been made a desolation, and when only a tenth part of the people are left, even that little tenth shall again be subjected to the purging fire of divine chastisement, until the Holy One of Israel shall have secured to himself "a holy seed." The surviving remnant will be like the stock or stump of a strong tree, which, though felled by the woodman's ax, still has its roots deep in the soil and retains germs of life from which shall come forth shoots and branches of glorious promise for the after time (comp. Isa. xi, 1–10).

This idea of an imperishable seed accords with many a Messianic promise and finds further expression in Isaiah's prophecies. The doctrine of "a holy seed," a surviving "remnant," was made prominent in the name Shear-jashub (*a remnant shall return*), which the prophet gave his son (vii, 3; x, 21, 22). It was significant that this child must be taken with him when he was sent to meet Ahaz, for the assurance that a remnant should survive all judgments was one ground of Isaiah's confidence and boldness before the king. In the symbolical name Immanuel of chap. vii, 15; viii, 8, we may discern another aspect of the same blessed hope. The virgin that was then about to bear a son might well call the newborn child GOD WITH US, for, before the child should become old enough to choose between good and evil, God would interpose in behalf of Judah, and overthrow the kingdoms of Damascus and Samaria. Again, in the name of Maher-shalal-hash-baz (viii, 4) we have another sign of the speedy coming of the Lord in judgment to carry into Assyrian exile "the riches of Damascus and the spoil of Samaria." And yet, again, the man child of the wonderful name in chap. ix, 6, is a symbolical word-picture of the highest ideal of the "holy seed," who is destined to bruise the serpent's head, draw all nations unto himself, redeem all Israel, reestablish "the throne of David," and "uphold it with judgment and righteousness forever." So all these symbolical names idealize some aspect of the holy seed referred to in Isaiah's opening vision. Like the lesson taught Moses at the burning bush; like the "still small voice" heard by Elijah after the wind, the earthquake, and the fire, they are so many signs that the true Israel of God will survive all the fires of judgment. Ephraim may vex, and Syria threaten, and Assyria roll in like a flood, and Babylon lead the daughter of Zion into captivity; but "Zion shall be redeemed in judgment, and be called the city of righteousness, the faithful city" (i, 26, 27).

The series of symbolical names ends with that of chap. ix, 6, in which the Messianic ideal is preeminent. But the thought of a surviving remnant as " a holy seed " is taken up again in chap. xi, 1, and the figure of a new shoot, springing out of an old stump, is, as already observed, another picture of the assurance given in chap. vi, 13. Near the close of the New Testament Apocalypse (Rev. xxii, 16), the great Revealer of the mystery of God announces himself as " the root and the offspring of David, the bright, the morning star."

II. ISAIAH XIII–XXIII.

1. In the collection of prophetic oracles against heathen nations which constitutes Isa. xiii–xxiii there are a few passages so apocalyptical in style as to deserve our attention. The first is the highly wrought picture of the day of Jehovah in chap. xiii, 4–13. That day is one of judgment upon Babylon, "the glory of kingdoms, the beauty of the Chaldeans' pride" (verse 19). The fiftieth and fifty-first chapters of Jeremiah should be read in connection with this entire oracle of the fall of the great Chaldean capital. So great an event as the overthrow of that terrible oppressor of many nations is as notable a judgment "as when God overthrew Sodom and Gomorrah" (verse 19). The prophet therefore portrays it in the following style :

Sound of a multitude in the mountains, as of a great people ;
Sound of a tumult of kingdoms of nations assembled !
Jehovah of hosts mustering a host to battle ;
Coming from a land afar, from the end of the heavens,—
Jehovah and the weapons of his fury, to lay waste all the land.
Howl ye, for the day of Jehovah is at hand ;
As a destruction from Shadday shall it come.
Therefore shall all hands become slack,
And every heart of man shall melt,
And they shall be dismayed ; writhing and throes shall seize them ;
As the travailing woman shall they twist in pain ;
Each at his neighbor they shall look aghast, their faces all aflame.
Behold the day of Jehovah cometh, cruel, with wrath and burning of anger,
To make the land a desolation, and destroy her sinners out of her.
For the stars of the heavens and their constellations shall not shed forth their light.
Dark is the sun in his going forth,
And the moon shall not cause her light to shine.
And I will visit evil on the world,
And on the wicked their iniquity.
And I will cause the arrogance of the proud to cease,
And the haughtiness of the lawless I bring low ;
And I will make men rarer than fine gold,
And mankind than the solid gold of Ophir.
Therefore will I make the heavens to tremble,

And the earth shall be shaken out of her place,
In the overflowing wrath of Jehovah of hosts,
And in the day of the burning of his anger (Isa. xiii, 4–13).

This concept of "the day of Jehovah" is an elaboration of what is briefly expressed in Amos v, 18, and is to be compared with Jer. xxx, 7; Zeph. i, 7, 14–17, and Joel i, 15; ii, 1, 2, 11; iii, 14–16. The day of Jehovah is the occasion when he executes his "sore judgment" (comp. Ezek. xiv, 21) upon a land or nation that deserves punishment for its sins. It may be a day of judgment on Israel as well as on a heathen city. "The day of Jezreel" (Hosea i, 11) was the momentous event of God's avenging the blood of Jezreel upon the house of Jehu and putting an end to the "kingdom of the house of Israel in the valley of Jezreel" (verses 4, 5). "The day of Midian" (Isa. ix, 4) was "the slaughter of Midian at the rock of Oreb" (Isa. x, 26), when "Jehovah set every man's sword against his fellow," and cut off the hosts of the Midianites (Judg. vii, 22, 25). In harmony with this conception the prophets regard the victorious armies which execute the judgment as a part of Jehovah's hosts, and the battle itself is Jehovah's as truly as if "the stars in their courses" (Judg. v, 20) and the sun and the moon took part in the terrible conflict.

2. Another passage in this collection of prophecies demanding our special attention is the oracle against Egypt in chap. xix. The prophecy exhibits the two sides of apocalyptic visions; first, the impending judgment upon Egypt (verses 1–15), and secondly, the salvation that shall come to Egypt afterward. The opening words of the oracle depict a coming of Jehovah in the clouds of heaven (comp. Psalm xviii, 9, 10; civ, 3; Dan. vii, 13; Matt. xxiv, 30; xxvi, 64; Rev. i, 7), and so assume the special language of an apocalypse.

Behold Jehovah riding upon a swift cloud and coming into Egypt,
And the idols of Egypt shall tremble at his presence,
And the heart of Egypt shall melt in the midst of it.
And I will stir up Egyptians against Egyptians,[1]
And they shall fight each man against his brother and each against his neighbor.
City against city, kingdom against kingdom.

The description goes on to detail the various ways in which Jehovah will overturn the power and wisdom of the Egyptians, all which are spoken of (in verse 16) as the swinging of Jehovah's hand

---

[1] Comp. Judg. vii, 22 ; 1 Sam. xiv, 16, 20 ; 2 Chron. xx, 23. Such a setting of the enemies to destroy one another is characteristic of Jehovah's warfare, and is made symbolical of "the valley of decision," or "valley of Jehoshaphat" in the Book of Joel. The valley of judgment to the foes becomes the valley of blessing to the friends of Jehovah.

against them. The last part of the chapter (verses 16–25) falls into six short strophes, each of which declares some remarkable result of the smiting of Egypt, and all of which together form a unique ideal of the Messianic future:

(1) Egypt shall thereafter be in awe of the land of Judah "because of the counsel of Jehovah of hosts" (16, 17).

(2) Five cities of Egypt shall speak the language of Canaan (18).

(3) An altar and pillar of witness shall be a sign in Egypt that Jehovah will deliver from oppressors (19, 20).

(4) The Egyptians shall know Jehovah, offer acceptable worship, and be healed (21, 22).

(5) There shall be a highway between Egypt and Assyria, and these rival nations shall have a common worship (23).

(6) Israel shall be a third with Egypt and Assyria, "a blessing in the midst of the earth" (24, 25).

In this remarkable picture of judgment on Egypt, and of such world-wide revolution and conversion that Assyria as well as Egypt shall become a part of Jehovah's inheritance, we are, of course, to understand the names as prophetico-symbolic. Egypt and Assyria disappeared long ago from among the nations; Israel is scattered to the four winds; but the Messianic ideal of the prophecy abides. The true Israel reappears in the Church of Jesus Christ, and Christianity is to-day bringing together the commerce and worship of the most distant nations, the antitypes of Egypt and Assyria.

3. A third passage to which we call attention in this connection is in chap. xxi. The fall of Babylon [1] is presented in this chapter as a "vision," and the picturesque and symbolical aspect of the entire oracle entitles it to consideration in the study of apocalyptics. The questions of date and authorship need not detain us, but the contents clearly imply the time when Babylon is about to perish at the hands of the Medes (Elam),[2] and this we know was true in the closing years of the Babylonian exile. The feast, depicted in verse 5, is well illustrated by Daniel's description of Belshazzar's revelry on the night when the city fell into the hands of the Medes and Persians (Dan. v), and the confirmatory statements of Herodotus (i, 191) and Xenophon

---

[1] Here called symbolically "the wilderness of the sea," as situate in the midst of lowlands often flooded by the great river Euphrates. So Nineveh and Thebes were situate among the rivers of waters (comp. Nahum ii, 8; iii, 8; Jer. li, 13; Rev. xvii, 1). It is noticeable that this oracle (verses 1–10) is the first of four which bear symbolical inscriptions (comp. verses 11, 13, and xxii, 1).

[2] This would not well suit the siege of Sargon, as Cheyne and others have thought; for, as Dillmann observes, Elam was at that time on the side of Babylon, and not against it. See also Delitzsch, *in loco.*

(*Cyrop.*, vii, 23). The destruction is first spoken of as a sweeping tempest from the south land,[1] such as might be supposed to rush up from a southeastern quarter to strike upon Babylon, which, according to Jer. li, 13, was dwelling upon many waters. The violence, treachery, and barbarity of the siege make it a severe vision to the prophet, and fill him for the time with anguish and terror (comp. Isa. xv, 5 ; xvi, 9, 11). He sees the nobles preparing the feast of revelry; they eat and drink, when suddenly comes the cry, "Arise, ye princes, anoint the shield!"

Then the picture receives another setting.[2] A watchman is set upon his tower to announce what he beholds. Troops of horsemen and asses and camels pass before him and disappear, and he waits and listens for some announcement of their mission until, weary of the long waiting, he cries and groans like a lion, and complains that he stands and watches continually, by day and by night, and hears nothing from the long line of troops that he had seen marching away into the distance. At length he sees a troop of men approaching, and soon comes the announcement, "Fallen, fallen is Babylon!" And this fall of Babylon and her idols is announced as a special message from "Jehovah of hosts, the God of Israel," to the people whom he has threshed and winnowed in the land of exile. The fall of Babylon is the signal of restoration for the exiled house of Jacob (comp. chap. xiv, 1, 2), and so, in the New Testament Apocalypse, the fall of Babylon the great prepares the way for the coming of the King of righteousness and the establishment of the New Jerusalem.

III. Apocalypse of General Judgment. Isaiah xxiv–xxvii.

These four chapters, which follow immediately after the group of oracles against the nations (Isa. xiii–xxiii), form one complete composition, and are regarded by all exegetes as an apocalyptic song. They occupy a front rank in Messianic prophecy, exhibit consummate art in their rhetorical structure, but furnish no clew for ascertaining the exact period of their composition.

Accordingly, on the questions of date and authorship critical opinion has been much divided. Those who maintain the Isaianic

---

[1] This no more implies that the armies of Elam would approach Babylon from the south than the word *northern*, in Joel ii, 20, implies that the armies of locusts in chap. i, 4–7, must have come from the north.

[2] The chapter divides naturally into two equal parts. The first (verses 1–5) presents the siege of Babylon in vision, as if impending, and ends with a call for the chiefs to arise from careless feasting and get ready for defensive battle. The second (verses 6–10) presents in true apocalyptic style a repetition of the vision under other symbols. Troops pass and disappear, and by and by comes the report of Babylon's fall.

authorship claim that the confusion and desolation consequent upon the Assyrian invasions furnish a suitable historical occasion. The overthrow and general ruin described in Isa. i, 7, 8, might well have afforded the prophet a sufficient ground for all this picture of ultimate salvation and triumph to be attained only through purging fires of judgment. Few recent critics, however, accept the Isaianic authorship. The language, the scope, and the entire range of conception and structure point to another age and another writer. According to Bleek[1] the author lived and wrote in Judea in the time of Josiah, and just after the overthrow of the Assyrian empire. In the fall of Nineveh, and the great world-power it represented, the prophet recognized the symbol of a general judgment on the earth, to be followed by the glorification of Israel. According to Gesenius, De Wette, and Umbreit, the author lived among the exiles of Babylon and wrote this oracle just before the overthrow of the Chaldean metropolis. Knobel and Davidson place the composition in Judea, soon after the destruction of Jerusalem by Nebuchadnezzar. Ewald[2] holds that the fall of Babylon is presupposed as complete, and that the prophecy belongs to the time when Cambyses was preparing for his Egyptian campaign. Dillmann also[3] seems inclined to favor this view, although he confesses that the exact point of time of the writer is very uncertain. Vatke and Hilgenfeld[4] also place the composition in the Persian period, the latter conjecturing that the destruction of Tyre by Alexander may be referred to. Stade and others have assigned the work to the Grecian period.

It must in all fairness be admitted that the data for determining the exact historical position of the writer do not exist. In the fourth edition of his commentary, even the conservative Delitzsch writes : "The author is not Isaiah himself, but a disciple of Isaiah's, who, in this case, surpasses his master. Isaiah is great in himself, greater still in his disciples, as rivers are greater than the source from which they issue. It must, however, always appear strange that tradition has been so careless as to let the name of a prophet who, like the author of Isa. xxiv–xxvii, played so important a part in the history of thought on the subject of salvation, sink into oblivion." But is this any more strange than that the Book of Job should be anonymous ?

The frequent reference to Zion and Jerusalem, and the words

---

[1] *Einleitung in das Alt. Test.*, p. 293. Berlin, 1886.

[2] *Prophets of the Old Testament*, English translation, vol. v, pp. 23, 24. London, 1881.

[3] *Der Prophet Jesaia*, p. 222. Leipzig, 1890.

[4] *Zeitschrift für wissenschaftliche Theologie*, 9 Yahrg., pp. 437, 438. Comp. Vatke, *Hist.-Krit. Einleitung in das Alt. Test.*, p. 623. Bonn, 1886.

"this mountain" (xxv, 6, 10), are evidence that the writer was an
inhabitant of Jerusalem, and the language of xxiv, 16, 17, imply
that he was dwelling in a land that was undergoing terrible spoliation. The fear of pit and snare was pressing hard upon all such as
should be left in the land. The exclamation "Behold" (הנה), followed by the active participle of the verb which introduces the
principal announcement, as in xxiv, 1, most naturally points to some
catastrophe which is about to come. There were times during Hezekiah's reign when these oracles would have found suitable occasion;
and also later, in the reign of Josiah, and especially in the days of
Jeremiah, when the Chaldean desolation was imminent. But the
scope of the prophecy so far transcended the immediate occasion as
to throw the latter comparatively out of sight. The judgments
and the salvation herein conceived seem rather ideal, and take in
the entire period of the Messianic reign. Only by a long series of
judgments and triumphs is the true Israel of God to attain glorification.

A satisfactory analysis of these chapters is difficult. There is
repetition of sentiment, but not so uniform as to help determine the
order of thought designed by the author. Briggs, in his *Messianic
Prophecy* (pages 295–308), divides the whole into twelve strophes,
but the theory of just so many lines to each strophe obliges him to
make points of division not in accord with the sentiment, and to
refer the last five lines to another writer. We do not find that in
all the great Hebrew poems (especially the prophetic) the successive
strophes contain an equal number of lines. But the principle of
dividing into strophes may lead us to the best analysis. 1. The
first twelve verses contain matter which may well come under one
caption. They portray a picture of widespread desolation. 2. The
next eleven verses present another picture, containing some repetition from the first (for example, verses 18–20), but noticeably
varied. We have, first, notes of joy, and songs in praise of the
righteous, coming from the ends of the earth (14–16). But over
against these songs the prophet sets the dismal situation in the
midst of which he lives (16–18), and then goes on to show that this
desolation is a judgment of heaven, to be consummated upon the
powers above and below, and result in bringing glory to Jehovah,
who reigns in Mount Zion (19–23). Here then we may observe two
passages of about equal length, the second repeating elements of
the first with such notable variations as we often find in apocalyptic
composition. 3. We find, moreover, that the next twelve verses
(xxv, 1–12) have a unity of thought, and are in fact a song of
triumph over the fall of the enemy of God and his people. 4. The

eleven verses which succeed (xxvi, 1–11) are another song of triumph, celebrating with varied thought and expression the same world-judgment as before. 5. Next follows a somewhat longer section of thirteen verses (xxvi, 12–xxvii, 1), a magnificent song of redeemed Israel, declaring how, through suffering and judgment, Jehovah will restore his people, and make that restoration even a resurrection of the dead. This analysis leaves yet another section (6) of about equal length (xxvii, 2–13), which takes on the prophetic form in which the writer speaks in the person of Jehovah, and concludes with the idea which is common to all the apocalypses— Jehovah and his people dwelling in the holy mountain and the city of God.

We accordingly divide into six sections of about equal length, each of which may, if one desires, be subdivided into minor strophes of from six to eight lines each. The first two announce the desolation and coming judgments; the next two are songs corresponding in sentiment to the suggestions of the judgment, and celebrate the certain triumph of God and his people; the fifth is the personified people of God, exulting in the glorious redemption as a life from the dead, and the sixth and last is the very word of Jehovah declaring the principles and results of his judgments, and assuring his people of ultimate glorification in the holy mountain.

I. The Coming Desolation.

1 Lo, Jehovah is about to empty the earth[1] and waste it,
And he will twist its face, and scatter its inhabitants;
2 And like the people so the priest shall be,
Slave like his lord, maid-servant like her mistress,
Buyer like seller, borrower like the lender,
Like him that takes so he that makes a loan.
3 All emptied is the earth, and spoiled, all spoiled,
For Jehovah has declared this very word.

4 Mourns, fades the earth; droops, fades the world away;
They droop—the lofty people of the earth;
5 And the earth has become foul under its inhabitants.
For they have transgressed laws, passed statutes by,
Broken an everlasting covenant;
6 Therefore a curse has eaten up the earth,
And guilty are the inhabitants therein.
Therefore the earth's inhabitants are burned,
And that which is left—a few feeble men.

---

[1] Or, *the land*. A Jewish prophet at Jerusalem would naturally associate this word with his own country, for that was virtually his world. But as his vision enlarges it must needs take in a wider world. Comp. verse 4.

7 The new wine mourns, the vine is drooping low,
   They groan within them all of merry heart.
8 The joy of tabrets rests, the proud exulters' noise has ceased,
9 The joy of harps rests, in the song they drink not wine.
   Bitter is strong drink unto them that drink it.

10 The city of chaos [1] has been broken down,
   Shut up is every house that none may enter.
11 An outcry o'er the wine is in the street,
   Dark is all mirth, the joy of the earth is gone into exile.
12 What is left in the city is a desolation,
   And into ruins is the gateway smitten.

II. Songs and Triumph through Judgment.

13 For thus shall it be in the earth, in the midst of the peoples,
   Like beating of olives, like gleanings [2] when vintage is ended;
14 Those will lift up their voice, they cry for joy,
   At Jehovah's grandeur shout they from the sea.
15 Therefore in east-lands [3] glorify ye Jehovah,
   In the isles of the sea the name of Jehovah, God of Israel.

16 From the edge of the earth have we heard songs—"Glory for the righteous." [4]
   But I say, Famine for me, famine for me, alas for me!
   Spoilers have spoiled, yea, spoil did spoilers spoil.
17 Fear and pit and snare are on thee, O dweller in the land!
18 And it shall be that whoso flees from the noise of the fear falls in the pit,
   And whoso rises from the pit is taken in the snare.

   For windows have been opened [5] from on high,
   And the foundations of the earth do shake.

---

[1] The allusion is to the chaos of Gen. i, 2. The "city of chaos" is so called in view of the confused mass of ruins into which it is about to be reduced by the impending judgment of Jehovah. The particular city intended would naturally be that one which, at the time of the prophet, stood as the most prominent representative of the hostile, godless world-power, exposed to the wrath of Jehovah of hosts. It may have been Nineveh or Babylon, according to the date of the prophecy. But in the true symbolical import of the oracle the "city of chaos" is every city which is hostile to Jehovah and therefore destined to be brought to nothingness.

[2] Here is another figure of the elect remnant, who are called a holy seed in Isa. vi, 13. They survive all the desolating judgments of the world. They are the ones who in the next verse are heard to shout for joy from the lands of their dispersion.

[3] Or, regions of light (אֻרִים). Others read אִיִּם, islands, as in close parallelism with what follows; but east and west are poetically contrasted.

[4] That is, honor and glory are for every righteous soul who exults in Jehovah's majesty. The words are not an ascription to the righteous God, nor to any one distinguished person (as Cyrus, whom Henderson here imagines). Then the seer suddenly checks himself, and remembers that he belongs to a generation destined to waste away and suffer from the violence of the spoiler.

[5] Allusion to the judgment of the flood (Gen. vii, 11). The entire passage (verses 18–20) is a sublime apocalyptic description of national catastrophe. Comp. Nahum i, 3–6.

19 Broken, utterly broken is the earth;
   Shattered, utterly shattered is the earth;
   Shaken, utterly shaken is the earth;
20 Reeling the earth reels like the drunken man,
   And dangles like the hammock to and fro;
   And heavy upon it is its transgression,
   And it is fallen and shall not rise again.

21 And in that day will Jehovah visit doom on the host of the high in the height,
   And on the kings of the ground on the ground,[1]
22 And they shall be assembled, captives for the pit,
   And they shall be imprisoned in the prison,
   And after many days be visited.
23 And the white moon shall blush, and the hot sun feel shame,
   For Jehovah Sabaoth in Mount Zion reigns,
   And in Jerusalem and before his elders is glory.

III. Song of Triumph over the Enemy.

xxv, 1 Jehovah, my God thou art, I will exalt thee,
   I praise thy name for thou hast wrought a wonder,[2]
   Counsels from long ago, truth, verity.
2 For from a city thou hast made a heap,[3]
   A fortified city—to a ruined pile,
   Palace of strangers—city now no more,
   Forever it shall not be builded up.

3 Therefore shall a strong people honor thee,[4]
   A city of the nations shall fear thee.

---

[1] 21-23. The judgment here portrayed is without parallel in the Old Testament. The host on high, as contrasted with "kings of the ground," seems obviously to refer to superhuman principalities and powers which have some kind of rule in the heavens. Such was the "prince of Persia" whom Michael and his associate angelic princes were wont to oppose (Dan. x, 13, 20). From this imagery the New Testament seer derived his symbols of the dragon and his angels (Rev. xii, 7-9), destined as in this vision to be imprisoned in the pit, and afterward visited and released a little season (Rev. xx, 2, 3, 7). Indeed, the harmony of these descriptions, with the final vision of Jehovah reigning on Zion, with his elders before him in glory (comp. Rev. iv, 4), is most striking. We recognize in this passage, therefore, a prophetic outline of the Messianic reign, which is destined to execute judgment on the ungodly of every class and grade, and to issue in the final glorification of the people of God. The ideal Jerusalem of Isaiah is also the golden Jerusalem of John.

[2] A wonder. The writer now occupies the visional standpoint suggested by what has just preceded, namely, the day of final triumph and glorification. The ruin of the wicked and the triumph of the godly constitute an unspeakable wonder. Therefore he turns to glorify in song the judgment of Jehovah.

[3] City heap. Babylon was perhaps the city first rising to the prophet's thought; possibly Nineveh, if Isaiah were the author. But in any case the scope of the vision transcends any local limitation, and contemplates the hostile city that stands in the way of Jehovah's triumph and of Israel's ultimate glorification. This entire passage is a celebration of the redemption of the true Israel.

[4] Honor thee. The address is to Jehovah.

4 For thou hast been a stronghold to the weak,
  A stronghold to the poor in his distress,
  A refuge from the storm, a shade from heat,
  For like a wall-storm [1] was the tyrant's blast.
5 As heat in drought thou quellest noise of strangers,
  As heat in shade of clouds the tyrant's song sinks low.

6 And Jehovah Sabaoth will make for all the peoples in this mountain
  A feast of fat things, feast of wines on the lees,
  Fat things rubbed over, wines on the lees strained off;
7 And he will swallow in this mountain the face of the veil that covers all the peoples,
  Even the covering that is spread o'er all the nations;
8 He swallows up forever death itself,
  And the Lord Jehovah wipes tears from all faces,
  And turns his people's shame from all the earth;
  For Jehovah has declared it.[2]

9 And one will say in that day, Lo, our God is this;
  We waited for him and he rescues us;
  This, this is Jehovah, we have waited for him,
  We will exult and joy in his salvation.
10 For in this mountain Jehovah's hand will rest,
   And Moab [3] shall be trodden under him,
   Like treading straw in the water of a dungpit;
11 And in its midst he will spread out his hands,
   Even as the swimmer spreads his hands to swim;
   But down he casts his pride with the plots of his hands.
12 And the high places of thy walls he hurls,
   Casts down, makes touch the earth, even to the dust.

IV. Celebration of God's Judgments.

xxvi, 1 In that day shall be sung this song in the land of Judah:
  A city strong [4] is ours; salvation he will set for walls and rampart.
2 Open, ye gates, and let a righteous nation enter,
3 Guardian [5] of faithfulness, in thought sustained.

---

[1] A sudden burst of rain and tempest against a wall that serves for a refuge from storm and a shade from heat. Perhaps, however, instead of קיר, *wall*, we should read קר, *cold*=cold wintry storm.

[2] This strophe (verses 6–8) contemplates a glorification which nothing less than the New Testament revelation enables us to understand. Three great thoughts are here, (1) the joyful feast, (2) removal of the veil that darkens the nations, and (3) the abolition of death, "the last enemy" (1 Cor. xv, 26). As a necessary consequence darkness, weeping, and shame are removed from the people of God.

[3] This ancient enemy is named as a representative of all tribes hostile to the people of God. Jehovah will tread all enemies under his feet.

[4] The "strong city" is the ideal Jerusalem, here set in striking contrast with the high fortress of the enemy which is to be hurled down to the dust. So habitually, in apocalyptic visions, the hostile city is cast down to give place to the city of God: Babylon, the harlot, falls, that the heavenly Jerusalem may appear in her glory.

[5] By ignoring the masoretic punctuation in verses 2 and 3, and arranging the parallelism as in our translation, we secure the more direct and simple idea that it is the

Thou [1] wilt keep peace, peace; for in thee they trust.
4 Put ye your trust forever in Jehovah:
   For in Jah Jehovah is the Rock of Ages.

5 For he has hurled down them that dwell on high;
   The lofty city, he will cast it down,
   To the earth will cast it, make it touch the dust.
6 A foot shall tread it down,—
   Feet of the wretched, footsteps of the weak.
7 The pathway for the just is evenness,
   Straight wilt thou smooth the highway of the just.

8 Also in the path of thy judgment, O Jehovah, we have waited for thee.[2]
   Toward thy name and thy memorial there is longing of soul;
9 In my soul have I longed for thee by night,
   Yea, in my spirit within me do I seek thee.
   For when thy judgments reach unto the earth,
   The world's inhabitants learn righteousness.

10 Let a sinner be favored, he learns not righteousness,
   In a land of right he will act wickedly,
   He will not see the majesty of Jehovah.
11 Jehovah, thy hand is high, (but) they will not see;
   Let them see,[3] and with shame, zeal for a people;
   Yea, even the fire of thy foes shall devour them.

V. ISRAEL'S RESURRECTION SONG.

12 Jehovah, thou wilt establish peace for us,
   For also all our works thou hast wrought for us.
13 Jehovah, our God, lords besides thee have ruled us;
   Alone in thee we celebrate thy name.
14 The dead ones [4] shall not live; the shades shall not rise up,
   Therefore didst thou visit and destroy them,
   And cause all memory of them to perish.

---

righteous nation that acts as guardian of the truth (אֱמֻנִים, *faithfulnesses*, or *faithful ones*), being itself divinely sustained and established in heart.

[1] Here the address turns directly unto Jehovah.

[2] The prophet here speaks for the devout Israel, who pray day and night for the triumph of righteousness. The great day of the manifestation of Jehovah is conceived as following upon the path of his judgments. Judgment opens and closes the period of the Messiah's reign.

[3] The construction and sense of verse 11 are obscure. Our translation is faithful to the Hebrew text. By taking יֶחֱזוּ and יֵבֹשׁוּ as jussives, and "zeal for a people" as accusative after these verbs, we have the wish that those who will not see may yet their eyes opened and be put to shame at the zeal of God in behalf of his people. That zeal is also a fire to devour Jehovah's enemies.

[4] These are to be understood of the dead lords who had ruled over Israel and oppressed them, but who are conceived as shades that shall not rise again. Observe the contrast in verse 19: These impious dead shall not live, but Jehovah's dead shall live and exult in triumph.

15 Thou hast, O Jehovah, added[1] to the nation;
   Thou hast added to the nation; thou art honored;
   Far hast thou set all limits of the land.
16 O Jehovah, in distress they visited thee,
   They poured out prayer when thou wast scourging them.
17 As one with child draws near the time to bear,
   She writhes, she cries out in her labor pains,
   So have we been away from thee, O Jehovah.
18 We were with child, we writhed; thus bore we wind;
   We could not work salvation for the land,
   Nor would the world's inhabitants fall forth.

19 Thy dead[2] shall live; my body—they shall rise;
   Awake and sing, O dwellers of the dust;
   For dew of lights is thy dew,[3] and earth shall cast forth shades.
20 Go thou, my people, enter in thy chambers,
   And fasten up thy double doors behind thee;
   Hide a small moment till the wrath be past.
21 For behold, Jehovah from his place goes forth,
   To visit the guilt of earth's inhabitants,
   And the earth shall disclose her mass of blood,
   And no more shall she cover up her slain.
xxvii, 1 In that day will Jehovah visit with his sword,
   The harsh, the mighty, and the violent,
   Upon Leviathan,[4] the flying serpent,
   And on Leviathan the crooked serpent,
   And slay the Dragon that is in the sea.

---

[1] That is, multiplied the nation (comp. Isa. ix, 3). In his address the prophet here turns away from the dead lords, whose memory is blotted out, and sets in contrast the glory of his people, who in their distress seek Jehovah, humble themselves, and through great pain and trial obtain as it were life from the dead.

[2] "Thy dead" are Jehovah's dead, and "my body" is the collective Israel, in whose name the prophet speaks. The thought running through the context is: Our writhings to produce a population and to save the land were all in vain; but thy power, O Jehovah, can make thy dead ones live again. So the nation is multiplied (verse 15) as by a resurrection from the dead, the boundaries of the land are enlarged, and the great body of God's people, the multitudinous dwellers in the dust, shall awake and sing (comp. Hosea vi, 2, and Ezek. xxxvii, 1–10).

[3] "Thy dew" is God's dew, and called "dew of lights," as if it were the product of heavenly luminaries, glittering in the beams of the morning, and suggesting the light and freshness of a new day. Such brightness quickens the dead into life and draws forth the shades from their secret places.

[4] Two Leviathans and the Dragon are named here as mystic designations of three hostile powers—probably Assyria, Babylon, and Egypt. The names thus used symbolically were appropriated from ancient myths of the monsters of the deep (comp. Psalm lxxiv, 13, 14; Isa. li, 9, 10; Ezek. xxix, 3; Job xli, 1, and Psalm civ, 26), but how far these Hebrew poets and prophets were acquainted with the origin and history of the myths it is now impossible to determine. For an interesting discussion of these names and their mythical significance see Gunkel, *Schöpfung und Chaos*, pp. 41–61 and pp. 69–81.

VI. Jehovah's Assuring Word for Israel.

2 In that day, a delightful [1] vineyard,—sing to it;
3 I Jehovah keep it,[2] water it each moment;
Lest any harm it, night and day I keep it.

4 Fury is not mine; [3] would that I had thorns and briers in battle,
I would rush in them, set them all ablaze.
5 Or—would one fasten upon my stronghold,
Let him make peace with me, make peace with me.
6 In coming times [4] shall Jacob strike deep root,
Israel shall blossom, and shall put forth buds,
And fill the surface of the world with fruit.

7 Like the smiting of his smiter did he smite him?
Or like the slaughter of his slayers was he slain?
8 In a measure didst thou in sending her off strive with her.
He growled with his rough blast in the day of the east wind.
9 Therefore by this he covers Jacob's guilt,
And this is all the fruit of putting away his sin;
In his making all the altar stones like shattered limestones;—
The Asherim and sun-pillars shall not rise.

10 For a fenced city [5] has become a waste,
A dwelling left, forsaken as the desert.
There feeds the calf, and then lies down, and ends her boughs.
11 When her twigs become dry they shall be broken;
Women will come and set them in a blaze.
For he is not a people of understanding;
Therefore his Maker will not pity him,[6]
And He that formed him will not show him mercy.

12 And in that day will Jehovah beat out (grain),
From the flood of the river unto Egypt's stream,
And one by one will [7] ye be gathered, O sons of Israel.

---

[1] Instead of חֶמֶר, *wine*, we here read with the Septuagint חֶמֶד, *delight*. The language of this verse is abrupt and obscure. It seems to be the heading of the song which begins with the next verse.

[2] In this prophetic song Jehovah is the speaker, but the song is one in which the people of Jehovah may be permitted to join "in that day."

[3] That is, against my vineyard; but the thorns and briers that grow up in it he would fain burn up.

[4] The Hebrew הַבָּאִים, *the coming* —, is indefinite. Days or years is the word to be supplied, and the period intended is that of the Messiah. Israel is destined to fill the face of the world with fruit. The ideal is like that of Isa. iv, 2–6.

[5] Allusion to the same hostile citadel of the world-power as in xxiv, 10; xxv, 2; xxvi, 5. It sinks into utter desolation, and becomes a place where calves may wander and lie down, and put an end to the few green boughs that may be found there.

[6] The hostile people, who persist in ignoring Jehovah, must ultimately perish without mercy. Such is the uniform lesson of divine revelation.

[7] In his adding to the nation (see xxvi, 15), and begetting an innumerable multitude, he acquires them one by one, every man according to his individual faith and

13 And it shall come to pass in that day that there will be blowing with a great
   trumpet,[1]
And those lost in Assyria's land shall come,
And those that were in Egypt's land dispersed,
And they will pay their homage unto Jehovah,
In the holy mountain, in Jerusalem.[2]

IV. Isaiah xxviii–xxxiii.

The apocalypse of general judgment is followed by another sub-
division of Isaiah, which Delitzsch calls the "Book of Woes," but
which Orelli entitles the " Book of Zion." Both headings may be
defended, for, as Delitzsch says, "all the independent and self-
contained discourses in this prophetic cycle begin with ' Woe,' " and
Orelli, while conceding this fact, observes that " as in chaps. vii–xii,
it was the person of the Messiah springing from David's house that
bound the whole closely together, so here it is the salvation established by God on Zion, more under local than personal aspects,
which serves as a leading idea to unite the several pieces together.
These two ideas (the Davidic kingdom and the abode of God on
the holy mount) were ever the pillars sustaining the prophecies
whose goal was the perfecting of God's kingdom."[3]

But as the greater part of these oracles is not strictly apocalyptic,
we attend only to two short passages, one of which (xxx, 27–33)
depicts a coming of Jehovah to execute judgment, and the other
(xxxiii, 20–24) his dwelling with his people upon Mount Zion, and
acting as their judge, lawgiver, and king. The coming of Jehovah
in punitive judgment upon Assyria is thus portrayed :

27 Behold, the name[4] of Jehovah cometh from afar,
   Burning in his wrath, and a heavy uplifting of smoke ;
   His lips are full of fury, and his tongue like devouring fire,
28 And his breath is like an overflowing torrent that divides even to the neck,
   To swing nations in a swing of nothingness,[5]

---

deeds. He gathers them in as one who beats out grain on many a threshing floor ;
and the regions from which they are gathered are as far apart as are the extremities
of the world known to the prophet—the boundaries of Assyria and Egypt. Comp. Isa.
xix, 23, 24.

[1] Note this apocalyptic symbol for the gathering of the elect of Jehovah, and compare Matt. xxiv, 31 ; 1 Thess. iv, 16 ; 1 Cor. xv, 52 ; Rev. xi, 15.

[2] Note how apocalyptic visions end with a glorification of Zion and Jerusalem, and
God and his people dwelling there. Comp. Isa. ii, 3 ; xxxv, 10 ; lxvi, 19–24 ; Jer. iii,
17 ; Ezek. xlviii, 35 ; Joel iii, 17, 21 ; Obad. 17, 21 ; Zeph. iii, 14, 15 ; Zech. ii, 10 ;
viii, 3, 22.

[3] Commentary on Isaiah, in loco.

[4] The name of Jehovah is the manifestation of Jehovah in signal judgments ; "that
side of Jehovah which is manifested to the world " (Cheyne).

[5] That is, one that swings nations into nothingness ; reduces to annihilation.

And a misleading bridle is on the cheeks of peoples.
29 Your song shall be as in a night when a feast is hallowed,[1]
  And a joy of heart like one marching with flutes,
  To go to the mountain of Jehovah, unto the Rock of Israel.
30 And Jehovah will cause the majesty of his voice to be heard,
  And the letting down of his arm will he display,
  In fury of anger and flame of devouring fire,
  Cloudburst, and rain storm, and hailstones.
31 For by Jehovah's voice shall Asshur be broken,
  With the rod[2] (with which) he will smite.
32 And every passing over of the rod of destiny,
  Which Jehovah shall cause to fall upon him,
  Shall be with timbrels and with lutes,
  And with battles of swinging[3] will he fight against them.
33 For set in order from of old is Topheth,[4]
  Even for Molech was it prepared; made deep and wide;
  Its pile is fire and wood in great abundance,
  The breath of Jehovah, like a torrent of brimstone, is burning within it.

The variety and force of the imagery employed in this short passage deserve studious attention. In all the displays of power and fury attendant upon the overthrow of the Assyrian empire the prophet beholds the parousia of Jehovah. The judgment executed is a manifestation of his Name. Accordingly, he portrays him as coming in furious anger, breathing out a torrent of fire, yet veiled in clouds of smoke, confounding and annihilating nations with the overpowering brightness of his coming. His majestic voice terrifies, the hand of his power is felt in flames of lightning, cloudburst, and hailstones; Assyria is broken by the rod of divine anger, and her king and all the host of oppressors are consigned to Topheth, the fires of which are kindled into fury "like a torrent of brimstone." How these figures of punitive wrath are appropriated and modified by later apocalyptists we shall see when we come to examine later prophecies.

The counterpart of the foregoing picture of judgment is found in the concluding verses of chap. xxxiii, where a vision of Zion is held up to view:

---

[1] Allusion to the first passover feast in Egypt, when Israel marched out of bondage toward the mountain of God.

[2] Jehovah employed Assyria as his rod to scourge Israel (Isa. x, 5), and now Assyria in turn feels the stroke of the rod of his anger.

[3] Battles in which Jehovah swings the rod of destiny.

[4] Topheth, the name of the place in the valley of Hinnom where abominable sacrifices were offered to Molech, is here used symbolically as a "place of burning," deep and wide enough to burn the king of Assyria and all his army. Jehovah's judgment will thus be shown to be consuming fire, burning to utter destruction the enemy of his people. Comp. Jer. vii, 31-33; xix, 6-15.

20 Behold Zion, the city of our festal assembly;[1]
  Thine eyes shall see Jerusalem a restful dwelling.
  A tent that shall not move about,[2] its pins shall never be pulled up,
  And none of its cords shall be broken.
21 But there majestic Jehovah will be ours;[3]
  A place of rivers, canals broad on both hands,
  In which there shall not go a boat with oars,[4]
  Nor shall majestic ship pass over it.
22 For Jehovah is our judge, Jehovah is our commander;
  Jehovah is our king; he will save us.
23 Loosed are thy cords,—[5]
  They hold not fast the socket of their mast,
  They cannot keep the flag outspread.
  Then is the spoil of plundering divided,
  The lame have seized upon the prey.
24 And no one dwelling (there) shall say, I am sick;[6]
  The people who dwell in it have their guilt forgiven (xxxiii, 20–24).

This vision of a glorified Zion is presented to the eyes of those sinners in Zion who are stricken with terror at God's judgment, and who ask,
  Who among us can sojourn in devouring fire?
  Who among us can sojourn in eternal burnings? (verse 14.)

They are answered that the consuming fires of Jehovah shall have no power on those who "walk righteously and speak uprightly," and keep themselves pure from all kinds of evil. Such are like the burning bush of Moses's vision (Exod. iii, 2), and the holy seed whose stump abides and ever sprouts anew (Isa. vi, 13). Their eyes shall see the king of Judah clothed in ideal beauty (verse 17),

---

[1] The ideal of the heavenly Zion and Jerusalem, the city of "the general assembly and church of the firstborn who are enrolled in heaven" (Heb. xii, 23).

[2] It is to be the antitype of the Mosaic tabernacle, the dwelling of God among men as declared in the vision of John (Rev. xxi, 3). Compare the chapter on the symbolism of the tabernacle, p. 81, *ff.*

[3] When the tabernacle of God is with men, "they shall be his peoples, and God himself shall be with them and be their God" (Rev. xxi, 3).

[4] The idea is that the place of Jehovah's dwelling with his people is so guarded by streams and canals on all sides that no kind of hostile vessels will venture to approach it.

[5] The cords or tacklings of the ship of Zion. The figure seems to have been suggested by the allusion to hostile vessels in verse 21. For now, as the prophet writes, Zion is like a ship in such ill plight as scarcely to be able to keep her mast in position; but *then*, in the certain triumphs of that coming time of the vision, in spite of all difficulties, they are seen dividing abundance of spoil. Even the lame take the prey. So they are "more than conquerors."

[6] Comp. Isa. xxxv, 5, 6; lxv, 19, 20; Rev. xxi, 4. Parallel with this freedom from sickness is deliverance from the guilt of sin. It is a Messianic ideal, in which body and soul are conceived as perfected in the presence of God. Comp. 1 Thess. v, 23.

and the land of Israel shall again appear as it once did in the
vision of Abraham, a land stretching as far as eye could see "northward, and southward, and eastward, and westward" (Gen. xiii, 14).
The fierce and barbarous people shall disappear (verse 19), and
Zion and Jerusalem shall be seen in glory, a restful dwelling for
the people of Jehovah. There Jehovah himself will dwell in majesty and keep it secure from all hostile assaults. Though Zion
now seems like a disabled vessel in the midst of storms, *then* shall
her people be victors over all calamity and divide a vast amount
of spoils. No sickness of body shall then be felt; no burden of
guilt shall then remain unlifted from the soul. All this is an Old
Testament prophetic parallel of what we read in more definite outline in Rev. xxi, 1–8.

V. Isaiah xxxiv and xxxv.

These two chapters present another apocalyptic picture of a
great national judgment followed by the redemption and glorification of Jehovah's people. Jehovah's wrath is declared against all
the nations, but the sword of his anger is drawn in fury against the
land of Edom.[1] The first ten verses of this description are so remarkable for boldness of conception and style that we present them
in the following translation :

> 1 Come near, ye nations, to hear, and ye peoples, attend;
>   Let the earth hear[2] and the fullness thereof,
>   The world and all things that come forth of it.
> 2 For Jehovah has wrath against all the nations
>   And fury against all their host:
>   He has laid them under ban, given them to the slaughter.
> 3 And their slain shall be cast out,
>   And the stink of their carcasses shall go up.
>   And mountains shall be melted[3] with their blood.
> 4 And all the host[4] of heaven shall molder away,

---

[1] "Edom here is what Moab is in chaps. xxiv–xxvii. By the side of Babylon the
world empire, whose policy of conquest led it to enslave Israel, Edom represents the
world which is hostile to Israel as the people of Jehovah. For Edom is Israel's brother
nation, and hates Israel as the people of the election. In this its unbrotherly, hereditary
hatred, it represents the enemies and persecutors of the Church of Jehovah as such in
their entirety. The specific counterpart to Isa. xxxiv is Isa. lxiii, 1–6."—*Delitzsch*,
Biblical Commentary on Isaiah, *in loco*.

[2] Compare the similar appeal in Isa. i, 2 ; Deut. xxxii, 1 ; and Psalm xlix, 1.

[3] The boldness of the thought is remarkable. Blood flowing in such abundance as
to dissolve the mountains may be compared with Ezek. xxxii, 6, and Rev. xiv, 20, and
contrasted with the hyperbole of Amos ix, 13.

[4] Compare the language of Ezek. xxxii, 7, 8 ; Joel ii, 31 ; iii, 15 ; Matt. xxiv, 29 ;
2 Peter iii, 10 ; Rev. vi, 13, 14.

And the heavens shall be rolled up as a scroll,
And all their hosts shall fade as fades the leaf from the vine,
And as a fading leaf from the fig tree.
5 For in the heaven my sword [1] has drunk its fill,
Behold upon Edom it shall come down
And upon the people of my curse, for judgment.
6 The sword of Jehovah is full of blood, besmeared with fat,[2]
From blood of lambs and goats, from kidney fat of rams.
For Jehovah has a sacrifice in Bozrah.
And a great slaughter in the land of Edom.
7 And the wild oxen shall come down with them,[3]
And bullocks with strong oxen.
And their land shall be drunken with blood,
And their dust with fat besmeared.
8 For it is a day of the vengeance of Jehovah,
A year of recompenses for the controversy of Zion.[4]
9 And its streams shall be turned to pitch and its dust to brimstone,
And its land shall become pitch, burning by night and by day,[5]
10 It shall not be quenched forever,
Its smoke shall go up [6] from generation to generation,
It shall lie waste forever and ever, none passing through it.

The rest of the chapter is filled with details of a picture of desolation, somewhat like Isa. xiii, 20–22. The imagery is notably of a
different character from that of the preceding verses, but it serves
to show impressively how Jehovah's vengeance upon Edom will
leave that land a scene of utter ruin and perpetual waste. The
thought and language of the first ten verses of the chapter are sublime in the extreme, and yet the judgment described is one that was
long ago executed on the land and people of Edom.

---

[1] This sword of Jehovah is no other than that which flamed in the Edenic Apocalypse (Gen. iii, 24), symbol of divine justice and judgment. Here the prophet speaks
of it as intoxicated with fury against the Edomites. Comp. Jer. xlvi, 10.

[2] Here Jehovah is depicted as one who offers a great sacrifice, and the lambs, goats,
and rams are the nations slain in such masses that the sword of their slaughter seems
to be full of their blood and their fat. Compare the similar figure in Jer. xlvi, 10 ;
Ezek. xxxix, 17–19 ; Zeph. i, 7 ; Rev. xix, 17, 18.

[3] That is, to the place of slaughter. Three kinds of horned cattle are here named
to correspond to the three kinds of smaller animals, lambs, goats, and rams, named in
verse 6.

[4] Recompense for the long strife of nations over Zion ; avenging of Zion's wrongs, to
the silencing of the reproaches which she has suffered from her enemies. Compare
the sentiment of Isa. lxi, 2, 3 ; lxiii, 4.

[5] We follow Cheyne in connecting these words with the preceding, and in observing
that the perpetuity of the desolation is thus four times asserted. This arrangement
of clauses is favored by the fact that adverbs denoting perpetuity usually in the Hebrew follow their verbs.

[6] Comp. Rev. xiv, 10, 11; xix, 3, and Gen. xix, 28.

The thirty-fifth of Isaiah presents an ideal of beauty and excellence in striking contrast to that of desolation in the preceding chapter. It is an apocalyptic picture of the new earth (comp. Isa. lxv, 17; lxvi, 22 ; 2 Peter iii, 13; Rev. xxi, 1), which the ransomed people of Jehovah shall inherit. All nature is to blossom in a glorious beauty and appear like a blessed garden of delight. No more will barren deserts and ravenous beasts be known. There will be no sickness (comp. xxxiii, 24), for the blind shall see, the deaf shall hear, the lame shall leap as a hart, and the dumb shall sing. A highway for God's released ones, and for them only, will lead them safely unto Zion, whither they shall come with joyful songs, and from them "sorrow and sighing shall flee away." This glorious future is Jehovah's "recompense for the controversy of Zion" (xxxiv, 8 ; comp. xxxv, 4). He thus comes to save (comp. xxxv, 4, and xxxiii, 22), and the salvation and glory implied in this thirty-fifth chapter is parallel with those of chap. xxxiii, 15–24.

When the Messianic hope took form in the prophet's soul as the full recompense and salvation of God it was fittingly portrayed as something far transcending the common joys of men. All that was conceived as baneful must pass away, and all that was beautiful and glorious in thought was assured. And so the Messianic hope was wont to connect with ideals of the transformation of nature, the absence of all evil, and the fruition of everlasting joy.

VI. Isaiah xl–lxvi.

The last twenty-seven chapters of Isaiah are not strictly apocalyptic, but they contain so many ideals of the redemption and future glory of Jehovah's people that we cannot pass them without some notice. Later apocalyptists have drawn from the metaphors and language of these chapters, and in no part of the Old Testament do we find more glowing conceptions of the Messiah's age and the future of the kingdom of God.

The writer's point of view is the time of the Babylonian exile. He refers to Cyrus as a well-known character, a conqueror whom Jehovah has stirred up from the sun-rising, and given peoples and kings to trample under foot (xli, 2, 25); he is moved to build God's city and send his exiles home (xlv, 13); he is God's eagle from a far country (xlvi, 11). In xliv, 28, and xlv, 1, Jehovah calls him his *shepherd* and his *anointed.* Cyrus did not know or worship the God of Israel, but was nevertheless employed in the providence of Him who "removeth kings and setteth up kings" (Dan. ii, 21), to conserve and advance the interests of the Jewish people. Hence he says, "I have called thee by thy name, I have titled thee (that is, called him *shepherd* and *anointed*), though thou hast not known me" (xlv, 4). It was of God that this remarkable Persian was called to perform all his pleasure, and to say of Jerusalem, "She shall be built; and to the temple, Thy foundation shall be laid " (xliv, 28).

When this great prophet wrote the Jewish people were in exile, Judah was a desolation, and Jerusalem and the temple were in ruins. "Thy holy cities are become a wilderness," he cries; "Zion is become a wilderness, Jerusalem a desolation. Our holy and beautiful house, where our fathers praised thee, is burned with fire: and all our pleasant things are laid waste" (lxiv, 10, 11). "Our adversaries have trodden down thy sanctuary " (lxiii, 18; comp. xlii, 22–25; xliv, 26–28).

From this standpoint the entire prophecy of Isa. xl–lxvi appears as a word of consolation. The first verses are a blessed oracle of assuring grace: "Comfort ye, comfort ye my people, saith your God. Speak ye to the heart of Jerusalem, and cry unto her, that her warfare is accomplished, that her iniquity is pardoned; that she hath received from the hand of Jehovah double for all her sins " (xl, 1, 2). Then Jehovah is spoken of as coming to accomplish the salvation of his people. His glory is to be revealed so that all flesh shall see it together. "Behold," he cries, "the Lord Jehovah as a mighty One shall come, and his arm ruling for him. Behold, his reward is with him, and his recompense before him. He shall feed his flock like a shepherd, he shall gather the lambs in his arm, and carry them in his bosom, and gently lead those that give suck." All this contemplates a divine parousia, and its outlook is realized only in the Messianic era.

Accordingly these twenty-seven chapters, summed up in a word or two, depict the glorification of Zion, as consequent upon the downfall of Babylon. Herein is the one great apocalyptic idea that runs through the oracle as a whole. Bel must bow down, Nebo must stoop. The idols of Babylon are to be carried off by beasts of burden as so much good-for-nothing rubbish. The proud daughter of Babylon is to be humbled in the dust and exposed to bitter shame (xlvii, 1–5). But the captive daughter of Zion is to awake and put on her beautiful garments (comp. Rev. xxi, 2), go forth out of Babylon, and flee from the Chaldeans (xlviii, 20; lii, 1, 2). She shall not, however, go out in haste as at the exodus from Egypt, for Jehovah will go before her and the God of Israel will be her rearward (lii, 11, 12). The great central figure of this redemption is Jehovah's servant, who is led as a lamb to the slaughter, and whose soul is made an offering for sin, but who shall see of the travail of his soul, and be satisfied (lii, 13–liii, 12). Along with this ideal sufferer the true Israel of God are destined alike to suffer and to triumph (comp. 2 Tim. ii, 11, 12).

> For a small moment have I forsaken thee;
> But with great mercies will I gather thee.
> In overflowing wrath I hid my face from thee a moment;
> But with everlasting kindness will I have mercy on thee (liv, 7, 8).

The mighty struggles of redemption are not the matter of a little time. They will involve danger and loss. It is the old and age-long conflict of the woman's and the serpent's seed. But the fall of Babylon is assurance that no proud oppressor will ultimately triumph. No weapon formed to oppose Jehovah shall permanently prosper.

For, behold, I create new heavens and new earth;
And the former things shall not be remembered, nor come into mind.
But be ye glad and rejoice forever in that which I create:
For, behold, I create Jerusalem a rejoicing, and her people a joy.
And I will rejoice in Jerusalem, and joy in my people:
And the voice of weeping shall be no more heard in her, nor the voice of crying (lxv, 17–19).

In all this magnificent picture we have an Old Testament ideal of what is more fully symbolized in the New Testament Apocalypse of the fall of Babylon, the harlot, and the glory of Jerusalem, the bride.

CHAPTER XIV

APOCALYPSE OF EZEKIEL

THE scope and style of Ezekiel's prophecies carry him over a broader field than that of any other apocalyptist of the Old Testament, for his forty-eight chapters are made up of vision, allegory, parable, symbolico-typical action, and formal prophesying. The formal apocalyptical elements in Isaiah are comparatively incidental and exceptional; those of Ezekiel are remarkably conspicuous, and detailed with such peculiar individuality of conception as to suggest a contrast between him and Isaiah very much like that which Macaulay has drawn between Dante and Milton. The most striking illustration of this is seen in the introductory vision, which occupies the entire first chapter, and should be compared with Isa. vi and Rev. iv.

This opening vision, though described in extensive detail, is remarkable for its majesty and impressiveness. St. Jerome says that the ancient synagogue treated the chapter as a record of secret theology concerning God and angels, and that the Jews did not permit their children to read it before the age of thirty, and even prohibited any attempt at a public exposition of it. But a careful study of its parts will show that its main purpose is essentially the same as that of Isaiah's vision which sealed his divine call to the prophetic office. The vision of Jehovah, seated on his throne, and surrounded with holy seraphim, produced in Isaiah an immediate sense of his own sinfulness (Isa. vi, 5); this vision of "the glory of Jehovah" caused Ezekiel to fall upon his face (Ezek. i, 28; comp. iii, 23 ; Dan. viii, 17 ; Rev. i, 17).

The place where Ezekiel received this first vision was "in the land of the Chaldeans by the river Chebar." This stream should not be identified with the Habor, "the river of Gozan" (2 Kings xvii, 6), which was in the land of the Medes, and two hundred or more miles from those rivers of Babylon by which the Jewish captives sat down and wept when they remembered Zion (Psalm cxxxvii, 1). It was more probably the great canal of Nebuchadnezzar, which, according to Abydenus, was called the royal river, and was dug so as to serve as a branch of the Euphrates. The date of the vision is definitely given as "the fifth year of King Jehoiachin's captivity." This Jewish monarch had reigned only three months when he and his mother and all the princes and mighty men of his kingdom, and all the craftsmen and smiths, were carried into exile, and none were left behind except the very poorest classes of the people (2 Kings xxiv, 8–16). This was to the exiles a memorable woe, a national calamity never to be forgotten, and therefore might well form an epoch in the thought of this prophet of the captivity, as "the thirtieth year" of his own life was also.

In the beginning of the prophet's description of his vision we notice the fourfold statement, "The heavens were opened, I saw visions of God, the word of Jehovah came expressly (or forcibly), the hand of Jehovah was there upon him." The first two suggest external presentations of the divine glory. The opening heavens indicate the source of all divine revelations, and visions are one method of communicating divine thoughts. The third statement conveys the idea of a moving revelation and message brought directly to the prophet's mind, and commissioning him for his ministry, while the fourth indicates the bestowal of a supernatural divine energy, by means of which all things became intensely vivid to his soul. As Ezekiel, in his thirtieth year, by the river Chebar saw heaven opened, received the word, and felt the hand of Jehovah, so Jesus, at the age of thirty, received by the river Jordan the wondrous anointing from on high; but in his case the Spirit, instead of presenting symbols of power and judgment, took rather the semblance of a dove.

In the vision the prophet beheld a stormy whirlwind sweeping down from the north (verse 4), and in its distant movement it seemed to be a great cloud. The whirlwind is naturally suggestive of God's desolating judgments (comp. Isa. xxix, 6; Jer. xxiii, 19; xxv, 32). The north is the natural region of clouds and storms. And so this stormy wind cloud forcibly symbolized a rapidly approaching calamity, a divine dispensation of judgment, from that quarter out of which all the bitter woes of Israel and Judah came (comp. Jer. i, 14; iv, 6; vi, 1)—that home of heathen gods upon whose mountains the ambitious monarch of Babylon would fain have set his throne (Isa. xiv, 13). From this direction the Assyrian and Chaldean armies had rushed down upon the land of the Hebrews.

The prophet further beheld "a fire unfolding itself," as if catching hold on itself, twisting in tongues of flame, and flashing continuously. We infer that this writhing fire appeared in the midst of the cloud. It was significant of God's presence and power, as in the burning bush (Exod. iii, 2), the pillar of fire (Exod. xiii, 21), and in the various representations of divine indignation against the wicked (comp. Deut. xxxii, 22; Isa. lxvi, 15; Heb. xii, 29). Round about the cloud was a circle of brightness, and in the midst of the fire something that resembled the glittering brilliancy of amber.[1] This latter was adapted to intensify in the prophet a sense of the living energy of that divine Power that was here revealing itself, while the circle of brightness was an appropriate emblem of the grace of God which always encompasses the dispensations of judgment. For love itself will chasten to reform the erring, and even punish with death in order to secure the ultimate peace and glory of the universal kingdom.

The next objects seen in the vision were "four living creatures," which seemed to come out of the midst of the fire (verse 5). In chap. x these living creatures are called the cherubim. Their general appearance bore preeminently "the likeness of a man;" that is, as appears from the context, the position of the head and the shape of the body of each resembled a man more than any other single creature. Each one of these living creatures had four faces and four wings (verse 6). The faces were those of a man, a lion, an ox, and an eagle (comp. Rev. iv, 7). The human and lion faces were on the right side, the face of the ox on the left side (verse 10), but the position of the eagle face is not told. We may infer, however, that the human faces were toward the prophet, and so the eagle faces, turned in the opposite direction, would naturally escape more particular designation. The wings were "divided above" (verse 11), so that, when the living creatures stood, the upper pair spread out horizontally, and the tips of the wings of one cherub joined the tips of the wings of another (verse 23), and the other pair were closed or let down so as to cover their bodies. When in motion the noise of the wings was awe-inspiring, like the sound of many waters, or the tumultuous tramping of a great host, or as the voice of the Almighty heard in the thunder's roar (verse 24; comp. Rev. xiv, 2; xix, 6). Under their wings these cherubs "had the hands of a man" (verse 8), which, according to chap. x, 7, each cherub could send forth at pleasure to perform the will of heaven. They also had "straight feet" (verse 7), that is, extending straight downward, and the sole or hoof was like that of a calf's foot, and "sparkled like the color of burnished brass." Thus extending straight downward, not turned horizontally as the human foot, they resembled those on the Babylonian monuments, which are round, and sometimes nearly square. Thus all was in keeping with the fourfold form of the creatures, and a peculiarity of their movements was that they could proceed in any direction without turning as they went.

---

[1] Hebrew, *as the eye of hashmal;* that is, according to Hävernick, as the brilliant spark that flies off from this kind of metal when beaten in the fire.

Viewed altogether, the appearance of these wonderful cherubs was like burning coals of fire and the appearance of lamps or torches (verse 13). Their entire composite form seemed to radiate as with flashes of lightning. The picture is climacteric, coals, lamps, lightning. When the creatures ran upon their mission or returned their movement seemed to the prophet like "the appearance of a flash of lightning" (verse 14).

But as the prophet continued to gaze upon the living creatures he beheld also "a wheel upon the earth beside the living creatures" so peculiarly formed as to present four faces or sides (verse 15). This was made to appear like one wheel in the middle of another, intersecting each other at right angles so as to run north or south, east or west, without needing to be turned about (verses 16, 17). These wheels were of the greenish color of the beryl stone, and of immense size. Their rings or rims were so high as to inspire the beholder with dread, and were "full of eyes round about" (verse 18). In the later vision of chap. x, 12, the wheels themselves, and also the backs, hands, and wings of the cherubim appeared full of eyes (comp. Rev. iv, 6). In their movements the wheels followed closely by the living creatures, so that they must have appeared somewhat like flaming chariots drawn by cherubic coursers. Their four sides corresponded with the four faces of the cherubim, and so they always went in the direction of some one of the four faces, and could move without turning to any one of the four points of the compass.

The living creatures and the wheels were alike governed in all their motions by a living principle called emphatically the Spirit (verse 30). It caused the wheels always to move in closest companionship with the living creatures, "for the spirit of the living creature[1] was in the wheels" (verse 20). One supreme, indwelling, potent, guiding spirit controlled them all.

Over the head and outstretched wings of the cherubim the seer observed "the likeness of a firmament like the color of the terrible crystal" (verse 22). From this firmament there came a voice, at which the living creatures dropped their wings in awe (verse 25). Gazing upward the prophet saw above the firmament "the likeness of a throne," refulgent "as the appearance of a sapphire stone; and upon the likeness of the throne was a likeness as the appearance of a man upon it above" (verse 26). It seemed impossible for Ezekiel to sketch the glory of this awful Being, for his style at this point is involved and obscure by reason of his labored efforts at comparison.

---

[1] The singular, *the living creature* (הַחַיָּה), in verses 20 and 21, as in verse 22, is to be understood as the entire cherubic group seen in the vision.

The appearance from the loins upward and downward resembled the glittering brilliancy of amber, or of fire, and this radiant form was encircled by the appearance of a rainbow. The unspeakable glory overwhelmed the seer, and he fell upon his face to the earth; but so far was he from identifying the things seen with God himself, as one that might be looked upon with direct and immediate view, that he says (verse 28) of all this manifestation of the supernatural, "It was the appearance of the likeness of the glory of Jehovah."

This vision of Ezekiel, as we have observed already, is for all essential purposes the same as Isaiah's sublime picture of the throne of God. It is an apocalyptic portrayal of "the chariot of the cherubim" (1 Chron. xxviii, 18), and has an obvious relation to the poetic concept expressed in Psalm xviii, 10:

> He rode upon a cherub and did fly,
> Yea, he sped swiftly on the wings of the wind.

Ezekiel was a priest (Ezek. i, 3), and accordingly familiar with the symbolism of the holy places in the temple and with the thought of Jehovah enthroned upon the cherubim (comp. Exod. xxv, 22 ; 1 Sam. iv, 4; 2 Sam. vi, 2; Psalm lxxx, 1; xcix, 1). His picture of the throne of God is elaborated according to the peculiarity of his own individual genius, and it differs from that of Isaiah much as Dante's poetic concepts differ from those of Milton. Isaiah speaks of Jehovah as sitting on a lofty throne, clothed with a majestic trailing robe, and surrounded by the six-winged seraphim. But Ezekiel takes pains to tell us that what he saw was only "a likeness as the appearance of a man." Both prophets, however, conceive Jehovah under the semblance of a man, remembering that man was created in the image and after the likeness of God (Gen. i, 26). His form, glowing with the brilliancy of amber and "the appearance of fire," suggests the consuming power of his judgments and his holiness which the flaming seraphs adore, while the brightness round about him like the appearance of the rainbow is a symbol of covenanted grace. The throne is suggestive of judgment and government, and, according to a frequent scriptural image, Jehovah is thought of as occupying a throne, and judging righteously (Psalm ix, 4). "Jehovah's throne is in heaven; his eyes behold, his eyelids try the children of men" (Psalm xi, 4). It was fitting that, at the beginning of his book, the prophet should set forth an impressive ideal of the most high God as the source of all divine revelation and the sovereign Ruler of the world.

Ezekiel's picture of the cherubim is peculiar, and was probably influenced to some extent by the grotesque forms of creature life which he had seen portrayed upon the monuments of Babylon. Winged lions and winged bulls, and human forms with the head of an eagle, were familiar objects in the lands of the exile. On a nature so sensitive to the strange and indescribable as his the gigantic symbols of Babylonian art must have made a deep impression. But that which notably differentiates Ezekiel's cherubim from those elsewhere described in the Scriptures is their position *under* the firmament which appeared to support the throne of God. This accords with the figure in Psalm xviii, 10, but differs from Isaiah's picture, which places the seraphim *above* the throne. Ezekiel's cherubim are further peculiar in having each four faces and four wings. The faces, representing beast, cattle, fowl, and man, comprehend all the higher forms of creature life on earth, and may appropriately symbolize the living presence and active agency of the Almighty in the entire domain of created life. But as man stands at the head of creation, and divine providence is most signally displayed in human life and history, so, altogether, the living creatures bore preeminently the likeness of a man. The wings are appropriate symbols of the rapidity with which the dispensations of God are often carried forth. Two wings of each cherub seem to have been continuously outspread (verse 11), as if scarce able to await the time when they were to speed away on some divine errand. The hands of a man under the wings show the alacrity with which, in particular events of providence, all divine commands are executed, and suggest that God makes use of human agency in the government of this world. In chap. x, 7, we observe the promptness with which a cherub's hand furnished an angel with the fire that was to burn Jerusalem. The straight, unbending feet may indicate the straightforward movements and irrevocable nature of the judgments of the Almighty.

Altogether, therefore, Ezekiel's cherubim are adapted to symbolize Jehovah in activity, not in repose. For this purpose also there is added the symbolism of the wheels. These wheels, with their four sides, like the four horsemen, the four horns, the four smiths, and the four chariots in Zechariah (i, 10, 19, 21 ; vi, 5), and the four horses and their riders in Rev. vi, 2–8, are symbols of the potent agencies of the divine government of the world. Whether they move against rebellious Israel or against heathen nations, they go at the command of the cherubim. So in Rev. vi, the symbols of conquest, bloodshed, famine, and aggravated mortality proceed on their solemn mission when one of the living creatures says, " Come." And herein is a profound intimation that all things work together for good to them who love God, and who are, accordingly, predestinated to be conformed to the image of his Son (Rom. viii, 28–30), and to be sanctified in his glory (Exod. xxix, 43). And so every agency of providence and judgment in all the world moves with a foreseen vital relation to the ultimate glory of God's elect (Rom. viii, 29 ; comp. i, 1, 2). Ezekiel's cherubim, therefore, like those at the gate of Eden, are indeed prophetic symbols of the gracious restoration of what was lost by sin, but they more particularly indicate the great truth that redeemed humanity has much to do in working out its own salvation (Phil. ii, 12, 13).

It should be added that the wheels, which seemed to form a sort of chariot of God, were called "the whirlwind"[1] in the hearing of Ezekiel. They may, therefore, be regarded as symbols of the forces of inanimate nature as distinguished from the animal creation. Winds and storms and pestilence and fire and hail obey the voice of Him who sits upon the circle of the heavens and fills all things by his Spirit (Psalm cxlviii, 8). And thus the revelation of God and nature here made known is inconsistent with any phase of materialistic pantheism. The innumerable eyes upon the wheels, symbols of infinite wisdom, admonish us that the laws and forces of nature are under the control of a personal Ruler, who, in the thought of prophet and psalmist, makes the clouds his chariot and walks upon the wings of the wind.

The symbolism of this vision was peculiarly appropriate both to the historical standpoint of Ezekiel and to the scope and contents of his prophecies. After Jehoiachin and the better part of the Jewish people had been carried into exile there was left at Jerusalem a remnant, which kept up the form of the kingdom of Judah, with Zedekiah at its head. But, after Nebuchadnezzar had withdrawn his armies from the land, this remnant continued their idolatrous abominations and mocked the messengers of God, and "Zedekiah rebelled against the king of Babylon" (2 Kings xxiv, 20 ; comp. Ezek. xvii, 15). All this resulted speedily in the utter overthrow of the kingdom of Judah, and the king of Babylon burned the temple and demolished the walls of Jerusalem. There was also among the exiles at Babylon a spirit of infatuation caused by lying prophets, who led the people to indulge in vain dreams of speedy deliverance from captivity (Jer. xxix).

Against this " rebellious house " Ezekiel was called to utter oracles of judgment, and it was fitting that his own soul, as well as those

---

[1] הַגַּלְגַּל. We translate Ezek. x, 13, literally : *As for the wheels, they were called the whirlwind in my ear.* This is the meaning of the word in Psalm lxxvii, 18, and is so rendered in the Anglo-American version.

to whom he prophesied, should be deeply impressed with the thought of Jehovah's power to make all forms of creature life and all the elements of nature serve him. The Chaldean army was one mighty agent of God by which the penal woes of sword and fire were to lay waste the land of Israel and make Jerusalem a heap of ruins, and the threatening features of Ezekiel's vision were terribly suggestive of the coming vengeance. The whirlwind coming out of the north, the compressed fire, the flashing lightnings, the sparkling feet, the noise of the wings, the rushing wheels so dreadful in their movements to and fro—all pointed significantly to the various aspects of that divine judgment which as a sore evil was about to break forth out of the north upon all the inhabitants of the land (Jer. i, 14–16). In accordance with this thought the first part of Ezekiel's prophecies abounds in announcements of judgment upon rebellious Israel and other nations (chaps. ii–xxxii). But the vision had also its background of hope and promise. The dark cloud from the north had a circle of brightness around it ; the fiery human likeness of the glory of God was encompassed by the appearance of a rainbow; and, in harmony with these hopeful symbols, the concluding portion of Ezekiel's prophecies (xxxiii–xlviii) is full of encouragement and consolation for the house of Israel. The first part is not without some gracious words of promise (xi, 13–20; xvii, 22–24), and the second announces the final judgment upon the enemies of God (xxxviii, xxxix); but viewed as a whole, Ezekiel's elaborate apocalypse magnifies the great doctrine that, while to the rebellious and perverse Jehovah is a consuming fire, to those who love him and keep his commandments his nature and his name are Love. So, in its deepest significance and suggestions, Ezekiel's opening vision is but another exhibition of the flaming sword and cherubim at the gate of the garden of Eden.

This apocalyptic vision, like its parallels in Isaiah and John, gives grandeur and sublimity to the book, and assures the prophet and his readers that the revelations are directly from God, and that "the word of Jehovah," so often mentioned herein, is truly a voice from the throne of Him who rules the heavens and the earth. It is immediately followed by an account of the prophet's divine commission (chaps. ii, 1–iii, 15).

Our purpose and limits require no elaborate exposition of this prophet of the exile. His book is so extensive, and contains so large an element of expostulation and rebuke, that we attempt only a clear analysis of its general plan and a brief exposition of the most remarkable apocalyptic portions.

In accord with most books of this class, the subject-matter falls in two principal divisions: the first (chaps. i–xxxii) announcing Jehovah's judgments upon rebellious Israel and the idolatrous nations, the second (xxxiii–xlviii) foretelling the restoration and final glorification of the people of God. We subdivide the first part into seven sections, and the second into three, as follows:

FIRST PART.—JUDGMENTS, I–XXXII.

1. *Chapters i, 1–iii,* 14. At the sight of Jehovah's glory, as revealed in the opening vision, the prophet fell upon his face in holy awe. But he was lifted up by the voice of one who spoke, and by the power of the Spirit, and commissioned to go and prophesy to the "rebellious house" of Israel and the nations, "whether they will hear or whether they will forbear." This divine commission was enhanced by a symbolical sign. He was told to open his mouth and eat what was given him, and, lo, a book-roll was spread out before him, "written within and without; and there was written therein lamentations, and mourning and woe." He was commanded to eat the roll, and then go and speak to the house of Israel, and he tells us that "it was in his mouth as honey for sweetness," for, as in the case of Jeremiah, such inner reception of Jehovah's word is a cause of "joy and rejoicing of heart" (Jer. xv, 16). But the contents of lamentation and woe could hardly fail to produce a sense of bitterness, and so, when the Spirit lifted him up and took him away on his mission, he went in bitterness and heat of soul (chap. iii, 14). In all this there is close analogy between Ezekiel and John. Comp. Rev. x, 8–10.

2. *Chapters iii,* 15–*vii,* 27. This section contains an account of the further commission of the prophet "at the end of seven days," during which he had been sitting among the exiles by the Chebar like one dumb with astonishment. Here also we read his first series of symbolico-typical and oracular announcements of the approaching desolation of Jerusalem.

3. *Chapters viii–xi.* These prophecies are dated "in the sixth year." Ezekiel is carried "in the visions of God to Jerusalem," and there beholds a fourfold picture of the abominations which constituted Judah's guilt and shame: (1) "the image of jealousy," (viii, 5, 6), (2) the seventy elders burning incense in the secret chambers of abominable imagery (verses 7–12), (3) "the women weeping for Tammuz" (13, 14), and (4) the worship of the sun "at the door of the temple of Jehovah, between the porch and the altar" (15–18). This vision is followed by that of the seven angels, six of whom were commanded to go through the city and smite all who had not the mark of God upon their foreheads (comp. Rev.

vii, 3; ix, 4, and the seven trumpet angels of Rev. viii, 2). Again the cherubim appear, and from between the wheels under them a man clothed in linen takes a double handful of coals of fire and scatters them over the doomed city (comp. Rev. viii, 5). After a word of hope has been spoken to the prophet (chap. xi, 16–20) the cherubim and the glory of Jehovah go up from the midst of the city, and stand upon the Mount of Olives on the east of the city (comp. Zech. xiv, 4), and the prophet is brought back again " in the vision by the Spirit of God into Chaldea, to them of the captivity."

4. *Chapters xii–xix.* This section belongs also to the cycle of prophecies of the sixth year (viii, 1), but the standpoint of the prophet is changed, and he appears among the captives in Chaldea, and there, by means of symbolico-typical action, allegory, parable, lamentation, warning, and expostulation, he exhibits the sins of Israel, and shows that rebellion against God is sure to bring misery and ruin upon the transgressors. Chap. xvi is specially noteworthy for its picture of Jerusalem under the figure of an abominable harlot.

5. *Chapters xx–xxiii.* These chapters contain the prophecies of " the seventh year," and repeat in other words and figures the catalogue of Israel's sins. Like other apocalyptic repetitions it brings out the ideas of the preceding section with more intense distinctness, and the figure of the harlot in chap. xvi becomes the more detailed allegory of Oholah and Oholibah in chap. xxiii.

6. *Chapter xxiv.* The date of this " word of Jehovah " is " in the ninth year, in the tenth month, in the tenth of the month," and is identical with the memorable day on which Nebuchadnezzar commenced the siege of Jerusalem (comp. 2 Kings xxv, 1). Under the figure of a boiling caldron we have the vengeance destined to come upon " the bloody city" most fearfully portrayed. In the evening of that day the prophet's wife, the desire of his eyes, was taken from him by death; but he was forbidden to mourn and weep that he might be a sign to the people of Israel of a grief too deep for tears (comp. Jer. xvi, 4–6).

7. *Chapters xxv–xxxii.* After having thus announced the woes on Judah and Jerusalem, Ezekiel proclaims the word of Jehovah against seven heathen nations, namely, Ammon, Moab, Edom, Philistia, Tyre, Sidon, and Egypt. These prophecies are to be compared with similar ones against the nations found in Amos i and ii, Isa. xiii–xxiii, Zeph. ii, and Jer. xlvi–li (comp. Jer. xxv, 15–32).

SECOND PART.—RESTORATION AND GLORIFICATION, XXXIII–XLVIII.

The second part of Ezekiel's prophecies is divisible into three sections, as follows :

1. *Chapters xxxiii–xxxvii.* After the renewal of the prophet's charge, which occurred on the day in which he heard of the fall of Jerusalem (xxxiii, 21), the word of Jehovah announces through him the restoration of Israel in six different forms: (1) As an offset to the work of the unfaithful shepherds who had caused the flock to be scattered abroad, Jehovah, like a good shepherd, will seek his scattered sheep and lead them into rich pastures upon the mountains of Israel (chap. xxxiv). (2) As an offset to the evils Israel suffered from the surrounding nations the doom of Edom is foretold as a specimen of the manner in which Jehovah will avenge his people on their heartless enemies (chap. xxxv). (3) As an offset to the prophecy against the mountains of Israel, in chap. vi, 1–7, there now comes a promise to restore and beautify all that was laid waste (chap. xxxvi, 1–15). (4) Thereupon follows the pledge of multiplied blessings to be showered upon the restored house of Israel (xxxvi, 16–38), and the section closes with the two symbolical signs of restoration, (5) the vision of the dry bones made to live again (xxxvii, 1–14), and (6) the symbol of the two sticks of wood, representing Judah and Ephraim united into one (xxxvii, 15–28).

2. *Chapters xxxviii and xxxix.* Here is a remarkable apocalyptic picture of the final overthrow of the hostile nations in their conflict with Jehovah. The highly wrought description is presented as fourfold : (1) Prophetic declaration against the army of Gog and its march against Israel (xxxviii, 1–13); (2) his fearful overthrow by the power of God (verses 14–23); (3) another prophetic declaration of the utter destruction of all the hostile multitude (xxxix, 1–10); (4) the seven months' burial in Hamon-gog, and the great feast of sacrifice upon the mountains of Israel (verses 11–29). This entire picture is manifestly ideal, and demands our more particular examination.

That this description of a last great battle and total defeat of God's enemies is an ideal apocalyptic picture, and not a literal account of some particular event yet to occur, appears from the following considerations :

(1) The proper names employed are taken for the most part from the table of nations in Gen. x (comp. Gen. x, 2, 3, 6, and 1 Chron. i, 5, 6, 8, 9), and are appropriated as most fitting symbolical designations of far-off and comparatively unknown peoples. They are conceived as immense hordes from " the uttermost parts of the north." The names Gog and Magog are employed in the same symbolical manner in Rev. xx, 8.

(2) As imaginary as these hordes is the feast of flesh and blood, "fatlings of Bashan," horses and chariots, and mighty men of war,

for which an invitation is given "to the birds of every sort and to every beast of the field" (xxxix, 17–20). The picture is no more a literal description of some actual event than are the parallel passages in Isa. xxxiv, 6; Jer. xlvi, 10, and Rev. xix, 17, 18.

(3) The burial of the dead bodies of the multitude during the space of seven months (xxxix, 12), and the burning of their weapons of war for seven years (xxxix, 9), are in keeping with the embellishments of symbolism, but inconsistent with a narrative of facts. If, moreover, this vast multitude of Gog is to be thus buried, why should the birds and beasts be invited to eat their flesh and drink their blood? The statement of xxxix, 15, is not consistent with the thought that the birds and beasts first devour the flesh, and the house of Israel subsequently spend seven months in burying the bones.

(4) The general style and range of thought accord with the highly wrought pictures of apocalyptic writing. The very extravagance of many of the statements is incompatible with actual reality. Witness the following passage :

And it shall come to pass in that day, when Gog shall come against the land of Israel, saith the Lord God, that my fury shall come up into my nostrils. For in my jealousy and in the fire of my wrath have I spoken, Surely in that day there shall be a great shaking in the land of Israel; so that the fishes of the sea, and the fowls of the heaven, and the beasts of the field, and all creeping things that creep upon the earth, and all the men that are upon the face of the earth, shall shake at my presence, and the mountains shall be thrown down, and the steep places shall fall, and every wall shall fall to the ground. And I will call for a sword against him unto all my mountains, saith the Lord God: every man's sword shall be against his brother. And I will plead against him with pestilence and with blood; and I will rain upon him, and upon his hordes, and upon the many peoples that are with him, an overflowing shower, and great hailstones, fire, and brimstone (xxxviii, 18–22).

Since, then, a literal interpretation of these chapters is inadmissible, we inquire after the true meaning of the ideal picture. This may best be ascertained by observing its relation to the restoration of Israel as outlined in chap. xxxvii, and by inquiry into the real significance of its several parts. Its relation to chaps. xl–xlviii is also to be studied.

(1) The relation of chaps. xxxviii and xxxix to chap. xxxvii is sufficiently indicated in xxxviii, 8, where the coming of the hostile hordes and their penal visitation of judgment are spoken of as occurring "after many days," and "in the end of the years" after Israel shall have been gathered out of the many peoples among whom they were dispersed, and are all of them dwelling securely upon the holy mountains. This naturally points to a period in Israel's history subsequent to the restoration and blessedness described in

the symbolical pictures of the resurrection of dry bones and the uniting of the two sticks of wood, as recorded in chap. xxxvii.

(2) In that future period of Israel's history a great leader, conceived as a prince of nations and called by the symbolical name Gog, will with his hordes come up like a vast storm-cloud "against the people that are gathered out of the nations." Many peoples will accompany him, and they will plot evil devices and aim to spoil the house of Israel. We understand that this great war is Ezekiel's prophetic outline of the final conflict between good and evil as represented respectively in the forces of God and Satan in this world. It is a struggle that follows the advent of God's "servant David," referred to in xxxvii, 24, and accordingly belongs to the period of the Messianic reign. The Messiah is to possess as his inheritance the uttermost parts of the earth (Psalm ii, 8; xxii, 27; lxxii, 8), and it is not supposable that the remote peoples will submit without a struggle. As his dominion extends more and more, and attracts attention among the most distant nations and tribes, there must needs come, some time, a decisive battle. It need not be supposed to be the struggle of a day or a year. It is rather a conflict of ages. The new David must rule, and his forces must struggle with the powers of evil until he shall have put all his enemies under his feet. This is essentially the doctrine of Psalm cx, and accords with the general Old Testament concept of the Messiah's reign.

(3) This world conflict is no new or exceptional thought with Ezekiel (xxxviii, 17), but only his peculiar manner of portraying the final battle against the kingdom of God. In Isa. xxix, 8, we are told of the dreamlike folly and futility of hostile devices of "the multitude of all the nations that fight against Mount Zion." The prophecy of Balaam had of old declared the ultimate failure of the enemies of Israel in their long conflict with the star and scepter out of Jacob (Num. xxiv, 17-24). In Joel iv, 2, 11-14; Zech. xii, 2, 3, and xiv, 2, 3, and Zeph. iii, 8, we find similar ideals, and Dan. xi, 40-45, and Rev. xx, 7-9, are other apocalyptic parallels. The conflict is a long one, but it must have its decisive day and hour (xxxviii, 18; xxxix, 8).

(4) The result of this last battle is the manifestation of God's glory and judgment among all the nations, and a revealing of himself to the whole house of Israel (xxxix, 20-29). The utter overthrow of all the enemies of God and his people involves, of course, the universal triumph of the kingdom of the Messiah. The final glory of perfect restoration, with God dwelling among his people, is symbolized in the visions of chaps. xl-xlviii, which appropriately

follow this picture of triumph and conclude the prophecies of Ezekiel.

Before passing to this last section of Ezekiel let us observe, even though it involve some repetition of things already stated, several characteristics of this prophecy against Gog and his hordes, which show that it belongs to the idealism of apocalyptics rather than to the realism of literal description.

(1) The fourfold structure of the passage, as given above in the analysis of the two chapters, is a formal element peculiar to apocalyptic prophecies.[1] The beginning of chap. xxxix is in substance a repetition of the beginning of chap. xxxviii, and the double picture of burial in Hamon-gog and feast of flesh upon the mountains of Israel (xxxix, 11–29) corresponds notably with the prophecy of judgment in xxxviii, 14–23. These artistic correspondencies in structure can scarcely be regarded as accidental or imaginary.

(2) The vagueness attaching to the names Gog, Magog, Rosh, Meshech, etc., makes them appropriate for symbolic usage. The place of Gog in "the uttermost parts of the north" suggests the mountain-throne of heathen gods (Isa. xiv, 13). This mystic Gog and the many peoples which join him in his campaign against Israel admirably symbolize the numerous foes, who, inspired and led on by Satanic power, make desperate assaults upon the kingdom of God. The imagery and perhaps some of the names were suggested by the inroads of the Scythians, who, when Ezekiel was a youth, swept in from the north and spread desolation and terror through all western Asia.

(3) Some final and decisive conflict between God and his enemies, the woman's seed and the serpent's seed (Gen. iii, 15), Christ and Antichrist, is a familiar concept of divine revelation, and this passage in Ezekiel is especially to be compared with the fundamental idea of Dan. xi, 40–45, and Rev. xx, 7–9. See our notes on those passages.

(4) It is important to note that the great result of this world-conflict is to establish the true knowledge of God among men. Over and over again is this divine purpose declared in the space of these two chapters (xxxviii, 16, 23; xxxix, 6, 7, 22, 23, 28). That this is the one highest purpose of all divine revelation, and includes the doctrines of redemption and salvation, is a commonplace of Christian theology. Its position in Old Testament prophecy is sufficiently indicated by the declarations of Isa. xi, 9, and Hab. ii, 14.

3. *Chapters xl–xlviii.* This last section contains the description of an ideal land and temple of "Israel restored." Ezekiel is carried

---

[1] See the Introduction, pp. 20–22.

away in the visions of God to a very high mountain in the land of
Israel, whence he beholds a new temple, new ordinances of worship,
a river of waters of life, a new land with new tribal divisions of territory, and a new city named Jehovah-shammah. The extent and
minuteness of detail in this description are characteristic of this
prophet, and no one would so naturally have portrayed the Messianic kingdom under the imagery of a glorified Judaism as one who
was himself a priest. From Ezekiel's point of view, as an exile by
the rivers of Babylon, smitten with grief as he remembered Zion
(Psalm cxxxvii, 1), no ideal restoration could have been more complete or glorious than that of an enlarged temple, a continual service, a holy priesthood in perfect harmony with a true Davidic king,
a magnificent city, and a land fully occupied by the twelve tribes
of Israel, and watered by a stream from the temple-mountain, deep-
ening and widening as it spread so as to make all the waste places
blossom as the rose, and even heal the waters of the Dead Sea
(comp. Joel iii, 18; Zech. xiv, 8).

An analysis of these nine chapters, sufficient for our purpose,
comprehends the entire description under three heads, as follows :

1. The temple as seen with its manifold parts and measures.
Chaps. xl–xlii.

2. The temple filled with the glory of God and provided with
ordinances for perpetual worship. Chaps. xliii–xlvi.

3. The river of life and the borders and tribe divisions of the
land. Chaps. xlvii, xlviii.

(1) That we may apprehend the true significance of this final
vision we should first of all observe that it is no mere appendix to
the prophecy to be treated as a section of no importance. Rather
it is the consummation and climax of all that has gone before. We
need not go to the extreme of declaring that these chapters of
Ezekiel "are the most important in his book," and "the key of the
Old Testament;"[1] but they are as significant and important at the
close of the book of prophecy as is the elaborate symbolism of the
cherubim at its beginning.

(2) The entire passage purports to be an apocalyptic vision, and
its symbolical import is not dependent upon the question of its
historical relation to the Levitical code as we now find it in the
middle books of the Pentateuch. One thing is certain, that in
numerous details Ezekiel's temple differs from that of Solomon before the exile, and that of Zerubbabel after the restoration, but in
its main features of court, holy place, and interior temple, or holy

---

[1] Wellhausen, *Prolegomena to the History of Israel*, p. 421. Edinb.

of holies, it follows the pattern of the tabernacle shown to Moses in the mount. We have already shown, in a previous chapter, the symbolical import of the Mosaic tabernacle, and here we need only observe that the Solomonic temple and the temple of Ezekiel's vision exhibit essentially the same mystic symbolism.

(3) But the notion that these chapters contain an accurate record of the plan of the Solomonic temple as it existed before the exile, or of the later temple of Zerubbabel, is justly rejected by the best exegetes. Aside from the extravagance of the measures given, and their incompatibility with the localities involved, it is very obvious that the vision of waters in chap. xlvii, and the divisions of the land in chap. xlviii, cannot be accepted as literal statements of fact. But if the last two chapters are explained as ideal pictures so must the others be, for they are all parts of one great symbolic vision. Ezekiel's temple is no more explicable as a model of real architecture than are his cherubim and wheels possible in mechanics.

(4) It is also to be noted that there is no description of the materials of this visional temple, nor any account of the process of its erection. It stands out simply as something seen "in the visions of God," and accordingly as a completed perfect structure. It is a composite visional symbol.

(5) What, then, is the real import of these concluding chapters? Our answer is that, like the corresponding conclusion of John's Apocalypse, this vision of restored and perfected temple, service, and land symbolizes the perfected kingdom of God and his Messiah. No time limit is set for the fulfillment of the vision, but it is naturally supposed to follow the battle of Gog, and be in fact the ultimate glorification of Jehovah and his people implied in chap. xxxix, 25-29. As the warfare of Gog is conceived as occurring many days after the restoration of Israel to their fatherland (xxxviii, 8), this perfection of Jehovah's triumph could not be expected immediately after the return from Babylonian exile. But of the times and the seasons of the completion of this Messianic kingdom Ezekiel utters no definite word. Like the descent of the new Jerusalem in the visions of John (Rev. xxi, 2), which was seen after the overthrow of Gog and Magog and their innumerable host (Rev. xx, 8, 9), this final glorification of Israel also follows the overthrow of the last enemies. This is the only natural, logical, and pictorial order consistent with the grand ideal of triumph.

(6) This interpretation of the symbolism necessarily excludes all Jewish-carnal theories of a literal restoration of Jerusalem and the Jewish state. The notion prevalent among some schools of Second Adventists that, at Christ's second coming, Jerusalem and the

temple will be rebuilt and become the throne-center of the kingdom of the Messiah, is inconsistent with a rational interpretation of the prophets and the spiritual nature of the kingdom of Christ. In like manner we reject all fanciful allegorizing of the several parts of this composite symbol. Any attempt to find a separate and distinctive significance of each wall, chamber, post, window, pavement, and gate would be as absurd and futile as to find like meaning for the boards, curtains, loops, rods, and rings of the Mosaic tabernacle. These are to be regarded as mere incidentals, designed to enhance the general impressiveness and perfection of the entire structure. In the number and extent of such minute references in Ezekiel's picture we simply recognize his personal and priestly peculiarities of thought and style.

(7) Several parts of this symbolic picture demand particular attention. We observe that the coming of "the glory of the God of Israel . . . into the house by the way of the gate whose prospect is toward the east" (xliii, 2, 4) is a coming to FILL the house (verse 5), and to abide perpetually. As John "heard a great voice out of the throne saying, Behold, the tabernacle is with men, and he shall dwell with them and they shall be his peoples, and God himself shall be with them and be their God" (Rev. xxi, 3), so Ezekiel heard a voice out of the temple, saying, "The place of my throne, and the place of the soles of my feet, where I will dwell in the midst of the house of Israel forever" (Ezek. xliii, 7). Here is expressed the fundamental thought embodied in the symbolism of the temple: God dwelling with man and man with God. Its perfection will be that union with God in Christ spoken of in John xvii, 21–24, "That they all may be one; even as thou, Father, art in me, and I in thee, that they also may be in us: . . . I in them, and thou in me, that they may be perfected into one."

(8) Another conspicuous feature of the vision is the position and extent of land apportioned to the temple, the city, the Levites, the priests, and the king. A central section, with seven tribes on the north and five on the south, is thus reserved and designated "a holy oblation unto Jehovah." It is twenty-five thousand reeds square, and the portions to be occupied by sanctuary, city, priests, Levites, and prince are carefully defined. The priests occupy the central portion, next to the sanctuary, and the prince has his possession on the east and west. This seems to make the prince somewhat subordinate to the priests who have the charge of the sanctuary, and raises the question whether we may suppose "the prince" of this vision to be the same as the Davidic king of chaps. xxxiv, 24, and xxxvii, 25. Some have thought the two ideals to be dis-

crepant and incompatible. But when we remember that the prophetic ideal of Israel's future was "a kingdom of priests and a holy nation" (Exod. xix, 6), we may discern in this picture of Ezekiel a most natural and appropriate relationship between prince and priest, and one peculiarly suitable for a priest-prophet like Ezekiel to portray. Nothing in his description necessarily implies subordination or conflict between priest and prince, but rather the most perfect harmony and equality of the two. As the Davidic prince of chap. xxxiv, 24, is conceived as a shepherd of the flock of Israel who shall feed them as a servant of God (verse 23), so the prince of this restored Israel is to "execute judgment and justice" (xlv, 9), see that "just balances" are in use (xlv, 10–12), and that the tribal territories are given to the house of Israel (xlv, 8). It is incumbent on the prince also "to give the burnt offerings and the meal offerings and the drink offerings in the feasts, and in the new moons, and in the sabbaths, in all the appointed feasts of the house of Israel: he shall prepare the sin offering and the meal offering and the burnt offering and the peace offerings, to make atonement for the house of Israel" (xlv, 17). This detailed statement shows the closest relationship between king and priest, and is Ezekiel's way of setting forth the doctrine of Psalm cx, 4, and Zech. vi, 13. Royalty and priesthood are to be so closely united that "the counsel of peace shall be between them both."

(9) But while this central section of the land is preeminently holy, and set apart for temple, city, priest, and king, the people of the whole land are to appear before Jehovah at the appointed feasts, and go in and out of the gates of the city (xlvi, 3, 9; comp. Zech. xiv, 16–21). The prince will no more appropriate any portion of the people's inheritance for his own or his son's private purpose (xlvi, 18), as the violent rulers of the former times had done or assumed the right to do (1 Sam. viii, 14; xxii, 7; 1 Kings xxi, 6, 7), but the land is to be equally divided among the twelve tribes, seven on the north and five on the south of the great central oblation, which, as containing the sanctuary and the city, is the common inheritance of all. The twelve gates of the city bear accordingly the names of the twelve tribes of Israel (xlviii, 31–34; comp. Rev. xxi, 12), as if each and all of the tribes were publicly honored with a monumental and memorial title to the freedom of the city. They would also have free and perpetual access to the living waters that issue from the sanctuary, and to the trees whose fruits serve for food and whose leaves are for healing (xlvii, 12). All this implies a redeemed and purified Israel, so that of these twelve tribes it might be said, as it is written in the New Testament

Apocalypse (xxi, 14) : "Blessed are they that wash their robes that they may have the right to the tree of life, and may enter in by the gates into the city."

(10) This central city, the delight of all the tribes, "the joy of the whole earth, the city of the great King" (Psalm xlviii, 2), is appropriately named in conclusion JEHOVAH-SHAMMAH (Ezek. xlviii, 35). In a like manner Isaiah says: "They shall call thee The City of Jehovah, The Zion of the Holy One of Israel" (Isa. lx, 14). This ideal holy city is no other than "the city of the living God, the heavenly Jerusalem," the eternal possession of "the general assembly and church of the firstborn who are enrolled in heaven" (Heb. xii, 23).

The prophecies of Ezekiel are thus seen to belong largely to the sphere of Apocalyptics, and not a few of the visions and symbols are reproduced in the later scriptures which we have yet to examine.

CHAPTER XV

APOCALYPSES IN ZECHARIAH

I. CHAPTERS I–VI.

THE first eight chapters of the Book of Zechariah constitute a body of prophecies remarkably unique, and the first six chapters are conspicuously apocalyptical. The author calls himself the "son of Berechiah, the son of Iddo." The name Iddo occurs in Neh. xii, 4, 16, among the priests who returned from Babylon with Zerubbabel, but the name of Berechiah does not appear in the same list, nor is it given in Ezra v, 1, and vi, 14, where this same prophet is called simply "the son of Iddo." Perhaps the father, Berechiah, died young and without distinction, and was not therefore mentioned by Ezra and Nehemiah, who name only the more distinguished grandfather. But our prophet may have been a different person from the son of Iddo mentioned in the genealogy of Neh. xii. The names Iddo, and Berechiah, and Zechariah are quite common in the Old Testament, and attach to a number of different individuals. We need not wonder that the personal history of even a distinguished prophet should not have been carefully preserved. It was the message, the revelation, not the personal history, of the prophet that was important for the purposes of Holy Scripture.

The main facts, important for us to know in the study of the first part of Zechariah, are recorded in the books of Ezra and Nehemiah. The short prophecy of Haggai, Zechariah's contemporary, is also helpful for a knowledge of the situation and for confirmation of the statements of Ezra v, 1, and vi, 14. The opposition of neighboring peoples delayed the completion of the temple until the second year of Darius Hystaspis. And not only the hostile feeling of enemies without, but disaffection within the Jewish community, ignorance of the law, abuses, and general disloyalty greatly embarrassed the noble leaders, who might well have felt discouraged in their efforts to restore the temple and city.

The Book of Haggai is an important aid to the study of Zechariah, and a brief outline of its contents will serve in part as an appropriate introduction to these prophecies. The first oracle of Haggai is dated two months earlier than the first date given in Zechariah (comp. Hag. i, 1, and Zech. i, 1). All the visions of Zechariah (including chaps. i, 7–vi, 15) appear to bear the date of the twenty-fourth day of the eleventh month of the second year of Darius (i, 7), which is two months later than the latest date mentioned in Haggai (Hag. ii, 10, 20). From Haggai we learn that by reason of the trials to which they were subjected many of the Jewish people at Jerusalem had become discouraged, lost confidence, and concluded that it was no suitable time to attempt the building of the temple. But many of them builded ceiled houses for themselves, and grew careless in matters of religion. As a consequence they were visited with the judgments of drought and scarcity. We have, accordingly, in Hag. i, 1–11, the prophetic word of rebuke, admonition, and command to gather material and build the house of God, and in verses 12–15 the happy result of this prophet's ministry. The second oracle is dated a month later (ii, 1), and is full of encouragement for Zerubbabel, and Joshua, and the people. The third oracle is two months later (ii, 10) and consists of further admonition and counsel, and the fourth and last oracle bears the same date (ii, 20) and is a prophecy of the overthrow of all enemies and the honor of Zerubbabel as Jehovah's chosen servant.

We must not leave this prophecy of Haggai without a comment on the remarkable picture of Jehovah's dominion over the world, as given in chap. ii, verses 6 and 7 and 20–23. Jehovah declares that he is about to "shake the heavens, and the earth, and the sea, and the dry land, and all the nations, and fill this house with glory, and overthrow the throne of kingdoms, and destroy the strength of the kingdoms of the nations." When Haggai and Zechariah prophesied, Assyria had fallen before the power of Babylon; Babylon in turn had fallen before the armies of the Medes and Persians; Egypt had succumbed to the forces of Persia, and the vast Persian empire, which then overshadowed the oriental world, was destined to be broken to pieces by the might of Alexander, the great Grecian conqueror from the west. In all these facts the prophets of Israel saw that the God who overthrew Pharaoh and his chariots in the days of Moses was the supreme Ruler of the nations, and was able to overthrow or build up according to his own infinite wisdom and pleasure.

Haggai's oracles thus prepared the way for the visions of Zechariah, and helped to intensify the expectations which they must have excited. We can now see the historical situation, without which we cannot appreciate the apocalypses of the son of Iddo. Recently returned from the lands of the exile, and distressed over the persistent opposition of the Samaritans and the feebleness of the Jews at Jerusalem, Zechariah may naturally have felt that his people had come to a desperate crisis in their history. How terribly had they been scattered and humbled by the great powers of the world! Jehovah had been sore displeased with their fathers (i, 2). Sword, and famine, and exile had visited them. The words of the former prophets had overtaken them, and proven beyond all cavil that Jehovah's oracles were sure. And now no human power, no forces at their command, could rationally hope for successful conflict with the nations. The contempt with which neighboring enemies looked upon them is seen in Neh. iv, 2, 3, where Sanballat says: "What are these feeble Jews doing? Will they fortify themselves? Will they revive the stones out of the rubbish?" And Tobiah the Ammonite replies, "Even that which they build, if a fox go up, he shall break down their stone wall!"

But God's thoughts and ways are not as man's. Zechariah was divinely commissioned to show his people that their triumphs were not to be brought about by the might and power of empire, but by the Spirit of Jehovah of hosts. Five times over in the short introduction of Zech. i, 1–6, does the prophet repeat the expression "Jehovah of hosts." The revelations of Zechariah are like the answer to Elisha's prayer for his young servant, when the horses and chariots and hosts of the king of Syria encompassed him, and caused him to cry out in despair, "Alas, my master, how shall we do?" In answer to the prophet's prayer, "The Lord opened the eyes of the young man, and he saw, and behold, the mountain was full of horses and chariots of fire round about Elisha!" (2 Kings vi, 17.) So the visions of Zechariah opened the eyes of his people to the invisible hosts of Jehovah, assuring them that the protecting ministries of heaven are more and mightier than all the forces of the kingdoms of the nations.

FIRST VISION.

The Angelic Horsemen, chap. i, 7–17.

After the mention of the date (verse 7) the first vision of Zechariah is recorded in a single verse (8), as follows: "I saw in the night, and behold a man riding upon a red horse, and he stood among the myrtle trees that were in the shady place; and behind him there were horses, red, sorrel, and white." The meaning of this vision of the night is to be derived mainly from what follows in verses 9–11, but the appeal of the angel of Jehovah in verse 12, and the gracious answer of Jehovah in verses 13–17, enable us to understand the import and significance of the revelation.

The prophet asked of his angelic interpreter, "What are these?" —that is, what do they signify? The man that appeared upon the red horse among the myrtles answered, "These are they whom Jehovah hath sent to walk to and fro through the earth" (verse 10). Whereupon the whole company of riders on the horses of different colors joined in and said, "We have walked to and fro through the earth, and, behold, all the earth sitteth still and is at rest" (11). These angelic riders were visional symbols of the "hosts" of Jehovah, who execute his will "in the army of heaven and among the inhabitants of the earth" (Dan. iv, 35). They symbolize the myriad agencies by which Jehovah shakes all nations and overthrows the thrones of the kingdoms, as Haggai had prophesied (Hag. ii, 7, 22). He controls the armies of heaven and of earth, and can at his word set the world in commotion or cause it all to sit still and be at rest (verse 11). The fact that these leaders of God's host had at that time brought about such conditions of quiet in all the earth showed that it was a most favorable time for the Jewish people to complete the temple at Jerusalem.

We need attach no mystical significance to "the myrtle trees" and "the shady place" where the riders were seen to stand (verse 8). They simply supply an appropriate background for the picture. The horsemen appear as if in a retired and quiet place, reposing after action. They have been marching to and fro through the earth, and have brought all things to a state of rest. Nor should we look for any special meaning in the different colors of the horses other than the general idea suggested by comparison with chap. vi, 2–7, and Rev. vi, 1–8. These do not naturally designate the different lands, kingdoms, and nations to which the riders were sent, but rather different kinds of agencies by which God executes judgment among the nations. A clew to this feature of the symbolism is found in Ezek. xiv, 21, where the Lord speaks of his "four sore judgments upon Jerusalem, the sword, and the famine, and the noisome beasts, and the pestilence." Compare the "wars, famines, earthquakes, and pestilences" of Matt. xxiv, 7, and Luke xxi, 11. With *white* we most naturally associate the idea of victorious wars; with *red*, bloodshed and slaughter; with *black*, pestilence and famine. But when several colors are mentioned together, as in Zech. i, 8, there is no occasion to attempt to discriminate and inquire into the distinct significance of each.

The comforting assurance of the vision is enhanced by the gracious promises of Jehovah, recorded in verses 13–17. They are noteworthy as given in answer to the prayer of the angel of Jehovah (in verse 12), and are called "good words, consolations" (verse 13). They consist of the three impressive thoughts : Jehovah's jealousy for Jerusalem and Zion (verse 14); his displeasure with the nations

(15); and his purpose to restore and enlarge Jerusalem (16, 17). "My house shall be built therein," he says. The former wrath has passed away, and Jehovah shall again "comfort Zion and choose Jerusalem." And so by direct promise as well as symbolic vision did Jehovah strengthen his people in their time of need. The prayer of Jehovah's angel availeth more than all the armies of the world, and the vision of angelic horsemen, like that of the mountain full of horses and chariots round about Elisha, gave assurance that Jehovah's hosts were more and mightier than all that could come against them.

SECOND VISION.

The Horns and the Workmen, chap. i, 18-21.

The prophet next beheld "four horns," whether of oxen or some other animals is not mentioned, and therefore needless to inquire. The horn is a symbol of power. Especially in a wild or furious animal does it suggest the idea of tossing and tearing that which comes in its way. These four horns were symbols of the hostile powers that had scattered Judah and Israel.[1]

The general apocalyptical significance of the number *four* is noticeable in this twofold vision of four horns and four smiths. In chap. ii, 6, the Jewish people are said to have been scattered or "spread abroad as the four winds of the heavens." This general concept of the four winds, or the four corners óf the earth (Isa. xi, 12; Ezek. vii, 2; Rev. vii, 1), warrants our calling four the symbolic number of the world (see Introduction, p. 20). Attempts to point out mathematical or literal significance in apocalyptic numbers are misleading. It matters not in the exposition of this vision whether the powers that scattered Israel were exactly four in number, or five, or seven, or ten.

Over against the four horns, the prophet saw "four smiths,"[2] coming to terrify them, to cast down the horns of the nations, which lifted up their horn against the land of Judah to scatter it" (verse 21). Here again the number four is to be understood in the same general way as in the vision of the horns. Some interpreters

---

[1] The perfect tense of the verb here employed (זֵרוּ, *have scattered*) points to something already accomplished, and may not naturally be referred to what was yet future when the prophet wrote. The construction of the names "Judah, Israel, and Jerusalem" is peculiar, and none of the common explanations are satisfactory. The text is perhaps corrupt.

[2] The Hebrew word translated *smiths* is חָרָשִׁים, *hewers*, and may refer to *workmen* of any kind. Some render *carpenters*. But the thought is that of *dehorning* cattle, and smiths or hewers would be most naturally thought of in the connection. Such were a terror to horned animals.

suppose that the four horns symbolize the four kingdoms of Daniel's prophecy; others understand Assyria, Babylon, Egypt, and Persia. The smiths have been explained as Nebuchadnezzar, Cyrus, Cambyses, and Alexander; or Zerubbabel, Joshua, Ezra, and Nehemiah. Some have found in them symbols of the four cherubim, and others of the four evangelists !

The great lesson of this double vision is to be seen, not in detailed efforts to find precisely four persons or powers to answer to that number of horns and of smiths, but in the fact that for every horn that ever scatters his people God will in due time provide a smith to terrify and cast down the oppressor. It may indeed be affirmed, by way of special illustration, that for every horn like Assyria, and Babylon, and Egypt, he raises up a hower like Nebuchadnezzar, and Cyrus, and Alexander to smite and overthrow the presumptuous power. So in Jer. li, 20, Jehovah thus addresses a nation that is employed to accomplish his work of judgment (it may be *any* nation or conqueror that serves such a purpose): "Thou art my battle-ax (or maul) and weapons of war: and with thee will I destroy kingdoms; and with thee will I break in pieces the horse and his rider; and with thee will I break in pieces the chariot and him that rideth therein."

The prophet and the people of Judah are thus further assured that their God will not leave them to be annihilated by the great powers of the world. Though Israel be scattered to the four winds, and mightily oppressed, Jehovah has abundant power "to cast down the horns of the nations," and to restore and vindicate those who have been for a while the spoil of their enemies. In its essential character, and in the lessons of comfort it furnishes, this vision is thus seen to have a very natural relation to the one that precedes it. It supplements and confirms the doctrine of the vision of the angelic horseman, and is to be compared further with the teaching of the vision of the four chariots in chap. vi, 1–8.

THIRD VISION.

The Measuring of Jerusalem, chap. ii.

The import of this vision and of the prophetic oracle attached to it (verses 6–13) may be best presented in a series of observations:

1. The word translated "measuring line" in verse 1 is not the same Hebrew word translated *line* in chap. i, 16, but it has the same general signification. It is a line of measurement intended to determine the limits of the city's breadth and length (verse 2).

2. The "young man" of verse 4 has been supposed by many to be the prophet himself. If we adopt this view the scene must be

explained as follows: The prophet sees a man with a line going forth, and asks him whither he is going; whereupon he receives the reply of verse 2. Then the interpreting angel (same as in i, 9; iv, 1, 4; v, 5) goes forth from the side of the prophet as if to speak with the man with the line, but is met by "another angel" (verse 3), who tells him (that is, the interpreting angel) to run back and speak to the prophet (="this young man") and say to him what is written in verses 4-13. I prefer, however, the view which identifies the "young man" of verse 4 with the "man with the measuring line" in verse 1, and regards the whole chapter as an object lesson depicted before the prophet's eyes. According to this view, the angel interpreter of verse 3 went forth and was met by "another angel," who presented himself as a subordinate, and who was commanded by the interpreting angel to run and speak to the young man who had the measuring line in his hand (that is, the man mentioned in verse 1), and who was about "to measure Jerusalem" (verse 2), and tell him that such a work of measurement would be a useless labor. For the new city was to "be inhabited as villages without walls, by reason of the multitude of men and cattle therein " (verse 4). Jehovah himself further declares that he will be "a wall of fire round about her and a glory in the midst of her " (verse 5). But, whichever of these views be adopted, the main lesson of the vision remains the same. We note the extent and variety of angelic ministrations in the visions of the prophet. He conceives heaven and earth as full of ministering spirits in the forms of men (compare the young man sitting in the tomb of Jesus, Mark xvi, 5), who do the will of "Jehovah of hosts."

3. The import of the vision is not difficult to understand. Jerusalem is to outgrow her former limits and be occupied as an unwalled town, without fear of molestation; for Jehovah purposes to defend his people, as in the exodus, by the pillar of fire. The "wall of fire round about " and the "glory in the midst " should also be compared with Isa. xxvi, 1, and lx, 19. But it is as little necessary to understand the wall of fire and the glory literally as it is to insist that the things seen in vision by the prophet were actual realities. The symbols and metaphorical language were the apocalyptic method of conveying the divine assurance of Jehovah's presence with his people and of his omnipotent protection.

4. The divine assurance thus symbolically revealed is the basis of the poetic oracle which immediately follows in verses 6-13. The scattered exiles are exhorted to "flee from the land of the north" (that is, Babylon and the adjacent regions), with the obvious implication that they come and help to rebuild and repeople Judah and

Jerusalem. These exiles are poetically addressed as "Zion that dwellest with the daughter of Babylon."[1]

5. Verses 10–13 are to be taken as a prophecy of the Messianic time. For while much that is promised or implied in the whole passage of verses 4–13 was actually fulfilled in the restoration of Jerusalem by the returned exiles, the full import of this inspiring oracle of promise is to be realized in the Gospel age. The restored and enlarged Jerusalem of the postexile time is but a symbol and type of the new Jerusalem that cometh down out of heaven from God, in which the nations of the saved shall walk. Comp. Rev. iii, 12; xxi, 2, 10, 24; comp. also Isa. ii, 2; lx, 3, 11, and especially Hag. ii, 7–9.

The concluding verse of this chapter (verse 13) is an outburst of inspired emotion, and very appropriately concludes the address to Zion which begins with verse 10. Comp. Hab. ii, 20, and Zeph. i, 7.

FOURTH VISION.

The Typical High Priest, chap. iii.

After the glorious word of promise for the fallen city and the captive daughter of Zion there immediately follows a vision of blessed hope for the fallen and dishonored priesthood. The chapter may be divided into three sections:

1. The high priest's humiliation depicted, verses 1–3.
2. The removal of the filthy garments and putting on of suitable apparel, verses 4, 5.
3. The testimony (הָעִיד) of Jehovah, verses 6–10.

In the first section we have a picture of the high priest in a condition of bitter humiliation; an object of derision for the adversary of God and his people. Satan is seen to stand as the accuser. We may imagine him saying, "See what a priest is here! How changed, how fallen from the dignity and holiness becoming one whose office is to minister in sacred things!"

We must bear in mind that in this vision of Zechariah we have only a symbolical picture. We are not to suppose that Joshua ever

---

[1] The sentiment of verse 8 is not easy to apprehend. "After glory hath he sent me unto the nations which spoiled you." The text as it now stands is probably corrupt. Jehovah is said to be the speaker, but who is the *me* sent to the nations? Some have thought the prophet means himself; but it nowhere else appears that Zechariah was ever sent unto the nations that spoiled Israel. Better to understand the speaker as the ministering angel, who speaks in Jehovah's name. The phrase "after glory" would then be best explained as glory to accrue to Jehovah by judgments on the nations that spoiled Israel, and also, as a consequence, by the joining of many nations to Jehovah as prophesied in verse 11.

actually stood before Jehovah or his angel in filthy garments,[1] or that Satan actually received the rebuke here recorded. The picture taken as a whole is a visional symbol of the people's representative before God, laden with their humiliation and reproach, and showing up the condition expressed in Isa. lxiv, 6 : "We are all become as one that is unclean, and all our righteousnesses are as a polluted garment."

The rebuke of Jehovah in verse 2 brings no "railing accusation" (comp. Jude 9), but calls attention to the fact that this is like "a brand plucked out of the fire." The Babylonian captivity had been a "furnace of affliction," by means of whose purging fires Jehovah purposed to refine his people (comp. Isa. xlviii, 10). The restored community at Jerusalem, represented before God in the person of their high priest, was as "a brand plucked out of the burning" (comp. Amos iv, 11), and to be pitied in its helplessness and lack of external beauty, not ridiculed by Satanic malice. The removal of the soiled garments and the putting on of "rich apparel and a fair miter" (or *turban*, verses 4, 5), such as became the high priest, was a symbolic prophecy of the restoration of the fallen priesthood to its former glory. And so the vision was a helpful word of Jehovah unto Joshua (comp. iv, 6). Though he might well feel at times that he was but a soiled brand, plucked from the fires of Babylonian exile, he was divinely assured that Jehovah would be his defender and redeemer. Satan is rebuked, and angels come and minister unto him. The abundant ministry of angels, noticeable especially in verses 4 and 5, is but the machinery, so to speak, of prophetic symbolism. They serve to vivify and deepen the impressiveness of the symbolism.

But the import of the vision is enhanced by the oracular testimony of Jehovah, which follows in verses 6–10. This *protestation*, or solemn testimony, furnishes Joshua and his associates in the holy office assurances of heavenly fellowship and participation in holiest mysteries. The passage is not easy of interpretation in its details, although the general purport of comfort and assurance is obvious to every reader.

Verse 7 assures Joshua that, on condition of obedience and fidelity to his sacred trust, he should be a judge of Jehovah's house and a keeper (guard or watchman) of his courts. It is further promised, "I will give thee a place of access among these that stand by."

---

[1] There is no evidence to support Ewald's fancy that Joshua was at that time fearing some formal accusation at the Persian court; nor for Stanley's statement that the splendid robe of the high priest had been detained at Babylon, and would not be restored until certain accusations had been cleared away.

By "the ones that stand by" we naturally understand the angels of this vision (comp. verses 4 and 5); but the significance in this place of the word (מהלכים) translated "a place of access," is not so apparent. The word itself is the plural form of either the intensive or causative participle of the verb (הלך) which means *to walk*. The common English version translates it "places to walk." The best interpreters incline to the view which recognizes in the word some *free access* to God, such as the angels are supposed to enjoy. The priest will thus be conceived as himself an angel of God, walking in and out before him on holy ministries, and, accordingly, in fellowship with the angels who "stand before Jehovah."

This lofty concept is still further enhanced by the statements of verse 8. Not Joshua only, but his "fellows" that "sit before" him, and are thus closely associated with him in the priestly office, are declared to be characters of typical significance : "For men of sign are they."[1] That is, they are persons of typical office and character, signs or types of a great Antitype who is destined in the plan of God to be brought forth in due time. This great Antitype is immediately mentioned as "my Servant Branch." There is no article before the word translated *Branch*,[2] and it seems clearly to be here intended as a proper name. This Branch is the Messiah, whom Jehovah promises to bring forth into manifestation. He will be the one final and all-sufficient high priest who, "because he abideth forever, hath his priesthood unchangeable" (Heb. vii, 24). The efficiency of this servant of Jehovah as priest is indicated further in the last statement of verse 9 : "I will remove the iniquity of that land in one day;" that is, "once for all" (ἐφάπαξ, as in Heb. vii, 27; ix, 12; x, 10), not on repeated days of atonement, occurring once a year and perpetually.

Verse 9 is notably obscure. "The stone," "seven eyes," and "the graving" are so many mysteries. Two opinions concerning "the stone set before Joshua" deserve attention. (1) According to some exegetes there is reference to some particular foundation stone of the new temple which had been laid in the presence of Joshua (comp. Ezra iii, 9, 10). Such stone is here conceived as typical or symbolical of the covenant people, who are builded up as lively

---

[1] The common version, "men wondered at," is misleading and without any relevant meaning. The Revised Version, "they are men which are a sign," is better, but scarcely suggests the real import of the passage. Perhaps the best translation would be, "For they are men of typical significance."

[2] The Hebrew word is צמח, and appears also in a Messianic sense in chap. vi, 12; Jer. xxiii, 5; xxxiii, 15, and Isa. iv, 2. Compare also the kindred words חטר and נצר in Isa. xi, 1.

stones into a spiritual house (1 Peter ii, 5), and "the graving" or carving must accordingly be understood as the ornamentations and inscriptions which Jehovah may be conceived as having set upon his people. This imagery would not be essentially different from that of *sealing* the elect of God (comp. 2 Cor. i, 22; Eph. i, 13; iv, 30; Rev. vii, 2; ix, 4). (2) According to others the stone is to be regarded as another symbol of the Messianic Servant of Jehovah. He is not only a Branch but a Stone. Compare the analogous imagery of Isa. xxviii, 16 : "Behold I lay in Zion for a foundation a stone, a tried stone, a precious corner of sure foundation " (comp. also Psalm cxviii, 22; Matt. xvi, 18; xxi, 42; 1 Cor. iii, 11; Eph. ii, 20–22; 1 Peter ii, 4). This view seems on the whole to be the more satisfactory interpretation. The word to Joshua would then in substance be : Not only will I bring forth my Servant Branch, but I will also make the stone which I have set before Joshua [1] a symbol of the living Stone and Rock of Israel, in whom is all my delight, and on whom I will continually keep my "seven eyes " (comp. iv, 10), and whom I will beautify and honor with the inscription of highest and holiest names (comp. Rev. xix, 16). "The seven eyes upon the stone" are most naturally explained as "the eyes of Jehovah" mentioned again in iv, 10. They symbolize the omnipresent oversight and care of God, which are ever turned upon his chosen Servant as well as on all his people.[2] The result of this allseeing providence will be the coming of one greater than Joshua, the son of Jozadak, even the Jesus of the New Covenant, who "saves his people from their sins " (Matt. i, 21), and, in the mystic language of our prophet, "removes the iniquity of the land in one day." The blissful state of peace and prosperity which is to follow this redemption is stated in verse 10 in a form of expression proverbial with the Hebrew prophets (comp. 1 Kings iv, 25; Isa. xxxvi, 16; Micah iv, 4).

Joshua appears again in chap. vi, 9–15, as a type of the future Messianic Branch. In the symbolico-typical act there portrayed we find the conclusion of the visions of Zechariah.

---

[1] In both interpretations "the stone set before Joshua " is best explained as some prominent stone in the temple, at the laying of which both Joshua and Zerubbabel were present. Compare "the head stone " in iv, 7, and the statement of iv, 9. Lowe translates הָאֲבֶן, *the stones ;* that is, collectively, the materials for rebuilding the temple.

[2] Others explain the phrase *upon one stone* as engraved upon the stone, and so serving as a symbol of the sevenfold Spirit mentioned in Isa. xi, 2 (comp. Rev. i, 4 ; v, 6), with which the Branch of Jehovah is to be anointed. Wright supposes that the seven eyes were seen as merely "drawn upon the stone," not yet cut or engraved—a work to be executed by divine power at a future period.

The Golden Candlestick, chap. iv.

This fifth vision is declared in verse 6 to be " a word of Jehovah unto Zerubbabel." It is, accordingly, to be understood as a counterpart of the fourth vision, which we have seen to be conspicuously a word of Jehovah unto Joshua, the priest, a word of encouragement and of glorious promise. The first five chapters of the Book of Ezra inform us how closely these two men were associated in the reorganizing of Israel after the Babylonian exile and in rebuilding the house of God at Jerusalem. Zerubbabel was the princely leader of the people, and the second temple is often called the temple of Zerubbabel, as the first was called the temple of Solomon. Zerubbabel was of the tribe of Judah, a descendent of David, and so represented the royal family. He is called, in Ezra i, 8, "prince of Judah," but he was never recognized as king, and made no pretension to the throne of David. He was the captain of the first band of exiles that returned to Jerusalem, and represented the regal and secular authority so far as such rule was allowed in the subject-condition of the Jewish people at that time. He must have seemed small and insignificant before such a monarch as Cyrus or Darius, and might well have felt discouraged over the fallen fortunes of Israel, as Joshua had reason to feel humiliation over the fallen condition of the priesthood. The vision of the golden candlestick was therefore adapted to cheer him as the foregoing vision was adapted to cheer Joshua, and both are to be recognized in " the two sons of oil " symbolized by the two olive branches in the vision.

In the main this vision is of easy interpretation. In the light of the foregoing observation we cannot fail to see how specifically it was Jehovah's word unto Zerubbabel. The chapter may be divided into three sections, as follows: (1) The candlestick and the trees as seen in the vision (verses 1–3;) (2) The explanation as a word for Zerubbabel (4–10); and (3) the special explanation of the two olive trees.

The candlestick was peculiar by reason of its connection with two olive trees, one upon the right and the other at the left side of it. A conspicuous "bowl upon the top of it " connected "its seven lamps " with the olive trees by means of a multitude of pipes[1] on the lower part, and " two golden spouts " above (verse 12), which latter received the golden oil from the two trees and poured the same into

---

[1] Whether there were seven pipes in all, one to each lamp, or seven pipes to each of the seven lamps, that is, forty-nine in all, is not quite clear. The Hebrew text favors the latter view. For an excellent illustration of candlestick and trees, see the picture in Wright's Commentary on Zechariah.

the bowl, while the former conveyed the same oil from the bowl into the seven lamps. The candlestick is an appropriate symbol of the Church (comp. Rev. i, 20). This particular candlestick was a symbol of the Jewish Church as existing in Jerusalem at that time. God's people, as a united community, are conceived as the light of the world. The candlestick, or lamp stand (מנורה), is the bearer (or holder) of that which gives forth the light ; and so the Church, as an organized community, affords a position and opportunity for each particular member of the body to give light "unto all that are in the house" (Matt. v, 14–16).

The " great mountain," addressed in verse 7, is a symbol of all the obstacles which confronted Zerubbabel in his work of rebuilding the temple. Compare illustrations of similar imagery in Matt. xvii, 20; xxi, 21. Such mountains melt and vanish away before the touch of God (Micah i, 4). The opposition of those "adversaries of Judah and Benjamin" (Ezra iv, 1), who "weakened the hands of the people of Judah, and troubled them in building" (Ezra iv, 4), was a mountain of difficulty in the way, but destined to be brought low by the authority of Darius, the king of Persia. Perhaps also we should see in this mountain an allusion to the great overshadowing might of worldly empire, under which Judah had been crushed for so many years, and before which at that time Zerubbabel and his community at Jerusalem must have appeared so insignificant and helpless. The prophetic oracle declares that all mountains of obstacle and threatening shall become "a plain," that is, disappear, "before Zerubbabel." The Spirit of Jehovah of hosts is mightier than all the empires and armies of the world.

After the address to the great mountain "the word of Jehovah unto Zerubbabel," given in verse 6, is resumed, and enlarged with specific application. In verse 6 the word is of the nature of a motto, an eternal truth of God. "Not by might, and not by power, but by my Spirit." The Spirit was symbolized by the golden oil (verse 12) which flowed from the olive trees to the candlestick, and is thus put in contrast with the "might" (חַיִל, wealth, resources, and military prowess) and "power" (כֹּחַ, force, strength in battle) on which men of the world are wont to rely. The prince of Judah is to know that Jehovah's Spirit is better for the mission of Israel in the world than all the resources and strength of armies in battle. He is therefore directly assured that he shall in due time "bring forth the headstone, with shoutings of Grace, grace unto it." That is, the topstone of the temple shall be laid and the work finished amid the public rejoicings of the people, who will shout and cry, "May the favor of God be on it!" All this is repeated in greater detail in verses 8 and 9. The same hands that laid the foundations of the house of God shall also finish it, and this fact will be a monumental witness that these visions and prophecies of Zechariah were a sure revelation of Jehovah of hosts.

Verse 10 is an additional word of comfort for Zerubbabel. It is in substance the proposition : Small beginnings are not to be despised when the eyes of Jehovah look on them joyfully. "These seven" are the same as the "seven eyes" of chap. iii, 9. The passage reads, literally: "And they shall rejoice and see the plummet[1] in the hand of Zerubbabel, even these seven, eyes of Jehovah; they are running to and fro in all the earth." That is, the eyes of Jehovah, which run all through the world, sparkle with joy at sight of Zerubbabel's triumph. What an affecting anthropomorphism !

The temple which Zerubbabel was building, like that of Solomon before it, and like the Mosaic tabernacle, was a material symbol of the Church of the living God, who dwelleth with his people. It was an embodiment of the overwhelming thought that "God will in very deed dwell on the earth" (1 Kings viii, 27), and commune with the human soul.[2]

The special explanation of the two olive trees, in verses 11–14, implies that they have an essential significance in the purpose of the vision. Although the candlestick was the central object, the prophet's attention was attracted to the trees, one on the right and the other on the left side of it. He is represented as asking a "second time" concerning their significance, and specifying two conspicuous "branches, which by means of two golden spouts empty the gold from above them." The question assumes that these two branches were clearly seen to be a medium of communicating the golden oil to the seven lamps of the candlestick. The answer of the angel, however, is not so clear but that his words have been understood variously : "These are the two anointed ones (Hebrew, *sons of oil*) who are standing by the Lord of the whole earth." We understand, in the light of the entire context, that these two anointed ones are Zerubbabel and Joshua. The preceding vision was Jehovah's word to the high priest Joshua; and this vision is declared in verse 6 to be Jehovah's word unto Zerubbabel. It was fitting, at the conclusion of these two closely related revelations, that the final word of explanation should include both of these highly honored servants of God, and show that they were divinely

---

[1] The *plummet* is in this connection simply the emblem of Zerubbabel's relation to the building of the temple. Jehovah sees the plumb-line in his hand as the sign of his successful execution of his task as builder.

[2] On the symbolism of the Tabernacle, see chap. xi, pp. 81–84.

appointed to minister and act as mediums of communicating the grace of God to his people.[1]

SIXTH VISION.

The Flying Roll, chap. v, 1-4.

Up to this point every vision has had a message of encouragement and promise for Zechariah and his people. But with this revelation of the "flying roll" there comes a change. This fifth chapter contains two messages of warning, the first of which admonishes the new community at Jerusalem that the curses of heaven move swiftly, and will smite a Jewish sinner as quickly and consumingly as any sinner of the Gentiles.

The size of the roll (20x10 cubits) was identical with the measures of the porch of Solomon's temple (1 Kings vi, 3), but need not be supposed to have any special significance in itself. The remarkable size alone would make it an impressive sight. Perhaps the size, as given, may suggest that judgment will begin at the house of Jehovah, and be meted out in full and exact measure. Comp. Ezek. ix, 6; 1 Peter iv, 17. The roll is explained in verse 3 as a symbol of "the curse that goeth forth over the face of the whole land" (that is, the land of Israel). A roll was an appropriate symbol of God's recorded statutes, and we are reminded of the roll on which Jeremiah wrote all the words of Jehovah against Israel (Jer. xxxvi, 2, f.). The king of Judah impiously cut that roll into pieces and cast it into the fire until it was entirely consumed (Jer. xxxvi, 23). This roll of Zechariah's vision is not to be so treated. It is a "flying roll," and seems to move forth on the wings of the wind. No impious hand is able to cast it into the fire, but Jehovah says in verse 4 : "I will cause it to go forth, and it shall enter the house of the thief, and the house of him that sweareth falsely by my name; and it shall abide in the midst of his house, and shall consume it with its timber and its stones."

---

[1] There are three other explanations of "the two anointed ones : " (1) They represent Jews and Gentiles to be incorporated in the Church. This view has no relevancy at this point, and confounds trees and candlestick. (2) They symbolize Church and State. But this view also confounds the symbolism of the candlestick and the trees. If the candlestick represents the Church, as all admit, why have another symbol of the same thought in such connection? (3) They represent the regal and priestly orders, which were to continue for communicating divine grace to the Church. The relevancy of such a doctrine in this connection might be questioned; but the fatal objection is that such a purpose for regal and priestly orders has no warrant in Scripture or in history. On such baseless assumptions one may argue the exploded doctrine of the divine rights of kings and priests.

It is obvious that we here have two notable sins, theft and perjury, marked out for the particular condemnation and curse of God.
The language of verse 3 most naturally conveys the idea that the
curse against stealing was written on one side of the roll and that
against false swearing on the other side, and by the judgment of God
both sins were destined to be quickly *cut off* or *purged out* of the
land. Others explain the words more generally: Everyone who
steals, on the one hand, and everyone who swears, on the other
hand, shall according to it be destroyed.[1] The main thought, on
either of these readings, is that the two sins specified are singled out
for special condemnation, and the two sins represent both tables of
the law. He who swears falsely takes the name of God in vain,
and so violates the third commandment. He lies to the Holy Spirit,
and is guilty of the great sin for which Ananias and Sapphira perished. He who steals violates the eighth commandment of the
decalogue. These two sins were conspicuous in Israel after the
exile, and Malachi (iii, 5, 8, 9) furnishes our best comment on this
vision: "I will come near to you to judgment; and I will be a swift
witness against . . . false swearers ; and against those that oppress
the hireling in his wages, the widow and the fatherless, and that
turn aside the stranger from his right, and fear not me, saith Jehovah of hosts. . . . Will a man rob God? Yet ye rob me, even
this whole nation (by withholding tithes and offerings). Ye are
cursed with the curse."

Our prophet sees the curse of God moving swiftly into the dwellings of the guilty thieves and perjurers, and burning even to the
timber and the stones. The law of Sinai is a consuming fire, and
will assuredly bring the curse of God upon sinners in the land of
Judah as well as upon those of heathen countries.

This vision connects closely with that of the flying ephah, which
immediately follows, and occupies the remainder of the chapter.

SEVENTH VISION.

The Ephah, chap. v, 5–11.

The ephah was a well-known Jewish measure, containing what
with us would be so nearly equivalent that it might be popularly
called a bushel. Such a measure the prophet saw "going forth,"
moving away, as if it were a thing of life. In the midst of it sat a
woman with "a talent of lead" apparently "lifted-up" before her.
This talent or "round piece of lead"[2] seems to have been so

---

[1] Thus reading נכה in the Hebrew text instead of נקה.
[2] So Revised Version, margin ; called also *weight* or *stone* of lead in verse 8.

"lifted up" and conspicuous as at first almost to hide the woman from view. The entire picture is a composite symbol, and its three most noticeable parts are the measure, the circular weight, and the woman.

The interpretation of the vision has been long obscured by a persistent adherence of most exegetes to a reading in the Hebrew text of verse 6, which is unquestionably corrupt. The word translated "resemblance" is the Hebrew word for *eye*, but it makes no sense in the connection, and no explanation of it as it stands here has been satisfactory. But the Septuagint version, a thousand years older than any Hebrew manuscript now known to exist, reads ἀδικία, *iniquity*. This is a correct translation of the Hebrew word עָוֹן, which differs from the word translated *eye* (עַיִן) only by a little prolongation of the letter *yod* (י).[1] The proper rendering of the last part of verse 6 is, accordingly, "This is their iniquity in all the land." This correction is confirmed by the parallel explanation given in verse 8, "This is the wickedness" (Hebrew הָרִשְׁעָה). That is, this composite symbol represents *the* particular form of wickedness and iniquity which now curses the land and should be removed.

The Revised Version has not improved on the common version in its construction of verse 7. I would begin a new and independent statement with verse 7, and conclude it with the first sentence of verse 8, as follows: "And behold, a talent of lead lifted up, and this one woman sitting in the midst of the ephah. And he said, This is the Wickedness."

That one woman, sitting in the bushel, appears as mistress both of the measure and the weight. These were the two symbols of the iniquity and wickedness then appearing in the land, and corresponding to the crimes of theft and perjury condemned in the previous vision. This woman's throne was an empty measure, and her sign an uplifted talent of lead. She thus appropriately portrayed the wickedness described in Amos viii, 4–6, of those who "swallow up the needy, and cause the poor of the land to fail; saying, When will the new moon be gone, that we may sell corn? and the Sabbath, that we may set forth wheat? *making the ephah small and the shekel great*, and dealing falsely with balances of deceit; that we may buy the poor for silver, and the needy for a pair of shoes, and sell the refuse of the wheat."

This, then, is "their iniquity in all the land." This is "the wickedness" which called for prophetic condemnation. It was the

---

[1] The reader unacquainted with Hebrew may observe the very slight difference between עֵינָם (*their eye*) and עֲוֹנָם (*their iniquity*), and how easily an ancient copyist might have written the one for the other.

iniquity of unrighteous traffic that was likely to become the easily
besetting sin of the postexilian Jew. This kind of wickedness has
its root and essence in covetousness. "The love of money is the
root of all kinds of evil" (1 Tim. vi, 10), and covetousness is idolatry (Col. iii, 5). Why a woman rather than a man appears in the
symbol is probably because of her peculiar power as a tempter.
The image symbolizes the sin rather than the sinner, and the en-
snaring images which have ever been most prominent in great
systems of idolatry have borne the female form.

The remainder of the chapter (verses 8–11) portrays the removal
of the ephah, the woman, and the leaden weight out of the land of
Israel far off into the land of Shinar. It is a symbolic picture of
retribution to be visited upon the wickedness of unrighteous traffic.
The woman was "cast down into the midst of the ephah," and the
round piece of lead, now conceived and spoken of as a heavy weight
of stone (Hebrew, *stone of lead*, verse 8), was "cast upon the mouth
thereof." The word *thereof* may refer either to the mouth of the
ephah or of the woman. Thereupon woman, ephah, and talent of
lead were "lifted up between the earth and the heavens," and carried off into a foreign land. The removal was seen to be accomplished by two other women, who "had wings like the wings of a
stork," and were helped by the force of the wind. The significance
of this complex symbolism is profound and far-reaching. It was
not a prediction of anything to be literally fulfilled, like the transportation of sinful Jews back to the land of Shinar. It is rather an
apocalyptic revelation of truths as sure and permanent as the kingdom of God. We may best indicate some of these truths by a series
of observations:

1. Such wickedness as this composite symbol portrays cannot
abide in "the holy land" (ii, 12), nor can it be tolerated in the
kingdom of God. There must be, and sooner or later there will be,
a removal by judicial separation. Comp. Mal. iii, 18.

2. The instruments of this woman's sin are made the means of
her punishment. What a suggestive picture of the narrow covetous soul! Cast into an empty measure, with a leaden stone upon
her mouth, cramped up into a little world of selfishness, this goddess
of covetousness knows nothing aside from weights and measures!
And thus the miser lives inside his own little bushel (or half bushel),
and talks of nothing but talents, and stocks, and bonds, and corner
lots. Sold to covetousness, he makes his own place and goes into
it; his heaven is made his hell.

3. But, further, by an irreversible law, such natures are taken out
of the fellowship of the pure and good and removed far away by

others of their own kind. The world loves its own, and when self-ish interests are at stake the men and women of an adulterous and sinful generation will naturally help those who have helped them. So this one woman was taken up and carried away by those of her own kind—her aiders and abettors in the mammon of unrighteous-ness. When the angel had cast her into the ephah and put the stone upon her mouth these other women come to her rescue, and remove her to a more congenial place. The stork is mentioned probably for no other reason than for being a well-known bird of passage, with notably large wings, and abounding in the land of Shinar in the valley of the Euphrates. The money-lovers of this world move rapidly and long distances in each other's selfish interests, as if borne upon the wings of the wind. Comp. Luke xvi, 8.

4. The "land of Shinar" is to be here understood as the opposite of the land of Israel, which in chap. ii, 12, is called "the holy land." It was that Babylonian plain where Noah's descendants settled after the flood and builded the city and tower which became the occasion of their being confounded and scattered by the curse of God (Gen. xi, 2). It was a land of prevalent idolatry, whither the Jewish people had, according to chap. ii, 6, been scattered as by the four winds of heaven. This vision might, therefore, serve as a warning to the returned exiles not to worship the goddess of weights and measures. Where the love of money is so strong as to employ the "balances of deceit," and make "the ephah small and the shekel great," there curse and exile are sure to come. He who persists in serving mammon rather than God must leave the holy land and go unto his own more appropriate place. Sordid, self-seeking friends may come to his help, and even build him a house on foreign soil, but that house, like the tower of Babel built by selfish ambition in the plain of Shinar, will prove a curse and confusion.

5. There is an important practical lesson in this vision of the ephah. The process of separating and removing the lovers of this world from real fellowship of the good is ever going on in the de-velopment of the kingdom of God. Judas loved silver, and was cut off and went to his own place. Demas forsook the apostle Paul, "having loved this present world." The first epistle of John speaks of those who went out from the godly "because they were not of them" (ii, 19), and Jude significantly mentions "the sensual, having not the Spirit," as those who "separate themselves," or "make separations."

So, by the necessary antagonism of opposite natures, the covetous must remove from the holy ; for the narrow-minded, self-centered worldling cannot inherit the kingdom of God. "Ye cannot serve God and mammon."

EIGHTH VISION.

The Four Chariots, chap. vi, 1-8.

This eighth and last vision of the series exhibits a noticeable correspondence with the first vision, in chap. i, 8-11, and also has its own different and peculiar imagery. The first scene was that of riders on horses of different color ; here we note that the horses are attached to four chariots, and are seen "moving forth from between two mountains." The colors [1] of some of the horses are here different from those of the first vision; but the most remarkable difference is that the chariots are seen to be "going forth," while the angelic horsemen of chap. i were "standing" still. The two visions are evidently of similar import, but by no means identical.

The meaning of this last vision may be best set forth by means of comparison and contrast with the first. It is common for apocalyptic writers to impress significant revelations by repetition and variety of symbols. Joseph's and Pharaoh's dreams were repeated under different imagery to show that "the thing was established of God, and God would shortly bring it to pass " (Gen. xli, 32). Daniel's vision of the four great beasts was in its import only a repetition of what Nebuchadnezzar saw in his dream of the colossal image.

"The two mountains " (verse 1) correspond to the shaded valley mentioned in the first vision (i, 8).[2] That retired place among the myrtles seemed a suitable spot for riders in repose, after having "walked to and fro in the earth ;" these mountains add impressiveness and grandeur to the picture of war chariots going forth to execute Jehovah's judgments. The mountains are said to have been "mountains of brass," and therefore not to be understood as real things, but as visional symbols. The exact meaning is doubtful,

---

[1] No special stress need be laid upon the different colors either here or in chap. i, except as there explained of a symbolic suggestion of God's "four sore judgments." The "grisled-bay horses " of the fourth chariot is a doubtful reading. ברדים means *spotted ;* אמצים, *strong,* is perhaps a corruption of אדמים, *red,* in verse 2.

[2] Some writers imagine these mountains to be those at Jerusalem which inclose the valley of the Kedron, and suppose that valley to be "the valley of Jehoshaphat " mentioned in Joel iii, 2, 12, where God gathers all the nations for judgment. But that "valley of judgment " appears to be rather a symbolical name, in allusion to Jehovah's judgment on the nations that combined in battle against Jehoshaphat, as recorded in 2 Chron. xx, 1-30.

and perhaps no special significance should be attached to this part of the picture, other than that suggested above, of adding grandeur to the scene. We may, however, understand that, as the "great mountain" addressed in chap. iv, 7, was a symbol of the over-shadowing power of worldly empire which awed Zerubbabel, and made him appear little and insignificant, so these two mountains may represent the might and power which are the glory, support, and strength of all great military expeditions. The war chariots, accordingly, proceed from between symbols of massive power and splendor.

As already observed the "going forth" of these chariots contrasts strikingly with the "standing among the myrtles" in chap. i, 8–10. Those angelic riders were in repose after having completed their walking up and down the earth; but these chariots are seen "going forth from standing before the Lord of all the earth." They appear to symbolize the same hosts of Jehovah as the riders, or, perhaps, another department of one and the same great army. In the first revelation the forces of God seem to have paused, and stood, as if waiting for new orders from their great Captain; but here they, or their fellows, are again in motion, going forth to execute the judgment of "the Lord of all the earth."

In the first vision only one rider was specifically mentioned (i, 8), and behind him were horses of various colors. Here no riders are mentioned, but only horses and chariots. In verse 5 we are told that, altogether, "these are the four winds [1] of heaven which go forth from standing before the Lord of all the earth." The word *winds* is to be understood as a synonym for swift messengers, as in Psalm civ, 4, and the symbolic chariots are not essentially different, therefore, from the angelic horsemen of the first vision. These agents of "Jehovah of hosts" execute his judgments on lands and peoples, and in their going forth may take on the forms of war, with the associated horrors of ruthless conquest, bloodshed, famine, and pestilence.

Verses 6–8 assume to designate the particular destination of some of the chariots. The black horses, which went "toward the north country"[2] are said in verse 8 to have wrought the will of God's

---

[1] The word רוחות, in the plural, is nowhere else used in the sense of *spirits*, as the common version here translates it. The plural always means *winds*, as in chap. ii, 6. Comp. also Jer. xlix, 36, and Psalm civ, 3, 4.

[2] The "north country" is the region of Babylon, the land of oppression and exile. See chap. ii, 6, and Jer. vi, 22; xlvi, 10. The oppressors from the east entered Palestine from the north, and so gave this association to the more distant region from which they came.

Spirit [1] on that land. For the Persian world-power, as a rod of God's anger, had already at the time of this vision subjugated Babylon, the oppressor of Judah. "The white went forth after them," or "unto the regions behind them," as the phrase may be translated ; but the meaning is quite indefinite. "The grisled went forth toward the south country," [2] but nothing is said as to what they accomplished. The bay ones went out, and sought, and obtained a commission to "go and walk to and for through the earth," and they did accordingly (verse 7). Altogether, they are to be thought of as a part of Jehovah's hosts, and, like the four living creatures of Ezekiel's vision, they were swift as the wings of the wind.

These four chariots of Zechariah's vision have been supposed to denote the same four world-powers as those symbolized by the four great beasts in the visions of Daniel. But there is no sufficient analogy to warrant the supposition. The chariots moved forth together, and nothing in their movements indicates chronological sequence, which is so prominent a feature of the prophecy of Daniel. No particular kingdoms or powers are designated in the visions of Zechariah. Like the four horns and the four smiths of the second vision (i, 18–21), these chariots symbolize any powers by means of which God executes his judgments in the world.

As we now pass from the last vision of the series to the symbolical crowning of Joshua, which occupies the rest of the chapter, we call attention to a notable analogy between these symbols and those of John's Apocalypse (vi, 1–8). In John's vision there went forth, in rapid succession, a white, a red, a black, and a pale horse, each bearing a rider. Those horses and riders seemed to prepare the way for the coming of the Lord, and in like manner these chariots that "go forth from standing before the Lord of all the earth" prepare us to appreciate the deep significance of the act which immediately follows (verses 9–15). That symbolico-typical act is a striking prophecy of the Messiah, the King-priest, who builds the true spiritual temple of God, and rules upon his throne.

The revolutions of empire in western Asia, which were the result of God's hosts marching to and fro through those lands, prepared the way for the coming and kingdom of the Lord Jesus Christ.

---

[1] "My spirit," in verse 8, is to be explained by Ezek. v, 12, 13 ; xvi, 42. For the Spirit of God, according to Isa. xliv, is a "spirit of judgment." In Judg. viii, 3, רוּחַ has the meaning of *wrath*, or anger. The ministers of judgment in the north country, Babylon, had executed God's wrath therein.

[2] The "south country" is the land of Egypt, occupying the quarter opposite Babylon.

The Crowned Priest, chap. vi, 9–15.

The last picture presented to our thought in this series of apocalyptic prophecies is called a "word of Jehovah," but it is not a vision like the preceding revelations. It is rather a prophetic action, which combines elements of the symbol and the type. It is symbolical so far as the persons and their acts stand forth as emblems of abiding truths ; it is typical so far as it points to a fulfillment in the future. Three returned exiles are named, who assist the prophet in making a crown of gold and silver and setting it upon the head of the high priest Joshua, concerning whom we have already had the vision and prophecy of chap. iii. In that former oracle we met the enigmatical statement about " my Servant Branch ; " the final picture seems to be an addition to the revelations of that former vision.

The word עטרות, *crowns* (verse 11), is in the plural but may be here understood as one composite crown. The same word in the same plural form is employed in Job xxxi, 36, as if it were singular. This coronet made for Joshua may perhaps have had the semblance of a double crown. In Rev. xix, 11, "the King of kings and Lord of lords " is represented as having many crowns upon his head.

Joshua, the priest, thus crowned, is a symbolical type of "the man whose name is Branch." He is destined to " grow up out of his place ; " that is, out of his own proper country and family ; for he is no other than the shoot, or "branch out of the stock of Jesse," referred to in Isa. xi, 1. In comparing this symbolic act with the vision of chap. iii we observe the habitual repetitions of apocalyptic prophecy. The Branch of chap. iii, 8, is mentioned less definitely, and not only Joshua, but his associates also are called "men of sign," that is, typical characters. Here Joshua is separately crowned and made preeminently a type of the Messiah.

One most notable statement of the prophecy is that of verse 13, that " he shall be a priest *upon his throne*." The coming Branch will be a *royal* priest, and so not " after the order of Aaron " (comp. Heb. vii, 11). Uniting in one and the same person the offices of kingship and priesthood, he will be a "priest forever after the order of Melchizedek " (Psalm cx, 4). It will be a new and blessed thing in Judah when the offices represented by Joshua and Zerubbabel are united in one person, and so harmoniously that "the counsel of peace shall be between them both." Then will there be no divided counsels, and no humiliation at the sight of king and priest at strife with each other. For the crowned and anointed Branch "shall bear the glory, and shall sit and rule upon his throne ; and he shall be a priest upon his throne."

Another statement of the most far-reaching significance is that "he shall build the temple of Jehovah," that mystic but real temple of the Messianic age, of which the temple of Joshua and Zerubbabel was but a symbol. This temple of the future is the structure of which Paul speaks in Eph. ii, 20, 21, as "built upon the foundation of the apostles and prophets, and growing into a holy temple in the Lord ; in whom ye also are builded together for a habitation of God in the Spirit." In this "temple of Jehovah," we are told in verse 15, "they that are far off shall come and build ;" not the dispersed of Judah only, but devout souls out of every kingdom, and tongue, and nation. All this is but a repetition, in substance, of what was spoken in chap. ii, 11 : "Many nations shall join themselves to Jehovah in that day, and shall be my people, and I will dwell in the midst of thee." The true explanation and fulfillment of these prophecies are found in the ministry of Jesus Christ, who is now King and Priest, and is steadily building the spiritual temple of the ever-living God.

II. Zechariah xii–xiv.

The last six chapters of the Book of Zechariah are quite generally believed to be of different date and authorship from the first eight chapters. A passage in chap. xi, 12, 13, is quoted in Matt. xxvii, 9, as a prophecy of Jeremiah. As long ago as in the seventeenth century Mede and Hammond maintained that these chapters were a lost or misplaced part of the prophecies of Jeremiah. Since that time an increasing number of critics have come to regard chaps. ix–xi as the work of an older prophet, perhaps the Zechariah named in Isa. viii, 2 ; and chaps. xii–xiv are attributed to still another writer, living after the days of Josiah (comp. xii, 11, with 2 Kings xxiii, 29 ; 2 Chron. xxxv, 24), and probably a contemporary of Jeremiah.[1]

The reasons for denying these last six chapters of Zechariah the same authorship as the first eight are various, such as (1) the remarkable difference of style and sentiment; (2) the absence of visions and symbols here, whereas in chaps. i–vi they are so abundant and conspicuous; (3) the different formulas in ix, 1, and xii, 1, as compared with i, 1, 7; vii, 1; (4) the different concept of the Messiah in ix, 9, and xiv, 1–11, as compared with iii, 8, and vi, 12; (5) the heathen powers as mentioned in ix, 1–7, and x, 10, are not

---

[1] A plausible theory is that which finds in Zech. ix–xi, xii–xiv, and the Book of Malachi three anonymous prophecies, each beginning with the word מַשָּׂא, *burden.* Malachi in that case is not a proper name, but *my messenger,* as translated in Mal. iii, 1. Three such anonymous prophecies may have been appended to the collection of the minor prophets before they were arranged into twelve.

thus naturally referred to by a postexile prophet; (6) the mention of the two kingdoms of Judah and Israel as in ix, 10; x, 6, 7; xi, 14, not natural after the exile; (7) the idolatry mentioned in x, 2; xiii, 2, did not exist in Israel after the exile; (8) the mention of "the house of David" in xii, 7, 10, 12; xiii, 1, more natural before the exile than after, and in like manner (9) the description of prophets in xiii, 2–6; (10) the allusion to the temple as yet standing in xi, 13.

Some of these arguments can be offset by others more or less plausible, and the mention of Greece in ix, 13, is thought to favor a postexile date. But, taken altogether, the reasons for denying the unity of authorship are more and weightier than all that can be said in favor of such unity. The time is happily past when such a judgment is seriously believed by intelligent biblical students to interfere in the least with the great religious purpose of the prophecies in question. Whenever and by whomsoever written, these "burdens of the word of Jehovah" contain a portion of the divine revelations of prophecy, which the Church will ever cherish as of superior value. The section in chaps. ix–xi is not sufficiently apocalyptical to detain us in these studies; but chaps. xii–xiv contain a revelation touching Jerusalem which must not be overlooked; for an analysis of these chapters discloses a fourfold picture of Jehovah's preservation, judgment, and glorification of that great city which figures so prominently in the biblical prophecies of the kingdom of God.

ANALYSIS OF ZECHARIAH XII–XIV.

1. Jerusalem impregnable against all the peoples, xii, 1–9.
2. The Repentance and Mourning of Jerusalem, 10–14.
3. The Purification of Jerusalem from Idolatry and False Prophecy, xiii, 1–6.[1]
4. The final Judgment and Glorification of Jerusalem, xiv.
   (1) Ruinous Judgment on the old Jerusalem, verses 1, 2.
   (2) The new Land and new Jerusalem, 3–11.
   (3) Overthrow of all enemies of Jerusalem, 12–15.
   (4) Worship of all nations and Holiness of all things in Jerusalem, 16–21.

The broad and general range which this entire oracle takes makes it impossible to confine its reference to any one particular event or period. The idea of Pressel that the prophecy best fits the period of Sennacherib's invasion of Judah has not a little in its favor, but closer study shows that, like the great prophecy of Isa. xxiv–xxvii, its lofty ideals transcend the particular circumstances of any one period of Jewish history. No particular siege of Jerusalem, before or after the exile, can be shown to accord so clearly with the

---

[1] I omit from this analysis chap. xiii, 7–9, as out of place in this connection, and belonging more properly at the end of chap. xi.

full significance of the terms of this prophecy that we can fix upon
one date rather than another, and insist on a definite historic fulfillment.   When, therefore, Wright urges that between the restoration
from Babylonian exile and the coming of Christ Jerusalem was a
bowl of reeling to various nations, and "Idumæans, Philistines,
Arabians, Ammonites, Moabites, Tyrians, Syrians, and Greeks made
vigorous attempts against the Jewish people and against Jerusalem,"
we may readily grant all he says, but add that the same statement
will hold in the main when applied to the long period before the
exile, as far back as the days of David.   And besides these neighboring tribes which were always hostile, and aside from all the
troubles with Assyria and Babylon, we recall the invasions of Shishak of Egypt and Zerah the Ethiopian, and Pharaoh-necho, who
defeated Josiah, deposed Jehoahaz, and made the whole country
tributary for three years to Egypt.   In fact, there was no time after
Jerusalem became the possession of Israel and Judah that it was not
an object of desire to the people and nations round about.   So
Wright, in finding notable fulfillments of the prophecy in the times
of the Maccabees, makes out no more certain a case than does
Pressel in referring it to the invasion of Sennacherib.   The oracle
has reference to all those repeated assaults which the heathen peoples made upon Judah and Jerusalem, and is essentially parallel with
the assurance given in Isa. xxix, 8: "The multitude of all the nations
that fight against Mount Zion" shall find their warfare as disap-
pointing as a deceitful dream.   For Jehovah has a great purpose of
grace to accomplish by that people whose name and interests are
identified with Jerusalem.   Hence the name "Israel" in the title
(xii, 1) is virtually synonymous with Jerusalem and Judah.

1. The import of the first section (xii, 1-9) is that all the hostile
attempts made upon Jerusalem shall fail, and the peoples that seek
her overthrow shall themselves be worsted and come to naught.
The two metaphors occurring in verses 2 and 3 are happily adapted
to suggest a double disappointment and damage.   The cup, or bowl
of reeling, implies that the peoples round about would attempt to
drink Jerusalem as so much spoil of wine, but would only become
shamefully intoxicated thereby, and reel and stagger in most
wretched plight.   They would also attempt to lift and carry
Jerusalem as a heavy stone, but would only find themselves bitterly
torn and wounded by the vain effort.   Every horse and rider that
moves against the city of God shall be so smitten as to be a pitiable
and helpless thing (verse 4).   The distinction of Jerusalem and
Judah in this passage may be regarded as mainly rhetorical, suggesting that all Israel is not confined within the walls of Jerusalem.

But the chieftains of Judah recognize, wherever they abide, that the inhabitants of Jerusalem are their strength, and all their national and Messianic hopes are bound up with the destiny of that holy city (verse 5). They shall be a consuming fire among all the heathen peoples, and, having destroyed their enemies, shall dwell triumphantly in Jerusalem. Jerusalem the people shall occupy Jerusalem the city (verse 6), and there shall be no glorying of the city, or even of the royal house, over the rest of the nation (verse 7). Under Jehovah's defending care the weak and wavering will become a strong man like the great hero David, and the royal house of David will be correspondingly exalted so as to serve "as the angel of Jehovah before them" (verse 8).

Thus this first section (xii, 1–9) of the oracle concerning Israel assures Judah and Jerusalem that their national city is impregnable against all the attacks of the peoples round about. Their defense is Jehovah, "who stretcheth forth the heavens, and layeth the foundation of the earth, and formeth the spirit of man within him" (verse 1). Who then can stand against his power? The significance of the passage is to be seen in the remarkable persistence of Jerusalem as the Jewish capital, in spite of all the sieges, oppressions, and captivities which her people suffered temporarily from the surrounding nations. As a nation the Jewish people were divinely protected, and their famous city of the holy hills was their central home and dwelling until the gospel of a new heavens and a new earth went forth from that place to disciple all nations.

2. The second section (xii, 10–14) presents a picture of striking contrast to that which has just been given. "The house of David and the inhabitants of Jerusalem" suddenly appear before us as a great house of mourners. This mourning is the result of an outpouring of "the spirit of grace and of supplication," and is as deep and bitter as that of one who "mourneth for his only son." The "mourning in Jerusalem" is compared to that of all Judah and Jerusalem for Josiah, who was slain "in the valley of Megiddo" (2 Chron. xxxv, 22–25). The families of the houses of David, Nathan, Levi, and the Shimeites are mentioned as mourning "apart, and their wives apart." Why these four families are specified is not, perhaps, an important question. It is one of those incidental features of biblical apocalyptics which have at most a subordinate suggestion.[1] The more important fact is that "all the families that remain" (verse 14) participate in the bitter sorrow.

---

[1] The most approved explanation is that the Nathan here mentioned is the son of David (2 Sam. v, 14), who is named in our Lord's genealogy (Luke iii, 31), and Shimei is the grandson of Levi (Exod. vi, 17; Num. iii, 18). Thus we have in David and

This great mourning is to be understood of the repentance of the Jewish people preparatory to their acceptance of the saving grace of Christ. Wright's comment seems fairly to cover the whole case : " The fulfillment of the prophecy took place when thousands, awakened to a sense of the sin they had committed in crucifying the Lord of life and glory, bitterly bewailed their transgression. The penitential sorrow of those days was not confined to Jerusalem, but pervaded the whole land of Judæa. Many thousands of the Jews believed (Acts xxi, 20); a fact too much lost sight of in the contemplation of the rejection of the Gospel by the majority of the Jewish people. If the Pentecostal outpouring of the Spirit was an event of such importance as to be predicted by Joel the mourning on account of our Lord's crucifixion was equally worthy to be noted by Zechariah. Both fulfillments were no doubt in some respects only inchoate ; both prophecies will yet have a grander, but not a more literal, fulfillment. . . . There never has been a period in the history of the Church when some believing Jew has not mourned because of the sin of his people, nor a time when such a penitential mourner has not found comfort in Christ." [1]

In that far-reaching, spiritual significance, in which the great prophecies transcend all local or particular reference, this " great mourning in Jerusalem " is a picture of the " grace and supplication " which must always and everywhere precede the cleansing and spiritual renewal of hearts that have willfully rejected the truth of God. But the context and scope of this passage most naturally turn the thought to the scattered tribes of Israel and warrant such a hope as Paul expresses in Rom. xi, 26, that " all Israel shall be saved." Just how, when, and where this hope is to be realized is left undetermined.

3. The third section (xiii, 1-6) refers, in appropriate logical and prophetical order, to the divine provision of a fountain of purification from sin and uncleanness for the inhabitants of Jerusalem. The particular forms of uncleanness specified are idolatry and false prophecy. These sins were so rare among the Jews after the exile, and so conspicuous before that date, that this passage has naturally been felt

---

Nathan two of the royal line, and in Levi and Shimei two of the priestly line, and the mention of two suggests the high and the low, or the famous and the more obscure families of each line. Another view is that David represents the royal family, Nathan the prophetic (referring, of course, to Nathan the prophet), Levi the priests, and Simeon (which the Septuagint reads instead of Shimei) the teachers. Perhaps, however, it would be better to understand " the family of the Shimeites," which name appears in many of the tribes, as comprehending all others not included in the regal, prophetic, and priestly families.

[1] Commentary on *Zechariah and his Prophecies*, p. 405.

to be inconsistent with a postexile origin. A sufficient answer to this may, perhaps, be found in the statement of Ezra ix, 1, and Mal. ii, 11, which indicate the presence of heathen abominations after the return from Babylon. The passage, however, need not be understood as affirming a prevalence of idolatry or false prophecy at the time of the writer. The two forms of sin specified are rather to be taken as typically representative of the perverse tendency of the Jewish people to forsake Jehovah and trust to their own wisdom (Jer. ii, 13; xvii, 13). The picture given us in xiii, 1-6, suggests that the cleansing fountain to be opened to the inhabitants of Jerusalem will prove so effectual in washing away the old idolatry, and removing "the unclean spirit" from the land, that no pretense or suspicion of idolatrous practices, or of soothsaying, will be practicable. Fathers and mothers will be so zealous to execute the law of Deut. xiii, 6-11, and xviii, 20, that they will even exceed the severity of the law itself and hasten to kill in the most violent way a son so daring as to presume to prophesy. The consequence of such a prevalent feeling will subject all false prophesying to lowest disrepute, and "the prophets shall be ashamed every one of his vision, when he prophesieth; and they shall not wear a hairy mantle to deceive" (verse 4). The hairy mantle, the outward garb of a professional prophet (comp. 2 Kings i, 8; Matt. iii, 4), would be a fatal display at the time of which Zechariah here speaks, for it would expose the one wearing it to the violence of the people, who would not tolerate the appearance of such claims.

The picture is intensified still further (verses 5 and 6) by representing a suspected person as protesting that, so far from being a prophet, he is a tiller of the soil and a bondman from his youth. It is assumed that prophets would not be found among such workmen and slaves. And yet so persistent is the search of suspicion that he is asked about the marks of smiting apparent between his hands or on his arms. His evasive answer that he was smitten in the house of his friends or lovers serves mainly to show that anyone suspected of idolatry or presuming to be a prophet will be put to the most trying examination. The entire description portrays an ideal day of purification, and by thus magnifying the extreme opposition to all that savors of an unclean spirit the writer seeks to make the deeper impression.

Three things have now been set forth by this apocalyptist of Israel's great future : (1) Jerusalem is to be divinely defended against all the nations that come against her; (2) the spirit of grace and of supplication shall be poured out upon her inhabitants; and (3) all idolatrous practices shall be cut off out of the land.

This is altogether a Messianic picture. We are not to look for a literal or special fulfillment of its several parts. The real fulfillment is to be seen in the remarkable survival of Jerusalem against all the nations that sought her ruin, and her preservation as the Jewish national capital until after the Christ appeared to pour upon the true Israel the spirit of penitence and prayer and cleansing from all unrighteousness.

4. The three ideals now presented are supplemented by another and more glorious picture. The final section (chap. xiv) is fourfold, and, according to our analysis and exposition, is an idealistic portraiture of the ruin of the old Jerusalem as Israel's national capital and the building up of the new Jerusalem, the true spiritual city of God.

(1) The first part of this fourfold oracle announces the capture of Jerusalem by the nations, the violence that will attend its fall, and the captivity of the half of it. Its fulfillment is to be seen in that overthrow of the Jewish capital by the Roman forces which marked the end of Jewish nationality and gave free outgrowth to the new Gospel of the kingdom of God in Christ. The prophet foretells no historical details of the capture of the city, but in the most general way declares as a word of the Lord that the usual plunder and violence of such an event will take place, and a part of the inhabitants will go into exile, but "a remnant of the people" will not be thus sent away. This remnant will be seen, in the next stage of the picture, to flee into the valley miraculously opened in the mountains of God.

(2) The second scene in this word-picture (verses 3–11) is a highly imaginative description of the coming and kingdom of Jehovah, so that he shall be, in a new and special sense, "king over all the earth." A literal interpretation of the passage is utterly out of the question. Jehovah's "going forth and fighting against the nations" is to be understood of that rule of the Most High in all the affairs of men, by which "he doeth according to his will in the army of heaven and among the inhabitants of the earth" (Dan. iv, 35). His cleaving the Mount of Olives so as to open a great valley of escape for his people is as ideal as Micah's concept of the temple mountain exalted above all the hills (Micah iv, 1). As God signally interposed to rescue his chosen people at the beginning of their national history, and both on their exodus from Egypt and their entrance into the land of promise opened for them a pathway through the waters (Exod. xiv, 22 ; Josh. iii, 14–17), so in the great day of their Messianic salvation will he cleave the mountains for their help (comp. Hab. iii, 6). The mention of Azel (verse 5), like that of

Geba, and Rimmon, and the tower of Hananel (verse 10), is but a poetic enhancing of the general picture by familiar local names. As Jehovah thus opens the way of escape for the remnant of his people he is conceived by the prophet as " coming with all his holy ones." We understand this coming as an Old Testament apocalyptic glimpse of what our Lord spoke of in Matt. xvi, 27, and xxv, 31. In accordance with this view of verses 3–5 we understand what follows in verses 6–11 as a highly wrought poetic representation of the millennial period of Messiah's reign. It is " one day which is known unto Jehovah," and ends with a luminous and blessed " evening time."

The details of the picture are quite difficult to define. The exact meaning of verse 6 is uncertain,[1] but the chief thought seems to be that the day shall be one of notable darkness. Such is the common prophetic concept of the day of Jehovah (comp. Zeph. i, 15 ; Amos v, 18 ; Ezek. xxxii, 7, 8). The next verse declares, however, that it should "not be day and not night." The entire conception is well adapted to set forth the general character of Messiah's day, a long period of mingled light and darkness ; a long conflict of light and darkness in the moral world. For the millennium, during which the mustard seed grows and the leaven operates (Matt. xiii, 31–33), is not a cloudless summer day. It opens amid clouds and darkness and with great opposition from the powers of evil ; but it is immediately added (in verse 7) that "it shall be one day ; it shall be known to Jehovah ; not day and not night ; but it shall come to pass at the time of evening it shall be light."[2] It is "one day " in its exceptional character. For, as Jeremiah (xxx, 7) portrays the troublous period of Israel's restoration,

---

[1] The simplest translation of the Hebrew text is, "And it shall come to pass in that day, there shall not be light; precious ones (that is, stars) shall be congealed." The Septuagint and Vulgate read, "There shall be no light, but cold and ice." The common English version, following Kimchi and others, reads, " The light shall not be clear, nor dark." The Revised Version has, "The light shall not be with brightness and with gloom."

[2] " The great period of the Messianic dispensation," says Wright, " seems to us to be signified by 'the day of Jehovah,' that dispensation which in some respects may be considered as having commenced in darkness and judgment for Israel, but which is to end in blessing for that people—its evening time will be a time of light. This day is not a period of darkness, for the light has come, and the glory of the Lord has risen, even upon Jerusalem with all her trials (Isa. lx, 1), by the advent of the Messiah. The darkness which covered the Gentile earth and the gross darkness which enveloped the peoples have been partially chased away. It is day, but not yet the perfect day, for though the Light of the world has come, the light shines in the darkness and the darkness comprehends it not (John i, 5)." *Zechariah and his Prophecies*, pp. 485, 486.

"that day is great, so that there is none like it: it is even the time of Jacob's trouble ; but out of it he shall be saved." It is the period of the Lord's making the kingdoms of the world his own, "for he must reign until he hath put all his enemies under his feet" (1 Cor. xv, 25), and at the blessed "time of evening" it shall issue in the creation of new heavens and new earth. For then shall all the nations walk in the light of the new Jerusalem (Rev. xxi, 24), and "God that said, Light shall shine out of darkness," shall shine in all hearts (comp. Jer. xxxi, 34), "to give the light of the knowledge of the glory of God in the face of Jesus Christ" (2 Cor. iv, 6). The eternal God *knows* this day from its beginning to its consummation in the ages of ages, and to him only is it thus perfectly known (comp. verse 7, and Matt. xxiv, 36).

The picture of living waters proceeding out of Jerusalem (verse 8) is the same apocalyptic ideal as that of Joel iii, 18; Ezek. xlvii, 1–12, and Rev. xxii, 1. This divine provision of heavenly grace is a familiar image of psalmists and prophets (comp. Psalm xxxvi, 8; xlvi, 4; Isa. xli, 18; xliii, 20; John iv, 14). It is a reminder of the river of the garden of Eden (Gen. ii, x).

The marvelous transformation of all the land of Judah from Geba and Rimmon, so as to become "like the Arabah" (verse 10), is also an apocalyptic figure like that of the exaltation of the temple mountain above all the hills in Isa. ii, 2, and Micah iv, 1. Geba and Rimmon are employed, like Geba and Beer-sheba in 2 Kings xxiii, 8, to designate the northern and southern limits of the territory of Judah, and the gates and towers of Jerusalem are named in a similar way to denote the entirety of the city from north to south and from east to west. The ideal is that of the whole land leveled into one extended valley or plain, in the midst of which Jerusalem "shall be lifted up and shall abide in her own proper place."

Verse 11 completes the glorious concept of the new land and the new Jerusalem by the brief but comprehensive statement: "And they shall dwell in her, and there shall be no more curse, and Jerusalem shall dwell securely." This is, in epitome, the same vision of glory which is written more fully in Isa. lxv, 17–25, and Rev. xxi, 1–xxii, 5. It is the lofty prophetic ideal of Messianic triumph and blessing which appears in Isa. xxxv, and which in all similar apocalyptic views depicts both the purpose and the consummation of the kingdom of God among men.

(3) But our author's fourfold apocalyptic method leads him now to turn a moment from his vision of Jerusalem dwelling securely, and, in order to enhance the final scene of "Jerusalem the holy" (verses 16–21), he describes "the plague wherewith Jehovah shall smite all

the peoples that have warred against Jerusalem." These are the same as the nations mentioned in verses 2 and 3 of this chapter, and the picture of the final overthrow of all the enemies of Zion is a prophetic parallel of such passages as Joel iii, 9–14; Ezek. xxxviii and xxxix, and Rev. xx, 7–10.

The plague or judgment-stroke (מַגֵּפָה) which the hostile peoples are to suffer consists of four distinct calamities: (1) Their flesh, eyes, and tongues "consume away;" (2) they fall into the confusion of fighting and destroying one another (comp. Judg. vii, 22; 1 Sam. xiv, 20; 2 Chron. xx, 23); (3) the wealth of all the nations shall be gathered as a spoil for triumphant Jerusalem, and (4) their beasts of burden shall, as in the case of Achan (Josh. vii, 24), be included in the penal curse.

This discomfiture of the enemies of Jerusalem may be regarded, in part at least, as a repetition of the picture given in xii, 1–9. It may be understood as a later phase of Jehovah's war against the nations, and also a repetition designed to show that the matter was established of God and sure to come to pass (comp. Gen. xli, 32). The repetition also serves the dramatic purpose of enhancing the picture of secure and blessed worship which next follows as the grand finale of this great oracle of Jehovah.

(4) Verses 16–21 declare the sanctity which shall be characteristic of the new Jerusalem. The passage contains four things of note: (1) Every survivor of all the nations which came up against Jerusalem shall be converted to the pure worship of "the King, Jehovah of hosts." (2) Any failure on the part of "the families of the earth" to conform to this worship shall be visited with a punishment for sin (חַטָּאת). (3) "Holiness unto Jehovah" shall be the motto and characteristic of every vessel of Jehovah's house, so that there be no distinctions of sacred and secular, holy and profane, or even holy and most holy, for all things will be holy. (4) "There shall be no more a Canaanite in the house of Jehovah of hosts." The word "Canaanite" here stands as the synonym of a profane person, a heathen, an enemy of God like those put under ban or curse. Everyone who "is left in Zion . . . shall be called holy" (Isa. iv, 3), and nothing shall thenceforth hurt or destroy in all the holy mountain.

All this glowing picture of the triumph and glorification of Jerusalem is a prophetic ideal of the future of the kingdom of God. It was introduced by the coming of the Christ and the overthrow of Judaism and the old Jerusalem. Its one long day is known unto Jehovah (verse 7); for nearly two thousand years it has been neither day nor night, but a conflict and mixture of both. The evening time cometh, and there shall be light. With this ideal agree all the great apocalyptists, and a fair and faithful comparison shows that these chapters of Zechariah are in substantial harmony with both the method and matter of the apocalyptic portions of Isaiah, Joel, and Ezekiel.[1]

---

[1] The grandeur and comprehensiveness of the ideal set before us by means of the apocalyptical imagery of Zech. xiv ought to be a sufficient defense against such disparagement as appears in the Expositor's Bible (*Book of the Twelve Minor Prophets*, by G. A. Smith, vol. ii, pp. 485, 486): "The language is undoubtedly late, and the figures are borrowed from other prophets, chiefly Ezekiel. It is a characteristic specimen of the Jewish Apocalypse. The destruction of the heathen is described in verses of terrible grimness; there is no tenderness nor hope exhibited for them. And even in the picture of Jerusalem's holiness we have really no really ethical elements, but the details are purely ceremonial." No matter what the date of the writing or the sources of the imagery, the outline and scope of the fourfold picture, as we have expounded it in the foregoing pages, show it worthy of rank among the other biblical apocalypses. The author, like Ezekiel, appropriates Jewish imagery, and so does the New Testament Apocalypse of John; and there are passages in Amos, and Hosea, and Jeremiah, which exhibit no more tenderness or hope for the enemies of God than does this Jewish Apocalypse. The legal and ceremonial concepts of holiness and triumph are but symbolical suggestions of the better things to come.

CHAPTER XVI

APOCALYPSE OF JOEL

THE Book of Joel is introduced by the simple statement, "The word of Jehovah that came to Joel, the son of Pethuel." Beyond this we have no knowledge of the author aside from what may be inferred from the prophecy itself. The frequent mention of Zion, Judah, and Jerusalem is sufficient reason for believing that Joel was a prophet of the kingdom of Judah, but the most diverse opinions have been maintained concerning the date of his oracles. Bunsen thought that the book was written within twenty-five years after Shishak's invasion (1 Kings xiv, 25), and imagined that Joel iii, 19, contained an allusion to that event. But the prophecy has been assigned to the time of Jehoshaphat (C. F. Bauer), and of Jehoram (Kimchi), and of Joash (Credner, Ewald, Keil), and of Uzziah (De Wette, Bleek), and of Hezekiah (Bertholdt), and of Manasseh (Drusius, Jahn), and of Josiah (Calmet), and to the period subsequent to the Babylonian exile (Vatke, Merx). The trend of the most recent criticism is to assign it to a postexile date.[1] In view of these remarkable differences of opinion, and the few data for forming a very satisfactory conclusion, it must be conceded that the occasion and date of the prophecy are quite uncertain.

The absence of historical data, however, does not conceal the great apocalyptic teachings of the book. These stand out in some sense as generic, and are of the highest value in the study of prophetic pictures of judgment and redemption. The language is characterized by originality of thought and great force and beauty

---

[1] The arguments in favor of the postexile date are: (1) The mention of Grecians as possessing Jewish slaves (iii, 6); (2) the "bringing again the captivity of Judah and Jerusalem," and the "scattering of Israel" (iii, 1, 2) are appropriate expressions if the book is postexilian; (3) there is no allusion to Syrians, Assyrians, or Chaldeans—a strange fact if written before the exile; (4) there is no allusion to Israel of the ten tribes; (5) there is no mention of a king in Judah; (6) there are no allusions to existing idolatry in Judah; (7) the picture of judgment upon all nations seems to have been drawn from Zeph. iii, 8, and Ezek. chaps. xxxviii and xxxix; (8) prominence given to fastings and offerings savors of the postexilian times; (9) the mention of ancient and long-standing enemies, like Egypt, Edom, Tyre and Zidon, suggests that these names are employed as typical of any and all hostile peoples; (10) Judah is spoken of as "a reproach among the nations" (ii, 19), more appropriate after the Babylonian exile than before. There are also other arguments, but of no greater force than these.

of expression, and seemed to Ewald to warrant the supposition that Joel was a voluminous writer, and that the beautiful passage which appears both in Isa. ii, 2–4, and Micah iv, 1–4, is a quotation from some lost work of his. The poetical spirit, sublime imagery, and intense emotion are everywhere apparent in the short series of oracles which bear his name.[1]

The unity, scope, and apocalyptic character of the book are seen in an analysis of its contents. Like all the biblical apocalypses, it embodies the twofold revelation of judgment and redemption. The habit of repetition is a conspicuous feature, and thereby the poet-prophet varies his pictures of woe and triumph, and emphasizes the certainty of what is destined to come to pass. The following analysis will show the formal structure of the prophecy, and help to its interpretation :

ANALYSIS OF JOEL.

I. JEHOVAH'S IMPENDING JUDGMENTS, i, 2–ii, 17.	II. JEHOVAH'S MERCY AND THE SALVATION OF HIS PEOPLE, ii, 18–iii, 21.
1. The Locust Plague and its dire Results, i, 2–12.	1. Assurance of Restoration, ii, 18–27.
2. Call to Repentance and Humiliation, i, 13–20.	2. Great Outpouring of the Spirit, ii, 28–32.
3. The Terrors of the great Day of Jehovah, which is nigh at hand, ii, 1–11.	3. Judgment upon all the Nations, iii, 1–17.
4. Second Call to Repentance and Humiliation, ii, 12–17.	4. The final Glory of Judah and Jerusalem, iii, 18–21.

There is noticeable an artificial correspondency between these two divisions of the prophecy, somewhat analogous to that which we observed in the division of the six days of creation (see p. 43). The locust plague in the first division is offset by the assurance of salvation in the second. The call to repentance has its counterpart in the great outpouring of the Spirit. The picture of the terrible judgment in ii, 1–11, is enlarged to the judgment upon all the nations in iii, 1–17 ; and the second call to repentance and humiliation has its counterpart in the apocalyptic picture of the final glory of Jerusalem. But whatever may be said of this correspondency of the parts of the analysis, the main doctrine of the book is the unfailing certainty both of the judgments and the mercy of Jehovah. The great and

---

[1] It is a remarkable illustration of the opposite extremes of criticism that while Ewald regarded the Book of Joel as a specimen of the oldest written prophecy, distinguished for vigor and originality of thought, Merx (*Die Prophetie des Joel und ihre Ausleger*, 1879) maintains that the book is singularly wanting in originality, being rather an awkward compilation out of materials appropriated mainly from Isaiah and Ezekiel. Some of his discussions seem like an anticipation of the most recent criticism of John's Apocalypse.

terrible day of the Lord comes at different times and in different forms. It is accompanied with signal manifestations of gloom and revolution in human affairs, but is always sure to result in the overthrow of the nations that fight against Mount Zion (comp. Isa. xxix, 8), and in the triumph and glory of the people of God. Comp. Amos v, 18 ; Zeph. i, 14–18 ; iii, 8 ; Isa. xiii, 6, 9 ; Mal. iv, 1, 5.

1. The prophet begins by calling the people to listen to the momentous announcements he is about to make. This style of exordium is like that of the blessing of Jacob (Gen. xlix, 2), the oracle of Balaam (Num. xxiii, 18), the song of Moses (Deut. xxxii, 1), and the prophecy of Micah (i, 2). After the manner of Moses in Exod. x, 1–6, he announces a fourfold plague of locusts, but in this case it is of a judgment that has already come, and left the land in mournful desolation. The like of it had not been known before.[1] The four classes of locusts here named are not correctly represented by the common version of " the palmer-worm, the locust, the cankerworm, and the caterpillar." The Hebrew names *gazam, arbeh, yelek,* and *chasil* may have been intended, as Credner and others think, to denote locusts at different stages of growth. We prefer, however, to understand the description as mainly rhetorical, and the fourfold plague as in formal accord with the apocalyptic habit of portraying penal judgments in fours (comp. Ezek. xiv, 21 ; Jer. xv, 3 ; Zech. i, 18, 20 ; vi, 1). These insects are also poetically called " a nation " (verse 6), just as in Prov. xxx, 25, 26, the ants and the conies are called " a people."

As the valley of Jehoshaphat is twice mentioned in the sequel of this prophecy (iii, 2, 12), it is well here to call attention to the sanctifying of a fast and the calling of a solemn assembly at the house of Jehovah, as enjoined in i, 14 ; ii, 15, and observe the obvious allusion to the acts of Jehoshaphat as recorded in 2 Chron. xx, 3, 4. At the time of Joel's prophecy it appears that the terrible plague described in chap. i, 4–12, had already visited the land, and was the immediate occasion of this apocalyptic picture of coming judgments. It was itself a beginning of sorrows, and the type or omen of a still more fearful day of Jehovah.

2. In chap. ii, 1–11, the prophet takes up and portrays in sublime style the terrors of the great day to which he had already made allusion in i, 15. The passage is worthy of transcription here:

---

[1] Comp. chap. ii, 2 : " There hath not ever been the like, neither shall be any more after them, even to the years of many generations." So in Exod. x, 14 : " Before them there were no such locusts as they, neither after them shall be such." Comp. Dan. xii, 1 ; Matt. xxiv, 21 ; Rev. xvi, 18. Such formulas of comparison are formal elements of poetic prophecy.

Blow ye the trumpet in Zion,
And sound an alarm in my holy mountain;
Let all the inhabitants of the land tremble:
For the day of Jehovah cometh, for it is nigh.
A day of darkness and of gloominess,
A day of clouds and thick darkness,
As the dawn spread upon the mountains.
A people multitudinous and strong,
Like them there have not been of olden time,
And after them there shall not be again,
Unto the years of many generations.
Before them a fire devoureth ;
And behind them burneth a flame.
Like the garden of Eden is the land before them,
And behind them a desolate wilderness;
And also there is nothing that escapes them.
The appearance of them is as the appearance of horses,
And as horsemen, so they run.
As the noise of chariots on the tops of the mountains they leap,
As the noise of a flame of fire that devours the stubble,
As a strong people set in battle array.[1]
At their presence peoples are in anguish :
All faces are waxed pale.
They run like mighty men ;
They climb the wall like men of war,
And each man in his way keeps marching on,
And they break not their ranks.
And each his brother does not push aside,
Every one in his pathway marches on,
And among the missiles they fall, and are not cut off.
They leap upon the city, they run on the wall,
They climb up into the houses ; around the windows they go like a thief.
Before them the earth quakes, the heavens tremble,
Sun and moon are darkened, and stars withdraw their shining.
And Jehovah utters his voice before his army,—
For his camp is very great,

---

[1] On this entire description we have a striking comment in the following testimony of one who saw a plague of locusts in Palestine in 1866: "From early morning till near sunset the locusts passed over the city in countless hosts, as though all the swarms in the world were let loose, and the whir of their wings was as the sound of chariots. At times they appeared in the air like some great snowdrift, obscuring the sun, and casting a shadow upon the earth. Men stood in the streets and looked up, and their faces gathered blackness. At intervals those which were tired or hungry descended on the little gardens in the city, and in an incredibly short time all that was green disappeared. They ran up the walls, they sought out every blade of grass or weed growing between the stones, and after eating to satiety, they gathered in their ranks along the ground, or on the tops of the houses. One locust found near Bethlehem measured more than five inches in length. It was covered with a hard shell, and had a tail like a scorpion."—*Journal of Sacred Literature for* 1866, p. 89. Comp. also the similar descriptions in G. A. Smith's *Book of the Twelve Minor Prophets*, pp. 399–403.

For strong is he that executes his word,
For[1] great is the day of Jehovah, and very terrible, and who can endure it ?

On this passage we remark three things: (1) The mighty army, so terrible in appearance and irresistible in its march, is not an army of locusts, as in chap. i, 4–7, but a multitudinous host of armed invaders, who enter the land of Judah from the north, and are therefore called in verse 20 "the northern" (הַצְּפוֹנִי).[2] But the general appearance and movements of this northern army are described in metaphorical style, and the imagery was suggested by the locust scourge referred to in i, 4–7. (2) The particular event referred to cannot be historically determined, and the description may, therefore, be best understood as an ideal picture based on the well-known fact that all the great invading armies that scattered Israel among the nations, and led Judah into captivity, entered the country from the north (comp. Jer. i, 13–15). (3) The great and terrible day of Jehovah is obviously this northern invasion, which reduces the land to a desolate wilderness, spreads anguish as it moves along, and works revolutions in human history. Any such signal event, that affects the destiny of a nation, is in apocalyptic language called the day of Jehovah.

The exposition of Joel has been confused and rendered unintelligible by some because of their dogmatic prepossession of the idea that "the day of Jehovah" can only mean one definite and formal act of judgment at the end of all human history. But a true prophet of Israel would see a great and terrible day of Jehovah both in a plague of locusts and a destructive invasion of hostile armies that spread the terrors of conquest over land and cities.

3. The statement made in ii, 18, 19, marks the transition from the first to the second part of the prophecy, as shown in the analysis, and the unity of the book is enhanced by this close and vital connection of its two main parts at this decisive turning point. Ewald

---

[1] Observe the *three* reasons for Jehovah's voice before the army, each introduced by the particle *for*. It is fitting that Jehovah's voice sound before this host, for (1) the camp is great, (2) the executor of his word is mighty, and (3) the day is great and terrible. A fearful thunder storm may have accompanied the recent locust plague of i, 4–7, and supplied the imagery of this passage. But the whole picture is poetical and apocalyptic, and therefore not to be explained as a literal narrative of facts.

[2] By understanding the allusion to refer to northern armies, which were wont to enter the land from the north, and not to swarms of locusts, which were rarely or never known to come from that quarter, we are relieved of the trouble which some expositors have experienced in trying to show that some armies of locusts might have entered Judah from the north. The notion that צָפוֹן, *northern*, is intended to denote the Egyptian *Typhon* is far-fetched and misleading.

regards these verses as a short historical explanation, standing between the two prophetical discourses which constitute the book.
Merx punctuates and translates the verbs as jussives, and explains
the verses as a continuation of the prayer to Jehovah begun in
verse 17. But in view of the ideal element, which is so prominent
throughout, it is better to understand the sequence (indicated by
the *waw consecutive* in the Hebrew text) as logical rather than historical. The form of statement implies that, upon the humiliation
and prayer called for in verses 12–17, the blessings promised in
verses 18–27 are certain to follow. That ideal sequence is a certainty of prophetic thought, and the prophet writes it down as if it
had been already bestowed.

The assurance of restoration and manifold blessings, given in
verses 18–27, is as ideal and poetical as is the picture of the day of
Jehovah in 1–11. The promise of fruitfulness and abundance in
verses 19–26 are parallel with such prophetic ideals as appear in
Isa. iv, 2 ; xxxii, 15–20 ; xxxv, 1,·2, 7 ; xli, 17–20 ; lv, 12, 13.
The description in verse 20 of the removal of "the northern"
plague is in rhetorical keeping with the well-known manner in
which the great armies of locusts are driven out of a land. Sometimes they are swept away by a strong wind into the barren desert,
and perish in the sands. Sometimes a strong east wind drives them
by millions into the Mediterranean Sea ; at other times a west wind
will sweep them into the Dead Sea, or some other waste. Comp.
Exod. x, 19.

4. The remarkable outpouring of the Spirit of Jehovah (verses
28 and 29) follows the restoration promised in verses 18–27, and
precedes the coming of the great and terrible day. In its nature it
is to be a fulfillment of Moses's devout wish that "all the people of
Jehovah were prophets, and that Jehovah would put his Spirit upon
them" (Num. xi, 29). This was fulfilled, according to Acts ii, 16–
21, in the great manifestation of spiritual power on the first Pentecost after the ascension of Jesus Christ. But we need not assume
that the event of that first Pentecost was the first, or last, or only
fulfillment of this prophecy. It was no more fulfilled in that one
outpouring of the Spirit than were the other great and noble things
foretold in connection with it. According to verse 32 "all who call
upon the name of Jehovah shall be delivered," and these delivered
ones are designated by two other words of much significance,
"those that escape," and "the survivors whom Jehovah calls."
But this calling, delivering, escaping, and surviving continue as
long as Jehovah continues to pour out his Spirit upon all flesh.

The "wonders in the heavens and in the earth" (verses 30, 31) are apocalyptic symbols of judgments and revolutions which determine epochs in human history. They are employed by the prophets as metaphorically descriptive of national catastrophes and great crises in the divine government of the world. This is abundantly shown by a comparison of Amos viii, 9 ; Micah i, 3 ; Isa. xiii, 10 ; xxxiv, 4, 5 ; Ezek. xxxii, 7 ; Matt. xxiv, 29.

5. The judgment upon all the nations, as depicted in iii, 1–17, demands our careful study. It is another picture of the great and terrible day of Jehovah, and shows how that day will ultimately affect all the nations who set themselves against Jehovah and his people. The allusions to the valley of Jehoshaphat (verses 2 and 12) must be studied in the light of what is written in 2 Chron. xx, 1–30. During the reign of Jehoshaphat, king of Judah, the Moabites and Ammonites, and with them some of the Maonites, joined forces to invade the land of Judah. When it was reported that the enemy had approached in great numbers as far as En-gedi a deep fear seized the soul of Jehoshaphat, and he at once proclaimed a fast, and the people out of all the cities of Judah assembled at Jerusalem, before the great court of the temple. After the king had offered an earnest prayer to God for help, and while all the people were standing there before Jehovah, the Spirit came upon Jahaziel, a Levite of the sons of Asaph, and he prophesied in the midst of the congregation, and declared that the battle was not one in which the forces of Judah and Jerusalem were to engage. It was God's battle, and they had only to stand and behold the salvation of Jehovah with them. Jehoshaphat and all the people received the message with profoundest awe, and early the next day they went into the wilderness of Tekoa, singing unto Jehovah, and praising his eternal mercies. While they were thus singing, an ambush, consisting probably of a band of daring marauders not belonging to either army, attacked the combined forces of Ammon, Moab, and the Maonites with such sudden fury as to put the whole host into confusion. The fight first turned against the Maonites of Mount Seir, and when they were utterly destroyed the Ammonites and Moabites fell to fighting each other, and like the Midianites when attacked by Gideon and his brave three hundred, " every man's sword was against his fellow " (Judg. vii, 22). Even the liers in wait who commenced the conflict seem to have perished with the rest.

Accordingly, when Jehoshaphat and his people came to the field of battle they beheld the valley covered with the dead bodies and immense spoil of their enemies, and they were three days in gathering up the booty. On the fourth day they all assembled in the valley, and blessed Jehovah for the wonderful triumph. It was like another singing of the song of Moses, when Jehovah had triumphed gloriously, and thrown the horse and rider into the sea (Exod. xv, 1), and that valley thereafter took the name of Berachah, that is, "valley of blessing." Jehoshaphat and his people returned to Jerusalem with joy, and entered the holy city with triumphal song and instruments of music, "and the fear of God was on all the kingdoms of the countries when they heard that Jehovah had fought against the enemies of Israel" (2 Chron. xx, 29).

Such a signal triumph could not fail to make a deep impression on all the devout in Israel. The "valley of Jehoshaphat" would thenceforth signify to the pious Hebrew an extraordinary judgment of the Lord upon the enemies of his people. The very name *Jehoshaphat*, meaning *Jehovah judges*, would help to preserve the lesson. The valley, which was the place of signal judgment upon their enemies, was to the people of Jehovah a valley of blessing, and later prophets would naturally allude to it in the name of the devout king of Judah, who was the great commanding figure in the congregation of Jehovah at that time, and call it "the valley of Jehoshaphat," "the valley of decision," in which it is God that pleads and decides the issue.

We are not, therefore, to think of "the valley of Jehoshaphat" in this prophecy as a particular locality, as, for example, the valley of the Kidron (which a worthless tradition has associated with the name). The name is symbolical, and in keeping with apocalyptic style. The meaning is that, in the judgment of the nations, Jehovah will interpose in the interests of his people, and by a wisdom and power infinitely above that of men bring to naught and destroy the plans of all who rise up as the enemies of his people. Compare the teaching of Psalm ii, 1–4, and Isa. xxix, 5–8. Jehovah rules the heavens and the earth, and can thwart the counsels of men and overthrow their organized forces as easily as he did in that famous valley which must ever be associated with the name of King Jehoshaphat.

It should be observed that according to the express statement of iii, 1 and 2 (Hebrew text iv, 1, 2) the "bringing again of the captivity of Judah and Jerusalem" is contemporaneous and coincident with the judgment of all nations in "the valley of Jehoshaphat." For "those days and that time" point to the period of Messianic rule, the millennial era during which Jehovah's Anointed restoreth all things and maketh all things new. While he is restoring his Israel and gathering his elect from the four quarters of the earth he is also at the same time reigning on his throne in the heavens, and putting all his enemies under his feet. Comp. Matt. xxiv, 29–31, and 1 Cor. xv, 25.

Let it be further observed that "the great and terrible day of Jehovah," conceived as the day of judgment, receives in this scripture one of its most significant illustrations. It is not to be thought of as a literal "day," any more than the *days* of God's creation as depicted in the first of Genesis. So far as the *time* of it is concerned it comes any day and hour when the sins of men and nations are ripe for punishment. It is a continual execution of divine judgments, repeated with every new occasion which demands its exercise. This conception inheres in the suggestive and emotional words of Joel iii, 14 :

> Multitudes, multitudes, in the valley of judgment!
> For near is the day of Jehovah in the valley of judgment.[1]

The apocalyptist's eye is here upon the great future of the people of God. He hears Jehovah say that he will gather the nations who have scattered his "heritage Israel," and *plead* with them in "the valley of Jehoshaphat." This *pleading* is expressed by a form of the Hebrew verb for *judging* (Niphal of שָׁפַט), which conveys the idea, not only of entering into a rational contention and prosecution as before a judge in court, but also of inflicting punishments as a means of conviction. So in a parallel picture in Ezek. xxxviii, 21–23, we have the following illustration of what God means by *pleading* with a nation: "And I will call for a sword against him unto all my mountains, saith the Lord Jehovah : every man's sword shall be against his brother. And *I will plead against him* with pestilence and with blood, and I will rain upon him, and upon his hordes, and upon the many peoples that are with him, an overflowing shower, and great hailstones, fire, and brimstone. And I will magnify myself, and sanctify myself, and I will make myself known in the eyes of many nations ; and they shall know that I am Jehovah."

Such is the nature of Jehovah's pleading with the nations that know him not, and the prophet Joel portrays it as a day of judgment and conviction. The mighty ones of Jehovah come down and enter into the contest (verse 11). Jehovah sits to judge the nations (verse 12). The following passage is unequaled for sublimity:

[1] These lines are an exclamation of profound emotion and awe. The prophet at this point is burning with sensations of holiest fervor. He sees how immanent in all the crises of history is Jehovah's power, and how he turns the multitudes at will to perform his judgments in the earth. The noisy crowds, the clashing of arms, the shock of battle, are invariable attendants upon decisive wars which turn the tides of history. So the symbolical "valley of Jehoshaphat" is preeminently a "valley of decision."

Put ye in the sickle, for the harvest is ripe,
Come, tread ye, for the wine press is full ;
The vats overflow, for their wickedness is great.
Multitudes, multitudes, in the valley of judgment !
For the day of Jehovah is near in the valley of judgment.
The sun and the moon are darkened,
And the stars withdraw their shining.
And Jehovah shall roar out of Zion,
And utter his voice from Jerusalem ;
And the heavens and the earth shall shake.
But Jehovah is a refuge for his people,
And a stronghold for the sons of Israel.
And ye shall know that I am Jehovah, your God,
Dwelling in Zion, the mountain of my holiness.
And Jerusalem shall be holy,
And strangers shall not pass through her any more (iii, 13–17).

All this is a highly wrought poetic picture, and is applicable to such desolations as befell Egypt, and Edom, and Assyria, and Babylon; such retributions as are alluded to in verses 4–8;[1] and such over-throw of dynasties and collapse of empires as we may read in the past history of nations. And thus must Jehovah and his Anointed judge and rule until the uttermost parts of the earth become his possession, and all things are made subject unto him. Comp. Psalm ii, 8; cx, 1; 1 Cor. xv, 25.

6. The final picture (verses 18–21), which follows the decisive judgment, and is enhanced by imagery adapted to charm the heart of " the children of Judah," receives its most captivating touch in JEHOVAH DWELLING IN ZION. It is a new and holy Jerusalem that the prophet sees. A living fountain pours its waters out of the house of Jehovah. The old enemies have disappeared. The land of promise is glorified in the vision, and mountains and hills and valleys abound with wine and milk and brooks of water. The blood

---

[1] The character, position in the context, and extent of contents of verses 4–8 are against construing them as a parenthesis (as do Hengstenberg and Pearson). The mention of " Tyre and Zidon and all the coasts of Palestine" (verse 4) affords no clew to the date or historical position of the prophet, for the reference is not to the peoples of these coasts at any particular period, but rather to the fact that these names desig-nate regions *contiguous* to " my heritage Israel " (verse 2), and were ever associated in Jewish thought with an outlying and closely encroaching heathendom. Similarly the "Javanim " and the " Shebaim " in verses 6 and 8 stand for peoples that are " far off," and should not be assumed to be a specific mention of some definite historical event. In like manner the mention of Egypt and Edom in verse 19 is not of a character to throw light upon the time of this prophecy, for those names are obviously employed in a general way for regions closely bordering on the land of Israel and associated in the national thought with ancient and perpetual enmity. So, too, the name Shittim, in verse 18, stands as a symbolical synonym of a dry and parched valley or country.

of innocence, shed in the long, long strife of ages, is finally avenged and pronounced innocent (comp. Deut. xxxii, 43; Rev. vi, 10; xix, 2). Judah and Jerusalem abide forever, dwelling with Jehovah in the holy mountain. All this but repeats the deepest thought in the symbolism of the tabernacle, and accords with the closing visions of Ezekiel and John. Comp. *Jehovah-shammar* in Exek. xlviii, 35.

7. Reviewing now the word of Jehovah to Joel, we may trace the course of the prophetic thought. Our analysis provides a clew. The terrible plague of locusts, which appears to have just visited the land of Judah, was the occasion of the prophecy and suggested not a little of the imagery employed by the writer. In this severe judgment on land and people Joel beholds the symbol of a still more terrible day of Jehovah close at hand. It will come like a "destruction from Shadday." It will take the form of a multitudinous host from the north, and spread anguish and desolation in its path. In view of this approaching calamity the people of Judah and Jerusalem are called to repentance and prayer; for "who knoweth whether he will not turn and repent, and leave a blessing behind him?"

If now we assume an early period for this prophet, and date this oracle before any of the great invasions from the north (for example, Assyria) had swept over the land of Judah, we may understand the picture of chap. ii, 1–11, as referring directly to one of the great invasions of the armies from beyond the Euphrates. But in the absence of anything sufficiently specific to prove such a reference of the prophecy, and in view of the many and strong reasons for assigning the book to a much later period, it is better to explain its portraitures of judgment in a more general way. We thus avoid committing the exposition to the maintenance of an historical position which cannot be fairly proven.

Assuming, then, on the other hand, that the author of this book was a prophet of Judah, living many years after the restoration from the Babylonian exile and filled with lofty concepts of divine judgment by the study of the visions of Ezekiel and Zechariah, we may easily apprehend the standpoint and significance of his poetic oracles. On this hypothesis, as on the other, the occasion of the prophecy was a plague of locusts, like that described in the footnote to page 172. But with the knowledge of all the invasions and marches and desolations of the armies of Egypt, and Assyria, and Chaldea, and Persia, and familiar with such prophetic pictures as appear in Amos vii, 1–6; Isa. v, 26–30; vii, 17–19; xiii, 4–13; Jer. i, 13–16; Ezek. xxxviii, 19–23; and Hab. i, 6–10, Joel sets forth an ideal of struggles and triumphs in which past events and a free use of prophetic imagery are made to contribute a true apocalyptic picture of the future of the kingdom of God.

From this point of view the judgment outlined in chap. ii, 1–11, is not any one particular event, but a vivid concept of such penal visitations as were continually disturbing the peace of Judah. From the first approach of the armies of the north until the overthrow of Jerusalem by the Romans " a day of darkness and gloom, a day of clouds and thick darkness," seemed to hang most of the time over that land. It was and has since been a battlefield of the nations. Such a day of Jehovah opened to the vision of the prophet and seemed nigh at hand. He painted its dark and terrible aspect in figures drawn largely from the horrors of the recent plague of locusts. But with all the anguish and terror foreseen, he also proclaims the divine mercy, that may even along with such judgments bring help and blessings to the people of God.

But after the transition at chap. ii, 18, 19, a more promising outlook is assured to the land and people of Jehovah. Not only shall the northern army be driven away, but great peace and prosperity shall be their portion ; they " shall eat in plenty and be satisfied, and shall praise the name of Jehovah " (ii, 18–27). Nor is this all; for afterward (verse 28) will Jehovah graciously pour out his Spirit, and along with the attendant wonders in heaven and earth a new era will open among the nations (ii, 28–32). Thereupon Jehovah will enter into judgment with all the nations, and all that act the part of his enemies will fare as did the nations that perished in the valley of Jehoshaphat. But the glorious issue of the momentous struggle will be the blessed triumph and security of the chosen people, dwelling in the new and holy Jerusalem with Jehovah forever.

CHAPTER XVII

APOCALYPSE OF DANIEL

The Book of Daniel is held by an increasing number of the leading biblical scholars of the time to be a pseudograph like the Book of Ecclesiastes. A Jewish writer, living in the time of the Maccabees, and inspired with the same devout zeal for the law and covenant of his fathers which fired the souls of Mattathias and his sons to "rescue the law out of the hand of the nations, and out of the hand of the kings" (1 Macc. ii, 48), is supposed to have conceived and written the book for the encouragement of his people in that time of fiery trial. Into the arguments for and against this view of the book it is no part of our purpose to enter. The controversy may be read in detail in the various critical introductions and commentaries. We proceed upon the supposition that the God of Israel may have inspired a holy man of the Maccabean times to set the magnificent apocalypses of this book in an idealistic background, and to publish them under the name of an ancient man (Ezek. xiv, 14; xxviii, 3) distinguished for his wisdom in the secret things of God. The miraculous narratives may, on this hypothesis, be regarded as sacred allegories, setting forth in sublime pictorial form the doctrine that there is a God in heaven, who reveals secret things to his prophets, defends and glorifies his faithful worshipers in times of bitter trial, does according to his will in the army of heaven and among the inhabitants of the earth, humbles those who walk in pride, and brings to confusion the counsels of wicked men. We are of opinion that no essential element of divine revelation is compromised by this supposition. Why may not an inspired apocalypse be cast in a framework of narrative as unreal as that of the Book of Job? Surely, its profitableness "for teaching, for reproof, for correction, for instruction in righteousness," would not be thereby destroyed. The lessons of Job are no less important and valuable as a part of Holy Scripture because of our inability to prove that its narrative portions are actual history. Nor does it detract from the parables of Jesus to say that they are all fictitious in their narratives. Parables, allegories, symbols, and fables are employed in the Scriptures for the purpose of instruction in righteousness, and it would seem that he has a self-imposed and needless task who presumes to say that no inspired prophecies of the Bible could have been set in a like idealistic background.

We accordingly feel no particular concern with the old question of "the genuineness of Daniel." The best possible defense of the book, as an important portion of Old Testament revelation, is a clear and self-consistent exposition of its prophecies. These are of such profound significance and imperishable worth that, when clearly apprehended in their relation to one another, and in their historical connection with the pre-Christian literature of the Jewish people, they carry with them their own self-evidencing apology. The apocalyptic sections constitute an original and most important body of divine revelation. Whether written during the exile, or in the times of the Maccabees, they contain a view of the kingdoms of the world and their ultimate subjection to the kingdom of God unsurpassed by any other prophecies of the Hebrew Scriptures. Nowhere else do we find, before the advent of Christ, such a magnificent conception of the kingdom of heaven.

The apocalyptic portions of the book consist mainly of (1) Nebuchadnezzar's prophetic dream, which was interpreted by Daniel (ii, 31–45); (2) the vision of the four great kingdoms, and the judgment executed by the "Ancient of days," who transferred "the kingdom, and the dominion, and the greatness of the kingdoms under the whole heaven to the people of the saints of the Most High" (chap. vii); (3) the vision of the ram and the he-goat (chap. viii); (4) the angelic oracle of the seventy weeks (ix, 24–27), and (5) that of the broken and divided kingdom, and the deliverance of "every one found written in the book" (xi, 2–xii, 4). These five distinct prophecies are found upon close examination to be so many phases of one grand ideal, and illustrative of the fundamental truth "that the Most High ruleth in the kingdom of men, and giveth it to whomsoever he will." The outcome of the mighty struggle is that judgment is to be given unto the saints of the Most High, and they shall possess the kingdom; "and they that be wise shall shine as the brightness of the firmament; and they that turn many to righteousness as the stars forever and ever."

The first and second prophecies, which present a picture of four great world-powers and their overthrow by the kingdom of heaven, are in substance closely parallel. With few exceptions interpreters of all schools agree that the four kingdoms represented in the great image of Nebuchadnezzar's dream are the same as those symbolized by the four beasts of Daniel's vision in chap. vii. The head of gold in the colossal image denoted the Babylonian empire as represented in the king Nebuchadnezzar (ii, 38), and the first beast, which was like a lion and had eagle's wings (vii, 4), is a symbol of the same splendid kingdom. The inferior kingdom, represented by the silver breast and arms (ii, 32, 39), and also by the bear "made to stand to one side" (vii, 5), is the Median rule which according to this book immediately succeeded the Babylonian, when "Darius the Mede received the kingdom" (v, 31), and "was made king over the realm of the Chaldeans" (ix, 1). The belly and thighs of brass (ii, 32) correspond with the symbolic leopard with four wings and four heads (vii, 6), and denote the great oriental monarchy which our writer conceives as beginning with "the reign of Cyrus the Persian" (vi, 28). The legs and feet of the image (ii, 33), and the terrible fourth beast described in vii, 7, 8, denote the Grecian subjection and domination of all western Asia by Alexander and his successors. Under the great Macedonian conqueror this monarchy more completely broke in pieces and obliterated the petty kingdoms of the Orient than any of the mighty monarchies which preceded it. The all-prevailing power of the Græco-Macedonian empire is witnessed in the fact that the Greek language was made the common dialect of all western Asia, and maintained itself long after Rome became victorious there. It should not be overlooked that the last royal representative of the successors of Alexander was the famous Cleopatra, whose death occurred about B. C. 30.

The four great kingdoms of these prophecies are, accordingly, the Babylonian, the Median, the Persian, and the Grecian. But it is a misapprehension of the purpose of apocalyptic prophecy to suppose it to be "history written beforehand." It is not to inform the people of one age what particular events of a racial, national, or secular character are to take place in a future period of the world's history, but rather to proclaim the supremacy of God over all the powers of this world, and the certainty that "he is the living God and steadfast forever, and his kingdom one which shall not be destroyed" (vi, 26; comp. vii, 13, 14, 27). It is not important, therefore, that the prophet enter into chronological details of the origin and growth of the different kingdoms to which he refers. Nor are the main lessons of the prophecy affected by the question of the different kingdoms to which the several symbols may refer. Many interpreters insist that the fourth kingdom must be the Roman empire. Others argue that we must distinguish between Alexander and his successors, and such exegetes as Grotius, Bertholdt, Moses Stuart, and Zöckler maintain that the fourth kingdom is to be understood as that of Alexander's successors. Any one of these views may be adopted, and yet the same great doctrine of God's dominion over all the kingdoms of the world will be seen to be the main purpose of the prophecies. Exegetical accuracy and self-consistency, however, require that we ascertain as closely as possible the apocalyptist's field of vision. It is nothing to the purpose to show that Daniel's portraiture of the fourth kingdom is applicable to Rome, or France, or England, or Russia, unless it can be as clearly shown that the kingdom referred to fell consistently within the scope of the prophet's vision. The book is to be interpreted by itself, and as a whole, rather than by tacit assumption of " what may be supposed too important for the prophet to have overlooked."

The following considerations go to show that the scope of this prophet's vision, so far as it concerns the kingdoms of the world, does not pass beyond the Grecian domination of Palestine. (1) Chaldean, Median, Persian, and Grecian are the only kingdoms mentioned by name in this book. (2) There is no sufficient reason for supposing that the "little horn" of vii, 8, represents a different king from that of viii, 9. The furious he-goat of chap. viii is but another symbol of the fearful fourth beast of chap. vii, and the variations in the subordinate parts of the symbolism of the two pictures are only such as comport with the repetitions of apocalyptic presentation. But the he-goat is expressly said to represent the Grecian kingdom (viii, 21). (3) The latest oracle of the prophet is dated in the third year of Cyrus (x, 1), and speaks of three kings yet to stand up in Persia (xi, 2), after which the Grecian power succeeds, and is depicted as a broken and divided kingdom. The kings of the north and the south (Seleucids and Ptolemies) war against each other, and out of these arises the " contemptible person " (xi, 21), Antiochus Epiphanes, who answers in all things to the " little horn" of vii, 8, and viii, 9, who magnified himself against the God of heaven and brought unspeakable trouble to the Jewish people. (4) The description of the fourth kingdom in ii, 40–43, and vii, 7, is a faithful and striking picture of the Grecian domination of western Asia, and is all the more impressive when we suppose the writer to have been living at the time when Antiochus Epiphanes was perpetrating his abominable acts of cruelty against Jerusalem and the Jewish people.[1]

Understanding, therefore, the four kingdoms of Daniel to be the Babylonian, the Median, the Persian, and the Grecian, we proceed to observe how they represent the hostile forces of this world as related to the kingdom of the God of heaven.

---

[1] For a fuller argument to show that Antiochus Epiphanes is the little horn of Dan. vii, 8, and viii, 9, and that the four kingdoms are best understood as Babylonian, Median, Persian, and Grecian, see my *Biblical Hermeneutics*, pp. 317–320 and 346–355. Also see my *Prophecies of Daniel Expounded*, for a more detailed exposition of the five prophecies of this book than is compatible with the purpose of the present work.

I. The Colossal Image and the Marvelous Stone.
Daniel ii, 31–45.

Great images cast in human form may be supposed to have been familiar sights to a Babylonian king like Nebuchadnezzar. In Dan. iii, 1, he is said to have made an image of gold, and to have called upon all the officers of his kingdom to fall down and worship it. There is, accordingly, a fitness in making this heathen monarch see the kingdoms of the world in the symbolism of such an image; and its exceeding brightness and fearful aspect (verse 31) were adapted to make a deep impression on his soul. The material of the image displayed a deterioration running from fine gold down to iron and clay. It is worthy of note that in Parsee tradition Zoroaster saw four trees, one of gold, one of silver, one of steel, and the fourth of iron; and he was told that they represented four successive ages of the world. Similarly Ovid and Hesiod speak of the ages of gold, silver, brass, and iron.

As already stated, these four parts of the image represented the Babylonian, the Median, the Persian, and the Grecian monarchies of western Asia. The scope of the visional dream does not take in Rome and western Europe any more than it does China and Japan. The first three of the kingdoms are rapidly passed over. The only statements of note are that the glorious, wide-ruling king Nebuchadnezzar is denoted by the head of gold, the next succeeding dominion was to be inferior, and the third kingdom was to bear rule over all the earth. The unwillingness of many expositors to allow the reign of Darius the Mede to count for a separate kingdom is due in part to a misapprehension of the nature of apocalyptic prophecy, and in part to an unwillingness to permit our author to explain himself, or, perhaps, to a failure to see how much the book itself affirms and implies touching the Median dominion of Babylon. They tacitly assume that we may expect to find in these prophecies an exact record of human history, and they have even gone searching among the petty kingdoms of modern Europe to find the ten toes of the colossal image! From their point of view it seems impossible that the prophet should have ranked an inferior regency, of which history knows little or nothing, among the great monarchies like those of Babylon and Persia. But such a method of procedure is virtually interpreting the scripture under the dictation of a dogma. The truer exegesis concerns itself only with what the prophet writes, not with an assumption of what he ought to have written. According to the book itself, "Darius, the son of Ahasuerus, of the seed of the Medes, was made king over the realm of the Chaldeans" immediately after the capture of Babylon by the

Medes and Persians (ix, 1). In vi, 28, "the reign of Darius" is distinguished from "the reign of Cyrus the Persian." This Darius is said to have been about sixty-two years old when, on the death of Belshazzar, he "received the kingdom" (v, 31). He "set over the kingdom a hundred and twenty satraps" (vi, 1), and signed and sealed royal statutes (vi, 7–ix, 17), and issued royal proclamations "unto all the people, nations, and languages that dwell on all the earth" (vi, 25). Let it be noted that this language implies the same absolute dominion as that which Nebuchadnezzar assumes in iv, 1. The silence of history touching this Median ruler does not in the least change the statements of the Book of Daniel, and it savors more of imposition than of exposition when overzealous apologists of "the genuineness of Daniel" ignore these numerous statements of the author of this book and construct suspicious hypotheses concerning what "he may be presumed to have had in mind." According to the passages cited above, the second and inferior kingdom is obviously the dominion of Darius the Mede. The inferiority is clearly implied in the statements that this Darius "received the kingdom" and "was made king" over the realm of the Chaldeans" (v, 31; ix, 1). These words most naturally suggest that the kingdom fell to him by some election or appointment. It seems to have been of the nature of a regency, confirmed by the suffrages of Medes and Persians. It may have been a stroke of policy on the part of Cyrus to set up a Median regency over Babylon, and so secure the good will of the Medes whom he had lately conquered.[1]

The fourth kingdom is the one which attracts the notice of the prophet more than all the rest. It is seen to be "strong as iron," and to break in pieces and crush whatever stands in its way. It becomes, however, a divided kingdom, and, as the iron and clay suggest, it is to be "partly strong and partly broken." The representatives of this divided kingdom also "cleave not to one another, even as iron does not mingle with clay." All this furnishes, as we

---

[1] It should also be noted that the writer recognizes Belshazzar as king of Babylon and successor of Nebuchadnezzar, his father (v, 1, 18). The name Belshazzar has been discovered in inscriptions as the son and associate of Nabonidus. This fact is hailed as a confirmation of the historical accuracy of Daniel, but it is conceded that the son was not sole ruler, nor was he a son of Nebuchadnezzar. From Daniel's point of view, however, and for his purpose in this book, the regency of Belshazzar and of Darius the Mede was as absolute and sufficient as that of Nebuchadnezzar or of Cyrus. If our book is the production of a writer living in the days of the Maccabees he would naturally have sought to conform to known historical fact so far at least as not to violate the truth; but it need not be assumed that he concerned himself about putting on record an exact account of the kings of Babylon or of the Medes.

have already shown, a notably truthful portraiture of the Græco-Macedonian empire, which was founded by Alexander the Great and lost its last royal representative in the death of Cleopatra, a descendant of Ptolemy, one of Alexander's generals. This fourth kingdom holds like preeminence in the visions recorded in chaps. vii and viii, and is the one so notoriously broken and divided by reason of the violent wars between the rival kings, as described in chap. xi.

The stone cut out of the mountain without hands, which broke the image in pieces, and became a great mountain (or rock), and filled the whole earth, is a most appropriate symbol of the kingdom of God. The prophet tells the king that "the God of heaven will set up a kingdom, which shall never be destroyed, nor shall the sovereignty thereof be left to another people; but it shall break in pieces and consume all these kingdoms, and it shall stand forever" (verse 44). This is the same kingdom of heaven of which Jesus speaks in Matt. xiii, 31–33, and which he compares to a grain of mustard seed, which grows from the least of seeds and becomes a tree wherein the birds of heaven may come and lodge. It is also like leaven hidden in the measures of meal until it is all leavened. This is the Messianic kingdom, founded by the advent and manifestation of the Lord Jesus. He declared that he "came not to send peace on the earth, but a sword" (Matt. x, 34). He now reigns, but his throne is in the holy heavens. We do not yet see all things broken in pieces and subdued before him, but we are assured that "he must reign till he has put all his enemies under his feet" (1 Cor. xv, 25). It may require a thousand times the number of years Christianity has been already operating in the world, but ultimately the psalmist's ideal is to be realized, and Jehovah will give his Son "the nations for his inheritance, and the uttermost parts of the earth for his possession" (Psalm ii, 8). But the times, and methods, and historic crises through which all this will come to pass it has been given to no prophet, nor angel, nor even to the Son of man himself to make known.[1]

---

[1] Literalistic interpreters expose their fallacious method in their treatment of the words "in the days of those kings," in verse 44. They insist that "those kings" are the ones denoted by the ten toes of the feet of the image, and they generally look for these toes among the smaller states or kingdoms of modern Europe. They strangely forget that, as a matter of fact, the head of gold (Babylon) was broken long before the kingdom denoted by the legs, feet, and toes came into existence. They stickle over the words "the days of those kings," but have no corresponding stress of literalism to make it clear how, as a matter of fact, the several kingdoms denoted by "the iron, the clay, the brass, the silver, and the gold," could, according to verse 35, be "broken in pieces together" (or all *at once*, כַּחֲדָה). Their trouble arises from the notion that all parts of a visional picture, and even incidental allusions, must be pressed

II. The Four Beasts and the Kingdom of the Saints.
Daniel vii.

It is a part of the art displayed in this Book of Daniel to make the first vision an impressive dream of Nebuchadnezzar, and introduce the prophet as a revealer of the secrets of the Most High. But in chap. vii the same mystery of the kingdom of God in its relation to the hostile world-powers is presented as a dream-vision of the prophet himself, and is interpreted by one of the angels that appeared in the vision.

The conception of violent barbaric world-powers as so many wild beasts coming up out of the wind-tossed sea is a figure of remarkable appropriateness and power.   Compare the suggestive language of Isa. xvii, 12, 13.   The number four applied to the winds as well as the beasts has its symbolic suggestion of revolutions and commotions in all parts of the world, out of which the mighty empires have from time to time arisen.

The four great beasts of this vision represent the same kingdoms as those which were symbolized in the dream of Nebuchadnezzar. In the imagery of a heathen monarch's dream the world-power appears in the brilliancy and grandeur of a colossal man; but from the prophet's point of view, and in the light of heavenly revelation, these powers of the world, controlled so notably by human ambition, pride, and passion, are rather monstrous beasts that tear and devour one another.

The first beast, representing the Babylonian monarchy, is appropriately likened unto a lion possessed with eagles' wings.   These symbols point to a combination of great power and great rapidity of movement.   In Jer. iv, 7, the destroyer of Judah and Jerusalem is compared to a lion that is gone up from his thicket; and in Hab. i, 8, the Chaldean cavalry are said to be "swifter than leopards," and "they fly as an eagle that hasteth to devour."   Comp. also Ezek. xvii, 3, 12.   The plucking of these wings, and the humanizing of this beast, as stated in verse 4, suggests an advance in civilization and an elevation of moral sense, and seems to refer to the remarkable experience of Nebuchadnezzar as recorded in Dan. iv, 28–37.

The second beast is the inferior kingdom of chap. ii, 39, and for reasons already given is to be understood of the reign of "Darius the Mede."   The prophet's statement (verse 5), literally translated, reads: "And behold another beast, a second, like to a bear, and it

---

into prophetic significance.   But, as we have seen again and again in these apocalyptic books, many things in such pictures are only the formal elements of imagery, and have no weight or importance in the interpretation.   See on this my *Prophecies of Daniel Expounded*, pp. 24–26.

was made to stand to one side, and three ribs were in its mouth between its teeth; and thus they said unto it: Arise, devour much flesh." The Median dominion was appropriately symbolized by a sluggish bear. The three ribs are the substance and living of the king, the revenues of the kingdom as collected and supplied by the three presidents whom Darius appointed for this purpose (Dan. vi, 2). Compare the statement of this custom in Ezra iv, 13, 16. But this "son of Ahasuerus, of the seed of the Medes," seems to have been without ambition for conquest. He entered upon no war for larger revenues, and although the presidents and satraps may be supposed to have urged him to "arise and devour much flesh," he does not appear to heed their counsel or pay any attention to such calls. As a ruling monarch he made no advances like " Cyrus the Persian," but rather, by reason of his inferior and subordinate position, " was made to stand to one side." Here we have the picture of an inferior power, sufficiently comfortable with its three ribs of revenue, and indisposed to rise up for any hazardous effort after other and greater prey.

The third beast, like a leopard, with four wings and four heads, is easily and naturally explained when understood to represent the Persian empire. The symbolical number four, applied to the wings and the heads, points to the world-wide extent of the conquests and dominion of the Persian kings. The leopard is noted for swiftness of movement (Hab. i, 8), and the wings (of an unnamed fowl) in this symbol, as in that of the lion (verse 4) intensify the thought of rapid marching in campaigns of victory. In Isa. xlvi, 11, Cyrus is referred to as "a ravenous bird from the east." He carried his conquests far and wide. The kings of Persia (comp. xi, 2) extended their empire beyond that of Nebuchadnezzar, overran Egypt and Greece, and in Esth. i, 1, one of them is said to have "reigned from India even unto Ethiopia, over a hundred and twenty-seven provinces." The four heads are to be understood as established seats of power in the four quarters of the earth. In apocalyptic symbolism the head of a beast is not representative of a king, but rather of established dominion out of which kings (horns) grow.

The fourth beast is portrayed as a nameless monster with ten horns. Like the fourth kingdom of chap. ii, 40–43, it is more fully described and has more importance for the prophet than any of the others. It is conspicuously terrible and strong, and has great iron teeth. "It devoured and broke in pieces and stamped the residue with its feet." All this fits the Græco-Macedonian kingdom, which, under the generalship of the great Alexander, terrified and crushed the kingdoms of the Orient with most astonishing displays of military power. The conqueror soon overcame all Asia Minor, Syria, Tyre and Sidon, Palestine, and Egypt, where he founded Alexandria. Thence he marched eastward and effectually subdued all the territory of ancient Babylon, Assyria, Media, and Persia, and carried his conquests as far as India. So effectual was his world-victory that a tradition says he wept for other worlds to conquer. Rome never succeeded in carrying her triumphs into Asia with anything like the crushing power displayed by Alexander. Unlike the Babylonian, Median, and Persian monarchies, the Grecian was of European origin, and so "diverse from all the beasts that were before it." It spread and established a western language and civilization over all western Asia and Egypt.

Not only in general outline but also in its details is this symbolism of the fourth beast seen to denote conspicuous facts of the Grecian domination of Asia. The ten horns are said to represent ten kings (verse 24), and chap. xi sufficiently indicates who the ten kings were. There we have an account of five Syrian and five Egyptian kings who controlled and terrorized all western Asia after the death of Alexander. That monarch left no posterity to inherit his wide domain (xi, 4), but "his kingdom was taken and divided toward the four winds of heaven." Our apocalyptist does not essay to write a history of all Alexander's successors, but takes the symbolic number ten and points out ten kings who terribly trampled under foot the holy land of Israel by their incessant wars. The ten kings who receive particular notice in chap. xi, 5–20, are the following :

SELEUCIDÆ.	PTOLEMIES.
Seleucus Nicator.	Ptolemy Soter.
Antiochus Theos.	Ptolemy Philadelphus.
Seleucus Callinicus.	Ptolemy Euergetes.
Antiochus the Great.	Ptolemy Philopator.
Seleucus Philopator.	Ptolemy Epiphanes.

The little horn described in verse 8 is explained in verses 24 and 25 as another king to arise after the ten and to be different from them. The description in all its details fits Antiochus Epiphanes. His elevation to the throne was secured by the assassination of his elder brother, Seleucus Philopator, the subtle superseding of his nephew Demetrius, the rightful heir (who was at the time held as a hostage in Rome), and the defeat of another nephew, Ptolemy Philometer, who had as good a claim to the throne of western Asia as Antiochus himself. These answer to the three kings whom he put down and humbled by his crafty measures. A fuller description of this notorious king is furnished in viii, 9–12, 23–25, and xi, 21–39, and these repeated portraitures of one and the same infamous persecutor of the Jewish people show how prominent he was in our prophet's thoughts. That which gave Antiochus Epiphanes such a despicable notoriety among the Jews is set forth in verse 25 : "He shall speak words against the Most High, and shall wear out the saints of the Most High; and he shall think to change the times and the law ; and they shall be given into his hand until a time, and times, and half a time." This is a strong prophetic style of depicting the daring and blasphemous impiety of this enemy of the Jews, and should be carefully compared with the parallels already referred to in chaps. viii and xi. The best commentary on all these prophetic statements of Daniel is, perhaps, the account of this Antiochus as given in the first book of Maccabees, and the corresponding narratives in the works of Josephus. The impious ruler is called in 1 Macc. ii, 62, ἀνήρ ἁμαρτωλός, sinful man, and doubtless furnished Paul with the concept of "the man of sin, the son of perdition, he that opposeth and exalteth himself against all that is called God or that is worshiped" (2 Thess. ii, 3, 4). The author of First Maccabees tells us that the servants of Alexander put diadems upon themselves after their great general's death, "and there came forth out of them a sinful root, Antiochus Epiphanes" (i, 10), who "after that he had smitten Egypt . . . went up against Israel and Jerusalem with a great multitude and entered presumptuously into the sanctuary and took the golden altar" and all the precious treasures of the temple, so that "there came great mourning upon Israel, and all the house of Jacob was clothed with shame" (i, 20–28). "He made a great slaughter, and spake presumptuously." At another time "he came unto Jerusalem with a great multitude, and he spake words of peace unto them in subtilty, and they gave him credence; and he suddenly fell upon the city, and smote it very sore, and destroyed much people out of Israel. And he took the spoils of the city, and set it on fire, and pulled down the houses and the walls thereof on every side. . . . And they shed innocent blood on every side of the sanctuary, and defiled the sanctuary" (i, 29–37). The same old Jewish writer further records that the devout Israelites were driven into secret places and forbidden to worship after the time-honored customs of their fathers. To complete the profanation the servants of Antiochus "builded an abomination of desolation upon the altar, and in the cities of Judah on every side they builded high places. And at the doors of the houses and in the streets they burnt incense. And they rent in pieces the books of the law which they found, and set them on fire" (verses 54–56). In 2 Macc. v, 11–14, it is written that this Antiochus, hearing that Judea was in revolt, became furious in mind and marched against Jerusalem, and "took the city by force of arms and commanded his soldiers to cut down without mercy such as came in their way, and to slay such as went up upon the houses; and there was killing of young and old, making away of boys, women, and children, slaying of virgins and infants. And in all the three days of the slaughter there were destroyed eight myriads (80,000), four myriads (40,000) in close combat, and no fewer were sold than slain." Josephus states (*Wars of the Jews*, book i, 1, 1), that Antiochus Epiphanes "came upon the Jews with a great army, took their city by force, slew a great multitude, spoiled the temple, and put a stop to the constant practice of offering a daily sacrifice of expiation for three years and six months."

These records show that in Jewish history and tradition this "sinful root," that sprang from the Græco-Macedonian kings, was remembered as a monster of impiety, a very incarnation of wickedness. He became a type of Antichrist, and, as already remarked, supplied the imagery of Paul's "man of lawlessness, who opposeth and exalteth himself against all that is an object of worship; so that he sitteth in the temple of God, setting himself forth as God." It is quite safe to say that only a mechanical notion of inspiration, and its correlated theories of biblical interpretation, have driven devout men to ignore the facts of Jewish history, and to go searching among the Goths, and Vandals, and Franks, and Britons, and Lombards, for the "ten kings" of Daniel's vision, and to find in the Pope of Rome the only true meaning of the "little horn."

The facts above mentioned show that the statements of Dan. vii, 25, and parallel passages were most strikingly fulfilled in the person of Antiochus Epiphanes. To a Jewish writer his entire career would appear most impious and contemptible. His order to abolish the worship of God at Jerusalem was a vile speaking against the Most High. His Jewish persecutions were designed to "wear out the saints of the Most High." His arbitrary prohibition of the "whole burnt offerings, and sacrifices, and drink offerings in the sanctuary," and his order to "profane the Sabbaths and feasts, and pollute the sanctuary and them that were holy" (1 Macc. i, 45, 46), were obviously a purpose "to change the times and the law;" and Josephus's statement that he "spoiled the temple and put a stop to the offering of a daily sacrifice for three years and six months," is a most significant explanation of the giving over of the sanctuary into his hand "until a time, and (two) times, and half a time."

The picture of the judgment and overthrow of all the beasts and their dominion, and the transfer of the kingdom to the saints of the

Most High (verses 9–14; comp. verses 22, 26, and 27), is unsurpassed for grandeur and sublimity. The Most High "who rules in the kingdom of men and giveth it to whomsoever he will" (Dan. iv, 25); "who doeth according to his will in the army of heaven, and among the inhabitants of the earth" (iv, 35); whose "dominion is an everlasting dominion, and his kingdom that which shall not be destroyed" (iv, 34, and vi, 26); the eternal Judge who rules through all the ages, is most appropriately called "the Ancient of days." His "raiment white as snow" reminds us of the psalmist's words, "Who covereth thyself with light as with a garment" (Psalm civ, 2). The "hair like pure wool" comports with the dazzling splendor of his presence and his everlasting years. His flaming throne and wheels of burning fire recall the vision of Ezekiel (Ezek. i, 16–26). The fiery stream which appeared to issue from before him accords with the psalmist's concept of "a fire going before him, and burning up his adversaries round about" (Psalm xcvii, 3), and also with the rhythmic couplets of Isa. lxvi, 15 :

> For lo, Jehovah with a fire shall come,
> And like the whirlwind shall his chariots be ;
> To recompense in angry heat his wrath,
> And his rebuke in flames of fire.

The "ten thousand times ten thousand" who stood and ministered before him should be compared with the heavenly host in Micaiah's vision (1 Kings xxii, 19), and the thousand upon thousand chariots of God extolled in Psalm lxviii, 17.

So far as I know, the statement in Dan. vii, 10—"the judgment was set, and the books were opened"—is the first instance in which the idea of God's judgment is set forth under the figure of a great assize, or formal session of a court of justice, and the opening of books of evidence. The idea is suggested in all those apocalyptic pictures of God taking counsel and expressing purposes of wrath or of mercy which we have repeatedly noticed. The statement of Eccles. xii, 14, is probably no older than the Book of Daniel. But the concept of a tribunal of formal judgment is found in Matt. xxv, 31–46 ; 2 Cor. v, 10, and Rev. xx, 12. In this picture of judgment God's holy ones are associated with him in counsel, and the innumerable thousands are ready to execute the sentence determined upon. Accordingly we note that the seer (in verse 9) "beholds thrones placed in view" (not "cast down" as the common version has it). In the similar picture of Rev. iv, 2–4, twenty-four thrones are seen arranged around the central throne of God. This all comports with the general concept, which we have noticed in Gen. i, 26 ;

iii, 22 ; vi, 3 ; xi, 5–7 ; that no events occur on earth which have not been duly considered in heaven. And so the execution of divine judgment upon the beasts and their dominion is shown to have the sanction of the court of heaven. The prophet "beheld even till the beast was slain, and his body destroyed, and he was given to be burned with fire " (verse 11). This destruction of the beast is to be understood as the direct result of the judgment just depicted. Because "the heavens do rule " (iv, 26), the beast of ungodly empire cannot forever prevail against the saints of the Most High, but must sooner or later go down under the fiery stream of God's judgment. The slaughter of the beast, the destruction of his body, and giving him over to be burned with fire, are symbolical descriptions of the retribution sure to come on all nations and governments that stand in opposition to the eternal truth of God.

The statements of verse 12 show that this execution of judgment is a matter of the providential government of this world. The rest of the beasts perish by the same fiery stream of divine judgment, but at different times. As the kingdoms represented by the head, breast, and belly of the great image perished before the fourth kingdom came to power, so also the lion, the bear, and the leopard had all lost their dominion before the terrible fourth beast with its little horn "made war with the saints, and prevailed against them." But all these things, when presented in the imagery of symbolism, must be so depicted as to form one coherent outline. A failure to observe this principle is the fallacy of many literalist expositors. As all parts of the image appeared to be "broken in pieces together" (ii, 35), by the stone that smote the image upon its feet, so in truth the fiery judgment, which destroyed the body of the fourth beast, destroyed also the rest of the beasts, "although their lives were prolonged for a season and a time." As the beastly kingdoms have existence only in this world their fiery judgments must be a matter of human history. Overwhelming judgments may visit a nation or a kingdom, and yet not totally end its existence. It may survive "for a season and a time," and become gradually defunct, or it may suddenly perish by the rod of a conqueror.

Accompanying or immediately following the judgment of the beasts, the apocalyptist " saw in the night visions, and behold, there came with the clouds of heaven one like unto a son of man, and he came even to the Ancient of days, and they brought him near before him. And there was given him dominion, and glory, and a kingdom, that all the peoples, nations, and languages should serve him: his dominion is an everlasting dominion, which shall not pass away, and his kingdom that which shall not be destroyed" (verses 13, 14).

This kingdom is obviously the same as that which was symbolized by the stone cut out of the mountain without hands (ii, 44, 45). It is described in the same terms as that of the Most High God in iv, 3, 34; vi, 26, and must be identical with the kingdom of the heavens which rule (iv, 26), the eternal dominion of Him "who changeth the times and the seasons; who removeth kings and setteth up kings" (ii, 21). It should not be overlooked that, according to these scriptures, the rule of the heavens may for long times tolerate the rule of tyrants on earth. There is no warrant in the volume of divine revelation for the assumption that God can have no kingdom in this world while glaring wickedness exists. The kingdom of God has its ages, its periods, and dispensations, and the figure of the stone becoming a mountain suggests its gradual development in the course of human history.

In verse 18 the angel interpreter tells Daniel that "the saints of the Most High shall receive the kingdom, and possess the kingdom forever;" and again, in verse 27, it is said, "The kingdom and the dominion, and the greatness of the kingdoms under the whole heaven, shall be given to the people of the saints of the Most High." But it is obvious from the words which immediately follow in verse 27, and from the whole teaching of this book, that the kingdom is still his. He does not abdicate by bringing others to share his kingdom and power and glory. But in verses 13 and 14 this kingdom is said to be given to "one like unto a son of man." The Aramaic text does not warrant the translation "the Son of man." The idea conveyed is that the one who was brought before the Ancient of days and received the dominion was like a human being rather than like a beast. In the dream of the heathen king the monarchy of the world was seen as a colossal image of gold and inferior metals, and the kingdom of God as a rude stone; but in the visions of Daniel the cruel world-powers are like so many wild and fearful beasts, seeking whom they may devour, and the kingdom of God is a dominion adapted to the glorification of humanity.

Inasmuch as the kingdom is, in verse 14, given to the "one like unto a son of man," and in verse 27 "to the people of the saints of the Most High," the title "son of man" may be here understood as an ideal personification or symbolizing of the people of God. It would thus be virtually equivalent to Isaiah's concept of "my servant, Israel, in whom I will be glorified" (Isa. xlix, 3), to whom kings and queens "shall bow down with their faces to the earth, and lick the dust of thy feet; and thou shalt know that I am Jehovah, and they that wait for me shall not be ashamed" (Isa. xlix, 23). A similar personification of "the Zion of the Holy One of Israel" appears

in Isa. lx, where the people of God are called upon to arise and
shine in the glory of Jehovah, and it is said that "nations shall
come to thy light, and kings to the brightness of thy rising." God
and his people are thus conceived as dwelling in one common glory
(comp. John xvii, 21), and with such a personification of "the people of the saints of the Most High" in his mind our prophet may
well have associated the idea of "all the peoples, nations, and languages serving him." This service, like that supposed in Isa. xlix,
23, and lx, 3, would not involve the idea of divine worship, but
rather of tribute and obedience.[1]

But this personification of the community of saints under the
symbol of "one like unto a son of man" does not exclude the Messianic reference of this passage. As Jehovah's "servant Jacob" in
the later Isaiah is, in the famous fifty-third chapter, idealized into
the vicarious sufferer, who "was wounded for our transgressions
and bruised for our iniquities;" and so became the prophetic type of
"the Lamb of God that taketh away the sin of the world;" so this
picture of one like unto a son of man, coming with the clouds of
heaven, and receiving the kingdom and the power and the glory of
God, is a remarkable prophecy of the coming and kingdom of Jesus
Christ. His coming with the clouds is, along with such scriptures
as Psalm xviii, 9–11; xcvii, 2; civ, 3; Isa. xix, 1, and Nahum i, 3,
the basis and source of such New Testament language as we read
in Matt. xxiv, 30; xxvi, 64; Mark xiii, 26, and Rev. i, 7. His
receiving the dominion is significantly explained by his own statement in Matt. xxviii, 18 : "There has been given unto me all authority in heaven and upon earth." There appears to be direct allusion
to this vision of Daniel in John v, 22 and 27, where Jesus says:
"The Father hath given all judgment unto the Son, . . . and he
gave him authority to execute judgment because he is a son of man."
So we recognize in this prophet Daniel a remarkable advance and
originality of Messianic conception. Here is the sublime idea of a
son of man receiving from the eternal God the dominion of an everlasting kingdom, and receiving the subjection and service of all the
peoples, nations, and languages. This conception is also in remarkable
harmony with the appointment of such persons as Belshazzar and Darius the Mede to the position of associate kings in the empire, a custom which certainly finds recognition in this Book of Daniel, and perhaps influenced the author in the construction of his Messianic ideal.

---

[1] Zöckler correctly observes that the word פלח in Dan. vii, 14, "is certainly not to
be limited to signify *religious* service (divine adoration, *cultus*), for in the extra-biblical
Chaldee, for example, in the Targums, it signifies also a purely secular service, and in
verse 27 of this chapter it is synonymous with אשׁתמע, to *obey*." Commentary on
Daniel, in the Lange series.

III. The Ram and the He-goat. Daniel viii.

In the vision of Daniel recorded in chap. viii we have an apocalyptic repetition of a portion of the things revealed in the previous chapter. The animals which appear as symbols in this vision are not wild beasts, but of the domestic kind. The ram represents the king of Media and Persia, and the rough he-goat represents the king of Greece. So the vision is a reproduction under other symbols of the third and fourth kingdoms of the foregoing prophecies.

The prophet represents himself as beholding the vision in the castle or citadel of Shushan. This change of place is an incidental element of the art of the writer, and was probably chosen with the idea that a vision of the fall of the Persian empire might be most appropriately seen from the throne-center and capital of the king of Media and Persia. His view of the Medo-Persian empire contemplated it at a period when, although still "pushing westward, and northward, and southward" (verse 4), its movements of conquest were less rapid and brilliant than at the first, and accordingly he now likens it to a ram, a slower and less powerful animal than a winged leopard. But as yet "no beasts could stand before him, neither was there any that could deliver out of his hand; but he did according to his will, and magnified himself." So as in chap. vii, 6, "dominion was still given unto him," and like the third kingdom of brass in ii, 39, he "bore rule over all the earth."

The two horns of the ram have been supposed to represent the union of the Median and Persian nationalities in the kingdom, and the common text of verse 20 seems at first reading to confirm this view. But all the ancient versions of that verse read *king*, not *kings of Media and Persia*, and the word *king* there, as in the next verse, is evidently used for the empire as represented in the ruling monarch. The analogies of biblical symbolism, moreover, show that horns represent individual kings rather than constituent nations and races which are incorporated in a kingdom. The Median and Persian elements went to form the body of the ram rather than his horns. Furthermore, in what is called the Medo-Persian empire, the Persian did not "come up last," but was preeminent from the first. The much more consistent and tenable view, therefore, is the ancient one maintained by Theodoret, according to which the two horns represent the dynasties of Cyrus and Darius Hystaspis. This exposition avoids the confusion of making the horns symbols of racial elements that entered into the body of the nation, and adheres to the analogies of biblical symbolism by making the horns represent kings, or a succession of kings.

As a fact of history the dynasty of Cyrus was of short duration.

His reign of some eight years was followed by that of his son Cambyses, whose foreign wars and tyrannical atrocities provoked insurrection and the usurping of his throne by a Magian priest. This led to the election of Darius, the son of Hystaspes, an Achæmenian prince, whose line continued until the overthrow of the Persian empire by the armies of Alexander, and was higher and mightier than the line of Cyrus. As the twelve or more kings of Persia, who followed Cyrus, had no separate or special importance for the prophecy of Daniel, the writer displays excellent art and skill in representing them all by two horns, inasmuch as the ram is by nature supplied with but two horns. In chap. xi, 2, the kings of Persia are represented as four, the last of whom "shall be far richer than they all." But in that chapter we have no symbolism except in the matter of numbers and the general outline of an angelic oracle.

The he-goat from the west is graphically described in verses 5–8, and is explained in verse 21 as "the king of Greece," just as the ram in the verse preceding is said to be "the king of Media and Persia." In these passages the word *king* evidently stands for kingdom, or dominion, as embodied and represented for the time in the ruling monarch.[1] The conspicuous horn between the he-goat's eyes was a symbol of the first king, and is admitted by all exegetes to denote Alexander the Great. The image of one notable horn between the eyes may have been suggested by pictures of the fabulous unicorn which appear on the monuments of Babylon and Persia. The size and power of this first horn attracted the seer's attention, and its might seemed greater than that of all the four that came up after it. But in the explanation of the vision the first great horn is passed over with little remark (verse 21), and the chief interest attaches to the significance of the "little horn" so fully described in verses 9–12, and interpreted in verses 23–25. When the great horn was broken there came up in its place "four notable horns toward the four winds of heaven" and out of one of these came forth the notorious little horn.[2] The main interest of the prophecy

---

[1] The peculiar interchange of the words *king* and *kingdom* in verses 22 and 23 is noticeable and somewhat confusing. The Hebrew text of verse 22 is probably in error, and should be corrected by the Septuagint and Vulgate, which read *four kings* instead of *four kingdoms*. For when it is immediately added in verse 23 that "in the latter times of *their* kingdom," etc., the pronominal suffix *their* properly requires the word kings in the preceding verse.

[2] The four horns have been commonly understood as four divisions of Alexander's empire, parceled out among the *Diadochi* after the battle of Ipsus. But it is better to understand the number four as symbolical, and indicating in a general way the breaking up of the empire "toward the four winds of heaven" (verse 8; comp. xi, 4). Each

centers in the "king of fierce countenance" who is represented by this little horn, and is permitted to inflict unparalleled calamity upon the sanctuary and "the people of the saints" (verse 24). That this fierce king is to be understood of the execrable Antiochus Epiphanes has been generally admitted. For, according to the context, he unquestionably springs from the line of Græco-Macedonian kings. That he is also the impious ruler denoted by the little horn of chap. vii, 8, has been already shown in the foregoing pages. He made his power felt in Egypt on the south, in Armenia on the east, and especially in Palestine, "the glorious land" (verse 9; comp. xi, 41, and Zech. vii, 14). His pride and self-conceit were like those of the king of Babylon, as portrayed in Isa. xiv, 13, who said in his heart, "I will ascend into heaven, I will exalt my throne above the stars of God." As in vii, 25, he is represented as speaking words against the Most High, so here (verses 11 and 25) he magnifies himself against the God of hosts, " the Prince of princes." He destroyed thousands of the people of the saints, made their sanctuary like a wilderness (1 Macc. i, 39), and, as Josephus says, "put a stop to the practice of offering a daily sacrifice for three years and six months." All this corresponds with what is written in vii, 8, 25, and what we shall find more fully detailed in xi, 21-45. The one word of doom which is pronounced upon him in this chapter is " he shall be broken without hand," that is, as one smitten by the judgment stroke of heaven, like the great image that was broken by the stone cut from the mountain without hands (ii, 45).

The meaning of the vision is thus clearly shown. The narrative portions of the chapter, which record the appearance and conversation of angels, are to be understood as the apocalyptic machinery of prophetic visions and dreams. The holy myriads, who act as God's ministers (vii, 10), are also conceived as supplying the angelic mediators of divine revelation. Comp. x, 5-11, and 18-21 ; Zech. i, 9 ; ii, 3 ; iv, 1-5. The 2,300 evenings and mornings of verse 14 are probably meant for so many successive morning and evening offerings, and would imply half that number of days (=1150). The number should be compared with the 1,290 and the 1,335 of chapter

---

section would thus be conceived as having its particular king or horn. But to make the first horn represent a kingdom by itself, and the four succeeding horns another and different kingdom or empire, works inadmissible confusion in the use of symbols. On the same principle the ten horns of vii, 7, might be held to represent a kingdom different from that of the beast to which the horns belonged. That the little horn comes forth from four horns in this vision, and from ten horns in the former vision, is simply owing to a different standpoint of prophetic view. Both views are true to facts in the history of the *Diadochi*.

xii, 11, 12. Like the " time, and times, and half a time " of vii, 25, and xii, 7, these several numbers suggest a period of about three years and a half. The approximation but inexplicable difference and variety of these numbers may itself be a symbolical suggestion that the prophetic times and seasons cannot be reckoned with mathematical certainty. The period might be approximately suggested, but it is not for prophet or reader " to know times or seasons which the Father hath set within his own authority " (Acts i, 7).

IV. THE SEVENTY HEPTADES. DANIEL IX, 24–27.

The prophecy of the seventy weeks occupies, aside from its introductory narrative, only four verses of the Book of Daniel, and is all but hopelessly obscure. The Hebrew text of verses 25–27 is in all probability corrupt, and no ancient or modern version affords substantial help in emending or explaining the language of the prophet. Conjectural emendations proposed by one class of interpreters are promptly rejected by those of another school, and it is not to be reasonably expected that any general agreement will soon be reached by expositors as to the exact meaning of this passage. The introductory statements of verse 24 have the form of Hebrew poetry, and are best presented as a series of synthetic parallelisms of cumulative significance. We make a few emendations, and translate quite literally as follows :

> Seventy heptades are decreed upon thy people and upon thy holy city,
> To close up the transgression and to consummate sins,
> And to expiate iniquity and to introduce eternal righteousness,
> And to seal up vision and prophet, and to anoint a holy of holies.

And thou mayest know and understand that from the going forth of a word to inhabit [1] and build Jerusalem unto an anointed one, a prince (there are) heptades seven and heptades sixty and two. It shall be inhabited [2] and builded, open court and narrow street. And in the end [3] of the times, and after the heptades sixty and two, there shall be cut off an anointed one, and no one for him. And the city and the sanctuary shall a people of a prince who is to come destroy, and his end in the flood. And until the end war ; determined are the desolations. And he shall strengthen a covenant for many one heptade, and the half of the heptade shall he cause sacrifice and oblation to cease. And on a wing of abominations a desolator, and, until the consummation and that which is determined, it shall be poured upon a desolate one.

As Daniel had been meditating "the number of the years, whereof the word of Jehovah came to Jeremiah the prophet, for the accom-

---

[1] Read הֵשִׁיב, or הוֹשִׁיב, instead of הָשִׁיב.

[2] Read תֵּשֵׁב instead of תָּשׁוּב.

[3] Read בְּקֵץ instead of בְּצוֹק. The word צוֹק occurs nowhere else, and as commonly construed at the close of verse 25 is awkward and unnatural.

plishing of the desolations of Jerusalem, even seventy years" (verse 2 ; comp. Jer. xxv, 11, 12 ; xxix, 10; xxxi, 38), the angel very appropriately employs the symbolical words "seventy heptades." The student of the Hebrew text will note that the masculine plural is here construed with a verb in the singular (*is decreed*). The seventy heptades are conceived as a unit, a round number, and are most naturally understood as so many sevens of years. It is as if the angel had said to Daniel : "The seventy years of the desolations of Jerusalem, on which thou hast been thinking, suggest another and longer period—a seven times seventy years, which must elapse before the consummation which is to introduce eternal righteousness." This mystic period of seven times seventy is no more to be pressed into the service of mathematical calculation than the "seventy times seven" of Jesus's response to Peter in Matt. xviii, 22. The main burden of the prophecy is that even restoration from Babylonian exile and the rebuilding of the holy city and the sanctuary will not consummate the desolations of Jerusalem. The seventy years of desolation then supposed to be about accomplished must be repeated seven times before the end. How noticeably this thought accords with the fourfold statement of Lev. xxvi, 18, 21, 24, 28, that disobedient Israel must needs be smitten "seven times" for refusing to obey Jehovah's commandments !

The statements of verse 24 are strikingly comprehensive, and to be understood in a lofty Messianic sense. The period of the seventy heptades is to end with the closing up, completing, and filling the measure of such transgressions and abominations as were referred to in chap. viii, 12, 13, 23. The end will be a time of judgment, when wickedness shall have come to its full (comp. Gen. xv, 16). But the judgment is to be accompanied and followed by marvelous provision for the expiation of iniquity and the introduction of eternal righteousness. The sealing up of vision and prophet implies the confirming and fulfilling of all the sacred oracles that had spoken of the great day of the Lord and the glorious age to follow, in which the earth would be full of the knowledge of Jehovah as the waters cover the sea (Isa. xi, 9). Such spread of knowledge would make further visions and oracles like these unnecessary. Finally, as the highest Messianic hope of Israel, a new holy of holies is to be anointed, which implies the institution of a "greater and more perfect tabernacle " (Heb. ix, 11). Into this holy of holies the saints of the Messianic age shall have boldness to enter by the new and living way (Heb. x, 19). And so in all its statements the introductory verse of this angelic oracle points to that kingdom of the God of heaven (comp. ii, 44 ; vii, 27), which is to follow the desolations which are determined upon Jerusalem. It is but another way of saying what is symbolized in vii, 11–14, by the beast slain, and his body destroyed and given to be burned with fire, in order that the dominion and glory of the kingdom of God may be given to the Son of man.

What follows in verses 25–27 is, in its particular references, far more difficult to explain. But the most obvious purport of the entire passage is that Jerusalem shall again be inhabited and built up, and after the lapse of times and seasons shall be again made desolate, the sanctuary shall be involved in the same calamity, and sacrifices and offerings shall be made to cease. All this may be most naturally supposed to be another picture of the desolation and impious desecration attributed to the "little horn" of chaps. vii, 25, and viii, 9–12. This general view of the passage accords with the methodic principle of apocalyptic repetition so conspicuous in the Book of Daniel, and it gives a remarkable unity and harmony to the five prophecies therein recorded. According to the first two revelations (chaps. ii and vii) the world-power ends with the fourth kingdom. According to the parallel descriptions of the little horn in chaps. vii and viii the culmination of beastly opposition to the people of the saints and their holy city is reached in the person of that notorious man of sin, Antiochus Epiphanes. The career of this "contemptible person" is taken up again and detailed in a fourfold picture in chap. xi, 21–45, where among other things it is declared that his armed forces "shall profane the sanctuary, and take away the continual offering, and set up the abomination that maketh desolate" (verse 31). What is more natural and self-consistent in the expositor of Daniel than to identify this profanation of the sanctuary with that spoken of in chap. ix, 27, where the destroyer for half of one heptade causes sacrifice and oblation to cease? This is also in noticeable accord with the "time, times, and half a time" of vii, 25, and the number of days mentioned in viii, 14, during which "the transgression that maketh desolate" is permitted "to give both the sanctuary and the host to be trodden under foot."

But when we come to the particulars of verses 25–27 we are far less certain of the meaning of the writer. The uncertainty is deepened by reason of the confused and probably corrupt condition of the scripture text. It is possible that much of the controversy of exegetes over words and phrases of this passage is based upon what was not originally written by the author of our books. There is, moreover, an indefiniteness in some of the main statements which may well make the careful expositor hesitate. "A word to inhabit and to build Jerusalem;" "an anointed one, a prince;" "a people of a prince who is to come;" "a desolator on a wing of abomination"—these are manifestly so indefinite that any reader must feel uncertain as to the particular person or event intended. There is also dispute over the punctuation of the latter part of verse 25. Instead of the division given in our translation, the masoretic text and many critics read : "From the going forth of a word to inhabit and build Jerusalem unto an anointed one, a prince, there are seven heptades. And sixty and two heptades it shall be inhabited and builded," etc.

All this indefiniteness cannot be attributed to corruption of text, nor to carelessness of author or copyist. The writer knew the use of the definite article, and when he wishes to specify or designate particularly he speaks of "the transgression," "after the sixty and two heptades," "the city and the sanctuary," "half of the (final) heptade." The absence of the article from words where we may expect or desire it may therefore be regarded as designed by the author, and intended to give an air of vagueness to the oracle.

The "word to inhabit and build Jerusalem" (verse 25) is most naturally understood of the proclamation of Cyrus, of which we have a double copy in 2 Chron. xxxvi, 22, 23, and Ezra i, 1-4. This allowed and even urged any so disposed "of all his people .'. . to go up to Jerusalem, and build the house of Jehovah." As this proclamation was issued in the first year of Cyrus it was an event of the near future in the first year of Darius the Mede, when Daniel says he received this oracle (ix, 1). For this reason, and also because of the preeminence of Cyrus the Persian, this proclamation is more naturally thought of than that of Artaxerxes given to Ezra some fourscore years later (Ezra vii, 11-26), or that of the same monarch given in the form of letters to Nehemiah commanding "the governors beyond the river" to assist in reconstructing the walls of the city (Neh. ii, 7, 8). These were of less importance than that which sounded the signal for the first return from Babylonian exile.

But many critical interpreters understand the "word to inhabit and build Jerusalem" as the "word of Jehovah to Jeremiah the prophet," mentioned in verse 2 of this chapter. As the seventy heptades are assumed to be seven times the seventy years of exile their *terminus a quo* may be supposed to be the same as that of the exile. No valid argument can be urged against this explanation except it be, perhaps, that the language of Jeremiah, which declares the desolations of seventy years (Jer. xxv, 11; xxix, 10), is not "a word to inhabit and build Jerusalem." His language in xxv, 12, does, however, involve the idea, and in xxix, 10, and xxxi,

38, it conveys the promise of return from Babylon, and a building
of the city unto Jehovah. The question, therefore, of the *terminus
a quo* of the seventy weeks is a matter of uncertainty on which the
best critical scholars have long been divided. But the proclamation of Cyrus seems to me to be the most natural and obvious
" word " (דָּבָר) referred to.

Similar difference of opinion prevails as to the person intended
in verse 25 by " an anointed one, a prince." He has been identified
with Zerubbabel, the prince; Joshua, son of Jozadak, the priest;
Ezra, the priest and scribe; Nehemiah, the governor; the priest
Onias III; Cyrus, who is called Jehovah's anointed in Isa. xlv, 1;
and Jesus Christ. The " anointed one " mentioned in verse 26 is by
some identified with the anointed prince of verse 25, and by others
referred to a different person. We shall not here enter into a discussion of these different opinions. The only two which seem to
us adapted to satisfy the meaning of the oracle are (1) that which
makes the anointed prince (verse 25) refer to Cyrus, and the
anointed one (verse 26) to Onias III; and (2) that which identifies
the two and refers both to the Messiah, who is here supposed to be
" cut off " amid the desolations of the end. If we adopt the first of
these views we should understand the " word " in verse 25 as Jeremiah's prophecy, and suppose that our prophet reckoned its " going
forth " as coincident with the ruin of Jerusalem under Nebuchadnezzar (about B. C. 588). Following the masoretic punctuation,
we should then read, " From the going forth of a word . . . unto an
anointed prince are seven heptades," and understand the period (forty-
nine years) to be an approximation of the time that elapsed between
B. C. 588 and the first year of Cyrus, B. C. 538 (588—538=50).
The sixty-two weeks are then to be understood of the whole period
during which the city was repeopled and builded and occupied until
the time Onias III was cut off by Antiochus Epiphanes. The final
heptade would then be the period of violence and desolation, depicted in verses 26 and 27, during half of which Antiochus put a
stop to offerings in the Jewish temple, and defiled the holy place.
This view is, in substance, adopted by many of the best critical
exegetes, but it confessedly fails to explain the sixty-two weeks in
harmony with the numbers designated by the prophet. If the forty-
nine years answer well to the time between the fall of Jerusalem and
Cyrus, the period between Cyrus and the death of Onias III was
not more than 365 years, whereas sixty-two heptades of years would
amount to 434. These discrepancies, however, will not weigh
heavily with those who do not recognize in the numbers literal accuracy but only a relative approximation, or a symbolical suggestion

of longer or shorter periods. We confess, however, a preference for the view which recognizes in the anointed prince a prophecy of the Messiah. The word may indeed be applied to a priest, as it often is in the Hebrew books; and it may be applied to a secular prince or king, as it is to Saul and Cyrus; but after the sublime picture we have already had in this book of "one like unto a son of man" brought before the Ancient of days and elevated to everlasting dominion and glory (vii, 13, 14), we are warranted in the opinion that our author sees a suffering Messiah manifest in the calamities of the holy people and city as truly as the author of Isa. liii discerned the same ideal in the suffering servant of Jehovah who was led as a lamb to the slaughter. We might even venture to treat the word מָשִׁיחַ in verses 25 and 26 as a proper name and read it *Messiah, prince,* in the first instance, and in verse 26 translate: "And in the end of the times and after the heptades sixty and two shall Messiah be cut off." In the overflowing destruction that is determined upon Jerusalem in the end of the times, Messiah himself will be cut off, and the prophet seems to see him carried down by the same flood that destroys city and sanctuary; but we shall see, in the further revelations of chap. xii, 1, that this anointed prince is to stand up again for the children of Israel, and "deliver everyone that shall be found written in the book."

It should be noted that this Messianic interpretation of the passage does not require us to refer the decreed desolations and the abominable desolator to any other period than that of Antiochus Epiphanes. As every other vision of the end of the world-power in this book connects that end with the overthrow of the fourth kingdom, and the last impious enemy to be destroyed is the "king of fierce countenance" who "shall stand up in the latter time of their kingdom" (viii, 23), so the desolating "prince who is to come," and who shall "destroy the city and the sanctuary" and himself also go down in the flood (verse 26), is the same Antiochus Epiphanes. In every case the apocalyptist connects the Messianic triumph with the decisive overthrow of the great enemy of the saints of God.[1]

In the prophecy of the seven heptades we, accordingly, find another portraiture of the vision of chap. viii, 9–14, with its dire

---

[1] In this particular the present exposition differs from that given in *The Prophecies of Daniel Expounded.* It violates the harmony of the five prophecies of this book, and transcends the scope of the author in every other vision, to explain "a people of a prince who is to come" as referring to the Roman army under Titus, and the destruction of the city and sanctuary to that effected by the Romans in A. D. 70. That event, as we shall see in New Testament prophecy, was the sign of the great transition to the new era of the kingdom of Christ, but it is not necessary to identify that desolation with the one here spoken of; but one may be regarded as a type of the other.

outline of "the transgression that maketh desolate, and gives both
the sanctuary and the host (of God's people Israel) to be trodden
under foot." The issue of the calamity and the time of trouble is
not told at the close of the picture, but is declared most emphatically at its beginning, in the statements of verse 24. The overthrow of Jerusalem and the cutting off of a Messianic Prince is
only to serve the purpose of closing up the multiplied transgressions, expiating iniquity, and introducing eternal righteousness.
This we have sufficiently explained above in our comments on these
profound utterances of judgment, redemption, and completed revelation.

It remains only to indicate our understanding of the divisions of
the seventy heptades into seven, sixty, two, and one $(7+60+2+1=70)$.
The entire period extends from the proclamation of Cyrus, which
authorized the restoration from Babylonian exile, unto the desolation of Jerusalem which the writer associates with Antiochus
Epiphanes. The seven heptades indicate approximately the first
period of the restoration, during which the temple was rebuilded,
and the new community of Israel was organized at Jerusalem.
This period is conceived as a jubilee of "seven sabbaths of years," a
"proclaiming of liberty throughout the land," and the "return of
every man unto his possession" (comp. Lev. xxv, 8–10).

The sixty and two heptades are united and reckoned as the
necessary intervening time between the restoration and the final
heptade of overwhelming disaster and transition to the new age
and kingdom of eternal righteousness. No scheme of interpretation, which looks for mathematical precision in the use of these
numbers, and assumes to find literal fulfillment, has yet succeeded in
commanding the confidence of the best scholars and exegetes. We
discard all such attempts, and treat all such apocalyptic designations of time as essentially symbolical, and not to be determined by
mathematical calculations. The one final heptade is the period of
consummation, when "the transgressors are come to the full"
(viii, 23), and during the latter half of which Antiochus caused the
daily sacrifice to cease.

It may be objected to this interpretation that the profanation of
the temple and city of Jerusalem by Antiochus Epiphanes was only
partial and temporary, and not of a character to be truly represented by such implication of utter desolation as verses 26 and 27
of this passage suggest. But such objection overlooks the fact that,
in apocalyptic prophecy, the vision of final consummation connects
with whatever great catastrophe stands out upon the near horizon of
the prophet. This is conspicuous in Isaiah's picture of the coming

of the Messianic King (Isa. xi) immediately after the fall of Assyria (Isa. x). We have noticed the same thing in the other apocalyptic portions of Isaiah, and in those parts of Joel and Zechariah where the ideal triumph of God's people follows immediately after the overthrow of all the nations that fight against Mount Zion and Jerusalem.

The final overthrow of the Jewish state by the Romans, and the coming of the kingdom of Christ which is, in the New Testament, associated with that great catastrophe, may be in like manner comprehended in the scope of this oracle of the seventy weeks. The bringing in of eternal righteousness and associate ideas mentioned in Dan. ix, 24, are a part of the Messianic ideal of this prophecy. But the time limit of prophetic outlook here, as in the preceding visions of the book, connects with the downfall of the last hostile world-power contemplated in the overthrow of the great persecutor of the saints of the Most High. The abomination that made desolate, "spoken of by Daniel the prophet" (Matt. xxiv, 15), was therefore a type of a later abomination, which stood in the holy place and destroyed city and temple so that "there should not be left one stone upon another" (Matt. xxiv, 2).

V. The Divided Kingdom and the Final Triumph of Michael and his People. Daniel xi, 2–xii, 4.

The fifth and final vision of our prophet is dated "in the third year of Cyrus, king of Persia." It is declared to be a revelation to Daniel, a word of truth, and a great warfare (צָבָא, x, 1). It came to him after a period of three weeks' fasting, when he "was by the side of the great river Hiddekel," and was communicated by "a man clothed in linen, whose loins were girded with pure gold of Uphaz ; his body was like the beryl, and his face as the appearance of lightning, his eyes as lamps of fire, and his arms and his feet like in color to burnished brass, and the voice of his words like the voice of a multitude." It is here worthy of note that this sublime description of the angels who seem to be identical with the " one like the similitude of the sons of men " in verses 16 and 18, is freely appropriated by John in Rev. i, 13–16, to set forth his vision of "the first and the last, and the Living One," who was dead, but is alive for evermore, and holds the keys of death and Hades. Whether this glorious angel were the Gabriel of viii, 16, and ix, 21, we are not informed, but he is said to hold the closest relation to " Michael, one of the chief princes " (verse 13), " your prince " (verse 21), " the great prince who stands over the children of thy people " (xii, 1). The doctrine of angels apparent in this Book of Daniel is more highly embellished than in any other part of the Old Testament. Each nation or people is supposed to have its guardian angel, and these are represented as contending with each other (verses 13–20). All this, however, may be understood as part and parcel of the art of apocalyptic writers. These superior beings are like the supernatural machinery of the great epic poets, and introduced like other symbolic creations to deepen impressions and convey rich thoughts of the all-observant providence of God. While on the one hand the angel of Jehovah encamps about them that fear him (Psalm xxxiv, 7), on the other, lying spirits are conceived as influencing the counsels of kings and prophets who perversely disobey the truth (1 Kings xxii, 19–23).

The entire narrative of chap. x is of the nature of a prologue to the revelation which is recorded in xi, 2–xii, 4 ; and what is written in xii, 5–13, is a corresponding epilogue, designed to give a suitable artistic finish to the book. The revelation itself surpasses all that has gone before it in the definiteness and fullness of its details. The writer seems to aim in this closing vision to set forth in particulars what had been more mystically pictured in the symbols of the ten horns of the fourth beast, and the little horn with "the eyes of a man and a mouth speaking great things " (vii, 8). If there were any doubt before what set of kings was intended in chap. vii, 24, and what particular king was denoted by the little horn, this final revelation ought to remove such doubt.

The first two visions (in chaps. ii and vii) took into view four great world-powers ; the third (chap. viii) limited itself to the last two of the four ; the fourth (chap. ix) was concerned only with the incoming of the eternal righteousness that was destined to follow the final desolation of Jerusalem. This last vision takes up the latter time of the kings of the fourth world-power only, "when the transgressors are come to their full " (vii, 23), and after a brief statement of the overthrow of the kings of Persia, and the breaking up and dividing toward the four winds of heaven of the dominion of the first mighty king of Greece (xi, 2–4), the angel sketches the feuds and wars of ten Greek kings, five in Syria and five in Egypt, who preceded the contemptible Antiochus Epiphanes (xi, 5–20), and then proceeds to devote the larger part of this communication (verses 21–45) to a fourfold description of that impious king.

As the vision is dated in the third year of Cyrus (x, 1), the three kings yet to stand up in Persia (xi, 2) are to be understood of so many successors of the great Persian conqueror. But there were in all at least twelve kings who ruled the so-called Medo-Persian empire. It is not to be assumed that the writer was ignorant of this fact, and we, therefore, most naturally conclude that he did not aim to supply us with a syllabus of history. These four kings, like the four wings and the four heads of the leopard in vii, 6, are best understood as symbolically representative of all the kings of Persia. The fourth, who "shall be far richer than they all," is commonly understood of Xerxes ; but we prefer the reference to the last king of Persia, Darius Codomannus, whose thousands of thousands vainly fought Alexander at Issus and Arbella, and whose immense treasures fell into the hands of his Grecian conqueror.

The "mighty king, who shall rule with great dominion, and do according to his will" (verse 3), is, of course, Alexander, who was symbolized by the great horn between the eyes of the rough he-goat in viii, 21. The breaking up of his kingdom and dividing it " toward the four winds of heaven " (verse 4) corresponds strictly with the picture of viii, 22, where the great horn was broken, and four came up in its place. But while from one point of view this Grecian empire was seen to be divided toward the four winds, another vision of our prophet has seen ten kings arising out of this same kingdom (vii, 24); and the angel now goes on to show who these ten were. He makes no attempt to tell us of all the successors of Alexander, nor even a complete list of either the Seleucid or the Ptolemaic kings. Such a minute writing of Grecian history was no more his purpose than to speak of all the kings of Persia between Cyrus and Darius Codomannus. And yet so great is his skill that he displays no mechanical effort to enumerate the ten, as if he would formally advise us that he is taking pains to mention just that number. But in verses 5–20 he refers distinctly to five Ptolemaic rulers of Egypt, whom he calls " kings of the south," and five of the Seleucidæ, who are called "kings of the north." There is little or no dispute among expositors that in verse 5 allusion is made to Ptolemy Soter and Seleucus Nicator; in verse 6 to Ptolemy Philadelphus and Antiochus Theos ; in verses 7–9 to Ptolemy Euergetes and Seleucus Callinicus; in verses 10 and 11 to Ptolemy Philopator and Antiochus the Great (whose career is sketched as far as verse 19) ; in verses 16 and 17 to Ptolemy Epiphanes, and in verse 20 to Seleucus Philopator. Here, then, we are told of ten Græco-Macedonian kings, who, during the period of their dominion, represented and controlled the vast domain of Alexander's empire. They were not of his posterity, nor did they rule "according to his dominion wherewith he ruled " (verse 4), but they were for the time monarchs of all western Asia and Egypt, and between them, as between upper and nether millstones, Jerusalem and Judea were most miserably bruised and crushed.

Those exegetes who look for the ten kings solely among the Seleucidæ fail to observe that those "kings of the north" represented
only a part of Alexander's empire, whereas the Ptolemies of Egypt
were, as truly as the Selucidæ of Syria, direct successors of Alexander.

Having sufficiently pointed out ten Græco-Macedonian kings
that succeeded Alexander and preceded Antiochus Epiphanes, the
writer proceeds through the rest of this chapter (verses 21–45) to
give an extensive picture of that "wicked root" (1 Macc. i, 10) of
whom so much was seen and said in chaps. vii and viii. This entire
passage is divisible into four distinctive paragraphs, which we
understand to be, not an historical and chronological account of the
career of Antiochus, but a fourfold apocalyptic revelation of this
man of sin and lawlessness. The four paragraphs present so many
phases or aspects in which his character and works are exhibited.

1. The first phase (verses 21–24) presents the general character
of the persecutor by naming him "a contemptible person," and
declaring that he obtains the kingdom dishonorably, sweeps his op-
posers away as with a flood, practices deceit, secures the friendship
of the powerful by lavish distribution of his spoils, and, in short,
forces his way by his cunning and devices.

2. The second paragraph (verses 25–28) presents him in his successful campaigns against the king of the south, his mischief and
lies, and his first outrages upon the Jewish people and "the holy
covenant."

3. In the third paragraph (verses 29–39) we have a picture of his
unsuccessful invasion of Egypt, his dejection and humiliating re-
treat, his profanation of the Jewish sanctuary and fortress, and his
taking away the continual burnt offering and setting up "the
abomination that maketh desolate," and other displays of his unparalleled impiety. In this passage he is also characterized as exalt-
ing himself above every god, speaking amazing words against the
Most High, and even disregarding the gods of his fathers. He is
thus made to appear as the very incarnation of wickedness.

4. The fourth and final picture of this vile person presents him
ideally as the leader of the last great battle of the world-power
against "the glorious holy mountain" (verses 40–45). It is a vision
of what shall occur "at the time of the end." No labors of critics
and expositors have been able to make the statements of these verses
agree with accredited facts in the career of Antiochus Epiphanes or
any other king. The mistake of most expositors is in assuming that
the statements of the prophet are historical. The paragraph is best
explained as an apocalyptic ideal of the overthrow of the last great

enemy of the holy people, and is to be compared with Ezekiel's picture of the destruction of Gog and his hordes "upon the mountains of Israel" (Ezek. chaps. xxxviii and xxxix).

The same ideal of the last great conflict of the world with the people of the saints of the Most High is portrayed in Rev. xx, 9, where Satan musters the hosts of Gog and Magog, marches up over the breadth of the land, and encompasses the camp of the saints and the beloved city, and fire suddenly comes down from heaven and devours the adversaries.

As the visions of chaps. vii, viii, and ix recognize no hostile king or world-power beyond Antiochus Epiphanes, so here the writer makes the last great battle against Mount Zion appear as if led by the same daring "king of the north" who has been so variously portrayed in the three paragraphs of verses 21–39. He first moves against his southern rival "like a whirlwind, with chariots and with horsemen and with many ships," and seems for a while to overwhelm all opposition. "Edom and Moab and the chief of the children of Ammon," however, are delivered out of his hand. These ancient hereditary enemies of Israel appear to be named symbolically (as in Isa. xi, 14) as indicating a number of peoples whom the fierce king will find himself unable to subdue. But the Libyans on the Egyptian coast and the Ethiopians of the upper Nile are conceived as following at his steps, and all the treasures of Egypt come into his power. These make up for him a great host like the hordes of Gog, and, excited by "tidings out of the east and out of the north," he marches "with great fury to destroy and to devote many to utter ruin," and, like the Antichrist of Rev. xx, 9, he pitches his palatial tent over against the glorious holy mountain of God, where he suddenly comes to his end with none to help him. So, as in chap. ix, 26, 27, "his end shall be with the flood" with which he aims to effect the utter ruin of city and sanctuary.

Out of these overwhelming desolations of the end God will deliver his people, and the vision of salvation presented in xii, 1–3, follows immediately after that of the ruin of the great enemy. "At that time," says the angel, "shall Michael stand up, the great prince that standeth for the children of thy people ; and there shall be a time of trouble, such as never was since there was a nation even to that same time ; and at that time thy people shall be delivered, every one that shall be found written in the book." This time of unparalleled trouble is the same as that with which the seventy heptades ended (ix, 26, 27). The vision of the seer penetrates amid the unspeakable sorrows of that day, and he is assured that no member of the true Israel of God will finally perish. There is to be a resurrection both of the just and the unjust, for some shall awake to everlasting life and some to everlasting shame. But the grand *finale* of the saints is declared in the concluding parallelism:

> They that be wise shall shine as the brightness of the firmament,
> And they that turn many to righteousness as the stars forever and ever.

All this final picture of glory for the people of God is but another and parallel representation of what we have seen in vii, 27, where the kingdom of God and all its greatness and triumph are "given to the people of the saints of the Most High." The apocalyptist entertains no thought of what events may intervene between the fall of Antiochus and the glorious triumph of the saints. The two things appear in his perspective as coincident. And this peculiarity of apocalyptic scenes we have noted again and again in the foregoing pages. The epilogue of this revelation (xii, 5–13) is in artistic harmony with the prologue of chapter x. The prophet inquires of the angels about the time of the end, but receives only the answer of symbolical numbers. These are sufficiently indefinite to admonish him that he need not expect to know the day or the hour. The times and seasons are definitely fixed by the Most High, and every faithful servant of God may rest assured that he will stand in his lot at the end of the days.

CHAPTER XVIII

APOCALYPSE OF THE SYNOPTIC GOSPELS

THE teaching of Jesus concerning " the end of the age," and the " Son of man coming in the clouds," as it is written in Mark xiii, Matt. xxiv, and Luke xxi, appears to have been given in the latter days of his ministry, and in connection with a prediction of the overthrow of the Jewish temple at Jerusalem. The entire prophecy as reported by all the synoptic gospels is so largely of an apocalyptic or eschatological character as to justify the title of " Apocalypse of the Gospels." A careful analysis of its composition, and an exposition of its occasion, scope, and meaning, are a necessary preliminary to the study of the Apocalypse of John.

I. THE DIFFERENT THEORIES OF INTERPRETATION. The variety of opinions on this eschatological discourse is very remarkable. It is difficult to classify the different views. There is, perhaps, no other scripture in the exposition of which we may observe a greater display of dogmatic prepossession. This last named fact is the chief obstacle to a calm and dispassionate study of the prophecy. The extreme rationalist, as well as the arrogant confessional theologian, has made so many unqualified assertions as to what Jesus could and could not have intended, what he knew and what he could not have known, that one may almost despair of arriving at any general consensus. The way to a scientific exposition is, accordingly, obstructed to an extent that is quite disheartening to the sober inquirer after the truth. Nevertheless, we submit the following exposition.

There are at least three different hypotheses which have been employed to explain this scripture. There is, first, (1) That which regards the discourse in its present form as a composition of incongruous materials. The writers who penned our synoptic gospels are supposed to have misapprehended much of what the Lord said, and to have united in one address various statements which were originally uttered on different occasions. (2) Another class of interpreters find in these words of Jesus teachings concerning two entirely different events, widely separated in time, namely, the destruction of Jerusalem and the end of the world. (3) A third method of interpretation maintains that the entire prophecy may be most simply explained as finding its fulfillment in the overthrow of the temple and the introduction of Christianity into the world.

1. The hypothesis of incongruous and contradictory elements comes before us in several forms. One class of critics affirms that the discourse contains the substance of a Jewish-Christian apocalypse which very early became confounded with the traditional sayings of Jesus. A considerable portion, accordingly, of what is here attributed to Jesus belongs to a different authorship. Keim tells us that "this piece of writing is to be ascribed unquestionably, not to Jesus, but to a Jewish Christian who lived toward the close of the apostolic period, and who, in view of the impending catastrophe of the temple and the holy city, dedicated to Christians and Jews the revelations, counsels, and consolations of Jesus, and did this evidently at once in writing and not orally." [1] This writer thinks it evident that this composition dates even before the investment of Jerusalem, and in this differs from several critics who hold views similar to his own but maintain that the writing belongs to a period later than the destruction of the Jewish capital. But this theory of an anonymous Jewish or Jewish-Christian document, which our gospels have incorporated without acknowledgment and complicated with some genuine sayings of Jesus, is destitute of any reasonable proof, and is obviously a mere critical conjecture. It creates more difficulties than it presumes to solve.

Another form of the hypothesis is that the evangelists have added to our Lord's words some things which he did not say. In the course of transmitting orally the many sayings of Jesus certain incongruous ideas were mixed up with them, and became so closely united that when the Logia were first written down it was impossible to separate the true original from its accretions. The result is that we have not an accurate or trustworthy report of what Jesus said on the occasion referred to. All this, however, is pure theory, and might be also applied, according to the varying notions of critics, to any other sayings of Jesus which are recorded in the three synoptic gospels.

Another and less objectionable form of the hypothesis is that which allows the genuineness of all these sayings of our Lord, but insists that they have become confused by the compilers of our gospels, and whole sections are here inserted out of their proper connection. Matthew records in xxiv, 17, 23, 27, 28, 37, 40, 41, what Luke refers to a different occasion (comp. Luke xvii, 20–37). Comp. also Matt. xxiv, 43–51, with Luke xii, 39–46.

---

[1] *History of Jesus of Nazara*, vol. v, p. 237, English translation. London, 1881.

Any attempt to discuss the relations of the parallel sections in the gospels must of course reckon with the critical results of the so-called "Synoptic Problem." We recognize the fact that the most ancient tradition of a compilation of *sayings* (λόγια, that is, of Jesus), written in Aramaic by Matthew, is well supported by internal evidence seen in the peculiar language and structure of our present gospels of Matthew and Luke, and is to be regarded as one of the chief sources of these two gospels. The same tradition reports that Mark's gospel was written under the oversight and dictation of Peter, and everything in the peculiar character of this gospel appears to be in harmony with the hypothesis of such an origin. Here then are at least two original sources of the contents of the synoptic gospels. That Mark is older than our present Matthew, and was used in its compilation, may be readily admitted, but the question may still remain an open one whether the Logia of Matthew were not older than Mark. Some do maintain that the author of the second gospel had Matthew's Logia before him, and made some slight use of it, but as it was not the purpose of that gospel to incorporate long discourses very little use of Matthew's work is traceable in it. Our purpose is sufficiently answered by accepting the now current hypothesis of two main sources, namely, Matthew's Logia and Mark's gospel. Which of these may best claim priority we shall not attempt to determine.[1] But our present Mark is the earliest of the synoptic gospels ; Matthew's gospel came next in time, and incorporated the original Logia into the historical framework of Mark. The gospel of Luke is latest of the three, and has made use of the other two, and also of other sources now unknown to us.

These things being so, it is simply a question of comparative criticism how far the discourse of Jesus, as written in Mark xiii, is trustworthy as a record of what our Lord said on the occasion referred to. It is the only example of a long discourse to be found in Mark's gospel. It agrees in the main with Matt. xxiv and Luke xxi. *So far as the three reports agree it is certainly the best authenticated of all the discourses of similar length now preserved to us in the synoptists.* We regard it, therefore, as great presumtion to insist that any of those sayings which all three of

---

[1] It is not improbable that this eschatological sermon, as embodied in Mark xiii, was copied from the original Aramaic Logia of Matthew. The fact that it is the only discourse of noticeable length in this gospel favors this view, and it seems more naturally accounted for by supposing it copied from a work like the Logia than to suppose it written from Peter's recollection and dictation. This hypothesis would ot course place the Logia before Mark's gospel.

the synoptists agree in attributing to Jesus on this occasion have been inserted out of their proper connection. Such a claim, to be of any value, must be supported by the most imperative kind of evidence.[1]

Our contention is, (1) that Mark xiii alone contains, aside from what is peculiar to Matthew and to Luke, all the elements of supposed incongruity in these eschatological sayings of Jesus, so that no real difficulty of this kind is removed from the discourse by the removal of sections which are peculiar to Matthew and Luke, or are by them placed in a different connection. For example, we may eliminate from Matt. xxiv the passages (verses 26–28 and 43–51), which Luke assigns to another occasion (Luke xvii, 22–37, and xii, 39–46), and all the real difficulties of the exposition remain in full force. We affirm (2) further that the parable of the ten virgins in Matt. xxv, 1–13, and the sublime picture of judgment in Matt. xxv, 31–46, though found in no other place, contain nothing inconsistent with the teaching of what is common to all the gospels, and nothing which is out of place in the connection in which we find it. The parable of the talents is essentially equivalent in its doctrine to that of the pounds (comp. Luke xix, 13–27, and Matt. xxv, 14–30), and the lesson of watchfulness taught in Matt. xxv, 1–13, is virtually expressed in similar imagery in Luke xii, 35–37. (3) Furthermore, it can be shown by valid exegesis that those words and phrases which are peculiar to either Matthew or Luke are not incongruous with what is written in Mark; and where we have reason, as in Luke xxi, 20, to believe that the writer has purposely changed the language of the Logia of Matthew from which he copied, it cannot be shown that he has introduced anything that materially changes the meaning and scope of the discourse as a whole.

---

[1] A recent work (*The Apostolic Gospel, with a Critical Reconstruction of the Text*, by J. F. Blair, London, 1896), remarkable for boldness and confidence of assertion, and the conjectural character of most of its contents, affirms that Mark xiii, 1–3, is purely editorial and unreliable, and that the corresponding passages in Matthew and Luke, which refer this apocalyptic discourse to the same occasion, are mere repetitions of Mark's mistake with sundry editorial modifications. The author offers a reconstruction of the original apostolic gospel, in which numerous explicit statements of the evangelists are arbitrarily set aside and a large portion of them is put down as untrustworthy. He declares that "the only permissible interpretation" of Luke xvii, 24; Matt. xxiv, 27, teaches that the coming of the kingdom "is an instantaneous, universal event," and cannot be preceded by any visible signs. The confident prepossession, which controls his judgment of things compatible and things incompatible for Jesus to have said, is noteworthy, and if his principles, methods, and conclusions be accepted we cannot see that our synoptic gospels are in the main trustworthy for ascertaining the real teachings of Jesus. What the Lord said is in the analysis determined by what the critic thinks he ought to have said.

We are, accordingly, shut up to the conclusion that no rearrangement of the material, and no theory of the composition of this discourse, which assumes that it is made up of incongruous elements, have so far succeeded in removing the difficulties of its exposition or providing a more satisfactory explanation of its words.[1]

2. The hypothesis which assumes two different events, namely, the destruction of Jerusalem and the end of the world, to be the subject of this prophecy, comes before us in two forms. Both accept the genuineness of the Gospel records and hold that they supplement each other; but with one class of expositors a dividing line is found between what refers to the fall of Jerusalem and what refers to the future coming of Christ, while with the other no such dividing line is recognized, but the entire discourse is interpreted on the theory of a double sense. When, however, the one school of interpreters attempt to point out the dividing line, there are as many differences of opinion as there are interpreters. In Matt. xxiv and xxv, for example, the transition from the one subject to the other is placed by Bengel and others at xxiv, 29; by E. J. Meyer at verse 35; by Doddridge at verse 36; by Kuinoel at verse 33; by Eichhorn at xxv, 14, and by Wetstein at xxv, 31. In view of these notable differences of judgment another class of writers reject all such attempts at finding a point of transition from one topic to the other, and imagine that the entire discourse may have a double significance. Lange thinks that the great future is depicted in a series of cycles, each one of which exhibits in its own way the course of the world and its various judgments down to the end.[2] Alford says that "two parallel interpretations run through the former part (of Matt. xxiv) as far as verse 28, the destruction of Jerusalem and the final judgment being both enwrapped in the words, but the former, in this part of the chapter, predominating. From verse 28 the lesser

---

[1] The attempt of a number of critics to reconstruct the original Logia of Jesus by means of what is written in our synoptic gospels may be a helpful service to New Testament study. But when the reconstruction goes to the presumption of convicting all the synoptists of downright error we may well pause and inquire if the procedure is truly scientific, rational, and trustworthy. When it is maintained that all the writers were mistaken in referring this discourse of Jesus to the time and place assigned, or that Mark made the mistake and Luke and Matthew copied it, we have a right to demand the most convincing kind of evidence. So, too, when a statement like that of Mark xiii, 30, and its parallel in Matthew and Luke is cast out as apocryphal, and Mark xiii, 24, and Matt. xxiv, 29, are divorced from their context on no other grounds than assumed incongruity, we ought to be furnished with the very strongest kind of proof of the incongruity. The result of such disruption of any writer's composition is to implicate him in almost incredible stupidity.

[2] *Commentary on the Gospel of Matthew* (Amer. ed., 1864), p. 418.

subject begins to be swallowed up by the greater, and our Lord's
second coming is the predominant theme, with, however, certain
hints thrown back, as it were, at the event which was immediately in
question; till in the latter part of the chapter, and the whole of the
next, the second advent, and at last the final judgment ensuing on
it, are the subjects." [1]

It is scarcely necessary to controvert the assumptions of a double
or a triple sense, as here put forward. The exposition built upon it
may be left to sink beneath its own weight. Few readers of the
gospels will at the present time rest satisfied with a theory of exegesis which makes Jesus palter in such a double sense with his disciples; and as for the attempts to show a dividing line between
what refers to the fall of Jerusalem and what refers to a yet future
coming of Christ, the remarkable differences of opinion as to the
point of transition from one subject to the other are of a nature
to make one suspicious of the hypothesis.

3. There remains the hypothesis which recognizes the substantial
unity of the discourse and maintains that all these sayings of Jesus
are capable of a self-consistent and satisfactory explanation as a
prophecy of what was in the near future when he uttered them.
The overthrow of the Jewish temple and the consequent going
forth of the new kingdom of Christ in the world are the main subject. We adopt this hypothesis as the only tenable explanation of
the language which all three synoptists ascribe to Jesus on the occasion of his concluding his teaching in the temple.[2] As for those
portions which are peculiar either to Matthew or to Luke, they are
to be treated according to their intrinsic merit and their relevancy
to the occasion.

This interpretation has the advantage of the unquestionable facts
that both the decisive overthrow of the Jewish national cult and
the triumphant establishment of Christianity in the world date from
about the close of the apostolic period. It was a part of the divine
order of the kingdom of Christ that its gospel should first be
preached to the nations and obtain an imperishable witness among
men before the end of the old age.

---

[1] Greek Testament with notes, *in loco*.

[2] Mark (xiii, 3) and Matthew (xxiv, 3) say expressly that the discourse was given on
the Mount of Olives; but Luke (xxi, 5-8) leaves the impression that it was spoken
while Jesus was yet at the temple, where his attention had been called to the costly
stones and gifts. Here, however, is no real discrepancy, for Luke xxi, 7, simply fails
to say whether the question of the disciples was asked *immediately after* his declaration in verse 6. Matt. xxiv, 3, and Mark xiii, 3, might be stricken out of their places,
and it would not alter in the least the occasion, scope, and import of the Master's
words.

II. Parallel Teaching in the Synoptic Gospels.

Before proceeding to the exposition of the main subject-matter we will first examine the various passages of similar teaching which have been recorded in a different connection.

The statements of Matt. x, 21–23, occur in connection with the Lord's instructions to the disciples when he sent them forth to preach the great message, "The kingdom of heaven is at hand " (verse 7). The language of verses 21 and 22 is identical with that of Mark xiii, 12, 13, and notably parallel with Luke xxi, 16–19. What is peculiar to Matthew is verse 23: "But when they persecute you in this city, flee into the next: for verily I say unto you, ye shall not have finished the cities of Israel, till the Son of man be come." The coming of the Son of man is to be understood here as in all other passages. To reject the passage as an interpolation of the evangelist or some later writer would certainly be arbitrary. It may be that the words are here inserted in a wrong connection, but of this there is no evidence. Whether we read them in connection with the first apostolic commission or as a part of the discourse on the Mount of Olives, their meaning is the same, and not unsuitable to either context. The Lord assures his disciples that before they shall have completed the work of their apostolic ministry in the cities of Israel the Son of man shall come. What the coming of the Son of man may signify he does not stop to say, and for anything that is said or implied to the contrary the apostolic ministry would go on after the coming of the Lord as well as before it.[1] On this point we shall have more to say in connection with Matt. xxiv, 14; but we may here premise that the true meaning of such phrases as " the coming of the Son of man " and the " coming in his kingdom" is to be learned in the light of Old Testament prophecies of the Messianic age.

The next passage to note is Matt. xvi, 27, 28, which must be compared with Mark viii, 38; ix, 1, and Luke ix, 26, 27. Here we observe some slight differences of phraseology, and Mark and Luke introduce before the passage the statement that when the Son of man shall come in his glory he will be ashamed of them that are now ashamed of him and his words. But it is to be observed that Matt. x, 32, 33, and Luke xii, 8, 9, report words of Jesus strikingly parallel with these. But all three synoptists agree in placing the main statement of this passage in the same connection, and imme-

---

[1] I have not considered it necessary in this exposition to entertain the theory that Jesus himself was in error either as to the time or the manner of his coming. His acknowledged ignorance of the day and the hour does not warrant us in supposing that he ever positively affirmed an error.

diately before their accounts of the transfiguration. The language
of Jesus, as it appears in each gospel, is as follows:

MATTHEW.	MARK.	LUKE.
The Son of man shall come in the glory of his Father with his angels; and then shall he render unto every man according to his deeds. Verily I say unto you, There are some of them that stand here, who shall not taste of death till they see the Son of man coming in his kingdom.	Whosoever shall be ashamed of me and of my words in this adulterous and sinful generation, the Son of man also shall be ashamed of him, when he cometh in the glory of the Father with the holy angels. And he said unto them, Verily I say unto you, there are some here of them that stand by, who shall not taste of death till they see the kingdom of God come with power.	Whosoever shall be ashamed of me and of my words, of him shall the Son of man be ashamed, when he cometh in his glory and that of the Father and of the holy angels. But I tell you of a truth, there are some of them that stand here, who shall not taste of death till they see the kingdom of God.

All sorts of efforts have been made to evade the simple meaning
of these words, but they all spring from the dogmatic prepossession
that the coming of the Son of man in his glory must needs be an
event far future from the time when the words were spoken. Some
have understood that the reference is to the transfiguration, which
all three synoptists record immediately afterward. But two decisive objections stand in the way of such a reference: (1) that
event occurred only six or eight days afterward, and (2) it could
not with any propriety be called a coming of the Son of man in the
glory of his Father with the angels, or coming in his kingdom.
Others have distinguished between Christ's coming in the glory of
his Father with the angels and his coming in his kingdom, or the
coming of his kingdom. But we incline to the belief that very few
can be fully persuaded, with the above Gospel-parallels before them,
that our Lord meant to be understood as speaking of two events
centuries apart. Had this been his intention he might certainly have
employed language less ambiguous and less likely to confuse the
minds of his disciples. The plain teaching of the passage is that before some of those who heard him speak should die the Son of man
would come in glory, and his kingdom would be established in
power. And this teaching is in strict accord with what is taught
in Matt. xxiv and its parallels in Mark and Luke.

No study of Mark xiii and its parallels in Luke and Matthew
should fail to compare what is written in Luke xvii, 20–37:

And being asked by the Pharisees, when the kingdom of God cometh, he answered
them and said, The kingdom of God cometh not with observation: neither shall they
say, Lo, here! or, There! for lo, the kingdom of God is in the midst of you.

And he said unto the disciples, The days will come, when ye shall desire to see one of the days of the Son of man, and ye shall not see it. And they shall say to you, Lo, there! Lo, here! go not away, nor follow after *them :* for as the lightning, when it lighteneth out of the one part under the heaven, shineth unto the other part under heaven; so shall the Son of man be in his day. But first must he suffer many things and be rejected of this generation. And as it came to pass in the days of Noah, even so shall it be also in the days of the Son of man. They ate, they drank, they married, they were given in marriage, until the day that Noah entered into the ark, and the flood came and destroyed them all. Likewise even as it came to pass in the days of Lot; they ate, they drank, they bought, they sold, they planted, they builded; but in the day that Lot went out from Sodom it rained fire and brimstone from heaven, and destroyed them all: after the same manner shall it be in the day that the Son of man is revealed. In that day, he which shall be on the housetop, and his goods in the house, let him not go down to take them away: and let him that is in the field likewise not return back. Remember Lot's wife. Whosoever shall seek to gain his life shall lose it: but whosoever shall lose *his life* shall preserve it. I say unto you, In that night there shall be two men on one bed; the one shall be taken, and the other shall be left. There shall be two women grinding together; the one shall be taken, and the other shall be left. And they answering say unto him, Where, Lord? And he said unto them, Where the body *is*, thither will the eagles also be gathered together.

It is to be first observed that verses 20 and 21 are peculiar to Luke, and have their occasion definitely assigned. They record Jesus's answer to the Pharisees who asked him, " When cometh the kingdom of God ? " They cannot, therefore, be a part of Jesus's discourse to his disciples on the Mount of Olives. Their teaching, moreover, concerning the coming of the kingdom of God seems also, at first sight, to lack harmony with what is written in Luke xxi, 27 : "Then shall they see the Son of man coming in a cloud with power and great glory." For Jesus tells the Pharisees that "the kingdom of God cometh not with observation," that is, in such a phenomenal manner that one can gaze upon it with the eyes of flesh. The word παρατήρησις, here translated *observation*, occurs nowhere else in the New Testament, but its cognate verb is employed three times in this same gospel of Luke (vi, 7; xiv, 1 ; xx, 20) to denote the unfriendly and even hostile manner in which the Pharisees observed the acts of Jesus. This fact should be taken into consideration when we interpret the language of Jesus as addressed to them. The purport of his answer is : "The kingdom of God does not come in such a way that it may be watched by men possessed of a hostile spirit. It is not to be thought of as a public spectacle on which men look and say, Lo, there it is! For even now the kingdom of God is in the midst of you,[1] and yet with

---

[1] Ἐντὸς ὑμῶν may certainly and most naturally mean *within you*, that is, in your souls. But as addressed to the Pharisees this meaning will not hold, and the phrase should be translated here *in the midst of you*, that is, among you, a meaning demanded by the context.

all your watching me you have not observed it." So his words were designed to have special reference to the attitude of the Pharisees toward himself, and their most obvious meaning is that, so far as a kingdom may be represented and be present in the person of its king, the kingdom of God was already among them in the presence of the Son of man.

But whatever we may think of the occasion and purport of Luke xvii, 20, 21, verses 22–37 form a section by themselves, and were addressed to the disciples, not to the Pharisees. They may or may not have been placed here in their proper connection. So far as the subject-matter of the passage argues anything to the purpose, these words to the disciples would be as appropriate in the eschatological discourse of Luke xxi as they are here. They are in closest harmony with what appears in Luke xxi, 29–36, and are actually interwoven with a series of statements made in Matt. xxiv, 26–28, and 37–41. Furthermore, the statements in Luke xvii, 22, 25, 28, 29, and 32, which are peculiar to the third gospel, contain no thought that is in the least inconsistent with what is found in Mark xiii, Matt. xxiv, and Luke xxi. The references to "the days of Lot" (verse 28) are, perhaps, more naturally connected with what Matthew writes in xxiv, 37, than they are in Luke's context. In either case the teaching of Jesus in Mark xiii and its parallels is in no way altered or made more simple and intelligible by hypothetical readjustment of particular passages. The doctrine of a coming of the Son of man in his kingdom and glory in the near future is common to all these passages, and Jesus's words to the Pharisees in Luke xvii, 20, 21, so far from teaching a far future coming of Christ, declare that the kingdom of God is already among them.

One other passage, common to all the synoptic gospels, deserves notice at this point. According to Mark xiv, 62, when Jesus was brought before the high priest and was asked, " Art thou the Christ, the Son of the Blessed ? " he answered, " I am : and ye shall see the Son of man sitting at the right hand of power, and coming with the clouds of heaven." Luke has (xxii, 69), " From henceforth (ἀπὸ τοῦ νῦν) shall the Son of man be seated at the right hand of the power of God." Matthew reads (xxvi, 64), " From this time (ἀπ' ἄρτι) ye shall see the Son of man sitting at the right hand of power, and coming on the clouds of heaven." We maintain that this language cannot be naturally interpreted as a reference to an event belonging to a far distant period of time. It is something that is to take place *from this time onward*, and something which the high priests and his associates are to see. We quote with great satisfaction the comment of Gould in the *International*

Critical Commentary on Mark (p. 252): "This settles two things : first, that the coming is not a single event, any more than the sitting on the right hand of power ; and second, that it was a thing which was to begin with the very time of our Lord's departure from the world. Moreover, the two things, the sitting on the right hand of power, and the coming, are connected in such a way as to mean that he is to assume power in heaven and exercise it here in the world. The period beginning with the departure of Jesus from the world was to be marked by this assumption of heavenly power by the Christ, and by repeated interferences in crises of the world's history, of which the destruction of Jerusalem was the first."

III. Occasion and Scope of the Discourse.

In passing now to the exposition of the apocalyptic discourse we observe the occasion of its utterance. In all the synoptists it follows soon after the controversy with the Pharisees, Herodians, and Sadducees, who watched him with an evil eye, and sought to ensnare him in his sayings. He warned the disciples against the scribes (Mark xii, 37–40 ; Luke xx, 45–47). Matthew in this connection adduces the series of oracular woes which fills up most of his twenty-third chapter. At the close of that chapter he introduces the terrible denunciation of Jerusalem, which Luke places in a different connection, but with substantial agreement in sentiment.

MATT. XXIII, 34–39.	LUKE XI, 49–51.
Therefore behold I send unto you prophets, and wise men, and scribes: some of them shall ye kill and crucify; and some of them shall ye scourge in your synagogues, and persecute from city to city: that upon you may come all the righteous blood shed on the earth, from the blood of Abel the righteous unto the blood of Zachariah son of Barachiah, whom ye slew between the sanctuary and the altar. Verily I say unto you, All these things shall come upon this generation.	Therefore also said the wisdom of God, I will send unto them prophets and apostles; and some of them they shall kill and persecute; that the blood of all the prophets, which was shed from the foundation of the world, may be required of this generation; from the blood of Abel unto the blood of Zachariah who perished between the altar and the house: yea, I say unto you, it shall be required of this generation.
	LUKE XIII, 34, 35.
O Jerusalem, Jerusalem, that killeth the prophets, and stoneth them that are sent unto her ! How often would I have gathered thy children together, even as a hen gathereth her chickens under her wings, and ye would not! Behold, your house is left unto you desolate. For I say unto you, Ye shall not see me from this time, till ye shall say, Blessed is he that cometh in the name of the Lord.	O Jerusalem, Jerusalem, that killeth the prophets, and stoneth them that are sent unto her ! How often would I have gathered thy children together, even as a hen her own brood under her wings, and ye would not! Behold, your house is left unto you ; and I say unto you, Ye shall not see me, until ye shall say, Blessed is he that cometh in the name of the Lord.

Whether now these words were uttered on the same day as the eschatological discourse, or on some other occasion, no sayings of Jesus are better attested, and no one can question their appropriateness in the context where Matthew places them. They certainly belong to the period of our Lord's latest appeals to his hostile countrymen, and most naturally to the last week of his teaching at the temple. The fact that both Mark and Luke insert the incident of the poor widow casting her farthing into the treasury (Mark xii, 41–44 ; Luke xxi, 1–4) immediately before the long discourse about the overthrow of the temple, and immediately after the denunciation of the scribes and hypocrites, is incidental evidence that Matthew has very properly distributed all these later sayings of Jesus. There is, moreover, every reason to suppose that some of the sayings of our Lord were in substance uttered on more than one occasion.

That which particularly called forth the apocalyptic discourse was the question of the disciples touching the time and the sign of the overthrow of the temple. Mark (xiii, 1–4) says that as Jesus " went forth out of the temple, one of his disciples saith unto him, Teacher, behold what manner of stones and what manner of buildings ! And Jesus said unto him, Seest thou these great buildings ? There shall not be left here one stone upon another which shall not be thrown down. And as he sat upon the mount of Olives over against the temple, Peter and James and John and Andrew asked him privately, Tell us, when shall these things be ? and what the sign when these things are all about to be accomplished ? " Matthew also locates the discourse on the Mount of Olives, but varies somewhat the form of the question of the disciples. Luke gives none of these details, but leaves the impression upon his reader that the discourse of Jesus was delivered in or at the temple. But the specific manner in which Mark records the details, and gives the names of four disciples who asked the question privately, bears its own internal evidence of accuracy, and is most like the vivid report of an eyewitness. Matthew confirms the statement that the sayings were uttered on the Mount of Olives, and one may appropriately call them " The Sermon on the Mount of Olives." The entire prophecy purports to be an answer to the question of the disciples. That question was twofold—*when* shall these things be, and *what the sign* of their accomplishment ? The Master responded directly, mentioned a number of things which must first take place, and a sign by which they might know the nearness of the impending catastrophe, and escape to the mountains. Immediately after the great tribulation which is to accompany the catastrophe, or in those very days, the Son of man is to be seen coming in the clouds with great power and glory. His coming is described according to the Hebrew apocalyptic style; and then it is solemnly affirmed with an emphatic *Amen* or *Verily,* "This generation shall not pass away till all these things be accomplished" (Mark xiii, 30; Matt. xxiv, 34; Luke xxi, 32). It would seem from all this that the occasion and scope of this prophecy are clear beyond controversy. It was preceded by many a word of rebuke and warning to the hypocritical scribes and Pharisees, and a terrible woe pronounced against Jerusalem, the murderess of saints and prophets. The time-limit so emphatically asserted accords perfectly with the assurance given on another occasion that some of those who listened to the great Teacher should not die till they had seen the Son of man coming in his kingdom.

These facts and considerations seem also to determine beyond reasonable controversy the meaning of the word *end* (τέλος) as used in this discourse by all the synoptists. It is the terminal point, or time limit at which all these things are to be accomplished (συντε-λεῖσθαι). It is, according to Matthew's phraseology, the end or "consummation of the age" (συντέλεια τοῦ αἰῶνος). It is the solemn termination and crisis of the dispensation which had run its course when the temple fell, and there was not left one stone upon another which was not thrown down.[1] That catastrophe, which in Heb. xii, 26, is conceived as a shaking of the earth and the heaven, is *the end* contemplated in this discourse; not "the end of the world," but the termination and consummation of the pre-Messianic age.[2]

---

[1] The claim that the temple was not *demolished* (καταλύω), but burned with fire, and that some of its foundation stones are yet standing firmly, does not in the least, even if the claim be true, invalidate the remarkable fulfillment of this prophecy. In prophetic speech such predictions of doom naturally take on a measure of hyperbole. Comp. Isa. xiii, 19, 20; Jer. xlix, 17, 18; comp. also Luke xix, 44; Micah iii, 12; Jer. xxvi, 18. It is not *literal* fulfillment that we are to expect in any of these prophecies.

[2] "Nothing can be more misleading to the English reader," observes Russell, "than the rendering, 'the end of the world;' which inevitably suggests the close of human history, the end of time, and the destruction of the earth—a meaning which the words will not bear. . . . What can be more evident than that the promise of Christ to be with his disciples to the close of the age implies that they were to live to the close of the age? That great consummation was not far off; the Lord had often spoken of it, and always as an approaching event, one which some of them would live to see. It was the winding up of the Mosaic dispensation; the end of the long probation of the theocratic nation; when the whole frame and fabric of the Jewish polity were to be swept away, and the kingdom of God to come with power. This great event, our Lord declared, was to fall within the limit of the existing generation."—*The Parousia*, p. 121. London, 1887.

IV. Analysis of Subject-matter.

Aside from verbal variations, the substance of teaching as presented in the three synoptic reports of the discourse may be thus summarized in outline:

MATTHEW XXIV.	MARK XIII.	LUKE XXI.
I.	**I.**	**I.**
Four things before the End, xxiv, 4–14.	*Four things before the End,* xiii, 5–13.	*Three things before the End,* xxi, 8–19.
1. False Christs and a great apostasy, 4, 5.	1. False Christs and a great apostasy, 5, 6.	1. False Christs, 8.
2. Wars, commotion of nations, famines, and earthquakes, 6–8.	2. Wars, commotion of nations, earthquakes, and famines, 7, 8.	2. Wars, tumults, commotion of nations, earthquakes, famines, pestilence, terrors and signs from heaven, 9–11.
3. Persecution, death, offenses, betrayals, hatred, false prophets, and great wickedness, 9–13.	3. Persecution, afflictions, betrayals, hatred, and putting to death, 9, 11–13.	3. Persecution, betrayals, putting to death, and hatred, 12–19.
4. Gospel in all the world —*ἐν ὅλῃ τῇ οἰκουμένῃ*, 14.	4. Gospel unto all the nations—*εἰς πάντα τὰ ἔθνη*, 10.	
II.	**II.**	**II.**
Three signs when the End (Consummation) is close at hand, 15–28.	*Three signs when the End is close at hand,* 14–23.	*Two signs when the End is close at hand,* 20–24.
1. The abomination of desolation, 15–18.	1. The abomination of desolation, 14–17.	1. Jerusalem compassed with armies, 20, 21.
2. The great tribulation, 19–22.	2. The great tribulation, 18–20.	2. The great tribulation, 22–24.
3. False Christs and prophets doing signs and wonders, 23–28.	3. False Christs and prophets doing signs and wonders, 21–23.	
III.	**III.**	**III.**
Apocalyptic picture of the End and the Parousia, 29–31.	*Apocalyptic picture of the End and the Parousia,* 24–27.	*Apocalyptic picture of the End and the Parousia,* 25–28.
1. Sun and moon darkened, stars fall, and powers of heaven shaken, 29.	1. Sun and moon darkened, stars fall, and powers of heaven shaken, 24, 25.	1. Signs in the sun, moon, and stars, distress and terror on earth, powers of heaven shaken, 25, 26.
2. Sign of Son of man in heaven, and coming in clouds with power and glory, 30.	2. Son of man in clouds with power and glory, 26.	2. Son of man in clouds with power and glory, 27.
3. Angel ministries, trumpet, gathering the elect, 31.	3. Angel ministries, gathering of the elect, 27.	3. Redemption at hand, 28.

IV.	IV.	IV.
Counsels and Warnings, 32–51.	*Counsels and Warnings,* 28–37.	*Counsels and Warnings,* 29–36.
1. Similitude of the fig tree, 32, 33.	1. Similitude of the fig tree, 28, 29.	1. Similitude of the fig tree, 29–31.
2. All to occur in this generation, 34, 35.	2. All to occur in this generation, 30, 31.	2. All to occur in this generation, 32, 33.
3. Day and hour unknown, 36.	3. Day and hour unknown, 32.	[Comp. Luke xvii, 26–35; and xii, 39, 40.]
4. Like the flood, 37–39.		
5. Sudden separations, 40, 41.		
6. Admonition to watch, 42–51.	4. Admonition to watch, 33–37.	3. Admonition to watch, 34–36.

There are at least four main divisions of this discourse common to all these gospels, and they stand in the logical order of (1) things to transpire before the end; (2) signs of the nearness of the catastrophe; (3) an apocalyptic portrayal of the coming of the Son of man, and (4) counsels and admonitions to the disciples.

V. Exposition of the Several Sayings.

I.

Taking up the four main divisions in their order, we now proceed to explain the prophecy and to show (1) that the three synoptic gospels are here in substantial agreement, and (2) that all these things came to pass within the time-limit of the prophecy.

(1) Matthew and Mark mention four things, or four classes of events, which are to take place before the end, while Luke mentions but three. The few changes in the order of the words which they have in common, and the few words and expressions which are peculiar to Luke, do not in the least militate against the substantial harmony of the three different writers.

(2) That all these things came to pass in that generation, that is, before the overthrow of the Jewish capital, is questioned by many exegetes. We must therefore make appeal (a) to well authenticated facts, and (b) then inquire how far the facts really fulfill the import of the prophecy.

It will scarcely be questioned that all the items named in the second and third classes of events in section I of the above analysis found abundant fulfillment in the course of the war which ended in the overthrow of Jerusalem. It is quite possible, however, for a modern reader to import into some of the words here employed much more than was understood by the writers, and much more than the usage of the New Testament justifies. The word *nation* ($\xi\vartheta\nu o\varsigma$), for example, must not be construed as meaning what modern usage so commonly associates with the term, namely, an independent body politic; an empire, or kingdom, exercising political sovereignty. We read in Acts ii, 5, that "there were dwelling at Jerusalem Jews, devout men, from every nation under heaven;"[1] but the kind of nations intended is explained in verses 9 and 10, where they are designated as Parthians, Medes, Elamites, dwellers in Mesopotamia, in Judæa, Cappadocia, Pontus, Phrygia, Pamphylia, Egypt, Libya, Rome, Crete, and Arabia. They were Jews or Jewish proselytes from these various tribes and provinces, which were all under the general dominion of the Roman empire. Accordingly, when mention is made of wars, rumors of wars, nations and kingdoms rising against one another, we are not to suppose the reference to other than the seditions, tumults, revolts, and bitter conflicts which occurred among these subject nations and kingdoms of the empire. We observe in Acts iv, 27, that Herod and Pontius Pilate are regarded as kings and rulers of the earth, fulfilling the import of a prophetic oracle concerning the rage of nations and peoples against Jehovah and his Anointed (Psalm ii, 1).

Nor should we ignore the tone and qualities of prophetic style in a discourse which assumes to be a prophecy of future events. A rigid literal interpretation of apocalyptic language tends to confusion and endless misunderstandings. We should bear in mind that words and phrases acquire in biblical usage a sort of conventional meaning. So all the synoptic texts contain the Hebraic couplet,

> Nation shall rise against nation,
> And kingdom against kingdom.

But this language is in substance a quotation from Isa. xix, 2: "City shall fight against city; kingdom against kingdom." Compare also the language of the chronicler (2 Chron. xv, 6): "Nation is dashed against nation, and city against city; for God has disturbed them with all affliction." Such language conveys a vivid impression of national tumult and civil strife, and is every way appropriate in the lips of Jesus when referring to the seditious, insurrections, revolts, and sectional wars which immediately preceded the conquest of Jerusalem, and spread famine, pestilence, and desolation through Palestine and adjacent regions.[2] These were but a

---

[1] Hackett observes on this passage: "A phrase of this kind has an aggregate sense, which is the true one, while that deduced from the import of the separate words is a false sense."—*Commentary on the Acts of the Apostles, in loco.*

[2] One has but to read the third and fourth books of Josephus's *Wars of the Jews* to find an appalling record of "wars and rumors of wars," continual revolts and plots of cities incited to rebellion by seditious leaders. Thousands perished in these wars before the siege of Jerusalem began, and the calamities of slaughter, and famine, and all

"beginning of travail-pains" (ἀρχὴ ὠδίνων), for it was the policy of Vespasian "first to overthrow what remained elsewhere, and to leave nothing outside of Jerusalem behind him that might interrupt him in the siege." [1]

In view of these facts it appears like an extravagance of fantasy to assert, as Lange does, that " here all wars are meant down to the end of the world." "The passage combines in one view the whole of the various social, physical, and climatic crises of development in the whole New Testament dispensation." Such bald assertions are destructive of all sober exegesis. Let it be granted that the phrase " beginning of travail-pains" is a designed allusion to the Jewish idea of the חֶבְלֵי הַמָּשִׁיחַ, *travail-pains of the Messiah;* [2] what is there in this thought or in the context to justify the notion that these birth-throes are to last for centuries? What is there in any of these statements about national wars, tumults, and their attendant woes to beget the idea of a long and indefinite period of time? How long must birth-pangs last? It was more than three years from the time when Vespasian marched for the subjugation of the Jews to the capture and ruin of Jerusalem by Titus, a period more than sufficient for all that the words of Jesus imply.

As for the persecutions and trial which the disciples were to undergo, we need no other witness of fulfillment than what is written in the Acts of the Apostles. They were hated, and beaten, and delivered up to councils, and brought before governors and kings, and delivered up to death, and a man's most dreadful foes were sometimes those of his own household. Among the Jewish people there was never a time of more desperate religious zeal and fanaticism than the decade preceding the fall of their great city and temple. The first Christian persecutions came mainly from Jews.

But it has been often affirmed that we have no record of false Christs before the destruction of Jerusalem. Here, however, we must first determine what is meant by "coming in my name." It cannot be supposed that he meant to say that many would come bearing the personal name of "Jesus of Nazareth." Nor does it necessarily mean the use of any one particular name or title. The

---

that makes a desperate conflict terrible, are detailed by the Jewish historian of this period with sickening minuteness.

[1] Josephus, *Wars of the Jews,* book iv, chap. vii, 3.

[2] That is, the agonies which the Jewish people were expected to undergo in the process of transition to the Messianic age. The idea of these *dolores Messiæ* was derived from Hosea xiii, 13, and accords with the figure of the *regeneration* (παλιγγενεσία) as used in Matt. xix, 28. For the great purpose of the Messianic reign is to regenerate the world and make all things new.

receiving little children *in his name* (Mark ix, 37) did not require the employing of a stereotyped formula or a set title. Already had the disciples reported to the Master that they had seen one casting out demons *in his name* (Mark ix, 38). The particular title or formula used was not of importance so long as the authority and power of Christ were assumed. Any impostor, therefore, who, like Simon of Samaria, declared " himself to be some great one," and whom the deluded people followed as " the Power of God which is called Great" (Acts viii, 9, 10), answered to the idea of a false Christ. But we are more naturally to think of one of those deceivers whose ideal of Messiah was that of a political chief who would liberate the people from the yoke of Rome. Josephus relates that after Nero became emperor "the affairs of the Jews grew worse and worse continually ; for the country was filled with robbers and impostors who deluded the multitude." He tells us how these " deceivers persuaded the multitude to follow them into the wilderness, and pretended that they would show wonders and signs that should be performed by the providence of God." He mentions an Egyptian who proclaimed himself a prophet, "and advised the multitude of the common people to go along with him to the Mount of Olives, and said that he would there show them how, at his command, the walls of Jerusalem would fall down."[1] Such a pretender, or one like Theudas (Acts v, 36), or Simon the sorcerer (Acts viii, 9), or Dositheus, or Menander, sufficiently fulfills the import of all that Jesus said about the coming of deceivers in his name " saying, I am."[2] But while we refer to these as illustrative examples we are not to point to this and that particular individual and say, " Here was the word of Christ literally fulfilled." We look for no such literal correspondencies. Such minuteness in prediction savors more of the nature of fortune-telling than of biblical prophecy. It is quite enough to show that the spirit and scope of Jesus's words were amply satisfied by well-attested facts, and find abundant fulfillment in the numerous impostors who, both before and during the Jewish war, led multitudes astray. " All those are essentially false Messiahs," says Lange, " who would assume the place which belongs to Christ in the kingdom of God. It includes,

---

[1] *Antiquities of the Jews*, book xx, chap. viii, 5 and 6. Comp. also *Wars of the Jews*, book ii, chap. xiii, 4 and 5. This Egyptian pretender is doubtless identical with the one referred to in Acts xxi, 38.

[2] It is to be noted that only Matthew (xxiv, 5) adds the words *the Christ*. Mark and Luke have simply the more indefinite *I am*, leaving us to supply from the context the idea of a deceitful pretender to divine authority. Any such pretender, whether he expressly call himself *the Christ* or not, lays claim to the same great power.

therefore, the enthusiasts who before the destruction of Jerusalem appeared as seducers of the people." [1]

But the statement which seems to many impossible to reconcile with the time-limit of this prophecy is that "the gospel must first be preached unto all the nations." The language of Matthew is: "This gospel of the kingdom shall be preached in the whole world (ἐν ὅλῃ τῇ οἰκουμένῃ) for a testimony unto all the nations; and then shall the end come." No corresponding statement appears in Luke, but its absence there cannot be fairly construed into an argument against its genuineness. Nor are the different forms of expression which appear in the texts of Matthew and Mark any sufficient reason for rejecting the statement, for they convey essentially the same idea and assure the disciples that the end shall not come until this preaching of the Gospel is accomplished. Mark makes the strong statement that the Gospel must (δεῖ) first be preached.

Two questions now arise : (1) What is the real import of these words? and (2) wherein lay the necessity for such preaching before the end? On both these questions opinions seem to vary. Alford sees in the language of Matthew's gospel an example of "the pregnant meaning of prophecy. The Gospel had been preached through the whole orbis terrarum, and every nation had received its testimony, before the destruction of Jerusalem (see Col. i, 6, 23; 2 Tim. iv, 17). This was necessary not only as regarded the Gentiles, but to give to God's people, the Jews, who were scattered among all these nations, the opportunity of receiving or rejecting the preaching of Christ. But in the wider sense the words imply that the Gospel shall be preached in all the world, literally taken, before the great and final end come. The apostasy of the latter days and the universal dispersion of missions are the two great signs of the end drawing nigh." [2] This exposition accords with this writer's well-known view of a double sense, or two parallel interpretations running through the twenty-fourth chapter of Matthew. But with those who reject such doctrine of a double sense his statements are without weight or value.

It is noticeable, however, that he admits and affirms that the Gospel had been preached through the whole world, and every nation had received its testimony before the destruction of the Jewish capital. This is a most important admission to come from such a source, for it shows that with a strict literalist the language of Jesus is seen, in the light of such statements as Col. i, 6, 23, to have been

---

[1] Commentary on Matthew xxiv, 5.
[2] *Greek Testament*, with notes, etc., *in loco*.

fulfilled before the close of the apostolic age. If this is so, why should anyone insist that it must mean the complete evangelization of the world in the widest sense ?

We maintain that the occasion, scope, and time-limits of this discourse forbid our construing these words into such absolute and universal import. For surely, if such a preaching of the Gospel of the kingdom as will effect the thorough Christianizing of the world as now known to us was intended by Jesus, the end was very far off from the apostolic times, and it is utterly inexplicable how, with any such thought in mind, our Lord could have said with the emphatic assurance which all the synoptists record, "This generation shall not pass away till all these things be accomplished." How much more reasonable and self-consistent to interpret the words in accordance with that more limited sense in which the New Testament writers use the terms *world* and *nations!* According to Luke ii, 1, "all the world" (οἰκουμένη) was enrolled by a decree of Augustus. In Acts xi, 28, mention is made of a great famine "over all the world; which came to pass in the days of Claudius." Paul and Silas were spoken of as those who had "turned the world upside down" (Acts xvii, 6), and Paul was accused as "a pest, and a mover of insurrections among all the Jews throughout the world" (Acts xxiv, 5). In all these passages the same word οἰκουμένη, *inhabited earth*, is employed. In 2 Tim. iv, 17, we read : "The Lord stood by me and gave me power, that through me the preaching might be fully proclaimed, and that all the nations might hear." In Col. i, 5, 6, the apostle speaks of "the word of the truth of the Gospel which is come unto you; even as it is also in all the world (ἐν παντὶ τῷ κόσμῳ), bearing fruit and increasing, according as it also does in you ;" and in verse 23 of the same chapter he says that the Gospel "was preached in all creation under the heaven" (ἐν πάσῃ κτίσει τῇ ὑπὸ τὸν οὐρανόν). Here are terms more comprehensive in their import than those employed by Jesus, and yet they are used in reference to the preaching of the Gospel as it had already been proclaimed in the apostolic times.

In view of these facts it seems like the persistent blindness of a dogmatic bias to insist that the "preaching of the gospel in all the world for a testimony to the nations" must needs include all the missionary operations of the Church during the Christian centuries. According to Matt. x, 23, as we have already noticed, Jesus declared to his disciples when he gave them their apostolic commission, "Ye shall not have finished the cities of Israel until the Son of man be come." Not even the cities and peoples of Palestine would be *completely evangelized* before the coming of Christ; much less may we suppose that all the other nations and regions of the world-empire of Rome must be *converted to Christianity* within the same period. The most natural and obvious meaning of our Lord's language is that during the latter days of the pre-Messianic era, and before the end of that age, the new Gospel must be proclaimed and witnessed among all the nations of what was commonly called "the inhabited earth" (ἡ οἰκουμένη). This "world" did not signify to Galilean fishermen or to learned Jewish rabbis what it does to a modern reader, familiar every day with telegraphic communications from remote continents and islands. Nor does Paul's comprehensive phrase, "all creation under heaven," require us to interpret it with any more rigid literalism than we do the statement at the close of John's gospel, that "the world itself would not contain the books that should be written." Such expressions are usually understood to contain an element of hyperbole and are common in all the languages of men. They are also of the nature of synecdoche, in which the whole is put for a part.

Such being the meaning of the words in New Testament usage, it remains for us to show the necessity of such a preaching of the Gospel before the end of the Jewish age. According to Mark xiii, 10, it was *necessary* (δεῖ) for the Gospel to be thus preached before the end, and we may reasonably look in such necessity for some intimation touching the divine order of the world. In the passing away of an old order and the introduction of a new we do not find a sudden and unlooked-for transition. God does not remove a system that has had a long career of usefulness until he has effectually provided and prepared the way for something better. Jesus had declared to the representatives of the Jewish people "that the kingdom of God should be taken from them, and be given to a nation bringing forth the fruits thereof" (Matt. xxi, 43). But the way must be duly made ready for such an historic change. It was necessary that the Gospel of Christ and the new teachings of his kingdom should be spread abroad beyond Jerusalem, and be immovably established in the civilized world, before the old system and worship which centered in the temple of Judaism were utterly broken down. The great apostle to the nations found Judaism an obstacle to the Gospel which he preached. Its persistent tendency was to "pervert the gospel of Chrsit" (Gal. i, 7); to teach that circumcision was essential to salvation (Acts xv, 1; Gal. v, 2); to "observe days, and months, and seasons, and years" (Gal. iv, 10; Rom. xiv, 5); to make much of meats, and drinks, and feast days, and new moons, and sabbaths (Col. ii, 16). The old temple-cultus which had begotten, and was striving to perpetuate, such external legalism became thus an old, useless, decaying thing, and was "nigh unto vanishing away" (Heb. viii, 13). Paul spoke of it as "the Jerusalem that now is, in bondage with her children, and bearing children unto bondage" (Gal. iv, 24, 25). He proclaimed in all the world that "the kingdom of God is not a matter of eating and drinking, but righteousness and peace and joy in the Holy Spirit" (Rom. xiv, 17).

It required the period of a generation for the thorough propaga- tion and establishment of this new gospel of the kingdom of God. Therefore before the temple be overthrown, so that "stone shall not be left upon stone," a new and better ideal of worship must first be established. The preaching of such good news was to serve "for a testimony unto all the nations," a witness (μαρτύριον) and evi- dence that a new light had come into the world. To use the lan- guage of the Epistle to the Hebrews, it was necessary that in all the world men should "taste the powers of the age to come," and receive the doctrines and life of "a kingdom that cannot be shaken," before the final overthrow and removal of a system which had already been fundamentally shaken and was tottering to its fall (Heb. vi, 5; xii, 28).

II.

In the second section of our analysis (see p. 226) there is little that calls for extended discussion. Here we are told of various signs by which the disciples might know when the end was close at hand. All that is mentioned hitherto might take place some time before the end; some of the things would require a considerable period; wars and rumors of wars and national tumults would occur in various places a considerable time before there would be occasion for special alarm for dwellers in Jerusalem; but when the invading armies began to make their appearance at the city and compass it about the great tribulation would begin, and those who would es- cape the calamities of those days must flee to the mountains with the utmost haste.

That what is here written refers to the siege of Jerusalem, and can by no sound principles of interpretation be otherwise explained, is quite generally conceded. The only questions of note are those concerning the meaning of several peculiar expressions.

(1) "The abomination of desolation" is a phrase appropriated from the Septuagint of Dan. xii, 11 (comp. Dan. viii, 13; ix, 27, and xi, 31), and refers there to the desolation and profanation of the sanctuary by Antiochus Epiphanes. There is no need to un- derstand it as referring to any particular *sign* or *symbol*, as the Roman eagles, or an imperial statue, or the sacrilege of the zealots

inside the temple. It is simply an appropriate prophetic phrase employed to denote here in a general way the same idea that it conveys in the Book of Daniel, namely, a presence of something abominable to Jewish thought. Its "standing in a holy place" (Matthew), or "where it ought not " (Mark), is to be understood in accord with the same general thought. Not the site of the temple only, but the mountains about Jerusalem, and indeed the whole land of Israel (comp. Zech. ii, 12), was to the Jew a holy place. When, therefore, the Roman armies began to encamp about Jerusalem, the abominable desolator occupied the places hallowed by the associations of more than a thousand years. The corresponding passage in Luke's gospel, " When ye see Jerusalem compassed with armies," is a confirmation of this exposition.[1]

(2) The admonition to flee to the mountains, and make such haste that one should not even go down from the housetop to take any of his goods, is to be interpreted as the emotional language of a prophetic oracle. Such language is never to be pressed into literal significance. The general thought is clear and impressive. They were to waste no time in making their escape from the doomed city. Fleeing for refuge to the mountains is an expression to be read in the light of such scriptures as Gen. xix, 17, and Zech. xiv, 5.

(3) The great tribulation and distress (Matthew and Mark, $\vartheta\lambda\tilde{\iota}\psi\iota\varsigma$, Luke, $\dot{\alpha}\nu\dot{\alpha}\gamma\kappa\eta\ \mu\epsilon\gamma\dot{\alpha}\lambda\eta$) are evidently the sufferings which must needs accompany a prolonged and bitter siege. The language of the first two gospels is appropriated in substance from Dan. xii, 1, and may be regarded as hyperbolical; but it is no more extravagant than that of the Jewish historian Josephus, who says that " the multitude of those that perished exceeded all the destructions which either men or God ever brought upon the world," and describes the horrors of famine and pestilence and suffering within the city in most appalling detail.[2]

(4) The mention of false Christs and impostors, in this section as in the preceding, is to be explained as we have already shown above. The repetition serves to make it emphatic that even up to the last such false pretenders would keep putting themselves forward, to deceive if possible the elect.

---

[1] These words of Luke may be understood as a substitution by the writer of what he regarded as the real meaning of the enigmatic prophetic words found in the Logia ; and they suggest that this third gospel was written after the destruction of Jerusalem ; while the parenthetic words of Mark and Matthew (" Let him that readeth understand ") imply that those gospels were written before this prophecy was fulfilled, and the parenthesis itself was not a part of the Lord's discourse, but inserted by the evangelists.

[2] See his *Wars of the Jews*, book vi, chap. ix, 3, 4.

(5) Luke's gospel has a passage in this connection which has no parallel in the synoptists : " There shall be great distress upon the land, and wrath to this people; and they shall fall by the edge of the sword, and shall be led captive into all the nations, and Jerusalem shall be trodden down by nations until times of nations be fulfilled." The only part of this which calls for discussion here is the phrase *times of nations* (καιροὶ ἐϑνῶν). We notice the absence of the article from the words. It is not *the times of the nations*, as if some definite and well-understood period or fact were referred to. And there is nothing in the text or context to determine absolutely the precise meaning of the words. The idea of " opportunities of grace allotted to the Gentiles " which some have found in Rom. xi, 25, and imported into this passage of Luke, has no relevancy to the context. "Times of the nations" are here much more naturally understood of times allotted to the nations for the treading down of the city, and thus executing the divine judgment of which the passage speaks. The closest parallel to this is seen in Rev. xi, 2, where the outer court of the temple is said to have been "given to the nations; and the holy city shall they tread under foot forty-two months." These καιροί are, accordingly, best understood as times of judgment upon Jerusalem,[1] not times of salvation for the nations. But who shall say how long a period these "times" are to cover ?

No answer to this last question can afford to overlook what is written in verse 22, a passage also peculiar to Luke: "For days of vengeance these are for the fulfilling of all things which are written." The words ἡμέραι ἐκδικήσεως, *days of vengeance*, are appropriated from the Septuagint of Hosea ix, 7, which reads: "The days of vengeance are come, the days of thy recompense are come; and Israel shall be afflicted as the prophet who has gone mad, a man who is carried away in spirit. Because of the multitude of thy iniquities thy madness (μανία) was made full." The Hebrew text of this passage reads: "The days of visitation are come, the days of recompense are come; Israel shall know; a fool is the prophet, the man of the spirit is mad; because of the abundance of thy iniquity, and great is the enmity." We cite the prophecy thus fully because of its obvious analogy with the context and scope of the passage in Luke where its leading words are appropriated. In Hosea and in Luke the " days of vengeance " are days of divine penal visitation on Israel; days of which prophets have spoken and written; days when the prophets themselves are gone mad and unworthy of trust; and the iniquities of the people have become so great and multitu-

---

[1] This is the view of Bengel, Meyer, and Van Oosterzee.

dinous that the nation is ripe for judgment. Now the "times" which are allotted the nations for executing judgment upon the city and people whose iniquities are full may be either an indefinitely long period or one short, sharp, and decisive. There is nothing in our gospels to determine this point. If we assume with Bengel that these times of judgment include the long period during which "Jerusalem has already been trodden down by the Romans, the Persians, the Saracens, the Franks, and the Turks," we must nevertheless acknowledge that the *terminus a quo* of this long-continued judgment dates from the overthrow of the city by the Romans. It would not in the least conflict with the definite time-limits of this prophecy to say that the desolation of the city would continue centuries after its fall. Such an incidental mention of continuous judgment cannot be fairly said to conflict with the emphatic assurance that all these things shall be accomplished before the passing away of this generation. Who would think of raising such a difficulty in the exposition of Isa. xiii, 20–22, where the perpetual desolation of Babylon is affirmed in immediate connection with the announcement that the day of her terrible judgment is at hand? "It shall never be inhabited," says the prophet; "wild beasts of the desert shall lie there, wolves shall cry in their castles, and jackals in the palaces; and her time is near to come, and her days shall not be prolonged." Surely, the positive declaration of the nearness of the catastrophe is not in the slightest degree invalidated by the statement that the doomed city will remain a ruin, or be for a long time trodden down by nations, or by wild beasts.

It may, however, be fairly claimed that the indefinite phrase "times of nations" is, like so much else in this part of the discourse, a prophetic term of limited significance. This is favored by the suggestions of the parallel passage already cited from Rev. xi, 2. The forty-two months there mentioned for the treading down of the holy city are a mystic designation, and seem to be an equivalent of the twelve hundred and sixty days mentioned immediately afterward (verse 3). The same period is again mentioned in Rev. xii, 6, and yet in verse 14 of the same chapter is apparently an equivalent of the prophetic phrase " a time ($\kappa\alpha\iota\rho\acute{o}\varsigma$), and times, and half a time." The phrase is taken from Dan. vii, 25 ; xii, 7. In every one of these texts it designates a period of suffering and disaster. In Daniel the obvious allusion is to the period of about three and a half years during which Antiochus Epiphanes despoiled the city and temple.[1] Why should it mean more here than a correspond-

---

[1] See the exposition of these words of Daniel on page 192 of this volume.

ingly short period during which Jerusalem was encompassed with armies, and "the abomination of desolation" remained standing and triumphing "in a holy place?"

III.

The third section of this prophecy consists of an apocalyptic picture of the end. It is set in the form of Hebrew parallelism, and, according to Mark, reads as follows:

> But in those days, after that tribulation,
> The sun shall be darkened, and the moon shall not give her light,
> And the stars shall be out of the heaven falling,
> And the powers which are in the heavens shall be shaken.
> And then shall they see the Son of man coming in the clouds with great power and glory.
> And then shall he send forth the angels,
> And shall gather his elect from the four winds,
> From the extremity of earth to the extremity of heaven.

The text of Matthew is substantially the same, but presents some verbal differences, which it is well to note:

> But immediately after the tribulation of those days,
> The sun shall be darkened, and the moon shall not give her light,
> And the stars shall fall from the heaven,
> And the powers of the heavens shall be shaken;
> And then shall appear the sign of the Son of man in heaven;
> And then shall all the tribes of the land mourn,
> And they shall see the Son of man coming on the clouds of heaven with power and great glory.
> And he shall send forth his angels with a great trumpet,
> And they shall gather his elect from the four winds,
> From the extremities of the heavens unto their extremities.

The corresponding passage in Luke has such peculiarities of its own that we defer our comments on it until after we have indicated what we regard as the true interpretation of the texts of the first two gospels. Our view of these apocalyptic sayings may be best set forth in a series of propositions, which seem to us so evident as scarcely to call for extended argument.

(1) The texts of Mark and Matthew are so closely parallel that we may safely accept them as in substance a portion of the best attested sayings of Jesus. The differences of phraseology are too slight to involve any important difference in the meaning.

(2) The language is appropriated in the main from the books of Isaiah and Daniel, but also from other prophets. The following passages are particularly in point:

For the stars of heaven and their constellations shall not shed forth their light;
Dark is the sun in his going forth,
And the moon shall not cause her light to shine (Isa. xiii, 10).

And all the host of the heavens shall be melted,
And the heavens shall be rolled together as a scroll,
And all their host shall fall,
As falls a leaf from the vine,
And as a fallen fig from the fig tree (Isa. xxxiv, 4).[1]

I was gazing in the visions of the night,
And behold, with the clouds of the heavens,
One like a son of man was coming,
And to the Ancient of days he approached,
And into his presence they brought him.
And to him was given dominion, and glory, and a kingdom;
And all the nations, and peoples, and tongues shall serve him (Dan. vii, 13, 14).

In that day great shall be the mourning in Jerusalem,
And the land shall mourn, families, families alone.
All the families [or tribes] that are left (Zech. xii, 11–14).

In that day there shall be a blowing with a great trumpet,
And they that are perishing in the land of Asshur shall come,
And those that are dispersed in the land of Egypt,
And they shall worship Jehovah in the holy mountain (Isa. xxvii, 13).

If thy dispersion be from extremity of the heaven to extremity of the heaven,
Thence shall the Lord thy God gather thee (Sept. of Deut. xxx, 4).

For from the four winds of the heaven will I gather you,
Saith the Lord (Sept. of Zech. ii, 6).

From these quotations it is apparent that there is scarcely an expression employed in Matthew and Luke which has not been taken from the Old Testament Scriptures.

(3) Such apocalyptic forms of speech are not to be assumed to convey in the New Testament a meaning different from that which they bear in the Hebrew Scriptures. They are part and parcel of the genius of prophetic language. The language of Isa. xiii, 10, is used in a prophecy of the overthrow of Babylon. That of Isa. xxxiv, 4, refers to the desolation of Edom. The ideal of "the Son of man coming in the clouds" is taken from a prophecy of the Messianic kingdom, which kingdom, as depicted in Dan. vii, 13, 14, is no other than the one symbolized in the same book by a stone cut out of the mountain (Dan. ii, 34, 35). It is the same kingdom of heaven which Jesus likened to a grain of mustard seed and to

---

[1] One should compare also the analogous language of Isa. xix, 1; xxiv, 23; Ezek. xxxii, 7, 8; Joel ii, 31; iii, 15; Micah i, 3, 4. Compare also our chapter on the apocalyptic elements in Hebrew song, pages 24–37.

the working of leaven in the meal (Matt. xiii, 31–33). The other citations we have given above show with equal clearness how both Jesus and his disciples were wont to express themselves in language which must have been very familiar to those who from childhood heard the law and the prophets "read in their synagogues every Sabbath" (Acts xiii, 27 ; xv, 21). A strictly literal interpretation of such pictorial modes of thought leads only to absurdity. Their import must be studied in the light of the numerous parallels in the Old Testament writers, which have been extensively presented in the foregoing part of this volume. But with what show of reason, or on what principle of "interpreting Scripture by Scripture," can it be maintained that the language of Isaiah, and Joel, and Daniel, allowed by all the best exegetes to be metaphorical when employed in the Hebrew Scriptures, must be literally understood when appropriated by Jesus or his apostles?

We sometimes, indeed, meet with a disputant who attempts to evade the force of the above question by the plea that if we interpret one part of Jesus's discourse literally we are bound in consistency to treat the entire prophecy in the same way. So, on the other hand, it is urged that if Matt. xxiv, 29–31, for example, be explained metaphorically, we must carry the same principle through all the rest of the chapter ; and if the words *sun, moon,* and *heavens* in verse 29 are to be taken figuratively, so should the words *Judœa,* and *mountains,* and *housetop,* and *field* in other parts of the chapter be explained metaphorically! It is difficult to understand how such a superficial plea can be seriously put forward by one who has made a careful study of the Hebrew prophets. Every one of the Old Testament examples which we have cited above stands connected, like these apocalyptic sayings of Jesus, with other statements which all readers and expositors have understood literally. The most prosaic writer may at times express himself through a whole series of sentences in figurative terms, and incorporate the extended metaphor in the midst of a plain narrative of facts. We have shown in previous pages how the Hebrew historians interweave poetic embellishment into their vivid descriptions, and, when the subject itself becomes grand and sublime, the language naturally rises into the style of poetic parallelism with its various properties of form and figure.[1] No set of mechanical rules can be drawn up for distinguishing between the language of prose and of poetry. The reader's common sense, united with a well-trained critical judgment, must needs be the court of final appeal in every case. It

---

[1] See especially the illustrations adduced in chap. ii, and pages 27–30.

would be sheer folly to attempt the construction of a vocabulary of prophetic metaphors for use in biblical interpretation.

(4) Our fourth and concluding proposition is that this apocalyptic passage is a sublime symbolic picture of the crisis of ages in transition from the Old Testament dispensation to the Christian era. The word-picture must be taken as a whole, and allowed to convey its grand total impression. The attempt, in a single passage like Mark xiii, 24, 25, to take each metaphor separately and give it a distinct application, ruins the whole picture. To say, with some of the older expositors,[1] that the heavens represent the Jewish theocracy, the sun is its religion, and the moon its civil government, while the stars that fall from this heaven are the judges and teachers, is to misapprehend the real nature of the aggregate impression designed to be made. As well might one take a rainbow into pieces, analyze each separate color, and point out its distinct significance, with the idea of thereby elucidating the real meaning of the sign set in the cloud as a token of God's covenant with Noah. The picture of a collapsing universe symbolizes the one simple but sublime thought of supernatural interposition in the affairs of the world, involving remarkable revolution and change. The element of time does not at all appear in the picture. So the Son of man coming on the clouds means here just what it means in Daniel's vision. It is an apocalyptic concept of the Messiah, as King of heaven and earth, executing divine judgment and entering with his people upon the possession and dominion of the kingdoms of the world. Here again the element of time does not enter, except it be the associated thought of Daniel's prophecy that "his dominion is an everlasting dominion" (Dan. vii, 14). It is the same coming of the Son of man in his kingdom which is referred to in Matt. xvi, 27, 28, the inception of which was to occur before some of those who heard these words of Jesus should taste of death. The mourning of all the tribes of the land is the universal wail and lamentation of Judaism over its national overthrow. In the fall of their city and temple the priests, scribes, and elders saw "the Son of man sitting at the right hand of power" (Matt. xxvi, 64), and thus it was made manifest to all who read prophecy aright that "Jesus the Galilæan" had conquered.[2] The gathering of Christ's elect

---

[1] Compare Lightfoot, *Horæ Hebraicæ in Evangelium Matthæi*, *in loco*.

[2] "The plain meaning of this is," says Dr. Adam Clarke, "that the destruction of Jerusalem will be such a remarkable instance of divine vengeance, such a signal manifestation of Christ's power and glory, that all the Jewish tribes shall mourn, and many will, in consequence of this manifestation of God, be led to acknowledge Christ and his religion."—*Commentary, in loco.*

from the four winds is the true fulfillment of numerous prophecies which promise the chosen people that they shall be gathered out of all lands and established forever in the mountain of God (comp. Amos ix, 14, 15 ; Jer. xxiii, 5–8 ; xxxii, 37–40 ; Ezek. xxxvii, 21–28). The time and manner of this universal ingathering of the elect ones cannot be determined from the language of any of these prophecies. As well might one presume to determine from Jesus's words in John xii, 32, where, when, and in what manner, when the Christ is " lifted up out of the earth," he will draw all men unto himself. The point made emphatic, in the eschatological discourse of Jesus, is that all the things contemplated in the apocalyptic symbolism employed to depict his coming and reign would follow " immediately after the tribulation of those days " (Matt. xxiv, 29) ; or, as Mark has it, " in those days, after that tribulation." That is, the coming of the kingdom of the Son of man is coincident with the overthrow of Judaism and its temple, and follows immediately in those very days.[1]

Whatever in this picture necessarily pertains to the continuous administration of the kingdom on the earth must of course be permanent, and continue as long as the nature and purpose of each work requires. When, therefore, it is affirmed that " this generation shall not pass away until all these things be accomplished," no one supposes that the kingdom and the power and the glory of the Son of man are to terminate with that generation. The kingdom itself is to endure for ages of ages. It is to increase like the stone cut from the mountain, which itself " became a great mountain and filled the whole earth." It is to grow and operate like the mustard seed and the leaven until it accomplish its heavenly purpose among men. The entire New Testament teaching concerning the kingdom of Christ contemplates a long period, and the abolishing of all opposing authority and power ; " for he must reign till he hath put all his enemies under his feet " (1 Cor. xv, 25). The overthrow of Jerusalem was one of the first triumphs of the Messiah's reign, and a sign that he was truly " seated at the right hand of power."

The corresponding passage in Luke's gospel (xxi, 25–28) is noticeable for its different forms of expression, not for anything that appears to be of different meaning. The language is as follows:

---

[1] Some expositors fall into the error of *identifying* the coming of the Son of man with the destruction of Jerusalem. These events are rather to be spoken of as coincident, in that the Messianic reign is conceived as following immediately after the tribulation of those days. The overthrow of Jerusalem was only one act of judgment of the King of glory, and should be so distinguished.

And there shall be signs in sun and moon and stars,
And upon the earth distress of nations,
In perplexity at the sound of sea and billows;
Men expiring from fear and expectation of the things which are coming on the world;
For the powers of the heavens shall be shaken.
And then shall they see the Son of man coming in a cloud with power and great glory.
But when these things begin to come to pass,
Look up and lift up your heads;
Because your redemption draweth nigh.

These lines are but a different version of the oracle as originally uttered by our Lord. They may be regarded as an example of Luke's peculiar manner of composition, and, like the parallels in Mark and Matthew, are an apocalyptic picture of the crisis of the pre-Messianic age. Let it be particularly noticed that the writer contemplates it as something which the contemporaries of Jesus might recognize, and lift up their heads in exultant expectation of their speedy redemption. There is nothing whatever that implies an event to be looked for in a distant age. The things of which he spoke were to "begin to come to pass" in the near future. But how long the Son of man would reign, "sitting at the right hand of power," before his enemies would all be put under his feet; how the Gospel would be preached in the world all through the period of his kingdom in the world; and how at other times and seasons the Son of man would be seen coming in his kingdom and coming in glory—these are matters on which Jesus spoke no definite word on that occasion.

IV.

The fourth section consists of counsel and warning, and calls for no special comment here. Luke has a part of these admonitions in another connection, and cites the example of Lot and Sodom as an illustration of the manner "it shall be in the day the Son of man is revealed" (Luke xvii, 30). But whether uttered on this occasion or some other, they have obvious reference to the same subject, and may have been repeated on many occasions. Three things, however, in this concluding section, it is of prime importance to note:

(1) The counsels and admonitions were addressed to the disciples. They, and not men of subsequent generations, were to see the signs by which they might know that he was nigh, even at their doors. What peoples of other lands and future times might see and know is nothing to the purpose in this context.

(2) These counsels, as well as what has gone before in this discourse, are in direct answer to the question of the disciples, WHEN shall these things be, and WHAT SIGN may we look for to indicate

when they are about to be accomplished? In the entire discourse he has uttered no word to inform them that the time is long after their day, and the sign of it something they shall not live to see. On the contrary, he mentioned a number of things which must first take place, and then he designated among other things one notable sign, at sight of which all of them yet left in Judæa should flee in greatest haste to the mountains. So significant and ominous would be "the abomination of desolation standing where it ought not," that the most ancient records attach to the words the parenthetic admonition, "Let him that readeth understand."

(3) But what ought to settle the question of time beyond all controversy is the most emphatic declaration : "This generation shall not pass away until all these things be accomplished." These words are clearly intended to answer the disciples' question, "WHEN shall these things be?" Their meaning is substantially the same as that of Mark ix, 1, and the parallels in Matthew and Luke. The words immediately preceding them show the absurdity of applying them to another generation than that of the apostles : "When YE SEE THESE THINGS coming to pass, KNOW YE that he [or it—'the kingdom of God'—Luke] is nigh, even at the doors. Verily I say unto YOU, This generation[1] shall not pass away," etc.

But not a few expositors presume to nullify the import of these words by affirming that they are glaringly inconsistent with what follows in Mark and Matthew : "But of that day or that hour knoweth no one, not even the angels in heaven, neither the Son, but the Father." It is difficult to understand how any interpreter, uninfluenced by a dogmatic prepossession, can insist on making one of these statements contradict or exclude the other. But it is not difficult to see that, when one has it already settled in his mind that the kingdom of Christ is not yet come, that the "Parousia" is an event yet future, and that "the end of the age" is not the close of the pre-Messianic age, but "the end of the world," such a weight of dogma effectually obliges him to nullify the simple meaning of

---

[1] The various meanings which, under the pressure of a dogmatic exigency, have been put upon the phrase "this generation," must appear in the highest degree absurd to an unbiased critic. It has been explained as meaning the human race (Jerome), the Jewish race (Dorner, Auberlen), and the race of Christian believers (Chrysostom, Lange). But what an insignificant platitude for anyone, and especially Jesus, to say that the human race, or the Jewish race, or Christian people, shall not pass away until all these things come to pass! Who would ever imagine the contrary? Nothing in New Testament exegesis is capable of more convincing proof than that γενεά means the great body of people living at one period—the period of average lifetime. Even in such a passage as Matt. xi, 16, or Luke xvi, 8, the class of persons referred to are conceived as contemporaries.

words as emphatic as Jesus ever spoke.[1] If the language of Mark xiii, 30, and its parallels in Matthew and Luke are to be arbitrarily set aside on such grounds we see not but it is just as proper a procedure to reject the statement of Jesus's ignorance of the day and the hour, which, indeed, does not appear in Luke at all. Why not reject Mark xiii, 32, which has no parallel in Luke, rather than verse 30, which appears in all the synoptic gospels? Such an arbitrary procedure is a two-edged sword which may smite in one direction as well as another.

But we find in these two associate statements of Jesus no inconsistency. The plain and obvious meaning of the two sayings is this: "I most solemnly assure you that all these things will occur before this generation shall have passed away, and I give you these signs by which ye may know when the end is close upon you; but the particular day and hour I do not know myself. Therefore, watch and be ready at every hour." Here is no contradiction of thought or sentiment; no inconsistency whatever. But to assume, as some do, that the day and hour intended may be centuries after that generation had passed away, would seem to be virtually implicating Jesus in a kind of preposterous trifling. For how would it differ from saying in substance: "All these things shall assuredly come to pass in your day, before some of you taste of death; but the day and the hour may be several thousands of years in the future! Watch, therefore, and be ye ready!!"

It is entirely self-consistent and every way rational to affirm positively that a foreseen event will take place inside of fifty years, and yet disclaim knowledge of particular year, month, week, day, and hour.[2] The only motive we can conceive for forcing a different construction upon the two statements is that already intimated above, namely, a belief that the Son of man has not yet come, and, consequently, that his prophecy of the end must be either a failure or else an event yet in the future. We think, on the contrary, that

---

[1] Meyer, who has no dogmatic theory to support, and seeks only the natural meaning of the words, observes: "The affirmation of Matt. xxiv, 34, does not exclude the fact that no one knows the *day and hour* when the second advent, with its accompanying phenomena, is to take place. It is to occur during the *lifetime of the generation then existing*, but no one knows on what *day* or at what *hour* within the period thus indicated."—*Critical and Exegetical Handbook on Matthew, in loco.*

[2] "To have specified the day and the hour," says Russell, "to have said, 'In the seven and thirtieth year, in the sixth month and the eighth day of the month, the city shall be taken and the temple burnt with fire,' would not only have been inconsistent with the manner of prophecy, but would have taken away one of the strongest inducements to constant watchfulness and prayer—the uncertainty of the precise time."— *The Parousia*, p. 90.

we have shown by a valid exegesis that the coming of the kingdom of Christ and the end of the pre-Messianic age were coincident with the overthrow of the Jewish temple at Jerusalem.

It remains to notice a few things peculiar to Matthew's report of this discourse of Jesus. According to his gospel the form of the disciples' question was, "When shall these things be, and what shall be the sign of thy coming (παρουσία) and of the consummation of the age (συντελεία τοῦ αἰῶνος)?" They seem to have already inferred or assumed that his coming and the consummation of the age would be connected in some way with the desolation of the temple. The closing words of chap. xxiii were of a nature to imply all this.[1] If it were not to be, and Jesus knew it, it is inconceivable that he should have confirmed them in such a belief as the language of Matt. xxiv was certainly adapted to do. What significance, then, are we to attach to the words *coming*, and *consummation of the age*?

The word παρουσία, commonly translated *coming*, is so constantly associated, in current dogmatics, with the ultimate goal of human history, that ordinary readers lose sight of its simple meaning in New Testament usage. The word means *presence* as opposed to *absence*. For example, we read in Phil. ii, 12, "So then, my beloved, even as ye have always obeyed, not as in my presence (ἐν τῇ παρουσίᾳ μου) only, but now much more in my absence (ἐν τῇ ἀπουσίᾳ μου), work out your own salvation with fear and trembling." But as the personal presence of anyone implies a previous coming, so this word is not improperly rendered *coming* in many passages, and the verb ἔρχομαι, to *come*, is often employed to denote the appearance and kingdom of Christ.[2] But to assume that this coming or presence of Christ must needs be spectacular in any physical sense, a literal display of his person in the atmosphere of this earth, is to involve the doctrine in great confusion. Why must the coming of the Son of man on the clouds to execute judgment on that generation be understood or explained in any other way than we explain Jehovah's "riding upon a swift cloud," and coming to execute judgment on Egypt, as prophesied in Isa. xix, 1? Whatever the real nature of the *parousia*, as contemplated in this prophetic discourse, our Lord unmistakably associates it with

---

[1] "The disciples assume as a matter of course," says Meyer, "that immediately after the destruction in question the Lord will appear, in accordance with what is said in xxiii, 39, for the purpose of setting up his kingdom, and that with this the current (the pre-Messianic) era of the world's history will come to an end."—*Critical and Exegetical Handbook on Matthew, in loco.*

[2] Comp. Matt. xvi, 27, 28 ; xxiv, 30; xxv, 31; John xiv, 3; Rev. i, 7; xxii, 7.

the destruction of the temple and city, which he represents as the signal termination of the pre-Messianic age. The coming on clouds, the darkening of the heavens, the collapse of elements, are, as we have shown above, familiar forms of apocalyptic language, appropriated from the Hebrew prophets.[1]

That other expression in Matthew, "the consummation of the age," is a phrase that has been much abused and widely misunderstood. The common translation, "end of the world," has been a delusion to many readers of the English Bible. It has helped to perpetuate the unscriptural notion that the coming and kingdom of Christ are not facts of the past, present, and future, but of the future only. The fundamental and distinguishing doctrine of all branches of the "Adventists," so-called, is that the coming of the Son of man to set up his kingdom in this world is solely an event of the future. *Christ has as yet no kingdom among men!* Even the parables of our Lord, illustrative of the spiritual character of the kingdom, are forced to harmonize with the concept of a spectacular advent and a political organization.[2] Those who maintain the doctrine, and, indeed, not a few who oppose it, fall into error and inconsistency by failing to apprehend the true meaning of the phrase "the end of the age."

For, first of all, they do not determine clearly what age (αἰών) is contemplated in such a text as Matt. xxiv, 3. They quite generally assume that the period of the Gospel dispensation is meant. But nothing is more familiar in the Jewish terminology of our Lord's time than the current phrases עוֹלָם הַזֶּה and עוֹלָם הַבָּא, *this age* and *the age to come.* The period which preceded the coming of the Messiah

---

[1] Acts i, 11, is often cited to show that Christ's coming must needs be spectacular, "*in like manner* as ye beheld him going into the heaven." But (1) in the only other three places where ὃν τρόπον, *what manner*, occurs, it points to a general concept rather than the particular form of its actuality. Thus, in Acts vii, 28, it is not some particular manner in which Moses killed the Egyptian that is notable, but rather the certain fact of it. In 2 Tim. iii, 8, it is likewise the fact of strenuous opposition rather than the special manner in which Jannes and Jambres withstood Moses. And in Matt. xxiii, 37, and Luke xiii, 34, it is the general thought of protection rather than the visible manner of a mother bird that is intended. Again (2), if Jesus did not come in that generation, and immediately after the great tribulation that attended the fall of Jerusalem, his words in Matt. xvi, 27, 28, xxiv, 29, and parallel passages are in the highest degree misleading. (3) To make the one statement of the angel in Acts i, 11, override all the sayings of Jesus on the same subject and control their meaning is a very one-sided method of biblical interpretation. But all the angel's words necessarily mean is that as Jesus has ascended into heaven so he will come from heaven And this main thought agrees with the language of Jesus and the prophets.

[2] See, for example, the excursus of Dr. E. R. Craven on *the Basileia* in the American edition of Lange's Commentary on the Revelation of John, pp. 93–100.

was spoken of as *this age;* that which followed his coming was
the age to come.[1] It is not important to consider what various and
often contradictory notions the rabbins associated with *the age to
come.* Their notions were as various as those concerning the character of the Messiah himself. But by *this age* they meant and
could mean nothing else than the current period in which they were
living, the then present age. The question of the disciples, as recorded, could therefore only refer to the pre-Messianic age, and its
consummation was, as we have seen, associated in their thought
with the overthrow of the temple. But even were it admitted that
their notion of "the consummation of the age" was erroneous, the
teaching of Jesus was emphatic beyond all rational question that
that generation should not pass away before all those things of
which they inquired should be fulfilled.

The age to come, the Messianic time, would accordingly be the
period that would follow immediately after the termination of the
pre-Messianic age. That time had not yet come when Jesus spoke.
According to the whole trend of New Testament teaching that age
and the Messianic kingdom were *near* or *at hand.* Christ's ministry
fell in the last days of an αἰών. The gospel of his kingdom must
be firmly established in the world before the end of that age. So
we read, in Heb. ix, 26: "Now, once, at the end of the ages (ἐπὶ
συντελείᾳ τῶν αἰώνων) hath he been manifested to put away sin by
the sacrifice of himself." Also in Heb. i, 1, it is written: "God . . .
hath at the last of these days spoken unto us in his Son." Similarly
Peter (1 Pet. i, 20) speaks of Christ as "foreknown before the foundation of the world, but manifested at the end of the times for
your sake." Paul, too, speaks of himself as living near the consummation of an age: "These things happened unto them by way of
example; and they were written for our admonition upon whom
the ends of the ages are come" (1 Cor. x, 11). The ministry both
of Jesus and his disciples must, therefore, be recognized as occurring in the latter days of an αἰών, or near the end of the pre-Messianic age. The New Testament writers, as well as Jesus, are clear
on this point. They never represent themselves as already entered
upon the first days, or the beginning of the age, but rather in the
last days.

If, now, we ask with the disciples, WHEN shall these things be?
or at what point are we to recognize the end of the pre-Messianic
age? we are to find the answer in the eschatological discourse of

---

[1] See Schürer, *History of Jewish People in the Time of Jesus Christ*, English translation, vol. ii, p. 177; Schoettgen, *Horæ Hebraicæ*, i, 1153–1158.

Jesus, and at some point before that generation passed away. "The ends of the ages" may have a definite point of contact and transition from one age to another. The coming age may, like the morning twilight, cast its beams into the foregoing night, and so the preceding age may partake in its last days of many things which belong to the age to come.[1] But such facts do not affect the question of the signal crisis which may conspicuously mark the end of one age and the opening of another. Was there such a crisis between the Jewish and Christian dispensations, that we can point to it and say, "That was preeminently and conspicuously an event which marked an epoch in the history of both Judaism and Christianity?"

Some writers find such a crisis or end in the crucifixion of Jesus, and at the moment when he said, "It is finished" ($\tau\epsilon\tau\acute{\epsilon}\lambda\epsilon\sigma\tau\alpha\iota$). Others say it was at the resurrection; some few designate the ascension; but many have taught that the outpouring of the Spirit on the day of Pentecost was the coming of Christ in his kingdom, the end of the old and the beginning of the new age. To all of these theories there are two insuperable objections: (1) They are irreconcilable with the statement of Jesus that the Gospel must first be preached "in all the habitable earth" ($o\grave{\iota}\kappa o\nu\mu\acute{\epsilon}\nu\eta$), and (2), long after the day of Pentecost, the apostles speak of their work as taking place in the last days, or near the end of the age.

Is it not strange that any careful student of our Lord's teaching should fail to understand his answer to this very question? The disciples asked, definitely, WHEN shall it be? And Jesus proceeded to foretell a variety of things which they would live to see— all preliminary to the end. He foretold the horrors of the siege of Jerusalem, and an intelligible sign by which they might know the imminence of the final catastrophe of Judaism. And having told them of all these things, and of his own coming in the clouds and its glorious significance, he added: "When ye see these things coming to pass, know that it is nigh, at the door. Verily I say unto you, this generation shall not pass away until all these things be accomplished." The ruin of the temple was, accordingly, the crisis which marked the end of the pre-Messianic age.

---

[1] And so we should note that many things which Jesus spoke by way of counsel and admonition are as applicable to one period as another. The exhortation to watch, while having a special historical motive and force with the disciples, has its abiding lesson as one of the things ever incumbent upon the servants of the heavenly King. So many particular exhortations and counsels of Old Testament prophets have permanent value. It is in this way that the scriptures of both Testaments are profitable for instruction in righteousness.

Matthew's gospel appends to the eschatological discourse three parables of admonition, which occupy the whole of the twenty-fifth chapter. The parable of the ten virgins and the picture of the judgment are peculiar to this gospel, but the parable of the talents appears to be in substance identical with that of the pounds ($\mu\nu\tilde{\alpha}\varsigma$, *minas*) in Luke xix, 11–27. The three parables as they stand in Matthew, whether originally uttered in this connection or not, are every way appropriate to the context. They are admonitions to watch and be ready for the coming of the Lord, and are not essentially different from the counsels already noticed in the fourth section of the preceding discourse (for example, Matt. xxiv, 32–51). The lesson of the parable of the virgins is, " Watch, therefore, for ye know not the day nor the hour." The great lesson of the parable of the talents is that the Lord's servants have also something more to do than merely to watch. They must be diligently employed in the service and interests of their owner during his temporary absence from them, whether the time be long or short. There is, then, no difficulty as to the import of these parables, and no question as to their relevancy to the subject of which Jesus spoke on the Mount of Olives.

Greater difficulty is supposed to attach to the sublime picture of judgment recorded in Matt. xxv, 31–46, and most expositors have thought that that picture must needs refer to a general and formal judgment of all nations of men at the conclusion of human history. But the language of Matthew is explicit in referring it to the time " when the Son of man shall come in his glory, and all the angels with him," and when " he shall sit on the throne of his glory." There would be obvious inconsistency in making this coming of the Son of man different from that of Matt. xxiv, 30, and xvi, 27, 28. How, then, it is asked, can this sublime ideal be brought within the time-limits of the prophecy of Matt. xxiv ?

The difficulties which are here suggested arise either from the assumptions of a literalizing exegesis or from a failure to keep in mind that the coming and kingdom of Christ are in their nature a *process*, which has definite historical beginning, but stretches on indefinitely into future ages of ages. Consequently, while most of the things enumerated in the foregoing discourse had fulfillment in the fall of Judaism and the beginning of Christianity, other things, from their very nature, are such as must needs be of repeated or continual occurrence. Such especially is the execution of judgment, a function of every reigning king. The scriptural doctrine of Messiah's reign is not that God, the Father Almighty, vacates his throne at the accession of the Christ. Neither the concept of Psalm ii,

7-9, nor Psalm cx, nor Dan. vii, 13, 14, implies that the eternal God is any less the ruler and sovereign of the world after he sets his anointed Son at his right hand, and "gives him dominion and glory and a kingdom." From thence onward he judges the world by Jesus Christ, and the sublime picture of Matt. xxv, 31–46, is a parable of this great fact. Hence the force and propriety of the words: "When the Son of man shall come in his glory, and all the angels with him, then shall he sit on the throne of his glory." But how long he shall continue to sit thus on his glorious throne of judgment—how long "he must reign until he hath put all enemies under his feet"—is not a matter of specific revelation. The ideal of judgment presented in Matt. xxv, 31–46, is therefore no single event, like the destruction of Jerusalem. It is not to be explained literally as a formal assize not to open until the end of human history on earth. It is, rather, a most impressive parabolic picture of the age-long administration of Jesus Christ, from the hour of the signal overthrow of Jerusalem until "he shall deliver up the kingdom to the Father" (1 Cor. xv, 24). The anointed King of glory is judge of the living as well as of the dead, and it is a grave error to represent "the day of the Lord" or "the day of judgment" as something deferred to the end of time. We have shown over and over again in the preceding portions of this volume that "the great and terrible day of the Lord" is a prophetic phrase of remarkable fullness of meaning. The Old Testament doctrine is that "the kingdom is Jehovah's, and he is ruler among the nations" (Psalm xxii, 28). "Say ye among the nations, Jehovah reigneth; he shall judge the peoples with equity. He cometh, he cometh to judge the earth ; he shall judge the world in righteousness, and the peoples in his truth" (Psalm xcvi, 10–13). The day of judgment for any wicked nation, city, or individual is the time when the penal visitation comes ; and the judgment of God's saints is manifest in every signal event which magnifies goodness and condemns iniquity.[1]

---

[1] We need not assume to say how far and in what manner Christ executes his judgments or gathers his elect by the ministry of angels. He who "makes the clouds his chariot, who walks upon the wings of the wind, making his angels winds, and his ministers a flame of fire" (Psalm civ, 3, 4; comp. Heb. i, 7), is present in all the great crises of this world's history, and he makes his angels ministering spirits to serve such as are to inherit salvation (Heb. i, 14). Our Lord represented Lazarus as carried away (ἀπενεχθῆναι) by the angels into Abraham's bosom (Luke xvi, 22). But there is no warrant in Scripture for the notion that when the angels are sent forth on missions of mercy or of judgment their operations must needs be visible to mortal eyes. When the impious Herod Agrippa allowed himself to be honored as a god, "immediately an angel of God smote him, and, becoming eaten of worms, he breathed out his spirit" (Acts xii, 22, 23). Human eyes saw nothing but the curse of a foul

But this divine administration of the world, which in the Hebrew Scriptures is the work of Jehovah, is portrayed in Dan. vii, 13, 14, and represented in the New Testament as committed unto Christ. The Father has given him "authority to execute judgment because he is Son of man" (John v, 27). And the Son of man came, in accord with the apocalyptic picture of Dan. vii, 13, and Matt. xxiv, 30, and executed judgment upon Jerusalem, guilty of "all the righteous blood shed upon the earth, from the blood of Abel the righteous unto the blood of Zachariah" (Matt. xxiii, 35, 36). That was the first conspicuous exhibition of his judicial power, and it marked the crisis and end of the pre-Messianic age. Christ is, therefore, now King and Judge; but all things are not yet subjected unto him, and he must reign until he shall have put all things in subjection under his feet. And this is no other than the decree,

> Jehovah has said to me, My Son art thou;
> I have this day begotten thee.
> Ask from me, and I will give nations for thine inheritance,
> And for thy possession the ends of the earth (Psalm ii, 7, 8).

We conclude, then, that the additions peculiar to Matthew's version of our Lord's discourse on the Mount of Olives contain nothing inappropriate to the occasion, and nothing inconsistent with the definite time-limit of the prophecy and the analogy of New Testament eschatology.

---

disease, or a terrible plague; but Scripture sees back of it the potent ministry of a destroying angel (comp. Exod. xii, 23; 2 Sam. xxiv, 16). So the visible *effects* of divine judgment were terribly manifest in the unparalleled miseries of Jerusalem. The righteous blood of unnumbered martyrs was visited upon that generation (Matt. xxiii, 35, 36); and where the Jewish historian saw and made record of appalling tribulation and woe the word of prophecy discerned a "revelation of the Lord Jesus from heaven, with the angels of his power [personal or natural] in flaming fire, rendering vengeance to them that know not God, and to them that obey not the Gospel" (2 Thess. i, 7, 8). In like manner the King of glory is continually judging and reigning among the nations, and he will not cease from his age-long work until "he shall have abolished all rule and all authority and power" (1 Cor. xv, 24).

CHAPTER XIX

THE APOCALYPSE OF JOHN

I. AUTHORSHIP.

THE different opinions respecting the authorship of the New Testament books commonly attributed to John may be stated as follows :

1. John, the son of Zebedee, the disciple and apostle of Jesus, was the author of the Apocalypse, the fourth gospel, and the three epistles.

2. John the apostle was the author of the Apocalypse, but not of the gospel and the three epistles.

3. John the apostle was the author of the gospel and the three epistles, but not of the Apocalypse. Those who adopt this third view attribute the Apocalypse either—

(1) To a Presbyter John, who is mentioned in early writings.

(2) To John Mark, the companion of Paul and Barnabas.

(3) To a John whose only monument is this Book of Revelation, and who is otherwise unknown.

Our purpose does not call for any extended discussion of these various opinions. But we have discovered no sufficient reason to reject the old and most current tradition that all these Johannean writings are the work of the disciple of our Lord. The external evidence is overwhelmingly in favor of this view, and Justin Martyr, Irenæus, Tertullian, Hippolytus, and Origen testify direct testimony that the Apocalypse is the writing of the apostle John. The contrary opinion rests mainly on negative considerations, such as its omission from the early Syriac version, and the statement of the Roman presbyter Caius, that it was written by the heretic Cerinthus and published under the name of John in order to obtain for it a claim to apostolic authority. The more noteworthy objections to the apostolic authorship are based on internal evidence, and were well stated by Dionysius of Alexandria (A. D. 250). They have been restated and enlarged by many later writers, and have always had weight with critical minds, so that as in the past there will probably ever in the future be not a few who will not be able to concede that the author of the Apocalypse was also the writer of the fourth gospel. The arguments are in substance as follow.

1. The apostle does not mention himself by name either in the

gospel or in the epistles. This fact, however, may be sufficiently accounted for by the nature and circumstances of each writing. In a book of prophecy, modeled so conspicuously after that of Daniel, there was special reason for using the forms of expression found in the older apocalyptist. As in the older book there is frequent occurrence of the phrase "I, Daniel" (comp. Dan. vii, 15, 28 ; viii, 1, 15 ; ix, 2), so the New Testament writer of an apocalypse appropriately employs the words "I, John."

2. He calls himself *servant, brother*, and *partaker* in the tribulation (i, 1, 9), but not apostle. It does not appear evident, however, that an apostle could not have appropriately used these expressions, and it may be affirmed with much emphasis that there was no other John in the early Church who could have announced himself simply as "John," and "I, John," without exposing himself to the charge of unseemly arrogance. Furthermore, he is simply bearing "the testimony of Jesus Christ" to the servants of God, and accordingly calls himself most appropriately a servant, brother, and fellow-partaker "in the tribulation and kingdom and patience in Jesus." This is in keeping, too, with the tender sympathy of John, the beloved disciple of Jesus.

3. We find in the Apocalypse no trace of apostolical authority, or of the paternal relation assumed in 1 John ii, 1; v, 21; 2 John i, and 3 John i. But such authority would have been notably out of place in a book of prophecy like this; and the epistles to the seven churches are in each case announced as coming from the glorified Christ, not from John, who is merely the reporter.

4. It has been urged by some that the names of the twelve apostles on the foundations of the heavenly city (xxi, 14) would have been incongruous in a vision seen by an apostle. But in view of what Jesus says of the twelve in Matt. xix, 28, and what Paul says of the apostles and himself in Eph. ii, 20, and 2 Cor. xi, 5 ; xii, 11, this objection seems trivial and far-fetched. The writer of the vision says nothing of himself personally, but simply states what was shown him.

5. But the most weighty argument is based on the language and style, which are acknowledged on all hands to be very different from what appears in the gospel and the epistles of John. The language of the Apocalypse is peculiarly Hebraistic, and Dionysius long ago said that it was notable for its solecisms and barbarous idioms. The book is distinguished for its numerous symbols and visions of things in heaven and on earth ; the addresses to the seven churches are stern and lordly, very unlike the manner of John's epistles. Instead of the profound, calm, and contemplative utter-

ances of the other Johannean writings we have vivid pictures and symbolic names and numbers. Instead of the spiritual worship taught in the fourth gospel we have magnificent pictures of cherubim, elders, angels, and glorified spirits, and all things in heaven and earth and under the earth and on the sea, giving glory to Him who sits upon the throne. The word of God, the Antichrist, the conception of the judgment and the resurrection are all in notable distinction from the same doctrines in the gospel and the epistles. From all these, it is claimed, we must conclude that the author of the Apocalypse is not to be identified with the author of the fourth gospel.

The weight and force of this argument cannot be ignored. But for the external testimony, no critic would think of ascribing the Apocalypse to the author of the fourth gospel and the three epistles. But this argument from the language and style of thought is largely nullified by three considerations :

(1) The subject-matter and scope of the Apocalypse place it in a totally different class of literature from that of the gospel and of the epistles. It is a book of prophecy. The addresses to the seven churches are not so much epistles as prophetic messages. The series of visions is not designed to inculcate lessons of Christian doctrine so much as to disclose things which were shortly to come to pass.

(2) Being essentially a book of prophecy, not a gospel nor an epistle, it is modeled after the apocalyptic portions of the Hebrew Scriptures. There is scarcely a symbol or figure employed that is not appropriated to some extent from the Old Testament. It is, therefore, not to be supposed that the language, or style of thought, or type of doctrine must needs resemble those of other productions of the same writer.

(3) The difference of language is further accounted for by the supposition that the Apocalypse was written by the apostle at an early period of his ministry, and the gospel and epistles some thirty or forty years later. We may easily believe that John, the Galilean fisherman, wrote just such rough Hebraistic Greek soon after he left Palestine ; but after thirty years of life in the midst of a Gentile community he would naturally have acquired such a command of the Greek language as the fourth gospel shows.

We are accordingly of opinion that the various arguments against the Johannean authorship of the Apocalypse are not conclusive or sufficient to set aside the best testimony of the early Church. It is not necessary, however, to insist upon maintaining the current tradition of the centuries. The exposition of the book is not dependent upon a certain knowledge of its authorship. The question of its origin is one of those problems of criticism on which there will probably never be uniformity of opinion. Dionysius of Alexandria, while disputing the apostolic origin of the Apocalypse, accepted the book as the production of a holy and inspired man of God. Not a few of the ablest exegetes of modern times adopt the views of Dionysius. It would be a singular infatuation to imagine that God could not have sent this "testimony of Jesus Christ" by some other John than the son of Zebedee.

II. Date.

Two different opinions have long prevailed respecting the date of the Apocalypse. One rests mainly on a statement of Irenæus, who seems to place the composition in the latter part of the reign of Domitian (A. D. 96) ; the other is based upon internal evidence, and maintains that the book was written before the destruction of Jerusalem. The most recent criticism, which finds documents of different authorship incorporated in the work, assigns some of the documents to an early and some to a later date. Deferring for the present the several hypotheses of the composite origin of the book, we may briefly state the arguments touching the date as follows :

1. Irenæus, Bishop of Lyons, says that in his boyhood he had conversed with Polycarp, and heard him tell of his personal fellowship with the apostle John.[1] In speaking of the name of the Antichrist which is concealed in the mystic number given in Rev. xiii, 18, he says : " If it were necessary to have his name distinctly announced at the present time it would doubtless have been announced by him who saw the Apocalypse ; for it was not a great while ago that [it or he] was seen (οὐδὲ γὰρ πρὸ πολλοῦ χρόνου ἑωράϑη), but almost in our own generation, toward the end of Domitian's reign."[2] Here the critical reader will observe that the subject of the verb ἑωράϑη, was seen, is ambiguous, and may be understood either of John or the Apocalypse. To assert, as some do, that the only grammatical and legitimate construction requires us to understand the *Apocalypse* rather than *John* as the subject of the verb is arbitrary and presumptuous. To say the least, in fairness, one construction is as correct and legitimate as the other. But why should he say that *the book* was recently seen ? The point he evidently aims to make is that the man who saw the visions of the Apocalypse had lived almost into the times to which Irenæus belonged, and had it been needful to declare the name of the Antichrist he would himself have done it. The time when John saw the Apocalypse was of no

---

[1] Eusebius, *Ecclesiastical History*, v, 20.
[2] *Adv. Hæreses*, v, 30.

consequence for determining the name of Antichrist so long as the apostle himself was yet alive. There is more reason for believing that the reference is to the Apocalypse in the fact that Irenæus elsewhere says that John lived on into the times of Trajan.

2. But admitting that Irenæus refers to the Apocalypse as having been seen near the close of Domitian's reign, his ambiguous statement is the only external evidence of any real value for determining the question. All other testimonies are later, and, like the numerous statements of Eusebius, seem to be either repeated from Irenæus or based on mere inferences. And it is notorious that even Eusebius, after quoting Irenæus and others, leaves the question of the authorship of the Apocalypse in doubt.

3. It has been claimed that the early date is incompatible with the existence of such heretical sects as the Nicolaitans mentioned in chap. ii, 6, 15, which must have required more time for their development. But the most rational explanation of the Nicolaitans indicates the very opposite; for these libertines were the first troublers of the Church, and the name itself is a symbolical designation for those *destroyers of the people*, who, like the Balaamites and Jezebelites of the same chapter (verses 14 and 20), taught the mischievous error of licentious freedom, even "to eat things sacrificed to idols, and to commit fornication." These evils were among the earliest with which the Church had to contend (Acts xv, 20, 29; 1 Cor. viii, 7–13, and vi, 13–20). There is no conclusive evidence that any sect of this name existed in the early Church, and all that writers like Irenæus, Epiphanius, and Tertullian say about their springing from the Nicolas of Acts vi, 5, is justly open to suspicion.

4. It is further argued that the churches of Asia must have existed some time, because some had, like Ephesus, and Sardis, and Laodicea, lapsed from their first love, had become lukewarm, and were ready to die. But such a plea can be allowed no weight in view of the abundant evidence of other defections in apostolic times. How long was it after Paul founded the churches of Galatia that he was compelled to write, "I marvel that ye are so quickly changing from him that called you in the grace of Christ unto a different gospel?" (Gal. i, 6.) How soon after his departure did false apostles and deceitful workers and heretical teachers arise in the church of Corinth? (1 Cor. v, 1, 7; xi, 18–21; xv, 12; 2 Cor. ii, 17; xi, 13; Phil. iii, 18; Rom. xvi, 17.) There is no apostasy or defection mentioned in connection with the seven churches which might not have arisen in any Jewish-Gentile church of apostolic times in less than two years after the date of its foundation.

5. The belief that the phrase "angel of the church," employed

at the beginning of each of the epistles, implies an advance in ecclesiastical organization beyond the simple constitution of the first period is based on the assumption that *angel* means *bishop*, and that the Church had no bishops before A. D. 68 who were different from presbyters. But there is no sufficient evidence that some churches were without a special bishop, or responsible pastor, even in apostolic times ; and, were this not the case, the opinion that "angel of the church " in the Apocalypse means the pastor, or bishop, is without authority. Much rather is it to be regarded as a symbolical title of the whole Church in its personnel (see our interpretation *in loco*); for the words both of praise and of censure are obviously intended, not for one individual like the pastor, but for the good of all; they are not addressed to the Church as an organic body (the candlestick), but to its personal constituents, who should all be like so many morning stars (Rev. ii, 28; comp. 1 Cor. xv, 41).

6. The overthrow of Laodicea by an earthquake (Pliny, *Hist. Nat.*, v, 41; Tacitus, *Annals*, xiv, 27) has been cited as bearing on this question of date. But, in the first place, it cannot be shown that the church there was destroyed by the earthquake, and further, the statement of Tacitus is that, having been overthrown by an earthquake, the city recovered from its fall in Nero's reign, and regained its former glory by means of its own resources. This corresponds notably with what is said in Rev. iii, 17, and shows that the place was in a flourishing condition in the time of Nero. Paul's reference to this church in Col. iv, 16, abundantly refutes all arguments against the early date which are based on the destruction of Laodicea by earthquake.

7. A fair weighing of the arguments thus far adduced shows that they all, excepting the statement of Irenæus, favor the early rather than the later date. The facts appealed to indicate the times before rather than after the destruction of Jerusalem; and this opinion is corroborated by the further consideration that the persecutions of the time proceed from the Jews (Rev. ii, 9; iii, 9). We know that the persecutions of the apostolic age came chiefly through Jewish instigation, and even at the time of Polycarp, we read in Eusebius (iv, 15), that the Christian martyr's death was secured by the fierce zeal of the Jewish population.

8. The mention, in chap. xi, 1–3, of the temple, the altar, and the court, and the mystical designation, in verse 8, of "the great city, which spiritually is called Sodom and Egypt, where also their Lord was crucified," implies that the city and temple of Jerusalem were not yet overthrown. It is singularly futile to plead that these expressions are symbolical; for, whatever the mystical significance,

the whole manner of statement supposes such a knowledge of the temple and the altar as would be unnatural and out of place if in fact the city and temple were then in ruins. But, on the other hand, if these were yet existing, and the time of their utter demolition was near at hand, the allusions would be most natural and impressive.

9. The early date is further supported by the emphatic statement, placed in the very title of the book, and repeated in various forms again and again, that the revelation was of "things which must shortly come to pass," and the time of which was near at hand (Rev. i, 1, 3 ; xxii, 6, 7, 10, 12, 20). If we adopt the early date, and the terrible catastrophe of the Apocalypse is understood of the ruin of that great city where the Lord was crucified, and on which the Lord himself charged the guilt of all the righteous blood of martyrs from Abel unto Zachariah (Matt. xxiii, 34–37), this prophecy has great force and significance in claiming to foretell things of the near future. The statements are thus seen to be true and appropriate. But it is impossible, without subjecting the language to the most unnatural treatment, to explain these time-allusions as referring to events which were not to take place until centuries after the book was written.

10. Another proof of the early date is found in the mystical number of xiii, 18, which can be legitimately explained as the number of the name NERO CÆSAR, when written in Hebrew characters. (See the exposition *in loco*.) This receives additional confirmation in the fact that the book assumes to belong to the period of the sixth king as mentioned in xvii, 10, ὁ εἷς ἔστιν, *the one that now is* ; and if we follow the most natural method of reckoning the Cæsars, and the one which appears in Suetonius and the Sibylline Oracles, we have (1) Julius, (2) Augustus, (3) Tiberius, (4) Caligula, (5) Claudius, (6) Nero. The reign of Nero extended from A. D. 54–68, and somewhere between these dates we may most properly assign the composition of this Apocalypse.

11. One of the most decisive arguments for the early date is based on the Hebraistic language and style of the author, and has been already mentioned in connection with the question of authorship. If the fourth gospel and the Apocalypse are from one writer the remarkable differences are most naturally explained by supposing the Apocalypse to have been composed many years prior to the gospel. To suppose the contrary is in defiance of all critical observation and experience.

12. There are, finally, several allusions to the Apocalypse in other New Testament writings which indicate that it must have been one

of the earliest written productions of the apostolic times. The contrast of "the Jerusalem that now is, and is in bondage with her children," with "the Jerusalem that is above, which is our mother" (Gal. iv, 25, 26), sums up in a few words a large portion of the Apocalypse, and may be most easily explained as an allusion to John's well-known visions of the new and heavenly Jerusalem. But it is difficult to suppose that the apocalyptic symbolism was drawn from Paul's brief allegory. A still more notable allusion appears in Heb. xii, 22–24, where the mention of "Mount Zion, the city of the living God, the heavenly Jerusalem, innumerable hosts of angels, the general assembly and church of the firstborn enrolled in heaven, and the spirits of just men made perfect," points to a number of the most familiar pictures of John's Apocalypse. To assume that John borrowed this from the Epistle to the Hebrews would involve a most violent literary judgment. Were it a mere question of citation, or the appropriation of a symbol or of a figure, we might readily believe that the apocalyptic writer borrowed from a New Testament source, as he frequently does from the Old Testament; but in this case it would be making John take the warp and woof of his whole book out of the half dozen expressions found in a single passage of the Epistle to the Hebrews.

Now, there is no contention that Galatians and Hebrews were written before the destruction of Jerusalem, and, to say the least, the most natural explanation of the allusions referred to is to suppose that the Apocalypse was already written, and that Paul and many others of his day were familiar with its contents. Writers who cite passages from the apostolic fathers to prove the priority of the gospel of John are the last persons in the world who should presume to dispute the obvious priority of the Apocalypse of John to Galatians and Hebrews. For in no case are the alleged quotations of the Gospel more notable or striking than these allusions to the Apocalypse in the New Testament epistles.

III. Recent Critical Theories of the Composition.

The unity of the Apocalypse is so apparent, and its language and style so uniform, that all schools of critics and interpreters have been, until quite recent times, practically unanimous in admitting its integrity. But since the year 1882 a large number of scholars have essayed to solve the mysteries of the book by a critical analysis and a distribution of its material among a variety of sources. Daniel Voelter led the way by his work on the *Origin of the Apocalypse* (1882, 2d ed. 1885), in which he maintained that the present book is the result of a series of redactions. The apostle John (or the presbyter) was the author of the original Revelation, written before A. D. 66, but supplemented by his own hand in subsequent years. The apostle's work underwent several revisions during the first half of the second century. In his *Problem of the Apocalypse* (Freiburg, 1893) this writer elaborates his theory with greater fullness, but with some minor modifications. He holds that the entire work, with all the revisions and supplements, is of Christian origin, while most of the recent critics recognize the Apocalypse as a composite of Jewish and Christian elements.[1]

In 1886 Eberhard Vischer published his important essay, in which he thought to show that the Revelation of John is a Jewish apocalypse translated into Greek and worked over with an introduction, some few additions in the body of the work, and a conclusion, by a Christian writer, near the close of the first century. Vischer argues that two completely different modes of viewing things run through the entire Apocalypse, and that these are so opposite that they cannot be supposed to come from one and the same author. For example, the vision of the innumerable multitude out of every nation (vii, 9–17) is opposed to that of the 144,000 out of the tribes of Israel (vii, 1–8); and the calling Jerusalem "the holy city" in xi, 2, is incompatible with the names Sodom and Egypt in verse 8. Aside from the introduction (chaps. i–iii) and conclusion (xxii, 6–21), the additions made by the Christian *Bearbeiter* appear, however, to be comparatively few. In the entire space of the six chapters (viii–xiii) the following only are attributed to the Christian editor : ix, 11, "in Hebrew" . . . "and in the Greek he has the name Apollyon;" xi, 8, "which is called spiritually Sodom and Egypt, where also their Lord was crucified;" xi, 15, "and of his Christ;" xii, 11, "and they overcame him because of the blood of the Lamb, and because of the word of their testimony, and they loved not their life unto death;" xii, 17, "Jesus;" xiii, 8, "the Lamb that has been slain;" xiii, 9, 10, "if any man hath an ear, let him ear. If any man is for captivity, into captivity he goeth; if any man shall kill with the sword, with the sword must he be killed. Here is the patience and the faith of the saints."

The hypothesis of Vischer begets distrust by its remarkable simplicity. It outdoes the minute elaborateness of Voelter by an opposite extreme of aiming to show how little the Christian editor has added to the original work. It seems strange that one who

---

[1] The theory of Voelter is so fanciful in many of its parts, and so minute in its analysis, as to fall by the weight of its own elaborateness. It assumes such a multitude of things which there is now no possibility of proving that one instinctively feels that its author can be no safe guide to trustworthy conclusions.

took in hand the task of adapting a Jewish apocalypse to a Christian revelation should have confined himself to so few additions, and should have retained the parts which this critic believes to be so irreconcilable with the Christian doctrine. Our exposition will show, it is hoped, that all those portions of the book which are supposed to be peculiarly Jewish are perfectly compatible with a Jewish-Christian authorship. The imagery throughout moves in the line of Old Testament modes of conception, and furnishes no doctrine of the Christ which is not warranted by some corresponding analogy in the gospels. Furthermore, it is exceedingly difficult to believe that a Christian writer, who added the portions which Vischer assigns him, would have taken it upon himself to record the solemn imprecation of xxii, 18, 19, against any man who should dare add upon or take away from the words of the prophecy of this book.

Weizsäcker, in his *Apostolic Age of the Christian Church*, maintains that the Apocalypse of John is a compilation out of a number of independent prophecies, made, not by the apostle, but by some member of his school a short time after his death. Its whole spirit, coloring, and view of the surrounding world make it certain that it all belongs to the first century of our era. Some parts (for example, xi, 1) are earlier than the destruction of the temple (A. D. 70), but other portions (i, 9) point rather to the time of Domitian, near the end of the century. He alleges that the first three chapters and the last two are obviously unsuitable to the main prophecies of the book, and the three sets of seven symbols (seals, trumpets, and vials) have no natural connection with the subject-matter of these prophecies. The so-called episodes in chaps. vii and x are interpolations without any natural relation to the context, and the contents of chaps. xvii and xviii have no connection whatever with the seven plagues of chap. xvi. The beast from the abyss (xi, 7) is an unintelligible anticipation of xiii, 1, 2, as is also the form of beast in xii, 3. The principal symbols, however, of chaps. xi, xii, xiii, and xvii are all indicative of historical matters, and furnish a clew to the times of the writer; the second beast (xiii, 11–17) cannot be regarded as historical, but is a creation of the writer's imagination.

Against these views of Weizsäcker it may be fairly affirmed (1) that he unreasonably underrates the unity of scope and plan apparent in the Apocalypse, (2) indulges in unwarranted assumptions of what the author ought or ought not to have done with his material, and (3) builds too many of his arguments on inferences drawn from doubtful, if not erroneous, interpretations of particular passages. In view of the unity of the book, which almost all exegetes acknowledge, and the manifest artistic finish which Weizsäcker himself

extols as evidence of the author's creative skill and tact, it is quite
insufficient to be told over and over that the visions lack homogene-
ity, the repetitions are self-contradictory, and the prophecies cannot
be fitted into harmony with the plan of the leading sets of symbols.
It is scarcely competent for one to declare without qualification
what the author ought or ought not to have said touching the three
woes referred to in viii, 13 ; ix, 12, and xi, 14 ; or touching the arrangement of any of his material. With other critics Weizsäcker
assumes as if it were something clearly settled that the wounded head
of xiii, 3, is Nero slain, and that the healing is his supposed return
from the dead. He also assumes as a matter of course that the list
of seven Cæsars must begin with Augustus, although Suetonius and
the Sibylline Oracle begin with Julius (book v, 12-14). The seven
mountains are also quietly assumed to be the *septem colles* of the
Latin writers, and the woman is the city of Rome, rather than the
same great city where the martyrs were slain and the Lord was
crucified. In view of the interpretations of these and other passages
given in the following pages we need not linger here to argue further against Weizsäcker's hypotheses.

These various theories of the composite structure of the Apocalypse have been taken up, modified, and elaborated by a large number of critics, but no one particular hypothesis has so far succeeded
in commanding the general assent of biblical scholars. There are
noticeable points of agreement, but no two writers fully agree.
Weyland argues for two Jewish apocalypses, both written in Greek,
one belonging to the time of Nero, the other to the time of Titus.
These were appropriated by a Christian writer in the time of Trajan,
and wrought into our present book. Pfleiderer supposes two (possibly three) Jewish sources, worked over by two different Christian
editors, who interpolated and added a number of passages. Sabatier
and his pupil Schoen find, on the contrary, that the groundwork,
consisting of chaps. i–xi, and the vision of the bowls in xvi, is of
Christian origin ; but the episode in x, 9–xi, 14, is an interpolation
from a Jewish source, as are also xii, 1–9, 13–17, and chaps. xiii
and xviii. Friedrich Spitta, in an elaborate volume on the *Revelation of John*, attempts to show that the three separate visions of the
seals, the trumpets, and the vials were originally independent apocalypses. The epistles to the seven churches and the vision of the
seals are the work of John Mark, written about A. D. 60 ; the vision
of the trumpets is a Jewish apocalypse of the time of Pompey, and
that of the vials another Jewish apocalypse of the time of Caligula.
These three, with their related matter, were combined by a Christian
compiler about the beginning of the second century, and worked

out into the plan and order in which the entire book now appears.
C. A. Briggs, in his work on the *Messiah of the Apostles*, adopts the
documentary theory of the Apocalypse, and argues that the conspicuous unity of the book is due to the skill of the final editor, who
combined and arranged in symmetrical form a collection of apocalypses of various dates. He thinks the earliest apocalypse is that
of the beasts, now distributed into x, 1b, 2, 8–11 ; xi, 1–13; xii,
18; xiii; xiv, 8–13 ; xviii; xix, 11–21.   Next in order was the
apocalypse of the dragon, which now appears in xii, 1–17 ; xx ; xxi,
1, 2, 16, 18–21 ; xxii, 3–5; xxi, 3–5.   The four apocalypses of the
sevens are supposed to have originated in the order of (1) the
trumpets, (2) the seals, (3) the bowls, which presuppose both the
trumpets and the seals ; and (4) the seven epistles, which were the
last of the series.   These several documents passed through four
successive editions, the first of which combined the three separate
apocalypses of the seals, the trumpets, and the bowls.   The second
edition added the seven epistles ; the third incorporated the apocalypses of the beasts and the dragon, which perhaps had already been
combined into one work ; and the fourth and final editing must
have been done near the end of the first century.

On all these critical theories it is to be observed that their differences are such as are natural to a literary problem of this kind.   In
any ancient work of a composite character it is not to be expected
that critical analysis will be able at once to solve all difficulties or
prove to be a task so simple that all critical minds will speedily ar-
rive at one and the same conclusion.   We need entertain no hostile
prejudice against the hypothesis of compilation and redaction.   It
is a notable fact that almost all works of this apocalyptic class (all
unless it be this Revelation of John and the Shepherd of Hermas)
exist under an assumed name, and the Greek Daniel, the Book of
Enoch, the Apocalypse of Ezra, and the Sibylline Oracles are unquestionably in their present form compilations or modifications of
various documents.   And it need be no disparagement of the real
value of such a production that it has made use of preexisting material.   A writer, inspired or uninspired, may perhaps best accomplish his aim by appropriating and combining various writings
which can be made to serve the particular occasion.

But the work of critical analysis may be easily overdone, and in
the schemes of several of the critics above named it appears to have
been carried to an unwarrantable extreme.   No theories of this
character can claim high regard which rest conspicuously upon
needless conjectures and unreasonable assumptions.   Any hypothesis which supposes original documents of diverse authorship and

date is bound, above all things, to show in the diverse sources differences of language, style, tone, method, and sentiment. But none of the critics have thus far produced what can be fairly claimed as real examples of incongruity between the different supposed sources. The alleged heterogeneous elements and inconsistencies are imaginary with the critic. In some cases they arise from a needless, not to say false, interpretation, and the varying critical theories suggest more difficulties than they seem able to explain.

We believe that no critic has proven or is able to prove that the Apocalypse is not a Christian work throughout. Its use of Jewish modes of thought and expression no more demand the hypothesis of exclusively Jewish documents than does the Epistle to the Hebrews. A Jewish Christian of the first century could hardly be thought of as incapable of any expression found in this Book of Revelation. It is nothing to the point to show that a Jew might have written much that now appears in this book; the real question is, Whether any portion of it could not have been written by a Jewish Christian? The following exposition will show, we trust, that the work in all its parts is capable of a rational interpretation, and that the Domitian date and the Nero legend have occupied far too prominent a place in the critical controversies. If our exposition is correct and defensible, the theories of compilation are both unnecessary and untenable.

IV. John in Patmos.

John's own testimony is that he "was in the island which is called Patmos on account of the word of God and the testimony of Jesus" (chap. i, 9). The phrase "on account of the word of God" (διὰ τὸν λόγον τοῦ θεοῦ), according to the well-established usage of διά with the accusative, means *for the sake of* the word. It gives the *ground* or *reason* for what is stated. So in chap. ii, 3, it is said: "Thou didst endure for my name's sake;" that is, the great objective reason for the endurance in the midst of trials was devotion to the name of Christ. So again in iv, 11: "On account of thy will they were and were created;" that is, all things were brought into existence because that was the will of God. The same meaning inheres in this formula in vi, 9; vii, 15; xii, 11, 12; xiii, 14; xviii, 8, 10, 15; xx, 4.[1] Now, according to i, 2, "the word of God and the

---

[1] Whether the reference be expressive of a *consequence* or a *purpose* must be determined from the context or the nature of the case. The examples in vi, 9 and xx, 4, are commonly cited as proofs of the former. These souls had been *slain* or *beheaded in consequence* of the word of God, etc. But in those passages, as Düsterdieck observes, the determinative expressions *slain* and *beheaded* occur, and may warrant a construction different from that of i, 9. After the writer so clearly defines in the immediate con-

testimony of Jesus" are no other than this Revelation concerning
all things which John saw. The most obvious meaning, therefore,
of verse 9 is that John was in Patmos for the sake of, or on account
of, this Revelation of Jesus Christ. The first and most emphatic
thing the writer tells us is that God gave this revelation (ἀποκάλυψις) to Jesus, and Jesus signified it through his angel unto John,
who witnessed it accordingly as God's word and Jesus's testimony
(verses 1 and 2). It was on this account, not on account of "the
tribulation and kingdom and patience" mentioned in the first part
of verse 9, that John "was in the island which is called Patmos."
But because John announces himself as a "brother and partaker"
in the tribulation of the times nearly all interpreters have jumped
to the conclusion that he must have been in Patmos because of such
tribulation. The fact, also, that criminals were banished to that
barren island by the Roman emperors has seemed to confirm the
tradition that John was dwelling there as an exile when he saw the
visions of this Apocalypse. There is certainly nothing improbable
in the tradition, but aside from what has been inferred from the
single statement of Rev. i, 9, there appears to be no convincing evidence that John was ever an exile in Patmos. The traditions of the
second and third centuries touching the movements of the first apostles are of very little value. Some of them may be true; but none
of them are to be accepted as well-attested facts of history. The tradition of John's banishment may be only a specimen of the manner
in which a statement like that of Rev. i, 9, was taken up a century
after it was written, given a particular meaning, and that meaning
propagated without contradiction until it came to be accepted as an
unquestionable fact. Aside from this passage there is no more authority for the tradition of John's exile than there is for the statement of Victorinus that he was sent to Patmos to work in a mine;
or of Tertullian that he was first plunged into burning oil at Rome,
and, having suffered no harm, was sent as a captive to Patmos; or
of Polycrates that he was a martyr and teacher, and also a priest
who bore the sacerdotal plate; or of Simeon Metaphrastes that he
was shipwrecked off the coast of Ephesus. These and a score of
other similar stories illustrate the tendency of early times to take up
a word or hint about an apostle and magnify it into a legend. Such
legends can have no real value as trustworthy history.

---

text what the "word of God and the testimony of Jesus" is, we are not at liberty to give
the expressions a different meaning, as that John was in Patmos *as a consequence of
his preaching the Gospel.* The exposition which takes διά in i, 9, as expressive of purpose, that is, for the sake or purpose of receiving the word of God, etc., has the strong
support of Lücke, De Wette, Bleek, and Düsterdieck.

The last reference to John in the Acts of the Apostles is in chap. xii, 2. It is not improbable that after the death of his brother James, there mentioned, John left Jerusalem, and proceeded to found Christianity in some of the cities of western Asia. Perhaps one reason why Paul was forbidden of the Spirit to preach in Asia (Acts xvi, 6) was because John was already on that field. Or possibly John made a journey to Rome, as Tertullian says, and was thence banished to Patmos at the time Claudius gave command for all Jews to depart from the imperial city (Acts xviii, 2). He may have subsequently visited Jerusalem as many times as Paul did. It is worthy of note that the "Muratorian Fragment," a very ancient and important document (A. D. 170), declares that "the blessed apostle Paul, *following the manner of his predecessor John*, wrote in like manner to seven churches expressly by name." This testimony clearly puts John before Paul in writing epistles to the churches, and tends to confirm the position taken above that Gal. iv, 25, 26, is an allusion to John's picture of the heavenly Jerusalem. The apostle John might have been quietly laboring in Smyrna, or in some neighboring parts of Asia Minor, while Paul was at Ephesus. To assume that in such case we must have had some allusion to it in Paul's writings, or in some other New Testament writing, is altogether baseless. The absence of any reference to John in the latter half of the Acts of the Apostles ought to be a sufficient admonition not to presume upon the silence of the New Testament on such matters.

Our object in giving so much space to this question about John's banishment to Patmos is to point out the worthlessness of much that has been written on such matters of little or no importance.[1]

---

[1] It is amazing what pages on pages have been written about matters of pure conjecture. Not a few writers on the Apocalypse discuss at great length the question whether John wrote his book while yet in Patmos or after he had returned to Ephesus! Perhaps the best comment one could make on such conjectures would be a travesty somewhat as follows: Assuming that John was in Ephesus when he received his divine call to go to Patmos for the word of God, he probably journeyed on foot to Miletus, over the same route subsequently traveled by the Ephesian elders when they went thither to meet Paul (Acts xx, 17). From this place a skillful sailor like the son of Zebedee could row a small boat in less than six hours to the isle of Patmos. Here, in the deep seclusion of the rocky island, he was in visions and revelations of God for forty days and forty nights, and was probably supplied with food by ravens, as was Elijah in the wilderness of the Jordan. In that lone spot he first wrote down what he saw; but not satisfied with his first composition, he made a journey to Jerusalem, and there revised it. After this he went to his old home in Capernaum, and there rewrote the whole book amid the associations of his early life, where he had so often seen the Lord and heard him speak. Then he returned to Asia, and published his prophecy first to the church of Philadelphia, probably for the reason that that church

Our contention is that the question of John's actual residence in Patmos, whether as an exile, or by reason of shipwreck, or otherwise, is of no importance in the exposition of the Apocalypse. But some interpreters seem to think that a whole scheme of exposition might be based upon an inference drawn from such an incidental statement as that of Rev. i, 9.[1] An impression is made to take the place of proof, and often magnified to the neglect of other statements or inferences of equal value. Whether the author of this book went to Patmos as an exile, or for the purpose of receiving this "word of God and testimony of Jesus," ought not to be treated as a question of any serious moment. One might even go further, and maintain that John's being in Patmos may, like Daniel's being "in Shushan the palace, which is in the province of Elam" (Dan. viii, 2), have been ideal only. So Ezekiel was "brought in the visions of God to Jerusalem" (Ezek. viii, 3). John immediately tells us that he was "in spirit," and as the visions he saw of seals, trumpets, beasts, and woman sitting upon many waters had no external reality in the physical world, so his being in Patmos might be understood as a symbolical expression equivalent to being apart in a lonely desert place.[2]

Whatever, then, the actual facts were, the great divine purpose of John's being in Patmos was to receive this revelation of things then about to come to pass. If he were banished to that desert place because he had made himself obnoxious to the authority of Rome, such fact was but incidental to the great purpose of God thereby effected, namely, the reception of the word of God and the testimony of Jesus Christ which are written in this book.

alone of all the seven stands without a word of blame in these epistles!!! Let no one now presume to say that these suppositions are a tissue of worthless and ridiculous conjectures. These conjectures, suppositions, assumptions, fancy-pictures, whatever one chooses to call them, are of as much real value as half the hypotheses which are employed in the critical discussions of the Apocalypse. All assumptions of determining the exact time, place, and method of the composition of this book are from their very nature to be regarded with suspicion. And we may venture to add that a considerable part of what has been written in recent years to show the diverse sources out of which the Apocalypse is compiled is of the same fanciful character.

[1] See, for example, Alford's *Greek Testament with Notes, in loco.*

[2] It might indeed be claimed that in a highly wrought apocalyptical composition like this such idealistic method of personal representation is to be presupposed. At the beginning of *The Pilgrim's Progress* Bunyan writes: "As I walked through the wilderness of this world, I lighted on a certain place where was a den, and laid me down in that place to sleep; and as I slept, I dreamed a dream." No well-informed reader ever understood this in its strict realistic import, for in an allegory, "delivered under the similitude of a dream," such formality of statement is part of the art and method of the writer. So, too, in apocalyptical literature, canonical and extra-canonical, the same usage appears.

V. Scope and Plan of the Apocalypse.

This remarkable book is the consummation and crown of all the apocalyptical prophecies. Its author has made a most discriminating use of figures, names, and symbols. His imagery belongs to Jewish modes of thought, and is appropriated mainly from the Hebrew Scriptures. It is, however, such as a Jewish Christian of the first century might naturally have employed. The originality of the author is not compromised by such a use of sacred symbols. It takes not from the perfection of the Lord's Prayer that its several petitions had been uttered in many ways before our Lord combined them in the inimitable model which the churches now possess and use. Originality may be seen in the grouping as well as in the invention of literary material. It is an old saying that "not every collection of straws makes a bird's nest." The highest genius may be displayed in the fresh setting of facts and ideals old as human thought. We feel obliged, in sheer justice, to award this Apocalypse a very high place as a literary composition. It contains the elements of a great epic, and every devout reader has been impressed with its sublime imagery as by few other books in the world. Some of the grandest poetry of the Christian ages owes not a little both of its thought and its inspiration to this remarkable prophecy. The language and style are often rough and Hebraistic, but the ideas are of the highest order, and the main subject is really the greatest event in human history—the coming and kingdom of the Christ of God.

According to the following exposition the prophecies of this book are an apocalypse of the fall of Judaism and the rise and triumph of Christianity. The old covenant had "become aged, and was nigh unto vanishing away" (Heb. viii, 13), but its removal involved a shaking, not only of the earth, but also of the heaven (Heb. xii, 26). That transition from the old to the new was an event of unspeakable moment, and is depicted as a world-convulsing revolution. The imagery and style of the Old Testament apocalyptists are most appropriately brought into use; sun, moon, and stars, and the heaven itself, are pictured as collapsing, and the crisis of the ages is signaled by voices and thunders and lightnings and earthquake. To insist on a literal interpretation of such imagery is to bring prophecy itself into contempt and ridicule. In our analysis and exposition we have been guided by the principles of interpretation which have already been tested and illustrated in the apocalyptic portions of the Hebrew Scriptures. We thus find that John's Apocalypse is but an enlargement of our Lord's eschatological sermon on the Mount of Olives. It takes up

the same line of thought and translates it into the more extended
and formal elements of apocalyptic symbolism. We have endeavored to support our exposition by abundant citation of illustrative
analogies from the older scriptures, and to show how the successive
revelations depict, in the most perfect harmony with apocalyptic
methods, the fearful overthrow of that great city which had become
a harlot, and the consequent descent from heaven of "the new Jerusalem, made ready as a bride adorned for her husband." The
corrupt and outcast Jerusalem, guilty of "all the righteous blood
shed on the earth" (Matt. xxiii, 35), is called Sodom, and Egypt,
and Babylon; but the heavenly kingdom which shall never be destroyed is appropriately called "the holy city, new Jerusalem."

That this Apocalypse is not a confused compilation of incongruous fragments, but a work of transcendent genius, remarkable for
its unity and the admirable symmetry of its arrangement, is made
evident in the following Analytical Outline of its contents.

ANALYSIS OF THE APOCALYPSE

FIRST PART

Revelation of the Lamb, i-xi

SECOND PART

Revelation of the Bride, the Wife of the Lamb, xii–xxii.

PART FIRST

REVELATION OF THE LAMB. I–XI

TITLE AND SUPERSCRIPTION. I, 1–3.

1   THE Revelation of Jesus Christ, which God gave him to show unto his
servants, *even* the things which must shortly come to pass: and he sent
2 and signified *it* by his angel unto his servant John; who bare witness of
the word of God, and of the testimony of Jesus Christ, *even* of all things
3 that he saw.   Blessed is he that readeth, and they that hear the words
of the prophecy, and keep the things which are written therein: for the
time is at hand.

1. The first three verses of this book serve the purpose of a title
and a superscription.   They declare the divine source and object of
the revelation, and pronounce a blessing on both reader and hearers.
We are emphatically told at the outset that this is a *Revelation of
Jesus Christ ;* which means, as the context shows, a revelation made
known by Jesus Christ.   It is not to be explained as a genitive of the
object—a revelation concerning Jesus, or belonging to him as a
peculiar possession; but a genitive of the subject; for Jesus is "the
faithful witness" (verse 5) who made the revelation known to John,
and through him to the churches.   The original source of this, as
of all heavenly revelations, is *God himself* (ὁ θεός).   He gave it to
Jesus Christ (as John vii, 16, 17, and xvii, 7, 8, affirm), and Jesus in
turn *sent and signified it by his angel unto his servant John.*   It
was designed to show unto all *his servants* (that is, servants of
Jesus Christ), as well as unto John, *the things which must shortly
come to pass ;* and so John reckoned himself as a fellow-servant
along with all who love and worship God and keep his commandments (comp. verse 9 and xxii, 9).   The word *signified* (ἐσήμανεν)
suggests that this heavenly revelation was communicated through
signs and symbols, and how God sent and symbolized it is indicated
in chaps. v–x, where the sealed book of divine mysteries, seen on
the hand of God, is taken by the Lamb, and, the seals having been all
opened by him, it is given as a little book to John, and eaten by
him so as to become a word of prophecy to many peoples.   For *his
angel* should here be understood as the angel of Jesus Christ, and
the particular reference is to the strong angel out of whose hand
John took the opened book, as recorded in chap. x, 8–10.   The

subject-matter of the Apocalypse is here said to be *things which must shortly come to pass*. The word *must* (δεῖ) indicates the writer's profound conception of the divine order of the world. The God who rules earth and heaven sees the end from the beginning, determines the times and seasons (Acts i, 7), and secures unfailingly those things which are necessary to the fulfillment of his purposes in the kingdoms of men. The things thus destined to come to pass soon after the composition of this book were in substance the same as those of which Jesus discoursed on the Mount of Olives, and which are written in Matt. xxiv, Mark xiii, and Luke xxi. They concerned the approaching end of that age, the overthrow of Jerusalem and with it the old covenant of Mount Sinai, and the coming of the kingdom which is to break in pieces and consume all other kingdoms, and never to be destroyed (Dan. ii, 44). It was necessary that these things *come to pass shortly*, for Jesus had repeatedly declared that the consummation of that age and his coming in his kingdom would take place before that generation passed away (Matt. xvi, 28 ; xxiv, 34).

2. It is next added that this servant John *witnessed the word of God, and the testimony of Jesus Christ.* The aorist tense here used suggests that this title and superscription were written, in the manner of a preface, after the rest of the book was completed ; and for the moment John contemplates the assembly listening to the reading of the words of the prophecy. To his own mind the entire revelation lies in a definite past, and he puts on record the fact that he *witnessed*, that is, bore testimony to *what he saw.* The command of verse 19 to write what he saw was strictly obeyed, and the book of this revelation is the result, and is here spoken of as already completed. *The word of God* is here to be understood of this revelation, considered as a word of prophecy originating with God as stated in verse 1 ; and *the testimony of Jesus Christ* is the same *word of God* as made known by him who in verse 5 is called "the faithful witness." It is the same word and testimony as in verse 9, for the sake of which John was in Patmos, and which are thought and spoken of as *whatsoever things he saw* (ὅσα εἶδεν).

3. The mention of *the reader and the hearers* contemplates a public reading and a devout assembly ; for *the words of the prophecy* are here commended as a genuine revelation from God, to be as much heeded as any book of inspired prophecy. For "the words of the prophecy of this book" (xxii, 10) do not only furnish a series of wonderful visions, which one may profitably meditate and keep in his heart (comp. Dan. vii, 28), but they are also full of command, exhortation, rebuke, and warning. And, therefore, the original

readers and hearers, and those of all time, may well *keep the things which are written therein.* One immediate motive for observing the words herein written was that *the time was at hand.* These words, like those of verse 1, and chap. xxii, 6, 10, 12, 20, declare the imminence of the events predicted in this book. The impending ruin of Judaism and its city and temple was but a few years in the future when John wrote, and that world-historical catastrophe was on the one hand a judging and avenging of the blood of the martyrs (chaps. vi, 10; xi, 18 ; Matt. xxiii, 31–36), and on the other a signal that the new word of Jehovah, the gospel of the kingdom, should thenceforth proceed from Jerusalem, untrammeled by the bonds of a local cultus, and grow until the kingdoms of the world become the possession of Jehovah and his Christ.

SALUTATION. I, 4–6.

4 JOHN to the seven churches which are in Asia: Grace to you and peace, from him who is and who was and who is to come; and
5 from the seven Spirits which are before his throne; and from Jesus Christ, *who is* the faithful witness, the firstborn of the dead, and the ruler of the kings of the earth. Unto him that loveth us, and loosed us
6 from our sins by his blood; and he made us *to be* a kingdom, *to be* priests unto his God and Father; to him *be* the glory and the dominion for ever and ever. Amen.

After the superscription of verses 1–3, which is of the nature of a short preface, or, perhaps, a title-page, the writer addresses himself to the seven churches of Asia after the manner of an epistolary salutation. He calls himself simply *John ;* in verse 9, *I John,* and so again in xxii, 8. No other John known to the early Church could have announced himself thus so well as the great apostle. "We instinctively feel," says Trench, "that for anyone else there would have been an affectation of simplicity, concealing a most real arrogance, in the very plainness of the title, in the assumption that thus to mention himself was sufficient to insure his recognition, or that he had a right to appropriate this name in so absolute a manner to himself." [1] The *Asia* in which *the seven churches* were located was what is commonly called " proconsular Asia," consisting of the provinces of Mysia, Lydia, Caria, and Phrygia. In these regions ancient tradition places the later life and ministry of the apostle John ; and there appears no good reason to doubt that, after the martyrdom of his brother James, which was so "pleasing to the Jews" (Acts xii, 2, 3), he left Jerusalem and repaired to the

---

[1] Commentary on the Epistles to the Seven Churches in Asia, *in loco.*

western part of Asia Minor. It is not improbable that he was the
founder of most, if not all, the churches named in verse 11.

The salutation of *grace to you and peace* is the same as that of
the Pauline epistles (see Rom. i, 7; 1 Cor. i, 3; Gal. i, 3; Eph.
i, 2); but the divine source of these mercies is immediately designated in
terms peculiar to this Apocalypse. They are from the Eternal One,
from the Seven Spirits, and from Jesus Christ. This mention of a
trinal fountain of grace and peace should be compared with Matt.
xxviii, 19, and 2 Cor. xiii, 13. The one *who is and who was and
who is to come* is "the God" of verse 1 and "the God and Father"
of verse 6, and *the Seven Spirits* are but an apocalyptic designation
of the Spirit who speaks to the churches in chaps. ii, 7, 11, 17, etc.
The threefold designation of God the Father is an allusion to Exod.
iii, 14, where God says to Moses that his name is I AM HE WHO IS.
This free appropriation and expansion of the words as a proper
name may account for the violation of grammar noticeable in the
Greek text (ἀπὸ ὁ ὤν). He is the God who is "from eternity unto
eternity" (Psalm xc, 2), the ever-living One. But the future
manifestation of his being is noticeably represented by the word
ἐρχόμενος, the one *who is to come*, rather than ἐσόμενος, who *is to be*.
For the God who is revealed in this Apocalypse is the one who
comes in judgment, continually carries on his plan of world dominion, and completes his covenants of promise. The *Seven Spirits*
are mentioned next, in order to leave the third place for the name
which is also to receive a threefold designation. The Holy Spirit is
appropriately given this symbolic title in allusion apparently to the
apocalyptic "seven eyes of Jehovah which run to and fro through
the whole earth" (Zech. iv, 10; comp. Rev. v, 6). The Spirit is
manifold in his gifts and operations (1 Cor. xii, 4), and the words
which are before his throne suggest the teaching of John xv, 26,
concerning "the Spirit of truth that goeth forth frőm the Father."
The name of *Jesus Christ* is brought in last for the purpose of a
special emphasis, and because the doxology with which the salutation closes is to be directed conspicuously to him. He is here called
the faithful witness, the words being appropriated from Psalm
lxxxix, 37 (38), where the seed of David is said to continue forever,
established as the moon, "even a faithful witness in the sky."
Christ came into the world to bear witness to the truth (John xviii,
37), and all the trustworthy testimony which we possess touching
God and life and immortality is through him. He is also *the firstborn of the dead*, and so has been "declared to be the Son of God
in power" (Rom. i, 4). Paul saw the fulfillment of Psalm ii, 7, in
the resurrection and enthronement of Jesus (Acts xiii, 33), and in

Col. i, 18, he employs the expression "firstborn from the dead." But in this book the apocalyptist probably uses the word *firstborn* as the chief representative and lord of such as live and reign with Christ in glory (chap. xx, 4, 6; xxii, 5). He was himself dead, but he says in verse 18, "I am alive for the ages of the ages, and I have the keys of death and of Hades." As the faithful witness he is "the truth," and as firstborn of the dead he is "the life" (comp. John xiv, 6). Having himself "been made perfect, he became unto all them that obey him the author of salvation eternal" (Heb. v, 9). The third title ascribed to him is *Prince* (or *ruler*) *of the kings of the earth*, and the manifest appropriation of the language of Psalm ii, 2; lxxxix, 27, implies a recognition of him as the Messiah, the anointed king of Zion, "highest of the kings of the earth." Compare his titles, "King of kings, and Lord of lords," in chaps. xvii, 14, and xix, 16.

The threefold designation of Jesus Christ prompts many a thought of the unspeakable riches of his grace, and naturally leads the writer to conclude his salutation with a doxology, ascribing *the glory and the dominion*, through all *the ages* to come, *unto him who loves us, and loosed us from our sins in his blood.* Observe that the word *loves* is in the present and *loosed* is aorist : the one pointing to the continual love which abides as a blessed experience, the other pointing back to the one great blood-atoning sacrifice for sin by which he "has perfected forever them that are sanctified" (Heb. x, 10, 14). At the beginning of the sixth verse the writer turns from the participial construction with which he began his doxology, and, after the Hebraistic manner so often noticeable in this book, proceeds : *And he made us* (*to be*) *a kingdom, priests unto his God and Father.* This second clause is in apposition with the first, and the sentiment is appropriated from Exod. xix, 6, where God promises Israel that they shall be a peculiar treasure to him above all people, and says, "Ye shall be unto me a kingdom of priests and a holy nation." John here conceives the promise as good as fulfilled, for the revelation of Jesus, communicated to him and the churches, has already assured him of all this. For he has heard "great voices in heaven" saying that Jehovah and his Christ have taken possession of the kingdom of the world (chap. xi, 15; comp. 1 Peter ii, 9), and his saints, made like himself to be both kings and priests, rule over the nations (chap. ii, 26; iii, 21; v, 10). Thus the members of this kingdom all become like Melchizedek, uniting the offices of royalty and priesthood, and live and reign with Christ, unto the glory of *his God and Father*, who is also the God and Father of them all. Comp. John xx, 17, and Rev. xxi, 3, 7.

APOCALYPTIC ANNOUNCEMENT. I, 7, 8.

7 Behold, he cometh with the clouds; and every eye shall see him, and
they who pierced him; and all the tribes of the earth shall mourn over
8 him. Yea, Amen. I am the Alpha and the Omega, saith the Lord God,
who is and who was and who is to come, the Almighty.

These two verses contain, first, a solemn declaration of the great
theme of the book, and second, a confirmation of it as a sure word
of God. In this twofold aspect the whole announcement follows
the style of Old Testament prophets who associate with their oracles
the assurance that Jehovah himself is the real speaker. It was the
word of Jehovah coming vividly to Ezekiel that enabled him to look
into the opened heavens and see the visions of God (Ezek. i, 1, 3, 4).
Amos's announcement that "Jehovah will roar out of Zion, and
wither the top of Carmel" is immediately followed by "thus saith
Jehovah" (Amos i, 2, 3 ; comp. iv, 12, 13, and Joel iii, 16, 17 ; Zeph.
i, 1, 2). The language of verse 7 is in substance identical with that
of Jesus in Matt. xxiv, 30 : "Then shall appear the sign of the Son
of man, and then shall all the tribes of the land wail, and they shall
see the Son of man coming on the clouds of heaven with power and
much glory." The image is repeated in Rev. xiv, 14, but is no
more to be understood of a visible phenomenon in the world of sense
than is the coming of Jehovah on a swift cloud to destroy Egyptian
idolatry, as prophesied in Isa. xix, 1. The emotional style conspicuous in the words *Behold, he cometh with the clouds,* shows that the
writer is in the element of spiritual vision, and it betrays a total
misconception of apocalyptics to insist that this language can only
mean that Christ is to come on a material cloud and display his
bodily presence to all men in the world at one moment of time.
Such a conception involves a manifest physical absurdity. The
coming is to be understood as we understand Micah i, 3, 4 : "Behold, Jehovah cometh forth out of his place, and he will come down
and tread upon the high places of the land ; and the mountains
shall melt under him." So, too, in Psalm xviii, 9-11, Jehovah is
described as bowing the heavens and coming down, making the
thick clouds a pavilion, and flying on the wings of the wind. The
language of Rev. i, 7, as well as Matt. xxiv, 30 ; xxvi, 64; Mark
xiii, 26, and Luke xxi, 27, is appropriated from Dan. vii, 13, and in
all these places alike is to be explained as apocalyptic metaphor,
and the *seeing* him by every eye must be understood in accord with
the same principle of interpretation. The great event, and all that
it involves from first to last, is conceived as a crisis of ages. The
words *they who pierced him* are from Zech. xii, 10, and should here

be understood, not so much of the soldiers who nailed Jesus to the cross, and pierced his side (comp. John xix, 37), as of those Jews upon whom Peter charged the awful crime (Acts ii, 23, 36 ; v, 30), and who had wantonly cried, "His blood be upon us and upon our children" (Matt. xxvii, 25). To the high priests, scribes, and elders who mocked and smote him Jesus himself said, "Hereafter ye shall see the Son of man sitting at the right hand of power, and coming on the clouds of heaven" (Matt. xxvi, 64). The phrase *all the tribes of the land* is from Zech. xii, 12-14, and here as there has reference to the families of the Jewish people, not to all the nations of the earth. The *mourning* is that of "the great tribulation" of those days of fearful woes when Jerusalem was brought to ruin (Matt. xxiv, 21). It is the long-continued wail of the scattered tribes who wander only to find a grave in foreign lands.

The words *Yea, Amen,* are best understood as spoken by the Lord himself, and in connection with verse 8. The *Yea* is Greek, and *Amen* is its Hebrew equivalent. As the writer combines Greek and Hebrew equivalents in chap. ix, 11, so he introduces the statements of verse 8 by a "verily, verily," expressed in each of these two tongues. But coming as they do between the prophetic words of verse 7 and the confirming response of verse 8, they ratify both, and give assurance that all these things shall certainly come to pass. In iii, 14, the faithful and true witness calls himself THE AMEN. Verse 8 is the avowed utterance of a *Lord,* (who is) *the God,* the "God and Father" of verse 6 and "the God" of verse 1, who gave this revelation to Jesus Christ to show unto his servants. This is further shown by his calling himself the one *who is and who was and who is to come* (comp. verse 4). He who perpetually exists sees the end from the beginning, and so can speak with definite authority and absolute knowledge of things past, present, and to come. All the glorious coming and future of his Messiah's kingdom is seen as in a moment of time, and we need not think it strange that he speaks through his prophets of some great events of that reign, which in their development will occupy centuries, as though they were the events of an hour. For he is ὁ παντοκράτωρ, *the All-Ruler.* This last word is the Greek equivalent and used in the Septuagint for "Jehovah of hosts" (צבאות יהוה). He calls himself also *the Alpha and the Omega,* which an ancient gloss has well translated "the beginning and the end." Comp. xxii, 13. The Eternal One is at the beginning and end of all the work of his Messiah. Like the "author and finisher of the faith" in Heb. xii, 2, he is first and last in all the outgrowths of the kingdom of heaven. He created all things, and on account of his will they were created (iv, 11). But he does all these things in and through Christ. Hence the adorable unity, traceable in this book as elsewhere in the New Testament, of Jesus Christ and God. In verse 17 it is the one like unto the Son of man who says, "I am the first and the last."

I. THE EPISTLES TO THE SEVEN CHURCHES. I, 9–III, 22.

INTRODUCTORY CHRISTOPHANY. I, 9–20.

9 I John, your brother and partaker with you in the tribulation and kingdom and patience *which are* in Jesus, was in the isle that is called
10 Patmos, for the word of God and the testimony of Jesus. I was in spirit on the Lord's day, and I heard behind me a great voice, as of a
11 trumpet saying, What thou seest, write in a book, and send *it* to the seven churches; unto Ephesus, and unto Smyrna, and unto Pergamum, and unto Thyatira, and unto Sardis, and unto Philadelphia, and unto La-
12 odicea. And I turned to see the voice which spake with me. And hav-
13 ing turned I saw seven golden candlesticks; and in the midst of the candlesticks one like unto a son of man, clothed with a garment down to the foot,
14 and girt about at the breasts with a golden girdle. And his head and his hair were white as white wool, *white* as snow; and his eyes were as a flame of
15 fire; and his feet like unto burnished brass, as if it had been refined in a
16 furnace; and his voice as the voice of many waters. And he had in his right hand seven stars: and out of his mouth proceeded a sharp two-edged sword: and his countenance was as the sun shineth in his strength.
17 And when I saw him, I fell at his feet as one dead. And he laid his right hand upon me, saying, Fear not; I am the first and the last, and
18 the Living one; and I was dead, and behold, I am alive for evermore,
19 and I have the keys of death and of Hades. Write therefore the things which thou sawest, and the things which are, and the things which shall
20 come to pass hereafter; the mystery of the seven stars which thou sawest in my right hand, and the seven golden candlesticks. The seven stars are the angels of the seven churches: and the seven candlesticks are seven churches.

As introductory to the epistles to the seven churches we have first a glorious vision of the Son of man, from whom all the messages proceed. The whole passage readily divides into four parts: (1) John in Patmos (9). (2) Words of the great voice (10, 11). (3) The vision of Christ (12–16). (4) The assuring word to John (17–20).

In the expression *I John*, the writer imitates the style of Daniel (comp. Dan. vii, 15; viii, 1; ix, 2; x, 2; xii, 5), the only other biblical writer who employs this form of address. But he takes to himself no special authority as an apostle or a prophet. He is profoundly conscious that he is but a bond slave of Jesus (comp. i, 1) in the communication of these wonderful messages. He accordingly calls himself *your brother and fellow-partaker in the tribulation and kingdom and patience in Jesus.* The three words, *tribulation, kingdom,* and *patience,* have notable relation to the prophecies of this book, but we need not look for any special significance in the order of the words as here written, nor (as Alford) regard the position of *kingdom* between the other two words as startling. For verse 6 has already assured us that John conceives the kingdom as good as come. The *tribulation* is the same as that foretold by Jesus in Matt. xxiv, 9. The *kingdom,* although yet to come, was already a mighty power with the disciples of Jesus. They conceived themselves, and all who with them were made partakers of the Holy Spirit, as having also "tasted the heavenly gifts and the powers of the age to come" (Heb. vi, 5). They were risen with Christ (comp. Eph. ii, 6; Col. iii, 1), and could be addressed as having already come to Mount Zion and the heavenly Jerusalem (Heb. xii, 22). But the situation was such that they could not expect to enter into the kingdom of God without many tribulations (Acts xiv, 22), and must meantime run with patience the race set before them (Heb. xii, 1). It is unscriptural to maintain that one cannot enter into the kingdom of God and be made a partaker in its heavenly powers, and yet speak of its glories and triumphs yet to come. One may be in *tribulation* and in the *kingdom* at one and the same time, and this very fact shows the necessity of *patience,* and the propriety of placing the word *patience* last in this enumeration.[1] The clause *in Jesus* qualifies the entire preceding part of the verse. It is only in Jesus Christ, as the personal friend and Saviour, that fraternal fellowship in the tribulation, kingdom, and patience is possible. On the fact and reason of John's being in Patmos, see above on pages 265–268.

Verse 10. *I was in spirit*—In the element of visional rapture, in which one obtains revelation of the heavenly mysteries. Comp. iv, 2; xvii, 3; xxi, 10. It involved the conditions of ecstasy (ἔκστασις) which fell upon Peter (Acts x, 10), and in which Paul had "visions and revelations of the Lord" (2 Cor. xii, 1). Its import is seen by help of the opposite idea expressed in Acts xii, 11, "When Peter

---

[1] There is much sound sense in the following words of Glasgow: "Those who stickle for a personal coming to Jerusalem in the future are only waiting in weak faith for what stronger faith would teach them that we have already; as the apostate Jews have lingered on for eighteen centuries waiting for the Messiah, not believing that he did indeed come. Personal presence in Jerusalem would not be presence to the saints in all the world. Corporeal visibility to men in the present life is a dream, altogether unsanctioned in the New Testament, and calculated from age to age to involve feeble believers in disappointment."—*The Apocalypse, Translated and Expounded,* p. 126. Edinburgh, 1872.

was *in himself*" (ἐν ἑαυτῷ): that is, when he had recovered his ordinary self-consciousness after the angelic visitation.

In the Lord's day—This expression has been usually explained as the first day of the week, the day of the Lord's resurrection, of which we read in the Epistle of Barnabas (xv, 9), "We observe the eighth day in cheerfulness, in which also Jesus rose from the dead." Ignatius, also, in his Epistle to the Magnesians, speaks of "no longer keeping Sabbath, but living κατὰ κυριακήν, *according to the Lord's* (day?), in which also our life sprung up through him and his death." But the critical reader will note that the expressions employed by Barnabas and Ignatius are not identical with this of John, and the New Testament phrase for the first day of the week is ἡ μία τῶν σαββάτων, or μία σαββάτου (Matt. xxviii, 1; Mark xvi, 2; Luke xxiv, 1; John xx, 1, 19; Acts xx, 7; 1 Cor. xvi, 2). But we do have the words ἡ ἡμέρα τοῦ κυρίου, and ἡμέρα κυρίου, as the frequent designation of the day of the Lord's coming (Acts ii, 20; 1 Cor. i, 8; v, 5; 2 Cor. i, 14; 1 Thess. v, 2; 2 Thess. ii, 2; 2 Peter iii, 10), and this is conspicuously the great theme of this book (see verse 7, and notes thereon). What remarkable difference is there between ἡμέρα κυρίου and κυριακὴ ἡμέρα, that any candid writer should feel called upon to say that the one could not be used as a substitute for the other?[1] We fail to see how any scheme of apocalyptic interpretation is affected by these words. The great subject of the book is the coming of the Lord to judge his enemies and reward his saints, and what difference could it make in the exposition whether John saw his visions on one day of the week rather than another? If he intended to say that his divine ecstasy placed him in the midst of the scenes of the great day of the Lord we do not see how he could have stated it more emphatically; but if ἐν τῇ κυριακῇ ἡμέρᾳ merely denotes the day of the week on which he saw the visions, it seems to occupy too prominent a place in the sentence and to receive too much emphasis for such an incidental matter. The only other passage in the New Testament where the word occurs is 1 Cor. xi, 20, in the phrase *Lord's supper* (κυριακὸν δεῖπνον). Will any of those who write so dogmatically on this subject show that the same thought could not have been expressed by τὸ δεῖπνον τοῦ κυρίου? Compare the word in Rev. xix, 9, 17. The truth is that this

---

[1] In Origen's Commentaries on John, tomus x, 20 (Migne, *Greek Patrol.*, vol. xiv, col. 372), where he discourses on John ii, 19, "Destroy this temple, and in three days I will raise it up," he makes the statement, πᾶς οἶκος Ἰσραὴλ ἐν τῇ μεγάλῃ κυριακῇ ἐγερθήσεται: *the whole house of Israel shall be raised up in the great Lord's* (day). Here certainly κυριακή does not mean the first day of the week. But in the *Teaching of the Apostles*, xiv, 1, the day of meeting to break bread is called κυριακή κυρίου.

whole controversy over the meaning of κυριακή in this passage has no more importance in determining the real meaning of the Apocalypse than the question whether John were corporeally or only in spirit in the isle of Patmos for the sake of this word of God. Trench very frankly concedes that it is a mistake to suppose "that ἡμέρα κυριακή was a designation of Sunday already familiar among Christians," although he thinks that "the name had probably its origin here." The plain facts are that the New Testament writers have a well-known phrase to designate the first day of the week; the phrase in question is not so used by them, and occurs nowhere else in the New Testament; but its equivalent and closest parallel, ἡμέρα κυρίου, is of frequent occurrence, and everywhere means the day of the Lord's coming, not the day of his resurrection. Since, therefore, this book is not an historical narrative but a record of visions and revelations of God, we incline to regard John's being in Patmos, as well as his being in the day of the Lord, as a matter of spiritual vision, not of objective reality. In the same manner we understand Daniel's presence in Shushan and by the river Ulai (Dan. viii, 2). While not denying that Daniel may have actually gone to Shushan, and John to the island Patmos, and that the latter may have seen this vision on a first day of the week, and called it the Lord's day, we think the other interpretation more in harmony with the genius of apocalyptic composition and the purpose of this book. Adopting this view, we do not, as Alford assumes, render John's language, "I was transported by the Spirit into the day of the Lord's coming." He says nothing about "transportation" either *into* Patmos or *into* the day of the Lord. He speaks rather of his visional presence there. He says, *I was in Patmos; I was in spirit* (not in THE SPIRIT); *I was in the Lord's day*. To say that, as a matter of visional experience, he *was ecstatically in the day of the Lord* is as proper and as grammatical as to say that one may "find mercy with the Lord in that day" (2 Tim. i, 18). It would no more be a violence to the language to say that one *was in spirit in the wilderness* than to say that he " was led in the Spirit in the wilderness " (Luke iv, 1). John simply says (not that he was carried away or transported into, but rather) that he *was in spirit* (that is, visionally) *in the Lord's day*. He found himself, so to speak, (not coming or going, lifted up or set down, but) *in the very midst* of visions of the things which were shortly to come to pass. He was visionally in that day as truly as the Lord himself is " glorified in his saints in that day " (2 Thess. i, 10). Compare " So shall the Son of man be in his day " (Luke xvii, 24).

When, therefore, it is asserted by Alford that " no such rendering

would ever have been thought of, nor would it now be worth even
a passing mention, were it not that an apocalyptic system has been
built upon it," it is perhaps sufficient to remark that it does not
appear to have been first suggested or ever pressed into notice by
the exigencies of a system of interpretation ; nor is it conceivable
how preterist, historical, or futurist expositor can show it to be
more helpful to one scheme than another. With greater sobriety
and reason may it be said that the large space given to the discussion of this point is out of all proportion to its importance in any
system of interpretation. Our apology for allowing it so much
space in these notes is that it is well, at an early stage of our investigation of this book, to expose the dogmatic air and one-sided
partisan pleading which has been the bane of much of the best literature on the Apocalypse. There is little hope of arriving at a
trustworthy treatment of such a book of prophecy until men show
a willingness to allow due weight to the relative claims of diverse
opinions. If one is given to arrogant and reckless assertion on
matters of no importance, what confidence can we have in his word
or his judgment on matters of fundamental character ?

I heard behind me—No occult meaning is to be sought in the
words *behind me,* but we recognize an obvious allusion to the phrase
as employed in Isa. xxx, 21, and Ezek. iii, 12. The *great voice* came
from a point toward which he was not looking; it therefore served to
awaken and attract the seer's attention. Many are the *great voices*
mentioned in this book (comp. v, 2, 12 ; vi, 10 ; vii, 2, 10 ; viii, 13 ;
x, 3 ; xi, 12, 15 ; xii, 10 ; xiv, 7, 9, 15, 18 ; xvi, 1 ; xviii, 2 ; xix, 1,
17 ; xxi, 3), and they all serve the art and purpose of apocalyptic
representation. In most cases we are told from whom the voices
proceed, but in this passage it is left indefinite. We might naturally suppose from what immediately follows that it was the voice
of the Son of man, but a comparison of iv, 1, and what follows
there, is not in accord with such a supposition. The voice was a
heavenly call, and it seemed to John *great as that of a trumpet.*
Voices, trumpets, angels, and various visional symbols are what
may be called the machinery of apocalyptics. The trumpet suggests the signal of a divine revelation or epiphany. Comp. Exod.
xix, 13, 16, 19 ; Joel ii, 1; Matt. xxiv, 31.

11. *What thou seest write*—So he is to be like Daniel, who wrote
his dream-visions (Dan. vii, 1). The writing is to take the form
of *a book* (βιβλίον), and to be what is called in verse 2 "the word of
God and the testimony of Jesus Christ." How this is related to
the sealed book of chap. v, 1, and the opened book of x, 2, 8–11, will
be interesting to observe in the study of those passages. *The seven*

churches call for no extended comment here. The names are those of seven well-known cities of western Asia Minor, and in the absence of any certain information to the contrary may be supposed to have all been visited, and most of them, perhaps, founded by the writer of this Apocalypse. Those who wish for detailed information concerning *Ephesus, Smyrna,* and the other cities here named, should consult the large Bible dictionaries under the several names. It has been commonly assumed that these seven were the only churches existing in Proconsular Asia at the time this book was written. Such a supposition is entirely unnecessary, and probabilities are against it. *Seven* seems rather to have been purposely selected in view of the symbolical significance of that number. There is no more reason for assuming that John must needs have addressed all the existing churches of Proconsular Asia than those of Antioch, and Derbe, and Lystra, or even those of Corinth and Rome. He writes to whom he is commanded to write, and that is all we need know.

The attempts which some have made to determine the *exact* time and place of John's writing are simply a specimen of exegetical folly. Why should anyone presume to settle such a question when neither the writer himself, nor anyone in a position to know, has put on record one word concerning it? "Whether he wrote it while yet in Patmos, or after he returned to Ephesus," is of no consequence whatever to us now. (See footnote on page 267.)

12–20. The vision which John beheld when he *turned to see the voice which spoke with* him, may be shown in its apocalyptic setting by the following arrangement of its contents :

1. Seven golden candlesticks.
2. One like a Son of man.
   (1) Clothed with a garment reaching to the feet.
   (2) Girded with a golden girdle.
   (3) Forehead white as snow.
   (4) Hair white as wool.
   (5) Eyes as a flame of fire.
   (6) Feet like burnished brass.
   (7) Voice like many waters.
3. Seven stars in his hand.
4. Sharp sword from his mouth.
5. Countenance like the sun.
6. Effect on John (prostration as one dead).
7. Words of the Living One.
   (1) Fear not.
   (2) I am the first and the last.

(3) The Living One.
(4) Was dead but alive for the ages.
(5) Hold the keys of death and Hades.
(6) Write the visions.
(7) The mystery of the stars and candlesticks.

Such an analytical tabulation of the contents of this vision is perhaps the best comment upon it. The sevenfold forms of statement have no recondite significance that we should seek for some special mystery in each allusion, but they altogether serve to impress the grandeur of the Christophany. The seven candlesticks represent the seven churches, and the messages about to be given originate with this most godlike Son of man. What could have been more impressive than such a picture of the Living One from whom the faithful testimony and admonitions to the churches come?

It is to be noted that nearly all the details of the picture are taken from Old Testament prophets. The candlesticks recall Zechariah's candlestick, all of gold, and seven lamps thereon (Zech. iv, 2). The phrase *one like unto a son of man* is taken from Dan. vii, 13 (comp. also Ezek. i, 26). The *clothing* and *golden girdle* are to be compared with Dan. x, 5; Ezek. ix, 2, 3, 11, and Isa. xi, 5. The *hair like wool* is from Dan. vii, 9, and the flaming *eyes* and burnished *feet* from Dan. x, 6 (comp. Ezek. i, 7). The *voice* like the *sound of many waters* is appropriated from Ezek. i, 24; xliii, 2, and Dan. x, 6. The figure of a *sword going out of his mouth* is found in Isa. xi, 4; xlix, 2 (comp. Heb. iv, 12), and the allusion to the *sun shining in his strength* is a reminiscence of Judg. v, 31. John's prostration, mentioned in verse 17, was also like that of Ezekiel and Daniel (Ezek. i, 28; iii, 23; Dan. viii, 17); the uplifting words *fear not* are from Dan. x, 12, and the declaration *I am the first and the last* is from Isa. xli, 4; xliv, 6; xlviii, 12.

All these various parts of the description constitute a composite picture, and its majesty is felt only as we contemplate it in the total impression it is designed to make. The author aims to represent this *Son of man* in all the glory in which Daniel beheld the "Ancient of days" (in Dan. vii, 9, 10), and he freely appropriates from any Old Testament prophet whatever helps to fill up the magnificent outline. When, therefore, interpreters presume to tell us that the girdle was the symbol of his prophetic office (Glasgow), and the white hair the sign of Christ's freedom from sin (Cocceius), and his feet the apostles and ministers of his word (Glasgow), the whole effect of such procedure is to divert attention from the one great purpose of the vision. The different parts simply serve to make up a symmetrical picture. A long flowing robe appropriately has a girdle, but no mystic significance is to be sought in either. The white head and hair are not naturally suggestive of "the beauteous flaxen locks of childhood, thus representing the man Jesus in perpetual youth" (Glasgow); rather as Dan. vii, 9, intimates, they suggest the ancient, the venerable and adorable. The flaming eyes may at once suggest his penetration and intelligence, and the sharp sword proceeding from his mouth reminds the biblical student of the Messiah who "shall smite the earth with the rod of his mouth" (Isa. xi, 4). Some of these parts have significance when specified separately, as we shall find in some of the messages to the churches; but in this opening Christophany it is better to leave them in their composite relationship, and not weaken the grand impression they make as a whole by undue attention to details.

The keys of death and of Hades (verse 18) is an obvious figure for authority over death and the realm of the dead. This glorious Son of man is lord of the citadel, so to speak, where Death seems to reign, and he can open and close the gates at will. The gates of this fortress lead to the underworld, the realm of departed souls, and over Death and Hades alike this ever-living One has power. Hence the force of the first words of verse 19: *Write therefore what things thou sawest.* Because the one who *placed his right hand upon* John, and assured him that he was the arbiter of life and death, is the divine revealer of this Apocalypse, *therefore* the inspired seer may cast off his sudden fear and with holy confidence write the vision which he has just seen. The words καὶ ἃ εἰσίν, *what things are*, may be understood in two ways, (1) *what things they signify*, that is, as explained immediately of the stars and the candlesticks, and (2) *what things are now existing*, as contrasted with what is to come to pass in the future. On the whole we prefer the latter. For ἃ εἰσίν followed immediately by καὶ ἃ μέλλει γίνεσθαι most naturally means *things which now are* as distinguished from *things which are yet to be.* If the writer meant to say "what things thou sawest and what they signify" would he not have used the word σημαίνουσι (as in chap. i, 1) rather than εἰσίν? As the language now stands we have the vision itself designated as past, things contemplated in the vision as present, and other things yet to follow *after these* (comp. iv, 1).

Verse 20 gives an explanation of *the mystery* of *the stars* and *the candlesticks.* The word *mystery* here means the mystical significance or symbolical meaning of these objects of the vision. The *candlesticks* or *lamp stands* (λυχνία; comp. מְנוֹרָה in Zech. iv, 2) are symbols of the churches. As organized bodies of Christian confessors the churches receive the light of the Lord and reflect the same so as to be the light of the world (comp. Matt. v, 14, 16; John viii, 12; ix, 5). But a deeper mystery seems to conceal the exact meaning of the *seven stars*; for, though said to be *angels of the seven churches*, the import of the word *angels* in such a definition is as difficult to determine as that of *stars*. We reject as unsatisfactory all those explanations which make the angels either messengers, delegates, officers, presbyters, or bishops of the churches. There is no evidence that the word *angel* was ever so employed in the early church, and what especially bears against this view is the fact that the addresses to the several churches are unsuitable for a mere officer, or bishop, or any one individual representative of the church. The responsible and characteristic *personnel*, embracing the church itself in the main body of its membership, seems to be contemplated in every address to the angel of the church designated. For this reason also we reject the notion that the guardian angel of each particular church is to be understood, for why praise or blame such an angel as personally guilty of the acts of the church itself? The old view of Andreas and Arethas that the angel of the church is the church itself seems on the whole to be the best supported, and in accord with the angel of the altar, the angel of the fire, and the angel of the waters (comp. chap. xiv, 18; xvi, 5, 7). The assumption of Alford that "as the *church* is an objective reality, so must the *angel* be, of whatever kind," is a fallacy in apocalyptic interpretation. One might as well maintain that the seals, and the trumpets, and the bowls of wrath are objective realities. That they have symbolic significance is clear, but that the angels that blow the trumpets have objective reality is as far from the truth as to say that all John's visions had objective reality. To discriminate between the symbol and the thing signified is the task of the interpreter, whose critical judgment should discern what is essentially real and what mere drapery or sign. The angels of the churches are best explained as an apocalyptic title for the churches, conceived not so much as organized bodies as in the characterizing personal elements and life which distinguish one church from another.[1] So when the Living One says to a church, "I know thy works, thy zeal, thy patience, thy failures, thy poverty and nakedness," the reference is to no one individual, least of all to a bishop or a guardian angel, but to the body of the church itself. Every member of a church so addressed is to feel himself intended, and to know that he personally, as well as the whole body associated with him in fellowship, is held in the right hand of him who also holds the keys of

---

[1] So Düsterdieck: "The angel of the church appears as the living unity of the one organism of the church, which, as it were, in mass clings to the Lord."

death and of Hades.[1] That right hand can lift him up and drive away his fears (verse 17) or in righteous judgment remove his candlestick out of its place (ii, 5).

In passing now to study in detail the messages to the seven churches we note especially the artificial symmetry of form in which they are all cast. Besides the introductory formula, *To the angel of the church write*, which is the same in all the epistles, we observe three main divisions in each epistle.

1. The divine source of the message, designated by one or more of the titles of the Son of man already given in the introductory Christophany (i, 12–18). The uniform beginning is, *These things saith*, virtually the equivalent of the prophectic "Thus saith Jehovah" (comp. Amos i, 3 ; ii, 1 ; Obad. 1 ; Zech. i, 4 ; Mal. i, 2, 9).

2. The message itself, declaring the speaker's knowledge (οἶδα) of the works, character, and condition of the church. With this declaration of knowledge are connected words of praise or blame, admonition or encouragement, according to the condition of each particular church.

3. The promise to him that overcomes (ὁ νικῶν), associated in each case with the solemn call, *He that hath an ear, let him hear what the Spirit saith unto the churches.* In the first three epistles (Ephesus, Smyrna, and Pergamum) these words precede, but in the other four they follow the words of promise.

We also observe a notable correspondence of the contents of these three parts, and a striking fitness to each other. The characteristic titles of the Lord who speaks seem to have been chosen with reference to the character of the particular church addressed, and the kind of reward promised to the victor.

1. The Church in Ephesus. II, 1–7.

Toiling, enduring, but fallen from her first love.

1 To the angel of the church in Ephesus write;
   These things saith he that holdeth the seven stars in his right hand, he
2 that walketh in the midst of the seven golden candlesticks: I know thy
   works, and thy toil and patience, and that thou canst not bear evil men,
   and didst try them which call themselves apostles, and they are not, and

---

[1] Hence the angel of a church is not to be explained as an "ideal reality," or an abstraction of thought, or a personification of the spirit of a community. The word *angel* here, as in analogous passages cited, is a mere apocalyptic title, a symbolical appellative ; but it denotes something that is real and conspicuous in each church addressed. "The angel of the church," says Gebhardt, "represents it as a unity, an organized moral person, a living whole, in which one member depends upon and affects the others, in which a definite spirit reigns, and by which one church is distinguished from another."—*Doctrine of the Apocalypse*, p. 39.

3 didst find them false; and thou hast patience and didst bear for my
4 name's sake, and hast not grown weary. But I have *this* against thee,
5 that thou didst leave thy first love. Remember therefore from whence
thou art fallen, and repent, and do the first works; or else I come to
thee, and will move thy candlestick out of its place, except thou repent.
6 But this thou hast, that thou hatest the works of the Nicolaitans, which
7 I also hate. He that hath an ear, let him hear what the Spirit saith to
the churches. To him that overcometh, to him will I give to eat of the
tree of life, which is in the Paradise of God.

1. The message is from him who holds the stars and walks in the
midst of the candlesticks (comp. i, 13, 16). In i, 16, the stars were
simply *had* in his hand (ἔχων), in i, 20, they were *seen upon* his
hand, but here they are held fast or *ruled* (κρατῶν) by his mighty
hand. So, too, in i, 13, he was seen in the midst of the candlesticks,
but no motion or activity was noted ; here he is *the one who walks*
in the midst of the candlesticks. He is a living and active power
in the churches, conversant with all that is going on among them.
2. The contents of the message consist of three main elements :
(1) A commendation of the *works, toil,* and *patience* of the church,
especially in the trial and conviction of false apostles. (2) Admonition and warning because of leaving their *first love.* (3) Their
relation to the *works of the Nicolaitans.* As an example of the *evil
men,* who were too heavy a burden for them to bear, mention is
made of *them who call themselves apostles and are not.* In what
particulars they claimed to be apostles, and on what grounds they
were proven to be *false,* we are not told. Compare Paul's words in
Acts xx, 29, 30, to the Ephesian elders about the "grievous wolves,"
and men of the church "speaking perverse things to draw away
the disciples after them."

The *first love* from which this church had fallen is to be understood of the first warm affection for Christ which it displayed.
There appears to be an allusion to the imagery of Jer. ii, 2, where
Jehovah says of Israel, "I remember thee, the goodness of thy
youth, the love of thy espousals." The notion that such a lapse
from the first Christian love and zeal implies a long period after the
foundation of the church is altogether untenable. The history of
individual churches for nearly two thousand years has shown many
an instance of deplorable leaving the first love within less than one
year after a most gracious quickening. Paul's epistle to the Galatians ought to silence the partisan pleading which has alleged that
this losing of first love by the Ephesians could not have taken place
before the end of Nero's reign. Those Galatians, whose first love
for Christ was such that they "would, if possible, have plucked out

their eyes and given them to" his apostle (Gal. iv, 15), fell away from that love so soon that he was obliged to write to them in sorrow, "I marvel that ye are so quickly removing from him that called you in the grace of Christ unto a different gospel" (Gal. i, 6). The admonition is threefold: *remember, repent,* and *do the first works.* The awakening of tender memories leads to repentance, and a genuine repentance is evinced by doing the same kind and quality of works as those which displayed the sincerity of the first warm affection. The warning that, in case of failure thus to *repent,* there would certainly follow a retributive removal of the candlestick itself was but the necessary announcement of him who is emphatically "the faithful witness."

The Nicolaitans are only mentioned here, as if their *works* were well known. Their *teaching* is mentioned in verse 15 in connection with that of Balaam, "who taught Balak to cast a stumbling-block before the children of Israel, to eat things sacrificed to idols, and to commit fornication." The fact that again in verse 20 "the woman Jezebel" is charged with the same evil teaching and deeds suggests that the names *Nicolaitans, Balaam,* and *Jezebel* are to be understood as symbolical, and represent different gradations of one and the same evil. The church in Ephesus is clear of the evil, and commended for *hating the works* of the Nicolaitans, for in this they have the mind of the Lord who also hates them. But the church in Pergamum had become complicated with the evil, and had some who held the *teaching of Balaam* and some who held the *teaching of the Nicolaitans;* that is, the church had different grades of these mischievous teachers, some being more notorious than others. In Thyatira, however, this evil was tolerated by the church, and seems to have assumed the boldness of an impious Jezebel, calling for fearful judgment from the Lord. That the *Nicolaitans* were no heretical sect of this name, as some of the fathers imagined, but that the name is symbolical, may be reasonably concluded from the following considerations.

(1) There is no trustworthy evidence of the existence of a sect of this name. The patristic testimonies from Irenæus downward exhibit a notable vagueness, are in several things self-contradictory, and are evidently based on this passage of the Apocalypse which they assume to explain. They trace the supposed sect to the Nicolas of Acts vi, 5 (apparently for the want of any other person of this name known to the early Church), and report various fanciful stories about the unhappy relations of Nicolas and his wife. The story grows with the lapse of time, until finally Epiphanius says that all the Gnostic sects sprung originally from this same "Nicolas,

a proselyte of Antioch." It has been well observed that the patristic knowledge of this sect grew in proportion to the remoteness of the several writers from the times when this Nicolas lived !

(2) The conjunction of Balaamites and Nicolaitans in verses 14 and 15 warrants the inference that if one is a symbolical name so is the other.

(3) The name *Nicolaitan* (from νικάω and λάος) is the Greek equivalent of the Hebrew *Balaam*,[1] and both alike denote *destroyer of the people*. They correspond as closely as Abaddon and Apollyon in chap. ix, 11, and the analogy of that passage in its use of a Greek and Hebrew name of like meaning tends to confirm the view here presented.

(4) But the fact that Balaamites and Jezebelites in these epistles are identical in their teachings and works, as seen by comparison of verses 14 and 20, makes it the more probable that the Nicolaitans are but another class of these same offenders. If this be true it is easy to trace the obvious gradation of the evildoers in three of these epistles. As dangerous foes of God's people they are hated in the church of Ephesus ; as successors of Balaam they injure the church of Pergamum, as that ancient soothsayer injured the children of Israel (Num. xxxi, 16). In the church of Thyatira they have become so rooted in the depths of Satan that they are tolerated as an impious harlot, who even claims to be a prophetess.

What hateful evil of the early Church, it may now be asked, is designated by these symbolic names ? The answer is furnished both in verses 14 and 20. The eating of things sacrificed to idols and fornication were evils over which the early churches composed of Jews and Gentiles had no little trouble. What Paul writes in Rom. xiv, 15-23 ; 1 Cor. viii, 7-13, about eating things sacrificed to idols, and his frequent condemning allusions to fornication and other sins of uncleanness (1 Cor. v, 1 ; vi, 13, 18 ; 2 Cor. xii, 21 ; Gal. v, 19 ; Eph. v, 3 ; Col. iii, 5 ; 1 Thess. iv, 3-7), is evidence of this. And the first great council of the apostles and elders at Jerusalem was convened to consider matters of this kind. There were two parties, one stickling over rites and Jewish laws, and insisting that the Gentile converts should observe circumcision and other laws of Moses (Acts xv, 5), while the other contended for greater liberty, and argued that the Gentile converts ought not to be brought under the yoke of Judaism. They compromised on four things which were to be enforced as necessary to the peace

---

[1] Balaam may be from בַל, *not*, or בְּלַע, to *destroy*, and עַם, *people*. If explained as *not the people*, it would still suggest hostility to the people, as a foe and an alien. Either derivation sufficiently meets the demands of nominal symbolism.

and prosperity of the Church, two of which were a total abstinence from things sacrificed to idols and from fornication (Acts xv, 29). The troubles over these things in churches to which Paul wrote show that the decrees of the Jerusalem council were not everywhere enforced. There were very naturally, as is always the case in such controversies, extremists on both sides. The rigid Jewish party doubtless provoked in many places, like Pergamum and Thyatira, a bold and lawless opposition which carried the liberty for which men like Paul pleaded into impious license, and commanded a following which might well have been likened to Balaam's teaching to cast a stumbling-block before Israel, and, in its worst forms, to an idolatry and presumption like that of Jezebel. Such presumptuous libertines may have given the envious Jews occasion to say that Paul's teaching of freedom from the law was responsible for these excesses. And it is notable that " Jews from Asia " excited the multitude against Paul at Jerusalem, and cried out, "This is the man that teacheth *all men everywhere against the people* and the law " (Acts xxi, 28). Such was virtually charging Paul with being a *Nicolaitan* (foe of the people) in the sense above explained. The charge was a vile slander against Paul, but it may have originated in confounding Paul's real doctrine with the wicked perversion of it in some of the churches of Asia.

3. The promise *to him that overcometh* is enforced and made quite general by the words which accompany all the promises in the seven epistles : *He that hath an ear, let him hear what the Spirit saith to the churches.* The Spirit is no other than "the seven Spirits which are before the throne" (i, 4), and what this universal Spirit here says is not merely for the church of Ephesus, but for all *the churches*. See more on this at the close of the epistles (iii, 22). The victor (ὁ νικῶν) in every case is the one who perseveres in all works, toil, patience, conflict, and suffering which the times and situation involve. He who is faithful to the truth of Christ, and maintains his cause unto the end of the struggle, is assured of glorious reward. In this first promise it is the heavenly gift of *eating of the tree of life which is in the Paradise of God.* This is a manifest allusion to the tree of life in the garden of Eden as mentioned in Gen. ii, 9 ; iii, 22–24. The lost Paradise and its tree of life are to be restored, and these Christian victors are to eat of that heavenly fruit. In the New Testament, Paradise is the name of the heavenly abode of disembodied spirits (Luke xxii, 43 ; 2 Cor. xii, 2, 4). Compare also what is said in chap. xxii, 2, of the river and "the tree of life, bearing twelve fruits, yielding its fruit every month: and the leaves of the tree were for the healing of the nations."

In studying the symmetry and inner congruity of the several parts of this first epistle of the seven we observe :

1. The propriety of designating Christ in this first epistle by the first and most conspicuous fact which arrested the eye of the seer, his position in the midst of the seven candlesticks, and his hold upon the seven stars.

2. He who holds fast, and has all power over, the seven stars takes occasion in this first address to say how thoroughly he knows all that is good and bad in the personnel of the church, and, walking in the midst of the candlesticks, and observing all that occurs among them, he will be sure to remove out of its place the candlestick whose representative stars persistently offend.

3. Paradise and the tree of life are a most fitting reward for those who, by toil and patience and doing the first works, recover and retain their first love unto the end. Such will find Paradise restored; they "wash their robes, that they may have the authority over the tree of life" (xxii, 14).

2. The Church in Smyrna. II, 8–11.

The martyr church.

8 And to the angel of the church in Smyrna write;
   These things saith the first and the last, which was dead, and lived
9 *again :* I know thy tribulation, and thy poverty (but thou art rich), and
   the blasphemy of them who say they are Jews, and they are not, but are
10 a synagogue of Satan. Fear not the things which thou art about to suffer: behold, the devil is about to cast some of you into prison, that ye
   may be tried; and ye shall have tribulation ten days. Be thou faithful
11 unto death, and I will give thee the crown of life. He that hath an ear,
   let him hear what the Spirit saith to the churches. He that overcometh
   shall not be hurt of the second death.

1. The message to this church comes from Him who is *the first and the last, who was dead and lived.* These are titles which he gave himself in i, 17, 18, when he laid his right hand upon John, and said, "Fear not."

2. This church is noted (1) for its *tribulation* and *poverty ;* (2) for the *blasphemy* of those who called themselves Jews, but were rather *a synagogue of Satan;* and (3) for encouragement in view of imprisonment and bitter trials in the near future. A part of their affliction may have been the *poverty* resulting from violent spoliation of their possessions (comp. Heb. x, 34), but they are cheered with the reminder that in spite of such poverty they were truly *rich* in heavenly treasure (comp. Matt. v, 10–12 ; vi, 20; 2 Cor. vi, 10). *The blasphemy of them who say they are Jews* is to

be understood of the calumnious and bitter opposition of fanatical Jews, who not only at Smyrna, but in all the provinces, were the leaders in the violent persecutions of the Christians (see Acts xiii, 50 ; xiv, 2, 5, 19 ; xvii, 5 ; xxi, 27 ; xxiii, 12; xxiv, 5–10 ; 1 Thess. ii, 14–16). Even the martyrdom of Polycarp at Smyrna, a generation later, was distinguished by the fierce zeal with which the excited Jewish calumniators urged it on. Such *Jews* were unworthy of the name. Bitterness so malevolent is conspicuously of the devil, and hence instead of representing a synagogue of God they are appropriately called *a synagogue of Satan.* We may well compare " the throne of Satan " in verse 13, and "the depths of Satan " in verse 24. We should note, too, that it is *the devil* who is *about to cast into prison* some of the church of Smyrna, so that, thus early in the book, "the old serpent who is called the Devil and Satan " (comp. xii, 9 ; xx, 2) appears as the great author of persecutions. The false and unworthy Jews are here his agents, as, at a later stage of the Apocalypse, other agencies appear as instigated and possessed by his infernal genius. The *ten days* are to be taken as a symbolical number, here indicative of a limited period of time (comp. Matt. xxiv, 22 ; Dan. i, 12, 14 ; Gen. xxiv, 55). The exhortation to *be faithful unto death* implies in this connection more than fidelity until the time of death ; it involves the idea of a martyr's death. Be thou continuously faithful even though that faithfulness subject thee to death. Compare the phrase *unto death* in xii, 11, and Acts xxii, 4. Such a death leads to a crowned life beyond. Comp. James i, 12 ; 1 Peter v, 4 ; 2 Tim. iv, 8. The *crown* is that of both victory and royalty.

3. The single promise to this martyr church is that *he that over-cometh shall not be hurt of the second death.* It is a notable feature of all the promises to the victors, made in these seven epistles, that they anticipate by their allusions the subsequent revelations of this book; and hence the probability that the epistles to the seven churches were written after the prophet had completed the subsequent portions of his Apocalypse. The seven epistles, therefore, are of the nature of an introduction prepared after all the visions and revelations had been fully formulated by the author. *The second death* is next mentioned in connection with the picture of the enthroned martyrs in xx, 4–6. "Over them the second death has no power." Their martyrdom leads to heavenly life and enthronement, so that they have a blessed resurrection by reason of their fidelity unto death.

As such a resurrection is a second life, so "the lake of fire " (xx, 14) is the eternal perdition of the wicked after death, and so a second death. The expression *second death* occurs in the Targum of Onkelos and also in the Jerusalem Targum of Deut. xxxiii, 6: "Let Reuben live in eternal life, and let him not see the second death." To say, therefore, that one *shall not be hurt of the second death* is equivalent to saying that with such a one "death shall be no more" (xxi, 4).

In the symmetrical composition of this epistle we observe:

1. How appropriately these words to the martyr church come from the ever-living One, who was dead but lived. It is equivalent to the assurance of John xi, 26, that "whosoever liveth and believeth on me shall never die."

2. How appropriately the words *fear not* in verse 10 come from him who laid his right hand upon John, and spoke the words recorded in i, 17, 18.

3. How appropriate that those who are subjected to great tribulation and trial for Christ's sake, and called to die a martyr's death, should be assured of no harm from the second death. Though death seem for a moment to reign over them, much the more gloriously shall they reign in life through Jesus Christ (comp. Rom. v, 17). For them no second death remains, but rather the crown of life, the living and reigning with Christ a thousand years (xx, 4).

3. THE CHURCH IN PERGAMUM. II, 12–17.

The church near Satan's throne.

12 And to the angel of the church in Pergamum write;
13 These things saith he that hath the sharp two-edged sword: I know where thou dwellest, *even* where Satan's throne is: and thou holdest fast my name, and didst not deny my faith, even in the days of Antipas my witness, my faithful one, who was killed among you, where Satan dwell-
14 eth. But I have a few things against thee, because thou hast there some that hold the teaching of Balaam, who taught Balak to cast a stumbling-block before the children of Israel, to eat things sacrificed to idols, and
15 to commit fornication. So hast thou also some that hold the teaching
16 of the Nicolaitans in like manner. Repent therefore; or else I come to thee quickly, and I will make war against them with the sword of my
17 mouth. He that hath an ear, let him hear what the Spirit saith to the churches. To him that overcometh, to him will I give of the hidden manna, and I will give him a white stone, and upon the stone a new name written, which no one knoweth but he that receiveth it.

1. To this church the message comes from him *who has the sharp two-edged sword.* In the vision of chap. i, 16, the sword was seen proceeding out of his mouth. This sharp sword is a symbol of that "sword of the Spirit, which is the word of God" (Eph. vi, 17), and

which, in Heb. iv, 12, is said to be "living and active, and sharper than any two-edged sword, and piercing even to the dividing of soul and spirit, of both joints and marrow, and skillful to judge (κριτικός) the thoughts and intents of the heart." It is therefore more especially a symbol of conviction and judgment (John xvi, 8–11). Compare the figure in Isa. xi, 4; xlix, 2; Hosea vi, 5. The Christ who speaks is therefore no other than the divine Judge and Ruler of the world.

2. The message shows (1) that this church was dwelling *where the throne of Satan* is; but (2) was a firm defender of the faith; yet (3) had some Balaamites and Nicolaitans; and therefore (4) is admonished to *repent* and avert the sword of judgment. *The throne of Satan* is undoubtedly to be understood as some notable stronghold of Satan's power. As another manifestation of Satan was a giving of "his power and his throne and great authority" to the beast out of the sea (xiii, 2), so at Pergamum the great adversary of Christ had in some way established his throne. The fact that the temple and "genuine sanctuary" of Æsculapius was at this place (Tacitus, *Annals*, iii, 63) may serve at least to suggest that Pergamum was at that time a stronghold of heathenish superstition and idolatry. This fact also helps to account for the pernicious *teaching of Balaam* and of the *Nicolaitans*, which had found some adherents even in the church. To *hold fast the name* of Christ and *not deny his faith* under such circumstances were high commendation. We know from Paul's epistles that the church of Corinth was near another throne of Satan, and some in that place were guilty of *eating things sacrificed to idols* and of *fornication* (1 Cor. v, 1; viii, 1). Such an evil leaven tends to "leaven the whole lump" (1 Cor. v, 6). As *Balaam* and *Nicolaitan* are symbolic names (see above on verse 6), so we most naturally infer that *Antipas* is but the mystic name of some one or more faithful witnesses and martyrs of Jesus in that place. The word means *against all*,[1] and may well denote a sufferer like the author of Psalm xxii (verses 12, 16), around whom the assembly of the wicked formed a circle like so many mad dogs or strong bulls of Bashan; or like another Jeremiah, who seemed at times to stand alone against a world of evil (Jer. xv, 10; xx, 10). Certain it is that we have no trustworthy

---

[1] The assertion of Winer (*N. T. Gram.*, § 16) and others that 'Αντίπας is a contraction from 'Αντίπατρος is of no force in discussing a word which occurs nowhere else in the New Testament, and which both the context and the usage of this Apocalypse suggest as a symbolical name. The word is certainly not *necessarily* a contraction, and, if designed as a mystic name, it expresses appropriately the idea of one or a few against many.

account of any early martyr of this name, for the later legends are manifestly fabulous; like those of the origin of the Nicolaitans, they have grown out of this word in the Apocalypse, and know nothing more than is here written.

The statement of verse 14, that Balaam *taught Balak to cast a stumbling-block before the children of Israel*, accords with the tradition which is recorded in Josephus (*Ant.*, iv, 6, 6), and is in substance warranted by what is written in Num. xxxi, 16, compared with Num. xxv, 1, 2. The teaching of Balaam, as well as that of the Nicolaitans, encouraged loose complicity with idolatrous heathenism. The Balaamites and Nicolaitans, as we have shown above, are best explained as symbolical names of different degrees of the same loose libertinism and freedom with the heathen world. The admonition to *repent* (verse 16) is intensified by the threat which follows, and is notable for the four words *come, quickly, war, sword.* The whole verse is remarkable as a potent expression of solemn warning.

3. The promise that follows in verse 17 is also remarkable for its mystic allusions and the correspondence of its symbolism with the situation and conditions of the church in Pergamum. Without detailing the various opinions concerning *the hidden manna, the white stone,* and *the new name,* we simply observe that the three terms together constitute a trinity of secret gifts. Trench has well admonished us not to look in the realm of heathen customs or in pagan symbolism for our explanation, and hence not beguile ourselves with the white pebbles of the Greek ballot box or the *tessara* of the Olympic games. *The hidden manna* is an allusion to the omer of manna which was deposited as a sacred treasure in the holy of holies in connection with the tables of the law (Exod. xvi, 32–34). *The white stone* suggests either the pure golden plate on the forefront of the high priest's miter, on which was graven HOLINESS TO JEHOVAH (Exod. xxviii, 36–38), or the URIM AND THUMMIM, which were "put in the breastplate of judgment" and worn "upon the heart" of the high priest (Exod. xxviii, 30). *The new name* is to be compared with chap. iii, 12, and xix, 12, where it appears to be the symbolic designation of some incommunicable secret known only to Christ and the believing soul. It implies a union and unity with Christ which only he whose life is hidden with Christ in God can know (Col. iii, 3, 4). We accordingly understand the threefold allusion of *manna, stone,* and *name* as designed to enhance the thought of the real priesthood of believers (comp. i, 6), to whom "it is given to know the mysteries of the kingdom of heaven" (Matt. xiii, 11). These victors dwell in the secret place of the Most

High; they eat even the treasured manna of the most holy place; they have direct revelations as by the sacred Urim, and they know the mysteries of the divine life and the name of their Lord, for that name is in their hearts, and they bear the image of the heavenly One (2 Cor. iii, 18).

The new name is a phrase appropriated from Isa. lxii, 2, and, like "new song," "new heaven," and "new earth," points to the new kind and quality (καινός) of things which characterize the heavenly kingdom of Christ and of God. Among "the things which must shortly come to pass" (i, 1) the Apocalypse gives prominence to the coming down of the "new Jerusalem" to the earth, and by that glorious *coming* the Lord will "make all things new" (xxi, 5).

Among the correspondencies of this epistle notice:

1. How appropriately the one who has the sharp two-edged sword is represented as making war on evil teachers with the sword of his mouth.

2. He that holds fast the name and faith of Jesus near Satan's throne is appropriately rewarded with the gift of knowing the hidden things of God.

3. The hidden manna, white stone, and new name suggest a bread of heaven, a prophetic priesthood, and a fellowship with Christ most inspiring to those who are beset with the snares and stumbling-blocks of a sensual libertinism. Such need and may well desire the gift of prophecy and a knowledge of "all the mysteries and all the *gnosis*" (1 Cor. xiii, 2).

4. THE CHURCH IN THYATIRA. II, 18–29.

The church burdened with Jezebel.

18 And to the angel of the church in Thyatira write;
These things saith the Son of God, who hath his eyes like a flame of
19 fire, and his feet are like unto burnished brass: I know thy works, and thy love and faith and ministry and patience, and that thy last works
20 are more than the first. But I have *this* against thee, that thou sufferest the woman Jezebel, which calleth herself a prophetess; and she teacheth and seduceth my servants to commit fornication, and to eat things sac-
21 rificed to idols. And I gave her time that she should repent; and she
22 willeth not to repent of her fornication. Behold, I do cast her into a bed, and them that commit adultery with her into great tribulation, ex-
23 cept they repent of her works. And I will kill her children with death; and all the churches shall know that I am he who searcheth the reins and hearts: and I will give unto each one of you according to your works.
24 But to you I say, to the rest that are in Thyatira, as many as have not this teaching, who know not the deep things of Satan, as they say; I
25 cast upon you none other burden. Howbeit that which ye have, hold

26 fast till I come. And he that overcometh, and he that keepeth my works
27 unto the end, to him will I give authority over the nations: and he shall
   rule them with a rod of iron, as the vessels of the potter are broken to
28 shivers; as I also have received of my Father: and I will give him the
29 morning star. He that hath an ear, let him hear what the Spirit saith to
   the churches.

1. Three things distinguish the author of the message to Thyatira : (1) He is called *the Son of God;* (2) his *eyes* are *as a flame
of fire;* (3) *his feet are like burnished brass* (comp. i, 13–15). The
title *Son of God,* rather than "Son of man," as in i, 13, is designed
to remind us of the anointed Son of Jehovah, whose enthronement
and world-wide triumphs are celebrated in the second psalm (see
especially Psalm ii, 7–9). To this there is obvious reference in verse
27, where see further comment.

2. The message itself contains three principal declarations : (1) A
commendation of the *works, love, faith, ministry, patience,* and increase (πλείονα) of good works; (2) a statement of the teaching,
acts, and doom of Jezebel; (3) a word of encouragement and exhortation to the burdened church. The chief concern of the exegete is
to determine the significance of *the woman Jezebel* (verse 20). The
reading *thy wife Jezebel* is now rejected from the leading editions of
the Greek Testament (as Tischendorf, Tregelles, and Westcott and
Hort, although the last named leaves it in the margin). The contents
of the message, which show the works, love, faith, ministry, and patience of " the angel of the church " to be on the whole increasingly
commendable, are utterly inconsistent with *conjugal* union with any
woman guilty of the crimes here charged and unwilling to repent.
Moreover, as the church itself is always conceived as bride or wife,
the consort should be represented as a bridegroom or husband. Accordingly, to speak of the wife of a church is preposterous. *The
woman Jezebel* is therefore not to be thought of as having conjugal
relation to the church or any of its representatives.

Four things characterize this woman : (1) She *calls herself a
prophetess;* (2) she is a seductive teacher; (3) she inculcates and practices *fornication* and eating *things sacrificed to idols;* (4) she persistently refuses to repent of her foul deeds. All these facts point
to an aggravated form of " the teaching of Balaam " mentioned in
verse 14. Balaam taught Balak to ensnare Israel in sensuality and
idolatry, but it does not appear that he himself participated in the
sins to which his evil counsels led (Num. xxxi, 16). But Jezebel
introduced and vigorously propagated Phœnician idolatry with its
abominable sensuality and witchcraft among the children of Israel
(1 Kings xvi, 31; xxi, 25, 26; 2 Kings ix, 22). She was " the daugh-

ter of Ethbaal, king of the Zidonians," and, according to Josephus (*Apion*, i, 18), her father was not only king but a priest of Astarte. Her marriage with Ahab was a turning point for evil in the history of Israel. Being the daughter of one who was both king and priest, she might naturally call herself *a prophetess* and feel that her mission was to teach Israel a new religious worship. As for boldness and commanding will-power Jezebel appears in Old Testament history as the embodiment of all that is terrible in the Clytemnestra of the Greek tragedians and the Lady Macbeth of Shakespeare. *The woman Jezebel* is, accordingly, best understood as a symbolic name for powerful heathen influences and customs which beset the church of Thyatira. These formed a controlling tendency toward the foul practices of licentious paganism which were a grievous burden to those who sought to propagate the virtues of the Gospel of Christ. The serious charge against the church of Thyatira was that it had let this woman too much alone in her seductive teaching. It was virtually tolerating a heathen prophetess and thus allowing her pernicious influences to damage many.

Verse 21. *She willeth not to repent*—There was a persistent willpower back of the Jezebelite leaven, which refused to forsake the customs of a fascinating heathenism and could only be overcome by the penal visitation of God. The persons guilty of the seductive teaching had *time* to *repent*, but would not heed the word of truth. They rejected the decree of Acts xv, 29.

22. *Cast her into a bed*—Instead of the bed of sensuality she shall be forcibly *cast into a bed* of pain. There may be an allusion to the casting of Jezebel down under the feet of the horses (comp. 2 Kings ix, 33). The language and connection show that a severe punishment for her sins is intended, and into a similar *great tribulation* those *who commit adultery with her* are also destined to be cast, *except they repent of her works.*

Verse 23 proceeds in the same strain, and emphasizes the truth that divine retribution is sure to come to every one according to his works. The killing of *her children with death* is, perhaps, another allusion to the history of Jezebel in the slaughter of the false prophets and the house of Ahab (comp. 1 Kings xviii, 40; 2 Kings x, 11, 25). But the great lesson is that all these offenders must reckon with him "who has his eyes like a flame of fire" (verse 18) and is the supreme judge of every man. The language of this verse is largely appropriated from Jer. xvii, 10; Psalm vii, 9; lxii, 12.

24. *To the rest.* The reference here is obviously to *those in Thyatira* who had not accepted the libertine *teaching* of Jezebel; those who were willing to accept and follow the judgment of the apostles

and elders touching things sacrificed to idols and fornication. *The deep things of Satan* has been quite generally understood as a caustic reference to the boasts of the Gnostic heretics that they knew the depths of divine mysteries. Incipient gnosticism and sorcery, as likely to show themselves in apostolic times, may naturally have pretended to such secret knowledge, and sorcerers like Simon of Samaria evidently assumed this much (Acts viii, 9–11). But such pretenders would hardly have claimed to *know the deep things of Satan.* They assumed to *know the deep things,* but the writer in sarcasm adds the words *of Satan,* as a condemning judgment of the real nature of their mysteries. And yet he charges this claim on the pretenders by appending the words *as they say.* The reference in the phrase *no other burden* seems best explained by comparison with Acts xv, 28, when the apostolic council imposes "no greater burden than those necessary things" on the Gentile churches throughout the world.

25. *What ye have hold fast*—That is, retain in firm grasp all the commendable qualities mentioned above in verse 19. *Until I come*—Which the whole trend and teaching of the book represents as an event near at hand. Comp. iii, 11.

3. The promise to them that overcome in the church of Thyatira is exceptional in its adding to the usual words, *he that overcometh,* the words *and he that keepeth unto the end my works.* The conjunction *and* which introduces the words of promise is also exceptional, and so links the promise to the exhortation of verse 25 as to show that *keeping my works* (contrast *her works,* verse 22) *unto the end* is equivalent to "holding fast what ye have until I come." The promise itself includes three things, (1) *authority over the nations,* (2) ruling *them with a rod of iron,* and (3) the gift of *the morning star.* The first two are allusions to the Messianic ideals of the second psalm, especially verses 7–9. *The morning star* is, according to xxii, 16, a title of Jesus himself, and there is no more impropriety in his saying that he will *give* himself as a bright life than that he will give his spirit to others. He is the morning star of a new era in the history of humanity, and all who, filled with his light and wisdom, let their light shine, become like him the light of the world (Matt. v, 14–16; comp. John viii, 12; xii, 46). The promise therefore in substance means that they who overcome shall be identified with the Lord in his kingdom and glory. They shall reign with him and shall be like him. Comp. Rom. v, 17; viii, 17; 2 Tim. ii, 12; Col. iii, 4; 1 John iii, 2. This same ideal of triumph and glory appears again in Rev. iii, 21; xii, 5; xx, 4. Comp. also Matt. xix, 28, and Luke xxii, 29, 30.

We observe among the notable correspondencies of this message to Thyatira :

1. How appropriately the title "Son of God" stands at the head of a letter in which occur such direct allusions to the enthroned Messiah as portrayed in Psalm ii, 7, 12.

2. "He who has eyes like a flame of fire" is a judge who will thoroughly "search the reins and hearts."

3. "His feet like burnished brass" suggest the terrible power with which he will tread down "in death" the impudent Jezebel and her children who do not "repent of her works" (comp. 2 Kings ix, 33).

4. He who triumphs over the guile and tyranny of such a Jezebel may well reign in authority with the Messianic Son of God, and become himself a "morning star."

5. THE CHURCH IN SARDIS. III, 1-6.

The nominal but dead church.

1 And to the angel of the church in Sardis write;
These things saith he that hath the seven Spirits of God, and the seven stars: I know thy works, that thou hast a name that thou livest, and
2 thou art dead. Be thou watchful, and stablish the things that remain, which were ready to die: for I have found no works of thine perfected
3 before my God. Remember therefore how thou hast received and didst hear; and keep it, and repent. If therefore thou shalt not watch, I will come as a thief, and thou shalt not know what hour I will come upon
4 thee. But thou hast a few names in Sardis which did not defile their garments: and they shall walk with me in white; for they are worthy.
5 He that overcometh shall thus be arrayed in white garments; and I will in no wise blot his name out of the book of life, and I will confess his
6 name before my Father, and before his angels. He that hath an ear, let him hear what the Spirit saith to the churches.

1. The message to this church is from him *who has the seven Spirits of God and the seven stars.* These *seven Spirits* are the same which in i, 4, are said to be "before the throne;" in iv, 5, they appear as "seven lamps of fire burning before the throne," and in v, 6, as "seven eyes sent forth into all the earth." These are all so many different apocalyptic conceptions of the one Holy Spirit, proceeding from God and Christ, whose operations are defined profoundly in John xvi, 7-14. The Christ possesses this sevenfold Spirit in all fullness (John iii, 34; Col. i, 19), and hence all spiritual life and activity in the churches must proceed from this divine source. He accordingly has also *the seven stars.* Comp. i, 16. Holding them in his right hand, he searches them through and through as by the

light of so many lamps of fire and with the intelligence of so many watchful eyes. Nothing, therefore, in the *personnel* of the churches can escape his gaze and his judgment. Comp. note on i, 20.

2. The message itself is a notable mixture of severe judgment, warning, exhortation, and promise. The church is charged with being (1) nominally alive but really dead ; (2) some remaining things (τὰ λοιπά) were about to die ; (3) no works complete before God ; (4) nevertheless, there were a few who had kept undefiled, and are pronounced *worthy* to *walk with* Christ *in white*. (5) The others are admonished (*a*) to be watchful, (*b*) to establish what good remains, (*c*) to *remember how* they had *received* and *heard* and *keep* it and *repent*. (6) In their failure to *watch*, the Lord *will come as a thief* in an unexpected hour. This last admonition is to be compared with chap. xvi, 15, and Matt. xxiv, 43, 44 ; 1 Thess. v, 2 ; 2 Peter iii, 10. In the *how* (πῶς) of verse 3 we note a vivid reminder of the hearty and joyful manner of their first reception of the Gospel, as contrasted with the spiritual deadness of their present condition (comp. 1 Thess. i, 5–10 ; Gal. iv, 13–15). A notable failure to go on to perfection results in spiritual stagnation. The gravest charge, perhaps, against the church of Sardis is, *I have found no works of thine perfected before my God*. Nothing had been brought to completion (πεπληρωμένα). There was such an apathy that any strong conflict with the irreligious world was impossible. There is no trouble at Sardis with Nicolaitans, Balaamites, or Jezebelites ; the church itself is but another world.

3. The promise to him that overcometh is threefold: (1) He shall be *arrayed in white garments*, (2) *his name* shall not be blotted out of *the book of life*, and (3) *his name* shall be confessed by Jesus before his Father and the angels. The *white garments* indicate that they are found worthy and "meet to be partakers of the inheritance of the saints in light" (Col. i, 12 ; comp. Matt. xiii, 43), and to enter upon the blessedness of heavenly life. *The book of life* is a familiar biblical figure (comp. Exod. xxxii, 32 ; Psalm lxix, 28 ; Dan. xii, 1 ; Luke x, 20 ; Phil. iv, 3 ; Heb. xii, 23), and the words of this promise are to be compared with the mention of "the Lamb's book of life" in Rev. xiii, 8 ; xvii, 8 ; xx, 12, 15 ; xxi, 27. The pure and good in the sight of God are conceived as having their names enrolled in a book, like a registry of citizens kept by the proper magistrate. From such rolls the names of deceased citizens are erased. The apocalyptist conceives the names of the true living citizens of heaven as "written in the book of life from the foundation of the world" (xvii, 8). The words *I will in no wise blot his name out* are analogous with "shall not be hurt of the second death" in ii, 11,

and both passages are to be compared with xx, 14, 15. The confession of *his name before my Father and before his angels* is a thought appropriated from Mark viii, 38; Luke ix, 26. "If any man serve me, him will the Father honor" (John xii, 26). Comp. Rom. ii, 10 ; viii, 17.

The correspondencies between the different parts of this epistle to Sardis are numerous and suggestive:

1. It is appropriate that a dead and dying church should be addressed by him who has the seven Spirits of God. Those lamps of, fire (comp. iv, 5) illumine the regions of death-shade, and have power to revive the dying and the dead.

2. He who holds the seven stars must needs be cognizant of everything about them, and knows alike the names of the dead, the dying, and the worthy, for the powers of his Spirit are as manifold as the stars.

3. Those who in the midst of such contagion of death keep their garments undefiled (compare "wash their robes" in xxii, 14) are fittingly rewarded with white garments and closest fellowship with Christ in heaven.

4. He who has a name to live while he is dead will find no registry of his name in heaven; but he who is bold to confess the name of Jesus before men will have his own name confessed by Jesus before God and the angels of heaven (comp. Matt. x, 32).

6. The Church in Philadelphia. iii, 7–13.

The faithful and stable church.

7 And to the angel of the church in Philadelphia write;
These things saith he that is holy, he that is true, he that hath the key of David, he that openeth, and none shall shut, and that shutteth, and
8 none openeth: I know thy works (behold, I have set before thee a door opened, which none can shut), that thou hast little power, and didst
9 keep my word, and didst not deny my name. Behold, I give of the synagogue of Satan, of them who say they are Jews, and they are not, but do lie; behold, I will make them to come and worship before thy
10 feet, and to know that I have loved thee. Because thou didst keep the word of my patience, I also will keep thee from the hour of trial, that *hour* which is to come upon the whole world, to try them that dwell upon the
11 earth. I come quickly: hold fast that which thou hast, that no one take
12 thy crown. He that overcometh, I will make him a pillar in the temple of my God, and he shall go out thence no more: and I will write upon him the name of my God, and the name of the city of my God, the new Jerusalem, which cometh down out of heaven from my God, and mine
13 own new name. He that hath an ear, let him hear what the Spirit saith to the churches.

1. The source of this message is (1) *he that is holy*, (2) *he that is true*, (3) *he that has the key of David.* These titles are not found in the Christophany of chap. i, but *the holy and the true* occur again in vi, 10 (compare "faithful and true" in xix, 11), and *the key of David* correlates with "Root of David" in v, 5, and "root and offspring of David" in xxii, 16. The latter part of the verse is appropriated from Isa. xxii, 22, and designates Jesus as the Messiah, the true son and successor of David, who holds the key as the symbol of power and authority. The true house of David is perpetuated in the new kingdom of God, and "the King of the ages" (xv, 3), who is "King of kings and Lord of lords" (xix, 16), not only inherits "the throne of his father David," but is also destined to "reign over the house of Jacob forever; and of his kingdom there shall be no end" (Luke i, 32, 33). He accordingly holds "the keys of the kingdom of heaven" (Matt. xvi, 19), and has all authority over its administration. His opening and shutting are final and decisive. For, as Trench well observes, "Christ has not so committed the keys of the kingdom of heaven, with the power of binding and loosing, to any other, but that he still retains the highest administration of them in his own hands."

2. The contents of the epistle to this church are notable for the absence of anything like rebuke or blame. The Lord seems to have found nothing against this church, the only one of the seven to receive such honor. (1) It is first of all distinguished for having set before it *an opened door.* The Lord has thus made use of the key of David just referred to, and opened a door of opportunity for that faithful church to make converts to the new kingdom of God. For the figure of an opened door compare Acts xiv, 27; 1 Cor. xvi, 9; Col. iv, 3. This great and effectual door no enemy of the truth was to close up. (2) Another fact to be noticed is the statement, *thou hast little power.* This is best explained as equivalent to 1 Cor. i, 26–28. This church made no show of "many wise after the flesh, many mighty, many noble;" it was not what the world would call a strong and influential church. But (3) its real strength consisted in *keeping* the *word* of Jesus, and in such faithful adherence to the truth that, when put to test, this church *never denied the name* of its Lord. (4) As a consequence and reward of such unwavering confession the Lord will bring some of their Jewish enemies to *worship before thy feet and to know that I have loved thee.* Thus shall be fulfilled in them the prophetic promise of Isa. xlix, 23; lx, 14; xliii, 4. *The synagogue of Satan* has been already mentioned in connection with the church of Smyrna (ii, 9), but in that case it was only presented as a persecuting power; here some of

that synagogue are made to come and worship along with the faithful servants of him who has the key of David. This shows further what a door is opened at Philadelphia, and how Satanic foes are made to come through it and acknowledge and worship Jesus Christ as Lord. Those who thus *come and worship* meet the condition imposed in Matt. xxiii, 39.

Verses 10 and 11 contain a most encouraging word of promise and of exhortation. *Because thou didst keep the word of my patience, I also will keep thee from the hour of trial.* We best understand *the word of my patience* as the word which reveals and inculcates the patience of Christ, namely, the Gospel itself. To *keep* that word is to abide steadfast in the same meekness and patience which were exemplified in the Lord himself ; and to be kept *from the hour of trial* is, not to be exempted from affliction and temptation, but to be saved from failure in that hour; not to be taken out of the world, but kept from the evil (John xvii, 15). *That hour which is to come upon the whole world, to try them that dwell upon the earth,* is the same as the " great tribulation" spoken of by Jesus in Matt. xxiv, 21, 29; Mark xiii, 19. In the midst of enemies and bitter persecution the disciples were counseled by the Lord to stand firm and true, and he assured them that not a hair of their heads should perish, but that in patience they should win their souls (Luke xxi, 18, 19). These of Philadelphia are given substantially the same assurance, and are exhorted to *hold fast* the good confession and noble record they had already made, so that no one might take their crown ; that is, get the better of them in good deeds and so obtain a crown of glory which might have been their own. Comp. Col. ii, 18. Here we have a foreglimpse of them who come out of the great tribulation (vii, 14).

3. The promise to the victor is worthy of special study. (1) *I will make him a pillar in the temple of my God.* (2) *He shall go out thence no more.* (3) *I will write upon him* (*a*) *the name of my God,* (*b*) *the name of the city of my God,* and (*c*) *mine own new name.* All this indicates that such steadfast confessors as in Philadelphia kept the word of Jesus and did not deny his name are to be builded into the living temple of God. With little change of imagery this promise is substantially like that of our Lord to Peter when, by revelation of God the Father, he confessed his name: "Thou art Peter, and upon this *petra* I will build my church" (Matt. xvi, 18). That promise was from him who held the keys of the kingdom of heaven, and could give authority to open and to shut. Zechariah's Messianic prophecy declared not only that "the man whose name is Branch" should "build the temple of Jehovah," but also that they

who were afar off should come and "build in the temple of Jehovah" (Zech. vi, 12, 13, 15). *The temple of God* is that "habitation of God through the Spirit," that "household of God," of which we read in Eph. ii, 19–22 ; 1 Cor. iii, 16. It is the church of the new dispensation conceived under the figure of a building. It is misleading to dispute, as some have here done, whether the reference in this promise is to the Church militant or the glorified Church in heaven; for the apocalyptist does not distinguish these two conditions of the temple, but thinks of it only as God's building for time and eternity. Those who are made pillars therein are to remain so, and *go out thence no more.* We cannot here anticipate the symbolism of the temple of God as measured off for preservation in xi, 1, and, after the sounding of the seventh trumpet, opened in the heaven (xi, 19); nor does the statement of xxi, 22, that the new Jerusalem contains no temple but the Almighty and the Lamb, conflict with the imagery of this promise to the church of Philadelphia; for, as Alford well says, "that glorious city is all temple, and Christ's victorious ones are its living stones and pillars." That *the temple of God* and *the new Jerusalem* are essentially one is inferred from the threefold *name* which the victors are to have written upon them, namely, of *God,* of the *new Jerusalem,* and *mine own new name.* This threefold inscription makes them citizens of heaven (comp. Phil. iii, 20), and those who stand with the Lamb on Mount Zion (xiv, 1) and serve God and the Lamb forever (xxii, 4) have his name written upon their foreheads. The *new name* here mentioned is to be compared with ii, 17, and xix, 12, and suggests the deep mysteries of the kingdom of God, which are hidden from the wise and understanding, but graciously revealed to babes (Matt. xi, 25).

In the inner correlations of this epistle we observe :

1. How appropriately the words of comfort and encouragement to a steadfast church come from him "who is holy and true."

2. He who holds the key of David speaks naturally of "a door opened" and of pillars fixed in "the temple of my God."

3. He who denies not the name of Jesus shall bear his "own new name."

4. The church before which is set an opened door may well bear the name of " the new Jerusalem which cometh down out of heaven," and whose gates of pearl are never closed (xxi, 25).

7. THE CHURCH IN LAODICEA. III, 14–22.

The lukewarm and self-conceited church.

14   And to the angel of the church in Laodicea write;
      These things saith the Amen, the faithful and true witness, the begin-

15 ning of the creation of God: I know thy works, that thou art neither
16 cold nor hot: I would thou wert cold or hot. So because thou art luke-
17 warm, and neither hot nor cold, I will spew thee out of my mouth. Because thou sayest, I am rich, and have gotten riches, and have need of
nothing; and knowest not that thou art the wretched one and miserable
18 and poor and blind and naked: I counsel thee to buy of me gold refined
by fire, that thou mayest become rich; and white garments, that thou
mayest clothe thyself, and *that* the shame of thy nakedness be not made
19 manifest; and eyesalve to anoint thine eyes, that thou mayest see. As
many as I love, I reprove and chasten: be zealous therefore, and repent.
20 Behold, I stand at the door and knock: if any man hear my voice and
open the door, I will come in to him, and will sup with him, and he
21 with me. He that overcometh, I will give to him to sit down with me
in my throne, as I also overcame, and sat down with my Father in his
22 throne. He that hath an ear, let him hear what the Spirit saith to the
churches.

1. The threefold title here is (1) *the Amen*, (2) *the faithful and
true witness*, and (3) *the beginning of the creation of God*. The first
occurs in i, 7, and is a frequent word in John's gospel (John i, 51;
iii, 3; x, 1); the second is found in part in i, 5, and the third has its
parallel in Col. i, 15. The first two are in substance one, and serve
to attest the trustworthy character of what is written. Compare
the statement of xxii, 6, "These words are faithful and true." The
words *beginning of the creation of God* are another way of saying
that Christ is the *Alpha*, "the first," as he is represented in i, 8, 18.
He is the beginning as well as the end, the first as well as the last.
While the language, considered by itself alone, may be construed to
mean, as the Arians teach, that Christ is himself a creature, such an
interpretation is inconsistent with the constant teaching of this
book, which so identifies God and the Lamb that what is predicated
of one is also attributed to the other. Jesus Christ is subordinate
to the Father, but not a creation of his power, for every created
thing in heaven and earth is represented as worshiping him (v, 13).
It is appropriate that titles which appear in the introduction of the
book (i, 5, 7, 8), and are repeated again at the close (xxii, 6, 13),
should stand at the head of this last of the seven epistles to the
churches.

2. The message to this church contains no word of commendation, but charges two offenses: (1) *Thou art neither cold nor hot;*
(2) Thou sayest, *I am rich, and have gotten riches, and have need
of nothing.* The lukewarmness which constitutes the first offense
is a condition of spiritual indifference and indecision. Such a moral
state is worse than hostile coldness, for there is more hope of win-
ning such an open-faced sinner to Christ than one who has tasted

some benefits of grace and then settled down into a feelingless indifference. If one is not *hot* (ζεστός), that is, glowing with fervent
love for Christ, it were better for him to be cold than to be void of
all keen spiritual sensibility. Hence the significance of the words
I would thou wert cold or hot. The imagery is from different conditions of water. Water either cold or hot may be pleasant to the
taste, but that which is *lukewarm* produces nausea, and one spews
it out of his mouth in loathing and disgust. But spiritual insen-
sibility begets pride and self-conceit. This lukewarm church boasts
of acquired riches and of having no sense of need. In this respect
it resembled Ephraim (Hosea xii, 8), and the Corinthians to whom
Paul wrote in a strain of holy irony (1 Cor. iv, 8). This fact shows
up still more clearly the fearful evil of indecision and unconcern
about one's relation to God. Such a one imagines himself rich,
when in fact he is of all men *the wretched one and miserable and
poor and blind and naked.* In view of this, their true condition, the
counsel (συμβουλεύω) which now follows is especially telling. Those
who say they are rich and *have need of nothing* are in perishing
need of some good counsel, and it here comes in the form of searching rebuke and condescending advice from the Lord. What they
need is a supply (1) of the true riches (comp. Luke xii, 21 ; 1 Cor.
i, 5); (2) of *white garments* to cover their spiritual *nakedness*, and
(3) of *eyesalve* that they may truly see. In their apathy and self-
conceit the Laodiceans had become really *miserable and poor and
blind and naked*, and the only power sufficient to supply their wants
was the Christ who was and is the *beginning of the creation of God.*
Those needy ones must come to him and *buy*, for though his mercies are without money or price the arrogant and self-conceited
must needs pay the heaviest of all prices—the humiliation and sur-
render of themselves. They must renounce their self-conceit and
pride, and be made to feel that they are indeed poor and needy.
When they acquire such a spirit they may obtain the pure *gold
refined by fire* (comp. 1 Peter i, 7), and be clothed in the *white garments* of a living and active righteousness (Col. iii, 10), and receive
that divine anointing which removes the blindness of one's spiritual
vision and teaches him all things (1 John ii, 11, 27).

Verses 19, 20. *I love. . .reprove. . .chasten*—The three things
go together. Comp. Job v, 17 ; Psalm xciv, 12 ; Prov. iii, 12 ;
Heb. xii, 6. This statement in connection with the other things
said to the lukewarm and self-conceited church shows how much
the faithful and true Witness loves and yearns to save those who
show indifference toward him. It becomes still more conspicuous
by the touching figure of the next verse: *Behold, I stand at the*

door and knock. To those who ought to be the suppliants, and to be themselves doing what is enjoined in Matt. vii, 7, he who was with God in the creation of the world approaches as a seeker and knocks for admission to their hearts. *I will come in*—Comp. John xiv, 23.

3. The promise to the victor is quite analogous to that in the epistle to the church in Thyatira (ii, 26, 27). They who overcome are to be associated with Christ on his throne. Having suffered with him, and triumphed through his grace, they shall also reign with him (comp. 2 Tim. ii, 12; Rom. v, 17; viii, 17; Col. iii, 4). And thus will be answered the prayer of Jesus in John xvii, 22–24. The resurrection, ascension, and enthronement of Jesus Christ are the last and highest ideals of triumph which the church may share. It is, accordingly, appropriate that this promise should come last in the manifold promises made to the seven churches.

The correspondencies of thought noticeable in this last of the seven epistles are the following:

1. He who is the *Amen* appropriately appeals to such as are false and self-deceived.

2. The faithful and true Witness imparts appropriate counsel, and fails not to expose the self-delusion of those who are really blind and naked.

3. He who is the first (as well as the last), and at the very beginning of the creation of God, appropriately concludes the promises to such as overcome with the final glory of reigning in triumph with Christ and God.

4. It is most encouraging counsel to know that the love which faithfully reproves and chastens is able to refine and clothe and enlighten the miserable and poor and blind and naked so as to make them meet to sit in the very throne of God.

At the conclusion of our notes on these seven epistles we record the following observations:

1. We find so much that is truly conspicuous and commanding in these messages that it seems like carrying interpretation too far into fanciful conjectures when we seek for deeper mysteries than those to which we have called attention. The notion that we have in these seven epistles a prophetic outline of seven chronological periods of Church history traceable through the Christian centuries may be safely discarded as the fiction of extremists, whose great error consists in spending more effort to discover what may possibly be made out of a sacred writer's words than to make sure of that which the scope and language most naturally require.

2. But it may be admitted that as the seven Spirits before the throne represent the one holy universal Spirit of God, so the seven churches represent in good measure the universal Church of Jesus Christ, and the conditions of life, labor, patience, trial, and hope are in substance such as may be seen somewhere in the Church of all time.

3. As the entire Apocalypse has much in common with our Lord's eschatological discourse in the synoptic gospels, so we notice in the personal addresses and appeals to the seven churches much that corresponds in substance to that which Jesus addressed personally to his disciples (for example, Matt. xxiv, 9, 11–13, 21, 42–51). The whole book has a purpose of comforting and encouraging the church of that first period—the apostolic age.

4. These epistles are so full of references to things which follow in subsequent portions of the Apocalypse that we may well believe they were not completed in their present form until the rest of the book was written. They appear on close analysis to be of the nature of a preface or introduction to the Revelation, but too thoroughly interwoven with its ideas and method to be attributed to a different authorship. If the interpretation we give of John's Revelation is correct there is no sufficient ground or reason for supposing that the book was constructed by combining two or more different apocalypses.

II. THE OPENING OF THE SEVEN SEALS. IV–VII.

The Heavenly Theophany. IV, 1–11.

1 After these things I saw, and behold, a door opened in heaven, and the first voice which I heard, *a voice* as of a trumpet speaking with me, one saying, Come up hither, and I will show thee the things which must 2 come to pass hereafter. Straightway I was in the Spirit: and behold, 3 there was a throne set in heaven, and one sitting upon the throne; and he that sat *was* to look upon like a jasper stone and a sardius: and *there was* a rainbow round about the throne, like an emerald to look upon. 4 And round about the throne *were* four and twenty thrones: and upon the thrones *I saw* four and twenty elders sitting, arrayed in white garments; 5 and on their heads crowns of gold. And out of the throne proceeded lightnings and voices and thunders. And *there were* seven lamps of fire 6 burning before the throne, which are the seven Spirits of God; and before the throne, as it were a glassy sea like unto crystal; and in the midst of the throne, and round about the throne, four living creatures 7 full of eyes before and behind. And the first creature *was* like a lion, and the second creature like a calf, and the third creature had a face as 8 of a man, and the fourth creature *was* like a flying eagle. And the four living creatures, having each one of them six wings, are full of eyes round about and within: and they have no rest day and night, saying,

Holy, holy, holy, *is* the Lord God, the Almighty, who was and who is
9 and who is to come. And when the living creatures shall give glory
and honor and thanks to him that sitteth on the throne, to him that
10 liveth for ever and ever, the four and twenty elders shall fall down before
him that sitteth on the throne, and shall worship him that liveth for ever
11 and ever, and shall cast their crowns before the throne, saying, Worthy
art thou, our Lord and our God, to receive the glory and the honor and
the power: for thou didst create all things, and because of thy will they
were, and were created.

The messages to the seven churches were appropriately introduced
by a sublime *Christophany;* for they were specific counsels of
Christ himself, the Son of man, to the churches of that time, and,
indeed, of every period and place which exhibit similar conditions.
But what follows, even to the conclusion of the book, consists
mainly of symbolic revelations, and they are appropriately introduced by a *Theophany,* seen in the opened heaven. The contents
of this vision, minutely analyzed, may be thus arranged :

1. Vision of the throne and the One sitting thereon, 1–3.
2. The twenty-four elders, 4.
3. The lightnings, voices, and thunders, 5.
4. The seven lamps of fire, 5.
5. The glassy sea, 6.
6. The four living creatures, 6–8.
7. The heavenly worship, 8–11.
8. The book with seven seals, v, 1–4.
9. The Lamb in the midst of the throne, 5–7.
10. The worship of God and the Lamb, 8–14.
    (1) Song of the living creatures and the elders, 8–10.
    (2) Song of myriad angels, 11, 12.
    (3) Song of the whole creation, 13.
    (4) Response of the living creatures and elders, 14.

Such heaven-scenes appear in the earliest fragments of apocalyptic
writing, as in Gen. i, 26; iii, 22; vi, 3, 7; but the most notable Old
Testament models, after which the visions of these two chapters
have been patterned, are the visions of Isa. vi, 1–4, and Ezek. i, 4–28;
x, 1–22. It detracts not from the inspiration and originality of John
that he made himself a profound student of the Hebrew prophets
and cast his own visions in the forms long consecrated to the purposes of holy revelation. The noblest human element as well as
the divine in sacred scripture is manifest in such appropriation of
metaphor and symbol.

1. *After these things*—After the visions and testimonies recorded
in the preceding chapters. How long after is not said, and is of no

importance in our study of this book. It is pitiable to note what long paragraphs and even pages have been written on such a trivial question. Whether it was "soon after," or "some time after," or "after he had written down the previous visions," matters not, and are all questions which probably never seriously occupied the thoughts of the sacred writer. *Door opened in heaven*—Heaven is the place of God's throne and the source of all true revelations. Therefore, in order to see and know the mysteries of God, the door of his heavenly temple must be *opened.* Comp. Gen. xxviii, 17; Ezek. i, 1; Matt. iii, 16; Acts vii, 56; x, 11; 2 Cor. xii, 1–4. The most exact translation of the words which follow is: *And the voice the first which I heard* (was) *as of a trumpet speaking with me;* and the obvious reference is, to the first voice heard after the vision of the opened door. John heard other voices after this first one. Comp. verses 5, 8, 10; v, 2, 9, 11, 13. Some think it was the same voice mentioned so similarly in i, 10, and to be understood as the voice of Christ. But it is only by inference that the "great voice" of i, 10, is supposed to be that of Christ, and, as Christ has been speaking continuously through the seven epistles of chaps. ii and iii, it is by no means so evident as some assume that *the first voice which I heard* is intended to refer to the voice spoken of in i, 10, or that it was the voice of Christ. There are many and great voices which are heard speaking in this Apocalypse, and it is not important to determine whether this *first voice* is the same as that of i, 10, or the first one heard after the heavenly door was opened. It is in any case the voice of heavenly authority, and may well be supposed to have come from him that sat upon the throne. *Come up hither*—Ascend into this realm of heavenly vision and revelation. John was thus caught away in spirit like Ezekiel to behold "visions of God." Comp. Ezek. iii, 12; viii, 3; xi, 1. This first verse of chap. iv begins and ends with the same words, *after these things* (μετὰ ταῦτα), and the reference seems to be in each case substantially the same. That which *must come to pass* is something to take place necessarily after the things thus far shown, and in the last occurrence the phrase may well be translated simply *hereafter.* In view of the meaning in i, 19, and the form of words in i, 1, we can hardly adopt the punctuation of Westcott and Hort, who connect the words with what follows in verse 2.

2. *I was in spirit*—As in i, 10. The language implies a new uplift of divine rapture, but need not be supposed to imply that the seer had meanwhile lost his inspiration, or lapsed from the state of ecstasy in which he beheld things already described. He must have been *in spirit* to see the "door opened in heaven," and to hear

the "voice as of a trumpet." But upon seeing and hearing these things *immediately* a special rapture seized him and enabled him to look through the opened door of heaven and behold the wonderful theophany about to be described. *A throne set in heaven*—It was in the same heaven (ἐν τῷ οὐρανῷ) the door of which he had seen already opened (verse 1). The *throne* was seen as *set*, or already placed in the heaven, when first the seer beheld it, and at the same time he saw *one sitting upon the throne*. Comp. Isa. vi, 1, and Dan. vii, 9. The one who sat upon the throne is not named, but he is described much after the manner of the unnamed one in Ezek. i, 26, 27.

3. *Like a jasper stone*—A precious stone of various colors, as purple, blue, green, yellow. *Sardius*—A similar stone of carnelian hue; red, or flesh-colored. These comparisons serve here, as in Ezek. i, 4, 26, 27, to give a powerful impression of the intense splendor of him who sat upon the throne. *Rainbow round about the throne*—Symbol of covenanted mercy (Gen. ix, 12-17). This rainbow was *in appearance like an emerald*, that is, a precious stone of a light green color, and, aside from its symbolic suggestiveness, serves in the picture as a screen or veil to soften the intense brightness proceeding from the throne.

4. *Thrones . . . elders*—These are ruling elders, for they occupy *thrones* after the manner of those who execute judgment (comp. xx, 4; Dan. vii, 9, 18, 22, 27). There are as many thrones as elders, so that each one sits upon his own separate throne. Here we naturally recall the words of Jesus to his disciples in Matt. xix, 28 : "In the regeneration, when the Son of man shall sit upon the throne of his glory, ye also shall sit upon twelve thrones, judging the twelve tribes of Israel." John, however, saw not twelve but *four and twenty thrones*, and the *four and twenty elders* who sat upon the thrones were *arrayed in white garments*, symbolical of their heavenly purity and glory (iii, 5); and *on their heads* were *crowns of gold*, additional emblems of their royal dignity. The whole picture indicates a glorious company of enthroned nobles. They sit on thrones as so many kings, and therefore cannot here be thought of as ministering angels or servants. The *twenty-four* may have been chosen in reference to the twenty-four courses of priests (1 Chron. xxiv), and in that case the enthroned elders may be regarded as a symbol of the kingdom which is constituted of those who are priests unto God (i, 6). But as the gates of the new Jerusalem bear the names of the twelve tribes of Israel, and the foundations the names of the twelve apostles (xxi, 12, 14), we may well believe that these twenty-four enthroned elders symbolize the glorified Church of the

Old and New Testaments as represented by the twelve tribes and the twelve apostles. All these are conceived as exalted into regal splendor, and associated like Daniel's "saints of the Most High" (Dan. vii, 18, 22, 27) with the King on the throne (comp. iii, 21) as so many heavenly princes.

5. *Lightnings . . . voices . . . thunders*—Signs of the terrors and omnipotence of the Most High in the heaven as well as of his manifested presence on earth (comp. xi, 19; Exod. xix, 16). The procession of these *from the throne* suggests that the throne of God is the source of all revelation and power. The *seven lamps of fire burning before the throne* are another symbol of *the seven Spirits of God* (i, 4)—that one universal Spirit from whose presence no man may hide (Psalm cxxxix, 7). They are like so many flaming eyes which search the whole world (v, 6; Zech. iv, 10; Prov. xv, 3), and bring every man's work into judgment before God.

6. *A glassy sea*—Not "a sea of glass," as translated in the common version; nor to be identified with the "glassy sea mingled with fire" in xv, 2; nor the same as the river of life in xxii, 1; but simply the broad open space before the throne, the polished floor, such as is to be seen in any great throne-chamber. This appeared in the vision to be so large, and so polished into the brightness of a precious stone *like unto crystal*, after the manner of a tessellated pavement, that the writer could not describe it more appropriately than by comparing it to *a glassy sea like unto crystal*.

6-8. The seer describes the position of the four *zoa*, or *living creatures*, as *in the midst of the throne, and round about the throne*. They do not appear to support the throne as in Ezekiel's vision (Ezek. i, 22, 26), but one stands at the middle point of each of the four sides of the throne, and so facing the throne (comp. Exod. xxv, 20, 22) that the seer could observe the multitudinous *eyes before and behind*—symbols of remarkable intelligence. The faces of these intelligent beings were like those of Ezekiel's vision (Ezek. i, 10), and resembled those of *a lion, a calf, a man*, and *a flying eagle*, thus representing the four highest types of animal life. As in Isaiah's vision (Isa. vi, 2), the living creatures had *each one of them six wings*, and they were *full of eyes*, not only *before and behind* as seen in their attitude toward the throne, but also *round about and within* when viewed in reference to the wings. Outside and under the wings they were also full of eyes, and like Isaiah's seraphim they are continually repeating the trisagion. In Isaiah they cry: "Holy, holy, holy, Jehovah of hosts : the whole earth is full of his glory." In our Apocalypse the formula is enlarged into a characteristic parallelism :

Holy, holy, holy Lord, the God, the Almighty,
He who was and who is and who is to come.

It is evident that this whole picture is modeled after the vision of
the seraphim in Isa. vi, 1-4, and of the cherubim in Ezek. i, 4-14. The
living creatures contribute largely to the glory and impressiveness
of the scene. They may be regarded simply as parts of a great
composite picture of the presence-chamber of the Almighty, not
having special symbolical import other than suggesting, perhaps,
the ministers and attendants suitable for a throne-chamber so heavenly and holy. Viewed in this light they are merely the bodyguard
or immediate attendants of the King, such as are to be seen about
the throne and person of every great sovereign when he appears in
state. Thus understood they would have no more symbolical meaning than the glassy pavement before the throne. But the detailed
description of their forms, and their essential identity with the
cherubim of the Old Testament, leave it hardly doubtful that, like
the four and twenty elders, these four *zoa* are symbols of some intelligent beings, or of the whole creation, as active and worshipful
in the presence of God. The name clearly indicates *living* creatures, their wings symbolize *rapidity* of movement, and their innumerable eyes suggest *wisdom* and continual *watchfulness*. With
good reason, therefore, have many of the best interpreters concluded
that the cherubim are symbols of the highest ideal of the living
creation in its relation to its God.

Any really satisfactory explanation of the cherubim must present
one predominant idea traceable alike in the Edenic symbols (Gen.
iii, 24), in those which spread their wings over the mercy seat (Exod.
xxv, 20), and in those which appear in the visions of Isaiah (vi), Ezekiel (i), and this Apocalypse of John. As the sword of flame at the
gate of Eden was a symbol of the righteousness which demands the
punishment of sin, the cherubim may well, on the other hand, symbolize the intelligent and active love that ever worships Him that
is holy. Whether hovering over the mercy seat in the holy of
holies, or appearing in the temple of heaven, or executing the divine
purposes of God, the cherubim represent the highest ideal of created
beings glorified before the holy One who rules the heavens and the
earth. While the twenty-four elders represent "the church of the
firstborn who are enrolled in heaven" the living creatures may
symbolize a still higher concept of the ultimate glorification of "the
spirits of just men made perfect" (Heb. xii, 23). The elders and
the cherubs may therefore represent, not different orders of created
beings, but the whole body of the redeemed at different periods of
glorification. The elders might well denote the saints of the Most

High as enthroned to receive and possess the Messianic kingdom
(comp. Dan. vii, 9, 18, 27), and the seraphim that glorified and perfected creation of God, including all saints, when the Christ "shall
have abolished all rule and all authority and power," and shall have
"delivered up the kingdom to the God and Father," and the Son
himself shall become so subjected "that God may be all in all"
(1 Cor. xv, 24-28). Then the last enemy shall have been destroyed,
and there shall be no more death, nor tears, nor pain, nor night, nor
curse (Rev. xxi, 4; xxii, 3, 5). In this symbolic portraiture of the
throne of God it certainly was fitting to introduce representations,
not only of such ideals of power and wisdom and judgment as are
ever traceable in the divine administration of the world, but also of
such progressive glorification of the saints as shall take place "unto
the ages of the ages." Hence, in accord with the explanation of
the cherubim we have suggested, these exalted and glorified beings
appropriately cry, without pause day or night:

> Holy, holy, holy Lord, the God, the Almighty,
> He who was and who is and who is to come.

9-11. The worship here recorded is to be compared with that
described in v, 8-14. Here it is solely from *the living creatures*
and *the four and twenty elders*. They act in concerted harmony, so
that when the cherubim lead off in ascribing *glory and honor and
thanks to him that sitteth on the throne, to him that liveth unto the
ages of the ages*, the elders also join in the worship, and *fall down
before him that sitteth on the throne*, and *cast their crowns before the
throne*. The worship of the four living creatures before the throne
of the Eternal is, like the cherubim at the gate of paradise and in
the holy of holies, a pledge of the final glorification of the creation
of God, and hence it is said in verse 11, *Thou didst create all things,
and because of thy will they were, and were created*. If we understand that the elders and the cherubim alike symbolize that which
is from the seer's point of view an ideal of the future ages of the
kingdom of God and his saints, the future tense of the verbs, *shall
give, shall fall, shall worship, shall cast* (δώσουσιν, πεσοῦνται, προσ-
κυνήσουσιν, βαλοῦσιν), has a noticeable significance. The falling
down and casting their crowns before the throne, as well as the
words of adoration and praise, are so many becoming forms of
humiliation before God. Thus the redeemed and glorified saints of
the Most High shall acknowledge his *glory and honor and power*
through all the ages to come. In this heavenly worship we note
the threefold forms of expression in the trisagion of verse 8, the
glory and honor and thanks of verse 9, in the *fall* and *worship* and

cast crowns of verse 10, and the *glory, honor,* and *power* of verse 11. A threefold allusion seems to be designed in the closing words of verse 11, *thy will, they were, and were created.* Back of all things, as the source and ground of their existence, is the will of God. It is *on account of* that will (not *by means* of it) that all things *were* and are. *They were* because God willed it. The ἐκτίσθησαν, *were created,* adds to ἦσαν the thought that *all things* (τὰ πάντα) not only were in existence by reason of God's *will,* but were also *brought into existence* because God so willed and brought it to pass by his act of creation.

The Book with Seven Seals. v, 1-4.

1 And I saw in the right hand of him that sat on the throne a book writ-
2 ten within and on the back, close sealed with seven seals. And I saw a
strong angel proclaiming with a great voice, Who is worthy to open the
3 book, and to loose the seals thereof ? And no one in the heaven, or on
the earth, or under the earth, was able to open the book, or to look
4 thereon. And I wept much, because no one was found worthy to open
the book, or to look thereon.

This sealed book is a part of the vision *of him that sat on the throne,* and is not to be thought of as a separate and independent revelation. The division of chapters at this point is unfortunate and tends to mislead the common reader. Having described the throne, and him who sat thereon as the Holy One, to be adored by crowned elders and living cherubim through all the ages, the seer proceeds to record additional features of the same adorable Theophany. *On the right hand* (ἐπὶ τὴν δεξιάν, that is, as if it were lying on the open palm of the enthroned Sovereign) appeared *a book written within and on the back, close sealed with seven seals.* This imagery is taken from Ezek. ii, 9, 10. Comp. also Isa. xxix, 11). The *book* is to be thought of as a scroll, a book-roll, like the Hebrew מְגִלָּה, and written on both sides. Just how the *seven seals* were adjusted we are not told, but from the opening of one seal after another, as described in chap. vi, it may be inferred that the roll was composed of seven leaves or sections, each one of which was fastened by a seal. The meaning of this sealed book appears from the opening of its several seals. It is a symbol of the mystery of God which is about to be revealed by the Lamb, consisting of "the things which must come to pass hereafter" (iv, 1). The unsealing of the book is the apocalypse itself, "the revelation of Jesus Christ, which God gave to him to show unto his servants the things which must shortly come to pass," and which "he sent and signified by his angel unto his servant John" (i, 1). For we shall see (what too many expositors have failed to note) that after the seals have been opened the revelation appears as "a little book opened" (x, 2), which John takes from the mighty angel's hand, and eats, and is commissioned to publish "over many peoples and nations and tongues and kings." The sealed βιβλίον of this vision thus becomes the opened book (τὸ βιβλίον τὸ ἠνεῳγμένον) in the hand of the angel, who gives it unto John and commands him to eat it (x, 8-11).

2, 3. *A strong angel proclaiming*—It must needs have been a *strong angel*, who was able amid "lightnings and voices and thunders" (iv, 5) to proclaim with such *a great voice* as to be heard *in the heaven*, and *on the earth*, and *under the earth*. The entire universe is thus denoted, and no one was found in heaven or earth or Hades *worthy to open the book*. There is a suggestiveness in the word ἄξιος, *worthy*, in this connection. He must needs be one of high rank and dignity who can take the book of mystery from the hand of God and open its secret things to the knowledge of others. He who is *worthy* to do a work like this must be possessed of something more than mere knowledge or intellectual ability.

4. *I wept*—As if in disappointment of what was promised by the voice of iv, 1.

THE LAMB IN THE MIDST OF THE THRONE. v, 5-7.

5 And one of the elders saith unto me, Weep not: behold, the Lion that is of the tribe of Judah, the Root of David, hath overcome, to open the
6 book and the seven seals thereof. And I saw in the midst of the throne and of the four living creatures, and in the midst of the elders, a Lamb standing, as though it had been slain, having seven horns, and seven eyes, which are the seven Spirits of God, sent forth into all the earth.
7 And he came, and he taketh *it* out of the right hand of him that sat on the throne.

5. *One of the elders*—It is appropriate that a representative of the exalted and glorious Church of God should comfort the weeping seer. *Lion . . . Judah . . . David*—All these terms are remarkably expressive of the Messianic hero, the hope and consolation of Israel (Luke ii, 25), the blessed Christ of God. Comp. Gen. xlix, 9; Isa. xi, 1, 10. *Overcame*—As in iii, 21. This Lion of Judah, this Root of David, *overcame, conquered* (ἐνίκησεν) by the passion of the cross and the power of his resurrection, so as to be worthy as well as able *to open the book and the seven seals thereof.* Compare the sentiment of verse 9.

6. We have an obvious Hebraism in the words *in the midst of the throne and of the four living creatures, and in the midst of the elders.* The meaning is : between the throne and the living creatures on the one side, and the elders on the other. But the *Lamb* here seen was so in mid-view of the throne, and so related to the throne, that in

xxii, 1, it is called the throne of the Lamb as well as of God. And so in the song of praise which here follows (verses 8–13) the Lamb is honored even as the one who sits upon the throne. It is all because he "overcame and sat down with his Father in his throne" (iii, 21). It is a most remarkable thing that when the seer looked to behold the conquering Lion of Judah, of whom the elder spoke, he saw *a little lamb standing as though it had been slain.* The word ἀρνίον is strictly a diminutive, and means *a little lamb.* It occurs nowhere in the New Testament outside this book except in the one instance of John xxi, 15, and there in the plural. The striking contrast between the lion and the lamb is further enhanced by representing the lamb *standing as slain.* The fact of his *standing* shows that he was truly alive; but something in the vision showed just as clearly that he *had been slain.* How this was made to appear we may not certainly determine; but the two descriptive participles (ἐστηκός—ἐσφαγμένον) taken together express the same great truth as the Lord himself proclaims in i, 18, "I was dead, and behold I am alive unto the ages of the ages." That which was seen was a symbol of the crucified and risen Lord, whom Paul set forth as "delivered up for our trespasses and raised up for our justification" (Rom. iv, 25). The great trouble with Judaism was that it looked for a mighty lion, and was scandalized to behold, instead, a little lamb. The "veil upon their heart" (2 Cor. iii, 15) hindered their seeing that the slain lamb was also the lion of Judah. This lamb, moreover, had *seven horns and seven eyes.* The *horns* are here, as elsewhere, symbols of power, and the *seven* suggests the perfection of power possessed by the lamb. The *seven eyes* are symbols of a corresponding perfection of wisdom, and are defined to be identical with *the seven Spirits of God,* which have already been described as so many "lamps of fire burning before the throne" (iv, 5). He who has these seven eyes is competent to "search all things, even the deep things of God" (1 Cor. ii, 10). It is especially worthy of notice that *the seven Spirits of God* are here identified with the eyes of the Lamb, and hence the inference that the Spirit as well as the throne of God is in some profound and wonderful sense the Spirit of the Lamb. Comp. also i, 4, and iii, i.

7. *He came and has taken*—This use of the perfect instead of the aorist may be charged to the inaccurate grammar peculiar to the Apocalypse. His coming and taking the book *from the right hand of him that sat upon the throne* evinced that though he had been slain he was now alive and active, and powerful to reveal the deep things of God. In the vision of chap. x we shall see how the book, when opened, is given to John to be eaten.

The Worship of God and the Lamb. v, 8–14.

8 And when he had taken the book, the four living creatures and the four and twenty elders fell down before the Lamb, having each one a harp, and golden bowls full of incense, which are the prayers of the 9 saints. And they sing a new song, saying, Worthy art thou to take the book, and to open the seals thereof: for thou wast slain, and didst purchase unto God with thy blood *men* of every tribe, and tongue, and peo- 10 ple, and nation, and madest them *to be* unto our God a kingdom and 11 priests; and they reign upon the earth. And I saw, and I heard a voice of many angels round about the throne and the living creatures and the elders; and the number of them was ten thousand times ten thousand, 12 and thousands of thousands; saying with a great voice, Worthy is the Lamb that hath been slain to receive the power, and riches, and wisdom, 13 and might, and honor, and glory, and blessing. And every created thing which is in the heaven, and on the earth, and under the earth, and on the sea, and all things that are in them, heard I saying, Unto him that sitteth on the throne, and unto the Lamb, *be* the blessing, and the honor, 14 and the glory, and the dominion, for ever and ever. And the four living creatures said, Amen. And the elders fell down and worshiped.

The act of taking the book out of the hand of the Most Holy One called forth at once the worship of all the hosts of heaven and earth, for the entire universe was interested in this sublime act of the Lamb. The worship as here described consists of four parts : (1) The song of the cherubim and the elders (verses 8–10). (2) The worship of myriads of angels (11, 12). (3) Worship of the entire creation (13). (4) Response of the cherubim and the elders (14).

8–10. The worship of *the four living creatures and the four and twenty elders* is represented as one, just as in iv, 9–11, they are seen to act in concert. Four different expressions serve to indicate the homage they pay, namely, *fell down, each one a harp, bowls of incense,* and a *new song.* Harps and bowls full of incense have been thought unsuitable for cherubim, and are supposed by some expositors to be understood only of the elders. But the text makes no such distinction, and predicates all that is here said alike of living creatures and elders. And this is perfectly consistent with the view of the cherubim and elders as presented in the foregoing notes. The symbolic representatives of redeemed humanity may, as kings and priests before the throne, present the symbols of *the prayers of the saints.* Comp. viii, 3, and Psalm cxli, 2. The *new song* they sing is something new in kind (καινή), as if prompted by a new and fuller revelation of the Lamb of God. His worthiness to open the sealed book is celebrated as resting upon three acts of unspeakable love: (1) *Thou wast slain,* (2) *didst purchase in thy blood,* (3) *and madest them a kingdom and priests.* And these three are virtually one, for the sacrificial death, the redeeming efficacy of the blood, and the consummation of this redemption in the heavenly kingdom constitute the infinitely meritorious work and triumph of the Son of God. The direct object of the verb *didst purchase* (ἠγόρασας) is not expressed except by implication (for the reading ἡμᾶς is omitted in the best accredited texts), but the redeemed ones are said to be *from every tribe, and tongue, and people, and nation.* This fourfold designation is frequent in this book. Comp. vii, 9; x, 11; xi, 9; xiii, 7; xiv, 6; xvii, 15. In the last part of verse 10 the words *they are reigning on the earth* show that the conquest and judgment are conceived as present and continuing. Comp. ii, 27; xx, 4–6; 1 Cor. xv, 25.

11, 12. The *many angels,* whom John both *saw and heard,* seem to have formed a kind of circle *round about the throne and the living creatures and the elders,* and their innumerable multitude is designated by the impressive but indefinite terms *myriads of myriads* and *chiliads of chiliads.* The expression is an imitation of Dan. vii, 10, but fuller and more striking. The angelic worship is notable for its sevenfold ascription to the Lamb of *power, riches, wisdom, might, honor, glory,* and *blessing.* How infinitely *worthy* must he be who receives from all the angels homage like this!

13. Finally, *every created thing* is *heard* to join in this worship; and the realms of their being are named under four heads, *heaven, earth, under the earth,* and *on the sea,* and then, by way of repetition and emphasis, it is added: *even all things that are in them.* Thus to the song of cherubim and elders, and the great voice of innumerable angels, the entire creation itself, with every part and portion of the same, is represented as responding with like words of adoration and addressing their worship *unto him that sitteth on the throne and unto the Lamb.* The previous strains of worship mention only the Lamb, but this response of all creation mentions first the enthroned Ruler of the universe, and ascribes to him and to the Lamb *blessing, honor, glory,* and *dominion,* which four terms should be compared with the seven of verse 12.

14. The antiphonal response of *the four living creatures,* who simply say *Amen,* is eminently fitting and impressive, and the last act noticed of *the elders* was apparently one of silent adoration, as they *fell down and worshiped.*

The contents of chaps. iv and v are thus seen to be an apocalyptic introduction to what follows in chaps. vi to xi, and, indeed, to the entire sequel of the book. Its most striking features are modeled after the visions of Isa. vi and Ezek. i, but the New Testament seer shows his own penetration and originality in the fullness and variety of his descriptions. What more magnificent introduction can be imagined than this elaborate picture of the throne of God and of the Lamb? From thence "proceed lightnings and voices and thunders," symbolic signs of momentous revolutions in the world. And while the vision of these two chapters is essentially a Theophany, the most conspicuous person revealed therein is the Lamb in the midst of the throne. It is worthy of note that in xxii, 1, 2, the last object seen by John is the river of life "proceeding out of the throne of God and of the Lamb."

In the artificial arrangement of the book we observe that the first four seals are closely related to each other and form a class by themselves. The fifth and sixth seals form a striking contrast, as if answering one to the other. Between the sixth and seventh seals comes a double vision of the salvation of God's servants and martyrs (chap. vii), and the seventh seal itself issues in the sounding of the seven trumpets (chaps. viii–xi), which are again capable of division into four and three, as will be pointed out in the proper place. The first four seals are rapidly opened one after another and disclose a fourfold picture of impending judgments. They reveal in each case what one of the four living creatures calls forth, and the imagery is evidently modeled after the four chariots and horses of Zech. vi, 1–8, with which Zech. i, 8–11, is also to be compared.

1. First Seal Opened (White Horse). vi, 1, 2.

1 And I saw when the Lamb opened one of the seven seals, and I heard one of the four living creatures saying as with a voice of thunder, Come.
2 And I saw, and behold, a white horse, and he that sat thereon had a bow; and there was given unto him a crown: and he came forth conquering, and to conquer.

1. *And I saw*—What he saw is stated in verse 2, and the words are repeated at the beginning of that verse by way of resumption, after having stated what he *heard when the Lamb opened one of the seals.* The word *come*, which each of the four cherubim utters *with a voice like thunder*, is not addressed to John, for he was already in position to behold (iv, 1, 2); nor to Christ, as Alford and Glasgow imagine by comparing xxii, 17, 20, for Christ is present as opener of the seals; but to that which, in the first four seals, at once responds and comes forth in obedience to the command, namely, first the white, next the red, third the black, and last the pale horse and his rider.

2. *A white horse*—Symbol of victorious war. The entire imagery of this first picture points suggestively to the opening of the Roman war against Jerusalem, which was irresistible in its movements (νικῶν), and destined to prevail (ἵνα νικήσῃ). The fact that the victorious rider *had a bow* suggests that in the first stages of this bitter and decisive war the fighting was at a distance, not a close hand-to-hand struggle, such as a use of the sword implies. The war began by capturing the outlying towns of Palestine, preparatory to the siege of the great central city, Jerusalem. *There was given unto him a crown*—It is a notable fact that Vespasian, who began, and Titus, who completed the Jewish war, both obtained the imperial crown.

2. Second Seal Opened (Red Horse). vi, 3, 4.

3 And when he opened the second seal, I heard the second living crea-
4 ture saying, Come. And another *horse* came forth, a red horse: and to
   him that sat thereon it was given to take peace from the earth, and that
   they should slay one another: and there was given unto him a great
   sword.

4. *A red horse*—One having the color of fire (πυρρός), or of blood—symbol of the terrible bloodshed inseparable from bitter and relentless war. Such bloody warfare necessarily *takes peace out of the land*, which is laid waste by its disastrous progress. The *great sword* is a fitting additional symbol, suggesting, as in contrast with the bow of the preceding rider, the closer and more bloody conflict of hand-to-hand struggle. Thus each successive symbol of the fourfold picture intensifies the terrible impression designed to be made.

3. Third Seal Opened (Black Horse). vi, 5, 6.

5 And when he opened the third seal, I heard the third living creature
   saying, Come. And I saw, and behold, a black horse; and he that sat
6 thereon had a balance in his hand. And I heard as it were a voice in
   the midst of the four living creatures saying, A measure of wheat for a
   penny, and three measures of barley for a penny; and the oil and the
   wine hurt thou not.

5. *A black horse*—Symbol of deadly famine. *Black* is naturally suggestive of something to be dreaded as a calamity, and the *balance in the hand* of the rider suggests the scarcity of times when the most necessary articles of food are difficult to obtain, and, when obtained, are to be weighed out with strictest care.

6. *I heard as it were a voice*—Observe how the art of the apocalyptist makes voices from a mysterious source help to intensify the import of his visions. "That the cry sounds forth *in the midst of the four living creatures* is, in itself, natural, since the unsealing of

the book occurs at the throne of God, which is in the midst of the four beings."—*Düsterdieck*. The prices of *wheat* and *barley* are extortionate when a *choinix* (about a quart measure) of the one is held for a *denarius* (a "penny"), the usual payment for a full day's work (Matt. xx, 2), and only three times that amount of the more common article, *barley*, for the same price. In a time of famine the most common and necessary articles of food become scarce and costly. The command not to harm or injure (ἀδικέω) *the oil and the wine* is supposed by some interpreters to be addressed to the rider on the black horse, and to put a limit to the famine. These luxuries are not to be injured, but rather to remain plentiful, as a mitigation of the suffering when the more common articles are cut off. But a more congruous explanation of the command is that which regards it as a general maxim for the time, addressed to any and all whom it might concern, not to waste and destroy that which, though commonly a luxury, may be the only food obtainable.

4. FOURTH SEAL OPENED (PALE HORSE). VI, 7, 8.

7 And when he opened the fourth seal, I heard the voice of the fourth
8 living creature saying, Come. And I saw, and behold, a pale horse: and he that sat upon him, his name was Death; and Hades followed with him. And there was given unto them authority over the fourth part of the earth, to kill with sword, and with famine, and with death, and by the wild beasts of the earth.

8. *A pale horse*—Χλωρός, a *pale-green;* compare the word as used in viii, 7, and ix, 4. The rider is named *Thanatos, Death,* and reminds one of Horace's familiar *pallida mors* in Odes i, 4, 13 :

> Pallida Mors æquo pulsat pede pauperum tabernas
> Regumque turres.

But in John's picture Death was not the only figure, for another personification, *Hades, followed with him,* as if the two were joined together in the appointed work of terrible judgment. *Hades* is here to be understood as *the underworld,* the realm of disembodied souls, which swallows down all those whom Death destroys. So Death and Hades are associates (comp. xx, 13). To both of these awful powers *was given authority over the fourth part of the land,* a notably large portion. Compare the "third part" in viii, 7–12, and the "tenth part" in xi, 13. The work of destruction for which these awful personages are sent out is accomplished by means of *sword, famine, death,* and *wild beasts.* These are no other than the "four sore judgments" of Jehovah, by which he threatened Jerusalem through the ministry of Ezekiel (Ezek. xiv, 21). Compare the language of Ezek. v, 12; vi, 11, 12; Jer. xiv, 12; xxi, 7;

xxiv, 10; xliv, 13.   We are not to understand the *sword* (ῥομφαία)
as referring back to the sword (μάχαιρα) of verse 4, nor the *famine*
as a designed allusion to what is symbolized in verses 5 and 6.   We
are rather to recognize in the symbolism of the fourth seal a general portraiture of the fearful consummation of all the preceding,
and a designed aggravation of them all.   The word *death*, in the
latter part of this verse, as associated with the other three destructive agencies, is best understood as corresponding with the דֶּבֶר,
deadly pestilence, in Ezek. xiv, 21 (so translated there by the Septuagint), and not as referring to the specific figure of the rider on the
pale horse.   Throughout the entire picture of the first four seals we
note the prominence of this symbolic number, and should keep in
mind the prevailing habit of biblical apocalyptics to represent wide-
sweeping judgments in a fourfold way.   The symbols of these seals
are to be understood as representing one combined set of events,
and not as prophecies of calamities far separated in time.   "It is
not war in one age of the world, famine in another, death and carnage in another, but war, famine, and death in dread combination, all conspiring to plague the men of some one generation.   For
these things *naturally go together*.   You cannot have the white horse
of victory and conquest through the bow without war; you cannot
have the red horse of war without having also the black horse of
famine and the pale horse, death, in his immediate train."—
Cowles.

The true interpretation of these first four seals is that which recognizes them as a symbolic representation of the "wars, famines,
pestilences, and earthquakes" which Jesus declared would be "the
beginning of sorrows" in the desolation of Jerusalem (Matt. xxiv,
6, 7; Luke xxi, 10, 11, 20).   The attempt to identify each separate
figure with some one specific event misses both the spirit and method
of apocalyptic symbolism.   The aim is to give a fourfold and most
impressive picture of that terrible war on Jerusalem which was destined to avenge the righteous blood of prophets and apostles (Matt.
xxiii, 35–37), and to involve a "great tribulation," the like of which
had never been before (Matt. xxiv, 21).   Like the four successive
but closely connected swarms of locusts in Joel i, 4 ; like the four
riders on different colored horses in Zech. i, 8, 18, and the four
chariots drawn by as many different colored horses in Zech. vi, 1–8,
these four sore judgments of Jehovah move forth at the command
of the four living creatures by the throne to execute the will of Him
who declared the "scribes, Pharisees, and hypocrites" of his time
to be "serpents and offspring of vipers," and assured them that
"all these things should come upon this generation" (Matt. xxiii,

33, 36). The writings of Josephus abundantly show how fearfully all these things were fulfilled in the bloody war of Rome against Jerusalem.

5. FIFTH SEAL OPENED (SOULS UNDER ALTAR). VI, 9–11.

9 And when he opened the fifth seal, I saw underneath the altar the souls of them that had been slain for the word of God, and for the tes-
10 timony which they held: and they cried with a great voice, saying, How long, O Master, the holy and true, dost thou not judge and avenge our
11 blood on them that dwell on the earth? And there was given them to each one a white robe; and it was said unto them, that they should rest yet for a little time, until their fellow-servants also and their brethren, who should be killed even as they were, should be fulfilled in number.

The fifth seal opens a martyr scene, and serves to relieve from the spell of horror begotten by the visions of the first four seals. Here again we note the studied method of the writer to vivify and enhance his prophecy by means of revelations of opposite character. We are not to regard this martyr scene as the prediction of an historical event to follow in chronological order after the events depicted in the first four seals. It serves rather for the encouragement and comfort of all who were exposed to martyrdom "in the tribulation and kingdom and patience in Jesus" (chap. i, 9), and corresponds to Jesus's words in Matt. xxiv, 9, and Luke xxi, 16, which admonished the disciples of the tribulation and death which many among them must suffer during the apostolic period. Again and again in this Apocalypse we shall notice visions of similar import and purpose.

9. *I saw under the altar the souls*—The vision finds its explanation in the custom of pouring out the blood of sacrificial victims at the basis of the altar (Lev. iv, 7; v, 9). "The life (or soul) of the flesh is in the blood," according to Lev. xvii, 11, and so in this vision the *souls* which went forth in the blood *of them that had been slain for the word of God* are conceived as so many sacrifices of life *for the testimony which they held* (*testimony* here in the same sense as i, 2, 9), and each life cries out from the blood "at the bottom of the altar," where the victim had been slain.

10. *They cried with a great voice*—Like the blood of Abel crying from the ground unto God (Gen. iv, 10). This cry of the martyr-souls may be understood as arising from "all the righteous blood shed upon the earth, from the blood of righteous Abel" to the last victim of Jewish persecution (comp. Matt. xxiii, 35–37). *How long* —Comp. Zech. i, 12. *O Master*—Observe that the word here employed is not the more common and general κύριος, *lord*, but the more specific δεσπότης, *master*, which implies the ownership of slaves. Compare the word σύνδουλοι in the next verse, and δοῦλοι

in chap. xi, 18.   The *Master* to whom these martyrs pray is God, *the holy and the true*, and the cry for judgment and vengeance is not to be understood as the expression of bitter and vindictive feelings, but a call for the Judge of all the earth to do that which is due to his holiness and truth.   He who forbids men to avenge themselves on one another declares that vengeance belongs unto him (Rom. xii, 19).   He will surely avenge his chosen ones who cry to him day and night (Luke xviii, 7, 8).

11.   *To each a white robe*—Comp. chap. vii, 9, 13–17.   The white robes and the rest assured the martyrs correspond with Jesus's pledge to his followers that in their patience they should win their souls (Luke xxi, 19), and that "whosoever shall lose his life for my sake and the gospel's shall save it" (Mark viii, 35).   *Yet for a little time*— Equivalent to the ἐν τάχει, *speedily*, of Luke xviii, 8; even before that generation passed away, for the accumulated vengeance was to come upon that same generation (Matt. xxiii, 36).   *Until their fellow-servants . . . should be fulfilled*—That is, until the number of martyrs *who were about to be killed even as they were* should be complete.   These others yet *to be killed* may be recognized in the two witnesses of chap. xi, 3–13, for when the seventh trumpet sounded "the time for the dead to be judged came, and the time to give the reward to the prophets and saints" (xi, 18).   Meanwhile, until that time should come, these martyr-souls are each one robed in the garment of heavenly victory, and, as we are to learn from subsequent visions, guided by the Lamb "unto fountains of waters of life," where "God shall wipe away every tear from their eyes" (chap. vii, 17).

6. Sixth Seal Opened (Shaking of Earth and Heavens).
VI, 12–17.

12   And I saw when he opened the sixth seal, and there was a great earthquake; and the sun became black as sackcloth of hair, and the whole
13   moon became as blood; and the stars of the heaven fell unto the earth, as a fig tree casteth her unripe figs, when she is shaken of a great wind.
14   And the heaven was removed as a scroll when it is rolled up; and every
15   mountain and island were moved out of their places.   And the kings of the earth, and the princes, and the chief captains, and the rich, and the strong, and every bondman and freeman, hid themselves in the caves and
16   in the rocks of the mountains; and they say to the mountains and to the rocks, Fall on us, and hide us from the face of him that sitteth on the
17   throne, and from the wrath of the Lamb: for the great day of their wrath is come; and who is able to stand ?

The opening of the sixth seal, as described in this passage, seems somewhat like an immediate answer to the cry of the souls under

the altar, and the imagery is in the main identical with that of
Matt. xxiv, 29–31, which describes the coming of the Son of man
"immediately after the tribulation" spoken of in the preceding context. The descriptions in both passages are an apocalyptic portraiture of the great and terrible day of the Lord, and the several
images and allusions are appropriated from Old Testament prophecy,
as the subjoined references show.

12. *A great earthquake*—Symbolic signal of divine visitations of
judgment. Comp. Isa. xxix, 6, and also this Rev. viii, 5; xi, 13, 19;
xvi, 18. *Sun became black . . . moon as blood*—Comp. Joel ii,
10, 31; iii, 15; Isa. xiii, 10; xxiv, 23; Ezek. xxxii, 7, 8; Amos viii, 9;
Matt. xxiv, 29.

13. *Stars fell*—Comp. Joel ii, 10 ; iii, 15 ; Isa. xiii, 10 ; Ezek.
xxxii, 7. *As fig tree*—Comp. Isa. xxxiv, 4 ; Nahum iii, 12.

14. *Heaven as a scroll*—Comp. Isa. xxxiv, 4. *Mountains and
islands moved*—Jer. iv, 24; Hab. iii, 6; Ezek. xxvi, 15, 18; xxxviii,
20; Nahum i, 5; Isa. lxiv, 1, 3; xl, 15; xli, 5.

16, 17. *Fall on us and hide us*—Comp. Hosea x, 8 ; Isa. ii, 19, 21;
Luke xxiii, 30. *Who is able to stand*—Comp. Nahum i, 6 ; Psalm
lxxvi, 7.

A careful comparison of these different Old Testament passages
in connection with the imagery and language of the sixth seal
shows how freely our author appropriates the older scriptures to suit
the purpose of his own book of prophecy. The great day of the
Lord is thus set forth after the manner of Isa. xiii, 6–9; Zeph. i,
14–18, and Joel i, 15; ii, 1, 2. And as the language of the older
scriptures referred to impending judgments of Jehovah on wicked
men and nations, so these verses 12–17 are to be understood as a
like description of fearful judgment impending at the time when
this book was written. And the appalling calamities involved in
the overthrow of Jerusalem, and their relation to the kingdom of
God, were surely of a magnitude equal to any of those depicted by
the apocalyptic writers of the Old Testament, whose language our
author appropriates.

We have now seen that the first six seals, as opened by the Lamb,
form a closely connected series and appropriate the apocalyptic
imagery of the Hebrew prophets. The first four find fulfillment in
the war which began about A. D. 66, swept over Galilee and Samaria, laid waste all the cities and villages of Palestine, and became
intensified with all those scenes of blood and famine and woe which
made the siege and final overthrow of Jerusalem by the Romans
one of the most horrible events of human history. It must be kept
in mind that these calamities of the Jewish people were announced

in most explicit terms by Jesus as a judgment upon that wicked generation for its guilt in shedding the righteous blood of saints and prophets (Matt. xxiii, 34–38). Hence the significance of placing the martyr scene of verses 9–11 in the midst of these pictures of retributive judgment. The first four seals disclose the conjoined forces of war, carnage, famine, and aggravated mortality, moving forth at the command of the four living creatures. But the opening of the fifth seal enables us to hear the cry of the martyrs for judgment and vengeance, and then, as if in immediate answer to that cry, the sixth seal is opened, and all the signs and terrors of the day of wrath appear. These are all apocalyptic disclosures of things which were to " come to pass quickly."

First Interlude. VII.

(1) SEALING OF GOD'S ISRAEL. VII, 1-8.

1 After this I saw four angels standing at the four corners of the earth, holding the four winds of the earth, that no wind should blow on the
2 earth, or on the sea, or upon any tree. And I saw another angel ascend from the sunrising, having the seal of the living God: and he cried with a great voice to the four angels, to whom it was given to hurt the earth
3 and the sea, saying, Hurt not the earth, neither the sea, nor the trees, till we shall have sealed the servants of our God on their foreheads.
4 And I heard the number of them who were sealed, a hundred and forty and four thousand, sealed out of every tribe of the children of Israel.
5   Of the tribe of Judah *were* sealed twelve thousand:
    Of the tribe of Reuben twelve thousand:
    Of the tribe of Gad twelve thousand:
6   Of the tribe of Asher twelve thousand:
    Of the tribe of Naphtali twelve thousand:
    Of the tribe of Manasseh twelve thousand:
7   Of the tribe of Simeon twelve thousand:
    Of the tribe of Levi twelve thousand:
    Of the tribe of Issachar twelve thousand:
8   Of the tribe of Zebulun twelve thousand:
    Of the tribe of Joseph twelve thousand:
    Of the tribe of Benjamin *were* sealed twelve thousand.

After the opening of the sixth seal, with its tremendous signs of judgment, one might naturally expect the seventh seal to be immediately opened and the final consummation to be told. But such is not the method of this Apocalypse. As between the fourth and sixth seals the heavenly victory and comfort of the martyrs were revealed, so between the sixth and seventh seals there intervenes a glorious vision of the sealing and salvation of the true servants of God. The martyr scene of the fifth seal is here enlarged so as to take in all the servants (δοῦλοι) of God, and brethren who have been "partakers in the tribulation and kingdom and patience which are in Jesus" (i, 9), and who "washed their robes and made them white in the blood of the Lamb" (verse 14).

In order to appreciate this method of the book the more clearly, we may here anticipate the subsequent revelations so far as to observe the seven instances in which the writer introduces such visions of triumph and glory between appalling scenes of woe.

1. The martyr scene of vi, 9–11, between the fourth and sixth seals.

2. The sealing and salvation of God's servants between the sixth and seventh seals (chap. vii).

3. Triumph and ascension of the two witnesses between the sixth and seventh trumpets (xi, 3–12).

4. The hundred and forty-four thousand with the Lamb on Mount Zion, and the world-wide proclamation of the Gospel, between the persecutions of the two beasts of chap. xiii, and the fall of Babylon and torment of those who worship the beast (xiv, 1–6).

5. The victorious company, singing the song of Moses and the Lamb, between the bloody scene of chap. xiv, 17–20, and the seven last plagues (xv, 2–4).

6. The great multitude, singing Hallelujah, between the fall of Babylon and the last great battle with the beast and his followers (xix, 1–10).

7. Vision of the enthroned martyrs between the binding and imprisonment of Satan and his release for final war against the saints (xx, 4–6).

Thus again and again, in the midst of scenes of tribulation and judgment, we are lifted up by some corresponding picture of glory and triumph. This feature of the book cannot reasonably be regarded as accidental, but is part of the plan and method of the inspired writer, who was divinely guided so as to set the several revelations in most telling form.

1. *After this I saw*—There was a pause in the progress of disclosures. The terrors of the sixth seal were adapted to appall, and leave the seer in a spell of amazement and confusion. The scenes which followed were of a nature to compose and cheer him. The contents of this seventh chapter are, in fact, an answer to the question with which the sixth chapter ends, "Who is able to stand?" We are herein assured that the awful judgments impending shall not harm those whom God seals as his own servants. How this corresponds with our Lord's words as recorded in Luke xxi, 18, 19, is noticeable: Some of them were to suffer death, and they were all to be hated and persecuted; but "not a hair of their head should

perish," for in their patience they should possess (κτάομαι) their
souls. Hence the blessed truth of Matt. x, 39: "He that loseth his
life for my sake shall find it." The entire picture of this seventh
chapter seems also to correspond with the words of Jesus in Matt.
xxiv, 31: "He shall send forth his angels with a great trumpet-
sound, and they shall gather his elect from the four winds, from
one end of heaven to the other." To interpret these words literally, and insist that this gathering of the elect is a visible phenomenon, taking place at one moment or brief period of time, is but to
perpetuate an error in biblical exegesis which results only in confusion. The same observation holds in respect to the visions of the
sealing of God's servants in verses 1–8, and the great multitude out
of all peoples in verses 9–17. The apocalyptic picture must needs
be instantaneous, like any object presented symbolically to our
thought, but the facts depicted are not therefore to be supposed as
occurring at any one particular period or place. Unless the time
and chronological order are expressly stated they need form no
essential feature of the vision. Consequently this sealing of God's
elect, and the glorification of the countless multitude before the
throne, are to be understood of events extended through an indefinite period, and designed to furnish a vivid picture of the glory of
those that inherit the salvation of God in Christ. The period which
the date and scope of this book imply is that of the first apostles
and servants of Jesus—the apostolic age.

Four angels. . . four corners. . . four winds—These three sets
of *fours* are noticeable, as accordant with a scheme of symbolical
numbers, but need not be supposed to have specific significance.
The irrelevant fancy which finds in the *four angels* the four emperors, Maximian, Severus, Maxentius, and Licinius, who hindered
the preaching of God's word (Lyra), is scarcely outdone by the
notion of Bengel that *the earth, the sea,* and *any tree,* mentioned in
this same verse, are to be understood, respectively, as Asia, Europe,
and Africa! We have had so many occasions to notice that world-
judgments and their agents move, so to speak, by fours that we
need not stop to emphasize this additional example. The *winds* are
God's messengers and agents to execute his will (Psalm civ, 4; Heb.
i, 7), and the four points of the compass are appropriately called
the four corners of the earth. The *earth, sea,* and *tree* are naturally
mentioned as objects affected by the wind, and also in anticipation
of the things to be smitten by the coming plagues (see viii, 7, 8).
It accords with the spirit and style of apocalyptics that all the
forces of the world should be conceived as committed to the charge
of angels. Compare "the angel of the waters" in xvi, 5.

2. *Another angel*—The ministry of innumerable angels constitutes what may be called the machinery of apocalyptic writings.
Comp. Zech. ii, 3. *Ascend from the sunrising*—"It is appropriate
and significant that the angel, coming for a victorious employment
which brings eternal life, should arise from that side from which
life and light are brought by the earthly sun. The angel himself,
who does not descend from heaven, but ascends from the horizon,
is represented after the manner of the rising sun."—*Düsterdieck.*
The seal of the living God is here conceived as a sort of signet ring
by which the name of God and the Lamb (comp. xiv, 1) was to be
stamped upon the foreheads of his servants (verse 3; comp. ix, 4).

This imagery of sealing God's servants in view of impending
calamities is taken from Ezek. ix, 4, where an angel is commissioned
to "go through the midst of Jerusalem, and set a mark upon the
foreheads of the men that sigh and that cry over all the abominations that are done in her midst." This mark was to save them
from the slaughter about to be executed on the guilty. In a similar
way the mark of the blood of the paschal lamb on the dwellings of
Israel turned away the destroying angel from the door (Exod. xii,
7, 13).

The purpose of the sealing was to preserve the true Israel of God
as a holy seed. It was not designed to save them from tribulation,
but to preserve them in the midst of the great tribulation about to
come and to glorify them thereby. Though the old Israel be cast
off, a new and holy Israel is to be chosen and sealed with the Spirit
of the living God. Though the old Jerusalem perish, a new and
heavenly Jerusalem will come forth to take its place, and the glory
of the new dispensation will be that the true Israelites will come,
not to fire, and blackness, and trumpet, and words of terror, but
to Mount Zion, the city of the living God, the church of those enrolled in heaven, and the spirits of just men made perfect (Heb. xii,
18–24).

4. *I heard the number*—The process of the sealing is passed over
without mention and the result announced. *A hundred and forty
and four thousand*—A symbolical number made up of twelve times
twelve, allowing each tribe an equal number. This number appears
again significantly in chap. xiv, 1, and the new Jerusalem has
twelve gates, guarded by as many angels, and bearing the names of
the twelve tribes (xxi, 12); it measures twelve thousand furlongs,
and its wall is a hundred and forty and four cubits (xxi, 16, 17).
Compare the "twelve pillars, according to the twelve tribes of
Israel" (Exod. xxiv, 4), the twelve cakes of showbread (Lev. xxiv,
5), the twelve memorial stones "according to the number of the

tribes" (Josh. iv, 5), and the "twelve bullocks for all Israel" (Ezra viii, 35).

5–8. Twelve names are here written after the manner and spirit in which the twelve tribes are often enumerated in the Old Testament. Comp. Gen. xlvi; Exod. i, 1–4; Num. i and xiii; Ezek. xlviii. No special significance is to be attached to the names or the order in which they occur. Judah was naturally placed first, as the great leader and prince from whom the "Root of David sprang" (v, 5), and Benjamin is named last because he was the youngest. Why Dan is omitted is now as impossible to explain as why Simeon is omitted in Deut. xxxiii. Some think the tribe of Dan had become extinct, for while mentioned in 1 Chron. ii, 2, his name does not appear in the lists of 1 Chron. iv–viii. Inasmuch as he would not omit Levi, nor fail to recognize the double portion of Joseph (whose name is substituted in verse 8 for Ephraim), he must needs omit some one name to secure exactly twelve, and who more suitable to be omitted than the firstborn son of Rachel's handmaid? The omission is of no significance.

The one hundred and forty-four thousand are thus far presented to our thought only as sealed of God and numbered. The purpose of the sealing was, at least in part, to preserve them from the judgments about to fall upon the earth. The relation of this sealed and numbered company to the "great multitude which no man could number" (verses 9–17) will be discussed at the end of the chapter.

(2) THE INNUMERABLE MULTITUDE WASHED IN THE BLOOD OF THE LAMB.   VII, 9–17.

9 After these things I saw, and behold, a great multitude, which no man could number, out of every nation, and of *all* tribes and peoples and tongues, standing before the throne and before the Lamb, arrayed in
10 white robes, and palms in their hands; and they cry with a great voice, saying, Salvation unto our God who sitteth on the throne, and unto the
11 Lamb. And all the angels were standing round about the throne, and *about* the elders and the four living creatures; and they fell before the
12 throne on their faces, and worshiped God, saying, Amen: Blessing, and glory, and wisdom, and thanksgiving, and honor, and power, and might,
13 *be* unto our God forever and ever. Amen. And one of the elders answered, saying unto me, These who are arrayed in the white robes, who
14 are they, and whence came they? And I say unto him, My lord, thou knowest. And he said to me, These are they who come out of the great tribulation, and they washed their robes, and made them white in the
15 blood of the Lamb. Therefore are they before the throne of God; and they serve him day and night in his temple: and he that sitteth on the
16 throne shall spread his tabernacle over them. They shall hunger no more, neither thirst any more; neither shall the sun strike upon them,

17 nor any heat: for the Lamb who is in the midst of the throne shall be
their shepherd, and shall guide them unto fountains of waters of life: and
God shall wipe away every tear from their eyes.

9. *After these things*—Another stage of the interlude (comp.
verse 1), so that the visions of verses 1–8 and 9–17 are to be recognized as distinct and successive. *Great multitude which no man
could number*—Obvious contrast with the twelve times twelve thousand who were sealed (verse 4). *Out of every nation and tribes
and peoples and tongues*—And therefore not confined to the "tribes
of the children of Israel" (verse 4). *Standing before the throne
and before the Lamb*—So this is a heavenly rather than an earthly
scene. The circumstances of sealing the one hundred and forty-four
thousand clearly implied that they were on the earth and exposed
to danger, but these before the throne have evidently passed all
such exposure to harm. *Arrayed in white robes*—Appropriate ves-
ture of those who have passed into heavenly triumph and blessedness (comp. iii, 4; vi, 11). *Palms in their hands*—Emblem of
triumphant peace and joy. The word φοίνικες, *palm branches*,
occurs only here and in John xii, 13. Comp. 1 Macc. xiii, 51;
2 Macc. x, 7; xiv, 4.

10. *Cry with a great voice*—The united audible worship of such
a countless throng must needs be with a great sound. *Salvation
unto our God*—The word in the Greek has the article, *the salvation*.
All the life, triumph, glory, and blessedness of their being and position are contemplated in this *salvation*, and they ascribe it all *to
God* and *to the Lamb*. In these two verses observe the fourfold
expressions :

> Nation, tribes, peoples, tongues;
> Standing, arrayed, palms, cry.

11. *All the angels were standing*—Comp. v, 11. The verb εἱστή-
κεισαν is strictly pluperfect, and if so translated, *had been standing*,
might perhaps suggest that the angels had been there before these
white-robed multitudes came (comp. 1 Peter i, 12), and now joined
in the heavenly worship by responding to the "great voice" of the
innumerable saints.

12. *Blessing . . . glory . . . wisdom . . . thanksgiving . . . honor . . .
power . . . might*—Seven chosen words of praise, and the same as
those employed by the angels in v, 12, except that *thanksgiving* is
here substituted in place of *riches*.

13. *One of the elders*—Just as in v, 5; a most appropriate one to
act as John's interpreter, being a representative of the Church of
the living God. *Answered*—Idiomatic use of this word, as in Matt.

xi, 25. The angel spoke relevantly to the occasion, and so answered the expectant inquiry of John's enraptured gaze. Comp. Zech. iii, 4; iv, 4, 11, 12. The question of the elder and John's answer in verses 13 and 14 are to be compared with those in Zech. i, 19, 21; iii, 2; iv, 11–13. This form of question and answer serves to give dramatic life to the description.

14. *These are they who come out of the great tribulation*—Not who *came* out, nor who *shall come out* of the tribulation, although this is necessarily implied by logical inference; but *they who come* (οἱ ἐρχόμενοι, *who are about to come*). The vision contemplates them as one great company already before the throne (verse 15). *The great tribulation*—Not to be understood as all the trials which may ever befall those who are counted worthy at last to enter the glory of God in heaven. This comforting assurance may indeed be allowed as a doctrine certainly tenable by reason of necessary inferences from such a picture of salvation and from other teachings of Holy Scripture. But our prophet's field of vision contemplates a definite *tribulation* of the near future, that bitter "hour of trial which was about to come upon the whole world, to try them that dwell upon the earth" (iii, 10). It is the same great tribulation spoken of by Jesus in Matt. xxiv, 21, immediately after which the "sign of the Son of man" is to appear in heaven (Matt. xxiv, 29). But from the tribulation thus definitely contemplated we need not exclude any of the trials incident to the apostolic period, such as those referred to in John xvi, 33; Acts xiv, 22. The entire period between John's writing and "the consummation of that age" (referred to in Matt. xxiv, 3) was for the Church a time of affliction, as Matt. xxiv, 9, implies. *Washed . . . white*—Comp. i, 5; xxii, 14; Eph. v, 26, 27; 1 John i, 7.

15. *They are before the throne*—Like ministers of his presence. *Serve him*—So that their heavenly glory is not a repose of idle inactivity, but a service of delight. *Day and night*—For day and night are alike to "the spirits of just men made perfect," so that, in fact, there is no such thing as night to them (xxi, 25). *In his temple*—So their service is that of "priests unto God" (i, 6). This temple of God is doubtless the same which, in xi, 19, is seen "opened in the heaven"—the triumphal outcome of what is measured in xi, 1, and destined to survive the ruin of the great city which crucified the Lord. In a later vision this temple is identified with "God the Almighty and the Lamb" (xxi, 22). And all this is intimated in the statement that *he who sits upon the throne shall spread his tabernacle over them*, so that they shall dwell with him and he with them (comp. xxi, 3; Exod. xxix, 45; Lev. xxvi, 11; Isa.

iv, 5, 6). This mention of *throne, temple,* and *tabernacle* in one verse is suggestive, and shows how all three are virtually one. The profoundest symbolism of tabernacle and temple points out how God will dwell with men and men with God. (See pp. 81–84.)

16. *Neither hunger . . . thirst . . . sun . . . heat*—Appropriated from Isa. xlix, 10; comp. also Psalm cxxi, 6. This implies utter absence of all plague and pestilence, and such calamities as were about to come at the sound of the first four trumpets of woe (viii, 7–12).

17. *The Lamb . . . their shepherd*—He shall act the part of a good shepherd, as suggested by such scriptures as Psalm xxiii, 1; Isa. xl, 11; John x, 11. *Life's fountains of waters*—Comp. Psalm xxiii, 2; xxxvi, 8; Isa. xlix, 10. *Wipe away every tear*—More expressive and tender than *all tears.* Comp. Isa. xxv, 8; xxxv, 10.

It remains for us here to inquire into the relation of the visions of verses 1–8 and 9–17 to each other. It is evident that the two companies are *represented* as distinct, but it does not therefore follow that they are of different nature and destiny. The distinctions are quite noticeable : (1) The one company are sealed with some stamp of the living God, while no such mark is mentioned of the others. (2) The one are out of every tribe of Israel, the other out of all nations and peoples. (3) The one comprise a definite number, the other is innumerable. (4) Nothing is affirmed of the first class except that they were "sealed out of every tribe of the children of Israel," but the other appear in white robes, with palms, and ascribe praise to God and the Lamb. The angels respond to their cry, and one of the elders tells who they are, and whence they come, in terms of description so closely analogous to those of chap. xxi, 3–7, and xxii, 1–5, as to show that the innumerable company of verses 9–17 are the same as those blessed ones who wash their robes and have the right of the tree of life and to enter into the new Jerusalem (xxii, 14). They are "the bride, the wife of the Lamb" (xxi, 9), and though here they are not spoken of as sealed, there they are "written in the Lamb's book of life" (xxi, 27) and "his name is on their foreheads" (xxii, 4).

We observe further that in chap. xiv, 1–5, we have a vision of "the Lamb standing on Mount Zion, and with him a hundred and forty and four thousand, having his name, and the name of his Father, written on their foreheads." They also sing "before the throne, and before the four living creatures and the elders." They are defined as "virgins," who "follow the Lamb whithersoever he goeth," and "were purchased from among men (as a kind of) first-fruits unto God and unto the Lamb." These as certainly correspond to the select and sealed Israel of vii, 4–8, as "the bride, the wife of the Lamb," in chaps. xxi and xxii, corresponds to the white-robed multitude of vii, 9–17.

If now we interpret vii, 4–8, in the light of xiv, 1–5, and vii, 9–17, in the light of what is seen in chaps. xxi and xxii to constitute the new Jerusalem, we need not suppose the sealed and numbered Israelites of the first vision to be excluded from the greater multitude of the second. If we adopt the view of many expositors in regarding the one hundred and forty-four thousand as Jewish Christians (the Church of the circumcision, Gal. ii, 9, 10), we need not thereby exclude them from the innumerable company "out of every nation, and from all tribes and peoples and tongues" (vii, 9), for these terms clearly include the Jewish as well as all other peoples.

It is most consonant with the language of the passage and the method of the book to understand these two companies as not so much composed of entirely different persons as contemplated in different relations and from different points of view. If we inquire how the souls under the altar to whom white robes were given (vi, 9–11) are related to this innumerable company arrayed in white robes, and palms in their hands, our problem would be very much the same. The greater number may well include the smaller, but the smaller are nevertheless to be regarded as constituting a special class, so distinguishable as to call for a separate description. The martyrs who "were slain for the word of God" (vi, 9) receive special recognition, and appear again as enthroned with Christ in exceptional glory (xx, 4–6), but no one would imagine them excluded from the company that inherit the new Jerusalem. So the hundred and forty-four thousand may be included in the innumerable multitude of vii, 9–17, but they are first viewed as a special class chosen out of the twelve tribes of Israel. We need not suppose them any more worthy, or noble, or exalted than others, but the definitions of xiv, 1–5, set them before us as the "first fruits unto God and unto the Lamb." We accordingly understand the company "sealed out of every tribe of the children of Israel" as an apocalyptic picture of that "holy seed" of which Isaiah speaks in Isa. vi, 13—that surviving remnant which was destined to remain like the stump of a fallen oak after cities had been laid waste and the whole land had become a desolation—that "remnant of Jacob," which was to be preserved from the "consumption determined in the midst of all the land" (Isa. x, 21–23). It is the same "remnant according to the election of grace" of which Paul speaks in Rom. ix, 27, 28; xi, 5. God will not destroy Jerusalem and make the once holy places desolate until he first chooses and seals a select number as the beginning of a new

Israel. The first Christian Church was formed out of chosen servants of God from "the twelve tribes of the dispersion" (James i, 1), and the end of the Jewish age was not to come until by the ministry of Jewish Christian apostles and prophets the gospel of the kingdom had been preached in the whole world for a testimony unto all the nations (Matt. xxiv, 14). The same great fact is again symbolized in xi, 1, 2, by the measuring of the temple of God.

Viewed in this light the contents of chap. vii are placed most impressively between the sixth and seventh seals. The old dispensation is about to come to an end; the city and temple are about to be destroyed by the judgment of God, as foretold by Jesus in Matt. xxiii, 36–38. But before the end is disclosed by the opening of the seventh seal with its trumpets of woe we have a vision, first, of that chosen remnant out of all Israel, composed of such Jews as were "sealed with the Holy Spirit of promise" (Eph. i, 13 ; iv, 30; 2 Cor. i, 22), and marked with that circumcision of the heart which is "in spirit, not in letter; whose praise is not of men, but of God" (Rom. ii, 28, 29). But the revelation does not stop with this vision of a new Israel, surviving as the nucleus of a new age and church, but adds the larger picture of vii, 9–17, as showing unto what that chosen first fruits will ultimately expand. The "remnant according to the election of grace" was but the beginning of a "holy seed," destined to become an innumerable company before the throne of God and of the Lamb, and thus fulfill in the highest sense the ancient promise made to Abraham (Gen. xv, 5; xxii, 17, 18).

The assertion that these correlated visions are so incongruous that they could not have originated with one author, but must needs be fragments of lost apocalypses, is thus seen to be without valid ground. It would reflect most unwarrantably on the literary sense of the final compiler or redactor of our book. The genius for symmetry and tact displayed in the arrangement of the contents of this entire book justifies us in the belief that what recent critics imagine to be dislocated fragments of divers preceding works are all well-considered and artistically planned portions of one great apocalypse, designed to encourage and comfort the earliest Christian churches.

7. Seventh Seal Opened. VIII, 1.

1 And when he opened the seventh seal, there followed a silence in heaven about the space of half an hour.

The opening of the seventh seal reveals seven angels, who proceed to sound seven trumpets as so many signals of the end. The imagery of the whole section which now follows (chaps. viii–xi) appears to have been suggested by the record of the seven trumpets which sounded the fall of Jericho.[1] Those trumpets sounded the doom of the first great Canaanitish city which stood in the way of the conquest of the promised land; these sound the doom of "the great city, which spiritually is called Sodom and Egypt" (xi, 8, 13), and which stood in the way of the free progress of the word of God and the testimony of Jesus Christ. Jerusalem and her temple, then " in bondage with her children," must give way before "the Jerusalem that is above and free" (Gal. iv, 25, 26).

The seven trumpets included in the seventh seal serve, after the manner of apocalyptic repetition, to intensify the terrors of the great day of wrath which were seen at the opening of the sixth seal (vi, 12–17). The revelation of that great and terrible day of the Lord here proceeds to bring forward a more exhaustive appropriation of Old Testament metaphor and symbol, in order to make a profounder impression upon the seer and his readers, and also to show that these judgments were ordained of God and shortly to come to pass (comp. Gen. xli, 32). So Daniel's apocalypse, in the vision of chap. viii, repeats in various details and with greater precision the latter portion of the vision of chap. vii.

1. *Silence in heaven about the space of half an hour*—How much learned folly has been displayed in fanciful expositions of this silence in heaven ! It has been made to signify the repose of the Church after the Diocletian persecution (Lord) ; the liberty granted the Church by Constantine (Daubuz) ; the silent forbearance of Christians under Jewish persecution (Alcazar); the thousand years' rest before the end of the world (Vitringa). The source of such far-fetched notions is in the main a failure to recognize a rhetorical element in Holy Scripture and the art of the sacred writers in their studied efforts to make impressions by means of analogies and contrasts which exist in the very nature of images. What is thus merely incidental and suggestive in a certain context is magnified into a mystic meaning of far-reaching significance. This *silence* is *in the heaven* where all these related visions appear, and, as all the preceding seals were accompanied by voices (comp. vi, 1, 3, 5, 7, 9, 12, 16), this last one is distinguished by the contrast of silence. It was simply the silent expectation and awful suspense before the final scene, and the mention of it by the writer serves to enhance the solemnity of the vision about to be disclosed. *About half an hour* would be a short time, but sufficiently long to enhance the awful solemnity of the occasion. Perhaps the idea of this *silence*

---

[1] Compare what is said on this subject above, pp. 85, 86.

was suggested by the cessation of singers and trumpets when King Hezekiah and those with him bowed themselves in reverent worship (2 Chron. xxix, 28, 29), and the *half hour* may have some reference to the offering incense described in verses 3 and 4, for that would be about the length of time necessary for a priest to enter the temple and offer incense and return (comp. Lev. xvi, 13, 14 ; Luke i, 10, 21).

III. THE SOUNDING OF THE SEVEN TRUMPETS. VIII-XI.

THE SEVEN ANGELS. viii, 2.

2 And I saw the seven angels which stand before God; and there were given unto them seven trumpets.

2. *The seven angels which stand before God*—The well-known presence-angels familiar to those versed in current Jewish angelology (see Tobit xii, 15). But no special significance attaches to these seven angels more than to the four angels of vii, 1. *Were given unto them seven trumpets*—By whom given is not recorded. In the corresponding vision of the seven bowls of wrath the bowls were given by one of the four living creatures (xv, 7). Each one of these angels received a trumpet, as in xv, 1, and xvi, 1, each angel had a bowl of plagues. The *trumpets* serve as signals of so many successive scenes of a terrible series of judgments, while the bowls are symbols of so many vessels of woe.

THE ANGEL WITH THE CENSER. viii, 3-6.

3 And another angel came and stood over the altar, having a golden censer; and there was given unto him much incense, that he should add it unto the prayers of all the saints upon the golden altar which was 4 before the throne. And the smoke of the incense, with the prayers of 5 the saints, went up before God out of the angel's hand. And the angel taketh the censer; and he filled it with the fire of the altar, and cast it upon the earth: and there followed thunders, and voices, and lightnings, and an earthquake.
6 And the seven angels which had the seven trumpets prepared themselves to sound.

3. *And another angel came* — Comp. vii, 2 ; Zech. iii, 2. All such ministration of angels is part of the machinery of apocalyptics, and the writer introduces as many angels as seem appropriate to perform the various parts of the symbolic picture. As the angel of the sunrise in vii, 2, had charge of the sealing of God's servants, so this one acts the part of an officiating priest in the offering of incense. *Stood over the altar*—Compare the vision of Amos ix, 1. The great temple of God in heaven is before the eye of the seer, and, like the earthly tabernacle and temple patterned after it (Exod. xxv, 40 ; xxvi, 30 ; Heb. viii, 5), has its golden altar of

incense *before the throne.* So in the tabernacle the position of the
altar of incense was immediately in front of the veil, behind which
was the ark, with its mercy seat and cherubim where Jehovah was
enthroned (Exod. xxx, 6 ; xxv, 21, 22 ; 1 Kings vi, 20, 22 ; Psalm
lxxx, 1 ; xcix, 1). The *much incense* is a fitting symbol of *the
prayers of all the saints,* and it is said that the incense was *given
to the prayers,* that is, *added to the prayers* as a sign that they were
presented and heard before the throne of God. Compare the mention of incense in v, 8, and Psalm cxli, 2. These *prayers of all the
saints* are to be understood as in harmony with the cry of the souls
under the altar (vi, 9, 10) and as superadded to them; also as of
the same character as the cry of God's elect ones referred to in
Luke xviii, 7, 8. In answer to these many prayers the judgment
and vengeance prayed for are about to be executed.

4. *The smoke . . . with the prayers*—The dative of ταῖς προσευ-
χαῖς may be translated *with the prayers,* as their accompanying
symbol ; or *for the prayers,* as indicative of their acceptability before the throne of God.[1]

5. *The angel has taken*—Apparently an inaccurate use of the perfect for the aorist, as in v, 7. *Filled it with the fire of the altar*—
The same fire of the altar which had burned the incense. So speedy
is the answer to the prayers that the same fire which consumes the
incense returns in burning coals of judgment upon the murderers of
the saints to destroy both their land and city. *Cast it upon the earth*
— A symbolic act, significant that God was about to answer the
prayers of his saints and would avenge them speedily (Luke xviii, 8).
Thunders . . . voices . . . lightnings . . . earthquake—Fourfold
sign of approaching judgments. These terminate the silence of half
an hour (verse 1), which was sufficiently long for the symbolic scenes
just described to make their full impression. The fourfold signals
serve also to notify the trumpet-angels to proceed.

The sounding of the seven trumpets occupies the rest of chaps.
viii-xi. As in the case of the seven seals, the first four form a class
by themselves and are noticeably distinguished from those which
follow. The seven trumpets correspond in substance to the seven
φιάλαι, *bowls,* or vials of wrath in chap. xvi, and the imagery is
appropriated in part from the plagues of Egypt. The entire picture
is to be understood as an apocalypse of the same woes referred to by
Jesus in Luke xxi, 25, 26 : "There shall be signs in sun and moon
and stars ; and upon the earth distress of nations, in perplexity for

---

[1] So Winer: "The ascending smoke had reference to the prayers, was designed to
accompany them and render them more acceptable."—*Gram. of N. T. Greek,* p. 270.
Edinb., 1882.

the roaring of the sea and the billows; men fainting for fear, and
for expectation of the things which are coming on the world : for
the powers of the heavens shall be shaken." Any attempt to interpret such language literally, or to find in each separate allusion
and figure an allegorical meaning, must end in confusion. The entire description moves in the element of apocalyptic symbolism, and
aims to produce an impression of the fearfulness of divine judgments on wicked men and nations. We find an Old Testament
parallel in Ezek. xxxviii, 18–23, where Jehovah speaks in fury
and jealousy and fire of wrath, and announces "a great shaking
in the land of Israel; so that the fishes of the sea, and the fowls
of the heaven, and the beasts of the field, and all creeping things that
creep upon the earth, and all the men that are upon the face of the
earth, shall shake at my presence, and the mountains shall be thrown
down, and the steep places shall fall, and every wall shall fall to the
ground. . . . Every man's sword shall be against his brother. And
I will plead against him with pestilence and with blood ; and I will
rain upon him, and upon his hordes, and upon the many peoples
that are with him, an overflowing shower, and great hailstones,
fire, and brimstone." As it would be an arbitrary and puerile dis-
tortion of this passage in Ezekiel to give distinct allegorical significance to the fishes, and fowls, and beasts, and men, and mountains,
and hailstones, and fire, so it seems equally absurd to search through
the history of modern Europe for events answering to the imagery
of the seven trumpets. The language and method of the biblical
apocalyptists, as seen in the Hebrew scriptures, abundantly warrant us in understanding all the trumpet-woes of chaps. viii–xi as
in substance identical with the great signs and terrors of Luke
xxi, 25, 26, which our Lord assured the disciples would all take
place before that generation passed away. The imagery of *trumpets*
is, as we have seen, constructed in allusion to the trumpets which
sounded the fall of Jericho (Josh. vi).

1. First Trumpet Sounded (Earth Smitten). viii, 7.

7   And the first sounded, and there followed hail and fire, mingled with
blood, and they were cast upon the earth: and the third part of the earth
was burnt up, and the third part of the trees was burnt up, and all green
grass was burnt up.

7. *Hail and fire, mingled with blood*—Hail and fire were mingled
together in one of the Egyptian plagues (Exod. ix, 23, 24), and our
author intensifies the picture by adding to the imagery thence derived the element of blood (comp. Ezek. v, 17; xxxviii, 22 ; Joel
ii, 30). *Third part*—As in the symbolic picture of Ezek. v, 2, 12,

each of the first four trumpet-plagues destroys a third of something. *Earth . . . trees . . . grass*—Comp. vii, 1, 3. Three objects naturally associated together are specified as the subjects of the plague; just as in the next plague (verses 8 and 9) sea, creatures of the sea, and ships are put together.

2. SECOND TRUMPET SOUNDED (SEA SMITTEN).   VIII, 8, 9.

8   And the second angel sounded, and as it were a great mountain burning with fire was cast into the sea: and the third part of the sea became
9   blood; and there died the third part of the creatures which were in the sea, *even* they that had life; and the third part of the ships was destroyed.

8, 9. *As it were a great mountain*—That is, something that looked like a great burning mountain. The image may have been suggested by Jer. li, 25 ; but the *mountain* has no significance here as a separate symbol. It merely appears a moment as the instrument employed by heaven to turn *the third part of the sea* into *blood*. Like the fire cast upon the earth in verse 5, it resulted in the bloody sea, and so brought a judgment like another one of the Egyptian plagues (Exod. vii, 20–25). The consequent death of *the third part of the creatures which were in the sea*, and the destruction of *the third part of the ships* finishes out the picture, just as the mention of trees and grass in verse 7 fills up the picture of destruction contemplated in the first trumpet-woe. To find special meanings in the living creatures of the sea and the ships is as uncalled for as to do the same in the trees and grass of the previous picture. The one plague affects the earth and what naturally belongs to it; the other affects the sea and what naturally belongs to the sea.

3. THIRD TRUMPET SOUNDED (RIVERS AND FOUNTAINS).   VIII, 10, 11.

10   And the third angel sounded, and there fell from heaven a great star, burning as a torch, and it fell upon the third part of the rivers, and upon
11   the fountains of the waters; and the name of the star is called Wormwood: and the third part of the waters became wormwood; and many men died of the waters, because they were made bitter.

10, 11. *A great star-burning as a torch*—An immense meteor glowing as with the luminous flame of a lamp (λαμπάς). The star in this plague served the same purpose as the burning mountain in the previous plague. The effect produced suggests that the star in falling burst into mineral fragments, and changed into poisonous bitterness *the third part of the rivers* and the *fountains* of which men were wont to drink. *Wormwood . . . bitter*—Comp. Exod. xv, 23. The effect of this plague is different from that on the sea, and more

disastrous to *men, many* of whom *died of the waters,* which were
rendered poisonous by the deadly wormwood.

4. FOURTH TRUMPET SOUNDED (SUN SMITTEN). VIII, 12.

12   And the fourth angel sounded, and the third part of the sun was smitten, and the third part of the moon, and the third part of the stars; that
the third part of them should be darkened, and the day should not shine
for the third part of it, and the night in like manner.

12. *Sun . . . moon . . . stars*—The effect of this fourth stroke was
like that of the ninth plague of Egypt (Exod. x, 21, 22), and this
completes the cycle of the first four judgments on land, sea, rivers
and fountains, and luminaries of heaven. Apocalyptic parallels of
this fourth trumpet-plague are found in Joel ii, 10, 30, 31; Ezek.
xxxii, 7, 8; Matt. xxiv, 29; Luke xxi, 25.

These first four trumpets sound the coming of sorrows and tribulation essentially like those symbolized by the first four seals (vi,
1–8). We need not seek to trace minute analogies between them,
but should rather look upon them as another set of symbols pointing to the same calamities. They foretokened the earthquakes,
famines, pestilences, terrors, and carnage which were to be a part
and parcel of the woes attendant upon the destruction of Jerusalem.
Thus by repetition under different symbols, and by means of all
analogous images of plague and wrath, the sacred writer aims to
make the most profound impression of the great and terrible day of
the Lord which is near at hand.

Eagle of Woe. VIII, 13.

13   And I saw, and I heard an eagle, flying in mid heaven, saying with a
great voice, Woe, woe, woe, for them that dwell on the earth, by reason
of the other voices of the trumpet of the three angels, who are yet to
sound.

13. *An eagle*—Not an angel, as in xiv, 6. The *eagle* is here introduced as the swift messenger of woe (Hosea viii, 1; comp. Deut.
xxviii, 49; Jer. iv, 13), and the *great voice,* with its awful notes of *woe,
woe, woe,* is a part of the art of this book to make use of every figure
and symbol which will serve to enhance the impressiveness of the
word of the prophecy. How fearful the plagues foretokened by the
sounding of the first four trumpets! But these are only a beginning of woes as compared with the things to come *by reason of the
other voices of the trumpet of the three angels, who are yet to sound.*
Expectation is thus raised to its highest pitch, and the three remaining woes may be supposed to reach the consummation of the age
and show its end.

5. Fifth Trumpet Sounded (Locust-plague). ix, 1–11.

1   And the fifth angel sounded, and I saw a star from heaven fallen unto
the earth: and there was given to him the key of the pit of the abyss.
2 And he opened the pit of the abyss; and there went up a smoke out of
the pit, as the smoke of a great furnace; and the sun and the air were
3 darkened by reason of the smoke of the pit. And out of the smoke came
forth locusts upon the earth; and power was given them, as the scor-
4 pions of the earth have power. And it was said unto them that they
should not hurt the grass of the earth, neither any green thing, neither
any tree, but only such men as have not the seal of God on their fore-
5 heads. And it was given them that they should not kill them, but that
they should be tormented five months: and their torment was as the tor-
6 ment of a scorpion, when it striketh a man. And in those days men
shall seek death, and shall in no wise find it; and they shall desire to die,
7 and death fleeth from them. And the shapes of the locusts were like
unto horses prepared for war; and upon their heads as it were crowns
8 like unto gold, and their faces were as men's faces. And they had hair
9 as the hair of women, and their teeth were as *the teeth* of lions. And
they had breastplates, as it were breastplates of iron; and the sound of
their wings was as the sound of chariots, of many horses rushing to war.
10 And they have tails like unto scorpions, and stings; and in their tails is
11 their power to hurt men five months.   They have over them as king the
angel of the abyss: his name in Hebrew is Abaddon, and in the Greek
tongue he hath the name Apollyon.

1. *A star from heaven fallen unto the earth*—Observe the perfect
πεπτωκότα, *fallen*, as indicating that the star was already fallen from
heaven when John first saw it. The personification of this *star
from heaven*, which is implied in *giving unto him the key of the pit
of the abyss*, warrants the interpretation according to which the star
denotes an angel. That it represents an evil and not a good angel
is inferred from the word *fallen*, as well as from his unloosing the
plague of infernal locusts upon the earth. We may well compare
Isa. xiv, 12 : "How art thou fallen from heaven, O brilliant star
(הֵילֵל, Septuagint, ἑωσφόρος, Vulgate, *Lucifer*), son of the morning !"
Also Luke x, 18 : "I beheld Satan fallen as lightning from heaven."
Alford well suggests a connection of imagery between this passage
and xii, 9. As the dragon drew after him "the third part of the
stars of heaven " (xii, 4), and the king of the infernal locusts is the
angel of the abyss (ix, 11), we may well infer that the king of these
locusts is designed to be thought of as a fallen star. *The pit of the
abyss* is here as elsewhere to be understood of the infernal world,
the prison of evil spirits. Comp. Luke viii, 31. In xx, 1, the key
is held by an angel, who also has a great chain to bind Satan.
2. *As the smoke of a great furnace*—Figure appropriated from

Gen. xix, 28, and Exod. xix, 18. *Sun . . . darkened*—Compare the similar effect of the locust-plague in Joel ii, 10.

3. *Locusts upon the land*—This woe corresponds to the Egyptian plague described Exod. x, 12–15, but the imagery descriptive of these locusts out of the abyss is appropriated from Joel i, 6; ii, 4–10. *As the scorpions of the earth*—We take the words *of the earth*, or *land*, not as serving to distinguish land-scorpions from sea-scorpions, but as a contrast with these scorpion-locusts from the abyss. Though coming out of the infernal world they have a power like that of the well-known creature of the land, which is a terror and torment to those who live in certain hot climates (Deut. viii, 15). The scorpion has many feet and eyes like the spider, but its deadly power is in its tail (comp. verse 10), which has many joints and is provided at the extremity with a crooked point with which it strikes its victim. This point of the tail is like the sting of a bee, secreting at its base a poisonous fluid, and when it strikes a man the poison, like that of a deadly serpent, is injected into the wound, and, if not fatal, causes unspeakable torment.

4. *Not hurt the grass*—So they would be quite unlike ordinary locusts, which are wont to devour *every green thing* and *every tree* which comes in their way. These had been sufficiently injured by the plague of the first trumpet (viii, 7 ; comp. vii, 3). *Such men as have not the seal of God*—Comp. vii, 3, and Ezek. ix, 4–6. The disciples were gifted with power over unclean spirits (Mark vi, 7), and all who received the Gospel were turned from the power of Satan unto God (Acts xxvi, 18).

5. *They should not kill*—Though armed with stings like scorpions these locusts were not permitted to take the life of their victims. *Five months*—The usual period, from May to September, during which locusts are wont to appear. We need seek no mystical time-reference here. If anything unusual is to be noticed it is that this infernal plague is continuous during the whole period of five months. Ordinarily they come in swarms during any of the five months, but soon pass away ; but these locusts, whose work is to torment men, not vegetation, continue their terrible work through the whole five months. *Their torment*—The torment of the men receiving the baneful stroke. *The torment of a scorpion*—Genitive of the subject : the torment inflicted by a scorpion *when it strikes a man*. The stroke of the scorpion's tail, like the sting of a great hornet, causes an intense pang of agony.

6. *Seek death, and shall in no wise find it*—Like those depicted by Job, who would prefer death to such miserable life (Job iii, 21).

7. *Shapes of the locusts like horses*—This comparison is from Joel

ii, 4. But our writer adds to Joel's picture and represents the infernal locusts as wearing golden crowns and human faces. These suggest the qualities of royalty and intelligence, and may well symbolize spiritual hosts of wickedness such as Paul describes by the words "principalities," "powers," and "world-rulers of darkness" (Eph. vi, 12 ; comp. Col. ii, 15).

8. *Hair as the hair of women*—So they were like the "hairy locust" mentioned in Jer. li, 27 (ילק סמר, a young devouring locust bristling with hair ; not "rough caterpillars," as A. V., nor "rough cankerworm," as R. V.). But the hair of these was long and flowing, and so arresting attention because of its unusual quantity (comp. 1 Cor. xi, 14, 15). *Teeth as of lions*—So in Joel i, 6.

9. *Breastplates*—The word so rendered (θώρακας) may mean either *breasts* or *breastplates*, but as "the shapes of the locusts were like unto horses prepared for war" (verse 7), it comports with the whole picture that they also wear what has the appearance of *breastplates of iron*, thus shielded by a strong coat of mail. Compare the breastplate of fire and hyacinth and brimstone in verse 17. *As the sound of chariots*—An eyewitness of a plague of locusts in Palestine writes : "The locusts passed over the city in countless hosts, as though all the swarms in the world were let loose, and the whirl of their wings was as the sound of chariots." Compare the same figure in Joel ii, 5, and the rest of the description given in the foot note of page 172 of this volume.

10. *Tails . . . stings . . . hurt men five months*—These statements reiterate in more specific form what has been already stated in verse 5. While most of the imagery is appropriated from Joel these features are peculiar to the picture created by our apocalyptist.

11. *Abaddon . . . Apollyon*—These words, appropriated from the two original languages of the Holy Scriptures, signify alike, *Destroyer*. They are each an appropriate title for the ruler of this monstrous army from the abyss.

We recognize in the woe of the fifth trumpet an apocalyptic symbolizing of the demoniacal possessions and mad fury which came upon the Jewish people, and especially upon their leaders, during the last bitter struggle with Rome. That this is the most obvious import of the symbols, and the most natural interpretation of the whole passage, may be seen in the following facts :

1. The abyss is the acknowledged prison of demons, or unclean spirits (comp. xx, 1–3, and Luke viii, 31).

2. The imagery of smoke, darkness, and tormenting of men fitly symbolizes the demoniacal possessions of New Testament times, and also all that infernal fury and rage which take possession of wicked

men when they yield to the power of the devil and give themselves over to believe a lie.

3. The angel-king of the abyss, who is called the Destroyer, is satisfactorily explained only of Satan, " the prince of the demons " (comp. Matt. xii, 24–27). He is the same evil angel that appears again in this book as the dragon, the old serpent, the devil, cast down with his angels to the earth, chained and shut up in the abyss, and finally cast into the lake of fire.

4. The words of Jesus in Matt. xii, 43–45, are a prophecy of woe to come upon that generation through the agency of unclean spirits. The fallen spirit which is cast out of a man is there represented as going and gathering to himself seven other evil demons, and with them entering into the house from which he had been ejected, and making it worse than ever before. " Even so shall it be also unto this wicked generation," said Jesus. That generation had been visited by the Saviour, and he had shown his power to cast out Satan. But the Jewish people rejected his teaching, continued empty of his truth, and persisted in Pharisaic washings and garnishing of self-conceit and hypocrisy. It remained, therefore, as a fitting work of the devil to call up a host of his kindred spirits and take possession of a house so vacant and inviting. We have only to change the figure slightly to make the allegory of Matt. xii, 43–45, a duplicate picture of the trumpet-woe of Rev. ix, 1–11.

5. Finally, we have in the writings of Josephus a remarkable confirmation of this interpretation. "No age," says he, " ever bred a generation more fruitful in wickedness than this from the beginning of the world." "I suppose," he observes in another place, " that had the Romans made any longer delay in coming against these villains, the city would either have been swallowed up by the ground opening upon them, or been overwhelmed by water, or else been destroyed by such thunder as the country of Sodom perished by; for it had brought forth a generation of men much more atheistical than were those that suffered such punishments ; for by their madness it was that all the people came to be destroyed." (Whiston's Josephus, *Wars*, bk. v, chap. x, 5, and chap. xiii, 6.)

Second Announcement of Woe. IX, 12.

12   The first Woe is past: behold, there come yet two Woes hereafter.

12. This verse, like viii, 13, is designed to enhance the expectation of the woes about to follow. The words, like those of xi, 14, are the words of the writer of the book, not those of an eagle or an angel; and the three announcements are an incidental evidence of the unity of plan in chapters viii–xi.

6. Sixth Trumpet Sounded (Euphrates-armies). ix, 13-21.

13 And the sixth angel sounded, and I heard a voice from the horns of
14 the golden altar which is before God, one saying to the sixth angel, who
had the trumpet, Loose the four angels which are bound at the great
15 river Euphrates. And the four angels were loosed, which had been prepared for the hour and day and month and year, that they should kill
16 the third part of men. And the number of the armies of the horsemen
was twice ten thousand times ten thousand: I heard the number of them.
17 And thus I saw the horses in the vision, and them that sat on them, having breastplates *as* of fire and of hyacinth and of brimstone: and the heads
of the horses are as the heads of lions; and out of their mouth proceedeth
18 fire and smoke and brimstone. By these three plagues was the third part
of men killed, by the fire and the smoke and the brimstone, which pro-
19 ceeded out of their mouths. For the power of the horses is in their
mouth, and in their tails: for their tails are like unto serpents, and have
20 heads; and with them they do hurt. And the rest of mankind, who
were not killed with these plagues, repented not of the works of their
hands, that they should not worship devils, and the idols of gold, and
of silver, and of brass, and of stone, and of wood; which can neither see,
21 nor hear, nor walk: and they repented not of their murders, nor of their
sorceries, nor of their fornication, nor of their thefts.

As the imagery of the fifth trumpet is taken largely from Joel's
picture of the fourfold locust-plague (Joel i, 4, 6), so also the imagery of the sixth trumpet corresponds notably to that of Joel ii,
1–11, in which we have the terrible picture of a rushing army of
horsemen spreading fiery destruction before them and behind them.
The two successive pictures have a close relation to each other both
in Joel and in this Apocalypse, and in the latter we note the mention of horses, heads, breastplates, and tails in both visions.

13. *Voice from . . . the golden altar*—And so like an answer from
before the throne of God to the prayers of all the saints. Comp.
viii, 3–5.

14. *Loose the four angels*—Notice *four angels* here as in vii, 1.
There they "hold the four winds of the earth;" here they are to
be let loose from the restraint which had so far *bound* them. The
number *four* in both cases has no other significance than that of
being the apocalyptic number of world-judgments. That the angels
are to be regarded as evil rather than good is inferred from the fact
of their having being *bound* and from the character of the army
which they lead. Compare the warlike angelology of Dan. x, 13,
20. *The great river Euphrates* is here employed as a symbolical
name in allusion to the well-known fact that from the regions of
that river came those rods of Jehovah's anger (Isa. x, 5), the great
armies of Assyrians and Chaldeans which swept over the land of

Israel like a destructive flood.   Comp. Isa. vii, 20; viii, 7, 8; Jer. xlvi, 10; Hab. i, 6–11.

15. *Prepared for the hour and day and month and year*—Notice the article with the first noun only, as if equivalent to *the hour of the day*, etc.   They have been held fast as in bonds, so to speak, only waiting for the appointed hour of summons to march forth upon their work of ruin.   *Kill the third part of men*—Compare the first four trumpets as destroying each a third (viii, 7–12).   The tormenting locusts were permitted only to *hurt men*, but there was no restriction to a third; now these angels of the Euphrates are sent forth to *kill men*, but in the same proportion as the earth, trees, sea, fountains, and sun were smitten at the sounding of the first four trumpets.

16. *The number of the armies*—Observe how suddenly the four angels assume the form of an immense army.   The angels of the army, like the angels of the seven churches, thus seem to be resolved into the army itself.   Comp. note on i, 20.   The idea of angelic princes or leaders of armies, however, is traceable in Dan. x, 13, 20, 21.   *Twice ten thousand times ten thousand*—Two hundred millions. An apocalyptic number, definite, as suggestive of an accurately numbered host, and yet so immense as to appear like an innumerable multitude.   Comp. Psalm lxviii, 17.   *I heard the number*—Some voice, therefore, must have proclaimed the number.

17. *Thus I saw the horses*—That is, in the manner about to be narrated.   *In the vision*—This word (ὅρασις) serves to admonish us that all this picture of woe is but a *vision*, and therefore not to be treated as a detailed record of material things.   As the symbolism of the sixth seal (vi, 12–17) is not to be interpreted literally, so the symbolism of this sixth trumpet is not to be subjected to such a method of exegesis as would find in horses, riders, breastplates, heads, and tails an accurate description of something to appear in actual life and form like these.   *Having breastplates*—These seem to have been so adjusted as to shield both the horses and the riders. The *fire, hyacinth, and brimstone* here denote the colors of the breastplates, and correspond to the *fire, smoke, and brimstone* which *proceed* out of the lionlike *mouths* of the horses.   The *fire* would represent red, the *hyacinth* a dark blue like that of smoke, and the *brimstone* a yellow color.   *As the heads of lions*—And so having the appearance of hideous monstrosities, like the beast of xiii, 1, 2, and that of Dan. vii, 7.

18. *These three plagues*—Namely, *the fire and the smoke and the brimstone*, a threefold symbol of the terrors of destructive war.

19. *The power . . . in their mouth and in their tails*—So that

they spread destruction before them and behind them; for the tails also *have heads*, the notable difference being that the heads of the horses resemble the heads of lions, and the heads of the tails are like those of *serpents*, having power to *do harm* not unlike the stings of scorpions (verse 10).   So the destructive work of this great army is like that depicted in Joel ii, 2 : "A fire devoureth before them, and behind them a flame burneth; the land is as the garden of Eden before them, and behind them a desolate wilderness."

20, 21. *They did not repent . . . and they did not repent*—These two verses thus make a double assertion of the impenitence and the wickedness of the survivors of *these plagues*.   Those *who were not killed* were two thirds of all the wicked men exposed to the terrors of this second woe.   *The works of their hands* are immediately defined as idolatrous objects of worship made out *of gold and of silver and of brass and of stone and of wood*, to do homage to which was no better, according to Lev. xvii, 7, Deut. xxxii, 17, than to *worship demons* (comp. 1 Cor. x, 20).   The language of our writer is here appropriated from such passages as Deut. iv, 28; Psalm cxxxv, 15–17; Isa. xvii, 8; Dan. v, 4.   The four crimes mentioned in verse 21 are to be noted as the flagrant crimes of Jezebel (comp. 1 Kings xxi, 14, 15; 2 Kings ix, 22), and are all violations of the second table of the decalogue, as the idolatry contemplated in verse 20 is a violation of the first table.   Thus *the rest of the men who were not killed in these plagues* are conceived and fittingly characterized as apostate Israelites, guilty of persistent violation of both tables of the law.   These sins are typically representative of apostasy from the law of God as promulgated at Sinai.   In the interpretation we are consistently to keep in mind that we are dealing with a complex symbol seen in vision, and, therefore, particular acts of idolatry or of crime are as little to be looked for in Jewish history (as a corresponding detailed fulfillment of the prophecy) as are horses with lions' heads, breathing fire from their mouths and destroying men with their tails.

The total picture presented in verses 20 and 21 is, accordingly, appropriate for the Jewish people, who "denied the Holy and Righteous One and killed the Prince of life" (Acts iii, 14, 15), became "full of hypocrisy and iniquity" so as to merit the title of "offspring of vipers" (Matt. xxiii, 28, 33), and among whom false prophets arose and led many astray (Matt. xxiv, 11, 24), so that in the latter time of the period which ended with the fall of Jerusalem, and even while yet the apostles lived to warn and admonish, some departed from the faith and gave heed to seducing spirits and doctrines of demons, and were guilty of all manner of wickedness (comp. 1 Tim. iv, 1; 2 Tim. iii, 1–6). To represent all such guilt and apostasy of the Jewish nation at that time as a flagrant violation of both tables of their fundamental law is in perfect accord with the methods of biblical apocalyptics.

In clearest harmony, therefore, with the scope and methods of this Apocalypse we understand the immense army of cavalry depicted in the symbols of the sixth trumpet to be no other than the overwhelming military forces of the Roman empire, which marched against Jerusalem and pressed the terrible siege to the utter overthrow of city and temple. A comparison of Matt. xxiv, 15, and Luke xxi, 20, shows that the compassing of Jerusalem with armies was a placing of "the abomination of desolation in a holy place" and a sign that her desolation was at hand. This abominable desolation was spoken of in Daniel the prophet, for it was of the same destructive character, if not the same calamity, as that which, in Dan. ix, 26, 27, is represented as overwhelming city and sanctuary in awful ruin, and bringing down a determined divine judgment "upon the desolate."

It is a well-attested fact that the Euphrates formed the eastern boundary of the Roman empire at the time of the Jewish war, and four legions of soldiers were stationed there (Tacitus, *Annals*, iv, 5; Dio Cassius, iv, 23); and Josephus states that Titus was followed by "three thousand drawn from the river Euphrates" (*Wars*, v, 1, 6). But to see in these facts a striking fulfillment of "the four angels at the great river Euphrates" (in verse 14) would be to follow the erroneous methods of those literalists who pay more attention to such an accidental correspondence of details than to the main purpose of a great symbolic picture. In the explanation of such a picture it is of the first importance to keep in view the one great total impression designed to be made. Undue attention to incidental features of the larger picture tends to divert from the main purpose of the whole.

As an exhibition of the incongruous and misleading interpretations which have been put upon this passage we give space to the following, which has been current with many of the "continuous historical" expositors for a century past. The armies described in Rev. ix, 17–19, are the Turkish hordes, which are said to have started out on a career of western conquests extending from Bagdad to Constantinople, and to have completed their work in the capture of the last named city. Great stress has been laid upon the following points as evidences of the truthfulness of the exposition:

1. These hordes went forth from the region of the Euphrates.
2. They were composed largely of cavalry.

3. Their myriads were so great that, according to Gibbon, they overspread a frontier of six hundred miles.

4. The breastplates represent the characteristic warlike apparel of the Turks, which is scarlet, blue, and yellow (that is, fire, hyacinth, and brimstone).

5. The heads like those of lions represent both the fierceness and the nominal titles of the leaders.

6. The fire, smoke, and brimstone out of their mouths is a reference to the use of powder in the siege of Constantinople.

7. The tails like unto serpents are the horsehair military ensigns, worn as symbols of authority by the Turkish pashas.

8. The hour, day, month, and year of verse 15 are resolved by mathematical calculation into three hundred and ninety-six years and one hundred and thirty days (from January 18, 1057, to May 16 or 20, 1453).

On this interpretation we make the following observations:

1. So far as the warlike imagery of the vision of verses 17–19 goes it may symbolize Turkish armies as well as any other armies; but one is left to wonder what the Turkish invasion and the capture of Constantinople had to do with John and his contemporaries, and how the events of 1057–1453 A. D. are to be truthfully included among "the things which must shortly come to pass" (Rev. i, 1). It is also singular that if the seer really attempted to foretell so many of the minute features of that Turkish war he should have mentioned the Euphrates by name, but made not the slightest allusion to Byzantium and the Bosporus.

2. It is a most remarkable use of symbolism to make *breastplates* of fire, hyacinth, and brimstone represent merely the colors of the apparel worn by the Ottomans.

3. To make the horses' heads emblematic of mere popular titles of the *leaders* (when the number of them is 200,000,000) is in the last degree far-fetched and incongruous. But if the lion heads represent the fierceness and strength of the *leaders* should they not have been put on the riders rather than on the horses?

4. If the horsemen especially represent cavalry, as is claimed, it is difficult to perceive the propriety of making the gunpowder used in the siege of Constantinople come from the horses' mouths.

5. To make the tails mere horsehair symbols of authority worn by chieftains is not only to involve the same incongruity as that noticed in respect to the heads (number 3 above), but also to allow no sufficient significance to the serpent form and heads of the tails.

6. To resolve "the hour and day and month and year" of verse 15 into a long period of centuries is not only to pay no proper respect

to the grammatical import of the language (see note on verse 15), but to make the entire picture involve the confusion of supposing one and the same army to continue in existence four hundred years. We need not here comment further on the exegetical jugglery which turns years into centuries and days into years.

Second Interlude. X, 1-XI, 13.

The visions of this passage are of the nature of an interlude between the sounding of the sixth and seventh trumpets. The writer thus displays consummate art in bringing forward a number of important revelations before the final stroke of doom. In this respect he follows the method of an epic poem or of a great tragedy, and brings in by way of episode all that can as well be introduced before the final crisis. In this way he enhances expectation, and makes the catastrophe of the end the more impressive when it comes. Accordingly, when he comes to record the sounding of the last trumpet (xi, 15-19), he is able to do so in few words, representing the end as signally decisive and unspeakably sublime.

By means of this interlude four things are presented to view: (1) The mighty angel coming down from heaven (x, 1-7); (2) the eating of the little book (viii, 11); (3) measuring the temple of God (xi, 1, 2); (4) the two witnesses (3-13).

(1) THE MIGHTY ANGEL COMING DOWN FROM HEAVEN. X, 1-7.

1   And I saw another strong angel coming down out of heaven, arrayed with a cloud; and the rainbow was upon his head, and his face was as
2 the sun, and his feet as pillars of fire; and he had in his hand a little book open: and he set his right foot upon the sea, and his left upon the
3 earth; and he cried with a great voice, as a lion roareth: and when he
4 cried, the seven thunders uttered their voices. And when the seven thunders uttered *their voices*, I was about to write: and I heard a voice from heaven saying, Seal up the things which the seven thunders uttered,
5 and write them not. And the angel which I saw standing upon the sea
6 and upon the earth lifted up his right hand to heaven, and sware by him that liveth forever and ever, who created the heaven and the things that are therein, and the earth and the things that are therein, and the sea
7 and the things that are therein, that there shall be delay no longer: but in the days of the voice of the seventh angel, when he is about to sound, then is finished the mystery of God, according to the good tidings which he declared to his servants the prophets.

1. *Another strong angel*—As one leading purpose of this angel is to deliver the little book to John, the most obvious reference of the word *another* is to the strong angel of v, 2, who made the proclamation there recorded concerning the sealed book. One strong

angel inquired in heaven and earth and underneath the earth (v, 3) for some one worthy to open the sealed book, and now *another strong angel* descends from heaven, with a little book laid open in his hand. *Arrayed with a cloud*—Not sitting on a cloud, as in xiv, 14, nor descending on a cloud, as one coming for the execution of judgment (Isa. xix, 1; Matt. xxiv, 30), but rather wearing a cloud as a garment, like the cloud of glory which filled the tabernacle and covered the appearance of Jehovah above the mercy seat (Exod. xl, 34-38; Lev. xvi, 2). Compare in xii, 1, "a woman *arrayed* with the sun." *The rainbow upon his head*—This symbol of covenanted mercy (comp. iv, 3; Ezek. i, 28) is another sign that the appearance of the strong angel is not for judgment, but for the announcement of good tidings (comp. verse 7). *His face*—Not his *countenance* (ὄψις) as in i, 16. *As the sun*—A source of light and life (comp. John i, 9; viii, 12). "It is God that said, Light shall shine out of darkness, who shined in our hearts unto illumination of the knowledge of the glory of God in the face of Jesus Christ" (2 Cor. iv, 6). *His feet as pillars of fire*—As if to give light to his ways, like the pillar of fire that illumined the way of Israel out of Egypt (Exod. xiii, 21, 22), and showed the presence and guidance of Jehovah's Angel (Exod. xiv, 19; xxiii, 20; xxxii, 34). Compare the "feet like unto burnished brass" in i, 15.

2. *In his hand a little book open*—In v, 7, the Lamb was seen to take the sealed book "out of the right hand of him that sat on the throne," and after a pæan that sounded through all the universe he proceeded to open the seals. They are all opened now, and the last trumpet is about to sound. The book of mystery is therefore no longer a sealed book, but now seems to John like *a little book* (βιβλαρίδιον) and *opened* (ἠνεῳγμένον), and it is about to be given to him as a word of revelation and prophecy. *Right foot upon the sea . . . left upon the land*—As if he were truly Lord of sea and land. *Cried with a great voice as a lion roareth*—Thus showing that the little Lamb (ἀρνίον) that took the book from the hand of God is truly the Lion of the tribe of Judah, who "conquered to open the book and the seven seals thereof" (comp. v, 4-7). So the revealer of the heavenly mysteries, who was first announced as the Lion of Judah, and then appeared as a slain Lamb, now comes down from the heaven as a glorious, mighty Angel to declare the nearness of the end (verses 6 and 7), and to transmit the opened book "unto his servant John" (comp. i, 1). *The seven thunders uttered their voices*—Signs of revolutions and wonderful events about to be inaugurated, but which John was forbidden to record. Comp. xii, 19.

4. *Seal up . . . the seven thunders*—This command is to be com-

pared with Dan. viii, 26; xii, 4, 9, where the seer is told that the
vision is shut up and to be kept concealed for many days, even to
the time of the end. This is an apocalyptic method of saying that
the thunder voices signified many "unspeakable words, which it is
not lawful for a man to utter" (2 Cor. xii, 4). What these voices
uttered, and why the thunders were seven in number, must remain
a mystery. He would be very presumptuous who should at this
time undertake to declare what John was forbidden to write.

But one might, perhaps, be permitted to suggest for the benefit
of a certain class of "continuous-historical" interpreters, who, like
Elliott, discern in the seven thunders a symbol of the papal bulls,
that these mystic thunders may much more probably have contained
"a complete revelation of the history of Christianity from the days
of Jesus on to the end of the world." And inasmuch as the long
periods of that history covered so many events which could not be
truthfully said to "come to pass shortly," the prophet was wisely
forbidden to attempt the impracticable task of writing them all
down!

5, 6. *Lifted up his right hand to heaven, and sware*—Compare the
notably analogous language of Dan. xii, 7. The objection that such
an oath is inconsistent with the idea that this strong angel is designed to represent Christ is nullified by the fact that the entire
vision of verses 1–7 is symbolical. If it is proper at all to represent
Christ under the form of a strong angel it certainly violates no law
of propriety to represent him as an angel lifting up his hand and
swearing according to the customary form. But even aside from
this consideration, why is it not as fitting for Christ thus to swear
as for Jehovah to swear by himself? Comp. Gen. xxii, 16 ; Isa.
xlv, 23; Jer. xlix, 13; Amos vi, 8. The form of lifting up the right
hand could hardly have been omitted from such a symbolic picture.
Who created the heaven . . . earth . . . sea—Comp. Psalm cxlvi, 6;
Neh. ix, 6 ; Exod. xx, 11. *Delay shall be no longer*—The immediate context, and comparison with vi, 11, warrants our translating
χρόνος in this passage by *delay*. The "yet a little time" (ἔτι χρόνον
μικρόν) of vi, 11, is now about to end, for the seventh trumpet is to
sound the ἐτελέσθη, *it is finished.* Compare the γέγονεν of xvi, 17,
and the τετέλεσται of John xix, 30. The prayers of the martyr-
souls and of all saints are now about to be answered, and so there
shall be *no more delay* in bringing in the long-expected consummation.

7. *The days of the voice of the seventh angel*—That is, the days
immediately preceding the blast of the seventh angel ; the last days
of the old dispensation, *when* the last trumpet *is about to sound, and*

(when) *the mystery of God was finished.* This *mystery of God* is the "gospel and the preaching of Jesus Christ, according to the revelation of the mystery which hath been kept in silence through times eternal, but now [in Paul's time] is manifested, and by the scriptures of the prophets, according to the commandment of the eternal God, is made known unto all the nations unto obedience of faith" (Rom. xvi, 25, 26). This *mystery* is further defined in Eph. i, 9; iii, 3–9, and Col. i, 26, 27. The verb ἐτελέσθη, *was finished,* is in the aorist tense, and thus conveys the idea that when the seventh angel sounds the last trumpet *the mystery of God* is to be thought of as a definite revelation of the past. The seventh trumpet, as we understand this book, is the symbolic signal of the end of the old dispensation and the consequent beginning of the new era of the kingdom of Christ on earth (comp. xi, 15). But the Old Testament *prophets* contemplated the appearance of the Messiah and the going forth of the new word of Jehovah as occurring "in the end of the days"—that is, the last days of the eon or dispensation under which they were living (comp. Isa. ii, 2; Micah iv, 1, and, for like use of the phrase, Gen. xlix, 1; Num. xxiv, 14; Dan. x, 14). In the same manner the New Testament writers consider themselves as living near the end of the age, and making known the mystery of God in Christ, "who was manifested at the end of the times" (1 Peter i, 20). This "end of the times" belongs, not to the era of the new dispensation, but to the concluding days of the old. So God spoke in fulfillment of Messianic promises "in the end of these days in his Son" (Heb. i, 1). The appearance of Christ and the first preaching of his Gospel are thus uniformly represented as occurring at a certain "fullness of times" (Gal. iv, 4; Eph. i, 10). Christ was manifested by the sacrifice of himself "once for all at the end of the ages" (Heb. ix, 26). Paul understood that he and his contemporaries were they "upon whom the ends of the ages have come" (1 Cor. x, 11). It is a serious error, therefore, when learned exegetes persist in assuming that the phrase "the last days," as employed in the Scriptures, means the period of the new Christian dispensation. Current chronology helps to perpetuate this error by dating the Christian era from the birth of Christ ; but our current chronology is no competent interpreter of the language or concepts of the prophets and apostles. *According to the good tidings which he declared to his servants the prophets*—This is a free but accurate translation of what the Greek idiom expresses much more briefly : *as he evangelized his servants the prophets.* But our English idiom does not employ this transitive use of the verb in the sense here intended. The prophets of the Old Testament are here referred to, and all

Messianic revelations made known to them were a declaration of good tidings, a gospel of good things to come.

(2) EATING OF THE LITTLE BOOK. X, 8-11.

8 And the voice which I heard from heaven, *I heard it* again speaking with me, and saying, Go, take the book which is open in the hand of
9 the angel that standeth upon the sea and upon the earth. And I went unto the angel, saying unto him that he should give me the little book. And he saith unto me, Take it, and eat it up; and it shall make thy belly
10 bitter, but in thy mouth it shall be sweet as honey. And I took the little book out of the angel's hand, and ate it up; and it was in my mouth sweet as honey: and when I had eaten it, my belly was made bitter.
11 And they say unto me, Thou must prophesy again over many peoples and nations and tongues and kings.

8. *The voice . . . again speaking*—The same voice as that mentioned in verse 4. *Go, take the book which is open*—Observe that it is called by the heavenly voice τὸ βιβλίον, *the book*, as in v, 1-5 ; but John calls it in this chapter (verses 2, 9, 10) the *little book* (τὸ βιβλαρίδιον). The imagery of taking and eating the book as detailed in this passage (verses 8-11) is based upon Ezek. ii, 9-iii, 7, 14. The Old Testament seer was commanded to take the roll of the book, which had been spread out before him, and eat it and go and speak unto the house of Israel. He found it in his mouth "as honey for sweetness," but when the Spirit lifted him up and took him away upon his mission he went in bitterness and heat of spirit.

9. *Eat it*—Compare the figure of eating the words of Jehovah and finding them a joy to the heart, in Jer. xv, 16.

10. *Sweet . . . bitter*—Notice the reverse order of these words in verse 9. The angel spoke of the bitterness first, but in the actual experience the seer tells us : *It was in my mouth sweet as honey: and when I had eaten it, my belly was made bitter.* The most natural explanation of this is that the reception of the word of prophecy is a sweet and precious experience ; the eating of this word, as in the case of Jeremiah (xv, 16), produced immediate joy and rejoicing of heart. But that word contained so many announcements fraught with "lamentations, and mourning, and woe," and destined to be treated in so many instances with derision and defiance (comp. Ezek. ii, 9; iii, 7), that the sympathetic heart would often be made bitter by reason of the burden.

11. *They say unto me*—Who those are who thus speak is not recorded ; but the plural suggests that the saying came from many voices. *Thou must prophesy again*—John's prophetic ministry is

not to end with the reception of this Apocalypse. He is *again* (πάλιν, *further* and *anew*) *to prophesy over* (or *concerning*) *peoples and nations and tongues and kings*. John was destined to survive the catastrophe of Jerusalem and to proclaim the passing away of the old darkness and the shining of the new and true light of the Gospel (1 John ii, 8). It is not in point to make the word *again* allude to one portion of this Apocalypse as contrasted with another part. John has not yet in this book prophesied at all. He has only been receiving revelations ; and the eating of the little book is but one symbolic act in the midst of many others, and not the end of the revelations he is to receive before he will go forth to resume his ministry as a servant and prophet of Jesus Christ. This apostle had, like Peter and other disciples (comp. Acts ii, 14–36 ; iii, 18–21), already proclaimed the coming and kingdom of Christ ; but after receiving these impressive revelations of the end of the old system, and the coming in of a new age, he will be able to preach and prophesy *again* a word of God concerning all nations and peoples.

We may now revert to what is observed in the note on v, 1, that the sealed book of that former vision is the opened book of x, 8–11. The Lamb took it out of the hand of him who sat upon the throne (v, 7); having opened the seven seals, he now has given it as a little book to John, who takes it out of the angel's hand and eats it as a word of prophecy (x, 10, 11). So when this servant of Jesus goes forth again to prophesy he will have become possessed of " the Revelation of Jesus Christ, which God gave him (that is, Jesus)," and which he in turn "sent and signified by his angel unto his servant John " (i, 1).

It remains to add a further word in defense of the position assumed throughout this chapter that the strong angel who gives the book to John is designed to represent Jesus Christ himself.

1. The description accords noticeably with that of the Christophany of i, 12–18.

2. He is the same as the Lamb who took the book out of the hand of him that sat on the throne, and now holds it open in his own hand.

3. He speaks as Lord in xi, 3, and throughout the vision appears to exercise a power and authority unsuitable to a created being.

4. It accords with the habit of apocalyptic repetition, and especially with the method of this book, to present Christ under various forms. First we are told the revelation is from Jesus Christ (i, 1); then we have the glorious Christophany of i, 12–18; then he is announced as the Lion of Judah and appears as a Lamb that had been

slain. After this angelophany he appears again as Michael (xii, 7); then again as the Lamb on Mount Zion (xiv, 1); then as the Son of man on a white cloud (xiv, 14); then as the rider on a white horse (xix, 11). In view of this variety of revelation the objection that he could not be presented under the form and name of an angel loses all its force.

5. Finally, the purpose of this interlude (x, 1–xi, 13) makes it particularly appropriate that the Christ's appearance should be under the symbolism of an angelophany; for he appears not as God, or as judge, but as the rainbow-crowned angel of the covenant, who commits the word of God to his servant and apostle.

(3) MEASURING THE TEMPLE OF GOD. XI, 1, 2.

1 And there was given me a reed like unto a rod: and one said, Rise, and measure the temple of God, and the altar, and them that worship
2 therein. And the court which is without the temple cast without, and measure it not; for it hath been given unto the nations: and the holy city shall they tread under foot forty and two months.

The first eleven verses of this chapter furnish a double picture, just as chap. x has done, and as it is impossible to disconnect the angelophany of x, 1–7, from the eating of the book in x, 8–11, so it is impossible for us to make the measuring of the temple in xi, 1, 2, independent of the figure of the two witnesses in xi, 3–12. The two pictures of the eleventh chapter stand also in most intimate relation to those of the tenth chapter. The appearance of Christ as the light of the world and the angel of the covenant announced the near end of the old age, and commissioned his disciples to proclaim his word to all the nations (Matt. xxviii, 19, 20; Mark xvi, 15). This was immediately followed by that apostolic ministry which gathered out of the Israelitish people the "remnant according to the election of grace," but was a ministry so hateful to the great body of the Jewish people that their testimony was despised and rejected, and they were persecuted unto death (comp. Matt. xxiv, 9). This intimate connection of the four pictures of the interlude will appear more fully further on.

1. *There was given me a reed*—It is noticeable that the seer himself is ordered to take part in this symbolical act, but no account is given of his doing what was commanded him. *Saying*—No new speaker has been introduced, and the close connection of what is here written with the preceding vision leaves us the most natural inference that the mighty angel who ordered John to take and eat the book is still the speaker. The command to *measure the temple of God*, and to cast the court without (verse 2), is followed in one

connected discourse with the account of the two witnesses, as if the one implied and involved the other, and so there was no particular opportunity to record the doing of what was commanded. It further displays the consummate art of the writer to concentrate attention upon the great thought intended by the symbol and to avoid narration of details. The *reed like unto a rod* was to serve as a measuring rod, like the "measuring reed" of Ezek. xl, 3, and the imagery here is taken in substance from Ezek. xl. The entire conclusion of Ezekiel's prophecy, from the fortieth chapter to the end, is a symbolic portraiture of the glorious future of God's true Israel, a detailed Jewish ideal of the restored church and kingdom of God. John appropriates only a few ideals. In his picture only the temple proper, the ναός, with its *altar* and *worshipers*, is measured off for preservation. The ναὸς τοῦ θεοῦ, translated *temple of God*, is strictly only that portion of the entire sanctuary (ἱερόν) which constituted the holy place and the holy of holies. *The altar* (τὸ θυσιαστήριον) which belonged to this part was the golden altar of incense which stood before the veil. The symbolical character of the passage is seen in the further command to measure *them that worship therein.* Only the consecrated priests were permitted to enter and minister in the holy place, but while the priest offered incense on the golden altar the devout people of Israel were wont to pray without (Luke i, 10), and the priest's act of offering the incense was an impressive symbol of their prayers (comp. viii, 3, 4, note), and truly represented all the devout worshipers among God's Israel. The holy places, and all that was symbolized by them and those who truly worshiped therein, are, accordingly, measured off for preservation from the impending destruction.

In these we have another symbol of "the remnant according to the election of grace." We have already shown how this was represented by the sealing of an elect Israel out of every tribe (comp. vii, 1-8, and notes there and at the end of chap. vii). As between the opening of the sixth and seventh seals a chosen number out of the tribes of Israel are sealed so as not to perish in the oncoming judgments, so between the sounding of the sixth and seventh trumpets a measured portion of the sanctuary of Israel is marked off for preservation from the impending woe. This chosen remnant is to be the nucleus of a new Israel of God, a temple of the Spirit ; and after the seventh trumpet sounds, and the destructive judgment falls, and the kingdom of Christ is inaugurated, behold, the temple of God is opened in the heaven, and in it once more appears the long-lost ark of his covenant (xi, 19).

2. *The court*—The uncovered courtyard (αὐλή) outside the temple

proper and inclosing it on all sides. *Cast without*—That is, treat it
as destined to destruction, and so already given over to be trodden
down. Compare the *casting off* (ἀπωθέω) of unbelieving Israel in
Rom. xi, 1, 2. As the activity of John is conceived as merely
symbolical he is appropriately addressed as if actually doing that
which is to come to pass by the judgment of God. *Measure it not*—
As those who received not the seal of God were given over to destruction, so likewise those who are represented by the portions of
the sanctuary not measured are, along with the holy places, given
over to the nations to trample under foot. For the unmeasured
portion is conceived as already *given unto the nations* by divine
decree, and John's not measuring it is therefore virtually a casting
it out as doomed. *The holy city*—Thought of and spoken of here
as *holy* because associated in the immediate context with the holy
remnant out of whom God is to build the new Jerusalem. So in
Isa. lxiv, 10, 11, the cities of Judah and the temple, although desolate and burned with fire, are called "holy cities" and "our holy
and beautiful house," because of their past association with saintly
fathers. *Tread under foot*—Comp. Isa. lxiii, 18 ; Luke xxi, 24.
Forty and two months—Compare xiii, 5, where the same number is
given for the period of the authority of the beast. Forty-two
months, resolved into days by reckoning thirty days to the month,
is the same as twelve hundred and sixty days ($42 \times 30 = 1260$), and
this latter is mentioned in the next verse as the period during which
the two witnesses prophesy. Comp. also xii, 6. The twelve hundred and sixty days appear in xii, 14, to be equivalent to the mystic
number "a time and times and half a time," which is appropriated
from Dan. vii, 25 ; xii, 7. There is no good reason to doubt that
these several designations are but examples of apocalyptic variety
in the use of terms, and all serve to denote, not so much the same
exact period of time as a period of one and the same character. In
every case, it should be observed, this mystic number points to a
period of apparent triumph for the enemy of God's people, and of
humiliation, trial, and persecution for the saints. Even the three
and a half days of verse 9 are of like character, being a period of
cruel exposure and shame. Seven is so often suggestive of something sacred that we may well think of three and a half as a broken
seven, a ruptured covenant, a temporary triumph of the enemy of
God (comp. Dan. ix, 27). We accordingly understand this mystic
number, not as a mathematical problem which we can reduce to a
specific chronology of times, and thence presume to tell the day and
hour of historical events, but as symbolical of a comparatively short
period of trial and disaster to the people of God. These *forty-two*

months during which *the nations shall tread the holy city under foot* are identical with the "times of the nations" referred to in Luke xxi, 24: "They shall fall by the edge of the sword, and shall be led captive into all the nations; and Jerusalem shall be trodden down by nations until the times of the nations be fulfilled." These "times of the nations" are obviously the period allotted to the nations to tread down Jerusalem, and those times are fulfilled as soon as the nations shall have accomplished their work of treading down the holy city. It is a misleading fancy, a catching at the mere sound of words, to confound these "times of the nations" with the "fullness of the nations" in Rom. xi, 25. The "times of the nations" in Luke are times of judgment on Jerusalem, not times of salvation to the Gentiles.

Verses 1 and 2, then, are a symbolical picture, quite analogous to the sealing of the one hundred and forty-four thousand in vii, 1–8, and the implied visitation of judgment on the unsealed Israel left out of the enumeration there detailed. There, however, the *people* of the twelve tribes are more particularly placed in view; here it is rather the *temple* and the *city* that are suggested as corresponding objects of thought.

(4) THE TWO WITNESSES. XI, 3-13.

3 And I will give unto my two witnesses, and they shall prophesy a thou-
4 sand two hundred and threescore days, clothed in sackcloth. These are the two olive trees and the two candlesticks, standing before the Lord of
5 the earth. And if any man desireth to hurt them, fire proceedeth out of their mouth, and devoureth their enemies: and if any man shall desire
6 to hurt them, in this manner must he be killed. These have the power to shut the heaven, that it rain not during the days of their prophecy: and they have power over the waters to turn them into blood, and to
7 smite the earth with every plague, as often as they shall desire. And when they shall have finished their testimony, the beast that cometh up out of the abyss shall make war with them, and overcome them, and kill
8 them. And their dead bodies *lie* in the street of the great city, which spiritually is called Sodom and Egypt, where also their Lord was crucified.
9 And from among the peoples and tribes and tongues and nations do *men* look upon their dead bodies three days and a half, and suffer not their
10 dead bodies to be laid in a tomb. And they that dwell on the earth rejoice over them, and make merry; and they shall send gifts one to another; because these two prophets tormented them that dwell on the earth.
11 And after the three days and a half the breath of life from God entered into them, and they stood upon their feet; and great fear fell upon them
12 which beheld them. And they heard a great voice from heaven saying unto them, Come up hither. And they went up into heaven in the cloud;
13 and their enemies beheld them. And in that hour there was a great

earthquake, and the tenth part of the city fell; and there were killed in the earthquake seven thousand persons: and the rest were affrighted, and gave glory to the God of heaven.

As the contents of verses 1 and 2 correspond to those of vii, 1–8, so the description of the Two Witnesses (xi, 3–13) has a corresponding relation to the vision of the great multitude who come out of the great tribulation and enter into the heavenly felicity of God and the Lamb (xi, 9–17). As this latter vision comes immediately before the opening of the seventh seal, so the picture of the Two Witnesses immediately precedes the sounding of the seventh trumpet. Compare note at the beginning of chap. vii.

3. *And I will give unto my two witnesses*—Note how the discourse of him who speaks in verse 1, and commands the seer to measure the temple, proceeds without interruption directly to the description of the witnesses. Neither the temple, city, nor witnesses of this chapter appear to John in vision, but all are presented as the word of the strong angel who has delivered the opened book to John. When, therefore, he speaks of MY *two witnesses* he assumes an authority and rank that virtually makes him equal with God. And we have already seen abundant evidence that, like the angel of the covenant, Jehovah's name was in him (Exod. xxiii, 21). *I will give*—This verb is not followed by a direct object, but it implies that to the witnesses will be imparted wisdom and ability to testify through their appointed time. As Moses, God's great prophet to Israel, was assured that Jehovah himself would be with his mouth and teach him what to say in the hour of trial (Exod. iv, 12), so the disciples of the Lord Jesus were told that, when brought before governors and kings for his sake and to bear witness against them and the nations, it should be given them in the very hour what they should speak (Matt. x, 19; Mark xiii, 11; Luke xii, 12). *They shall prophesy*—So these witnesses are essentially *prophets*, and do the very work to which the seer himself was appointed (x, 11) after he had eaten the book of the revelation of Jesus. The apostolic prophesying "over many peoples, and nations, and tongues, and kings" was one of the most important things of the closing period of the old dispensation, for the end of that age was not to come until "the gospel of the kingdom should have been preached in all the world *for a witness unto all the nations*" (Matt. xxiv, 14). The *thousand two hundred and threescore days* is not to be identified with the forty-two months of verse 2, as if covering the same chronological period of time, but, as explained above, is symbolical of *a like period* of persecution and suffering among the saints of God. During an appointed time of trial, and while many souls under the

altar of sacrifice cry out, "How long, O Lord, dost thou not avenge our blood?" (vi, 10,) these witnesses and prophets of Jesus are faithfully to declare the whole counsel of God. Compare Dan. ix, 26, 27, where the Messiah is to confirm a covenant with many for one week, in the midst of which the desolating abomination pours its destructive flood upon the city and the sanctuary. *Clothed in sackcloth*— The appropriate garb of prophets at a time of impending woes (Jer. iv, 8; Isa. xx, 2; Zech. xiii, 4).

4. *These are the two olive trees*—This is a direct allusion to the symbols of Zech. iv, where the golden candlestick was seen to be fed with oil by two olive trees standing one upon the right and the other upon the left of the candlestick. In that vision the candlestick represented, as always, the Church or people of God, whose defense and triumph are not to be sought by means of the might and power of the world, but by the Spirit of Almighty God. The two olive trees or olive branches represented Zerubbabel and Joshua, who for their time were declared to be "the two anointed ones that stand by the Lord of the whole earth." Through those two anointed leaders God for the time communicated his divine power to his people, and it was a time of peril. Appropriating these symbols in their broader import, the speaker here calls the Two Witnesses both *olive trees and candlesticks*. They represent what was symbolized by the one candlestick and the two trees. They are in some sense both the light of the world and the builders and defenders of God's true temple. That there should be *two candlesticks* as well as *two olive trees* is probably owing to the fact that the witnesses are spoken of as TWO. The *two* is thus emphasized as a symbolic number, the number of witnesses always necessary to establish testimony (Deut. xvii, 6; xix, 15; Matt. xviii, 16; 2 Cor. xiii, 1). But these Two Witnesses, being candlesticks as well as olive trees, are representative of the Church itself, the whole body of God's people, as well as their anointed leaders. The original New Testament Church constituted the true "household of God, being built upon the foundation of the apostles and prophets, Christ Jesus himself being the chief corner stone; in whom each several building, fitly framed together, groweth into a holy temple (ναόν) in the Lord" (Eph. ii, 20, 21). And that which was the distinguishing character and glory of the first Christian household of God was the fact that it was A WITNESSING CHURCH, a Church of martyrs (μάρτυρες).

5, 6. These two verses describe the Two Witnesses as gifted with miraculous power and divinely defended from harm until their work is done. The allusions are to well-known facts in the lives of Moses and Elijah, so that for the time of their ministry the Two Witnesses

are as potent to repel harm, smite their enemies, and do wonderful
works as were those two most distinguished prophets of the olden
time. *If any one wills to hurt them*—So as to act toward them like
the hostile forces which in successive companies marched against
Elijah (2 Kings i, 9, 12) as if to do him harm. *Fire proceedeth out
of their mouth and devoureth their enemies*—In Elijah's case "the
fire of God came down from heaven and consumed the enemy"
(2 Kings i, 10, 12). This is conceived as a terrible and real fulfilling of what Jehovah said to his prophet Jeremiah: "Behold, I will
make my words in thy mouth fire, and this people wood, and it shall
devour them" (Jer. v, 14; comp. Jer. i, 10; Psalm xcvii, 3). But
in accord with the symbolism of i, 16; ii, 12, the language may be
taken metaphorically, suggesting how the word of these prophetic
witnesses was as a savor of death unto death unto the enemies of
God and his people. *In this manner must he be killed*—That is, by
the devouring judgments of God, as announced by the witnesses.
Power to shut the heaven—As Elijah in 1 Kings xvii, 1. *Power
over the waters to turn them to blood*—Like Moses and Aaron in
Exod. vii, 17, 19. *With every plague*—Allusion to all the other
plagues of Egypt, as brought on by Moses and Aaron. Comp. 1 Sam.
iv, 8. Compare also Christ's promise to his disciples in Luke x, 19;
Mark xvi, 17, 18.

7. *When they shall have finished their testimony*—Observe that
no power in earth or hell is able to prevail against them until their
work is done. But, although the supernatural powers above referred
to interpose to aid them in their work, they fall at last and die the
death of martyrs. *The beast that cometh up out of the abyss*—This
beast has not yet been described, but the reference is an anticipation of what is written in xiii, 1, 2, and xvii, 8; just as in iii, 12, the
writer anticipates "the new Jerusalem which cometh down out of
heaven." But this beast is no other than the kingly angel of the
abyss mentioned in ix, 11, and whose name and nature there pointed
him out as the Destroyer. *Make war . . . overcome*—The language
in which he is here described is suggested in Dan. vii, 3, 21. As
the dragon from the abyss appears later to take possession of the
Roman power (xiii, 1, 2), it may, perhaps, be well to note that capital punishment, even when demanded by Jewish law, must be executed by authority of the empire. This is seen in the case of Jesus
(John xviii, 31). In cases of violence, where an offender was put
to death by a Jewish mob, as in the case of Stephen, we may still
believe that the Roman power winked at the illegality and was thus
in fact to blame. The Roman empire was thus chargeable with
executing the penalty of death, and so, like the beast of chap. xiii,

may be said to have made war on the early Christians and killed them. But the inspiration of all such cruel persecutions and death came from the prince of hell.

8. *Their dead bodies upon the street*—So that they were made an open spectacle of shame. The mad vindictiveness of their enemies has often thus exhibited itself on the dead bodies of martyrs; but their deadly hate could only "kill the body" (Matt. x, 28). *The great city*—The same great city as that mentioned in xiv, 8; xvi, 19; xvii, 5, 18. *Called spiritually*—As indicating its spiritual or moral character. *Sodom and Egypt*—A double name, employed symbolically to designate the great city under description as characterized by what the words *Sodom and Egypt* would most naturally suggest to a Jewish mind. Those words in biblical history are synonymous with flagrant wickedness and oppressive persecution. In Gen. xviii and xix we read of the enormous sin of Sodom, that cried to heaven for judgment, and the whole story of the exodus of Israel out of Egypt shows the bitter oppression of that "house of bondage." In Isa. i, 10, the prophet addresses the leaders of the Jewish people of Jerusalem as "rulers of Sodom." In Jer. xxiii, 14, the prophets of Jerusalem and all the people are said to be unto God as Sodom and Gomorrah. In Ezek. xvi, 46–52, Jerusalem is charged with corruption and sins even worse than those of Sodom. Egypt figures frequently in the Old Testament as the house of bondage and the seat of abominable idolatry (Exod. i, 13, 14; xiii, 3; xx, 2; Deut. xv, 15; Jer. xliii, 12, 13; xlvi, 25; Ezek. xx, 7; xxiii, 3, 8). No more suitable names, therefore, could have been employed, *spiritually*, to designate that great city upon which Jesus charged the crimes specified in Matt. xxiii, 34–37; Luke xiii, 34. Comp. also Acts vii, 52. But, to put the matter beyond all question, it is further added that the city in which the witnesses were exposed to shame was the same city *where also their Lord was crucified.* There is only one city that comes to mind at this specific statement, and that answers perfectly to the description of this verse. Jesus himself said to his disciples "that he must go unto Jerusalem and suffer many things of the elders and chief priests and scribes, and be killed" (Matt. xvi, 21; xx, 18; Mark x, 33; Luke xviii, 31). It was he who said, "It cannot be that a prophet perish out of Jerusalem" (Luke xiii, 33). It was the people of Jerusalem that madly cried, "His blood be on us and on our children" (Matt. xxvii, 25). In view of these statements and the well-known facts it is a remarkable exhibition of partisan pleading to allege, as does Alford (Greek Testament, *in loco*), that Christ "was crucified, not in, but outside the city, and by the hands, not of Jews, but of Romans!" And yet this expositor, and

others who like him have much to say about our duty to be governed by the obvious import of the language of Scripture, can thus presume to nullify the statement that Jerusalem was the place where the Lord was crucified, and insist that this "great city" must be understood of some unknown and unnamed city, "which will be the subject of God's final judgments." And Lange can gravely write that the city where the Lord *was crucified* (ἐσταυρώθη) means a "divine establishment, embracing Church and State, as a mock-holy fallen theocracy!" (Commentary, *in loco.*)

One chief trouble with those interpreters who try to explain away this obvious reference to Jerusalem is that they consider it impossible to identify this "great city, which spiritually is called Sodom and Egypt," with "the holy city" of verse 2. These, they insist, cannot be the same. But others will incline to think that half the ingenuity employed on their own visionary expositions of the place where the Lord was crucified might have shown them that, in strict accord with Old Testament usage, both designations suit Jerusalem. How is it that Isaiah could call this same Jerusalem a "faithful city" and a "harlot" in one breath? The answer is very simple : Once "righteousness lodged in her, but now murderers" (Isa. i, 21). Similarly Jeremiah speaks in chap. ii, 20. The simple fact is that in verses 2 and 8 of this chapter Jerusalem is viewed in different relations. The mention in the first instance of "the temple of God and the altar and them that worship therein," as measured off for preservation (comp. 2 Sam. viii, 2), made it proper in that connection to speak of the city which was about to be trodden down by the nations as "the holy city," for he is contemplating it there as a place of hallowed associations about to be ruined. The wickedness of the city does not in that connection come into view at all, but rather the destruction of a venerable shrine. Hence the designation of the city is naturally and properly like that of Isa. lxiv, 10, 11, where the prophet cries : "Thy holy cities are a wilderness, Zion is a wilderness, Jerusalem a desolation. Our holy and beautiful house, where our fathers praised thee, is burned up with fire, and all our pleasant things are laid waste." Furthermore, in verses 1 and 2 of this chapter the thought is primarily directed to that reserved and chosen remnant out of whom God is to build a new Jerusalem, and hence there is a touch of pathos in the accompanying allusion to the desecration of "the holy city." But after the description of the death of the Two Witnesses and the shameful exposure of their dead bodies, and in immediate connection therewith, the place and people guilty of their blood may well be called Sodom and Egypt. That "great city" was enormously great in wickedness, and doomed to a judgment of retribution for "all the righteous blood shed on the earth, from the blood of righteous Abel unto the blood of Zacharias" (Matt. xxiii, 35). A city or a people is great or small in proportion to its importance from the prophet's point of view.

9. *From among the peoples and tribes*—Jerusalem was often thronged with such (comp. Acts ii, 5–13). *Three days and a half*— As their ascending to heaven in a cloud (verse 12) is after the manner of the ascension of their Lord and a symbol of their triumph, so this subjection of their dead bodies to their enemies for *three days and a half* accords proximately with the period when his dead body lay in the grave. Compare the sign of the prophet Jonah, Matt. xii, 39, 40. But the three and a half days are as truly a symbolical number as the forty-two months of verse 2, and not to be understood as a specific designation of computable time. Like the "time, times, and half a time" (see note on verse 2), it seems to be intended to suggest a broken seven and to indicate a short period of calamity and shame. It is something worthy of note in this connection that Jesus himself speaks, in Luke xiii, 33, in a like singularly mystic way, when, before addressing Jerusalem as the murderer of prophets, he says : "I must walk to-day, and to-morrow, and the day following : for it cannot be that a prophet perish out of Jerusalem."

10. *Rejoice . . . make merry . . . send gifts*—Customary expressions of great hilarity. The enemies of God show great rejoicing when they imagine they have gained a victory. But their triumphing is usually short. *Tormented them*—Wicked men, like demons, are usually tormented by the presence and word of Christ and his true prophets. So the words of Peter and Stephen cut to the heart when they, as witnesses of Jesus Christ, declared his truth to their Jewish enemies (Acts v, 32, 33 ; vii, 54).

11. *Breath of life . . . and they stood*—The language is mainly from Ezek. xxxvii, 10, and appropriately pictures a resurrection of dead bodies. *Great fear fell*—Notable change from the merriment described in verse 10. Their rejoicing is suddenly turned into trembling.

12. *They went up to heaven in a cloud*—Comp. Acts i, 9. As they had suffered like unto their Lord, so also are they glorified with him (Rom. viii, 17 ; 2 Tim. ii, 11). The imagery and allusions are throughout to the ascension of Jesus, but the similar ascension of Elijah is not to be excluded. As Elijah's power as a prophet is alluded to in verses 5 and 6, so his final glorification may also be naturally associated with that of Jesus. We observe that (according to the best sustained reading) the witnesses *heard a great voice from*

the heaven, calling them up on high; but it is not said that *their enemies* heard that voice, but rather that they *beheld them.* Contrast the companions of Saul who heard the heavenly voice but beheld no one (Acts ix, 7). In all this description of the power, prophesying, death, resurrection, and ascension of the Two Witnesses we recognize an apocalyptic picture of the work, sufferings, and triumph of the apostles and prophets of Jesus, who laid the foundations of the Christian Church.

The careful reader of the foregoing notes on the Two Witnesses will have seen that the exposition has led naturally and logically to the conclusion just announced. A very large proportion of those who founded and builded the New Testament Church were called to seal their work and testimony with their blood. That these apostles and prophets are truthfully portrayed in verses 3–12 of this chapter may be more clearly seen by the following considerations:

1. They were preeminently WITNESSES ($\mu\acute{\alpha}\rho\tau\upsilon\rho\varepsilon\varsigma$). Comp. Luke xxiv, 48; Acts i, 8; ii, 32; iii, 15; v, 32; x, 39, 41; xiii, 31.

2. They are represented as Two Witnesses rather than any other number because of the analogy of the two olive trees, and especially because it requires two witnesses to establish testimony (Deut. xvii, 6; xix, 15; Matt. xviii, 16; 2 Cor. xiii, 1).

3. They were anointed, like Joshua and Zerubbabel, to build the new Church, and they were in fact the candlestick that was destined to supplant and supersede the old defunct Judaism.

4. They were notably gifted with power to work miracles, and were divinely supported until their work was finished (Mark xvi, 17, 18; Luke x, 19; Acts v, 12; xxviii, 5). Hence the obvious allusions in verses 5 and 6 to the miraculous power exercised by Moses and Elijah.

5. Their resurrection and triumphant going up into heaven is an apocalyptic picture of what Jesus had repeatedly assured his followers (Matt. x, 16–32; xxiv, 9–13; Luke xxi, 12–19), and corresponds to the triumph of the martyrs in chap. xx, 4–6, which is there called "the first resurrection."

As this account of the Two Witnesses concludes the fourfold picture of what we have entitled the second interlude (x, 1–xi, 13), we do well to pause here, before proceeding to the grand finale, and, even at the risk of some repetition, emphasize the relations and significance of this section of the Apocalypse. We have explained the four parts of the section as (1) a manifestation of Christ as the great covenant angel; (2) a revelation and commission given to John to prophesy to the nations; (3) a calling of the chosen remnant of true Israelites to be the nucleus of the future Church; and

(4) the work, power, suffering, and glory of the **founders** of Christianity.

The significance of these revelations, as coming between the sixth and seventh trumpets, must be studied as a part of the artistic scheme of the Apocalypse. Their position here may be seen to indicate that the manifestation and ministry of Christ and the witness of his new Gospel in the world must precede the overthrow of Jerusalem and of the cultus which centered in the temple. Christ's proclamation of the approaching end of the age and of his own kingdom at hand was magnificently symbolized in this strong angel from heaven, who declared the mystery of God about to be finished.

Interpreters and theologians have in general strangely failed to note the uniform teaching of the Scriptures that both the incarnation of Christ and the apostolic ministry took place in the end of the age. Christ's own testimony was that "the kingdom of heaven is at hand," and that the Gospel of his kingdom must be preached " in the whole world for a witness unto all the nations " before the end should come (Matt. xxiv, 14). Peter at Pentecost recognized that the outpouring of the Spirit was to be "in the last days" (Acts ii, 17). God spoke in the last days by his Son (Heb. i, 1); for though Christ was foreknown before the foundation of the world he was manifested "at the last of the times" (1 Peter i, 20). In Heb. ix, 26, the manifestation and sacrifice are said to occur " at the end of the ages." It is therefore a serious error of exegesis to maintain that the centuries of Christian history belong, in the biblical sense of the words, to "the last days" or "the end of the age."

This Apocalypse depicts the end of the Old Testament cultus and the consequent beginning of the new kingdom of God among men. It was, therefore, in striking harmony with the scheme of the book that a manifestation of Christ and the commission and prophetic witnessing of the first generation of martyrs should be set forth in appropriate symbols before the sounding of the seventh trumpet. Hence we may well admire the consummate genius and art displayed by the writer in presenting all these things in an impressive episode between the sixth and seventh trumpets.

With this view of the plan and purpose of the writer observe now the fitness of the four pictures as presented in this interlude. The appearance of the strong angel, his holding a book opened, his authority over sea and land, his lionlike cry and the response of the seven thunders (comp. John xii, 23–32), the declaration that there shall be no more time-delay in finishing the mystery of God as spoken by the prophets—all this is a wonderful setting forth of the substance of Jesus's testimony to the world. Nothing is more

firmly fixed in the common record of the synoptic gospels than the
assertion of Jesus that the generation then living should not pass
until all these things should be fulfilled.

The giving of the book to the seer and the assurance that he
must prophesy over all the nations is a most admirable symbolizing
of the apostolic commission of Matt. xxviii, 19, 20; Mark xvi, 15,
and Acts i, 8. The measuring of the holy places and true worshipers of the temple, and the casting out of the rest, depicts the
election of the true Israel, around which the new building of God
would grow into a holy temple (Matt. xvi, 18 ; 1 Cor. iii, 9 ; Eph.
ii, 21), and abide in heavenly places after the old one had passed
from human view.

The foregoing notes have sufficiently shown how the Two Witnesses symbolize the witnessing Church of the apostolic age. As
the innumerable multitude in chap. vii, 9–17, may include the sealed
Israel of vii, 4–8, so these witnesses may also include the measured
worshipers of xi, 1.

13. *In that hour*—The hour of the triumph of the witnesses, the
last lingering hour of the sixth trumpet, when it became evident to
the most desperate Jewish zealots that their city was doomed. *A
great earthquake . . . tenth part of the city fell*—A literalist might
well appeal here to the narrative of Josephus : "There broke out a
prodigious storm in the night, with the utmost violence, and very
strong winds, with the largest showers of rain, with continued
lightnings, terrible thunderings, and amazing concussions and bel-
lowings of the earth, that was in an earthquake. These things were
a manifest indication that some destruction was coming upon men,
when the system of the world was put into this disorder, and anyone would guess that these wonders foreshowed some great calamities that were coming " (*Wars,* bk. iv, 4, 5). But we need no such
exact correspondences of statement or description in order to show
the fulfillment of apocalyptic symbols. The figures point to a great
political upheaval, a signal revolution in human affairs. *Tenth part
of the city fell*—A conspicuous portion. The number is to be taken
symbolically, like the fourth part in vi, 8, and third part in viii, 7, 8.
Seven thousand names of men—Another symbolical number, indicative of a noticeably large number of persons, and amounting to
a calamity so great that overwhelming fear begins at once to take
possession of *the rest* of the populace. The fact here recorded that
the rest were affrighted shows that there is a notable change from the
picture presented in ix, 20, 21. The effect produced is like that upon
the centurion at the earthquake which accompanied the death of
Jesus on the cross (Matt. xxvii, 54), and the statement that they

gave glory to the God of heaven (comp. Dan. ii, 19) affords a gleam of light and hope amid the gathering darkness, prophetic of what the seventh trumpet will inaugurate.

Announcement of Third Woe. XI, 14.

14   The second Woe is past: behold, the third Woe cometh quickly.

14. *The third woe cometh quickly*—The final catastrophe, toward which all things have been moving on, is now about to be reached. With inimitable art the sacred writer has heightened expectation and prepared the way for this great consummation. As epic and dramatic poets, who arrange all that can enhance the final scene in episodes and statements that beget expectation and awe, so this writer has prepared us for the sublime finale. This enables him to state the outcome in a few effective sentences.

7. Seventh Trumpet Sounded (the End). XI, 15–19.

The preceding revelations have sufficiently indicated what we are to expect at the sounding of the seventh and last trumpet. The mighty angel also expressly declared in x, 7, that the sounding of the seventh trumpet would serve to announce the finishing of "the mystery of God, according to the good tidings which he declared to his servants the prophets." The completion of that mystery was the special mission of Christ and his apostles, and occupied the transition period between the old dispensation and the full inauguration and establishment of the kingdom of Jehovah and his Messiah. With the fall of Jerusalem and the ruin of the temple Christianity became thoroughly liberated from the fetters of effete Judaism and entered upon its world-wide career of leavening the civilizations of the earth with a higher spirit and of bringing the kingdoms of the world into subjection to the law of Christ. Having prepared the way for the signal announcement of the end of the old age and the beginning of the new, our author displays the highest art in making the sublime description very brief. The great word-picture consists of (1) the heavenly announcement that the kingdom is become Christ's, (2) the heavenly song of triumph, and (3) the vision of the opened temple of God in the heaven.

(1) THE KINGDOM BECOMES CHRIST'S. XI, 15.

15   And the seventh angel sounded; and there followed great voices in heaven, and they said, The kingdom of the world is become *the kingdom* of our Lord, and of his Christ: and he shall reign forever and ever.

15. *Great voices in heaven*—It is not said from whom these voices came, but they seem to have been a united chorus of all the hosts of

heaven. It is the art of the writer to make voices from heaven declare the issue of the seventh trumpet. *The kingdom of the world*
—That is, "the kingdom and dominion, and the greatness of the
kingdom under the whole heaven," spoken of by Daniel the prophet
(see Dan. vii, 14, 27). *Is become that of our Lord*—Compare the
language of Psalm xxii, 28, and Obad. 21. *And of his Christ*—
An imitation of the language of Psalm ii, 2. *Shall reign unto the*
ages of the ages—Compare the language of Exod. xv, 18 ; Psalm
x, 16 ; Dan. ii, 44 ; vii, 14, 18, 27. There is joy in heaven that the
kingdom of Jehovah and of his Messiah is now at last established.
The witnesses (of verses 3–12) have already made it known " in all
the world," where it has for a generation been " bearing fruit and
increasing ; " for already in Paul's day it " was preached in all creation under the heaven " (Col. i, 6, 23). This is the " kingdom that
cannot be shaken," spoken of in Heb. xii, 28, where there seems to be
a reference to the shaking of earth and heaven by these last trumpets, and " the removing of those things that are shaken " (the old
covenant of Sinai, represented in the Jerusalem that was in bondage
with her children ; comp. Gal. iv, 25), " that those things which
are not shaken may remain " (Heb. xii, 27). The shaking down of
obsolete Judaism by the thunders of God made way for the complete inauguration of the kingdom of Christ.

(2) THE SONG OF TRIUMPH. XI, 16-18.

16   And the four and twenty elders, who sit before God on their thrones,
17 fell upon their faces, and worshiped God, saying, We give thee thanks,
      O Lord God, the Almighty, who art and who wast; because thou hast
18 taken thy great power, and didst reign. And the nations were wroth,
      and thy wrath came, and the time of the dead to be judged, and *the time*
      to give their reward to thy servants the prophets, and to the saints, and
      to them that fear thy name, the small and the great; and to destroy them
      that destroy the land.

  16. *Elders which sit before God on their thrones*—Comp. note
on iv, 4. It is very appropriate that these enthroned representatives
of the Old and New Testament Church should utter forth the pæan
of thanksgiving and triumph contained in verses 17 and 18. From
their exalted position at the throne of God they see as it were the
end from the beginning, and like the voices of verse 15 contemplate the kingdom as fully come.

  17. *Who art and who wast*—Or, *the one who is and who was.*
Observe the omission of the ὁ ἐρχόμενος, *who is to come*, of i, 8, and
iv, 8 ; for the mystery of God is now conceived as finished. From
the elders' point of view the kingdom has come; and so they say,

Thou hast taken thy great power and didst reign. The kingdom is no longer "at hand," but has appeared.

18. *The nations were angry, and thy wrath came*—An allusion to Psalm ii, 1, 2, 5, as having now been fulfilled. Comp. also Acts iv, 24–30. All the strifes and jealousies and ambitious self-seeking; all the threatenings and oppressions and persecutions ; all the mad revolts and sedition of "Herod, and Pontius Pilate, and the nations, and the people of Israel," were overruled to the glory of God and the accomplishment of his purposes. *The time of the dead to be judged*—The time to avenge by divine judgments of wrath those dead martyrs who "had been slain for the word of God" (vi, 9–11), and the faithful witnesses whose dead bodies were exposed in that great city where their Lord was crucified (xi, 7, 8). The "little time" of vi, 11, is now finished ; the martyr-blood is now avenged (comp. Matt. xxiii, 35), and it only remains, as the elders say, *to give their reward to thy servants the prophets, and to the saints and to them that fear thy name.* Observe, the apocalyptist does not stop to picture the ruin of the rest of the city (comp. verse 13) and to narrate details of the final woe. These have been all sufficiently implied, and it would detract from the power of this concluding passage to thrust such details in. The higher art is shown by making the glorified elders say or sing the assured triumph and eternal glory of God's *servants the prophets.* This phrase is appropriated from Dan. ix, 6–10 ; Amos iii, 7 ; Zech. i, 6, and the additional words, *the small and the great,* are taken from Psalm cxv, 13 : "He will bless them that fear Jehovah, the small along with the great." *Destroy them that destroy the land*—Namely, those "inhabitants of Jerusalem and men of Judah" who had so culpably neglected the vineyard of the Lord intrusted to their care (comp. Isa. v, 1–7, and Matt. xxi, 33–46). Jesus warned the chief priests and elders of the Jewish people that the Lord of the vineyard would "miserably destroy those miserable men, and let out the vineyard to other husbandmen."

(3) GOD'S TEMPLE IN HEAVEN OPENED. XI, 19.

19 And there was opened the temple of God that is in heaven; and there was seen in his temple the ark of his covenant; and there followed lightnings, and voices, and thunders, and an earthquake, and great hail.

19. *There was opened the temple of God that is in the heaven*—This temple is the heavenly reproduction of what was measured off for preservation in xi, 1, 2. It is "the true tabernacle, which the Lord pitched, not man" (Heb. viii, 2 ; comp. Heb. ix, 8–13, and x, 9). The writer does not stop here to describe this heavenly

temple, for he proposes by a second series of revelations to present the same subject from another point of view and by means of other symbols. This temple will appear again at the close of the book as Jerusalem the golden, which has for its temple "the Lord God the Almighty and the Lamb" (xxi, 22), and in which dwell forever "those who are written in the Lamb's book of life" (xxi, 27). *The ark of the covenant*—Nothing could more effectively enhance this vision of God's temple in the heaven than to behold in it that most precious and holy of all the treasures of the old tabernacle and temple, "the ark of the covenant of Jehovah." This was not mentioned in verse 1. It had long been lost, and the Jewish temple of John's time contained no ark within the veil. But in that temple of the living God, which was to supersede the temple made with hands, there appears again this holiest symbol of the mystery of God in Jesus Christ. In this temple the saints are given to know the mysteries of the kingdom of heaven.

The statement that *there followed lightnings, and voices, and thunders, and an earthquake, and great hail* is a sign that the revelations now made to John are not all that he is to behold. These great signs may be regarded as echoes of the great crisis just past, but they are no less intimations that there is much more to follow. The reader also is thus admonished that the heaven of these visions is yet open (comp. iv, 1), and he may expect to see and hear yet other things pertaining to the coming and kingdom of Christ.

PART SECOND

REVELATION OF THE BRIDE, THE WIFE OF THE LAMB
XII–XXII.

As Joseph's second dream of the sun, moon, and stars bowing down to him was in its essential import only a repetition, under other symbols, of his first dream of the sheaves in the field (Gen. xxxvii, 5–11), and as Pharaoh's double dream of the kine and the ears was explained as but one in significance, but repeated unto the king twice in order to deepen the impression and assure him that the matter was established of God and destined to come to pass quickly (Gen. xli, 18–25, 32), so the second half of this Apocalypse is another portraiture of the same great subject which has been set before us in the foregoing chapters. The great red dragon (xii, 3) is not to be regarded as different from the angel of the abyss (ix, 11). The hundred and forty-four thousand on Mount Zion (xiv, 1) are the same as the sealed Israelites of vii, 4–8. The seven last plagues (chaps. xv and xvi) correspond noticeably to the seven trumpets of doom. "Babylon the great" is the same as the great city where the Lord was crucified (xi, 8), and the new Jerusalem, filled with the glory of God and the Lamb, is but another symbol of the temple of God in the heaven (xi, 19). In all this elaborate recapitulation John follows the manner of the prophet Daniel, whose vision of the four beasts in chap. vii is but another presentation of the same four kingdoms symbolized in Nebuchadnezzar's dream (chap. ii). Similar repetitions, as we have pointed out in previous pages of this volume, appear in the apocalyptic portions of Zechariah and Joel, and constitute a notable feature of the biblical apocalypses.

Part First has revealed the Lamb of God under various symbols, glorious in power, opening the book of divine mysteries, avenging the martyred saints, and exhibiting the fearful judgments destined to come upon the enemies of God. Everything is viewed as from the throne of the King of heaven, who sends forth his armies and destroys the defiant murderers of his prophets and burns up their city (comp. Matt. xxii, 7). Part Second reveals the Church in conflict with infernal and worldly principalities and powers, surviving all persecution, and triumphing by the word of her testimony, and, after Babylon the harlot falls and passes from view, appearing as the wife of the Lamb, the tabernacle of God with men, glorious in her beauty and imperishable as the throne of God.

I. THE WOMAN AND THE DRAGON. XII.

1. The Woman in Travail. XII, 1, 2.

1　And a great sign was seen in heaven; a woman arrayed with the sun,
and the moon under her feet, and upon her head a crown of twelve
2　stars; and she was with child: and she crieth out, travailing in birth,
and in pain to be delivered.

1. *A great sign was seen*—That is, a symbolical figure of remarkable attributes, such as the seer proceeds immediately to describe.
In the heaven—This phrase, which locates so many visions of the
Apocalypse, may well be understood as a mystic designation of that
element of exalted life and fellowship in which the things of God
are spiritually discerned.　True Christians have their citizenship
(πολίτευμα) in this heaven (Phil. iii, 20), and sit together with Christ
and one another "in the heavenlies" (ἐν τοῖς ἐπουρανίοις, Eph. ii, 6).
In a similar way we are to think of the New Testament Church
as in some sense the kingdom of heaven.　Into this same element
Satan and his angels carry war (verses 3 and 7).　*A woman*—Here
to be understood as a symbol of the apostolic Church, which Paul
in Gal. iv, 26, calls "Jerusalem which is above, which is our mother."
Arrayed with the sun—That is, clothed with the glory of God, who
covers himself with light as with a garment (Psalm civ, 2; comp. Isa.
lx, 1).　*The moon under her feet* serves to enhance our conception
of her exalted position, and the *crown of twelve stars*, while being a
possible allusion to the twelve apostles, is intended rather to give
additional splendor to the vision.　Compare Cant. vi, 10, and the
description of the Son of man in i, 13–16.　Any attempt to find
distinct allegorical meanings in the *sun, moon*, and *stars* as here
presented tends to obscure the vision.　The picture is composite,
and these luminaries are naturally mentioned as giving their glory
to the appearance of the woman *in the heaven*.　The sun enrobes
her; the moon, not the earth, appears as her footstool, and the stars
form for her head a crown.

2. *She was . . . travailing and in pain to bring forth*—This
language and imagery are in substance from Isa. lxvi, 7, 8, where
the reference is expressly to Zion : "As soon as Zion travailed,
she brought forth her children.　Before she travailed she brought
forth; before her pain came, she was delivered of a man child."
As the Old Testament Church thus brought forth children, so the
New Testament Church, but not without many outcries of pain.

2. The Great Red Dragon. XII, 3, 4.

3　And there was seen another sign in heaven; and behold, a great red
dragon, having seven heads and ten horns, and upon his heads seven dia-

4 dems. And his tail draweth the third part of the stars of heaven, and did cast them to the earth: and the dragon standeth before the woman who is about to be delivered, that when she is delivered, he may devour her child.

3. *Another sign in heaven*—Another symbol, as in verse 1, and in the same element of vision. This *sign* was seen in the same *heaven* from which Jesus beheld Satan fall (Luke x, 18). *A great red dragon*—In verse 9 he is said to be " the old serpent, he that is called the Devil and Satan, the deceiver of the whole world." Representing "the old serpent," he may well be pictured as a *dragon*, a monster which in ancient sculpture and painting is often represented as a winged crocodile. But this monster of John's vision is not said to have been supplied with wings, but has *seven heads and ten horns*. The *redness* of his appearance may suggest that, like the red horse of vi, 4, his work was to take away peace from the earth. In John viii, 44, he is said to have been a *man-slayer* from the beginning. It is added that there were *upon his heads seven diadems*. These heads, horns, and diadems are thought by some to be here mentioned in anticipation of what is written in xiii, 1, and to be interpreted by means of xvii, 9–12. But such a procedure is scarcely necessary at this stage of our exposition. It is, rather, to be remembered that the Lamb was seen to have seven horns and seven eyes (v, 6), and why should not his great antagonist, the Antichrist, appear with like symbols of power? The *ten horns* of this dragon may be regarded as symbols of his great power, just as we have explained the seven horns of the Lamb ; and the *heads* and *diadems* are in like manner symbols of the regal resources and splendor of the prince of the devils. He is thought of as presuming to sway authority and power like the King of heaven, and to say like the proud Babylonian oppressor : "I will exalt my throne above the stars of God. I will ascend above the heights of the clouds ; I will be like the Most High" (Isa. xiv, 13, 14).

4. *His tail draweth the third part of the stars*—This imagery, like that of ix, 10 and 19, shows him to have a great power for destruction behind him, so that with his tail he accomplishes what the little horn of Dan. viii, 10, did with his whole strength. No special importance is to be attached to the fact that the dragon's tail does this work of dragging down the stars, for like the infernal locusts (ix, 10), and many another monster of the dragon type, the tail is a most potent weapon of their power to do harm. Such a dragon in the heaven might naturally be expected to sweep down many of the stars with the angry lash of his tail and *cast them to the earth*. The whole picture is to be treated as a highly poetic description of

Satan's presumption and power, and not to be taken in pieces with
the idea of finding some separate allegorical significance in each
particular part. *The third part of the stars* is, accordingly, to be
understood in the same general way as in viii, 12. A large proportion of the luminaries of the heaven seemed to be dragged down by
the power of the dragon's tail. But he is not especially aiming to
destroy the stars ; the object of his deadly rage is rather the woman
and the child about to be born of her ; for now the seer beholds
that *the dragon is standing* (ἔστηκεν, has taken his position and remains there waiting) *before the woman who is about to bring forth,
that when she brings forth he may devour her child.* His attitude
is therefore like that of the king of Egypt watching to destroy
every male Israelite as soon as born (Exod. i, 16, 22).

3. THE CHILD CAUGHT UP TO GOD AND THE WOMAN NOURISHED IN THE WILDERNESS. XII, 5, 6.

5   And she was delivered of a son, a man child, who is to rule all the
      nations with a rod of iron: and her child was caught up unto God, and
6   unto his throne. And the woman fled into the wilderness, where she
      hath a place prepared of God, that there they may nourish her a thou-
      sand two hundred and threescore days.

5. *A son, a man child*—The Greek υἱόν, ἄρσεν, is peculiar in making the appositive ἄρσεν (*man child*, neuter) a kind of additional
definitive of υἱόν, *son.* Like the change from masculine to feminine
in Matt. xvi, 18 (πέτρος to πέτρα), it may suggest that the *man child*
here, as in Isa. lxvi, 7, is not an individual, but a collective body.
It has been the error of many interpreters to insist that this man
child represents the Messiah, but the *son* in this symbol is no more
a single person than the mother. Like the seed of the woman in
Gen. iii, 15 (comp. verse 17 of our chapter), it need not exclude the
Messiah, but it certainly does include those who are Christ's. The
time-limits and scope of this book require us to refer it particularly
to the firstborn or first fruits of the apostolic Church ; so that, while
the woman's seed in Gen. iii, 15, most naturally includes the Messianic victor, the man child of this symbol most naturally excludes
the person of the Messiah. Those who think that the man child is
the Christ seem to be misled by the statement that he *is to rule all
the nations with a rod of iron,* forgetful of what was said to those
in Thyatira : "To him that overcometh will I give power over the
nations, and he shall rule them with a rod of iron " (ii, 26, 27). The
language and imagery here, as there, are taken from Psalm ii, 9.
Compare also the picture of the enthroned martyrs reigning with
Christ a thousand years (xx, 4–6). So also the two witnesses, like

their Lord, went up to heaven in a cloud (xi, 12). These symbolic representations were given as a comfort and assurance to all those in the early Church who were called to suffer with their Lord, and who were wont to say, "If we suffer, we shall also reign with him" (2 Tim. ii, 12). Moreover, the statement that *her child was caught up unto God and unto his throne,* as from before the face of the dragon, does not accurately describe the ascension of Christ ; but it does appropriately symbolize the triumph of the martyrs who "overcame because of the blood of the Lamb, and because of the word of their testimony, and loved not their lives unto death" (verse 11). The apocalyptist here makes no account of physical death. The fact that the dragon did kill the children of the Church (xi, 7) amounts to nothing in this vision in view of their immediate exaltation to the throne of God. They realize what Jesus said of himself as "the resurrection and the life," and that "he that believeth on me, though he die, yet shall he live: and whosoever liveth and believeth on me shall never die" (John xi, 25, 26). Compare also Luke xxi, 18, 19 : "Not a hair of your head shall perish. In your patience ye shall win your souls."

6. *The woman fled into the wilderness*—Appropriate symbol of the scattering of the church in Jerusalem by reason of great persecution (Acts viii, 1). Jesus himself commanded a similar flight in Luke xxi, 21; Matt. xxiv, 16. According to Eusebius (bk. iii, chap. v), "the whole body of the church in Jerusalem, commanded by a divine revelation," fled to Pella, beyond the Jordan, which place at that time, according to Josephus (*Wars,* bk. iii, 3, 3), was mostly a desert. But we should err in confining the symbolic flight of this *woman* to any such single event of the time before the fall of Jerusalem. It is rather the general scattering abroad of all those who were driven by persecution to forsake their homes and go into greater retirement. Like the prophets that fled from the persecutions of Jezebel many of the early Christians hid themselves in caves and dens of the earth (comp. 1 Kings xviii, 4, and Heb. xi, 38). *Where she has a place prepared by God*—Like the Israelitish people when they fled out of Egypt before the persecution of Pharaoh and became "the church in the wilderness" (Acts vii, 38). *A thousand two hundred and threescore days*—The same symbolic number as that which denoted the period during which the two witnesses prophesied (xi, 3), a notable period of oppression and trial (comp. verse 14).

Verses 7-12 constitute a side picture to show that the dragon would not be permitted to maintain his position "in the heaven." It is not to be thought of as a chronological sequel of what has been presented in verses 1–6, but rather as designed to furnish additional information concerning the character and history of the dragon.

4. WAR IN HEAVEN. XII, 7, 8.

7 And there was war in heaven: Michael and his angels *going forth* to
8 war with the dragon; and the dragon warred and his angels; and they prevailed not, neither was their place found any more in heaven.

7. *War in heaven*—In the same element in which the woman and the dragon have thus far appeared. *Michael and his angels*—These are obviously the heavenly antagonists of *the dragon and his angels*. As the one class represents the powers of darkness, the others must represent the forces of light. It would have been incongruous to introduce Christ, or the Lamb, by name, as the great opponent of the dragon, and equally so to have portrayed the seed of the woman as going to war with the dragon as soon as they were born. But while incongruous in the apocalyptic imagery and scheme, it is still true in fact that Christ and his holy angels are the real antagonists of Satan; and the mention of the rest of the woman's seed in verse 17, and the statement of verse 11 that they who overcame the great adversary "loved not their life even unto death," are evidence that the redeemed "first fruits unto God and the Lamb" (xiv, 4) also take part in this great war. We accordingly understand *Michael and his angels* to be here a symbolic designation of Christ and his apostles, together with all the angelic forces in sympathy and co-operation with them. The name *Michael* is taken from Dan. x, 13, 21; xii, 1, where he is spoken of as "the great prince who standeth over the children of thy (Daniel's) people." We compare also with this "the prince of the host of Jehovah" (Josh. v, 14), who assisted the children of Israel in the overthrow of Jericho. As we have shown in the note at the close of chap. x, it accords with the apocalyptic scheme of this book to introduce Jesus Christ under various names and symbols. Having appeared in x, 1, as the strong covenant angel of light, he now appears as Michael the archangel, the great leader of the hosts of heaven against the prince of hell. The anomalous infinitive construction, τοῦ πολεμῆσαι, is apparently appropriated from the Septuagint of Dan. x, 20, but is without proper grammatical connection with the preceding phrase. The ἐπολέμησαν of the *textus receptus*, translated *fought against* in the Authorized Version, is destitute of manuscript authority, and evidently an attempted emendation. Probably the best solution of the solecism is the supposition that some word corresponding to the ἐπιστρέψω of Dan. x, 20, has fallen out of the text, and the Anglo-American revisers have done well to supply the words *going forth*.

8. *They prevailed not*—Namely, the dragon and his angels prevailed not, but were cast down, as the next verse states. *Their place no more in the heaven*—The ministry of Christ and his apostles was to clear the spiritual heaven and effectually break Satan's power.

5. THE DRAGON AND HIS ANGELS CAST OUT. XII, 9.

9 And the great dragon was cast down, the old serpent, he that is called the Devil and Satan, the deceiver of the whole world; he was cast down to the earth, and his angels were cast down with him.

9. *The great dragon was cast down*—We interpret these words and the whole passage in the light of Luke x, 18, where Jesus said to the seventy who returned with joy and declared that the demons were subject unto them in his name, "I beheld Satan fallen as lightning from the heaven." We are not to suppose that Jesus beheld this sight as an objective fact in the physical world. As little to the purpose would it be to suppose a reference to the original fall of Satan as an angel of light. Rather, in the ministry and triumph of the seventy Jesus was beholding (ἐθεώρουν) as in vision the glorious outcome of the apostolic ministry. He exulted with them, not so much in what they had already done, as in the anticipation of greater works to follow. He accordingly said to them that they should rejoice, not so much in the subjection of the evil spirits as in the assurance that their names were written in the heavens (Luke x, 20). They were already enrolled in the heavenly army of the great Captain of their salvation, and might therefore understand, not only that the God of peace would bruise Satan under their feet shortly (Rom. xvi, 20), but that they should be partakers with the Lord in his work, sufferings, triumph, and glory.

Another passage to be cited in this connection is John xii, 31: "Now is there a judgment (κρίσις, a *crisis*) of this world : now shall the prince of this world be cast out." Here we recognize another anticipation of triumph on the part of Jesus. His exaltation through suffering and death was destined to draw all men unto him. As the dragon's tail drew many stars down and cast them to the earth, so on the opposite side would Christ and his angels cast out Satan and draw all men up from the earth into the heaven, there to become the stars of God. In his comments on John xii, 31, Alford says : "Observe, it is *shall be cast out*, not *is cast out*, because the casting out shall be gradual, as the *drawing* in the next verse. But after the death of Christ the casting out *began*, and its first fruits were the gathering of the Gentiles into the Church."

This apocalyptic "war in heaven" may also be understood to

include all such "wrestling against the principalities, against the powers, against the spiritual hosts of wickedness in the heavenlies," as is referred to in Eph. vi, 12. To be "able to quench all the fiery darts of the evil one " (Eph. vi, 16) is to partake in the spiritual and supernatural triumphs which all Christly souls enjoy in vital fellowship with their Lord.

6. JOY IN HEAVEN. XII, 10-12.

10 And I heard a great voice in heaven, saying, Now is come the salvation, and the power, and the kingdom of our God, and the authority of his Christ: for the accuser of our brethren is cast down, who accuseth
11 them before our God day and night. And they overcame him because of the blood of the Lamb, and because of the word of their testimony;
12 and they loved not their life even unto death. Therefore rejoice, O heavens, and ye that dwell in them. Woe for the earth and for the sea: because the devil is gone down unto you, having great wrath, knowing that he hath but a short time.

10. *I heard*—The art of description is displayed by turning from further detail of the " war in the heaven " and presenting the outcome of the struggle by means of *a great voice in the heaven.* This one *great voice* celebrates the victory much like the many " great voices " in xi, 15, and the exclamation, *now is come the salvation,* should be compared with " now is there a crisis of this world " in John xii, 31. In both passages there is a prophetic anticipation of the glorious result, a welcome of it as if already come. Notice the fourfold expression, *the salvation, the power, the kingdom,* and *the authority.* These come to view whenever the power of Satan is broken, and his character as κατήγωρ, *accuser,* is exposed. The word *Kateegor* (קטינור) is found in rabbinical writings as a designation of Satan, as *Sabeegor* (סביגור) is of Michael. When he is called *the accuser of our brethren* it is implied that the heavenly voice represents all brethren and partakers in the tribulation and kingdom and patience of Jesus (i, 9). It may have proceeded from the twenty-four elders, representatives of the glorified Church. In the statement that he *accuseth them before our God day and night* there is a reference to the persistent going up and down of Satan and acting the part of a destructive enemy of such servants of God as Job (comp. Job i, 7 ; ii, 2 ; 1 Peter v, 8, and Matt. xii, 43).

11. *They overcame*—The *they* (αὐτοί) are " our brethren " of the preceding verse, but the fact that they are here contemplated as having already conquered (ἐνίκησαν), and witnessed *even unto death,* warrants our including them all in the great host of Michael. *Because of the blood of the Lamb, and . . . the word of their testi-*

mony—Not *by the blood*, as the common version, although it may seem every way proper to conceive their victory as accomplished *by means of the blood* of Jesus, and especially by means of *the word of their testimony*. But the writer views both the blood and the testimony as the *ground* or *reason* of their triumph rather than the means. It was for the sake of the Lamb, and for the sake of their testimony, and for what these were destined to accomplish in the world, that they overcame. The telic idea attaches to the language here as in i, 9, and the inspired apocalyptist is subjectively controlled with the idea of divine purpose to be accomplished in accord with the words of this book of prophecy. *Unto death*—By not *loving their lives* unto death they evinced the wisdom presented in Matt. xvi, 25, and displayed the fidelity which, according to ii, 10, insures "the crown of life." All those who are included among these conquerors follow the Christ in conquest and glory, and as we contemplate their heavenly triumph we may well recall the promise of iii, 21 : "To him that *overcometh* I will give to sit down with me in my throne, as I also *overcame*, and sat down with my Father in his throne."

12. *Rejoice, O heavens*—These words are appropriated from Isa. xlix, 13, or Psalm xcvi, 11. The heavenly places are delivered of the evil spirits, so that now they are contemplated as a tabernacle in which all who " sit together in the heavenlies " have blissful fellowship (comp. Eph. ii, 6 ; Col. iii, 1). *Woe for the earth and the sea*—For these, instead of the heavens, are now about to become the scene of Satan's new activity and mischief (see xiii, 1, 11). *Having great wrath*—By reason of his failures and his being cast down to the earth. Such defeats intensify his rage. *He hath but a short time*—For the binding of the dragon and the casting of him into the abyss (xx, 1-3) are among the things which, according to this book, must shortly come to pass (i, 1).

7. Persecution of the Woman and the Rest of her Seed. xii, 13-17.

13 And when the dragon saw that he was cast down to the earth, he per-
14 secuted the woman who brought forth the man *child*. And there were given to the woman the two wings of the great eagle, that she might fly into the wilderness unto her place, where she is nourished for a time,
15 and times, and half a time, from the face of the serpent. And the serpent cast out of his mouth after the woman water as a river, that he
16 might cause her to be carried away by the stream. And the earth helped the woman, and the earth opened her mouth, and swallowed up the river
17 which the dragon cast out of his mouth. And the dragon waxed wroth with the woman, and went away to make war with the rest of her

seed, who keep the commandments of God, and hold the testimony of Jesus: and he stood upon the sand of the sea.

13. *When the dragon saw*—Resumption from verse 9. *He persecuted the woman*—The triumphs in the heavenly places do not prevent continued persecution and trials of the Church of God.

14. *The two wings of the great eagle*—The metaphor of Exod. xix, 4 (comp. also Deut. xxxii, 11, 12), is more fully expressed. As Jehovah bore his people away from the face of Pharaoh and the Egyptians, and carried them as on the strong wings of an eagle to himself, so he cares for this persecuted woman. Contrast "the wings of a stork," by which the woman called Wickedness was carried to the land of Shinar (Zech. v, 9). This flight of the woman into the wilderness is not different from that mentioned in verse 6, but the matter is here again presented to show the further action of the serpent toward her. The *time and times and half a time* is equivalent to the twelve hundred and sixty days of verse 6, and like it denotes a period of humiliation and trial, like that of exile. This mystic number seems to have been resolved by reducing 1260 days into *times* approximating a year of 360 days each. See note on xi, 2.

15. *Serpent cast out . . . water as a river*—The one figure from the story of the Exodus seems to have suggested another, and the host of Pharaoh which pursued the flying Israelites out of Egypt (Exod. xiv, 8, 9), and were swallowed up in the Red Sea (Exod. xiv, 28), served to construct the image of a stream of water cast forth out of the dragon's mouth. The waters are here a symbol of the forces at the command of the serpent, just as the chariots and horsemen were at the command of Pharaoh, and sent forth to overtake and overwhelm the flying Israelites. Others, however, may prefer to explain the figure of overwhelming waters more generally, as in Psalm xviii, 16, 17, and cxxiv, 2-5. If one prefer this more general allusion there is certainly no controlling reason for insisting on the more particular reference. The imagery is no more to be explained literally or allegorically than the two wings of the eagle.

16. *The earth helped the woman*—In the development of the figure it is naturally the earth, not the sea, that *opened her mouth and swallowed up the river*. The earth helped the woman by opening her mouth and swallowing the stream of water that issued from the dragon's mouth. Here again we may see an allusion to Num. xvi, 32, where it is written that "the earth opened her mouth and swallowed" the wicked men who rebelled against Moses and against God. The great thought in all these images is that the divine power is put forth to deliver and sustain the New Testament Church of God in the day of her persecution—the same power that of old

wrought the miracles of Egypt, and of the Red Sea, and of the wilderness.

17. *Waxed wroth with the woman*—The wrath mentioned above in verse 12 became intensified because of the obvious divine help by which the Church was defended. *Went away to make war with the rest of her seed*—Went up and down in the earth, as he is wont, and sought new devices by which to carry on his Satanic *war*. The words *the rest of her seed* refer to those other children of the Church who had not yet been caught up to the throne of God (comp. verse 5), and this reference serves to show that the man child of verse 5 is not to be understood as the Christ-child, Messiah, but rather the special "first fruits unto God and the Lamb," who receive pre-eminent attention in this book.

Thus far the symbol of the woman and her offspring has exhibited three things, which are to be discriminated as follows :

1. The woman, a symbol of the mother church at Jerusalem.

2. The man child, the first fruits ($\dot{a}\pi a\rho\chi\acute{\eta}$), consisting of such apostles and martyrs as the two witnesses of chap. xi, 3–12, and the martyr souls of vi, 11, and xx, 4, who receive exceptional distinction and glory.

3. The rest of the woman's seed, who suffer persecution and great tribulation, but are not slain for the testimony of Jesus, which they in common with the others hold.

These distinctions are easily made and maintained. The Church, considered as an institution and an organic body, is distinguishable from her children, as Isa. lxvi, 7, 8, and Gal. iv, 22–26, clearly show. The children of the Church, the individual members, are here thought of as two classes, (1) the first fruits of martyrs and witnesses, caught up unto God and sitting on his throne (comp. ii, 26, 27; iii, 21), and (2) the rest who suffer persecution on the earth. We accordingly observe that the Church is in one point of view the totality of all her members or children ; in other ways, familiar to the Scripture, her individual members are thought of as related to her as children to a mother.

Verse 17 of this chapter ends with what appears in the common text as a part of verse 1 of chap. xiii : *And he* (the dragon) *stood upon the sand of the sea.* He stood as if looking for some new ally or instrument by means of which he might the better persecute the rest of the woman's seed.

The entire symbolism of chap. xii may thus be seen to have a rational and satisfactory explanation by means of suggestions and parallels found in the Old Testament. A New Testament writer, familiar as was Paul or the author of the Epistle to the Hebrews with the Scriptures, could have developed all this symbolism from that divine storehouse of apocalyptic ideals. But current Jewish thought may also have taken up some elements of ancient mythology, and the images of leviathan and the dragon in such passages as Psalm lxxiv, 13, 14; Isa. xxvii, 1, and Ezek. xxix, 3, are doubtless to be understood as allusions to mythical monsters of the deep. But the New Testament apocalyptist need not be supposed to have sought for his imagery outside the Scriptures of the Jewish people.

II. THE TWO BEASTS. XIII.

The symbolism of the two beasts is appropriated in great part from Daniel's vision of the four great beasts from the sea (Dan. vii). But while in Daniel the beasts represent separate and successive world-powers, the two beasts of John's vision are contemporaneous, and the second is a mere satellite of the first, exercising the authority of the first beast as if in his immediate presence. Hence while appropriating the symbols from Daniel our author shows his independent mastery of the materials by his construction of a symbolic picture quite distinct from any of those in Daniel.

1. THE BEAST OUT OF THE SEA. XIII, 1–10.

And I saw a beast coming up out of the sea, having ten horns and seven heads, and on his horns ten diadems, and upon his heads names of
2 blasphemy. And the beast which I saw was like unto a leopard, and his feet were as *the feet* of a bear, and his mouth as the mouth of a lion: and the dragon gave him his power, and his throne, and great authority.
3 And *I saw* one of his heads as though it had been smitten unto death; and his death-stroke was healed: and the whole earth wondered after
4 the beast; and they worshiped the dragon, because he gave his authority unto the beast; and they worshiped the beast, saying, Who is like
5 unto the beast? and who is able to war with him? and there was given to him a mouth speaking great things and blasphemies; and there was
6 given to him authority to continue forty and two months. And he opened his mouth for blasphemies against God, to blaspheme his name,
7 and his tabernacle, *even* them that dwell in the heaven. And it was given unto him to make war with the saints, and to overcome them: and there was given to him authority over every tribe and people and
8 tongue and nation. And all that dwell on the earth shall worship him, *every one* whose name hath not been written from the foundation of the
9 world in the book of life of the Lamb that hath been slain. If any man
10 hath an ear, let him hear. If any man *is* for captivity, into captivity he goeth: if any man shall kill with the sword, with the sword must he be killed. Here is the patience and the faith of the saints.

1. *A beast*—Here, as in Daniel's visions, the symbol of a great world-power inimical to the Church of God. *Coming up out of the*

sea—The conclusion of the preceding picture, where the dragon was seen standing upon the sands of the sea, prepared the way for this new vision. As in Dan. vii, 1–3, the beasts were seen to come up from the storm-tossed sea, and as the many waters of chap. xvii, 1, 15, represent " peoples, and multitudes, and nations, and tongues " it is legitimate to trace the analogy of great kingdoms arising out of the commotion and strife of nations. Thus the great empires of the world have arisen and come to power. But the reference to the sea here and to the earth in verse 11 follows also appropriately after the woe for earth and sea pronounced in xii, 12. Sea and land thus appear to represent all the world over which the authority of the beast is exercised. *Ten horns . . . seven heads . . . ten diadems*— Like the great dragon in xii, 3, except that the *diadems* are *ten* in number and placed, not on his heads, but *on his horns.* We look for no secret mystery in such incidental variations. In general we regard the *beast* as a symbol of worldly empire ; the *horns* represent kings (comp. Dan. vii, 24), and the *diadems* upon them are the natural symbol of royalty and rank belonging to a king. The *heads* most naturally suggest the different seats or centers of the royal resources and power. The numbers *ten* and *seven* are symbolical here as in v, 6, and xii, 3, and need not be pressed into definite significance ; for nothing in the context calls for any such search after seven periods, or seven forms of government, or ten kings, as many expositors have presumed to find in these numbers. They serve here to denote the extent and completeness of the beast's power and authority. *Upon his heads names of blasphemy*—In all the seats of his power he perpetrates and encourages such blasphemy as is referred to in verses 5 and 6. Comp. xvii, 3.

2. *Leopard . . . bear . . . lion*—A monstrosity made up of different parts of the first three beasts of Daniel's vision (Dan. vii, 4–6), but stated in reverse order. Altogether it was somewhat like the fourth beast of Daniel (Dan. vii, 7, 8). As the fourth beast of Daniel represented the empire of Alexander and his successors, this first beast of the New Testament Apocalypse represents the Roman empire. We are immediately told that unto this Roman beast *the dragon gave his power, and his throne, and great authority,* and, accordingly, we should keep in mind that in all this prophetic symbolism we have before us *the Roman empire as a persecuting power.* This Apocalypse is not concerned with the history of Rome. It is as irrelevant to its scope to search among its revelations for a synopsis of the history of mediæval Europe as to look therein for mystic prognostications of the history of the Church in India or China. We do not find anywhere in the book a reference even to " the eternal

city " by the Tiber. The beast is not a symbol of the *city of Rome*, but of the great *Roman world-power*, conceived as the organ of the old serpent, the Devil, to persecute the scattered saints of God. The empire was represented in the reigning Cæsar. Having failed in the struggle of the spiritual forces of wickedness in the heavenly places (chap. xii, 7-9, 13), the dragon is now represented as appropriating the forces of worldly empire to further his Satanic plans. The empire, possessed of the *power* and *throne* of Satan, must needs wield *a great authority* for evil in the world.

3. *One of his heads as smitten unto death*—Observe, it is *one of his heads*, not one of his horns, that is thus smitten. Hence we infer that it is no one king, emperor, or ruler that is referred to. Were the reference to an individual ruler we should, according to all analogies of biblical symbolism, have had one of the *horns* smitten and subsequently restored. We are told that though this head was smitten with a stroke that seemed likely to result in death *his death-stroke was healed.* The heads of a symbolic beast are best understood as the chief seats of power and dominion. The four heads of the third beast of Daniel's vision seem to have implied the dominion it possessed in the four quarters of the earth (Dan. vii, 6), and especially the rule and authority it maintained in the different places. We accordingly see in the wounded head of this Roman beast a reference to some temporary loss of power in one of its many seats of authority. According to xiii, 14, it was a " stroke of the sword " by which the wound was given, indicating that it was some military conquest (comp. vi, 4). As the Roman dominion over Palestine is especially within the scope of this book it was not irrelevant for the author to make a symbolical recognition of the grievous wound the empire received in this quarter during the civil wars and troubles that followed the assassination of Julius Cæsar. At this time the Parthians overran all western Asia and Palestine and captured Jerusalem (see Josephus, *Ant.*, bk. xiv, chap. xiii, and *Wars*, bk. i, chap. xiii). This was truly a smiting one of the strongholds of Roman supremacy as if it were unto death, and erecting over Jerusalem for the time the dominion of a totally different world-power. " For a full year," says Rawlinson, " western Asia changed masters ; the rule and authority of Rome disappeared, and the Parthians were recognized as the dominant power " (*Sixth Oriental Monarchy*, p. 189). But the subsequent conquests of the Roman armies healed this notable wound of the empire, and her power over that land was restored to her again. *The whole earth wondered after the beast*—So widespread was the dominion of the empire, and so complete its control of all the nations under its sway, that every

subject land might well be filled with admiration and awe in the thought of a world-power so apparently omnipotent.

4. *They worshiped the dragon . . . and they worshiped the beast—* They worshiped the one in the other, and the reverence required to be paid to the image of the reigning emperor was, from the standpoint of our apocalyptist, a blasphemous idolatry. According to Josephus the honors which were demanded by the Cæsars included among other things that all subjects of the empire, in all the provinces, should build altars and temples unto him, treat him as they would treat the other gods, and even swear by his name (*Ant.*, bk. xviii, 8, 1). It is matter of well-known record that Julius Cæsar was apotheosized after his death (Suet., *Cæs.*, 88; Dio, xlvii, 18). Augustus had temples and altars erected to his honor (Suet., *Octav.* 52). Caligula called himself the brother of Capitolian Jupiter (Josephus, *Ant.*, bk. xix, 1, 1), and had an image of his own head placed upon a statue of Olympian Jupiter (Suet., *Calig.*, 22). Nero received the most abject worship of the senate and the people of Rome. Pliny's letter to Trajan evinces the extent to which the worship of the emperor's image was required in the provinces (Plin., *Epist.*, bk. x, epist. 96). See also Tacitus, *Annals*, bk. xv, 29, 74.

5. *A mouth speaking great things and blasphemies*—This description is taken from Daniel's portraiture of the impious Antiochus Epiphanes (comp. Dan. vii, 8, 20, 25; xi, 36). It applies with even greater force to such impious representatives of empire as Caligula and Nero. *Authority to do*—The ποιῆσαι of the Greek text here seems to have been modeled after the Theodotion version of Dan. xi, 28, where the same form appears without any direct object following. The verb in its connection implies some such object as *his own will.* Comp. also Dan. viii, 12, 24; xi, 36. The beast had power and *authority to do* what he pleased for the mystic period of *forty and two months*, the same or a similar time of calamity as in xi, 2.

6. The *blasphemies against God*, besides all other forms they may have taken, were directed also against *his name and his tabernacle*, (even) *them that dwell in the heaven.* There seems to be an allusion here to "the temple of God, and the altar, and them that worship therein," mentioned in xi, 1. This idolatrous world-power, which commanded the armies destined to "tread down the holy city forty and two months" (xi, 2), and execute divine judgment on an apostate nation, made little or no distinction between Jews and Christians. The "holy seed," chosen out of all Israel to be the nucleus of "God's tabernacle with men" (xxi, 3), and exalted to dwell in the heavenlies in Christ Jesus (Eph. ii, 6), suffered many things

from the blasphemous impiety and persecutions of the Roman power. "No blasphemy can surpass that of arrogating the homage due to God alone. This was practically blaspheming God and his worshipers. To receive such worship from men is most emphatically to decry both God and all his true worshipers in heaven."—*Cowles*.

7. *It was given unto him to make war with the saints*—In this respect he was another manifestation of persecuting power like the little horn of Daniel's vision (comp. Dan. vii, 21, from which passage these words are taken). *The saints* here are to be understood as equivalent to "the rest of her seed" in xii, 17. The dragon is conceived as having usurped the powers of worldly empire in order to make war upon the children of the Church. *Authority over every tribe. . . people. . . tongue. . . nation*—This is equivalent to universal empire.

8. *All shall worship him*—Repetition in substance of what has been stated in verses 3 and 4. *Not written in the book of life*—The book referred to in iii, 5, and xx, 12, 15; comp. Dan. xii, 1. *From the foundation of the world*—Whether this clause is designed to connect with *slain* immediately preceding, or with *written* near the beginning of the sentence, is an open question. Either construction is possible. The former is favored by the nearness of the word *slain* to the qualifying clause; the latter by the statement of xvii, 8, and, perhaps, the general sense and scope. Doctrinally considered both sentiments are true; for 1 Peter i, 20, sustains the one, and Eph. i, 5, 11, and Rom. viii, 29, confirm the other. The context favors the connection with *written*, for it is not particularly relevant to speak here of the slaying of the Lamb from the foundation of the world, but it does notably enhance the exceptional glory of those who worship not the beast to be admonished that their names were written of old in heaven (comp. Luke x, 20).

9. *Let him hear*—This admonition calls attention to what is about to be said, after the manner of ii, 7, 11, 17.

10. *For captivity . . . sword*—The language and sentiment are mainly from Jer. xv, 2, and Matt. xxvi, 52. Two forms of persecution are specified, as those wherein *the patience and the faith of the saints* are to be chiefly exhibited, and at the same time the admonition is given not to resort to the use of carnal weapons for the propagation of God's truth. Herein the counsel of Jesus in Matt. xxvi, 52, is affirmed. At the same time the words give assurance that retribution will come in due time to the persecuting power. *Here is the patience*—That is, here is the opportunity for the exercise of *the patience and the faith of the saints* who will be called to suffer by captivity and sword.

2. The Beast out of the Land. XIII, 11–18.

11 And I saw another beast coming up out of the earth; and he had two
12 horns like unto a lamb, and he spake as a dragon. And he exerciseth
all the authority of the first beast in his sight. And he maketh the
earth and them that dwell therein to worship the first beast, whose
13 death-stroke was healed. And he doeth great signs, that he should even
make fire to come down out of heaven upon the earth in the sight of men.
14 And he deceiveth them that dwell on the earth by reason of the signs
which it was given him to do in the sight of the beast; saying to them
that dwell on the earth, that they should make an image to the beast,
15 who hath the stroke of the sword, and lived. And it was given *unto
him* to give breath to it, *even* to the image of the beast, that the image
of the beast should both speak, and cause that as many as should not
16 worship the image of the beast should be killed. And he causeth all,
the small and the great, and the rich and the poor, and the free and the
bond, that there be given them a mark on their right hand, or upon their
17 forehead; and that no man should be able to buy or to sell, save he that
hath the mark, *even* the name of the beast or the number of his name.
18 Here is wisdom. He that hath understanding, let him count the number of the beast ; for it is the number of a man : and his number is
Six hundred and sixty and six.

The distinguishing features of this second beast are somewhat
numerous and seemingly sufficient to identify the power intended
without much difficulty. The chief points to be noted are (1) that
he comes up out of the land rather than the sea, (2) that he has two
horns like a lamb, (3) but he speaks as a dragon, (4) he exercises
all the authority of the first beast as if he were the mere agent and
representative of the same, (5) he compels the worship of the first
beast, and (6) works all sorts of lying wonders to secure the most
thorough subjection to his authority. So it is particularly noticeable that this second beast is but a satellite of the great power denoted by the first beast.

The two most current explanations of the beast from the land
are (1) that which sees in it a description of the pagan priesthood as
allied to the Roman state and including all its divination, witchcraft, and various magical arts, and (2) that which identifies it with
the Latin Church, the Roman papacy, considered especially as a
priestly persecuting power. But neither of these views seems in
perfect accord with the analogous symbolism of *beasts*, which everywhere stand for some organized world-power. The rise of the
Roman papacy, moreover, was far beyond the scope of this revelation which was of " things shortly to come to pass." Aside from
the great unspeakable future of the kingdom of God and of Christ,
the beginnings of which are celebrated in this book (for example,

xi, 15 ; xx, 4 ; xxi, 2, 3), our prophecy makes no note of particular
events of the distant future. Why should John have been gifted
to foretell the rise and fall of the papacy rather than the discovery
of America and the founding of the great western republic of religious liberty ?

But the best way of setting aside an erroneous interpretation is to
present a better one in its place. Some elements of truth attach to
that view which recognizes in the symbol the witchcraft and magical arts of paganism ; but faithful adherence to the analogies of
biblical symbolism requires that this second beast be a real political
power, an organized dominion, not a mere function or attribute of
such power and dominion. We find all the requirements of the
symbol met in the provincial governments of Judæa and Palestine
by the procurators (commonly called *governors* in the New Testament, ἡγεμόνες). Thus Pilate is called *the governor* (ἡγεμών) in
Matt. xxvii, 2, 11, 27 ; Luke xx, 20, and the authority of Rome, as
exercised by him in the crucifixion of Jesus, is an example of the
power of such a provincial ruler. Felix and Festus also bear the
same title (Acts xxiii, 24, 26 ; xxiv, 27 ; xxvi, 30). These rulers
were the immediate representatives of the emperor, and held from
him the power of life and death over their subjects (Josephus, *Wars*,
bk. ii, 8, 1). How the dominion exercised by these provincial
governors meets all the conditions of the beast described in verses
11–17 will appear in the following notes.

11. *Another beast . . . out of the land*—Observe that *land* (or *earth*)
here is contrasted with *sea* in verse 1. In view of the fact that
Jerusalem is the main center of operations in this book we may
most naturally understand the reference to the land of Judæa—the
particular *land*, or province, with which this Apocalypse is concerned.
If, however, one sees in the *sea* of verse 1 a symbol of the confusion
and strife out of which great empires rise, the *land* of this verse may
be supposed to denote the more quiet and established conditions
under which local governments with delegated powers have their
origin. *Two horns like a lamb*—No special significance need be
sought in these *two horns*, inasmuch as a horned lamb would
naturally have two horns. But if particular significance is sought
we should expect to find it in two kings or governors of exceptional
notoriety. These, in fact, appear in Albinus and Gessius Florus,
the last two procurators of Judæa. Josephus says of them : " Albinus concealed his wickedness, and was careful that it might not
be discovered to all men ; but Gessius Florus (who was sent by
Nero as successor to Albinus), as though he had been sent on purpose to show his crimes to everybody, made a pompous ostentation

of them to our nation, as never omitting any sort of violence, nor any unjust sort of punishment ; for he was not to be moved by pity and never was satisfied with any degree of gain that came in his way. . . . It was this Florus who necessitated us to take up arms against the Romans, while we thought it better to be destroyed at once than by little and little" (*Ant.*, bk. xx, 11, 1 ; comp. *Wars*, bk. ii, chaps. xiv and xv). *Spake as a dragon*—For the same infernal spirit possessed this second beast as that which prompted the blasphemies mentioned in verses 5 and 6. The beast which has the horns of a lamb and the speech of a dragon is also a striking symbol of the false prophet, who is like a ravenous wolf in sheep's clothing (Matt. vii, 15).

12. *All the authority of the first beast in his sight*—He is therefore the subordinate and servant of the higher power of Rome, and all he does is under the oversight of his master, as if in his immediate presence. He exercised all local power in the name and authority of the empire. Such exercise of power on the part of the provincial governor of Judæa is illustrated by the statement of Tacitus : "While Tiberius was reigning emperor, Christ was put to torture by the procurator Pontius Pilate" (*Annals*, xv, 44). *Maketh the land* (which is put under his power) *and them that dwell therein to worship the first beast*—How procurators and proconsuls enforced the worship of the empire in the image of the reigning emperor is especially witnessed by the famous letter of Pliny to Trajan (bk. x, epist. 97). He declares to the emperor that he gave over to capital punishment those Christians who persisted in their faith, but adds : "When at my instance they would call on the gods, and by incense and wine would supplicate thy image, which for this purpose I had ordered brought along with the likenesses of the deities, and would besides curse Christ, . . . I thought that they ought to be dismissed."

13. *Doeth great signs*—In this respect the beast made use of such lying wonders as the magicians of Egypt employed when they opposed the ministry of Moses and Aaron (comp. 2 Tim. iii, 8). As regards the *great signs* mentioned in this verse and the following, they may be supposed to include those foretold by Jesus in Matt. xxiv, 24 (comp. 2 Thess. ii, 9, 10). Nor is it improbable that men like Gessius Florus, intent on carrying out the imperial mandates of such a beast as Nero, would have turned to their nefarious purposes the magical arts of impostors like Simon (Acts viii, 9) and Elymas (Acts xiii, 8), for such sorcerers seem to have been numerous in all the provinces of the empire (comp. Acts xix, 19).

14. *He deceiveth*—Compare the statement of 2 Thess. ii, 11, where

it is said in connection with "the signs and lying wonders, and all deceit of unrighteousness" practiced by the Satanic Antichrist, that "God sendeth them a working of error (πλάνη), that they should believe a lie." *Make an image to the beast*—This was one of the ways by which he deceived *them that dwell on the land.* The image of the reigning emperor was virtually the image of the beast as represented by that emperor. Düsterdieck observes that "all images of deified emperors must have appeared to the Christian conscience as images of the beast, the more certainly as all those individual emperors were possessors of the same antichristian secular power."

15. *To give breath to the image of the beast*—Or, *to give a spirit to the image;* that is, make it appear to be alive. It was the work of the local governors to make the Roman authority a very living thing to all its subjects, and the vigorous exercise of such power might in symbolic description be spoken of as a giving of life to the image of imperial sovereignty. There may also in this connection be an allusion to such well-known claims and feats of miraculous power as Simon Magus puts forth in the *Recognitions of Clement* (iii, 47), where he is represented as saying : "I have flown through the air ; I have been mixed with fire, and been made one body with it ; I have made statues move ; I have animated lifeless things."

16. *Causeth all. . . mark on their right hand*—This verse and the following describe in a form suitable to the symbolical portraiture of the entire passage (verses 11-17) the absolute power and rigor with which Rome enforced her claims on all the subject provinces. All who failed to conform to the imperial orders and receive the mark (χάραγμα) of such passive submission were proscribed, and the procurators were charged with enforcing the interdict.

18. *Here is wisdom*—That is, here is opportunity for the exercise of wisdom, namely, in the solution of the riddle about to be propounded. Compare the like form of expression in verse 10. *The number of the beast*—It is obviously the number of the first beast which is here intended, for the reference is continually to that beast in verses 12, 14, 15, and 17. This fact shows still more clearly that the second beast has no independent authority of his own, but is at most the minion and satellite of the first beast. He is a subordinate power through whom the beast out of the *sea* exercises his authority on the *land*, and the spirit of the old serpent, the dragon, possesses and actuates them both. *It is the number of a man*—This most naturally means that the number about to be given, when set in the proper numerical letters, will represent the name of a man. The apocryphal apocalypses contain numerous examples of such desig-

nations of proper names.[1] Less satisfactory is the explanation, which, citing xxi, 17, and Isa. viii, 1, as parallels, makes the *number of a man* equivalent to "according to human reckoning" or "counted as men are wont to count." In either case it is agreed that the number is to be resolved into letters that will spell out the name intended. It is a question what alphabet, Hebrew or Greek, is to be understood. The assumption of some that we must look to the Greek alphabet because the book is written in Greek is quite untenable in view of ix, 11, where the Hebrew name of the angel of the abyss is placed first. The Hebrew cast and style of the whole book makes it further probable that the tongue of the Hebrews would be the language specially appropriate for such a mystic riddle as is here propounded to the wise. But if a double designation, one Hebrew and one Greek, both pointing out the same great beast, can be produced, the solution will be all the more entitled to credit. We have such a solution in the Hebrew appellation NERO CÆSAR (נרון קסר), and in the Greek word Λατεῖνος, long ago propounded by Irenæus. The plea sometimes made that these names were sometimes written with one letter more or less is worthless in view of the fact that they were also written as above. The further fact that scores of names in many different languages can be made to represent numerically *six hundred and sixty and six* ought to admonish us that *not any possible solution* of the name, but rather *a relevant solution*, is required. Having already shown that the Roman empire is the beast described in verses 1–8 of this chapter, we naturally look for some name that gives specific designation of that power. In xvii, 11, we observe that the beast is conceived as identical with any one of the reigning kings, who for the time represents the empire and commands its forces. It will be further shown in our notes on that passage that Nero was the sixth of the list of Cæsars there referred to. Hence it would seem that no solution of this *number of the beast* could be more conclusive or relevant than the name נרון קסר, *Nero Cæsar*, a form of the name actually found in rabbinical writings. The numerical value of the Hebrew letters forming this name is as follows: נ=50; ר=200; ו=6; נ=50; ק=100; ס=60; ר=200; which seven numbers added together = 666. It is also worthy of note that Irenæus mentions the number *six hundred and sixteen* (616) as the reading of some of the ancient manuscripts of his time; and another form of writing the name

---

[1] See *Sibylline Oracles*, Terry's English translation, bk. i, lines 167–171, 383–387. In bk. v, lines 15–70, the emperors from Julius Cæsar to the Antonines are similarly designated. Compare also the frequent use of numbers and letters in this enigmatical way in bks. xii and xiv.

Nero Cæsar, נרו קסר, gives this very number. The fact that both
forms are legitimate ways of spelling Nero's name in Hebrew characters suggests that this ancient diversity of readings arose from a
current understanding that Nero was the man intended; but some
spelled the name one way and some another. No interpreter ought
to demand a more fitting solution of this mystic number.

The Greek word Λατεῖνος is also entitled to consideration, because
it also points to the great *Latin* world-power. It is less specific
and therefore less satisfactory than the Hebrew name above given;
but it was the ancient and current appellation of the great empire
which had its chief seat in ancient Latium.

III. SEVENFOLD REVELATION OF TRIUMPH AND JUDGMENT. XIV.

The revelation of the three great foes, the dragon, the beast from
the sea, and the beast from the land, is followed immediately by a
sevenfold disclosure of victory and judgment in the heavens. The
purpose of these visions and voices from heaven is obviously to
show that the powers of the heavens are mightier than those of the
infernal serpent and his associates. The trinity of hostile forces,
armed with many lying wonders, might seem from a human point
of view invincible. But John, like the young servant of Elisha
when confronted with the horses and chariots and immense host of
the king of Syria, is here admonished that they which are with the
persecuted Church are more and mightier than they which make war
against her (comp. 2 Kings vi, 15–17). The contents of this chapter
are a vivid apocalyptic setting of much that is written in the second
psalm : the enemies may rage and do their worst, but he that sitteth
in the heavens shall have them in derision (see additional note after
verse 5).

1. The Lamb and his Thousands on Mount Zion. xiv, 1-5.

1   And I saw, and behold, the Lamb standing on the mount Zion, and
with him a hundred and forty and four thousand, having his name, and
2 the name of his Father, written on their foreheads. And I heard a voice
from heaven, as the voice of many waters, and as the voice of a great
thunder: and the voice which I heard *was* as *the voice* of harpers harping
3 with their harps: and they sing as it were a new song before the throne,
and before the four living creatures and the elders: and no man could
learn the song save the hundred and forty and four thousand, *even* they
4 that had been purchased out of the earth. These are they which were
not defiled with women; for they are virgins. These *are* they which
follow the Lamb whithersoever he goeth. These were purchased from
5 among men, *to be* the first fruits unto God and unto the Lamb. And in
their mouth was found no lie: they are without blemish.

1. *The Lamb*—The same Lamb who received the divine worship of v, 9-13, and opened the book of seven seals. *Standing on the Mount Zion*—The Mount Zion is here to be understood as the heavenly Zion, the seat of the new Jerusalem which is above, and which is our mother (Gal. iv, 26). On this holy mountain is to rise the new temple of God in the heaven (xi, 19), and the *hundred and forty and four thousand* are not different from "them that worship therein," as measured in xi, 1. Being the "first fruits unto God and unto the Lamb" (verse 4), they are the same as the twelve times twelve thousand of vii, 4-8. In that earlier vision they were represented as sealed on their foreheads as the servants of God ; here they appear as standing with the Lamb on Zion, *having his name, and the name of his Father, written on their foreheads.* The purport of the vision is to show that while the old dragon is making war with the woman's seed (xii, 17), and even employing the proscriptive force of worldly empire to secure his foul designs, a new and holy congregation is gathering on Mount Zion and learning there to sing a new song known only to the redeemed, or to that select "first fruits" whose excellency is here extolled.

2. *A voice from heaven*—Three comparisons are given to enhance in our minds the wonderful qualities of this *voice:* it was like *many waters,* like *a great thunder,* and like *harpers harping with their harps.* Its loudness did not seem to take anything from its charming melody, and altogether it was a sound of heavenly song so magnificent and harmonious as to imply new triumphs of God and of the Lamb.

3. *They sing as it were a new song*—New triumphs, new revelations, new eras in the kingdom of God call for new songs. Comp. v, 9 ; Psalm xxxiii, 3 ; xl, 3 ; cxliv, 9. *Before the throne*—So the new song was sung in that holy heaven where John had previously seen the throne, and him that sat on it, and *the four living creatures and the elders* (iv, 2-11), and heard the sound of the worship that was wont to be there paid to God and the Lamb. It is not here written by whom this new song was sung, but it is said that *no man could learn the song save the hundred and forty and four thousand.* Only the skilled ear and the understanding heart that were versed in the mysteries of the kingdom of God were competent to *learn* the song of redemption. The thought here suggested is that the one hundred and forty-four thousand comprised a select company, whose common trials, dangers, and final triumphs enabled them to appreciate and learn the heavenly song. They *had been purchased out of the earth,* and therefore they belonged to heaven ; and hence the reason why they alone could learn the new song. Observe that

when one is *purchased out of the earth* he becomes an associate of the heavenly host that worship one common Lord.

4. *Not defiled with women . . . virgins*—To be understood figuratively of spiritual purity. These are free from all that is associated in thought with carnal uncleanness. As fornication, harlotry, and adultery stand in this book (ii, 20–22 ; xvii, 2, 4 ; xviii, 3 ; xix, 2) for all abominations of idolatry and uncleanness, so these undefiled ones are called *virgins* to denote their separateness from all such contaminations. The word for *virgins* (παρθένοι) is here masculine, and is used also in other Greek writings for men as well as women. *Follow the Lamb*—Through all exposure and trial in this life, and to the living fountains in the heavenly glory (comp. vii, 17). Their abiding and intimate relations with the Lamb are thus emphasized here after the statement of verse 1 above that they were " with him." *Purchased from among men*—Repeated in substance from verse 3, but defined more particularly as *from among men* rather than "from the earth" to indicate their elect and precious character as a *first fruits unto God and unto the Lamb*. The confessors and martyrs of the apostolic Church, who overcame by reason of their testimony and the blood of the Lamb, are thus declared to be a *first fruits* (ἀπαρχή), a choice selection out of the innumerable company of saints. The purpose of this Apocalypse was to give special comfort and encouragement to these virgin spirits.

5. *In their mouth was found no lie*—For, like their Lord, they are holy and true (iii, 7). There seems here to be an appropriation of language and thought from Zeph. iii, 13 : " The remnant of Israel shall do no iniquity, nor speak lies ; neither shall a deceitful tongue be found in their mouth." Comp. also Isa. liii, 9. *They are without blemish*—This completes the description and gives it a most admirable finish. No spot of any kind is found in them. Contrast the murders, sorceries, fornication, and thefts of ix, 21.

The question which expositors have raised as to whether the foregoing picture of Mount Zion was in heaven or on earth may well be answered by reference to Heb. xii, 22–24, a passage which seems to us clearly to have been written with this vision of the Apocalypse in mind. THE HEAVEN of our apocalyptist is the visional sphere of the glory and triumph of the Church, and no marked distinction is recognized between the saints on earth and those in heaven. They are conceived as one great company, and death is of no account to them. So the writer of Heb. xii, 22, says, " Ye are come unto Mount Zion ; " that is, ye who have entered into the life of faith, and are made " partakers of a heavenly calling " (Heb. iii, 1), have already come (προσεληλύθατε) to Zion, the mountain and city of the living God, the heavenly Jerusalem, on which John saw the one hundred and forty-four thousand with the Lamb. Ye have come as so many additional members of the general assembly and Church of the firstborn, who are enrolled in heaven. Ye have also come to the innumerable company of angels, whose voices John heard like the sound of many waters, and of a great thunder, and of harpers singing a new song. "The spirits of just men made perfect" in Heb. xii, 23, is but another designation of the undefiled, who are without blemish, and are therefore called virgins. Thus the entire passage serves to illustrate how saints " dwelling in heavenly places in Christ Jesus " are all one in spirit and triumph, no matter what physical locality they may occupy. The entire picture is one of vision, and therefore questions of physical locality are out of place. Hence we are to understand the vision of xiv, 1–5, as we do the visions of xi, 19, and xii, 1, and indeed all the other pictures by which the apocalyptist discloses the real position and victories of those "who follow the Lamb whithersoever he goeth." The redeemed children have passed from death into life. They live though they die, and their life of faith and hope is so hidden in God that they are conceived and spoken of as never dying (John xi, 25, 26).

> " The Church triumphant in thy love,
>   Their mighty joys we know :
> They sing the Lamb in hymns above,
>   And we in hymns below."

2. The Eternal Gospel. xiv, 6, 7.

6 And I saw another angel flying in midheaven, having eternal good
   tidings to proclaim unto them that dwell on the earth, and unto every
7 nation and tribe and tongue and people; and he saith with a great voice,
   Fear God, and give him glory; for the hour of his judgment is come:
   and worship him that made the heaven and the earth and sea and fountains of waters.

6. *Another angel*—In distinction from the angelic harpers mentioned in verse 2. *Flying in midheaven*—Contrast the flying eagle and his message of woe in viii, 13. *Having an eternal gospel to proclaim*—The order of the words in the Greek is worthy of note : *having good tidings eternal to announce as good tidings* ($\varepsilon\dot{v}\alpha\gamma\gamma\varepsilon\lambda\dot{\iota}$-$\sigma\alpha\iota$). Although without the article this *gospel eternal* is no other than " the gospel of the kingdom " which Jesus declared should be " preached in the whole world for a testimony unto all the nations " before the end of the Jewish cultus and temple should come (Matt. xxiv, 14). It is appropriately called *an eternal gospel*, for it was declared of old as a blessed hope to the fathers and prophets (x, 7),

it "was preached in all creation under heaven" by the apostles
(Col. i, 23), and its saving truths are the comfort and joy of the
Church through all ages. The proclaiming of the Gospel *unto them
that dwell on the land* seems to be a reference to the first preaching
of the apostles to the Jews of Palestine, as distinguished from the
later proclamation of Christ *unto every nation and tribe and tongue
and people*, after it became manifest that "to the Gentiles also God
granted repentance unto life" (Acts xi, 18). Compare also the
seer's commission in x, 11, of this book.

So we are assured, in the face of all the dragon's persecution of
the woman's seed, not only that the Lamb and his followers triumph
on Mount Zion, but also that the Gospel of the kingdom is proclaimed among all the nations.

7. *Fear God, and give him glory*—Comp. xi, 13. The Gospel has
its message of *fear* as well as of joy. The terrors of the Lord are
one means of persuading men (2 Cor. v, 11), and the near approach
of *the hour of his judgment* was an important part of the preaching
of the apostolic age (Acts x, 42; xvii, 31; xxiv, 25). *Worship him
who made the heaven*—Not the beast and his image (comp. verse 9,
and xiii, 12, 15). He alone who created all things is worthy to
receive the glory and honor (comp. iv, 11, and Isa. xl, 12). The
division of the physical universe into *heaven, earth, sea*, and *fountains* is characteristic of the writer of this book. Comp. v, 13; viii,
7-12, and xvi, 2-8.

3. The Fallen Babylon. xiv, 8.

8   And another, a second angel, followed, saying, Fallen, fallen is Baby-
     lon the great, which hath made all the nations to drink of the wine of
     the wrath of her fornication.

8. *Another, a second angel*—Each announcement has its special
angel. Scarcely has the angel of the eternal Gospel made his proclamation than another *followed*, announcing the fall of *Babylon the
great*. This *great Babylon* is mentioned here proleptically, as was
the beast out of the abyss in xi, 7; but the fuller portraiture is
reserved for a special revelation in chaps. xvii and xviii. A similar
proleptic allusion is again made in xvi, 19. The language is appropriated from Isa. xxi, 9, and Jer. li, 7, 8, and is to be understood
here as a decree of doom, announced with prophetic assurance as if
the fall had already occurred. The name *Babylon* is employed
symbolically, and, like Sodom and Egypt in xi, 8, must be explained
by means of the historical associations which the great city of the
Euphrates would most naturally suggest to Jewish thought. Babylon is depicted in the Old Testament prophets as the proud oppressor,

the insolent persecutor, full of abominable idolatries and of all manner of wickedness.   The name is, accordingly, employed in this
book to designate the woman of xvii, 3, 4, "the mother of harlots
and of the abominations of the earth" (xvii, 5), "drunken with the
blood of saints," committing fornication with the kings of the earth,
and becoming a "habitation of demons and a hold of every unclean
spirit and of every unclean and hateful bird" (xviii, 2), and "having
dominion over the kings of the land" (xvii, 18).   That this great
city is no other than Jerusalem, the murderer of prophets, full of
hypocrisy and extortion and all uncleanness, the hold of a generation of vipers, and drunken with superstition and spiritual idolatry
and schemes of worldly power, will be shown in the notes on chap.
xvii.   As Jesus in Matt. xxiv, 14, said that the end of this city and
the pre-Messianic age would follow the preaching of the Gospel
among the nations, so in this Apocalypse the proclamation of the
fall of *Babylon the great* follows immediately after that of the
eternal Gospel.   *The wine of the wrath of her fornication*—This
peculiar expression is an addition to Jeremiah's language.   That
prophet speaks of "Babylon, a golden cup in Jehovah's hand, that
made all the earth drunken : the nations drank of her wine; therefore the nations are mad" (Jer. li, 7).   Some accordingly explain
the words *wine of the wrath of her fornication* as equivalent to
inflammatory wine of her fornication.   Her foul sins are conceived
as so much heating and inebriating wine which made others drunken
as herself.   But it is better to understand the word *wrath* ($\vartheta \nu \mu \acute{o} \varsigma$)
here as in verse 10 of the *wrath of God*, so that we have the double
thought that the wine of her fornication is also the wine of God's
wrath.

4. THE SOLEMN ADMONITION. XIV, 9–12.

9   And another angel, a third, followed them, saying with a great voice,
     If any man worshipeth the beast and his image, and receiveth a mark
10 on his forehead, or upon his hand, he also shall drink of the wine of the
     wrath of God, which is prepared unmixed in the cup of his anger; and
     he shall be tormented with fire and brimstone in the presence of the holy
11 angels, and in the presence of the Lamb: and the smoke of their torment
     goeth up forever and ever; and they have no rest day and night, they
     that worship the beast and his image, and whoso receiveth the mark of
12 his name.   Here is the patience of the saints, they that keep the com-
     mandments of God, and the faith of Jesus.

9. *Another angel, a third*—Comp. verses 6 and 8.   The announcement of Babylon's fall is appropriately followed by a warning
against the worship of the beast, as if that sort of idolatrous worship had been the ruin of the great city.   The warning is emphasized

with a great voice, so that all may hear and be duly admonished. The worshiping of the beast and his image, and receiving his mark, are direct allusions to what has been written in xiii, 12–17. It was the work of the second beast to enforce this worship of the first beast upon "the land and them that dwell therein" (xiii, 12). Now the warning is sounded aloud that anyone who participates in this worship must needs come to fearful judgment as surely as did Babylon the great.

10. *Drink of the wine of the wrath of God*—Compare the language of Isa. li, 17 ; Jer. xxv, 15, 16 ; Psalm lxxv, 8. *Prepared unmixed in the cup of his anger*—Figure suggestive of anger in its most intense fury, like a cup of strong drink undiluted with any mixture of water. *Tormented with fire and brimstone*—Comp. xx, 10. This is the writer's way of designating the gehenna of fire. *In the presence of the holy angels and . . . of the Lamb*—The torment is conceived as inflicted before the eyes of the angels and of the Lamb, and this accords with the concept of Mark viii, 38; Luke ix, 26; xvi, 23. Thus the dire punishment is depicted as an act of judgment to be administered in the very presence of the Lamb and the angels of his power.

11. *Smoke of their torment*—The smoke of the fire and brimstone which causes their torment. *Goeth up forever and ever*—This statement, which is designed to add horror to the thought of the torment, and is repeated again in xviii, 18, and xix, 3, is appropriated from Gen. xix, 28, where Abraham is said to have looked toward Sodom and Gomorrah, "and, behold, the smoke of the country went up as the smoke of a furnace." The figure is enlarged and intensified in Isaiah's prophecy of the desolation of Idumea in the day of Jehovah's vengeance (Isa. xxxiv, 9, 10). The doctrinal significance of this passage is not to be overlooked. So far as it has any bearing on the question of the duration of the punishment of the wicked it speaks without any hint of limitation. It accords with the teaching involved in Matt. xxv, 46, and also with the "certain fearful expectation of judgment and a fierceness of fire which shall devour the adversaries," spoken of in Heb. x, 27. A *torment* that runs through *ages of ages* is a most fearful conception. *They have no rest*—That is, from their torment; no release or recreation from their doleful lot. Comp. xx, 10.

12. *Here is the patience of the saints*—Comp. xiii, 10. Here is opportunity for the exercise and display of saintly patience. The refusal to worship the beast and his image demanded the martyr's firmness and a patience in persecution which only a true keeping of God's commandments and faith in Jesus could secure.

5. The Blessed Dead. xiv, 13.

13 And I heard a voice from heaven saying, Write, Blessed are the dead
who die in the Lord from henceforth: yea, saith the Spirit, that they
may rest from their labors; for their works follow with them.

13. *I heard a voice from heaven*—The precious revelation of this
verse is given through *a voice from the heaven*, not by a vision, and
the special commandment to *write* serves to enhance the value of
this particular communication. *Blessed are the dead who die in the
Lord*—This comes as a most encouraging word immediately after
the admonition of verses 9–12, for that solemn warning implied the
putting to death of multitudes who counted not life on earth so dear
that they would keep it by violation of "the commandments of God
and the faith of Jesus." Dying in vital fellowship with the Lord
Jesus involved with many a martyr's death of violence and torture,
but the Lord had already instructed his followers that " whosoever
would save his life shall lose it ; and whosoever shall lose his life
for my sake and the Gospel's shall save it " (Mark viii, 35). It is
worthy of note, perhaps, that the only other beatitude of the Apocalypse is that pronounced on him that "has part in the first resurrection " (xx, 6). The special emphasis of the sentence lies in the
closing words ἀπ' ἄρτι, *from henceforth,* which most obviously mean
from this time onward, and are best construed with μακάριοι, *blessed:*
Blessed from now onward are the dead who die in the Lord. They
are immediately introduced into the presence of the Lord himself,
so that, as in the case of Paul, for them " to die is gain " (Phil. i,
21). The consolation afforded by this assurance of immediate and
continuing blessedness is like that which Paul writes to the Thessalonians " concerning them that fall asleep." So far from losing any
glory or blessedness, those fallen asleep in Jesus have the prece-
dence, being already with the Lord, and so occupying a position of
preeminence in every signal manifestation of his presence (1 Thess.
iv, 13–18). Those who die in the Lord are blessed at once and forever thereafter. They are not required to wait until the dragon and
the beast have finished their persecution of the Church on earth, nor
do they linger in longing expectation of some future reward, but,
having fallen asleep in Jesus, they find him to be the resurrection
and the life, and though dying, they live (John xi, 25), and are
blessed from henceforth, that is, from the moment of death onward,
forever. The blessedness is indicated by the further statement that
they shall rest from their labors. The Greek word for *labors* (κόπων)
involves the idea of fatiguing toils, and may include that of sufferings. The blessed dead rest from all such labor, and are blessed in

that they may and shall thus rest. *For*—This is the best attested reading, and is less likely to have been substituted for δέ than *vice versâ*. It introduces another reason for pronouncing them *blessed* and at the same time enhances the thought of their *rest* from the toils of earthly life and persecution. *Their works* (ἔργα) *follow with them*—All the good works they have wrought in fellowship and suffering with Christ are conceived as accompanying them, like so many attendants and witnesses of their keeping "the commandments of God and the faith of Jesus." They rest *from their labors*, but *their works* abide with them as things of precious memory. Comp. 1 Thess. i, 3.

6. The Harvest of the Earth. xiv, 14–16.

14 And I saw, and behold, a white cloud; and on the cloud *I saw* one
   sitting like unto a son of man, having on his head a golden crown, and
15 in his hand a sharp sickle.   And another angel came out from the temple,
   crying with a great voice to him that sat on the cloud, Send forth thy
   sickle, and reap: for the hour to reap is come; for the harvest of the
16 earth is over-ripe.   And he that sat on the cloud cast his sickle upon the
   earth; and the earth was reaped.

Verses 14–20 contain two distinct visions, the one, verses 14–16, showing a son of man reaping "the harvest of the earth;" the other, verses 17–20, showing an angel gathering "the vintage of the earth." But the two pictures have so much in common that they seem to have been designed to accompany and supplement each other. Their relevancy to what precedes is seen in that they are an assurance that God will bring every work into judgment, whether good or evil, and will thus vindicate his own servants "in the presence of the holy angels and in the presence of the Lamb" (verse 10 above). The two descriptions present the following notable correspondences:

The Harvest.	The Vintage.
1. Son of man on a white cloud.	1. Angel from the temple in heaven.
2. Having a sharp sickle.	2. Having a sharp sickle.
3. Another angel from the temple crying with a great voice to send forth the sickle and reap.	3. Another angel from the altar calling with a great voice to send forth the sickle and gather the clusters of the vine.
4. The harvest is over-ripe.	4. The grapes are fully ripe.
5. He that sat on the cloud cast his sickle upon the earth, and it was reaped.	5. The angel cast his sickle into the earth, gathered the vintage, and cast it into the wine press of God's wrath.
[Nothing is said as to the character of the harvest.]	6. The wine press when trodden overflows with blood amounting to a vast sea—symbol of fearful retribution.

The two closely related figures of harvest of grain and vintage of grapes appear in Joel iii, 13 : "Put ye in the sickle, for the harvest is ripe: come, get you down; for the press is full, the vats overflow; for their wickedness is great." This association of the two illustrations of judgment warrants us in referring both the harvest and the vintage to the impending judgment of God upon the wicked. The habit of apocalyptic repetition for the purpose of showing that the vision is established of God, and shortly to come to pass (Gen. xli, 32), also allows us to refer these visions of harvest and vintage both alike to the execution of the wrath of God upon his enemies. It may also be argued that if the harvest of verses 14–16 represents an ingathering of saints rather than a judgment on the wicked something ought to have been added after verse 16, or elsewhere, in order to acquaint us with a distinction so important.

It may, however, be maintained that in such apocalyptic symbolism too many formal definitions are out of place and much is left to inference. The harvest reaped may alone be sufficiently suggestive of gathering the wheat into the garner (comp. Matt. iii, 12 ; xiii, 30), and after the benediction on the blessed dead and the reference to their rest and works there was no need of further specification to inform us that the ingathering of the ripe harvest is symbolic of the blessed reward of the saints.

We incline, therefore, to the view of verses 14–16, which makes the harvest represent the ingathering and blessed reward of the saints. The double picture of harvest and vintage may well be regarded as an apocalyptic amplification of the parable of the wheat and the tares (Matt. xiii, 24–30, 37–43). The harvest gathered by the sickle (comp. Mark iv, 29) corresponds to the gathering of the wheat into the storehouse (Matt. xiii, 30); but the vintage trodden in the wine press corresponds to the binding of the tares and the casting of them into a furnace of fire. Everything in language and allusion fits this interpretation of the double vision.

14. *A white cloud*—Compare the white horse of vi, 2, and xix, 11, as symbolic of a triumphant procedure. *On the cloud . . . one like a son of man*—Comp. Dan. vii, 13; Matt. xxiv, 30. This *son of man* is no other than the Christ of i, 7. His heavenly royalty is further indicated by his *having on his head a golden crown.* The *sickle* is the instrument alike of reaping and of vinedressing.

15. *Another angel came out from the temple*—The machinery of apocalyptics, as elsewhere observed, makes use of any number of angels which the various visions may require. The word *another*, as in verse 6, refers in a general way to angels mentioned or implied in the preceding context. The fact that this angel cried with a loud

voice to the son of man to thrust in the sickle and reap does not necessarily imply his superiority, for he is himself but a messenger out of God's temple, serving to utter a signal cry. *Send forth thy sickle*—Language from Joel iii, 13. Compare the expressions, *cast the sickle* and *send out the sickle* in verses 16, 19, and Mark iv, 29. The allusion is to the reaper's habit of putting forth his sickle with a swing of the arm in the act of reaping. *The harvest is over-ripe*— Or, as the aorist implies, *was dried up.* But the word here seems to have no other meaning than that the harvest was fully ripened for the sickle. The time of harvest was fully come.

7. The Vintage of Judgment. xiv, 17-20.

17 And another angel came out from the temple which is in heaven, he
18 also having a sharp sickle. And another angel came out from the altar,
he that hath power over fire; and he called with a great voice to him
that had the sharp sickle, saying, Send forth thy sharp sickle, and gather
19 the clusters of the vine of the earth; for her grapes are fully ripe. And
the angel cast his sickle into the earth, and gathered the vintage of the
earth, and cast it into the wine press, the great *wine press*, of the wrath of
20 God. And the wine press was trodden without the city, and there came
out blood from the wine press, even unto the bridles of the horses, as far
as a thousand and six hundred furlongs.

17. *Another angel . . . from the temple*—The same *temple* as that mentioned in verse 15 and which was opened to the seer's vision in xi, 19. These angels come forth from *the temple which is in the heaven,* for there is the throne of God, and they are the ministers of his judgments. The Son of man does his will by the angels of his power. Comp. Matt. xiii, 30, 41 ; xxv, 31 ; 2 Thess. i, 7, 8.

18. *Another angel . . . from the altar*—Compare the angel " over the altar " in viii, 3-5, who added incense to the prayers of the saints, and cast the fire of the altar into the earth, as if in answer to the prayers of the souls under the altar to avenge their blood (vi, 10). The same angel seems to be here denoted by the statement that it was *he that hath power over the fire ;* that is, the one who in the former vision filled the censer with the fire of the altar and cast it down upon the earth. It was fitting that the same angel should now *sound forth* (φωνέω) *with a great voice* the signal for the thrusting in of the sickle into the clusters of grapes *fully ripe* for the wine press of bloody judgment.

19. *The great wine press of the wrath of God*—Compare " wine of the wrath of God " in verse 10. These words, together with what is added in the next verse, show that the entire picture of verses 17-20 is one of terrible retributive judgment. But the extent of

the judgment, or the particular objects of the divine wrath, are not specified. We may think of the dragon and of the two beasts and of Babylon the great, for they were all acting the part of enemies of God and the Lamb. But the repeated mention ·of *the land* (verses 15, 16, 18, 19) and *the city* in verse 20 point us most naturally to the land and city of the Jewish people, which are throughout this book the most notable objects of the wrath of God.

20. *Trodden without the city*—We understand the city here referred to as the " Babylon the great " of verse 8 and identical with the city which is called " Sodom and Egypt " in xi, 8. Without and around this city the Roman armies gathered to tread down Judah and Jerusalem until her times of judgment were fulfilled (Luke xxi, 20–24). Those armies were under God the agents of divine retribution, and by them was the wine press of his wrath trodden. On this figure of treading the wine press comp. Isa. lxiii, 3, from which the imagery is partly drawn. Comp. also Lam. i, 15. *Blood . . . even unto the bridles*—The picture of blood is made purposely appalling by the extravagance of the hyperbole. It seemed to the seer as if *the horses* (comp. ix, 16, 17, and xvi, 12–16) that trod the land of this vine waded in a sea of blood and the sea extended *as far as a thousand and six hundred furlongs.* This number, like all others in the book, is symbolical, made up of forty times forty, the number of judgment and penalty (Num. xiv, 34 ; Gen. vii, 12), and thus suggestive of a retribution fearfully intensified. The distance thus indicated being equivalent to two hundred miles, approximately the length of Palestine from north to south, may incidentally point to the fact that this whole land was, figuratively speaking, deluged with blood during the Jewish war which ended in the destruction of Jerusalem. This fearful vision of judgment stands in relation to the seven last plagues of chaps. xv and xvi as does the symbolism of the sixth seal (vi, 12–17) to that of the seven trumpets.

IV. THE SEVEN LAST PLAGUES. XV, XVI.

The contents of chap. xv are of the nature of an introduction to the pouring out of the seven bowls of wrath (chap. xvi), which will be found to correspond strikingly to the seven trumpets. After the announcement of the seven last plagues in verse 1 there is a vision of victors singing a song of triumph (verses 2–4), and this artistic feature corresponds to the introduction of the multitudes, sealed by the living God and arrayed in white robes, singing with the angels round the throne (chap. vii), which was brought in between the opening of the sixth and seventh seals and just before the seven angels were sent forth to sound the seven trumpets of woe.

The Seven Angels. xv, 1.

1   And I saw another sign in heaven, great and marvelous, seven angels
having seven plagues, *which are* the last, for in them is finished the
wrath of God.

1. *Another sign in heaven*—Allusion to the great signs seen in xii,
1, 3.   *Seven angels having seven plagues*—Compare the opening of
the seventh seal which issued in the seven trumpets (viii, 1, 2).
Compare also the language of Lev. xxvi, 21.   *The last*—So called
because in them is finished the wrath of God.   In them is consummated the utter overthrow of "Babylon the Great" (xvi, 19).   Immediately after the seventh plague (xvi, 17–21) one of the seven
angels that had the seven bowls of plagues showed John the special
apocalypse of the fall of this Babylon the harlot (xvii, 1); and, still
further on, one of the same seven angels showed him the corresponding vision of the new Jerusalem, the bride, the wife of the Lamb
(xxi, 9).

Song by the Glassy Sea. xv, 2-4.

2   And I saw as it were a glassy sea mingled with fire ; and them that
come off victorious from the beast, and from his image, and from the
number of his name, standing by the glassy sea, having harps of God.

3 And they sing the song of Moses the servant of God, and the song of the
Lamb, saying, Great and marvelous are thy works, O Lord God, the
Almighty; righteous and true are thy ways, thou King of the ages.

4 Who shall not fear, O Lord, and glorify thy name? for thou only art
holy; for all the nations shall come and worship before thee; for thy
righteous acts have been made manifest.

2. *A glassy sea mingled with fire*—And so quite different from the
"glassy sea like unto crystal" (iv, 6) which formed the open space
before the throne.   This had, like that, a smooth, glittering surface,
as if it were of glass, but it had also the appearance of being *mingled
with fire,* as if reflecting the vast sea of blood from the wine press of
God's wrath mentioned just before (xiv, 20).   This allusion, as well
as the immediate mention of "the song of Moses the servant of
God," and the entire picture of the triumphant host show that the
imagery is drawn from the triumph of Israel at the Red Sea.   There
the hosts of Israel, standing upon the further shore, safe from pur-
suit and persecution by Pharaoh, " saw the Egyptians dead upon the
seashore " (Exod. xiv, 30).   *Them that come off victorious from the
beast*—How like the victory of the Israelites who had escaped the
persecutions of Egypt and, having made the passage of the Red
Sea, triumphed gloriously as the saved people of Jehovah.   In chap.
xii, 4, 15, 16, we have already noted allusions to this period of Israel's trial and triumph.   *From his image and from the number of*

his name—Reference to xiii, 17. *Standing by the glassy sea*—Just as Israel stood by the Red Sea, or on its further shore, and saw God's vengeance on their enemies. The preposition ἐπί, with the accusative in the sense of *by* or *at*, is used here as it was in iii, 20, and vii, 1. *Having harps of God*—Like the multitude of exultant singers in xiv, 2. So the Israelitish song of triumph was accompanied with the sound of timbrels (Exod. xv, 20).

3. *They sing the song of Moses*—That is, a song of victory like that of Moses in Exod. xv, 1-18: "Then sang Moses and the children of Israel this song unto Jehovah, saying, I will sing unto Jehovah, for he hath triumphed gloriously: the horse and his rider he hath cast into the sea." But this strain of triumph is something more than that old song of Moses: it is also *the song of the Lamb,* who stood on Mount Zion with his redeemed Israel (xiv, 1). These lofty designations of the song enhance in our minds the idea of its superior excellence and glory. The language of the song is a combination from Psalm cxi, 2; cxxxix, 14; Exod. xxxiv, 10; Amos iv, 13 (Septuagint); Deut. xxxii, 4; Jer. x, 7, 10; Psalm lxxxvi, 9; cxlv, 17; Mal. i, 11.

THE PROCESSION OF THE ANGELS. xv, 5-8.

5 And after these things I saw, and the temple of the tabernacle of the
6 testimony in heaven was opened: and there came out from the temple the seven angels that had the seven plagues, arrayed with *precious* stone,
7 pure *and* bright, and girt about their breasts with golden girdles. And one of the four living creatures gave unto the seven angels seven golden
8 bowls full of the wrath of God, who liveth forever and ever. And the temple was filled with smoke from the glory of God, and from his power; and none was able to enter into the temple, till the seven plagues of the seven angels should be finished.

5. *After these things*—The song of verses 3 and 4 is supposed to have occupied some time. Verse 1 serves to announce the entire subject of chaps. xv and xvi, and after the preliminaries of verses 2-4 the subject of the "seven angels having seven plagues" is formally taken up, and their procession from the temple in heaven is described. *The temple of the tabernacle of the testimony in heaven was opened*—This can be no other than the temple of xi, 19, which was seen to contain the ark of the covenant of God. From the same temple went forth the angels of xiv, 15, 17. The phrase *the tabernacle of the testimony* appears in Acts vii, 44 (comp. Septuagint of Exod. xxix, 10, 11), and was so called because it contained as its most precious treasure the ark with the "two tables of testimony" (Exod. xxv, 16; xxxi, 18). *The temple of the tabernacle of the*

testimony is so called because it contained and represented all that
was symbolized in the ancient tabernacle of the wilderness made
after the pattern shown to Moses in the mount (Exod. xxv, 40).

6. *There came out from the temple the seven angels*—So in xiv,
17, the angel with the sharp sickle came out from the temple to
execute his work of judgment. *Clothed with a pure bright stone*—
This remarkable reading seems on the whole best attested, and is to
be explained by comparison with Ezek. xxviii, 13, where the glory
of the king of Tyre is set forth as a perfection of beauty, not the
least of which was his covering of every precious stone. If, however, one prefer the reading *linen* (λινον instead of λιϑον), he may
find analogy in xix, 8, and think of these angels as clothed in priestly
array (comp. Exod. xxviii, 39) and performing a work as holy as
the angel of the altar in viii, 3-5. *Golden girdle*—Like the Son of
man in i, 13. The "angels of his power" (2 Thess. i, 7) are in
apocalyptic symbolism appropriately arrayed in a glory like that of
the Lord himself.

7. *One of the four living creatures gave*—The last recorded act
of these living creatures was to call out the horses of the first four
seals (vi, 1-8). It was appropriate that one of these also give *unto the
seven angels* the bowls of wrath now about to be poured out into the
earth. The stability both of the temple and the throne of God in
the heaven calls for many judgments of wrath; and hence the fitness of this act of one of the living creatures before the throne, as well
as of the procession of the seven angels from the temple in heaven.

8. *The temple was filled with smoke*—This accords with Isaiah's
vision of Jehovah's glory in his temple (Isa. vi, 4). It was a sign
of the invisible presence of God in his temple, and the imagery is
from Exod. xl, 34, where it is written that "a cloud covered the
tent of meeting, and the glory of Jehovah filled the tabernacle." So
this cloud of *smoke* proceeded *from the glory of God and from his
power.* Comp. 1 Kings viii, 10, 11. *None was able to enter*—For
the same reason that "Moses was not able to enter into the tent of
meeting, because the cloud abode thereon, and the glory of Jehovah
filled the tabernacle" (Exod. xl, 35).

No student can fail to see that the bowls of wrath, as depicted in
chap. xvi, correspond in a striking manner to the seven trumpets in
the first part of the book. Thus the first bowl like the first trumpet
affects the earth, the second the sea, the third the rivers and fountains, the fourth the sun, the fifth the throne of the beast, the sixth
the Euphrates, and the seventh the air, as if to clear the way for the
kingdom of the heavens. But these correspondences are not exact
repetitions, or a *recapitulation*, as some of the older expositors main-

tained.   No apocalyptic repetitions of symbolism are exactly parallel.   The later imagery always adds somewhat to the earlier, so that
the repetition is of the nature of a new and additional illustration.
Thus it will be seen that the seven last plagues are more completely
destructive than the trumpet woes.   They are not limited to a third
part of earth and sea and sun, but effect a total ruin.   Nor are they
divisible into groups of four and three, as the seven seals and the
trumpets, nor is any room allowed for side pictures and episodes
between; but the sevenfold tragedy moves right on without interruption until a great voice from the throne says, "It is done."   The
climax is reached and the object of the plagues declared when it is
said that "Babylon the great was remembered in the sight of God,
to give unto her the cup of the wine of the fierceness of his wrath"
(verse 19).

The seven last plagues are therefore to be regarded as an intensified picture of consuming judgment.   The imagery moves entirely
in the realm of symbolism and metaphor, and "literal interpretation" is not to be thought of.   As the seven trumpets have obvious
suggestions of the trumpets that sounded the fall of Jericho, and
derive thence their general idea, so the seven plagues derive much
of their imagery from the plagues of Egypt, to which a number of
the allusions are apparent.   By means of these rapidly successive
pictures of consuming wrath the same penal judgments are exhibited as in the seven trumpets.   We are no more to seek different
historical events to answer to these plagues than we are to suppose
that Joseph's dream of the sun, moon, and stars depicted something
entirely different from his dream of the sheaves of the field that
bowed down to him.

1. First Plague (Grievous Sore).   xvi, 1, 2.

1   And I heard a great voice out of the temple, saying to the seven angels,
Go ye, and pour out the seven bowls of the wrath of God into the earth.
2   And the first went, and poured out his bowl into the earth; and it
became a noisome and grievous sore upon the men which had the mark
of the beast, and which worshiped his image.

1. *Voice out of the temple*—The temple is the one just mentioned
(xv, 8), and, as it was so filled with the cloud of the glory of God
that none was able to enter, the *voice* must be understood as from
God himself.   *Pour out the seven bowls*—On the figure of pouring
out of divine wrath compare Psalm lxix, 24; Jer. x, 25; Ezek. xiv,
19; Zeph. iii, 8.   The *bowls*, or *vials* (φιάλας), are conceived as containing ingredients of penal woe, like the *cups* of xiv, 10, and xvi,
19.   Comp. also Isa. li, 17, 22 ; Ezek. xxiii, 32, 33.

2. *The first* . . . *a noisome and grievous sore*—Although the first bowl was poured directly *into the earth*, so corresponding to the first trumpet (viii, 7), it resulted like the ashes and small dust of the land of Egypt in producing a malarious *sore*, or *ulcer* (ἕλκος), *upon the men who had the mark of the beast.* In this it was like the sixth Egyptian plague (Exod. ix, 8–10), which brought boils and blains on man and beast and tormented the magicians as well as all the other Egyptians. The first trumpet was followed by hail and fire, mingled with blood, which, like the seventh plague of Egypt (Exod. ix, 22–25), smote the land and herb and tree. But in both cases the sphere of operation was *the earth* as distinct from sea, and waters, and abyss, and heavens.

2. Second Plague (Sea Turned to Blood). xvi, 3.

3   And the second poured out his bowl into the sea; and it became blood as of a dead man; and every living soul died, *even* the things that were in the sea.

3. *The second* . . . *into the sea* . . . *blood*—This plague and the following one result in the same calamity as that of the first Egyptian plague (Exod. vii, 19–21), and is in noticeable analogy with the effects which followed the sounding of the second trumpet (viii, 8, 9). But the trumpet woe affected only a third part of the sea and its creatures; this affects the whole sea so that *every living thing* therein *died.* Another notable feature was that the sea *became blood as of a dead man;* that is, says Düsterdieck, "not a great pool of blood, as of many slain, but the horribleness of the fact is augmented in that the sea seems like the clotted and already putrefying blood of a dead man."

3. Third Plague (Rivers and Fountains Turned to Blood). xvi, 4–7.

4   And the third poured out his bowl into the rivers and the fountains
5 of the waters; and it became blood. And I heard the angel of the waters saying, Righteous art thou, who art and who wast, thou Holy One, be-
6 cause thou didst thus judge: for they poured out the blood of saints and prophets, and blood hast thou given them to drink: they are worthy.
7 And I heard the altar saying, Yea, O Lord God, the Almighty, true and righteous are thy judgments.

4. *The third* . . . *rivers and fountains* . . . *blood*—This third plague maintains the same distinction between the sea and the rivers and fountains as was observed in the third trumpet (viii, 10, 11); but while the result of the third trumpet was to make the waters bitter so as to cause the death of them that drank, the third plague, like the second, turns the waters into blood. This difference

was designed, as is seen from what is added in verses 5–7; for in all this blood " the angel of the waters " recognizes righteous retribution for " the blood of saints and prophets."

5. *The angel of the waters*—Everything in apocalyptic vision appears to have a superintending angel, but the angel is to be conceived as the ideal personification of that which he represents. As the angel of a church is but a figure for the church itself, so *the angel of the waters* is but a personification of the waters themselves. It is as if the very waters cried out in acknowledgment of the righteous judgments of God. *Righteous art thou*—Comp. Psalm xix, 9. As usual in such ascription of praise the language is made up of choice selections from current expressions of devout worship. Comp. xv, 3, 4. *Thus judge*—Or, *because thou didst judge these things*, namely, this judgment of blood, because it seemed so fitting a retribution for the shed blood of the saints.

6. *They poured out the blood of saints*—Who are *they* who *poured out* this *blood of saints and prophets?* The unmistakable answer is : They who are represented by the woman of xvii, 6, who was " drunken with the blood of the saints and with the blood of the witnesses of Jesus," that is, " Babylon the great " (xiv, 8 ; xvi, 19), whose judgment is symbolized in all these plagues. *And blood hast thou given them to drink*—Thus fulfilling the prophecy of Jesus against the murderous Jerusalem, " that killeth the prophets and stoneth them that are sent unto her " (Matt. xxiii, 34–37). *Worthy are they*—That is, richly deserving such bloody retribution, and therefore it was said that upon them should come " all the righteous blood shed upon the earth " (Matt. xxiii, 35).

7. *I heard the altar saying*—The same as if he had written *the angel of the altar*, for in this symbolism the one represents the other, as the " angel of the waters " in verse 5 above is the same as the waters themselves. Not only do the waters cry out in praise of God's *true and righteous judgments*, but the altar at which the prayers of all the saints were mediated (viii, 3–5) utters the same acknowledgment before *the Lord God, the Almighty.* Compare the voices from the altar in ix, 13, and xiv, 18.

4. Fourth Plague (Sun Smitten). xvi, 8, 9.

8 And the fourth poured out his bowl upon the sun; and it was given
9 unto it to scorch men with fire. And men were scorched with great heat: and they blasphemed the name of God who hath the power over these plagues; and they repented not to give him glory.

8, 9. *The fourth . . . upon the sun*—Compare the result of the fourth trumpet (viii, 12). In the trumpet woe other luminaries were smitten and the third part was darkened, but the object of this plague was *to scorch men with fire*. This was the direct opposite of the ninth plague of Egypt (Exod. x, 21–23), but both were adapted to produce horror and torment, and the result of the judgment was that the tormented ones *blasphemed the name of the God who has the power over these plagues*. Compare the corresponding impenitence of those " who were not killed with these plagues " (in ix, 20, 21).

5. Fifth Plague (Throne of Beast Smitten). xvi, 10, 11.

10   And the fifth poured out his bowl upon the throne of the beast; and his kingdom was darkened; and they gnawed their tongues for pain,
11 and they blasphemed the God of heaven because of their pains and their sores; and they repented not of their works.

10, 11. *The fifth . . . upon the throne of the beast*—Compare the fifth trumpet and the torments which followed it (ix, 1–11). The tormenting locusts, which came out of " the pit of the abyss," have a king over them whose name is Abaddon and Apollyon. This king of the abyss is no other than the great red dragon of xii, 3, " he that is called the Devil and Satan " (xii, 9), and he " gave his power and his throne and great authority " to the beast that came up out of the sea (xiii, 2). Now, by the pouring out of the fifth bowl of wrath, *his kingdom was darkened*, and the consequent torment was even worse than that caused by the ninth Egyptian plague, which brought thick darkness over all the realm of Pharaoh (Exod. x, 21–23). Being poured upon the throne of the beast, this bowl of wrath seems to have tormented Satan himself and his fallen angels, as well as all the subjects of his infernal power (comp. Matt. viii, 29 ; Mark i, 24 ; v, 7). *Gnawed their tongues for pain*—This refers to all those subjects of Satan and the beast, who had been given over to believe a lie and who persisted in their impiety in spite of all previous warnings and judgments. In pouring out the blood of saints (verse 6) they had inflicted many and great tortures ; now they are visited with demoniacal torment. *Blasphemed the God of heaven*— Like the victims of the preceding plague (verse 9). *Because of their pains and their sores*—Each additional plague seems to increase the *pains* and *sores* (comp. verse 2) of all that went before. For these seven last plagues, like those of Egypt, increase in power as they advance, and no respite is allowed between the successive strokes. *Repented not*—Their hearts, like the heart of Pharaoh, became hardened and impenitent beyond recall. They had persistently hardened themselves until they had become " vessels of wrath fitted unto destruction."

6. Sixth Plague (Euphrates-armies). xvi, 12–16.

12 And the sixth poured out his bowl upon the great river, the *river*
Euphrates; and the water thereof was dried up, that the way might be
13 made ready for the kings that *come* from the sunrising. And I saw *com-*
ing out of the mouth of the dragon, and out of the mouth of the beast,
and out of the mouth of the false prophet, three unclean spirits, as it
14 were frogs: for they are spirits of devils, working signs; which go forth
unto the kings of the whole world, to gather them together unto the war
15 of the great day of God, the Almighty. (Behold, I come as a thief.
Blessed is he that watcheth, and keepeth his garments, lest he walk
16 naked, and they see his shame.) And they gathered them together into
the place which is called in Hebrew Har-Magedon.

12. *The sixth . . . upon the great river Euphrates*—Compare the
sixth trumpet and the armies from the Euphrates which it summoned for destructive war (ix, 13–19). The symbolic significance
of *Euphrates* is the same here as in ix, 14, where see note. The
imagery is here changed to fit it to another point of view. Instead
of four angels bound with their immense hosts, and loosed at the
divine mandate, we have the *water* of the great river *dried up, that*
the way might be made ready for the kings that come from the sun-
rising. Thus the procedure of these *kings* is as truly under divine
control as the march of Israel across the Red Sea and across the
Jordan (comp. Josh. iv, 23, 24). As the Assyrian was employed as
the rod of Jehovah's anger to execute his wrath upon a hypocritical
nation (Isa. x, 5, 6), so are these *kings from the sunrising* to execute like judgment upon the same nation, now utterly apostate and
doomed to the fearful punishment here portrayed. Kings and armies that marched from the far East toward the West would naturally be spoken of as coming from the rising of the sun, and they
must needs cross the Euphrates on their western march. The analogy and self-consistency of the symbolism require that, though these
are in some sense "the kings of the whole world" (verse 14), they
march from that quarter whence the most terrible kings and armies
came that of old desolated the land of Israel.

13, 14. *Three unclean spirits as frogs*—As so many of these
plagues show a manifest reference to the plagues of Egypt we may,
perhaps, see in this mention of *frogs* an allusion to the second Egyptian plague (Exod. viii, 5, 6). But the allusion is at most only
incidental. The *unclean spirits* constitute a trinity by proceeding
from the *dragon, beast,* and *false prophet,* each being represented
by a spirit, and yet the three are "in demoniac concord joined."
The false prophet is but another name for the second beast out of
the land (xiii, 11), and so called on account of the deceitful signs

and teaching ascribed to him in xiii, 13, 14. The trinity of Satanic forces are said to be *spirits of demons, working signs, which go forth upon the kings of the whole world, to gather them together unto the war.* Here we see an obvious allusion to the vision of Micaiah, who saw "a lying spirit" go forth and speak through the mouth of the false prophets of Ahab, persuading the kings to undertake a disastrous war (1 Kings xxii, 19-23). For though this *war of the great day of God, the Almighty,* be a means of pouring out a bowl of wrath upon his enemies, his infinite wisdom and power can employ the agency of demons and military hosts to execute his punitive judgments. *The great day of God* is any day in which he executes the fearful judgments of his almighty power on wicked men and nations. Comp. Joel ii, 1, 11, 31; Isa. xiii, 6, 9; Z ph. i, 14-18; Amos v, 18. This was the great day of wrath foreshadowed by Jesus in the parable of the marriage of the king's son, when "the king was wroth, and sent forth his armies and destroyed those murderers, and burned up their city" (Matt. xxii, 7). These *kings* are the same as those more particularly described in xvii, 16, 17.

15. *Behold, I come as a thief*—Comp. iii, 3; Matt. xxiv, 42-44; Luke xii, 35-40; 1 Thess. v, 2. *Blessed is he that watcheth*—An echo of Matt. xxiv, 46, and Luke xii, 37. *Keepeth his garments*— As suggested in iii, 18, and vii, 9, 14; comp. xxii, 14. A failure to watch and keep their garments undefiled will expose to nakedness and shame at the coming of the Lord. This verse is a parenthesis, and of the nature of an admonition occasioned by the mention of "the great day of God the Almighty" (verse 14). Compare the exclamation in Jacob's prophecy immediately after the mention of Dan as a serpent, biting the heels of the horse and throwing the rider (Gen. xlix, 18).

16. *They gathered*—The subject of the verb is the same as that of *go forth* (ἐκπορεύεται) in verse 14, namely, the unclean spirits, who go forth *to gather* (συναγαγεῖν) the kings together. The subject is there a neuter plural (ἅ) construed with a verb in the singular, and hence the propriety of translating the συνήγαγεν of this verse *they gathered.* *The place which is called in Hebrew Har-Magedon*—The symbolical import of this name is to be sought in its Old Testament associations. Megiddo is first mentioned in Deborah's song as the place where the kings of Canaan came and fought (Judg. v, 19). It is again mentioned as the place where Josiah went up to war against the king of Egypt and was slain (2 Kings xxiii, 29), a calamity so great that all Judah and Jerusalem mourned and perpetuated the lamentation for a protracted period (2 Chron. xxxv, 24, 25; comp. Zech. xii, 11). It seems therefore to have been

associated in the songs of Israel with the great battlefield of nations, the plain of Esdraelon, and that battlefield came to be thought of in the later times as connected with sore lamentation in Jerusalem. But the prefixed *Har*, or *Ar*, as some read it, is more difficult to explain. It may mean *mountain* (הר) or *city* (עיר = ער) according as it is pronounced with a rough or smooth breathing. So we have the two readings *Har-Magedon* and *Ar-Magedon*. If we read *Har-Magedon*, that is, *Mount Magedon*, we have a noticeable contrast with " valley of Megiddo" in Zech. xii, 11, and " waters of Megiddo" in Judg. v, 19. If we read *Ar-Magedon*, that is, *city* of Magedon, we may, perhaps, see a designed pointing to the great city Babylon, against which these armies march to make war. May not both meanings be allowed, and be suggestive that the great war of these kings is to be fought in a mountain and about a city, the very city where the Lord was crucified (xi, 8)? That war which destroyed the murderers and burned up their city (Matt. xxii, 7) caused " a great mourning in Jerusalem" like that of Zech. xii, 11, and to it a reference may be seen in i, 7.

It is to be noted that no account is here given of the actual " war of the great day of God," for which these kings are gathered together. In the woe of the sixth trumpet " the third part of men was killed" (ix, 18), and we might naturally look for a complete slaughter to be wrought by these kings from the sunrising, actuated by the foul spirits of demons. But it appears to be the plan of the writer to hasten on so rapidly to the end of these plagues that he does not pause to record separately the execution wrought by the kings alone, but combines it with the catastrophe consummated by the pouring out of the seventh bowl of wrath, when earthquake and hailstones from heaven shake not only the great city, but the cities of the nations. The earth and the heavens thus are shown to unite with the forces of the kings, and the elements take part in this war against the enemies of God. The art of the apocalyptist is notably displayed in thus reserving what will make the seventh and last judgment stroke the more tremendous.

7. Seventh Plague (Babylon Doomed). xvi, 17–21.

17 And the seventh poured out his bowl upon the air; and there came forth a great voice out of the temple, from the throne, saying, It is done:
18 and there were lightnings, and voices, and thunders; and there was a great earthquake, such as was not since there were men upon the earth,
19 so great an earthquake, so mighty. And the great city was divided into three parts, and the cities of the nations fell: and Babylon the great was remembered in the sight of God, to give unto her the cup of the wine
20 of the fierceness of his wrath. And every island fled away, and the

21 mountains were not found. And great hail, *every stone* about the weight
of a talent, cometh down out of heaven upon men: and men blasphemed
God because of the plague of the hail; for the plague thereof is exceeding great.

17. *The seventh . . . upon the air*—The elemental home of the
lightnings and voices and thunders, and the source of the great hail
about to come down upon men. The sounding of the seventh
trumpet was followed by " great voices in the heaven " announcing
the beginning of the reign of Christ (xi, 15); but the sounding of
that trumpet was delayed by the revelation of many things which
must come to pass before the end. Here, on the contrary, the plan
of the writer is not yet to introduce the coming of the kingdom of
Christ, but to depict the signal judgments by which the end of the
pre-Messianic age was consummated. The two events were essentially simultaneous, but the apocalyptic symbolism first portrays the
fall of Babylon the great and shows how much was represented and
implied in God's " giving unto her the cup of the wine of the fierceness of his wrath." Hence the seventh plague displays the fearful
end of these judgments, and it is not until after the writer has amply
described the fall of the bloody harlot and after the multitudes in
heaven have sung their song of hallelujah over her righteous retribution that the " King of kings and Lord of lords " moves forth to
his world-wide conquests and the new Jerusalem descends from
heaven to earth. *Great voice out of the temple from the throne*—
The same voice which had commanded the seven angels to pour out
the bowls of wrath (comp. verse 1 above). *It is done*—Γέγονεν.
Not the same as the ἐτελέσθη (*it is finished*) of x, 7, but referring
more particularly to the completion of the seven plagues. This
picture of sevenfold judgment is now done.

18. *Lightnings . . . voices . . . thunders . . . earthquake*—Comp.
xi, 19. The *earthquake* is here emphasized as something exceptional and unparalleled. All these movements of the elements are
symbolic of a great revolution in the state of the world, and here,
as in xi, 19, they imply that the revelations of this book are not yet
all given. Other and great apocalypses are to follow, and the book
itself, with its golden outlook into the future, is not to close with
earthquakes and thunders and lightnings.

19. *The great city was divided into three parts*—This city is here,
as elsewhere in the book, identical with *Babylon the great*. Already
an apocalyptic angel has announced its fall (xiv, 8), but the scheme
of the book contemplates repeated pictures of its overthrow, and the
purpose of the repetitions is the same as that of Pharaoh's doubled
dream (Gen. xli, 32). The division *into three parts* is to be com-

pared with the fall of the tenth part in xi, 13, and shows a more
effectual ruin. The triple division of Ezekiel's symbolical act (Ezek.
v, 2–12) seems to have been in the writer's mind, for that was a
prophecy against Jerusalem, whom God " set in the midst of the
nations." For, according to the prophet's oracle, " she hath changed
my judgments into wickedness more than the nations that are round
about her. . . . Therefore the fathers shall eat the sons in the midst
of thee, and the sons shall eat their fathers ; and I will execute judgments unto thee. . . . A third part of thee shall die with pestilence,
and with famine shall they be consumed in the midst of thee : and
a third part shall fall by the sword round about thee; and I will
scatter a third part unto all the winds, and I will draw out a sword
after them." Thus, in the fullness of time, was this once favored
city, having made herself an abominable *Babylon, remembered in
the sight of God to give unto her the cup of the wine of the fierceness of his wrath.* Compare the language of xviii, 5, and Psalm
ix, 12. On the figures of cup of wrath and wine of wrath see notes
on xiv, 8, 10, and xvi, 1. All these figures set forth the doctrine of
unfailing righteous retribution.

20. *Every island fled . . . mountains were not found* —Apocalyptic metaphors like those of vi, 14, designed to produce an impression of the awful force and fierceness of the judgment.

21. *Great hail about the weight of a talent*—Th incredibly great
size of these hailstones is in keeping with the metaphorical picture
of verse 20. The Jewish talent weighed more than a hundred
pounds troy, so that every hailstone is to be conceived as a huge
bowlder as heavy as a man could well lift. Compare the Egyptian
plague of hail (Exod. ix, 23–26). In the statement that this *great
hail cometh down out of heaven upon men* we may see a sign of
" the war of the great day of God, the Almighty " (verse 14 above).
There is an allusion here to the war at Gibeon, where Jehovah discomfited the enemies of his people, and " slew them with a great
slaughter . . . and cast down great stones from heaven upon them "
(Josh. x, 10, 11). Similarly the stars of heaven fought against
Sisera and his host (Judg. iv, 15; v, 20). Comp. also Psalm xviii,
13, 14; Isa. xxviii, 2; xxx, 30. It may be worthy of a passing notice that Josephus (*Wars,* vi, 3) speaks of stones of a talent weight
hurled by the Romans on the men of Jerusalem. But to find in
such a fact the fulfillment of our prophecy would be to belittle the
sublime apocalyptic picture. The mind that is taken captive by
such analogies, and sees in them striking confirmations of prophecy,
fails to appreciate the spirit of prophecy and misconceives both its
purpose and method. *Men blasphemed*—As they did under the

fourth and fifth plagues (verses 9 and 11). This statement in connection with the last plague sets in the strongest possible light the
unchangeable obduracy of the people's hearts, upon whom these
bowls of plagues were poured.

V. BABYLON THE GREAT HARLOT. XVII–XIX, 10.

Although the seven angels have poured out the bowls of wrath
they have not yet finished their mission in this book. For the purpose of a fuller disclosure of "Babylon the great" one of these
seven angels carries John away in the wilderness and shows him a
vision of the great harlot, whose destruction must be accomplished
before the Messianic King can fully introduce his kingdom and
bring the new Jerusalem to the earth. For Babylon the Harlot and
Jerusalem the Bride are the two great figures in the concluding
portion of the Apocalypse. The one must be overthrown before
the other can appear in her full glory. And as in the sequel one of
these same seven angels carries John away to a mountain and shows
him the Bride, the wife of the Lamb (xxi, 9), so it serves the scheme
of the whole revelation that one of these angels first shows the
character and judgment of "Babylon the great, the mother of the
harlots and of the abominations of the earth."

1. VISION OF THE HARLOT. XVII, 1-6.

1 And there came one of the seven angels that had the seven bowls, and
   spake with me, saying, Come hither, I will show thee the judgment of
2 the great harlot that sitteth upon many waters; with whom the kings of
   the earth committed fornication, and they that dwell in the earth were
3 made drunken with the wine of her fornication. And he carried me
   away in the Spirit into a wilderness: and I saw a woman sitting upon a
   scarlet-colored beast, full of names of blasphemy, having seven heads
4 and ten horns. And the woman was arrayed in purple and scarlet, and
   decked with gold and precious stone and pearls, having in her hand a
   golden cup full of abominations, even the unclean things of her fornica-
5 tion, and upon her forehead a name written, MYSTERY, BABYLON THE
   GREAT, THE MOTHER OF THE HARLOTS AND OF THE ABOMINATIONS OF
6 THE EARTH. And I saw the woman drunken with the blood of the
   saints, and with the blood of the witnesses of Jesus. And when I saw her,
   I wondered with a great wonder.

1. *One of the seven angels*—It is fitting that one of these minis-
ters of the judgments already symbolized *show the judgment of the
great harlot.* The foregoing notes have already pointed out that
"Babylon the great" is no other than the apostate "Judah and
Jerusalem," more execrable now than when Isaiah cried over her,
"How is the faithful city become a harlot!" The entire arraign-

ment of the "sinful nation, a people laden with iniquity," found in
the first chapter of Isaiah, might have been repeated against Jerusalem at the time this Apocalypse was written, and, in fact, the
twenty-third chapter of Matthew is virtually such an arraignment by
the Lord himself. A *harlot* in the prophetical sense is one who has
broken the vows and bonds of the marriage covenant by any infidelity to the obligations of such union. The idolatries of the older
Jerusalem were one of her most infamous offenses against Jehovah,
but extortion, and falsehood, and violation of many laws and ordinances of divine authority were also charged against her. But
while idolatry in the strict sense was not the crying sin of the Jewish people in the time of Christ and his apostles, they were guilty
of so many violations of the true spirit of God's law (comp. Acts
vii, 53) that the charge of infidelity to their covenanted bonds could
be most justly made against them. But their most flagrant crime
was the open rejection of their Lord, who "came unto his own, and
they who were his own received him not" (John i, 11). They not
only cast him off by such refusal, but were his "betrayers and murderers" (Acts vii, 52). The crime of Clytemnestra in the betrayal
and murder of her husband was not so enormous as that of the
people who "denied the holy and righteous one, and killed the
Prince of life," preferring a murderer to him (Acts iii, 14, 15), and
crying in blasphemous defiance, "His blood be on us, and on our
children" (Matt. xxvii, 25). The Jerusalem and Judah which thus
rejected the Christ of God were therefore guilty of the most criminal apostasy, and are appropriately called *the great harlot.* The
shameful repudiation of her Lord was but the filling up of a long
history of apostasy from the holy law, which was recognized as having been given by the ministry of angels. *That sitteth upon many
waters*—This is added to maintain the harmony of the figure with
ancient Babylon, which is described by Jeremiah as "dwelling
upon many waters" (Jer. li, 13). But as these waters, according
to verse 15, symbolize "peoples and multitudes and nations and
tongues," so this harlot had her commerce with all the nations of
the Roman empire and derived her revenues from them. She would
not even hesitate for the sake of gain to make Jehovah's temple "a
house of merchandise" (John ii, 16).

2. *Kings committed fornication*—The same kings as those described in verse 12, but the reference is here without specific limitation. The language of this verse is in substance from Isa. xxiii, 17,
and has allusion to a widespread commerce resembling that of ancient Tyre. Such commercial and political intercourse with heathen
lands and rulers was inconsistent with the spirit of Mosaism (comp.

Lev. xviii, 2; xx, 23; Exod. xxxiv, 12), and is here figuratively called *fornication*. Compare also Jer. li, 7, for the figure of being *drunken with the wine of her fornication*. Much intercourse with foreign peoples, and ambition to be like them in power and glory, always produced among the Jewish people an infatuation like that of drunkenness, and was the fruitful cause of their backslidings and calamities.

3. *A woman sitting upon a scarlet-colored beast*—Observe that the words *sitting upon* are the same as, in verse 1, are followed by "many waters." Not only does this harlot depend upon "peoples and multitudes and nations and tongues" for revenue and support, but also and most notably upon the *beast having seven heads and ten horns*, as described in xiii, 1; for his heads bore many *names of blasphemy*, and he received "his power and his throne and great authority" from the "great red dragon" of xii, 3. Hence he may well be here called *a scarlet-colored beast*, and *full of names of blasphemy*. The Jewish people, at the time this Apocalypse was written, had been dependent for their national existence a hundred years on Rome.

4. *Arrayed in purple and scarlet*—Notably the attire of a harlot. Contrast the array of the woman of xii, 1. *Gilded with gold . . . stone . . . pearls* — The corresponding extravagance of outward ornamentation befitting a harlot. *Golden cup full of abominations* —Comp. Jer. li, 7. This allusion keeps up and complements the figure of uncleanness in verse 2.

5. *A name written, a mystery*—That is, a name that involved mystical significance symbolic of the woman's character. *Mother of harlots*—Allusion to Hosea's symbolical portraiture of the apostate Israel of his day. Comp. Hosea i, 2; ii, 1-5. *Abominations of the land*—All the evils of the land of Israel were the offspring of the people's apostasy from the Lord that bought them. The Lord Jesus came to the house of Israel and the men of Judah, and, as in the times of Isaiah, "looked for judgment, but behold oppression; for righteousness, but behold a cry" (Isa. v, 7).

6. *Drunken with the blood of saints*—No clearer or more conclusive comment on these words could be asked than is furnished in the language of Jesus in Matt. xxiii, 29-39; Luke xiii, 33-35. *Witnesses of Jesus*—To be understood as a direct reference to the μάρτυρες in xi, 3. For these *witnesses* are no other than those slain by "the beast that cometh up out of the abyss," and whose dead bodies were exposed "in the street of the great city . . . where also their Lord was crucified" (xi, 7, 8). *I wondered with a great wonder*—Because he did not understand the mystery of the

vision, and the mystery seemed so very great. In this he was like Daniel, who confesses his astonishment in Dan. viii, 27.

2. THE MYSTERY EXPLAINED. XVII, 7–18.

7 And the angel said unto me, Wherefore didst thou wonder? I will tell thee the mystery of the woman, and of the beast that carrieth her,
8 which hath the seven heads and the ten horns. The beast that thou sawest was, and is not; and is about to come up out of the abyss, and to go into perdition. And they that dwell on the earth shall wonder, *they* whose name hath not been written in the book of life from the foundation of the world, when they behold the beast, how that he was, and is
9 not, and shall come. Here is the mind which hath wisdom. The seven
10 heads are seven mountains, on which the woman sitteth: and there are seven kings; the five are fallen, the one is, the other is not yet come;
11 and when he cometh, he must continue a little while. And the beast that was, and is not, is himself also an eighth, and is of the seven;
12 and he goeth into perdition. And the ten horns that thou sawest are ten kings, which have received no kingdom as yet; but they receive author-
13 ity as kings, with the beast, for one hour. These have one mind, and
14 they give their power and authority unto the beast. These shall war against the Lamb, and the Lamb shall overcome them, for he is Lord of lords, and King of kings; and they *also shall overcome* that are with him,
15 called and chosen and faithful. And he saith unto me, The waters which thou sawest, where the harlot sitteth, are peoples, and multitudes, and
16 nations, and tongues. And the ten horns which thou sawest, and the beast, these shall hate the harlot, and shall make her desolate and naked,
17 and shall eat her flesh, and shall burn her utterly with fire. For God did put in their hearts to do his mind, and to come to one mind, and to give their kingdom unto the beast, until the words of God should be accom-
18 plished. And the woman whom thou sawest is the great city, which reigneth over the kings of the land.

7. *I will tell thee*—All this is modeled much after the manner of Dan. viii, 15–19. It is designed to introduce an angel interpreter to make known the mystery.

8. *The beast was, and is not*—The interpretation of the angel is itself cast in the form of an enigma, and the demand for *wisdom* to comprehend it (see next verse) is like that prefixed to the riddle of xiii, 18, concerning the number of the beast. In his explanation the angel seems to point our attention particularly to the spirit which actuated the dragon, the beast from the sea, and the false prophet alike; and so what is here affirmed of the beast has a special reference to the different and successive manifestations of Satan himself. He has his hour, when he wields the power of darkness (comp. Luke xxii, 53), now in one form, now in another. He was shown in the previous visions to have been in heaven (xii, 3); but being cast out

thence he seemed to disappear for a time (xii, 17), but anon incarnated himself in the beast that came up out of the sea (xiii, 1, 2), and yet again in the beast that came up out of the land, in whom he acted as the prophet of lies (xiii, 13–15). Hence we understand by the beast that *was and is not* an enigmatical portraiture of the great red dragon of xii, 3. He is the king of the abyss in ix, 11, and the beast that killed the witnesses in xi, 7. He appears for a time in the person of some great persecutor, or in the form of some huge iniquity, but is after a while cast out. Then he again finds some other organ for his operations and enters it with all the malice of the unclean spirit who wandered through dry places, seeking rest and finding none until he discovered his old house, empty, swept, and garnished as if to invite his return (Matt. xii, 44). So we are told this same beast *is about to come up out of the abyss*, and we can therefore but believe that he is in some sense identical with the angel of the abyss, whose name is Abaddon and Apollyon (ix, 11), that is, "the old serpent, he that is called the Devil and Satan, the deceiver of the whole world" (xii, 9). His destiny is, as the sequel of the book will show, *to go into perdition ;* for the beast and the false prophet and the devil himself are all ultimately to be " cast into the lake of fire and brimstone" (xx, 10). Such also was the fate of the terrible beast of Daniel's vision (Dan. vii, 11). *They that dwell on the earth shall wonder*—As they did in the case of the beast whose deathstroke was healed (comp. xiii, 3–5). The power and signs and lying wonders of Satan, however manifested, have never failed to attract wondering crowds and to command the admiration of such as have *not been written in the book of life.* For the ungodly world will 'love its own and bestow an idolatrous worship on that which panders to its lust of the flesh, and lust of the eye, and pride of life. The Roman world-power, filled with Satanic pride, possessed much to be thus admired, and the apocalyptist saw in this perpetual command of idolatrous admiration the power of the infernal spirit, who *was, and is not, and shall come.* Disappearing with one imperial monster, who acts the part of a persecutor of the saints, he by and by reappears in another, but always displays the same Satanic spirit and power.

9. *Here is the mind that hath wisdom*—An admonition that he is speaking in enigmas and furnishing occasion and subject-matter on which the wise mind may exercise its skill. Comp. xiii, 18. *The seven heads are seven mountains, on which the woman sitteth*—This statement has led most interpreters to believe that the *woman* must be Rome, the great city of the Tiber, because that city is said to have been builded on the seven hills, known as the Palatine,

Capitoline, Quirinal, Viminal, Æsquiline, Cœlian, and Aventine. But such a specific designation of Rome is not in harmony with the enigmatical character of the angel's interpretation. Glasgow well remarks : " The mountains are, like other terms, to be understood symbolically. If the woman is not literal why should the mountains be so thought ? And to call the woman a literal city, built on seven hills, is equally gratuitous, whether a Protestant says it of Rome or a Romanist of Constantinople." And, we may add, if literal mountains are to be understood, we may find them at Jerusalem as well as at Rome. There were Zion, Moriah, Acra, Bezetha, Millo, Ophel, and the rocky eminence fifty cubits in height (see Josephus, *Wars*, v, 5, 8) on which the tower of Antonia was erected. But these seven heads of the beast no more represent literal mountains than do the seven heads of the dragon in xii, 3. And unless we insist on understanding the *waters* of verses 1 and 15 and the *scarlet-colored beast* of verse 3 as literal waters and a literal beast we cannot consistently maintain that the mountains must be understood literally. For the woman sitteth on many waters, on a beast, and on seven mountains. Rather do mountains symbolize seats of power and political and governmental resources. Compare note on xiii, 3. This great Babylon had her seats of power and resources of various kinds and in various places, as well as did the beast on which she was seated, so that for dependence and support, as far as she needed, the heads of the beast were her heads. She rested on them.

10. *And there are seven kings*—Not *they are seven kings*, as if referring to the mountains, for such a rendering would work confusion in the whole picture. Kings are represented by the horns of a beast (see verse 12, below), not by its heads. Hence we should punctuate and read the beginning of this verse as a new and independent statement. The *seven kings* here referred to are generally understood as the first seven Cæsars, and this we believe to be the true interpretation. *Five* of these *fell* and passed away before John wrote. These were (1) Julius Cæsar, (2) Augustus, (3) Tiberius, (4) Caligula, (5) Claudius. *The one* then reigning was Nero, the sixth of the list, and *the other*, the seventh, had *not yet come* when this book was written, and nothing is said about him, except that *when he cometh* he, like all the rest, *must continue a little while*. So we are not concerned to know more about him, and the controversies of exegetes over what emperors were the real successors of Nero is irrelevant and of no value in the true interpretation of John's Apocalypse. All that it concerns us here to know is that the succession would go on, and not to a seventh only, but also "an eighth," as the next verse declares.

11. *The beast that was, and is not*—The same as in verse 8 above.
The king of the abyss (ix, 11), who comes up out of the abyss to
make war on the witnesses of Jesus (xi, 7), and gives his throne
and power (xiii, 2) to every agent and system of organized force
that will advance his foul purposes, *is himself also an eighth*, as he
is also the inspiring genius *of the seven*. He is the same red dragon,
the same old serpent and deceiver of the whole world, that appears
in one imperial persecutor after another. But his destiny is decreed, as we have seen in verse 8, for *he goeth into perdition*, and
will drag thither all his subjects and satellites along with him. So
while *the beast* is the great Roman world-power as symbolized in
chap. xiii, 1–8, the angel interpreter of this vision of the great harlot
points us especially to the Satanic spirit which gave the beast its
great authority (xiii, 2).

The superstitious fiction of *Nero redivivus*, found in many early
writers, has been brought forward by some interpreters to explain
"the beast that was, and is not, and shall come." Nero is held to be
the wounded head of xiii, 3, and the healing of the stroke is supposed to be the reappearance of that monster after his death. The
rumor was to the effect that Nero was not dead, but had only disappeared from Rome, and was for the time dwelling among the Parthians, whence he would return again to the empire of the West.
But this theory not only requires us to understand that Nero had
already disappeared when this book was written, but it also involves
the utterly improbable, not to say preposterous, supposition that
the writer of this sublime Apocalypse gave so conspicuous a place
in his work to a fabulous and superstitious rumor. Düsterdieck
well remarks : "The writer of the Apocalypse in no way betrays
such impurity and limitation of faith and Christian culture that
without injustice a superstition dare be ascribed to him which the
Roman authors already had derided" (*Com.* on xiii, 3). It is far
more likely that the rumor itself arose from an early misapprehension of this passage in John's prophecy. It could not have acquired
its current form in Nero's time, when this Apocalypse was written;
and therefore with him it would have been an unthinkable anach-
ronism. But the notion may have started from an early misunderstanding of the beast which was, and is not, and yet shall come
again as an eighth, and be *also of the seven*. Once started, the fear
of Nero and the superstition of the times might have easily spread
it through many parts of the empire; and many of the early writers
affirm that it originated with an oracle of the soothsayers.

12. *The ten horns . . . are ten kings*—The number ten is to be
taken here as elsewhere symbolically, and we need not cast about

for ten particular persons to satisfy the import of the symbol. It is the *totality* of those allied or subject kings who aided Rome in her wars both on Judaism and Christianity. *Have received as yet no kingdom*—They possessed no independent royalty, and as yet exercise no kingly dominion. There seems to be here an appropriation of Daniel's language concerning the "ten kings that shall arise" (Dan. vii, 24). *They receive authority as kings one hour with the beast*—All which goes to show that these kings are not independent sovereigns, but exercise only a temporary authority, after the style of kings, in conjunction *with the beast.* Apart from the beast they held no power.

13. *These have one mind*—Beast and kings all have one and the same judgment, feeling, and purpose (γνώμην) in the war against the Lamb (verse 14), and also in the destruction of the harlot (verse 16). So, in giving *their power and authority unto the beast,* these kings are not performing an altogether compulsory service. They are in full sympathy with the operations of the beast, for they are all alike inspired by the angel of the abyss, and are in fact so many incarnations of his power. The ten horns, therefore, of this vision appear to represent the same power that was symbolized by the beast out of the land in xiii, 11–17 ; but they may include also the heads of all the allied tribes and nations which were associated with Rome in her acts of persecution, and especially such as hated the harlot and helped to destroy her (verse 16).

14. *These shall war against the Lamb*—Even as the dragon and his angels warred against Michael and his angels in xii, 7. For having lost in that war the dragon was wroth and went away to war with the rest of the woman's seed (xii, 17), and this war against the Lamb and *those who are with him, called and chosen and faithful,* is one phase of that war on the seed of the woman. But in their war on the Lamb and his followers *the Lamb shall overcome them* as triumphantly as Michael prevailed in the war of xii, 7–9, *for he is Lord of lords and King of kings,* as will be more fully brought out in chaps. xix and xx, after the destruction of the harlot has been fully shown. The *chosen and faithful* associates of the Lamb shall also overcome, as was in xii, 11, announced by a great voice in heaven. Here as there we understand that they overcome " because of the blood of the Lamb and because of the word of their testimony." "They conquer though they die," but not so the harlot, as the sequel shows.

15. *The waters*—See verse 1. *Peoples . . . multitudes . . . nations . . . tongues*—Fourfold designation, suggestive of the many and extensive affiliations of Jerusalem with the mixed populations

of the Roman empire. The Jewish people had manifold connection with the provinces of the empire, as is seen in the fact that the devout from all these parts were wont to come up to Jerusalem to the great feasts (Acts ii, 5-10).

16. *These shall hate the harlot*—The bitterness of neighboring tribes and nations toward Jerusalem is noticed by Josephus (*Wars*, ii, chap. xviii), and their union with the armies of the empire in the final war against the hated city was an acceptable service. In this they displayed one mind with the beast (verse 13). The destruction of *the harlot* is set forth under the fourfold picture of making her *desolate and naked, eating her flesh* and *burning* her utterly *with fire.* This is a vivid apocalyptic portraiture of the terrible judgments inflicted on Jerusalem by the Roman armies.

17. *God put it into their hearts to do his mind*—That is, as verse 13 above has already implied, God put it into the hearts of the ten kings to do the mind and will (γνώμην) of the beast. So they readily *give their kingdom,* that is, contribute whatever their several dominions afford of a nature to assist *the beast* in executing on the harlot the judgments which had been foretold. *Until the words of God should be accomplished*—Such words as were uttered by the Son of God in Matt. xxiii, 35, 36.

18. *The woman . . . is the great city*—Here, at the conclusion of the vision and its explanation, we have the most specific and formal definition of the import of the harlot. The term *great city* has already been applied to the place called in mystic language Sodom and Egypt, where the Lord of the two witnesses was crucified (xi, 8). That city is allowed by the best exegetes to be Jerusalem, and Josephus calls Jerusalem in one passage (*Wars*, vii, 8, 7) "that great city." But it has generally been supposed that the concluding words, commonly translated *which reigneth over the kings of the earth,* cannot be appropriately applied to Jerusalem. Hence this verse, as well as the "seven mountains" of verse 9, are held by many to be conclusive that the *great city* intended must be Rome. But we believe that opinion to be erroneous and the following reasons to be conclusive of the soundness of the exposition given in these pages:

1. If our position is correct that the latter half of the Apocalypse (chaps. xii–xxii) is in the main a repetition of the first half (chaps. i–xi) under different symbols, "the great city" of this verse is presumably the same as that of xi, 8. It comports with the variety of symbols employed that other symbolical names also be introduced; hence "Babylon the great," instead of "Sodom and Egypt."

2. The latter part of the verse (18) should be translated *which*

has dominion over the kings of the land. The meaning is, not that this city reigns over all the kings and kingdoms of the habitable world, but that it is the capital city of the land in which the great catastrophe of this book centers. "The kings of the land" is a phrase to be interpreted in the light of Acts iv, 26, 27, where it is evident that in the early Church "Herod and Pontius Pilate, with the Gentiles and the peoples of Israel," were the sort of kings and rulers of the earth contemplated in the second Psalm, there quoted. Such kings are represented by Josephus as subject "to the royal city Jerusalem," which, says he, "was supreme and presided over all the neighboring country as the head does over the body" (*Wars*, iii, 3, 5); and he goes on to designate ten "inferior cities," which were in the land of Judea. In another place he speaks of Jerusalem in the identical language of our writer, and calls it "that great city" (*Wars*, vii, 8, 7).

3. If the beast is the Roman empire, the harlot must be something else than the city of Rome. For it cannot be said that the emperors or the chief princes of the empire hated Rome or ever sought to destroy that great city. For the empire to destroy its own capital is incongruous in thought and untrue in fact.

4. It contravenes the analogy of biblical symbolism and usage to call pagan Rome a harlot. The imagery, according to this scripture, implies that she had been in covenant relations with God, but this is totally untrue of any heathen city. The imagery of this whole section of the Apocalypse is appropriated from Ezek. xvi, xxii, and xxiii, where the apostate people of Judah and Jerusalem are depicted. But they were a people unto whom Jehovah sware and entered into covenant (Ezek. xvi, 8), and their sins were accordingly like those of "a woman that breaketh wedlock" (Ezek. xvi, 38). But such imagery is wholly inapplicable to Rome. How unsuitable it would have been for Ezekiel to have employed the imagery of those chapters in reference to Assyria, or Babylon, or Egypt!

5. Many expositors have held that this great harlot is the Church of Rome, depicted as an apostate Church. In that case the imagery employed would not be inconsistent, and the political affiliations and claims of the Roman papacy and the bloody persecutions of which that Church has been guilty correspond well with the picture here drawn of "Babylon the great." But it is not true that the Roman empire or any kings or powers of earth have hated and destroyed that Church in any such sense as the statements of verse 16 require.

6. Finally, we may well discard any views which carry our thoughts far away from that great metropolis, the fall of which was

the sign of the end of the old dispensation and the complete introduction of Christianity. Rome is but incidentally connected with
this, and figures only as one of the agents operating with other
forces at the time. This revelation is not particularly concerned
with the fall of the Roman empire as such, but only as it rises and
passes from view as an instrument used by the Almighty to accomplish what his own wisdom and counsel determined to have done. Its
beastliness as symbolized in vision, together with all that works
abomination and makes a lie, is destined to go into perdition ; but
this overthrow of "the mother of harlots and of the abominations
of the land" is the fulfillment of what Jesus so emphatically foretold in Matt. xxiii and xxiv, and is in perfect harmony with the
scope of the Apocalypse.

The eighteenth chapter introduces no new subject, but is a continuous part of the apocalyptic portraiture of the fall of the harlot-
city. Having described in prophetic form the judgment of the
great harlot, and given an interpretation of the "mystery," the
writer aims to intensify the vividness of his picture by what follows
as far as xix, 8. The dirges over this fall of Babylon, and the exul-
tations of the holy heavens over such righteous judgment of God,
are largely of the nature of rhetorical embellishment. It is therefore unnecessary to enlarge on these symbolic pictures. They are
a combination of the imagery and language which the author has
carefully selected from the Old Testament. No better commentary
can be furnished the student than a patient study for himself of the
passages (referred to in the notes which follow) from which the
imagery is drawn.

3. ANGELIC PROCLAMATION. XVIII, 1–3.

1   After these things I saw another angel coming down out of heaven,
    having great authority; and the earth was lightened with his glory.
2   And he cried with a mighty voice, saying, Fallen, fallen is Babylon the
    great, and is become a habitation of devils, and a hold of every unclean
3   spirit, and a hold of every unclean and hateful bird. For by the wine
    of the wrath of her fornication all the nations are fallen; and the kings
    of the earth committed fornication with her, and the merchants of the
    earth waxed rich by the power of her wantonness.

1. *Another angel*—That is, one different from the angel mentioned in xvii, 1, 7, 15. *Having great authority*—No special significance is to be seen in this statement, or in the fact that *the earth
was lightened with his glory*, other than that his authority and glory
were in keeping with the great proclamation he was commissioned
to make "with a mighty voice." Compare the announcement of
the "strong angel" of v, 2.

2. *Fallen, fallen is Babylon*—Already in xiv, 8, has this word of doom been sounded forth, and it is now repeated with even greater impressiveness. The language is from Isa. xxi, 9, and Jer. li, 7, 8. *Devils . . . spirit . . . bird*—The imagery is traceable to Isa. xiii, 21; Jer. ix, 11; l, 39; li, 37, and indicates a scene of utter desolation. How Jerusalem became infested with demoniacal exhibitions of wickedness, even before her fall, has been shown in notes on the woe of the fifth trumpet (ix, 1–11).

3. *Wine of the wrath of her fornication*—See note on this expression in xiv, 8, and for the imagery compare Jer. xxv, 27; li, 7.

4. Another Voice from Heaven. xviii, 4-8.

4 And I heard another voice from heaven, saying, Come forth, my people, out of her, that ye have no fellowship with her sins, and that ye
5 receive not of her plagues: for her sins have reached even unto heaven,
6 and God hath remembered her iniquities. Render unto her even as she rendered, and double *unto her* the double according to her works: in the
7 cup which she mingled, mingle unto her double. How much soever she glorified herself, and waxed wanton, so much give her of torment and mourning: for she saith in her heart, I sit a queen, and am no widow,
8 and shall in no wise see mourning. Therefore in one day shall her plagues come, death, and mourning, and famine; and she shall be utterly burned with fire; for strong is the Lord God who judged her.

4. *Come forth, my people*—Comp. Isa. xlviii, 20; lii, 11; Jer. l, 8; li, 6, 9, 45. There was something analogous to this in Christ's command for the disciples to flee from Jerusalem when they should see the signs of her impending ruin (Matt. xxiv, 16).

5. *Her sins have reached even unto heaven*—So in substance Jeremiah said of Babylon (Jer. li, 9).

6. *Render unto her even as she rendered*—Comp. Jer. l, 15, 29; Psalm cxxxvii, 8. *The cup*—See on xiv, 10. *Double*—Comp. Isa. xl, 2; Jer. xvi, 18; xvii, 18.

7. *I sit a queen*—Comp. Isa. xlvii, 5, 7, 8.

8. *In one day*—That is, suddenly. So in Isa. xlvii, 9: "These two things shall come to thee in a moment in one day, the loss of children, and widowhood: they shall come upon thee in their perfection for the multitude of thy sorceries, the great abundance of thine enchantments." *Strong is the Lord God*—Comp. Jer. l, 34: "Their avenger is strong; Jehovah of hosts his name."

5. Dirges and Rejoicing over her Fall. xviii, 9-20.

9 And the kings of the earth, who committed fornication and lived wantonly with her, shall weep and wail over her, when they look upon the

10 smoke of her burning, standing afar off for the fear of her torment, saying, Woe, woe, the great city, Babylon, the strong city! for in one hour
11 is thy judgment come. And the merchants of the earth weep and mourn
12 over her, for no man buyeth their merchandise any more; merchandise
of gold, and silver, and precious stone, and pearls, and fine linen, and
purple, and silk, and scarlet; and all thyine wood, and every vessel of
ivory, and every vessel made of most precious wood, and of brass, and
13 iron, and marble; and cinnamon, and spice, and incense, and ointment,
and frankincense, and wine, and oil, and fine flour, and wheat, and cattle, and sheep; and *merchandise* of horses and chariots and slaves; and
14 souls of men. And the fruits which thy soul lusted after are gone from
thee, and all things that were dainty and sumptuous are perished from
15 thee, and *men* shall find them no more at all. The merchants of these
things, who were made rich by her, shall stand afar off for the fear of
16 her torment, weeping and mourning; saying, Woe, woe, the great city,
she that was arrayed in fine linen and purple and scarlet, and decked
17 with gold and precious stone and pearl! for in one hour so great riches
is made desolate. And every shipmaster, and every one that saileth any
whither, and mariners, and as many as gain their living by sea, stood
18 afar off, and cried out as they looked upon the smoke of her burning,
19 saying, What *city* is like the great city ? And they cast dust on their
heads, and cried, weeping and mourning, saying, Woe, woe, the great
city, wherein were made rich all that had their ships in the sea by reason
20 of her costliness! for in one hour is she made desolate. Rejoice over
her, thou heaven, and ye saints, and ye apostles, and ye prophets; for
God hath judged your judgment on her.

9. *Kings of the earth*—The entire picture of the wailing of kings,
merchants, shipmasters, and sailors (verses 9-19) is taken from
Ezekiel's prophecy of the fall of Tyre (Ezek. xxvi, xxvii). But it
is not thence to be urged that this great city of the Apocalypse
must needs be as celebrated for commercial enterprise as ancient
Tyre. The imagery of the older prophet is appropriated in order
to give the utmost sublimity and completeness to the picture of her
fall. *Look upon the smoke of her burning*—This imagery has its
origin in such passages as Gen. xix, 28, and Isa. lxvi, 24.

11. *The merchants. . . weep and mourn*—Comp. Ezek. xxvi, 16,
17; xxvii, 24, 36.

12, 13. *Merchandise of gold. . . purple. . . ivory. . . spice*—This
specification of various kinds of articles of commerce is in imitation
of Ezek. xxvii, 12-22.

17. *Shipmaster. . . sailors*—Comp. Ezek. xxvii, 26-33.

20. *Rejoice over her, heaven*—This sudden call for *heaven, saints,
apostles,* and *prophets* to exult over the fall of Babylon is in striking
contrast with the weeping and wailing of the earthly associates of
the ruined harlot. Comp. Isa. xliv, 23; xlix, 13, and Jer. li, 48.

This exultation, like the hallelujahs of xix, 1–7, is the utterance of
joy over the triumph of righteousness, and the *judgment* celebrated
is that for which the martyrs prayed (vi, 10).

6. SYMBOLIC ACT AND WORD OF DOOM. XVIII, 21–24.

21   And a strong angel took up a stone as it were a great millstone, and
cast it into the sea, saying, Thus with a mighty fall shall Babylon, the
22 great city, be cast down, and shall be found no more at all. And the
voice of harpers and minstrels and flute-players and trumpeters shall be
heard no more at all in thee; and no craftsman, of whatsoever craft, shall
be found any more at all in thee; and the sound of a millstone shall be
23 heard no more at all in thee; and the light of a lamp shall shine no more
at all in thee; and the voice of the bridegroom and of the bride shall be
heard no more at all in thee: for thy merchants were the princes of the
24 earth; for with thy sorcery were all the nations deceived. And in her
was found the blood of prophets and of saints, and of all that have been
slain upon the earth.

21. *Cast it into the sea . . . thus shall Babylon be cast down*—
The main figure in this symbolic act of doom is taken from Jer. li,
63, 64, where Seraiah is commanded by the prophet to bind a stone
to the book of the woes of Babylon and cast it into the Euphrates,
and say, " Thus shall Babylon sink, and shall not rise from the evil
that I will bring upon her." *Shall be found no more*—Comp. Ezek.
xxvi, 21.

22, 23. *Voice of harpers . . . no more*—Comp. Ezek. xxvi, 13;
Jer. xxv, 10. Observe the fourfold picture, *harpers, minstrels,
flute-players, trumpeters.* The immediate mention of *craftsmen,
sound of the millstone, light of the lamp*, and *voice of the bridegroom*, forms a corresponding set of images of prosperity and joy.
Comp. also Jer. vii, 34; xvi, 9. *Thy merchants were princes*—Comp.
Isa. xxiii, 8. *Thy sorcery*—Comp. Isa. xlvii, 9; Nahum iii, 4.

24. *Blood of prophets and of saints*—Comp. Matt. xxiii, 34, 35;
Luke xi, 49–51; xiii, 33, 34. Needlessly do some expositors, in spite
of Jesus's words, go outside of Jerusalem to find this martyr-blood.

7. THE HEAVENLY HALLELUJAHS. XIX, 1–8.

1   After these things I heard as it were a great voice of a great multitude
in heaven, saying, Hallelujah; Salvation, and glory, and power, belong
2 to our God: for true and righteous are his judgments; for he hath judged
the great harlot, which did corrupt the earth with her fornication, and
3 he hath avenged the blood of his servants at her hand. And a second
time they say, Hallelujah. And her smoke goeth up forever and ever.
4 And the four and twenty elders and the four living creatures fell down
and worshiped God who sitteth on the throne, saying, Amen; Hallelujah.

5 And a voice came forth from the throne, saying, Give praise to our God,
6 all ye his servants, ye that fear him, the small and the great. And I
heard as it were the voice of a great multitude, and as the voice of many
waters, and as the voice of mighty thunders, saying, Hallelujah: for the
7 Lord our God, the Almighty, reigneth. Let us rejoice and be exceeding
glad, and let us give the glory unto him: for the marriage of the Lamb
8 is come, and his wife hath made herself ready. And it was given unto
her that she should array herself in fine linen, bright *and* pure: for the
fine linen is the righteous acts of the saints.

The fall of the mystic Babylon, which we have shown to be identical with the great city called Sodom and Egypt (xi, 8), is the
great catastrophe of this book, and chap. xviii is a solemn prophetical dirge over that fearful fall ; but now, in contrast with her
"harpers, and minstrels, and flute-players, and trumpeters" which
have become silent (xviii, 22), there is heard the sound of heavenly
song, as if in answer to the call of xviii, 20. In sentiment it corresponds to the song of xii, 10–12, over the casting out of Satan.
The position of this song between the fall of the great Babylon and
the going forth of the King of kings to smite the nations and destroy the beast and false prophet is also worthy of note as a part
of the artificial arrangement of the book. See note at the beginning of chap. vii. The fall of the blood-stained Harlot is essential
to the manifestation of the Bride, the wife of the Lamb. Hence
this heavenly song serves not only to celebrate the righteous judgment of God on the great Harlot, but also to open the way for the
concluding visions of the triumph of the Lamb over all his enemies,
and his marriage with the beloved Bride.

1. *After these things*—Comp. xviii, 1. *Hallelujah*—Here first
occurring in this book, and repeated four times in verses 1–6. The
Hebrew הַלְלוּ יָהּ means *Praise ye Jehovah*, and occurs in Psalm civ,
35, and frequently thereafter, especially at the beginning and end
of the last five psalms.

2. *True and righteous are his judgments*—Comp. Psalm xix, 9;
cxix, 137. *Judged . . . avenged*—Comp. Deut. xxxii, 43.

3. *Her smoke goeth up forever*—Comp. Isa. xxxiv, 10.

4. *The four and twenty elders*—As in v, 8, 14; xi, 16–18.

5. *A voice from the throne*—Distinct from that of the elders and
the living creatures, but by whom uttered is not said. We see in
this no special mystic significance, but only the art of the writer to
give a profound impression of the number and variety of voices in
the heaven. *Give praise . . . ye his servants*—Comp. Psalm cxxxiv,
1; cxxxv, 1. *Ye that fear him*—Comp. Psalm xxii, 23. *The small
and the great*—Comp. Psalm cxv, 13.

6. *Voice of a great multitude*—Comp. Dan. x, 6.   *Voice of many waters*—Comp. Ezek. i, 24; xliii, 2.   *The Lord reigneth*—Comp. Psalm xciii, 1; xcix, 1.

7. *The marriage of the Lamb is come*—In verse 9 below mention is made of "the *supper* of the marriage of the Lamb." The song being cast in a prophetic mold, things future are conceived as already complete, and hence the aorists of this verse, *came* (ἦλθεν) and *made ready* (ἠτοίμασεν). *The marriage of the Lamb* is the union of Christ with believers, and is therefore essentially a fact of spiritual life. The *feast* or *supper* of that marriage is a figure for the delightful fellowship, the blessed entertainment and fruition of such vital union with the Prince of life. The marriage of the Lamb is a process continually going on as long as such unions of Christ and his beloved and elect ones continue to be consummated. The glory and blessedness of life with Christ in heaven are but the perpetuation of the union formed by faith and love in this world. The marriage and feast of this apocalyptic song are accordingly to be understood as referring to the same spiritual fact as the parables of the marriage of the king's son in Matt. xxii, 2–13, and the great supper in Luke xiv, 15–24. *His wife hath made herself ready*—In apocalypse as in parable facts or great truths which continue for ages are necessarily pictured in harmony with the figure employed. The union of one believer with Christ is a representative of all such unions of all time. But to conserve the figure of a marriage feast the entire process of ages is conceived as complete.

8. *Fine linen, bright and pure*—Compare the "bright pure stone" of xv, 6. The fine, soft, white *linen* (βύσσινος) array, we are told, *is the righteous acts of the saints*. It is a symbol of that outward beauty and purity which must distinguish all who are truly Christ's, and which shows itself in all labors of love and acts of righteousness (δικαιώματα) which *the saints* perform in their devotion to their Lord. Compare the lesson of the wedding garment in Matt. xxii, 11–13.

The Angel's Words to John. XIX, 9, 10.

9 And he saith unto me, Write, Blessed are they who are bidden to the marriage supper of the Lamb. And he saith unto me, These are true
10 words of God. And I fell down before his feet to worship him. And he saith unto me, See thou do it not : I am a fellow-servant with thee and with thy brethren who hold the testimony of Jesus : worship God : for the testimony of Jesus is the spirit of prophecy.

The words immediately following the heavenly song (verses 9 and 10) are analogous to those of x, 8–11, and are addressed personally to the seer. Compare also xxii, 6–9. He is admonished by the angel that he is the honored recipient of divine revelations of God. Before the closing scenes of the first part of the Apocalypse he was commanded to eat the book received from the angel's hand and was told that he must " prophesy again over many peoples and nations and tongues and kings." So now, before the closing scenes of the second part, he is admonished that vital union with Christ is unspeakably blessed, and the witness of that holy fellowship is the very life and soul of all true prophecy. The angels have no higher honor.

9. *Blessed are they who are bidden*—Compare the beatitude of Luke xiv, 15. Compare also the other two beatitudes of this book (xiv, 13, and xx, 6), which are, in their essential blessedness, the same perpetual fruition as the marriage supper of the Lamb. *And he saith unto me*—Observe the double statement. Twice over in this verse he repeats the fact that the angel addressed him thus personally. It was the same angel of xvii, 1, who had shown him the judgment of the great Harlot and now bids him *write* the heavenly blessedness of those who are in fact the wife of the Lamb. Here is the mystery within a mystery. " The wife " that "made herself ready " (verse 7) is truly no other than those blessed ones who are bidden to the marriage supper of the Lamb. *These are true words of God*—Strictly, *these words* may refer to the beatitude which John has just been told to write, for that utterance of blessedness contained no conjecture or hope of the angel, but *true words of God* himself. The reference, however, is generally understood of all the foregoing communications of this angel from xvii, 1, onward to this point. And, indeed, all the words of this book of divine revelation will bear this commendation. Comp. xxi, 5 ; xxii, 6.

10. *I fell down . . . to worship him*—It seemed to him as if God himself had spoken, and in the deep emotion of the moment he would have worshiped the messenger instead of the one who sent him. Comp. xxii, 8. *Fellow-servant of thee am I, and of thy brethren*—This is not equivalent to saying, " I am one of thy brethren ; " but he assures John that he is also himself a servant. He serves the same God that John and his brethren serve. So every created intelligence of heaven capable of serving God is a *fellow-servant* along with men on the earth who love God and keep his commandments. *That hold the testimony of Jesus*—The same form of words as in xii, 17, and to be explained here, as there, of those who hold fast the word which Jesus had witnessed of himself. There is no sufficient reason for making *the testimony of Jesus* mean anything else in this passage than it means in i, 2, 9, where it is coordinate with " the word of God." The genitive is that of the

subject, that is, the testimony which Jesus himself gives. He is pre-eminently " the faithful witness " (i, 5), and his testimony in this book consists of " true words of God." This testimony proceeding from Jesus and received and apprehended as God's truth in the heart of John or any of his brethren *is the spirit of prophecy.* With-out it there can be no New Testament prophecy. It is the vital element, the life and soul and essence of prophecy. It is also a part of the office and work of the Holy Spirit to take this testimony of Jesus and make it clear to the consciousness of every true disciple of the Lord (John xvi, 14). Possessed of such inspired testimony one becomes gifted for the work of prophesying.

The last statement is not to be understood as an appended word of John, but a part of .the personal announcement of the angel to John, and is therefore an intimation, like x, 8–11, that he is yet to prophesy and publish this testimony of Jesus to the world. As a part of that testimony, and one of its most inspiring words, he was commanded to write, " Blessed are they who are bidden to the mar-riage supper of the Lamb."

VI. THE MILLENNIAL CONFLICT AND TRIUMPH. XIX, 11–XXI, 8.

In this section of the book we have a series of seven visions, each beginning with the words Καὶ εἶδον, *and I saw.* It opens with the picture of a heavenly Conqueror going forth, in company with white-robed armies, to smite the nations with the sword of his mouth, and after a series of wonderful victories it concludes with the picture of a new heaven and a new earth, from which all evil-doers are cast out. From the seer's point of view it is an apoca-lyptic outlook into the Messianic era, the millennial age, during which " the law shall go forth out of Zion, and the word of Jehovah from Jerusalem " (Micah iv, 2 ; Isa. ii, 3). While disclosing an ideal outline of future Messianic triumphs the prophet does not transcend the main purpose of his book, which is " to show the things which must shortly come to pass " (i, 1). That purpose is accomplished when he depicts the overthrow of Judaism, the end of the old temple dispensation, and the consequent opening of the new era, the Messianic age, which is destined, according to the prophets, to make all things new. His task is complete when he shows forth the beginning of the new age and a visional outline of what that age will bring. He furnishes no " continuous historical " record of the progress of Christianity in the Roman empire. We should no more look in the prophecies of this book for a syllabus of the petty feuds of mediæval Europe than for an account of modern missions in India, China, and Japan. Too long have false presumptions led men to search in apocalyptic pictures for predictions of such events as the French Revolution, the fall of Napoleon Bonaparte, the Protestant Reformation, and the Wars of the Roses. One might as well expect to find in scripture predictions of the discovery of America and the invention of the steam engine and the electric telegraph. The mind that gives itself to discover such things in biblical prophecy misapprehends the mind of the Spirit. The fallacy of such procedures in exegesis lies in a total misconception of the nature and scope of apocalyptic writing.

1. THE HEAVENLY CONQUEROR. xix, 11–16.

11 And I saw the heaven opened; and behold, a white horse, and he that sat thereon, called Faithful and True; and in righteousness he doth judge
12 and make war. And his eyes *are* a flame of fire, and upon his head *are* many diadems; and he hath a name written, which no one knoweth but
13 he himself. And he *is* arrayed in a garment sprinkled with blood: and
14 his name is called The Word of God. And the armies which are in heaven followed him upon white horses, clothed in fine linen, white *and*
15 pure. And out of his mouth proceedeth a sharp sword, that with it he should smite the nations: and he shall rule them with a rod of iron: and he treadeth the wine press of the fierceness of the wrath of God, the
16 Almighty. And he hath on his garment and on his thigh a name written, KING OF KINGS, AND LORD OF LORDS.

11. *I saw the heaven opened*—Compare the language of Ezek. i, 1. We are about to have a new apocalyptic picture of the Son of man coming in the clouds of heaven (i, 7), but it is the picture of an æonic struggle upon which he sets out, not a single historical event to which one can point and say, Lo here! or, Lo there! *A white horse*—The symbol of victorious procession here as in vi, 2, but *he that sat thereon* is not the same as the rider on the white horse in the earlier vision. His title of *faithful and true* is sufficient to designate him as the Christ of i, 5, and iii, 14, and the additional statement that *in righteousness he judges and makes war*, appropriated from Psalm xcvi, 13; Isa. xxxii, 1; Jer. xxiii, 5, 6, shows that he is no other than the Messiah of Old Testament prophecy.

12. *His eyes a flame of fire*—Comp. i, 14, and Dan. x, 6. *Many diadems*—Symbols of many a triumph and of highest royalty. He is the Conqueror of Psalm cx, 6, who " has smitten the heads (chiefs) over many a land." *A name written which no one knoweth but he himself*—So that he is a high priest of the holiest mysteries. Comp. ii, 17, and iii, 12.

13. *Arrayed in a garment sprinkled with blood*—This, in connection with the figure of treading the wine press of God's wrath in verse 15, makes it evident that Isa. lxiii, 1–6, is before the mind of

the writer. The victor has sprinkled his garments with the blood of his enemies, as he trod on them in his anger and trampled them in his fury (comp. Isa. lxiii, 3). *His name is called the Word of God*—He is the same WORD which is so sublimely presented to our thought at the beginning of John's gospel (John i, 1–18). He is the beginning of the *revelation* as well as of the *creation* of God (iii, 14).

14. *Armies which are in the heaven followed him*—These are identical with the " called and chosen and faithful " associates of the Lamb spoken of in xvii, 14. His saints are with him in this glorious war, and like the bride, the wife of the Lamb, are *clothed in fine linen, white and pure.* Comp. verse 8 above.

15. *Out of his mouth a sharp sword*—As in i, 16. *That with it he should smite the nations*—This is the same figure that we find in Isa. xi, 4, where it is said of the Messiah that " he shall smite the earth with the rod of his mouth, and with the breath of his lips shall he slay the wicked." *Rule them with a rod of iron*—Comp. ii, 27 ; xii, 5; and Psalm ii, 9. *Treadeth the wine press*—Comp. xiv, 19, 20, and Isa. lxiii, 1–6. In all these allusions the great Conqueror is described as executing righteous judgment upon the enemies of *the Almighty God.* It is the picture, not of a judge sitting on his throne and formulating a sentence, but of a fierce warrior who goes forth to execute judgment by treading the enemies of God under his feet.

16. *King of kings, and Lord of lords*—This is the lofty title of the Messianic ruler and judge of the nations. Comp. xvii, 14 ; 1 Tim. vi, 15 ; Deut. x, 17 ; Dan. ii, 47. All the kingdoms of the world are to become the kingdom of Jehovah and his anointed (xi, 15 ; Psalm ii, 2–8).

The foregoing vision (verses 11–16) is a most sublime apocalypse of the conquering Messiah, who "must reign until he has put all his enemies under his feet" (1 Cor. xv, 25). The struggle may consume a million years. The details and chronology of its age-long history no prophet has foretold, but this unrivaled portraiture presents the conquering King, with his names, his insignia, and his works. Its comprehensiveness may be seen by tabulating the contents as follows :

I. HIS NAMES.

(1) Faithful and True ; (2) Written but known only to himself; (3) The Word of God ; (4) King of kings and Lord of lords.

II. HIS INSIGNIA.

(1) Sitting upon a white horse ; (2) Many diadems ; (3) Blood-sprinkled garments ; (4) Eyes of flame.

29

III. HIS WORKS.

(1) In righteousness he judges and makes war ; (2) He smites the nations with the sword of his mouth ; (3) He rules them as with a rod of iron ; (4) He treads the wine press of the wrath of God.

There can surely be no question but that this glorious personage is the Christ of Old Testament prophecy and of New Testament revelation.

2. THE GREAT SACRIFICIAL SUPPER OF GOD. xix, 17, 18.

17　And I saw an angel standing in the sun; and he cried with a loud voice, saying to all the birds that fly in midheaven, Come *and* be
18　gathered together unto the great supper of God; that ye may eat the flesh of kings, and the flesh of captains, and the flesh of mighty men, and the flesh of horses and of them that sit thereon, and the flesh of all men, both free and bond, and small and great.

The symbolism of this passage is appropriated from Ezek. xxxix, 17–20, where the prophet is commanded to "speak unto every feathered fowl, and to every beast of the field," and to say unto them : "Assemble yourselves, and come; gather yourselves on every side to my slaughter which I sacrifice for you, even a great slaughter upon the mountains of Israel, that ye may eat flesh and drink blood. Ye shall eat the flesh of the mighty, and drink the blood of the princes of the earth, of rams, of lambs, and of goats, of bullocks, all of them fatlings of Bashan. And ye shall eat fat till ye be full, and drink blood till ye be drunken, of my sacrifice which I have sacrificed for you. Thus shall ye be filled at my table with horses and chariots, with mighty men, and with all men of war, saith the Lord Jehovah." A literal interpretation of such a metaphorical passage must needs lead to absurdity and confusion. It is a symbolic picture of the fearful visitation of divine wrath on wicked men and nations, and quite analogous to the figure of the wine press in verse 15.

17. *An angel standing in the sun*—The most appropriate place in the visible heavens for an angel to take his position for the purpose of addressing *all the birds that fly in midheaven.* Hence we need not look for special allegorical significance in this statement. It is but an incidental feature of the vision. *The great supper of God*—The idea is that of a sacrificial feast, in which the victims slain are so many propitiatory offerings to God.

18. *Eat the flesh of kings*—Six kinds of *flesh* are specified, but it seems to be mainly a human sacrifice. *Kings, captains,* and *mighty men* are specifications which show how largely the slaughter is to take the mighty ones. No kings or princes of the earth will be able

to withstand the power of "the King of kings and Lord of lords." The other three are *horses*, and *them that sit thereon*, and *all men*. The enumeration is less comprehensive than that of Ezek. xxxix, 17–20, where mention is made of drinking blood as well as of eating flesh; also rams, lambs, goats, bullocks, and horses and chariots, as well as mighty men and princes are eaten. But in both pictures the idea of a fearful slaughter is conveyed, and the addition in this verse of the words *free and bond, and small and great*, is designed to show that no class or condition of men will be able to escape the judgment of the great Conqueror of verses 11–16.

3. The Beast and the False Prophet Destroyed.   xix, 19–21.

19   And I saw the beast, and the kings of the earth, and their armies, gathered together to make war against him that sat upon the horse, and
20   against his army.   And the beast was taken, and with him the false prophet that wrought the signs in his sight, wherewith he deceived them that had received the mark of the beast, and them that worshiped his image: they twain were cast alive into the lake of fire that burneth with
21   brimstone: and the rest were killed with the sword of him that sat upon the horse, *even the sword* which came forth out of his mouth: and all the birds were filled with their flesh.

This picture stands in closest possible connection with the preceding one, and in fact is the result of the angel's call to eat the flesh of kings and mighty men.   It shows in few words the necessary and certain outcome of the conflict between Christ and his white-robed armies on the one side, and the beast and his army on the other.   The imagery is substantially identical with that of the overthrow of the beast in Daniel's vision (Dan. vii, 11, 12), but it is notably expanded and enhanced with various incidental features which show the genius of the New Testament apocalyptist.

19. *Beast . . . kings . . . armies*—This beast is obviously the one portrayed in xiii, 1–7, and *the kings of the earth* may be understood of the ten kings of xvii, 12.   But in a general way beast, kings, and their armies also represent all hostile earthly forces which in any way "set themselves" (in the spirit of Psalm ii, 2, 3) "against Jehovah and against his Messiah, saying, Let us break their bands asunder, and cast away their cords from us."

20. *The false prophet*—Already mentioned in xvi, 13, and to be understood as another designation of the "beast out of the land" described in xiii, 11–16.   *That wrought the signs*—See xiii, 14. *They twain were cast alive into the lake of fire*—Daniel saw the beast slain "and his body destroyed and given to the burning flame" (Dan. vii, 11); but our author gives a more fearful touch to the

picture by representing both beast and prophet as burned *alive*. *The lake of fire which burneth with brimstone* is a figure peculiar to this book. Comp. xx, 10, 14, 15; xxi, 8. It is doubtless to be understood as "the gehenna of fire" (Matt. v, 22; Mark ix, 43–48). But when in apocalyptic symbolism a beast is seen to be "cast into a lake of fire," or "given to the burning flame," coherency of figure requires us to interpret the entire statement on some general principle. If the beast is not a literal beast the lake of fire is not to be explained literally. The idea conveyed is rather that of complete destruction.

21. *The rest*—Referring to the kings and armies of verse 19, and to all supposable allies that engage in war against Jehovah and his Christ. *Killed with the sword*—Thus verifying the prophetic word of xiii, 10, and also confirming the saying of Jesus that "with what judgment ye judge, ye shall be judged, and with what measure ye mete, it shall be measured unto you" (Matt. vii, 1). *All the birds were filled*—This completes the picture outlined in verse 18; the two visions, introduced by "I saw" in verses 17 and 19, constitute but one actual judgment. The vision of verses 17 and 18 is but an introduction to the vision of verses 19–21, but they are nevertheless presented as two separate visions.

4. SATAN CHAINED AND IN PRISON. xx, 1–3.

1 And I saw an angel coming down out of heaven, having the key of
2 the abyss and a great chain in his hand. And he laid hold on the
   dragon, the old serpent, which is the Devil and Satan, and bound him
3 for a thousand years, and cast him into the abyss, and shut *it*, and sealed
   it over him, that he should deceive the nations no more, until the
   thousand years should be finished: after this he must be loosed for a
   little time.

The harlot has fallen; the beast and false prophet are cast into the lake of fire; it remains to show that Christ's victory is not complete until the great dragon, the old serpent, the deceiver of the whole world, is not only cast down to the earth (comp. xii, 9), but cast into the abyss, his appropriate place.

1. *An angel coming down out of heaven*—Quite different from "a star fallen out of heaven" (ix, 1). No particular description of this angel is given, but it is evident that he is able to bind the strong adversary of God and man (comp. Matt. xii, 29). *Having the key of the abyss*—For it is no longer in a fallen angel's hand (comp. ix, 1). *A great chain*—This chain, like the key, is a figure to be compared with the statement of Jude 6 and 2 Peter ii, 4.

2. *Dragon . . . serpent . . . Devil . . . Satan*—Observe this nota-

ble accumulation of titles and names, and comp. xii, 9. The old deceiver has made himself a name for evil. *Bound him for a thousand years*—The period of the Messianic reign (comp. verses 4 and 5). Observe that nothing is here said of the angels of Satan, who, according to xii, 9, were cast down to the earth with him. They seem to have been left at large in the earth.

3. *Cast him into the abyss*—Where the demons dread to go (Luke viii, 31), but where they properly belong. *Shut and sealed over him*—Thus making his imprisonment secure and authoritative (comp. Matt. xxvii, 66). *Deceive the nations no more*—So that no more beasts or false prophets, of the character and likeness of those depicted in chap. xiii, shall appear to persecute the saints and trample down the rights of men.

This symbolic picture of the binding of Satan has been greatly misapprehended by supposing it to imply the cessation of all evil among men. It is too readily assumed that if Satan be shut up and sealed in the abyss the angels of Satan and wicked men can have no more place in the world—a most unauthorized assumption. The passage presents only one phase of the triumph of Christ over all his enemies. The final defeat of the devil is described in verse 10, and the Messiah's triumph over the last enemy, Death and Hades, is told in verses 13 and 14. Hence it is of the first importance to a correct interpretation of these closely related visions to note that they constitute a series of victories which run through the entire period called symbolically *a thousand years.*

We must keep in mind that we are dealing with symbols, not pragmatic events marked off by definite chronological dates. The symbolism of xx, 1-3, points to a suppression of personal Satanic agency. It is to be studied in the light of such sayings of Jesus as "I beheld Satan fallen as lightning from heaven" (Luke x, 18); "Now is the judgment of this world; now shall the prince of this world be cast out" (John xii, 31); "The prince of this world has been judged" (John xvi, 11). None of these declarations imply the sudden and permanent cessation of wickedness among men. But in some of them, and especially in the symbolism of this passage of the Apocalypse, we may understand the cessation of demoniacal possession, so conspicuous in the time of our Lord, and of which we have so vivid a picture in ix, 1-11. After the overthrow of Jerusalem the Harlot, and the full inauguration of the kingdom of heaven, with the triumphant going forth of the Gospel that followed that momentous crisis of ages, no well-authenticated instance of such demoniacal possession is to be found. That crisis, moreover, marked a transition from the old barbaric civilizations to a new and better order of affairs in the world. All this is represented, symbolically, as a binding of Satan, the deceiver of the nations.

5. MILLENNIAL REIGN AND FINAL OVERTHROW OF SATAN. xx, 4–10.

4 And I saw thrones, and they sat upon them, and judgment was given
unto them: and *I saw* the souls of them that had been beheaded for the
testimony of Jesus, and for the word of God, and such as worshiped
not the beast, neither his image, and received not the mark upon their
forehead and upon their hand; and they lived, and reigned with Christ
5 a thousand years. The rest of the dead lived not until the thousand
6 years should be finished. This is the first resurrection. Blessed and
holy is he that hath part in the first resurrection: over these the second
death hath no power; but they shall be priests of God and of Christ, and
shall reign with him a thousand years.
7 And when the thousand years are finished, Satan shall be loosed out of
8 his prison, and shall come forth to deceive the nations which are in the
four corners of the earth, Gog and Magog, to gather them together to
9 the war: the number of whom is as the sand of the sea. And they went
up over the breadth of the earth, and compassed the camp of the saints
about, and the beloved city: and fire came down out of heaven, and de-
10 voured them. And the devil that deceived them was cast into the lake
of fire and brimstone, where are also the beast and the false prophet;
and they shall be tormented day and night forever and ever.

4. *I saw thrones*—So Daniel beheld thrones set and the kingdom
and dominion under the whole heaven given to the saints of the Most
High (Dan. vii, 9, 18, 27; comp. Matt. xix, 28; 1 Cor. vi, 2). *They
sat upon them*—Who they were that sat upon the thrones is not expressly said, but the most natural inference from the context is that
they were *the souls of them that had been beheaded for the testimony
of Jesus, and for the word of God, and such as worshiped not the
beast, neither his image, and received not the mark upon their forehead and upon their hand.* It was one part of the purpose of this
book to encourage the martyr spirit in the early Church, and to portray again and again the triumph and glory sure to come to them
that "loved not their life even unto death" (xii, 11). It is pledged
in the martyr scene of vi, 9–11, and symbolized in the triumph of
the witnesses of xi, 11, 12, and of the man child caught up to the
throne of God (xii, 5). The further statement that *they lived, and
reigned with Christ a thousand years*, shows that the thrones were
set for them to occupy. It is one essential part of the office and
work of a king to exercise judgment (comp. Psalm lxxii, 2 ; Isa. xi,
2–4 ; xxxii, 1), and reigning with Christ is to participate in the
judgments which he makes and executes. So in xix, 14, his white-
robed armies follow with the King of kings as he goes forth to smite

the nations and to rule with a rod of iron. So in ii, 18, 26, 27, "the Son of God, who hath his eyes like a flame of fire, and his feet like unto burnished brass," promises to him "that overcometh" that he shall have "authority over the nations, and shall rule them with a rod of iron." Comp. also iii, 21. These martyrs do not reign on the earth in the forms of flesh and blood, as some have grossly imagined, but they are enthroned along with Christ in the place of his glory, and are not only with all other saints permitted to behold his glory (John xvii, 24), but are also given to sit down with him in his throne, as he also overcame by not loving his life unto death, and sat down with his Father in his throne (iii, 21). Hence the encouragement given in 2 Tim. ii, 11 : "If we died with him, we shall also live with him : if we endure, we shall also reign with him." The statement that *judgment was given unto them* is capable of a double meaning. It may signify that these souls now received a judgment in their favor and were vindicated and avenged (comp. xi, 18). But the context here favors the idea that to those who sat upon thrones was given the authority of exercising judgment—the power and right to judge. To them was given power to pass condemning sentence on the enemies of their Lord, as if they were constituted a jury or were made associate judges with the Christ himself. *The thousand years* is to be understood as a symbolical number, denoting a long period. It is a round number, but stands for an indefinite period, an æon whose duration it would be a folly to attempt to compute. Its beginning dates from the great catastrophe of this book, the fall of the mystic Babylon. It is the æon which opens with the going forth of the great Conqueror of xix, 11–16, and continues until he shall have put all his enemies under his feet (1 Cor. xv, 25). It is the same period as that required for the stone of Daniel's prophecy (Dan. ii, 35) to fill the earth, and the mustard seed of Jesus's parable to consummate its world-wide growth (Matt. xiii, 31, 32). How long the King of kings will continue his battle against evil and defer the last decisive blow, when Satan shall be "loosed for a little time," no man can even approximately judge. It may require a million years. But during all this time the enthroned martyrs, whose blood and ashes were the seed of the Church, live and reign with their glorified Lord. They are conceived as risen with Christ (comp. Rom. vi, 5 ; Eph. ii, 6 ; Col. ii, 12 ; iii, 1), seated with him in glory, sharing his triumphs, and exercising judgment with him as associate kings.

But those who live and reign with Christ during the thousand years are not the martyrs only. All *such as worshiped not the beast*, whether called to a martyr's death or not, share in the millennial

glory. All those who overcome on account of the blood of the
Lamb may expect to realize the blessed answer to the prayer and
will of Jesus "that, where I am, they also may be with me, that
they may behold my glory" (John xvii, 24).

5. *The rest of the dead*—Those not belonging to the class who
live and reign with Christ. The benediction pronounced in the
next verse on those who have part in the first resurrection, and the
fact that the judgment scene of verses 11-15 is concerned mainly,
if not altogether, with the final doom of everyone who "was not
found written in the book of life" leave us very naturally to infer
that *the rest of the dead* are those who held not the testimony of
Jesus, nor the word of God, but rather worshiped the beast and his
image, and in some way received his damning mark. *Lived not
until the thousand years should be finished*—They came not into the
apocalyptist's field of vision until he "saw the dead, the great and
the small, standing before the throne," and "the sea gave up the
dead which were in it, and Death and Hades gave up the dead
which were in them" (verses 12 and 13). Those thus held under
the dominion of Death and Hades are not they who are " dead unto
sin and alive unto God through Jesus Christ " (Rom. vi, 11), and of
whom it may be said, as it is said of Christ himself, that "death
has no more dominion over him " (Rom. vi, 9; comp. John xi, 26).
This is the first resurrection—That is, the living and reigning with
Christ a thousand years is the first resurrection. This *resurrection*
is evidently to be understood and explained as a part of a series of
great symbolical pictures. Nothing is said, either here or in verses
12 and 13, of a rising up from the dust of the earth or a resuscita-
tion of mortal bodies. Although the word *resurrection* may ordinarily imply this, and what is here written does not necessarily
exclude the thought, still it is simply a fact that these apocalyptic
pictures do not represent " the general resurrection of the last day,"
as commonly apprehended, but the millennial living and reigning of
the blessed with Christ on the one hand and the appearance of all
the rest of the dead for judgment on the other. All the dogmatic
deliverances about " the plain literal sense" which interpreters like
Alford have made concerning the " two resurrections" of this passage are irrelevant. The word *resurrection* is here no more to be
pressed into a literal significance than the words *thrones* and *books*
and *lake of fire*, but *the first resurrection* is expressly shown in the
context to be a LIVING AND REIGNING WITH CHRIST.

6. *Blessed and holy is he that hath part in the first resurrection*—
Compare the beatitude of xiv, 13, and the note thereon. This benediction implies that those only who partake in *the first resurrection*

are preeminently *blessed and holy ;* but when it is immediately added
that *over these the second death hath no power* we cannot but infer
that those not partaking in the first resurrection are under the dominion of sin and of death, and consequently exposed to the power of
the second death, which, according to verse 14, is "the lake of fire."
But all the *blessed and holy* that overcome the powers of evil "shall
not be hurt of the second death" (ii, 11), *but they shall be priests
of God and of Christ,* as already shown in i, 6, and v, 10.

The five scenes of the millennial period thus far presented form
a closely connected series, and are to be thought of, not as chrono-
logically successive, but rather as simultaneous and supplementary
in their logical relations. Thus, the moving forth of the great
Conqueror (xix, 11–16) results in the great slaughter of the numerous enemies of God (xix, 17, 18); this involves at the same time
the destruction of the beast and the false prophet (xix, 19–21), and
the binding of Satan (xx, 1–3). These are different aspects of a
world-wide conquest, for the Messianic King of Old Testament
prophecy is to "have dominion from sea to sea, and from the river
unto the ends of the earth" (Psalm lxxii, 8). But the great events
symbolized are not sharply separated from each other in ·time.
Most of them, if not all, are coetaneous, and extend through the
entire period of the Messianic era, the symbolical *thousand years.*
Through what historic stages the conflict is to pass ; what particular forms of government may arise and exhibit more or less of the
spirit of the beast and the dragon; what mysteries of iniquity may
work against Jehovah and against his Anointed during the thousand years—these and such like are not written, and their details do
not seem to come within the scope of prophetic revelation. But
the millennial era of conflict and triumph is prophetically presented
in one great field of view.

7, 8. *When the thousand years are finished Satan shall be loosed*—
The millennial era is to end with the utter defeat and destruction of
the old serpent, the Devil, thus fulfilling at the last the prediction
of Gen. iii, 15. With this final defeat of Satan all his allied forces
are also destined to perish (comp. Matt. xxv, 41). In order to enhance the final and decisive character of this victory over Satan the
writer represents him as *loosed out of his prison,* in which he had
been shut up for the long period (comp. verse 3). The old enemy
is thus granted a second probation in order to show that "the deceiver of the whole world" (xii, 9) is at the end, as from the beginning, "a liar and the father thereof" (John viii, 44). His going
forth once more *to deceive the nations which are in the four corners
of the earth* implies that the millennial era, with all its world-wide

triumphs, is not destined so to eliminate all evil from among men but that at the very last there will be found in all quarters of the earth those who can be deceived and led by Satan into conflict with the people of God. These nations, which are thus marshaled *to the war* against the Most High, are called by the symbolical names *Gog and Magog*, taken from a similar prophetic picture in the Book of Ezekiel (comp. Ezek. xxxviii, 2). Any attempt to find in these symbolical names and pictures of battle a reference to particular peoples and provinces of the earth must needs be utterly futile. Both here and in Ezekiel we have an ideal scene. *The number* of those gathered for the final battle *is as the sand of the sea*. In Ezekiel they are represented as "many people," "a great company, and a mighty army." They come up "against my people of Israel, as a cloud to cover the land." They are "gathered out of many people against the mountains of Israel." The corresponding passage in Ezekiel (xxxviii, 18–23) deserves transcription here, as showing beyond question its metaphorical character : "It shall come to pass in that day, when Gog shall come against the land of Israel, saith the Lord Jehovah, that my fury shall come up into my nostrils. For in my jealousy and in the fire of my wrath have I spoken. Surely in that day there shall be a great shaking upon the land of Israel ; so that the fishes of the sea, and the fowls of heaven, and the beasts of the field, and all creeping things that creep upon the earth, and all the men that are upon the face of the earth, shall shake at my presence, and the mountains shall be thrown down, and the steep places shall fall, and every wall shall fall to the ground. And I will call for a sword against him unto all my mountains, saith the Lord Jehovah : every man's sword shall be against his brother. And I will plead [1] against him with pestilence and with blood ; and I will rain upon him, and upon his hordes, and upon the many peoples that are with him, an overflowing shower, and great hailstones, fire, and brimstone. And I will magnify myself, and sanctify myself, and I will make myself known in the eyes of many nations ; and they shall know that I am Jehovah " (Ezek. xxxviii, 18–23).

9. *Went up over the breadth of the land*—The language has allusion to Hab. i, 6, where the Chaldean armies are spoken of as "marching through the breadth of the land to possess the dwelling places which are not their own." *Compassed the camp of the saints about*—The imagery here is of a fortified camp rather than of a

---

[1] This is the same word as that employed in Joel iii, 2. The pleading is an execution of judgment (נישפט) in vindication of God and his people.

moving army, as in xix, 14, thus affording variety of description, and at the same time conforming to the corresponding picture in Ezekiel of Israel dwelling safely in the day when the armies of Gog come up against their land (comp. Ezek. xxxviii, 14). *And the beloved city*—The figure is that of a city with a camp outside of it, as if set there for defense. The *city* is the new Jerusalem, already mentioned in iii, 12, but to be more fully described in following visions. It is called *the beloved city* in allusion to such scriptures as Jer. xi, 15; xii, 7, and Psalm lxxviii, 68. In point of fact this beloved city is to be understood as descending from heaven to earth (xxi, 2, 3, 10) DURING THE ENTIRE PERIOD OF THE MILLENNIAL ERA; but the artistic proprieties of the book required that the full description of the city of the saints follow the record of the overthrow of all her foes. *Fire came down . . . and devoured them*—Allusion to the event in Elijah's history (2 Kings i, 10, 12), which has been already referred to in these visions (comp. xi, 5). Thus these saints have only to stand still and see the miraculous judgment of God upon their enemies. Thus will God ultimately crush Satan under their feet (Rom. xvi, 20).

10. *Devil . . . cast into the lake of fire*—Not now "cast down to the earth" (xii, 9, 13), where he may still persecute the saints of God, but cast into final and irretrievable perdition, and visited with the terrible fury which Ezekiel thus portrays: "I will rain upon him, and upon his bands, and upon the many people that are with him, an overflowing rain, and great hailstones, fire, and brimstone" (Ezek. xxxviii, 22; comp. also Gen. xix, 24). *Where are also the beast and the false prophet*—As described in xix, 20. *Tormented day and night unto the ages of the ages*—Another form of expressing the perpetual torment so vividly portrayed in xiv, 10, 11. See the notes on those verses.

These verses 7–10 depict the last great struggle of Satan and his forces to overcome the saints of God, and their overwhelming defeat before the manifested power of heaven. The obvious purpose is to show the final and decisive victory of the seed of the woman over their ancient foe. It is a great symbolic picture, and its one great teaching is clear beyond the possibility of doubt or misunderstanding, namely, that Satan and his forces must all ultimately perish. This is written for the comfort and confidence of the saints. But that final victory is in the far future, at the close of the Messianic age, and it is here simply outlined in apocalyptic symbols. Any presumption, therefore, of determining specific events of the future from this grand symbolism must be regarded as in the nature of the case a species of worthless and misleading speculation.

6. The Final Judgment. xx, 11–15.

11 And I saw a great white throne, and him that sat upon it, from whose
face the earth and the heaven fled away; and there was found no place
12 for them. And I saw the dead, the great and the small, standing before
the throne; and books were opened: and another book was opened,
which is *the book* of life: and the dead were judged out of the things
13 which were written in the books, according to their works. And the
sea gave up the dead which were in it; and death and Hades gave up
the dead which were in them: and they were judged every man accord-
14 ing to their works. And death and Hades were cast into the lake of fire.
15 This is the second death, *even* the lake of fire. And if any was not found
written in the book of life, he was cast into the lake of fire.

Although the kings and their armies have been defeated and the
beast and the false prophet and Satan himself are cast into the lake
of fire, the apocalyptic scheme is yet incomplete, and we have here
a further vision of " the rest of the dead " (comp. verse 4) and of the
destruction of the last enemy, even death itself (1 Cor. xv, 26).
According to apostolic teaching, "we must all be made manifest
before the judgment seat of Christ, that each one may receive the
things done through the body according to what he hath done,
whether good or bad " (2 Cor. 5, 10). We have been shown a glorious picture of the judgment and honor of the martyrs and of all
those who kept themselves untainted by any mark of the beast ; it
remains for us to be shown the judgment which will try every man's
work, of what sort it is (1 Cor. iii, 13). This final judgment shows
that not one of all the dead, whether hidden in earth or sea or the
vast realm of Hades, is to escape the retribution which tests "every
man according to his works." The vision, like all the rest of this
sevenfold series, is set in the form of apocalyptic symbol.

11. *I saw a great white throne*—Comp. Isa. vi, 1 ; Dan. vii, 9. So
far as the symbolism of the color points to anything, it may, as in
the white horse and the white robes, suggest an ideal of divine
triumph. This throne of judgment is associated with the thought
of the final victory and vindication of righteousness. *Him that sat
upon it*—The same " King of kings and Lord of lords " who was
seen sitting upon a white horse (xix, 11). *From whose face the earth
and the heaven fled away*—The concept is an enlargement of Psalm
cxiv, 3, 7, and designed to give an awful impression of the majesty
of the judge. The earth and the heaven above it are thought of as
so terrified that they vanish utterly, and so *there was found no place
for them.* They disappeared from view.

12. *The dead, the great and the small*—These are most naturally
understood as " the rest of the dead " referred to in verse 5, and the

words *the great and the small*, repeated from xix, 18, seem to classify
them in general character with those there mentioned. It is notable
that in this entire passage (verses 11–15) there is no word indicative
of blessedness to accrue to these dead, as in the case of those "that
have part in the first resurrection" (verse 6). These dead of various
grades do not sit on thrones and "live and reign with Christ," but
are seen *standing before the throne* as so many culprits, and there is
no evidence apparent that any one of them was found written in
the book of life (see on verse 15). *The books were opened*—The
record of their works is conceived here, as in Dan. vii, 10, to have
been written in books or scrolls, and the accurate record assures us
that they are to be judged strictly according to their works. *And
another book was opened*—To afford them every possible means of
evidence. It is implied in this description, when taken altogether,
that no name was to be found written in the book of life which had
a record in the other books. The book *of life*, or of the living, in
which the names of God's approved ones are written, is a familiar
figure in the Scriptures (comp. Exod. xxxii, 32 ; Psalm lvi, 8 ;
lxix, 28 ; Dan. xii, 1 ; Luke x, 20 ; Phil. iv, 3). But *the dead*,
whose judgment is here depicted, do not seem to have been written
in *the book of life*, for it is immediately added that they *were judged
out of the things which were written in the books*, that is, the other
books first mentioned above. *According to their works*—Comp.
Rom. ii, 6 ; 2 Cor. v, 10.

13. *The sea . . . Death and Hades gave up the dead*—The reference is to all supposable places where the dead could be found.
The enumeration of *the sea* in the same category with *Death and
Hades* (see on vi, 8) forbids any dogmatic inference from this text
touching the resurrection of bodies from the grave. It is noticeable,
also, that no mention is here made of the dust of the earth giving up
its dead. For the thought conveyed is not so much of a resurrection of bodies from their graves as of a gathering together of all
the dead (exclusive of those contemplated in verse 4) in conscious
personality before the throne of final judgment. But as it is immediately added that *they were judged, every man according to
their works*, it is evident that we have here a picture of resurrection
unto judgment, and we may well call attention to the analogy of
John v, 28, 29, where Jesus declares that "the hour is coming, in
which all that are in the tombs (ἐν τοῖς μνημείοις) shall hear his
voice, and shall come forth ; they that have done good, unto the
resurrection of life ; and they that have done ill, unto the resurrection of judgment." The first resurrection, as depicted in verses
4–6, is conspicuously a resurrection of life, and this of the rest of the

dead is as conspicuously a resurrection of judgment. The fourth gospel and the Apocalypse of John thus supplement each other.

14. *Death and Hades were cast into the lake of fire*—This is the apocalyptic equivalent for the statement of 1 Cor. xv, 26: "The last enemy that shall be abolished is Death." Comp. also Isa. xxv, 8; Hosea xiii, 14. But taken in connection with what follows, and compared with xxi, 8, the words *Death and Hades* seem also to be used by synecdoche for the subjects of these infernal powers. But the entire picture of judgment and perdition is wrapped in mystic symbolism, and the one certain revelation is the final overthrow in remediless ruin of all who live and die as subjects of sin and death. *This death is the second, the lake of fire*—Observe that there is no specific designation of *the second resurrection*, as distinct from the first ; but in contrast therewith we have *the second death*, which involves the doom of being cast into *the lake of fire*. It was promised to the martyr church of Smyrna, "he that overcometh shall not be hurt of the second death" (ii, 11). It was also written of those blessed and holy ones who have part in the first resurrection that the second death has no power over them (verse 6). But those who come to the judgment scene here described are impliedly of the characters enumerated in xxi, 8, whose "part is in the lake that burneth with fire and brimstone, which is the second death."

15. *If any was not found written in the book of life*—This statement is to be understood as a principle governing the judgment of the dead, and not as implying that numbers of them were found written in the book of the living. There is nothing to indicate that any of those dead, great and small, seen standing before the throne in verse 12 were found written in the book, but the whole passage and context imply the contrary. Their works (which seem to have been of the character specified in xxi, 8, and which accordingly made them the slaves of Death and Hades) were written in the other books that were opened, and condemned them ; and, as a further evidence against them, the book of life was also opened, and no record of their names was found therein. It will be seen that the foregoing exposition of "the first resurrection," and of the judgment before "the great white throne," removes this entire section of the Apocalypse (which has ever been regarded as the most difficult in the book) from what may be cited as specific revelation touching the question how the dead are raised and with what manner of body they come (1 Cor. xv, 35). The doctrine of the resurrection of all the dead, as enunciated in John v, 28, 29, is evidently assumed, but these apocalyptic pictures of "the first resurrection" and "the second death" are given, not to furnish a doctrine of resur-

rection from the dead, but to serve the purpose of showing most impressively the heavenly glory, on the one hand, of those who "overcome," and the certain judgment and final perdition, on the other, of all who are not found "written from the foundation of the world in the book of life of the Lamb that hath been slain" (xiii, 8). A faithful and true interpretation must follow the scope and artistic method of the entire book, and not be concerning itself with specific dogmas about "the general resurrection of the last day," and efforts to reconcile "two resurrections a thousand years apart" with other teachings of Christ and the apostles on the general subject. For the apocalyptist employs the concept of resurrection of the dead only metaphorically and with special reference to the rewards awaiting the blessed and holy and the retribution sure to come on the unbelieving and unholy, whose names are not written in heaven.

7. New Heaven, New Earth, and New Jerusalem. xxi, 1-8.

1 And I saw a new heaven and a new earth: for the first heaven and the
2 first earth are passed away; and the sea is no more. And I saw the holy city, new Jerusalem, coming down out of heaven from God, made ready
3 as a bride adorned for her husband. And I heard a great voice out of the throne saying, Behold, the tabernacle of God is with men, and he shall dwell with them, and they shall be his peoples, and God himself
4 shall be with them, *and be* their God: and he shall wipe away every tear from their eyes; and death shall be no more; neither shall there be mourning, nor crying, nor pain, any more: the first things are passed
5 away. And he that sitteth on the throne said, Behold, I make all things
6 new. And he saith, Write: for these words are faithful and true. And he said unto me, They are come to pass. I am the Alpha and the Omega, the beginning and the end. I will give unto him that is athirst
7 of the fountain of the water of life freely. He that overcometh shall in-
8 herit these things; and I will be his God, and he shall be my son. But for the fearful, and unbelieving, and abominable, and murderers, and fornicators, and sorcerers, and idolaters, and all liars, their part *shall be* in the lake that burneth with fire and brimstone; which is the second death.

This last vision of the series commencing at xix, 11, is appropriately placed after the great judgment scene of xx, 11-15, although the "making of all things new" (verse 5) is a process going on through all the thousand years of the Messiah's reign. The new earth and heaven are never to pass away, and the felicity of God's servants, as portrayed in this section, contemplates not only the life that now is, but also the eternal life of a glorified existence before the throne of God and of the Lamb.

1. *New heaven and new earth*—This ideal of a new creation is appropriated from Isa. lxv, 17, 18: "Behold, I create new heavens and a new earth: and the former shall not be remembered, nor come into mind. But be ye glad and rejoice forever in that which I create: for behold, I create Jerusalem a rejoicing, and her people a joy." In this book, as in Isaiah, the reference is to the renovation of the world by the coming and reign of the Messiah. This new creation is "the regeneration" (παλινγενεσία) referred to in Matt. xix, 28, and the "restoration of all things" (ἀποκατάστασις πάντων) mentioned in Acts iii, 21. This renovation, as Heb. xii, 26, 27, shows, involves a removal or passing away of that which is old and shaken. *And the sea is no more*—To interpret this statement literally would be to bring confusion into the whole picture. *Heaven, earth,* and *sea* are mentioned as including all the "elements" (comp. 2 Peter iii, 10), and symbolic of what Paul calls "the fashion (σχῆμα) of this world" (1 Cor. vii, 31). The new creation, wrought by the truth, and word, and sword, and rod of the great Conqueror of xix, 11-16, will not be shaken by the wild restlessness and trouble which the Hebrew mind associated with *the sea* (comp. Isa. lvii, 20, 21). There will be no more such sea as that from which the beast came forth (xiii, 1).

2. *The holy city, new Jerusalem*—Jerusalem is called "the holy city" in Isa. xlviii, 2; lii, 1, and here is called also *new* in order to harmonize with the new heaven and earth to which it belongs. The old Jerusalem became a harlot, and is called "Babylon the great" (xvii, 5). The seer has witnessed and recorded her miserable fall, and now is permitted to behold a new and holy city, *coming down out of heaven from God, made ready as a bride adorned for her husband.* Comp. Isa. lxi, 10. How beautiful is the conception of the bride descending in glory from heaven after the abominable harlot has "fallen, fallen!" (xiv, 8; xviii, 2, 21!) This *new Jerusalem* is the same as that which Paul in Gal. iv, 26, calls "the upper Jerusalem, our mother." Comp. also Heb. xii, 22. It is a symbol of the new covenant and those embraced therein, including all which the redeeming work of Christ secures to them that believe in his name, and by implication stands for "the general assembly and church of the firstborn, who are enrolled in heaven" (Heb. xii, 23). For the *bride* is indeed the Church of Christ (Eph. v, 25-32).

3. *A great voice out of the throne*—Best understood as the voice of God and of the Lamb, who are so united as to possess one throne (xxii, 1). *The tabernacle of God is with men*—The old tabernacle served its highest purpose when it conveyed to the true worshiper the profound uplifting thought that God would indeed dwell with

men on the earth and commune with them. Comp. Exod. xxix, 42–
46; 1 Kings viii, 27; Ezek. xxxvii, 27; Zech. ii, 10, 11.[1] The New
Testament dispensation brings the symbolism of the tabernacle
into blessed realization, for the believer now enters with boldness into the holy places by the blood of Jesus (Heb. x, 19),
and knows by the witness of the Spirit that he has passed from
death into life, is an adopted child of God, and dwells in God (Rom.
viii, 14–16 ; 1 John iii, 24 ; iv, 13–16). In view of these facts of
the new covenant how significant the words, *he shall dwell with
them, and they shall be his peoples, and God himself shall be with
them.* Thus they become the temple and tabernacle of the living
God.

4. *Wipe away every tear*—Comp. vii, 17, and Isa. xxv, 8. With
this comforting assurance is also connected the promise that the
fourfold army of earthly woe and trial, *death, mourning, crying,
pain, shall be no more.* This promise finds fulfillment in the believer's immortality and eternal life in Christ.

5. *He who sitteth on the throne*—The judge seen in xx, 11, "from
whose face the earth and the heaven fled away." He is also the
ruler of the ages, the great Conqueror of xix, 11–16, and his throne
is "the throne of God and of the Lamb" (xxii, 1). In the renovation of the world, as in its original creation, God and his Word are
one (comp. John i, 1–3). *I make all things new*—Comp. Isa. xliii,
19, and 2 Cor. v, 17. In establishing and carrying out the provi-
sions of the new covenant "he hath made the first old. But that
which becometh old and waxeth aged is nigh unto vanishing away"
(Heb. viii, 13). It required a shaking of heaven and earth to effect
the change from the old to the new, and a "removing of those
things that are shaken, that those things which are not shaken may
remain" (Heb. xii, 26, 27). The crisis hour of transition from the
old to the new was that of the ruin of the old Jerusalem, but the
renovation of the world is the work of the millennial age. The
words may well apply to what the Christ is doing during all this
period, and should be translated *I am making all things new*, that
is, a new heaven and a new earth, according to verse 1. *Write*—
Comp. xiv, 13. Things of special note and comfort are thus emphasized by a definite command to put on record. *These words are
faithful and true*—For they proceed from the great Conqueror who
is "called Faithful and True" (xix, 11).

6. *They are come to pass*—Γέγοναν. Compare the γέγονεν of
xvi, 17. The vision and prophetic work treat the restoration of all

---

[1] See the chapter on the symbolism of the Mosaic tent of meeting, pages 81–84.

things as already accomplished in the purpose of God. For the divine speaker immediately adds, *I am the Alpha and the Omega, the beginning and the end.* He is the one who "calls the generations from the beginning," inasmuch as he is "the first and the last" (Isa. xli, 4; xliii, 10; xliv, 6; xlviii, 12), the one "who is and who was and who is to come" (i, 4). He accordingly beholds all the purpose both of judgment and of grace as accomplished from the very beginning. Comp. i, 8. *Unto him that is athirst . . . water of life*—Comp. Isa. lv, 1; Zech. xiv, 8. The promise is not, after the manner of verse 4, "there shall be no more thirst;" but rather the bounteous provision for the satisfaction of thirst is named, for *the water of life* is *freely* given. Comp. xxii, 17. This pledge virtually implies that there will be no more thirst because of the ample and free provision; and hence the passage is not essentially different from vii, 16, 17.

7. *He that overcometh*—Compare the promises appended to each of the epistles to the seven churches (ii, 7, 11, 17, etc.). The victor (ὁ νικῶν) is kept prominent in this Apocalypse as the associate of Christ and the sharer of his glory. "These are they who follow the Lamb whithersoever he goeth" (xiv, 4), and they constitute the white-robed armies of xix, 14. They know the felicity of "the first resurrection" and "live and reign with Christ a thousand years" (xx, 4–6). *Shall inherit these things*—That is, all the blessedness and glory mentioned or implied in the preceding verses. For if children, sons of God, as is said immediately after, then are they "heirs of God and joint heirs with Christ" (Rom. viii, 17). *I will be his God, and he shall be my son*—Compare the language of 2 Sam. vii, 14; Psalm lxxxix, 26, 27, and Zech. viii, 8. The one who overcomes along with Christ is thus honored as a son of God and sits down with him on his throne as an associate prince and ruler (comp. iii, 21; ii, 26, 27).

8. *But as to the fearful and unbelieving*—Observe how the series of visions, begun with the εἶδον, *I saw*, of xix, 11, concludes with the solemn statement of the doom of all who have no inheritance in the new Jerusalem. The statement may be regarded as a solemn warning. The *fearful* are those timid souls who shrink away from the bloody struggle required of them that overcome, not willing to dare fierce conflict with the enemies of God. The *unbelieving* are those of perverse hearts who refuse to accept and act upon the truths of divine revelation. The *abominable* are all such as are in love with the "golden cup full of abominations" referred to in xvii, 4. The *murderers* are especially those who killed the prophets and stoned the messengers of God (Matt. xxiii, 37; Acts vii, 52).

The *fornicators and sorcerers and idolaters* refer especially to such as made the harlot Babylon "a hold of every unclean spirit" (comp. xviii, 2, 3, and ix, 20, 21). *All the liars*—Comp. verse 27 and xxii, 15. He that "loveth and maketh a lie" is last named as a character which is made up of the sum of all evils, for he shows himself to be a worthy son of the devil, who was a liar and a murderer from the beginning (John viii, 44). Observe how the eight words of this category of evildoers compose four sets of two in each : 1. Fearful and unbelieving; 2. Abominable and murderers ; 3. Fornicators and sorcerers ; 4. Idolaters and liars. *Their part is in the lake that burneth with fire and brimstone*—They belong to the great body of enemies represented by the beast and the false prophet (xix, 20) and Satan and his angels (xx, 7-10). Compare with this the language of Matt. xxv, 41, 46.

At the risk of some repetition we again call attention to the general character and scope of the seven visions, beginning with xix, 11, and ending with xxi, 8. These are seven closely related pictures of the triumph of the holy heavens over the powers of earth and hell, and furnish a vivid outline of the entire period of the Messiah's reign. As a series of triumphs over all evil, preceding and introducing the everlasting fruition of the heavenly Jerusalem, they correspond in the apocalyptic scheme to the seven last plagues which issued in the fall of the great Babylon. Those plagues were of the nature of seven judgments on the corrupt and abominable harlot ; these visions are of seven victories over the various allied forces of the old serpent, the devil. After the rapid narration of the seven last plagues there followed a detailed picture of the ruin of the great harlot, the mother of abominations of the land (xvii, 1–xix, 10); and we shall note the artistic formality with which these seven triumphs are followed by a detailed vision of the glorious bride, the wife of the Lamb (xxi, 9–xxii, 5).

But we shall miss the great purpose of John's Apocalypse if we presume to treat these seven last visions of triumph as a literal record of historic events. They are to be recognized as symbolical pictures, designed to indicate the ultimate victory of the Christ, "who must reign till he hath put all his enemies under his feet" (1 Cor. xv, 25). Accordingly, the first (xix, 11–16) is a magnificent representation of the coming and kingdom of the Christ of God, set in such symbolic figures and allusions as indicate his character and work. It is an ideal picture of what the Messiah is and what he does during the whole period of his reign ; not of any one particular event of his coming. To render the more impressive the certainty of his triumph we next have the call to God's great sacri-

ficial feast (xix, 17, 18), set in a symbolical form which is appropriated from the prophet Ezekiel. This call is appropriately followed
by the vision of the overwhelming destruction of the beast and the
false prophet, along with the kings and armies gathered to war
against the King of kings (xix, 19–21). Then this victory is made
the more signal by the vision of Satan chained and imprisoned for
a thousand years (xx, 1–3). But during all this period the witnesses
of Jesus, who overcome for the word of God, keep themselves un-
spotted from the beast, live and reign with Christ in his glory; and
when at the end Satan is loosed and makes one more assault upon
"the camp of the saints" he and his hosts are consumed by fire
from heaven (xx, 4–10). Thereupon two additional pictures are
given, the one (xx, 11–15) descriptive of final judgment upon all
who are not found written in the book of life, and the other (xxi,
1–8) giving a brief outline of the renovation of heaven and earth
and the descent of the new Jerusalem as a bride adorned for her
husband. These are all millennial pictures, set in one broad field
of vision, but involving also the eternal issues of the Messiah's reign.

The coming and kingdom of Christ are accordingly to be conceived as continuing through the long indefinite period symbolized
by "a thousand years." It is no sudden product of a night ; no
local scenic display of a day and an hour, as literalist interpreters
have vainly imagined. But it was no part of John's purpose to
write a detailed history of Christianity beforehand. He wrote of
things destined to come to pass shortly, namely, the fall of Judaism,
the ruin of Jerusalem, and the passing away of the old cultus ; and
he accordingly compassed all that was given him to know of the
great future of the kingdom of God in a few vivid pictures, set in
symbolic forms which the Old Testament prophets had already employed.

VII. THE HOLY JERUSALEM, THE BRIDE. XXI, 9–XXII, 5.

After the pouring out of the seven bowls of the wrath of God,
the seventh and last of which was accompanied by "a great voice
out of the temple, from the throne, saying, It is done" (γέγονεν),
"and Babylon the great was remembered in the sight of God"
(xvi, 17–19), there followed a vision of "Babylon the great, the
mother of harlots and of the abominations of the earth," so detailed
and comprehensive as to occupy two full chapters of the book.
The detailed portraiture was introduced by "one of the seven angels
that had the seven bowls" (xvii, 1). In notable analogy as an
artistic counterpart the seven visions of Messianic triumph (xix, 11–
xxi, 8) concluded with a picture of the new Jerusalem, and a voice

from the throne, saying, Γέγοναν, *they are done ;* and now there follows (xxi, 9–xxii, 5) a vision of the new Jerusalem, the wife of the Lamb, set in an elaborate symbolic framework corresponding to that of Babylon the harlot. That this was a definite design of the writer appears further in the statement that one of the same seven angels showed him this picture of a woman so opposite in character and destiny. So, after the manner of apocalyptic repetition, the seer now proceeds to take up the last preceding vision (xxi, 1–8), and expand it with manifold details appropriated largely from the abundant metaphors and symbols of the Hebrew scriptures.

1. VISION OF THE NEW JERUSALEM. XXI, 9–14.

9 And there came one of the seven angels who had the seven bowls, who were laden with the seven last plagues; and he spake with me, saying,
10 Come hither, I will show thee the bride, the wife of the Lamb. And he carried me away in the Spirit to a mountain great and high, and showed me the holy city Jerusalem, coming down out of heaven from God,
11 having the glory of God: her light was like unto a stone most precious,
12 as it were a jasper stone, clear as crystal: having a wall great and high; having twelve gates, and at the gates twelve angels; and names written thereon, which are *the names* of the twelve tribes of the children of
13 Israel: on the east were three gates; and on the north three gates; and
14 on the south three gates; and on the west three gates. And the wall of the city had twelve foundations, and on them twelve names of the twelve apostles of the Lamb.

9. *There came one of the seven angels*—Compare the identical language employed in xvii, 1. *I will show thee the bride*—This is to be a vision of glory, not of penal judgment (as in xvii, 1); a sight of *the wife of the Lamb,* not of a " great harlot sitting upon many waters." This figure of the Church and people of God or of Christ as wedded in holy covenant relationship is a familiar Old Testament image, and may be profitably studied in the light of Eph. v, 23–32.

10. *He carried me away . . . to a mountain great and high*—Not "into a wilderness" where the harlot was seen (xvii, 3). Ezekiel's corresponding vision of the temple of God was seen from " a very high mountain " (Ezek. xl, 2). *The holy city Jerusalem*—This is the conspicuous contrast of Babylon the mother of harlots and abominations (xvii, 5). This holy city is the symbol of the Church of the new covenant, and Paul seems to refer to this apocalyptic vision when he writes about " the Jerusalem that is above, which is our mother " (Gal. iv, 26). Once united in living fellowship with Christ, believers are his own beloved for time and eternity. Hence the vision of the heavenly Jerusalem makes no distinction between

those who are in the flesh and those who are perfected in heavenly glory. They all belong to one great family, and constitute the one body of Christ. This idea, together with this whole picture of *the holy city Jerusalem,* appears to have prompted the language of Heb. xii, 22-24. *Coming down out of heaven from God*—As already stated in verse 2. The renovation of the world is to be accomplished by this *coming down* of the holy city. Thus is the prayer to be answered, "Thy kingdom come; thy will be done, as in heaven, so on earth." The infusion of heavenly truth and life into the hearts of men on earth is the great aim of the kingdom of Christ.

11. *Having the glory of God*—Allusion to the *shekinah,* the cloud of glory which covered and filled the tabernacle in the day of its erection (Exod. xl, 34-38). Comp. also Isa. lviii, 8; lx, 1, 19; Zech. ii, 5. *Her light was like unto a stone most precious*—In iv, 3, we were told that he who sat upon the throne was "to look upon like a jasper stone and a sardius." Here the comparison of the *light,* or brightness (φωστήρ), of the holy city to a most precious stone is suggestive of the light of the glory of God himself. Comp. verse 23.

12. *A wall great and high*—So as to be proof against all assaults or reproach of enemies. Comp. Neh. ii, 17. *Twelve gates . . . twelve angels*—Hence so guarded that the powers of Hades cannot prevail against her (Matt. xvi, 18), or take her by surprise. *The names of the twelve tribes*—This agrees with the vision of Ezek. xlviii, 30-34, from which the statements of this verse and the following are fashioned.

14. *Twelve foundations*—The three gates on each side divided the entire circuit of the wall into twelve great sections, of which the four corner sections would be most prominent. Each of these twelve sections was supported by a massive foundation stone, the quality and material of which are enumerated in verses 19 and 20 below. *On them twelve names of the twelve apostles*—In Eph. ii, 19-22, it is written, "Ye are fellow-citizens with the saints, and of the household of God, being built upon the foundation of the apostles and prophets, Jesus Christ himself being the chief corner stone; in whom each several building, fitly framed together, groweth into a holy temple in the Lord; in whom ye also are builded together for a habitation of God in the Spirit." If now, in connection with this general figure, we compare what Jesus said to Peter about building his church upon the rock (πέτρα) of a confessing disciple, and what Peter says (in 1 Peter ii, 5) about being built up as living stones into a spiritual house, we may obtain a more complete conception of the new Jerusalem as the Church of Christ. The Church

of the prophets and apostles bears the names of the twelve tribes of Israel as well as the twelve apostles of the Lamb. Hence, as we have observed elsewhere, the twenty-four elders before the throne of God (iv, 4).

2. MEASURE OF CITY AND WALLS. XXI, 15–17.

15 And he that spake with me had for a measure a golden reed to measure
16 the city, and the gates thereof, and the wall thereof. And the city lieth
 foursquare, and the length thereof is as great as the breadth: and he
 measured the city with the reed, twelve thousand furlongs: the length
17 and the breadth and the height thereof are equal. And he measured the
 wall thereof, a hundred and forty and four cubits, *according to* the
 measure of a man, that is, of an angel.

15. *Had for a measure a golden reed*—This measurement of the city with a reed is modeled after Ezek. xl, 3, 5. The measurement is not carried out to the extent that is detailed in Ezekiel's successive chapters, but is said to have compassed *city, gates,* and *wall.* The result of the measurement is announced in the next verse, and is there seen to serve a symbolic purpose.

16. *Twelve thousand furlongs*—About fifteen hundred miles. But the number, as well as the measure, is symbolical, and it is of no great importance to determine whether the *twelve thousand stadia* are the measure of the entire circuit of the city or only of one of the four sides. The main result of the measurement is to show that the city was immense, and that *the length and the breadth and the height thereof are equal.* Its form is accordingly shown to be a perfect cube, like the holy of holies in the tabernacle. The symbolism thus suggests that this holy city was to the new earth and heavens what the holy of holies was to the congregation and camp of Israel.

17. *The wall . . . a hundred and forty and four cubits*—That is, the height of the wall was twelve times twelve cubits, about two hundred and sixteen feet; so that we have the picture of a vast city, in the form of a perfect cube, surrounded by a comparatively low wall. *The measure of a man, that is, of an angel*—The only natural meaning these words can bear is that the angel who showed these things to John, and measured the city and wall, employed the measure commonly adopted by men. The measure reckoned by man and angel were alike.

3. MATERIALS OF THE STRUCTURE. XXI, 18–21.

18 And the building of the wall thereof was jasper: and the city was pure
19 gold, like unto pure glass. The foundations of the wall of the city were

adorned with all manner of precious stones. The first foundation was
jasper; the second, sapphire; the third, chalcedony; the fourth, emer-
20 ald; the fifth, sardonyx; the sixth, sardius; the seventh, chrysolite;
the eighth, beryl; the ninth, topaz; the tenth, chrysoprase; the eleventh,
21 jacinth; the twelfth, amethyst. And the twelve gates were twelve
pearls; each one of the several gates was of one pearl: and the street of
the city was pure gold, as it were transparent glass.

18. *The building of the wall*—That is, the material of which the
wall was constructed. *Jasper*—Like the appearance of him who sat
upon the throne (iv, 3). *The city was pure gold, like unto pure glass*
—This is designed to enhance the splendor of the city to the uttermost in the thought of the reader. The comparison with glass implies that the gold was so pure as to be even transparent as glass.

19. *The foundations of the wall*—Mentioned in verse 14 as twelve
in number and bearing the names of the twelve apostles. Already
Isaiah had prophesied of Zion that God would lay her foundations
with sapphires (Isa. liv, 11). The enumeration of *all manner of
precious stones* in this verse and the following is modeled after the
four rows of similar stones which were set in the breastplate of the
high priest (Exod. xxviii, 17-21) and which also bore the twelve
names of the tribes of Israel. No special and separate significance
attaches to each stone, but the enumeration as a whole is designed
to produce the effect of something beautiful and exquisite in the
extreme. All the precious stones referred to in Holy Writ are
named to give the impression of the superior glory of the heavenly
city. Is there not a profound symbolical suggestion in foundations
that bear both the names of the twelve apostles and the precious
stones of the ephod? "The city which hath the foundations"
(Heb. xi, 10), being a symbol of "the church of the firstborn who
are written in heaven," is builded upon the apostles and prophets,
to each of whom is given to know and publish the mysteries of the
kingdom of heaven, even as the high priest learned the will of Jehovah by means of the precious stones of the ephod.

21. *The twelve gates were twelve pearls*—Most appropriate portals
of a city, of which the foundation stones were of jasper and amethyst and the city itself pure gold. The Talmud has a saying that
" God will give gems and pearls thirty cubits long and just as broad,
and will hollow them to the depth of twenty cubits, and the breadth
ten, and place them in the gates of Jerusalem." *The street of the
city*—The singular is employed for the entire street system of the
city. All the streetways were of *pure gold transparent as glass*, as
if forming a part of the solid material of the city itself (comp.
verse 18).

4. Its Temple and its Light. XXI, 22, 23.

22 And I saw no temple therein: for the Lord God the Almighty, and the
23 Lamb, are the temple thereof. And the city hath no need of the sun,
  neither of the moon, to shine upon it: for the glory of God did lighten
  it, and the lamp thereof *is* the Lamb.

22. *No temple therein*—For this golden city is in fact the reality
of which the old temple and tabernacle were outward symbols.
They were fashioned after the pattern shown to Moses in the mount
(Exod. xxv, 40), but this holy city is itself the true Israel dwelling
in God. For all that the temple symbolized in its highest ideal is
realized by those whose lives are hidden with Christ in God (Col.
iii, 3), and who understand the blessed truth that "God is love ; and
he that abideth in love abideth in God, and God in him " (1 John
iv, 16). Hence the announcement that *the Lord God the Almighty,
and the Lamb, are the temple* of this new Jerusalem. When God is
all and in all there is no place for outward symbol, for the saints
behold the glory of God, like cherubim in the holy of holies.

23. *No need of the sun*—Thus realizing the fulfillment of Isa. lx,
19, 20 : "The sun shall be no more thy light by day ; neither for
brightness shall the moon give light unto thee; but Jehovah shall
be thine everlasting light, and thy God thy glory. Thy sun shall
no more go down; neither shall thy moon withdraw itself ; for Jehovah shall be thy everlasting light, and the days of thy mourning
shall be ended." Not only is God Almighty the giver of light to
the new Jerusalem, but *the lamp of it is the Lamb*. This association of the Lamb with God as the source of heavenly light, and also
as the temple of heaven itself, exalts him to the dignity and glory
of Jehovah himself.

5. Character of its Inhabitants. XXI, 24–27.

24 And the nations shall walk amidst the light thereof: and the kings of
25 the earth do bring their glory into it. And the gates thereof shall in no
26 wise be shut by day (for there shall be no night there): and they shall
27 bring the glory and the honor of the nations into it: and there shall in
  no wise enter into it anything unclean, or he that maketh an abomination
  and a lie: but only they who are written in the Lamb's book of life.

24. *The nations shall walk by means of its light*—Comp. Isa. lx, 3:
"The nations shall come to thy light, and kings to the brightness of
thy rising." This statement implies that the new Jerusalem coexists
with *nations*, and is not essentially different from "the mountain of
Jehovah's house," unto which " all the nations flow " (Isa. ii, 2). This
is the "desire of all the nations," to which "all the nations shall
come " and bring their precious things (Hag. ii, 7, 8).

25. *The gates shall in no wise be shut by day*—So Isaiah's picture of the future of Zion : " Thy gates shall be open continually ; they shall not be shut day nor night ; that men may bring unto thee the wealth of the nations " (Isa. lx, 11). *No night there*—Repeated in xxii, 5, as an important feature of the city of everlasting light.

26. *Bring the glory and honor of the nations into it*—So that it will be a treasure city of all that can contribute to its glory and beauty. Comp. Isa. lx, 5–10; lxvi, 12 ; Hag. ii, 7, 8.

27. *There shall in no wise enter into it anything common*—Comp. Isa. lii, 1, when " Jerusalem, the holy city," is told that " henceforth there shall no more come into thee the uncircumcised and the un- clean." The last part of this verse is in substance a repetition of verse 8 and xx, 15.

6. RIVER AND TREES OF LIFE. XXII, 1, 2.

1 And he showed me a river of water of life, bright as crystal, proceed-
2 ing out of the throne of God and of the Lamb, in the midst of the street
thereof. And on this side of the river and on that was the tree of life,
bearing twelve *manner of* fruits, yielding its fruit every month: and the
leaves of the tree were for the healing of the nations.

1. *A river of water of life*—Here the imagery is taken from Ezek. xlvii, 1, and Zech. xiv, 8, but the picture furnished by John is most choice and beautiful. The river as seen by him was *bright as crystal*, a most entrancing sight; and it was seen *proceeding out of the throne of God and of the Lamb*. Hence it must be from an inexhaustible fountain and a most sacred stream. Comp. John iv, 14. It is also seen to flow *in the midst of the street of* the city, for these words are best connected with the preceding, and show the position of the river, not the tree of life, as many have read it.

2. *On this side of the river and on that*—That is, on each bank of the river. The language is equivalent to that of Ezek. xlvii, 7, 12, and Dan. xii, 5. *A tree of life*—Thus suggesting that paradise is to be fully restored (Gen. ii, 9). Comp. ii, 7 : " To him that over- cometh will I give to eat of the tree of life, which is in the midst of the paradise of God." The words *tree of life* may here be taken as a collective, like the street of the city (see note on xxi, 21), and de- note a collection of trees. *Bearing twelve fruits*—That is, yielding twelve crops of fruit, because of its *yielding its fruit every month.* Compare the like statement in Ezek. xlvii, 12. *The leaves . . . for the healing of the nations* — Comp. Ezek. xlvii, 12 : "The fruit thereof shall be for food, and the leaf thereof for a medicine." As the nations walk by the light of this golden city, so also have they their bruises and diseases cured by the leaves of its tree of life.

7. Eternal Reign in Glory. xxii, 3-5.

3 And there shall be no curse any more: and the throne of God and of
4 the Lamb shall be therein: and his servants shall serve him; and
5 they shall see his face; and his name *shall be* on their foreheads. And
there shall be night no more; and they need no light of lamp, neither
light of sun; for the Lord God shall give them light: and they shall
reign forever and ever.

3. *There shall be no curse any more*—As Zechariah also prophesied
(Zech. xiv, 11). The original *curse* brought on the world of man
by sin (Gen. iii, 16–19, 23) is thus removed, and all the nations have
access to the tree of life. This truly points to the regeneration and
restoration of all things (Matt. xix, 28 ; Acts iii, 21), a heavenly
paradise regained. *Throne of God and of the Lamb shall be therein*
—So that all who enter may stand before the throne, like the elders
and the cherubim of iv, 4–6, and like so many royal ministering
servants shall they not only worship him but *do him service.*

4. *They shall see his face*—Comp. Psalm xvii, 15 ; Matt. v, 8 ;
1 Cor. xiii, 12 ; 1 John iii, 2. This beatific vision of the saints of
God supplants the cherubim. For as this city has no temple, so, as
the holy of holies is in heaven, it has no symbolic cherubim. For
the glorified servants of God and the Lamb, who have washed their
robes and obtained authority over the tree of life (verse 14), now
take the places of " the living creatures," and realize all the life and
glory which those forms of living being symbolized. *Name on their
foreheads*—Comp. iii, 12 ; xiv, 1.

5. *Night no more*—Therefore eternal day. *Need no light of lamp
and light of sun*—For the same reason as that given in xxi, 23.
Comp. Psalm xxxvi, 9. *They shall reign for the ages of the ages*—
So that the reign of the thousand years (xx, 4–6) is but the beginning of a regal life and felicity which are to continue through all
the æons to come. And so the kingdom of the saints of the Most
High will be most truly, as Daniel wrote, "an everlasting kingdom "
(Dan. vii, 27). This is the "eternal life" of Matt. xxv, 46, just as
the second death, the lake of fire, is the "eternal punishment " into
which the "cursed" go away. But no curse shall come any more
to those who stand before the throne and inherit the kingdom prepared for them from the foundation of the world.

Thus ends the vision of the new Jerusalem, the wife of the Lamb.
What follows is of the nature of a conclusion to the book.

This glorious picture of the new Jerusalem, the Bride, the wife
of the Lamb, is the New Testament Apocalypse of what the last
nine chapters of Ezekiel portray in a more minute and detailed
description peculiar to that prophet. Taken as a whole, it is a

symbolical picture of the Church of Christ in time and eternity, but especially in its ultimate glorification. We have repeatedly called attention to the fact that the New Testament conception of the believer's life in Christ leaves the matter of death quite out of account. He who lives and believes in Christ never dies (John xi, 26). Having died with Christ, he is also raised with him, and, as in the case of his risen Lord, he conceives that "death no more hath dominion over him" (Rom. vi, 8–11; Col. iii, 1). So the entire Church is also conceived as the living body of Christ, and all the ideals of triumph and glory which the Old Testament prophets associated with the Messianic reign are in the New Testament Apocalypse associated with the Church and kingdom of Christ. The members of this sanctified body "have already come unto Mount Zion, and unto the city of the living God, the heavenly Jerusalem, and to the innumerable hosts of angels, to the general assembly and church of the firstborn who are enrolled in heaven, and to God the Judge of all, and to the spirits of just men made perfect, and to Jesus the Mediator of the new covenant, and to the blood of sprinkling that speaketh better than that of Abel" (Heb. xii, 22–24). Such a vivid conception of identification with God and Christ and all the holy leaves for the moment all other things out of sight, and associates with the blessed life in Christ the vision of eternal fellowship in his glory.

CONCLUSION. XXII, 6–21.

The conclusion of the Apocalypse appears upon close analysis to be a sevenfold epilogue, affirming and confirming at the close the fact that this is truly the book of the revelation and testimony of Jesus Christ, as announced at the beginning (i, 1–3). For we have (1) the angel's testimony to the truthfulness of the words of this book (verses 6 and 7). Then follows (2) John's own testimony of his intercourse with the angel (verses 8 and 9). (3) Verses 10–15 contain a testimony of solemn admonition and counsel, in view of the revelations given. (4) Next we have Jesus's own personal testimony (verse 16), followed (5) by the great invitation to partake of the water of life freely (verse 17), and then (6) comes the final prophetic warning, confirmed by the Lord himself (verses 18–20), and (7) the brief benediction of verse 21.

1. ANGEL'S TESTIMONY. XXII, 6, 7.

6   And he said unto me, These words are faithful and true: and the Lord, the God of the spirits of the prophets, sent his angel to show unto
7 his servants the things which must shortly come to pass. And behold, I come quickly. Blessed is he that keepeth the words of the prophecy of this book.

6. *He said unto me*—That is, the angel of xxi, 9, who has just shown him the vision of the new Jerusalem. *These words*—The entire prophecy of this book. Comp. verse 7 and xxi, 5. *Faithful and true*—Like the Lord from whom they came (i, 5; iii, 7). *God of the spirits of the prophets*—The God who inspired the spirits of the ancient prophets, and made them the vehicles of communicating his truths to men. *Sent his angel*—As stated in i, 1, and shown repeatedly during the progress of the revelations.

7. *Behold, I come quickly*—Everything relative to the great catastrophe of this book, and the coming and kingdom of the Christ, is represented as about to come to pass. The great event is in the immediate future. Comp. verses 10, 12, 20, and i, 1, 3, 7. Of this same momentous crisis and its related signs and woes Jesus spoke most solemnly to his disciples on the Mount of Olives and assured them that their generation should not pass till all these things were fulfilled (Matt. xxiv, 34). It was coincident with the collapse of Judaism and its temple, for the kingdom of God, as represented in the Gospel of Jesus, was destined to supersede the old covenant, grow like the mustard seed, and fill the whole earth like the stone of Daniel's prophecy (Dan. ii, 35). The judgment of Judah and Jerusalem and the consequent coming and kingdom of Christ were events near at hand when John wrote. *Blessed is he that keepeth the words*—Compare the like beatitude in i, 3.

2. John and the Angel. XXII, 8, 9.

8 And I John am he that heard and saw these things. And when I
heard and saw, I fell down to worship before the feet of the angel which
9 showed me these things. And he saith unto me, See thou do it not: I
am a fellow-servant with thee and with thy brethren the prophets, and
with them who keep the words of this book: worship God.

8. *I John am he that heard and saw*—We repeat here what we have said elsewhere (on i, 4, 9), that no other John known to the Church could write these words so properly as the well-known apostle and disciple of Jesus. *I fell down*—As recorded in xix, 10. The repetition of this attempt *to worship before the feet of the angel* shows what a profound impression the revelation made upon the seer. Notwithstanding the previous rebuke and admonition to worship God only, the abundance of the revelations and their magnitude so overwhelm him that he forgets for the moment that it is only an angel that shows him the visions.

3. Solemn Admonition. XXII, 10–15.

10 And he saith unto me, Seal not up the words of the prophecy of this
11 book; for the time is at hand. He that is unrighteous, let him do

unrighteousness still: and he that is filthy, let him be made filthy still:
and he that is righteous, let him do righteousness still: and he that is holy,
12 let him be made holy still.   Behold, I come quickly; and my reward
13 is with me, to render to each man according as his work is.   I am the
Alpha and the Omega, the first and the last, the beginning and the end.
14 Blessed are they that wash their robes, that they may have the right *to
come* to the tree of life, and may enter in by the gates into the city.
15 Without are the dogs, and the sorcerers, and the fornicators, and the
murderers, and the idolaters, and every one that loveth and maketh a lie.

10. *Seal not up the words*—Quite unlike the command given to
Daniel (Dan. xii, 9), for the Old Testament prophet's revelations
were not to come to pass shortly, but "closed up and sealed till the
time of the end."   But of the fulfillment of John's revelation he is
assured that *the time is at hand.*

11. *He that is unrighteous, let him do unrighteousness still*—The
language and sentiment of this verse are those of exhortation, mixed
with a conspicuous element of judicial declaration.   The passage is
to be studied and understood in the light of scriptures of similar
tone and spirit in Isa. vi, 10 ; Ezek. iii, 27 ; Matt. xxvi, 45.

12. *My reward is with me to render to each man according to his
works*—So that much of that judgment which is depicted in xx,
11-15, is a continual process, coming *quickly* and certainly to every
man.   Neither Lazarus nor Dives wait indefinite ages to receive,
each according to his works.   Often in this life, but always after
death sure judgment comes (Heb. ix, 27).

13. *I am the Alpha*—Thus he repeats at the end what he declared
at the beginning (comp. i, 8).

14. *Blessed are they that wash their robes*—Like those beatified
ones described in vii, 14-17, for besides the glory there mentioned
they also *have the right to come to the tree of life,* or, more literally,
that their authority may be over the tree of life.   This implies a
restoration of all that was lost in Eden and an elevation to the position and glory of the cherubim (Gen. iii, 24).   *Enter in by the
gates*—Which are ever open to those whose names are written in the
Lamb's book of life (xxi, 25-27).

15. *Without are the dogs*—The dog being an abomination according to the law (Deut. xxiii, 18), and an animal of many odious habits,
was naturally associated in the Jewish mind with that which is vile.
Hence the word is used metaphorically for the vicious and the unclean.   In oriental cities dogs are notorious for prowling in the darkness of the night and for fighting and devouring one another.   Hence
the horror of the thought of "the outer darkness, where is gnashing
of teeth" (Matt. xxii, 13).   Düsterdieck suggests that in view of

the prominence of the word *without* (ἔξω), and standing as it does in
the true text without a connecting particle, we should translate,
Let dogs be without. The other impious characters named in this
verse are the same as those of xxi, 8.

4. Jesus's Personal Testimony. XXII, 16.

16   I Jesus have sent mine angel to testify unto you these things for the
churches. I am the root and the offspring of David, the bright, the
morning star.

16. *I Jesus have sent mine angel*—Here is the self-testimony of
Jesus to the fact stated in i, 1. *To testify unto you*—Unto all
you who read and hear the words of this prophecy (i, 3). *For the
churches*—For the good of the churches. Compare the sending of
the book to the seven churches (i, 11). Instead of *for the churches,*
other authorities read *in the churches.* The book is not to remain
a sealed one, but to be read in the churches for their comfort and
hope. *The root and the offspring of David*—The word *offspring* is
here but epexegetical of *root*, which is to be understood in the light
of Isa. xi, 1, 10. See on v, 5. *The bright, the morning star*—Introducing the eternal day, in which there shall be no more need of
lamp or sun, "and there shall be night no more" (verse 5). Comp.
2 Sam. xxiii, 4 ; Num. xxiv, 17.

5. The Great Invitation. XXII, 17.

17   And the Spirit and the bride say, Come. And he that heareth, let
him say, Come. And he that is athirst, let him come: he that will, let
him take the water of life freely.

17. *The Spirit*—Who is no other than the seven spirits before the
throne (i, 4), omniscient and omnipresent. *The bride*—The whole
body of Christ's beloved people, whom he has purchased with his
own blood. The general assembly and church written in heaven
are ever inviting to " come unto Mount Zion, and unto the city of
the living God, the heavenly Jerusalem " (Heb. xii, 22). *He that
heareth*—The one who hears the Spirit and the bride say, Come,
and who hears this book read in the churches, is not only to come
himself, but to extend the invitation to others. *He that is athirst*
—Comp. xxi, 6, and John vii, 37. And when he is guided by the
Lamb "unto fountains of waters of life" he shall thirst no more
(vii, 16, 17). The fullness and freeness of this invitation, intensified further by the words *he that will, let him take the water of life
freely*, represent the spirit of the everlasting Gospel. These good
tidings are to be announced during the entire millennial age.

6. Prophetic Testimony of Warning. XXII, 18–20.

18   I testify unto every man that heareth the words of the prophecy of this
book, If any man shall add unto them, God shall add unto him the
19 plagues which are written in this book: and if any man shall take away
from the words of the book of this prophecy, God shall take away his
part from the tree of life, and out of the holy city, which are written in
this book.
20   He who testifieth these things saith, Yea: I come quickly. Amen:
come, Lord Jesus.

18, 19. *I testify*—These are most naturally understood as the
words of John himself, but he speaks as the prophet of God, and
his testimony is also that of Jesus and the Spirit. *If any man
shall add*—The solemn warning given in these two verses is in substance like that of Moses in Deut. iv, 2 ; but it is cast in an impressive form, after the apocalyptic style and spirit of the whole book.
The writer thus most solemnly guards against any unlawful adding
to or taking from *the words of the book of this prophecy*, that is,
this book of Revelation (as in verses 7, 9, and i, 3, 11).

20. *He who testifieth these things*—That is, Jesus Christ himself;
so that the Apocalypse is, as announced at the beginning, the "testimony of Jesus Christ" (i, 2). *Yea: I come quickly*—Thus em-
phasizing in conclusion the great theme of the book as announced in
i, 7. And we know that he did come in that generation to which
John belonged, and the great Conqueror of nameless secret power,
but called Faithful and True, The Word of God, and King of
kings and Lord of lords (xix, 11–16), is also now *coming*, and
will continue to come in his kingdom and power and glory, until he
shall have put all his enemies under his feet. To his words, *I am
coming*, the seer at once responds, *Amen: come, Lord Jesus*. This
prayer is but another form of saying, "Thy kingdom come. Thy
will be done, as in heaven, so on earth." This is the continual
prayer of every true servant of God and of Jesus Christ, and in
answer to it Jehovah shall give unto his Anointed the heathen for
an inheritance and the uttermost parts of the earth for a possession.

7. Benediction. XXII, 21.

21   The grace of the Lord Jesus be with the saints. Amen.

21. *The grace of the Lord Jesus be with the saints*—This final
benediction is a brief repetition of what is more fully and rhetor-
ically drawn out in i, 4, 5. It is not strange that very early copies
contain also the words *Christ* and *all: The grace of the Lord Jesus
Christ be with all the saints*. In either form the benediction appropriately closes this word of God and testimony of Jesus.

CONCLUDING OBSERVATIONS.

Having now reached the end of our exposition of the biblical apocalypses, we deem it important to recapitulate briefly the fundamental positions of this volume and the principles of interpretation which have largely governed in our treatment of the several books.

1. The inspired prophet of God may receive and declare a divine revelation without full apprehension of the time and manner of its fulfillment. A great fact of the future may be proclaimed with all assurance, while the way it shall come to pass is left in obscurity or veiled in figurative forms of speech. This is the teaching of 1 Peter i, 10, 11, where it is said that the prophets who foretold the grace of salvation in Christ made anxious and diligent search "into what or what manner of time the Spirit of Christ which was in them did point when it testified beforehand the sufferings of Christ and the glories that should follow them." Even the contemporaries of Jesus were remarkably slow to perceive how the Messianic prophecies were fulfilled in him. It is, perhaps, too commonly assumed that the actual fulfillment of predictive prophecy is the certain and final interpreter of the same. But every critical scholar knows what modifications of interpretation many of the Messianic prophecies have undergone in recent years. Meyer's comment on Matt. i, 23, is worthy of attention. "This Messianic method of understanding the Old Testament in the New," he observes, "had its justification, not merely in the historically necessary connection in which the New Testament writers stood to the popular method of viewing the Old Testament in their day and to its typological freedom of exposition, but as it had its justification also generally in the truth that the idea of the Messiah pervades the prophecies of the Old Testament and is historically realized in Christ. . . . Although the New Testament declarations regarding the fulfillment of prophecies are to be presupposed as generally having accuracy and truth on their side, nevertheless the possibilities of erroneous and untenable applications in individual instances, in accordance with the hermeneutical license of that age, is thereby so little excluded that an unprejudiced examination upon the basis of the original historical sense is always requisite." Hence it is that we may still search the ancient Messianic prophecies with the presumption of finding new light on what was long ago fulfilled.

2. The manner in which the disciples and contemporaries of Jesus understood and repeated his eschatological sayings is, therefore, no conclusive determination of their real meaning. The most favored

of the disciples " questioned among themselves what the rising again from the dead should mean " (Mark ix, 10). Our Lord did not take pains to correct all the misapprehensions of those who heard him speak. He spoke in parables, " because seeing they see not, and hearing they hear not, neither do they understand " (Matt. xii, 13). On one occasion, when he said, " He that hath no purse, let him sell his cloke, and buy a sword " (Luke xxii, 36), his disciples in blind misapprehension observed, " Lord, behold, here are two swords ; " but Jesus did not stop to correct their error, but, as Meyer observes, " gently turned aside further discussion with a touch of sorrowful irony." All his words of parable and prophecy could be safely left to find their true interpretation in the progress of his Gospel and kingdom in the world. Inasmuch as he took no pains to correct the mischievous allegorical exegesis of his day we cannot reasonably presume that he would accompany his use of the language of Old Testament prophets with public or private instruction on principles of literary composition and interpretation.

3. It is now generally conceded that the apostles and the Church of the first century expected the parousia, or coming and kingdom of Christ, in that generation. This earnest expectation and blessed hope found frequent expression in the apostolic epistles, and we have shown above (in chap. xviii) that there are no sayings of Jesus better attested than those in the synoptic gospels which affirm an epochal crisis of ages certain to come to pass before that generation passed away. Unless Jesus were himself in error there was no mistake about the TIME of his coming again. He assured those that stood by and heard him speak that some of them should in no wise taste of death till they had seen the kingdom of God come with power. It was not given him to know or declare the day and the hour, for such minute specification would have been inconsistent with honorable seriousness in the command to watch and be in constant readiness (see above, pp. 244, 245). But the fact thus stated cannot be rationally construed to nullify Christ's most explicit asseveration that the crisis would occur in that generation. If now we must conclude that the apostles and their contemporaries misapprehended the teaching of Jesus touching his coming again, it is far more reasonable to suppose that their mistake was *not in the approximate* TIME, *but in the* MANNER *in which they imagined* all those things were destined to come to pass.

4. Our contention is that our Lord probably employed the apocalyptical language of the Hebrew scriptures in its true original import, but made it no part of his mission to deliver lessons on the proper interpretation of figures of thought and of speech. To

correct a literal exposition of Isa. xxxiv, 4, or of Dan. vii, 13, would have been as remote from his methods as to correct a current literal exposition of the first chapter of Genesis. He would as little anticipate the results of modern literary criticism as those of natural science. And as modern scientific research has quite effectually exploded the literal interpretation of the first of Genesis, so it is in a fair way to accomplish the like wholesome effect in exposing the essential absurdities of a literal explanation of apocalyptic prophecy. And it ought not to excite surprise or alarm to find that the apocalyptic scriptures have in many parts been persistently misapprehended. Happily the essential truth of these scriptures is generally perceptible in spite of erratic expositions. Indeed, the real nature and true religious purpose of some scriptures may be imperfectly understood for thousands of years and yet minister profit to their readers by reason of fundamental truths embodied in them so clearly that a child cannot mistake them. The first chapter of Genesis is at once an example and illustration. Century after century has it been understood literally as a prosaic historical narrative, and men believed that God made the entire universe—the heavens, the earth, the sea, and all that is in them—in six days of twenty-four hours each. We have shown in chap. iii of this volume that the great fundamental truths of that apocalypse of creation may be discerned underneath the pictorial garb with which poetic genius has clothed them. They have always been obvious to old and young, learned and unlearned readers, while in the interpretation of the language employed there has been most remarkable diversity. In like manner it may be said that the visions of the prophets and the language of Jesus touching the coming and the kingdom of God have been the subject of persistent misapprehension in the questions of times and seasons and manner of manifestation, while the great facts and fundamental truths have always been accepted.

5. The assumption that we have anywhere in the Scriptures a literal description of the realities of the unseen world is the source of many fallacious notions concerning the doctrines of eschatology. The real manner of Christ's coming and the full import of his " sitting at the right hand of power " (Mark xiv, 62) are as imperfectly revealed as is the mode of the resurrection of the dead and the possibilities of eternal life in the heavens of God. A rigid analysis of the language of Paul touching the parousia, the resurrection, and the future life (for example, in 1 Thess. iv, 13–v, 4 ; 2 Thess. ii, 1–10 ; 1 Cor. xv, 35–55 ; 2 Cor. iv, 16–v, 8 ; Phil. i, 20–25 ; 2 Tim. iv, 6–8) exhibits on the one side a most positive conviction of the reality and fundamental truth of the subject under discussion, and on the other

side a singularly obscure method of statement. In 1 Thessalonians he speaks of God bringing with Jesus (he does not say from whence) those who had fallen asleep, and also of their rising up at the voice of the archangel and the trump of God. In 2 Corinthians he writes as if expecting his new tabernacle from heaven immediately after putting off his earthly tabernacle. In Philippians he says that for him to die is to depart and be with Christ. A collation and analysis of all these statements and others of like character leaves the impression that the apostle himself had no very clearly defined conceptions as to the *manner* of the resurrection or of the future life with Christ. But of the fact itself he had no shadow of doubt.

6. The great truth embodied in the biblical apocalypses can be truly discerned and set forth only by a rational interpretation of the literary peculiarities of this class of composition. We have seen how large a place such pictorial representation affords for the use of metaphor and symbol, and how essentially the poetical element enters into the concepts of an apocalyptist, as well as into his distinctive forms of expression. We have felt it safe to assume that our Lord, in appropriating the Old Testament apocalyptic language, employed it in its true meaning, and that "his servant John," uplifted by the illuminating power of his Spirit, amplified the eschatological teachings of Jesus in strict harmony with the spirit and methods of the older Hebrew prophets. The task of the faithful interpreter of the divine revelations thus given from heaven is to discriminate between substance and form, between the essential fact or truth and its apocalyptic setting.

7. Finally, it is important to observe that the preterist and historical method of interpretation followed in this volume conserves the substance of every fundamental doctrine of the Gospel of Christ. It may helpfully modify some current conceptions of "the great and notable day of the Lord;" for it treats the imagery of collapsing skies, and falling stars, and sounding trumpets, and dissolving mountains, and great white throne, and scores of similar figures of thought as expressing great realities, but not spectacular physical phenomena. Our interpretation no more denies or sets aside the doctrines of eternal judgment, of heaven and hell, of resurrection of the dead, and the coming and kingdom of Christ than does the refusal to affirm the literal "fire and brimstone" of future retribution deny or invalidate the doctrine of eternal reward and punishment beyond this mortal life.

Nearly nineteen centuries of the manifested power and glory of Christianity in the world ought to have thrown some light on the nature of the coming and the kingdom of Christ. It can scarcely

be a question among intelligent believers in Christ that the
beginning of the era of our Lord and Saviour was the most signal and significant epoch in the history of mankind. It marked
a " fullness of times," a crisis of ages. The exact point of transition
from the old to the new may be with many an open question. But
whether we place it at the birth of Jesus or at the time of his crucifixion, when he cried, " It is finished," or at his resurrection, or at
his ascension, or at Pentecost, or at the fall of Jerusalem, the great
commanding fact is still before us that the manifestation of the
Christ, with which all those events must ever appear in vital relation, opened a new era in human civilization.

We now submit the thought that these nineteen centuries of Christian light and progress are relatively but the misty morning twilight
of the great day of Christ. It may be that he must reign a thousand
times a thousand years before he shall have put all his enemies
under his feet (1 Cor. xv, 25). The coming of Christ in his kingdom and power and glory is not one instantaneous act or event. It
is a long-continuing process comprehensive of his entire work both
of redemption and of judgment. He comes in the power of his
Spirit to convict the world respecting sin and righteousness and
judgment (John xvi, 8); he comes in like manner to forgive the sins
of the penitent and to lead the disciple into all the truth ; he comes
and is present wherever two or three are gathered together in his
name. He has been coming through all the Christian centuries to
receive unto himself the faithful souls who have looked for his
heavenly appearing and glory (John xiv, 3 ; xvii, 22–24). As truly
as Jehovah came of old in the clouds of heaven to execute judgment
on the Egyptians (Isa. xix, 1), so did the Son of man come in the
clouds and with the angels of his power to execute judgment on the
great city that was guilty of his blood and drunken with the blood
of his saints and martyrs. He sitteth at the right hand of Power
and sendeth forth continually his innumerable company of angels
to minister for them that shall inherit salvation. Such triumphal
administration of judgment, mercy, and truth has been, is now, and
shall for ages be the work of his Messianic reign. And in full accord with these revelations of his power and glory we cry out with
the Hebrew psalmist :

> The Lord cometh, he cometh to judge the earth :
> He shall judge the world with righteousness,
> And peoples with his truth.

And we also respond with the Christian apocalyptist:

> Amen : come, Lord Jesus.

APPENDIX

THE Apocalypse of John is the consummation of all the biblical apocalypses, and the most complete in form and construction. But it belongs essentially to a vast literature of like character which grew up and flourished during the period from about B. C. 175 to A. D. 400. The pseudepigraphical character of nearly all this literature is remarkable. The books of Daniel and Jonah appear to have produced so powerful an impression, and to have evinced so clearly the fitness of pseudonymous prophecy to illustrate the dominion of God over all the world, that a host of writers followed in the ideal method of these great models. We have seen, however, in the first half of this volume that the formal elements of apocalyptic writing are found in the older Hebrew literature, and that the books of Isaiah, Ezekiel, Zechariah, and Joel contain some of the finest specimens.

The apocryphal apocalypses, though of inferior rank, demand the attention of exegetes and theologians. Our limits and aim do not call for a detailed discussion of these books, but it seems entirely appropriate to include in this volume at least a brief notice of the most important of them. Our main purpose in this appendix, while supplying a short account of these pseudepigrapha and informing the English reader where he may find fuller knowledge, is to point out the inferior character of all this extra-canonical literature. It may be said that our exposition of the Apocalypse of John ignores the help that may be derived from the apocryphal apocalypses; and therefore it is one purpose of this chapter to show that the New Testament Apocalypse was not in any perceptible degree dependent upon or influenced by the pseudepigraphical writings which are now known to us.

THE BOOK OF ENOCH.

Among all the Old Testament pseudepigrapha the Book of Enoch holds highest rank.[1] It is now generally believed to be a compila-

---

[1] The English reader may find this book in three different translations. The first and oldest is that of Laurence (Oxford, 1821), the title page of which is: "The Book of Enoch the Prophet: an apocryphal production, supposed for ages to have been lost;

tion out of a variety of ancient Jewish writings, of different authorship, which once circulated as apocalypses of Enoch and of Noah.
Critics differ as to the number and dates of the several sections of
the composite work, some supposing three, others four or more independent writers. The entire book as it has come to us in its
Ethiopic version consists of one hundred and eight chapters (Laurence made one hundred and five), and, according to R. H. Charles,
who has furnished us with the latest and best English translation
and commentary, it may be analyzed into six constituent elements,
as follows : 1. Chaps. i–xxxvi, written before B. C. 170 ; 2. Chaps.
lxxxiii–xc, written before B. C. 166 ; 3. Chaps. xci–civ, written before
B. C. 134–94 ; 4. Chaps. xxxvii–lxx, written before B. C. 94–79, or
70–64 ; 5. Chaps. lxxii–lxxviii, lxxxii, and lxxix, date uncertain ;
6. A large number of interpolations, most of which are supposed to
have been taken from a lost Book of Noah.

Taking up these sections separately, it is sufficient to say, first of
all, that nothing in the large number of scattered fragments, supposed to have come from an Apocalypse of Noah, and perhaps from
other sources also, can reasonably be brought into a rival comparison with the apocalyptic portions of the biblical canon. They are
in part a grotesque enlargement of the story of the apostate angels,
and in part a collection of Jewish speculations and fancies touching
the secrets of the lightnings and thunder and various cosmical phenomena. The same may be said of the section which Charles entitles
" The Book of Celestial Physics " (chaps. lxxii–lxxxii). It assumes
to be a revelation made to Enoch by the angel Uriel, and to explain
" the courses of the luminaries of the heaven and the relations of
each, according to their classes, their dominion, and their seasons,
according to their names and places of origin, and according to
their months, and how it is with regard to all the years of the world
and till the new creation is accomplished which dureth till eternity." The author declares that " the moon brings in all the years
exactly, so that their position is not prematurely advanced or delayed
by a single day unto eternity ; but (the moons) complete the changing years with perfect justice in three hundred and sixty-four days "

---

but discovered at the close of the last century in Abyssinia ; now first translated from
an Ethiopic manuscript in the Bodleian Library. By Richard Laurence." A great
improvement on this is " The Book of Enoch: translated from the Ethiopic, with
Introduction and Notes. By George H. Schodde." Andover, 1882. These have both
been superseded by "The Book of Enoch: translated from Professor Dillmann's Ethiopic text, emended and revised in accordance with hitherto uncollated Ethiopic manuscripts and with the Gizeh and other Greek and Latin fragments which are here published in full. Edited with Introduction, Notes, Appendices, and Indices, by R. H.
Charles." Oxford, 1893.

(lxxiv, 12). The translator fittingly remarks that nothing but the writer's Jewish prejudices, and possible stupidity, could have prevented him from seeing that a year of three hundred and sixty-four days could not effect such a result.

The other sections contain passages of a higher religious type, and emphasize in true apocalyptic spirit the doctrines of reward for the righteous and retribution for the wicked. But taken as a whole the work is easily seen to belong to a lower order of thought and composition than the biblical apocalypses. Its highest ideals are not infrequently puerile and fantastic enlargements of something recorded in the Hebrew Scriptures. The larger portion of the first thirty-six chapters, which appear to be the oldest section of the book, is made up of a detailed account of the sin and punishment of the angels, the "watchers of the heaven who abandoned the high heaven and the holy eternal place, and defiled themselves with women." They are charged with having "taught all unrighteousness on earth and revealed the secret things of the world which were wrought in the heavens." These fallen watchers are said to have besought Enoch to draw up a petition for them, and to seek their forgiveness in the presence of God in heaven. The saintly patriarch is represented as acting for them as intercessor, and his testimony is :

I composed their petition and the prayer on behalf of their spirit, and for their individual deeds for which they besought forgiveness and forbearance. And I went off and sat down by the waters of Dan, in Dan, to the right of the west of Hermon, and I read their petition till I fell asleep. And behold a dream visited me and visions fell down upon me, and I saw the vision of a chastisement to the intent that I should recount it to the sons of the heaven and reprimand them. And when I awaked I came to them, and they were all sitting together weeping with their faces covered at Ublesjael, which is between Lebanon and Seneser. And I recounted to them all the visions which I had seen in my sleep, and I began to recount those words of righteousness, and to reprimand the heavenly watchers (xiii, 6-10).

As an example of the heavenly visions of Enoch the reader will do well to study the following, which purports to be the answer to Enoch's intercession, and the manner in which the revelation was made known. After declaring to the fallen watchers that God will not grant their petition throughout all the days of eternity, he thus describes the vision :

Behold in the vision clouds invited me and a mist invited me: the course of the stars and the lightnings drove and impelled me, and the winds in the vision gave me wings and drove me. And they lifted me up into heaven and I came till I drew nigh to a wall which is built of crystals and surrounded by a fiery flame : and it began to affright me.   And I went into the fiery flame and drew nigh to a large house which was built of crystals : and the walls of that house were like a mosaic crystal floor, and its ground-work was of crystal.   Its ceiling was like the path of the stars and light-nings, with fiery cherubim between in a transparent heaven.   A flaming fire surrounded the walls of the house and its portal blazed with fire.   And I entered into that house, and it was hot as fire and cold as ice : there were no delights of life therein : fear covered me and trembling gat hold upon me.   And as I quaked and trembled, I fell upon my face and beheld in a vision.   And lo! there was a second house, greater than the former, all the portals of which stood open before me, and it was built of flames of fire. And in every respect it so excelled in splendor and magnificence and extent that I cannot describe to you its splendor and its extent.   And its floor was fire, and above it were lightnings and the path of the stars, and its ceiling also was flaming fire.   And I looked and saw therein a lofty throne : its appearance was like hoarfrost, its circuit was as a shining sun and the voices of cherubim.   And from underneath the great throne came streams of flam-ing fire so that it was impossible to look thereon.   And the great Glory sat thereon and his raiment shone more brightly than the sun and was whiter than any snow.   None of the angels could enter and could behold the face of the honored and glorious One, and no flesh could behold him.   A flaming fire was round about him, and a great fire stood before him, and none of those who were around him could draw nigh him : ten thousand times ten thousand were before him, but he stood in no need of counsel.   And the holiness of the holy ones, who were nigh to him, did not leave by night nor depart from him.   And until then I had had a veil on my face, and I was trembling : then the Lord called me with his own mouth and spake to me : Come hither, Enoch, and hear my holy word.   And he made me rise up and approach the door : but I turned my face downwards.

And he answered and spake to me with his voice : I have heard ; fear not, Enoch, thou righteous man and scribe of righteousness : approach and hear my voice.   And go, say to the watchers of heaven, who have sent thee to intercede for them : You should intercede for men and not men for you. Wherefore have ye left the high, holy, eternal heaven, and lain with women, and defiled yourselves with the daughters of men and taken unto yourselves wives, and done like to the children of earth, and begotten giants as (your) sons ?   Whilst you were still spiritual, holy, in the enjoyment of eternal life, you have defiled yourselves with women, have begotten (children) with the blood of flesh, and have lusted after the blood of men, and produced flesh and blood, as those produce them who are mortal and shortlived. Therefore have I given them wives also that they might impregnate them, and children be borne by them, that thus nothing might be wanting to them on earth.   But you were formerly spiritual, in the enjoyment of eternal immortal life, for all generations of the world.   Therefore I have not ap-pointed wives for you ; for the spiritual have their dwelling in heaven.   And now the giants, who are produced from the spirits and flesh, will be called evil spirits upon the earth, and on the earth will be their dwelling.   Evil spirits proceed from their bodies; because they are created from above, and from the holy watchers is their beginning and primal origin; they will be evil spirits on earth, and evil spirits will they be named. . . . And the spirits of the giants will devour, oppress, destroy, attack, do battle, and cause destruction on the earth, and work affliction: they will take no kind of food, nor will they thirst, and they will be invisible. And these spirits will rise up against the children of men and against the women, because they have proceeded from them. In the days of murder and of destruction and of the death of the giants when the spirits have gone forth from the souls of their flesh, in order to destroy without incurring judgment—thus will they destroy until the day when the great consummation of the great world be consummated over the watchers and the godless. And now as to the watchers who have sent thee to intercede for them, who had been aforetime in heaven (say to them), You have been in heaven, and though the hidden things had not yet been revealed to you, you knew worthless mysteries, and these in the hardness of your hearts you have recounted to the women, and through these mysteries women and men work much evil on earth. Say to them therefore: You have no peace (chap. xiv, 8–xvi, 4).

Here now is one of the finest passages of the oldest section of the Book of Enoch ; but, to say nothing of the prolixity of the composition as a piece of literature, what are we to think of the value of its subject-matter as compared with any corresponding passages or pictures in the biblical apocalypses ? The detailed account here given of the fallen angels and of their propagation of demons in the world moves in a very different realm of thought from that of the brief ideal in Gen. vi, 1–4, out of which it was evidently developed. If we allow the statements in Genesis to be a fragment of an ancient myth, it is to be observed that the author of the Book of Genesis briefly touches it with the hand of a master word-painter in order to enhance the picture of human wickedness. Not so the writer or writers whose crass imagination elaborated the story as it appears in the Book of Enoch.

Another of the most remarkable passages is that part of " The Similitudes " which describes the Elect One of the Lord of spirits, and speaks of him as—

the Son of man who hath righteousness, and who reveals all the treasures of that which is hidden, because the Lord of spirits hath chosen him, and his lot before the Lord of spirits hath surpassed everything in uprightness forever. . . . And he will put down the kings from their thrones and kingdoms because they do not extol and praise him, nor thankfully acknowledge whence the kingdom was bestowed upon them. And he will put down the countenance of the strong and shame will cover them: darkness will be their dwelling and worms their bed, and they will have no hope of rising from their beds because they do not extol the name of the Lord of spirits (xlvi, 3, 5, 6).

And in those days I saw the Head of days when he had seated himself on the throne of his glory, and the books of the living were opened before him, and his whole host which is in heaven above and around him stood before him. And the hearts of the holy were filled with joy that the number of the righteous had drawn nigh, and the prayer of the righteous was heard, and the blood of the righteous required before the Lord of spirits. And in that place I saw a fountain of righteousness which was inexhaustible: around it were many fountains of wisdom, and all the thirsty drank of them and were filled with wisdom, and had their dwellings with the righteous and holy and elect. And at that hour that Son of man was named in the presence of the Lord of spirits and his name before the Head of days. And before the sun and the signs were created, before the stars of the heaven were made his name was named before the Lord of spirits. He will be a staff to the righteous on which they will support themselves and not fall, and he will be the light of the Gentiles and the hope of those who are troubled of heart. All who dwell on the earth will fall down and bow the knee before him, and will bless and laud and celebrate with song the Lord of spirits. And for this reason has he been chosen and hidden before him before the creation of the world and for evermore. And the wisdom of the Lord of spirits hath revealed him to the holy and righteous, for he preserveth the lot of the righteous, because they have hated and despised this world of unrighteousness, and have hated all its works and ways in the name of the Lord of spirits: for they are saved in his name and he is the avenger of their life (xlvii, 3–xlviii, 7).

So far now as the author of this passage (and of others like it) has presented us a unique ideal of the Son of man, modifying the sources from which he derived his suggestions and stamping them with the cast and color of his own individuality, we give him all due credit for the sublime picture he has made. But it is scarcely open to question that in its main elements it is modeled after what is written in Dan. vii, 9–14. The doctrine of preexistence here set forth is traceable to the well-known portraiture of Wisdom in Proverbs viii, 22–30, and has further parallels in the apocryphal Wisdom of Solomon vii, 25–27, and the Fourth Book of Ezra xii, 32; xiii, 26. It is also probable, as some of the best scholars hold, that all these more striking Messianic passages have been enlarged or colored by the hand of some Christian translator. But, taken at their best and made the most of, they are still exceptional portions of the Book of Enoch as a whole; and are mixed up with much that is of an inferior cast and with some things that are puerile.

In his Introduction to the Book of Enoch, Charles maintains that the influence of the book on the New Testament writers "has been greater than that of all the other apocryphal and pseudepigraphal books taken together" (p. 41). There can be no reasonable doubt of this in the composition of 2 Peter and Jude, and there appears

no good reason to suppose that the book was unknown to any of
the New Testament writers. But how far any of them, except
the two just named, made direct use of it or consciously quoted it
is a very open question. It requires more than mere analogy of
ideas and language to establish such a position, especially when it
can be shown that such ideas and language are traceable to other
and older written sources. Whatever influence the book may
have had on other writers, there is no conclusive evidence that the
author of John's Apocalypse made any direct use of it whatever.
The statement that "the writer or writers of this book are steeped
in Jewish apocalyptic literature" (p. 42) is very true if it is understood that by "Jewish apocalyptic literature" we include the
apocalyptic portions of the biblical canon. For our notes on the
Apocalypse have shown that there is scarcely a figure or symbol of
the book that is not traceable to some corresponding idea in the Old
Testament. The list of passages in the Book of Revelation which
Charles refers to (pp. 43–45) as having been derived from the
Book of Enoch cannot be fairly pressed for such a purpose. Most
of them are obviously traceable to the Old Testament, as his own
notes sufficiently show, and not one of them is of a nature to prove
beyond question that the New Testament writer made use of the
apocryphal Enoch. What propriety is there in citing John's sublime ideal of "the seven spirits which are before the throne" (Rev.
i, 4; comp. iv, 5; viii, 2), as if it were drawn from the "seven first
white ones" of Enoch xc, 21? Much rather may we suppose it to
have been taken from Zech. iii, 9; iv, 10, especially as Rev. v, 6,
is seen to be a direct allusion thereto. The doctrine of seven chief
angels, moreover, was so current in the Jewish thought of the time
(see Tobit xii, 15) that we have no need to suppose that the author
of the Revelation was in the least dependent for it on the Book of
Enoch.

Equally futile for his purpose is Charles's assumption that the
ideals of the tree of life in Rev. ii, 7; xxii, 2, 14, 19, have any necessary connection with Enoch xxv, 4, 5. For all these allusions go
back originally to the story of Gen. ii, 9, and the apocalyptic picture of John is clearly modeled after that of Ezek. xlvii, 12. How
anyone can believe that the four living creatures full of eyes before
and behind, as seen around the throne in Rev. iv, 6, are an ideal
drawn from Enoch xl, 2, rather than from Isa. vi, 2, 3, and Ezek.
i, 5–13, is difficult to comprehend. The same may be said of the
implication that the star fallen from heaven (Rev. ix, 1) was suggested by Enoch lxxxvi, 1, rather than by Isa. xiv, 12 ; and that
the mention of the opened books in Rev. xx, 12, is indebted to

Enoch xc, 20, and xlvii, 3, when in his notes on those passages of
Enoch the writer admits that the idea is clearly expressed in Dan.
vii, 10, and also underlies several other passages in the Old Testament. The picture of terrible judgment in Rev. vi, 15, 16, seems
at first sight to be a striking parallel of Enoch lxii, 3–5; but careful
examination shows that all the essential elements of the picture in
both places are to be found in Isa. ii, 17–19; xi, 2–4; xiii, 6–8, and
Hosea x, 8, combined with Dan. vii, 13, 14. In his own note on
Enoch lxii, 5, Charles says, "This shows that Isa. xiii, 8, was in the
mind of the writer."

It is needless for us to go further over the list of supposed parallels. Those already cited are among the most noticeable.[1] It is
not improbable, as we have already observed, that the author of
John's Apocalypse was acquainted with the Book of Enoch, and it
need not be denied that he was to some extent influenced by a few
of its apocalyptic ideals; but if so the influence was of no considerable weight in shaping either the plan or the details of his own
superior prophecy.

Another book of the same general cast of thought, entitled "The
Book of the Secrets of Enoch" (one manuscript bears the title, "The
Secret Books of God which were shown to Enoch"), has lately been
brought to the attention of English readers.[2] It has been preserved
in a Slavonic version, and proves to be an independent pseudepi-
graph rather than a version of the Book of Enoch as we find it in
the Ethiopic. It exhibits a much greater unity, and is scarcely less
valuable for critical and historical purposes than its older and better
known rival. The translator, Mr. Morfill, and the editor, Mr.
Charles, are of opinion that its author was a Hellenistic Jew and
that it was written in Egypt, probably at Alexandria, sometime
during the period A. D. 1–50. The discovery of this new pseudep-
igraph is an additional evidence of the magnitude of apocryphal
literature that in ancient time gathered around the name of the
saintly patriarch who "walked with God, and was not, for God
took him" (Gen. v, 24). The character and style of the book may
be seen in the following paragraph, which constitutes its first
chapter:

Hardly had I accomplished a hundred and sixty-five years [here the
Septuagint is followed], when I begat my son Methusal; after that I lived

---

[1] Compare the observations of Deane, *Pseudepigrapha :* An account of certain apocryphal sacred writings of the Jews and early Christians, pages 84–88. Edinburgh, 1891.

[2] *The Book of the Secrets of Enoch.* Translated from the Slavonic, by W. R. Morfill,
M.A., and edited with Introduction, Notes, and Indices, by R. H. Charles, M. A. Oxford, 1896.

two hundred years and accomplished all the years of my life, three hundred and sixty-five years. On the first day of the first month I was alone in my house, and I rested on my bed and slept. And as I slept a great grief came upon my heart, and I wept with mine eyes in my dream, and I could not understand what this grief meant, or what would happen to me. And there appeared to me two men very tall, such as I have never seen on earth. And their faces shone like the sun, and their eyes were like burning lamps; and fire came forth from their lips. Their dress had the appearance of feathers; their feet were purple, their wings were brighter than gold, their hands whiter than snow. They stood at the head of my bed and called me by my name. I awoke from my sleep and saw clearly these men standing in front of me. I hastened and made obeisance to them and was terrified, and the appearance of my countenance was changed from fear. And these men said to me: Be of good cheer, Enoch, be not afraid; the everlasting God hath sent us to thee, and lo! to-day shalt thou ascend with us into heaven. And tell thy sons and thy servants, all who work in thy house, and let no one seek thee till the Lord bring thee back to them.

The book goes on to tell how Enoch was taken up through the seven heavens, which doctrine of seven heavens, Charles observes, " is set forth by our author with a fullness and clearness not found elsewhere in literature." The patriarch was shown in the first heaven the secrets of the world, the treasuries of the snow and ice and dew, and the angels that guard them. In the second heaven he saw the prison of the apostate angels, who asked him to intercede for them. The third heaven is described as a beautiful and blessed paradise, with the tree of life in the midst, and the picture corresponds remarkably with the ideal of the third heaven into which Paul was caught up, and heard unspeakable words (2 Cor. xii, 2, 4). In the seventh heaven, the writer says:

I saw a very great light and all the fiery hosts of great archangels, and incorporeal powers and lordships, and principalities and powers; cherubim and seraphim, thrones and the watchfulness of many eyes. There were ten troops, a station of brightness, and I was afraid, and trembled with a great terror. And those men took hold of me and brought me into their midst and said to me: Be of good cheer, Enoch, be not afraid. And they showed me the Lord from afar sitting on his lofty throne. And all the heavenly hosts having approached stood on the ten steps, according to their rank, and made obeisance to the Lord. And so they proceeded to their places in joy and mirth, and in boundless light singing songs with low and gentle voices, and gloriously serving him.

Into this glorious heaven Enoch was welcomed by the Lord, anointed with holy oil, clothed in shining raiment, and put in charge of the wisest among the archangels, who instructed him for thirty days and thirty nights in the secrets of the world and of men and of angels, the results of all which were written down accurately in three hundred and sixty-six books (chaps. iii–xxiii).

There follow after this revelations of the creation of the heavens and the earth, a fanciful and, in part, grotesque elaboration of the creation narratives of Genesis. One is reminded of Milton's poetic description (*Paradise Lost*, bk. vii), and may observe that in taste and power of expression the Hellenistic dreamer is far surpassed by the English poet. In the creation of man the Jewish apocalyptist represents the Lord as saying: " On the sixth day I ordered my Wisdom to make man of seven substances: his flesh from the earth; his blood from the dew; his eyes from the sun; his bones from the stones; his thoughts from the swiftness of the angels, and the clouds; his veins and hair from the grass of the earth; his spirit from my Spirit and from the wind. And I gave him seven natures: hearing to his body, sight to his eyes, smell to the perception, touch to the veins, taste to the blood, the bones for endurance, sweetness for thought."

The foregoing specimens are sufficient to show that, while the apocryphal Enoch literature was very popular and widespread at the beginning of our era, it is conspicuously inferior to the biblical apocalypses, and could have exerted little or no influence on the composition of John's Apocalypse. The New Testament writer drew from a deeper fountain, and his entire range of thought moves in a higher plane.

The Fourth Book of Ezra.

Hardly second in importance to the Book of Enoch is that apocalyptic production which is generally known among readers of the Apocrypha in the Authorized English version as " Second Esdras." [1] Among modern scholars it is, perhaps, most commonly known as " The Fourth Book of Ezra." The first two and last two chapters (i, ii, xv, xvi) are obvious additions to the original work, and in a majority of the manuscripts are detached and designated as separate books. A very common arrangement in the manuscripts is to reckon the canonical Ezra and Nehemiah as First Ezra ; chaps. i and ii of our book as Second Ezra ; the Greek apocryphal *Esdras* as Third Ezra ; chaps. iii–xiv of our book as Fourth Ezra, and chaps.

---

[1] The Latin version of this book, believed to be the oldest and best of the versions, was revised and edited by Professor R. L. Bensly, of the University of Cambridge, with an Introduction by M. R. James, and published by the Cambridge University Press as number 2 in vol. iii of *Texts and Studies: Contributions to Biblical and Patristic Studies*, Cambridge, 1895. The revision of the Authorized Version of the Apocrypha (1895) presents this book in much better form than that of the old version of 1611.

xv and xvi as Fifth Ezra. As the book consisting of chaps. iii–xiv, called Fourth Ezra in this arrangement, is the earlier and independent work, and is conspicuously apocalyptical in style, we shall examine these chapters only as a possible source of some of the contents of John's Apocalypse, and as having a rank in literature coordinate with that of the Book of Enoch. Aside from all questions concerning the original title of this production, the contents would justify our calling it the "Apocalypse of Ezra." [1]

This apocalypse consists of a series of seven revelations, purporting to have been made known to Ezra in the thirtieth year after the overthrow of Jerusalem by the Chaldean army. In answer to the appeal and prayer of the prophet, who argues that the Most High Lord, that beareth rule, has preserved his enemies, the Babylonians, and destroyed his people, and who implores that the iniquities of Israel and those of the nations be weighed by an impartial balance to show "which way the scale inclineth," the angel Uriel is sent unto him to show him three ways and to set forth three similitudes before him (iv, 3). He is asked, much after the manner of Jehovah's answer to Job out of the whirlwind (Job xxxviii), if he can weigh fire, or measure the wind, or call back again a day that is past. If a man know so little of fire and wind and day through which he has passed, how can he expect to comprehend the way of the Most High? Ezra, however, protests that "it were better that we were not here at all than that we should come hither and live in the midst of ungodliness, and suffer and know not wherefore" (iv, 12). Whereupon the angel answers him by a fable of the woods of the field and the waves of the sea, showing that each has its own place and bounds, that they who dwell on earth can understand only what is on the earth, and that things above the heavens are known only to the Most High. But the prophet persists in his questioning: "Wherefore is the power of understanding given unto me? For it was not my mind to be curious of the ways above, but of such things as pass by us daily; because Israel is given up as a reproach to the heathen" (iv, 23). What purports to be an answer to this question runs on through a similar succession of questions and answers unto v, 13, but leaves the subject in as deep obscurity as before, save that the general doctrine is announced that "the world

---

[1] There is, however, another apocryphal book which bears the title of Apocalypse of Ezra. The Greek text is published in Tischendorf's *Apocalypses Apocryphæ*, pp. 24, *ff.* Leipsic, 1866. An English translation of this appears in the *Ante-Nicene Christian Library*, vol. xvi, pp. 468–476. It is a late production, by a Christian hand, and a very weak imitation of our Fourth Book of Ezra.

hasteth fast to pass away," and a time is coming when all wrongs shall be righted.

After fasting and weeping for seven days, and again asking in his prayer the same question—why the one chosen people had been given over to the violence of the many—the angel Uriel communicates further instruction to the prophet. All things and all seasons of the world have their natural order, but there shall come times of momentous change.

The trumpet shall give a sound, which when every man heareth, they shall be suddenly afraid. . . . And it shall be that whosoever remaineth after these things that I have told thee of, he shall be saved, and shall see my salvation, and the end of my world. And they shall see the men that have been taken up, who have not tasted death from their birth; and the heart of the inhabitants shall be changed, and turned into another meaning. For evil shall be blotted out, and deceit shall be quenched; and faith shall flourish, and corruption shall be overcome, and the truth, which hath been so long without fruit, shall be declared (vi, 23–28).

A like repetition of prayer, question, and answer runs on through the third revelation, which extends from vi, 35, to ix, 25, and yields the same general result. In this section occurs the passage touching the places of torment and of rest set opposite each other, the furnace of gehenna and the paradise of delight. This passage does not appear in the common version, but was preserved in the Ethiopic and Arabic versions, and has in recent years been found in an old Latin manuscript, and has added a new chapter to our Old Testament Apocrypha.[1] Its main doctrine is the certainty of reward and punishment in the world to come, and the unchangeableness of the final judgments of God. The outcome is that "the Most High hath made this world for many, but the world to come for few. I will tell thee now a similitude, Ezra: As when thou askest the earth, it shall say unto thee, that it giveth very much mold whereof earthen vessels are made, and little dust that gold cometh of : even so is the course of the present world. There are many created, but few shall be saved " (viii, 1–3).

The fourth, fifth, and sixth revelations are in the form of visions, and maintain the methods and style of apocalyptic symbolism. In the first of these visions (ix, 26–x, 59) the prophet is in "the field which is called Ardat " (or Arphad), and is sitting among the flowers and eating the herbs of the field. As he vexes his soul over

---

[1] *The Missing Fragment of the Latin Translation of the Fourth Book of Ezra,* discovered and edited, with an Introduction and Notes, by Robert L. Bensly. Cambridge University Press, 1875. In all recent versions of the book this fragment is inserted in its proper place between verses 35 and 36 of the seventh chapter.

the miseries of Israel and cries unto God he beholds in a vision a woman bewailing the death of her son, and refusing to be comforted. While Ezra expostulates with her and exhorts her to throw off her excessive sorrow she suddenly disappears, and in her place he beholds a city builded up upon large foundations. The angel explains to him that the woman is Zion, and the death of her son the destruction that came to Jerusalem. For his comfort he is told to enter and look upon the beauty and greatness of the building (x, 55), and he is assured that he shall see and hear things of great moment, and receive from the Most High visions of what shall befall " them that dwell upon the earth in the last days."

Next follows (in xi and xii) the vision of the great Eagle that came up out of the sea, and had twelve feathered wings and three heads. In the interpretation, which is given in chap. xii, the eagle is said to be " the fourth kingdom which appeared in vision to thy brother Daniel." The symbolism of this vision is detailed, confused, and difficult to explain. Most interpreters understand by the eagle the Roman empire. The twelve wings are twelve Cæsars, the eight smaller wings over against them (Authorized Version, "contrary feathers ") represent so many dependent and tributary kings, and the three heads are the Flavian emperors, Vespasian, Titus, and Domitian. But there is obvious incongruity in thus making the heads as well as the wings represent emperors. We should more naturally understand by the heads some territorial seats of power, distinctive sources of revenue, and constituent elements of the body of the kingdom; not temporary rulers, but prominent parts of the empire, like those lying in Europe, Asia, and Africa. The roaring lion out of the wood is said to be the Anointed One of the Most High, who "shall set them alive in his judgment, and when he has reproved them, he shall destroy them " (xii, 33).

In the next vision the prophet sees a man ascend from the midst of the sea and fly with the clouds of heaven, and cause all things to tremble before him (xiii, 3). Against him a great multitude of men from the four winds of heaven make war; but " as he saw the assault of the multitude that came, he neither lifted up his hand, nor held spear, nor any instrument of war, but he sent out of his mouth as it had been a flood of fire, and out of his lips a flaming breath, and out of his tongue he cast forth sparks of the storm. And these were all mingled together, and fell upon the assault of the multitude, and burned them up every one, so that upon a sudden of an innumerable multitude nothing was to be perceived, but only dust of ashes and smell of smoke " (xiii, 9–11). Afterward this man came down from the great mountain which he had made for himself, and called unto him another multitude which was peaceable. This man is shown to be one "whom the Most High hath kept a great season, and who by his own self shall deliver his creature" (xiii, 26). He is the Son of God (verse 32), and "he shall stand upon the top of the mount Zion. And Zion shall come, and shall be shown to all men, being prepared and builded" like the mountain which Ezra saw graven without hands (verses 35, 36). The peaceable multitude, to be gathered to this Messiah after the destruction of his enemies, are the ten tribes of Israel, who are preserved beyond the river Euphrates, and destined to be called back again and shown very many wonders.

The seventh and last revelation of the series is a communication of God to Ezra, which came as a voice out of a bush after the manner in which Moses received revelations in the days of old (xiv, 1–3). He is told that the world has lost its youth, and that the times begin to wax old; for of the twelve parts into which the period of the world is divided ten have already passed and only two remain. Worse evils are to happen in the future than in the past; as there will be no prophet to instruct the people, and the law is burnt, Ezra is commanded to withdraw from the people for forty days, and with five assistant scribes write down the things which should be revealed unto him. When they were thus alone in the field Ezra drank of a full cup which was given him, and forthwith his "heart uttered understanding and wisdom grew in his breast" (xiv, 40). By means of such supernatural revelation ninety-four books were written during the forty days. Seventy of these were to be kept in secret, and delivered only to the wise; but the other twenty-four (books of the Old Testament canon?) were to be published openly, so that the worthy and the unworthy might alike have the liberty of reading them.

Here now we have an apocalyptic composition of unquestionable merit, but whether it can be shown to antedate the Apocalypse of John is a question not likely to be soon determined. It is generally believed that the work was originally written in Greek, but that original is now lost, and existing translations are so overlaid with additions of later writers that the exact contents of the book as it first appeared are quite uncertain. The notable Messianic passages are in all probability colored by the hand of editors and Christian translators. The oldest witnesses to its existence are citations from it in the Epistle of Barnabas (xii), and in the *Stromata* of Clement of Alexandria (iii, 16); but these citations cannot prove it to be older than the close of the first century. This being the case, it cannot be fairly maintained that the author of John's

Apocalypse made use of this Ezra-Apocalypse for anything which the two works have in common.

To test any such claim by direct appeal to the books themselves, we compare the cry of the souls in their chambers (Fourth Ezra iv, 35) with that of the souls underneath the altar in Rev. vi, 9.

FOURTH BOOK OF EZRA.

Did not the souls of the righteous ask questions of these things in their chambers, saying, How long are we here? [so Syriac; Latin: How long shall I thus hope?] when cometh the fruit of the threshing time of our reward? And unto them Jeremiel the archangel gave answer, and said, Even when the number is fulfilled of them that are like unto you.

APOCALYPSE OF JOHN.

I saw underneath the altar the souls of them that had been slain for the word of God, and for the testimony which they held: and they cried with a great voice, saying, How long, O Master, the holy and true, dost thou not judge and avenge our blood on them that dwell on the earth? And there was given to each one a white robe; and it was said unto them, that they should rest yet for a little time, until their fellow-servants also and their brethren, which should be killed even as they were, should be fulfilled.

Here in both cases are souls inquiring how long before they shall obtain redress. It can hardly be claimed that there is any necessary dependence of one of these passages on the other. Their apparent likeness may be only accidental. The familiar frequency of the cry, " How long, O Lord! " in the Psalms and the Prophets may be sufficient to account for two apocalyptic writers composing the above passages independently of one another. Comp. Psalm vi, 3, 4; xiii, 1, 2; xxxv, 17; Hab. i, 2. But if one of these writers borrowed from the other the presumption would be that the Ezra Apocalyptist is the borrower. For his language is an appeal to what certain souls of the righteous had aforetime asked, as something already known, or assumed to be known. The vision in John's Apocalypse, on the contrary, is altogether unique, and immeasurably superior in language and imagery. Even if it were clear that the passage in Ezra had suggested the vision of the cry of the martyr-souls in John, it must be conceded that the latter has amplified and exalted the ideal far beyond any imagery which was before the apocryphal writer.

The vision of an innumerable multitude gathered together to fight against the Messiah, who stands on Mount Zion and destroys them by the fiery flame out of his mouth (Fourth Ezra xiii), has obvious likeness to that of Rev. xx, 7–9. But the two pictures are not strictly parallel, and we have seen in our notes on Rev. xx, 7–9, that the New Testament writer has drawn his imagery and in part his language from Ezek. xxxviii and xxxix. In such parallels as Fourth Ezra xiv, 32, and ix, 3, and Matt. xxiv, 7, it may be questioned (1) whether the parallel is real or only apparent; (2) whether, in case it be real, the evangelist or the apocryphal writer is the borrower; and (3) whether, after all, the similarity of language is not due to the Christian translator and editor of Ezra rather than to the original work. A number of such verbal parallels can, therefore, in the absence of the Greek original of Ezra, prove nothing as to the age of this apocryphal apocalypse.

The book is unquestionably of great importance to the biblical scholar. One may study with much interest its doctrine of the Messiah, of rewards and punishments, of the small number of the saved, of resurrection and judgment, of the efficacy of good works, and of the relations of mankind to Adam the first. The chief value of this entire body of apocryphal literature is in thus showing the beliefs of the Jewish people of the time.

The apocalyptic character of the book may be seen not only in its formal elements of angelic revelations and visional dreams, but in the dark background of suffering and oppression which is implied in the oft-repeated cry, How long shall the wicked triumph? How long shall Israel, the chosen people, be trampled down by the heathen nations that are more sinful than they? The author was evidently a Jew, and his most elaborate symbol, that of the great Eagle in chaps. xi and xii, is confessedly an attempt to enlarge upon the vision of the fourth kingdom in the Book of Daniel. But his work as a whole lacks the originality of Daniel, and moves in a line of thought and imagery far below the Apocalypse of John.

The Apocalypse of Baruch.

A number of apocryphal books attach to the name of Baruch, the son of Neriah, who was famous for being the close companion and amanuensis of the prophet Jeremiah. The Book of Baruch, which appears in the Old Testament Apocrypha along with the attached Epistle of Jeremiah, is well known. Other works ascribed to the same author are mentioned by several of the early fathers; but the most important of all, and a production worthy to rank with the Book of Enoch and Fourth Ezra (which latter it much resembles), was lost to the world for more than a thousand years, and discovered by Ceriani in a Syriac version and published in 1871. A Latin translation of the Syriac was published in 1866, soon after the discovery of the manuscript in the Milan Library. The Syriac version appears to have been made from a Greek text, and the Greek probably from a Hebrew original. It has been made the subject of most thorough study by a large number of eminent critics, and has recently been translated into English and elaborately annotated by R. H. Charles.[1]

The book may be divided into two large sections, the first (chaps. i–lxxvii) of which contains various revelations and prayers of Baruch ; the second (chaps. lxxviii–lxxxvii) being an epistle to the nine and a half tribes. The first of these greater sections is artificially divided into seven parts, each division being denoted by a fast of the prophet, which in most cases lasted seven days. The main burden of the apocalypse consists of anxiety on the part of the seer to know God's purposes concerning Jerusalem and the people of Israel, and of revelations of the Lord given in answer to his servant's prayers. A few selections from the finest passages of the book will best exhibit the character of the writing. In chap. vi the prophet says :

I was grieving over Zion, and lamenting over the captivity which had come upon the people. And lo! suddenly a strong spirit raised me, and bore me aloft over the wall of Jerusalem. And I beheld, and lo! four angels standing at the four angles of the city, each of them holding a lamp of fire in his hands. And another angel began to descend from heaven, and said unto them: Hold your lamps, and do not light them till I tell you. For I am first sent to speak a word to the earth, and to place in it what the Lord the Most High has commanded me. And I saw him descend into the holy of holies, and take from thence the veil, and the holy ephod, and the mercy seat, and the two tables, and the holy raiment of the priests, and the altar of incense, and the forty-eight precious stones wherewith the priest was adorned, and all the holy vessels of the tabernacle. And he spake to the earth with a loud voice: Earth, earth, earth, hear the word of the mighty God, and receive what I commit to thee, and guard them until the last times, so that, when thou art ordered, thou mayest restore them, so that strangers may not get possession of them. For the time comes when Jerusalem also will be delivered up for a time, until it is said that it is again restored forever. And the earth opened its mouth and swallowed them up.

In chap. xxvii (comp. also chap. lxx) the travail pains which usher in the time of the Messiah are described, and may be compared with the corresponding parts of the apocalypse of the synop-

---

[1] *The Apocalypse of Baruch*, translated from the Syriac, edited, with Introduction, Notes, and Indices, by R. H. Charles, M.A. London, 1896. It should be stated that the last section of the book (chaps. lxxviii–lxxxvi), entitled "The Epistle of Baruch which he Wrote to the Nine and a Half Tribes," had been known to scholars long before Ceriani's discovery of the complete manuscript of the Apocalypse. These chapters were published in Syriac and Latin in the Paris and London Polyglots, and were translated into English by William Whiston in his *Collection of Authentic Records* (1727). It was not until after the discovery of the complete Syriac manuscript that this epistle was proven to be a portion of a larger work.

tic gospels (comp. p. 229 above), and the opening of the seals in Rev. vi :

Into twelve parts is that time divided, and each one of them is reserved for that which is appointed for it. In the first part there will be the beginning of commotions. And in the second part there will be slayings of the great ones. And in the third part there will be the fall of many by death. And in the fourth part the sending of desolation. And in the fifth part famine and the withholding of rain. And in the sixth part earthquakes and terrors. (Seventh is wanting.) And in the eighth part a multitude of portents and incursions of the Shedim (demons). And in the ninth part the fall of fire. And in the tenth part rapine and much oppression. And in the eleventh part wickedness and unchastity. And in the twelfth part confusion from the mingling together of all those things aforesaid.

In chap. xxix it is written :

It will come to pass when all is accomplished that was to come to pass in those parts, that the Messiah will then begin to be revealed. And Behemoth will be revealed from his place, and Leviathan will ascend from the sea, those two great monsters which I created on the fifth day of creation, and I kept them until that time; and then they will be food for all that are left. The earth also will yield its fruit ten thousandfold, and on one vine there will be a thousand branches, and each branch will produce a thousand clusters, and each cluster will produce a thousand grapes, and each grape will produce a cor of wine.[1]

The vision of the white and black waters and the great lightning in chap. liii is noteworthy. The writer says :

I fell asleep and saw a vision, and lo ! a cloud was ascending from a very great sea, and I kept gazing upon it, and lo! it was full of waters white and black, and there were many colors in those selfsame waters, and as it were the likeness of great lightning was seen at its summit. And I saw that cloud passing swiftly in quick courses, and it covered all the earth. And it came to pass after these things that the cloud began to pour upon the earth the waters that were in it. And I saw that there was not one and the same likeness in the waters which descended from it. For in the first beginning they were black exceedingly for a time, and afterwards I saw that the waters became bright, but they were not many, and after these things again I saw black waters, and after these things again bright, and again black and again bright. Now this was done twelve times, but the black were always more numerous than the bright. And it came to pass at the end of the cloud, that lo! it rained black waters, and they were darker than had been all those waters that were before, and fire was mingled with them, and where those waters descended they wrought devastation and destruction. And I saw after these things that lightning which I had seen on

---

[1] This passage is cited in Irenæus (*Adv. Hær.*, bk. v, chap. 33) as a part of the teaching of the Lord.

the summit of the cloud, that it held it fast and made it descend to the earth. Now that lightning shone exceedingly, so as to illuminate the whole earth, and it healed those regions where the last waters had descended and wrought devastation. And it took hold of the whole earth and had dominion over it. And I saw after these things, and lo! twelve rivers were ascending from the sea, and they began to surround that lightning and to become subject to it. And by reason of my fear I awoke.

In the interpretation which follows, given by "the angel Ramiel who presides over true visions" (chap. lv), Baruch is told that the black and bright waters symbolize successive periods of good and evil between the time of Adam and the consummation of the world ; and the bright lightning which is to come at the end is the Messiah, in whose days "healing will descend in dew, and disease will withdraw, and anxiety and anguish and lamentation will pass from amongst men, and gladness will proceed through the whole earth. And no one shall again die untimely, nor shall any adversity suddenly befall" (chap. lxxiii).

These extracts are enough to show that this pseudograph is an invaluable monument of the later Jewish literature. But it contains nothing which can be shown to have influenced the composition of the Apocalypse of John. The mention of opening books "in which are written the sins of all those who have sinned" (xxiv, 1) is parallel with Rev. xx, 12, but the source of the imagery is Dan. vii, 10. The allusion in li, 11, to "the living creatures which are beneath the throne," reminds us of Ezek. i, 26, and x, 1, rather than of Rev. iv, 6. Taken as a whole, the book falls far below the New Testament Apocalypse. In range of thought, symmetry of arrangement, power of description, and magnificence of execution the Revelation of John is immeasurably superior.

The date and composition of the Baruch Apocalypse are yet matters of discussion. The analogy between it and the Fourth Book of Ezra is very striking, and the relations of these two pseudographs is a complicated problem of criticism. Into these questions we have no occasion here to enter. Mr. Charles, who has given the subject a very thorough investigation, believes that this Apocalypse of Baruch is a composite work put together about the close of the first century of our era, and compiled out of five or six independent writings. In the Preface of his recent edition of the work he observes: "In this Apocalypse we have almost the last noble utterance of Judaism before it plunged into the dark and oppressive years that followed the destruction of Jerusalem. For ages after that epoch its people seem to have been bereft of their immemorial gifts of song and eloquence, and to have had thought and energy

only for the study and expansion of the traditions of the fathers.
. . . The Apocalypse of Baruch has had a strange history. Written
by Pharisaic Jews as an apology for Judaism, and in part an im-
plicit polemic against Christianity, it gained, nevertheless, a larger
circulation amongst Christians than amongst Jews, and owed its
very preservation to the scholarly cares of the Church it assailed.
But in the struggle for life its secret animus against Christianity
begat an instinctive opposition in Christian circles, and so proved a
bar to its popularity.   Thus the place it would naturally have filled
was taken by the sister work, Fourth Ezra.   The latter work having
been written in some degree under Christian influences, and forming, in fact, an unconscious confession of the failure of Judaism to
redeem the world, was naturally more acceptable to Christian readers, and thus, in due course, the Apocalypse of Baruch was elbowed
out of recognition by its fitter and sturdier rival."

THE ASSUMPTION OF MOSES.

An apocryphal book, called variously the *Assumption*, the *Ascen-*
sion, and the *Reception* of Moses, is frequently referred to by the early
Christian fathers, and according to Origen (*De Princip.*, iii, 2, 1)
was the source of information concerning Michael's contention with
the devil about the body of Moses mentioned in the ninth verse of
the Epistle of Jude.   The book was supposed to be lost until Ceriani, in 1861, published a considerable fragment of it in a Latin version which he discovered in the Ambrosian Library at Milan.   The
manuscript of this version is a palimpsest of the sixth century,
illegible in many passages, the beginning and end missing, and the
style of the Latin barbarous and irregular.   The Latin version
was evidently made from the Greek, as a slavish dependence on a
Greek original is apparent in numerous words and phrases; but
the Greek is believed to have been a translation from a Hebrew or
Aramaic original.   The work has recently been made accessible to
English readers by R. H. Charles, who supplies a faithful translation from the Latin into English with extended notes and critical
discussions.[1]   This translator maintains that the work was written
in Hebrew shortly after the beginning of our era, between A. D. 7
and 29, and that a Greek version of it appeared during the first
century.   The version was made to embody a composite work of
two originally distinct books, namely, the "Testament of Moses" and

---

[1] *The Assumption of Moses*, translated from the Latin sixth century manuscript, the
unemended text of which is published herewith, together with the text in its restored
and critically emended form.   Edited with Introduction, Notes, and Indices, by R. H.
Charles, M.A.   London, 1897.

the "Assumption of Moses," both of which titles appear in lists of apocryphal books. Mr. Charles thinks that the fragment preserved in the Latin is not the Assumption but the Testament of Moses, and that it "was designed by its author to protest against the growing secularization of the Pharisaic party through its fusion with political ideals and popular Messianic beliefs. Its author, a Pharisaic Quietist, sought herein to recall his party to the old paths, which they were fast forsaking, of simple unobtrusive obedience to the law. He glorifies, accordingly, the old ideals which had been cherished and pursued by the Chasid and early Pharisaic party, but which the Pharisaism of the first century B. C. had begun to disown in favor of a more active rôle in the life of the nation. He foresaw, perhaps, the doom to which his country was hurrying under such a shortsighted and unspiritual policy, and labored with all his power to stay its downward progress. But all in vain " (Preface, p. vii).

That it is referred to in the Epistle of Jude is not doubted, and that a few sentences have been appropriated from it in Matt. xxiv, 29; Acts vii, 35, need not be disputed. That it was known to the author of the New Testament Apocalypse of John is neither affirmed nor denied. But a very brief survey of its contents, so far as this fragment goes, must show every unbiased reader that its rank as an apocalypse is unworthy of any serious attempt at comparison with the Revelation of John.

The work is arranged in twelve chapters, and purports to be a communication of Moses to Joshua. He tells him that the Lord

has created the world on behalf of his people. But he was not pleased to manifest this purpose of creation from the foundation of the world, in order that the Gentiles might thereby be convicted, yea, to their own humiliation might by their arguments convict one another. Accordingly he designed and devised me, and prepared me [Moses] before the foundation of the world, that I should be the mediator of his covenant. And now I declare unto thee that the time of the years of my life is fulfilled, and I am passing away to sleep with my fathers even in the presence of all the people. And receive thou this writing that thou mayest know how to preserve the books which I shall deliver unto thee.

Chaps. ii–vii purport to be a prediction in brief outline of the history of Israel from their entrance into the promised land under Joshua until the time of Herod the Great, and the suppression of a Jewish rebellion by Varus, Roman governor of Syria. Charles offers valid reasons for transposing chaps. viii and ix so as to place them between vi and vii; for internal evidence shows that they treat of the time of Antiochus Epiphanes. They accordingly form a part of the picture of the fortunes of the Hebrew people which it is the purpose of this pseudograph to foretell. Chap. x reads as follows:

> And then his kingdom will appear throughout all his creation,
> And then Satan will be no more,
> And sorrow will depart from him.
> Then the hands of the angel will be filled
> And he will be appointed chief,
> And he will forthwith avenge them of their enemies.
> For the heavenly One will arise from his royal throne,
> And he will go forth from his holy habitation,
> And his wrath will burn on account of his sons.
> And the earth will tremble: to its confines will it be shaken:
> And the high mountains will be made low,
> And the hills will be shaken and fall.
> And the horns of the sun will be broken and he will be turned into darkness;
> And the moon will not give her light, and will be turned wholly to blood.
> And the circle of the stars will be disturbed.
> And the sea will retire into the abyss,
> And the fountains of waters will fail,
> And the rivers will dry up.
> For the Most High will arise, the eternal God alone,
> And he will appear to punish the Gentiles,
> And he will destroy all their idols.
> Then thou, O Israel, wilt be happy,
> And thou wilt mount upon the necks and wings of the eagle,
> And the days of thy mourning will be ended.
> And God will exalt thee,
> And he will cause thee to approach to the heaven of the stars,
> And he will establish thy habitation among them.
> And thou wilt look from on high and wilt see thy enemies in gehenna,
> And thou wilt recognize them and rejoice,
> And thou wilt give thanks and confess thy Creator.

The rest of the fragment consists of a conversation between Joshua and Moses, in which the former bewails his insufficiency to be a leader of Israel, and asks his "lord Moses, What will be the sign that marks thy sepulcher? Or who will dare move thy body from thence as a man from place to place? For all men when they die have according to their age their sepulchers on earth; but thy sepulcher is from the rising to the setting sun, and from the south to the confines of the north: all the world is thy sepulcher." Moses's response (chap. xii) is in substance that all things are in the hand of God, who will certainly prosper the righteous and punish the wicked.

The Ascension of Isaiah.

This book is a compilation of Jewish and Christian documents, and may, like the analogous Assumption of Moses, be said to treat of two different subjects, namely, the Martyrdom and the Ascension of the prophet Isaiah. The Jewish section was probably written some time in the first century A. D., and the Christian portion in the second century. It is preserved to us in an Ethiopic translation which was made from the Greek. It was long lost, but discovered and published in 1819 by Laurence with a Latin and English translation. A revised edition of the Ethiopic with a Latin translation and notes was published by Dillmann in 1877. The only English version aside from that of Laurence (which is very scarce and rare) is one by Schodde, published in the *Lutheran Quarterly* of October, 1878 (Gettysburg). The book records the tradition that Isaiah was sawn asunder with a wooden saw, and appears to be referred to in the Epistle to the Hebrews xi, 37, and in Justin Martyr (*Trypho*, cxx).

The apocalyptic portion of the books (chap. vi–xi) details a vision of the seven heavens through which Isaiah was taken. It was written by a Christian who makes the Hebrew prophet foretell the descent of Jesus Christ, unrecognized, through the seven heavens, and then his ascent again glorified by all. The trinitarian form of worship in the sixth heaven, where "all called by name the first Father, and his beloved One, Christ, and the Holy Spirit, all with one voice" (viii, 18), betrays the late origin of the work, and forbids the thought that the Apocalypse of John could have derived anything from it. On the contrary, there are several passages in this Pseudo-Isaiah which appear to have been appropriated in substance from John's Apocalypse. The mention of heavenly clothing and thrones and crowns in ix, 9–12, remind one of Rev. iii, 4; iv, 4; vi, 11; vii, 14 ; xx, 4. The contention in the firmament in vii, 9–12, is not unlike what we read in Rev. xii, 7–9 ; and the coming of the Lord with his angels and hosts of saints to put Berial (Belial) and his hosts into gehenna (iv, 14) is a sort of combination of Rev. xii, 9, and xx, 1–3. Isaiah's falling on his face to worship the angel who acted as his guide (vii, 21) is like that which is written in Rev. xix, 10. The impious matricide, who becomes possessed of Berial and works wonders in the world (iv, 2–12), is a picture of Nero made up of ideals derived both from Daniel (vii, 25; viii, 10–12) and the Revelation (xiii, 2–7, 12–16 ; xvii, 8). These correspondencies show how early and how profoundly John's Apocalypse influenced the pseudepigraphic productions of ancient Christian writers.

THE SIBYLLINE ORACLES.

The collection of Greek hexameters in twelve books now known as the Sibylline Oracles contains a great variety of prophetic utterances cast in pretentious poetical form. In the opening lines of the first book the Sibyl says :

> Beginning with the generation first
> Of mortal men down to the very last
> I'll prophesy each thing, what has been erst,
> And what is now, and what shall yet befall
> The world through the impiety of men.[1]

In different parts of the work the author represents herself as a daughter-in-law of Noah, and a sister of the Egyptian goddess Isis. These variations, however, may be due to the diverse authorship of the several books ; for the collection of oracles which make up the twelve books exhibits a mixture of Jewish and Christian elements, and some portions of possible pagan origin. But most of the books as we now find them are of Christian authorship and of a date later than that of the Apocalypse of John. There are some passages that appear to have been derived from John's Apocalypse, and the numerous references to Nero and the notion that he would come again from the East may be regarded as evidences that these portions were written not long after the death of that impious Cæsar. It is generally conceded that the oldest part of the collection is that portion of Book iii which begins with line 114 (Greek text 97) and comprises nearly all the rest of that book. The reference to the tower of Babel and the confusion of tongues at the beginning of this section is cited by Josephus (*Ant.*, i, 4, 3). The fourth and fifth books also contain passages which may antedate the Christian era, and there are several fragments, one known as the Proem, which are among the oldest portions. These Sibylline Books are referred to and quoted by Justin Martyr, Athenagoras, Clement of Alexandria, Lactantius, and other Christian fathers, and are treated by some of them as if they were as authoritative as the Holy Scriptures.

In the fifth, twelfth, and fourteenth books we find a prophetico-poetic enumeration of the Roman emperors, and a designation of each by the numerical equivalent of his initial letter. This habit of pointing out a person by a mystic number of his name is seen in Rev. xiii, 18, and need not be supposed to be original either with the author of John's Apocalypse or the unknown writers of the

---

[1] The only English translation of all these books is that rendered into English blank verse by M. S. Terry, New York, 1890. A new and thoroughly revised edition, based upon the Greek text of Rzach (Vienna, 1891), is about to be issued.

Greek Sibyllines. As analogous with the mystery of Rev. xiii, 18, observe the following from Book i, 167–172 (Greek text 141–146):

> Nine letters have I, and four syllables;
> Mark me. The first three have two letters each,
> The other has the rest, and five are mutes;
> Of the whole sum the hundreds are twice eight,
> And thrice three tens, with seven. Know who I am,
> And be not unacquainted with my lore.

The name or word intended is doubtful. Some suggest ἀνέκφωνος, shortened from ἀνεκφώνητος, *unutterable;* others propose θεὸς σωτήρ.

Another passage of similar character is found in Book i, lines 382–391 (Greek text 324–331):

> Then also shall a child of the great God
> To men come clothed in flesh and fashioned like
> To mortals in the earth; and he doth bear
> Four vowels, and two consonants in him
> Are twice announced; the whole sum I will name:
> For eight ones, and as many tens on these,
> And yet eight hundred will reveal the name [1]
> To men insatiate; and do thou discern
> In thine own understanding that the Christ
> Is child of the immortal God most high.

Wherever and at whatever time this method of designating names began in prophetic writings, it will hardly be claimed that the author of John's Apocalypse borrowed from these Sibylline Oracles. He doubtless made use of the method which was current in his time, just as he appropriated numerous figures and symbols from the Old Testament and gave them the masterly touch of his own genius. But certainly these Oracles as a whole could have had no influence upon the composition of the New Testament Revelation.

The Testaments of the Twelve Patriarchs.

Under this title we have a most interesting production of the early Christian times, purporting to be the last words of the twelve sons of Jacob to their children, after the manner and spirit of Jacob himself as recorded in Gen. xlix.[2] So far as these utterances assume

---

[1] The name Jesus in its Greek form, Ἰησοῦς, has four vowels, and the two consonants are the same, σ appearing twice, and the numerical value of all the letters when added into one sum is 888.

[2] The English reader may find an accurate English translation of the Testaments of the Twelve Patriarchs in vol. xxii of the Ante-Nicene Library. Edinburgh, 1871. It was made by Robert Sinker, of Cambridge, who is also the editor of the best Greek text, published in Cambridge, 1869.

to foretell the future they take on the nature of an apocalypse. But the work is so obviously a production of the second century of our era that we need not take space for any comparison with the biblical Apocalypses. In the Testament of Levi (15) there is mention of the destruction of the temple and of the dispersion of the Jews; and the numerous references to the various books of the New Testament show that the composition must date not only subsequent to the fall of Jerusalem by the Romans, but some considerable time thereafter, when most if not all the writings of the New Testament were in circulation. Being cited by Tertullian and Origen, these Testaments must have been known before the close of the second century.

Direct use of the Revelation of John seems to be made in Levi (18), where it is said, "He shall give to his saints to eat from the tree of life" (comp. Rev. ii, 7); in Naphtali (5), where Judah appeared in vision "bright as the moon, and under his feet were twelve rays" (comp. Rev. xii, 1); and in Joseph (19), where we read that "the Lamb overcame them, and destroyed them, and trod them under foot" (comp. Rev. xvii, 14). But should these allusions to John's Apocalypse be disputed no one would for a moment seriously suppose that the New Testament writer drew from these pseudepigraphic Testaments.

THE BOOK OF JUBILEES.

This ancient Jewish writing is apocalyptic so far as it purports to be a revelation given to Moses on Mount Sinai. But in contents it is merely a repetition of the narratives of the Book of Genesis and so much of Exodus as concerns the call and ministry of Moses. It is sometimes called *Leptogenesis*, or "Little Genesis," because of its narration of many little matters not recorded in the first Book of Moses. But the name *Jubilees* is the more appropriate, since the author so adjusts his narrative as to set the events from the creation to the time of Moses in fifty jubilee periods ($49 \times 50 = 2450$).

The author made use of the Book of Enoch, and has introduced into the stories of the patriarchs numerous rabbinical legends. He was probably a Palestinian Jew, and wrote the book sometime before the destruction of Jerusalem by the Romans ; but there is no evidence that any New Testament writer has made use of it. The composition moves in a relatively low plane of thought, has a semi-apologetic tone about it, and belongs to the midrashic literature of decaying Judaism.[1]

---

[1] See *The Book of Jubilees*, translated from the Ethiopic, by George H. Schodde. Oberlin, O., 1888. A later translation from a revised and improved Ethiopic text, by R. H. Charles, may be found in the *Jewish Quarterly Review*, vol. vi (October, 1893, and July, 1894), pp. 184–217 and 710–745.

There are other less important apocalyptic writings of which we have no need to speak in detail. A fragment of the "Apocalypse of Peter" was discovered in Egypt in 1886, and aroused no little attention and interest at the time. An English translation of it is published in the supplemental volume of the American edition of the Ante-Nicene Fathers. The translator observes that it is "the earliest embodiment in Christian literature of those pictorial presentations of heaven and hell which have exercised so widespread and enduring an influence. It has, in its imagery, little or no kinship with the Book of Daniel, the Book of Enoch, or the Revelation of John. Its only parallels in canonical Scripture, with the notable exception of the Second Epistle of Peter, are to be found in Isa. lxvi, 24, Mark ix, 44, 48, and the parable of Dives and Lazarus in Luke xvi, 19." With this witness before us we have no occasion here to consider this interesting fragment further.

The same volume of the Ante-Nicene Library contains also " The Vision of Paul," another and quite different version of the "Revelation of Paul," which appears in the Edinburgh edition of this library (vol. xvi), in the volume of "Apocryphal Gospels, Acts and Revelations." There are also "The Apocalypse of the Virgin," "The Apocalypse of Sedrach," and the "Testament of Abraham," of which we have no space or need to speak. There is also a spurious Apocalypse of John, and, in his Prolegomena to the Greek Apocryphal Apocalypses, Tischendorf mentions Apocalypses of Bartholomew, Mary, and Daniel. An Apocalypse of Elijah is mentioned in the Apostolical Constitutions (vi, 16), and Moses Buttenwieser has recently published the first part of a German translation and exposition of a Hebrew Apocalypse of Elijah, which appears to have been written some centuries later than any New Testament book. None of these, however, are entitled to a rival comparison with the New Testament Book of Revelation.

This rapid survey of apocryphal apocalyptic literature is sufficient for the purpose of this volume. It has proven, I trust, that no one of these pseudepigraphic books can fairly claim to have been either a source or a direct help in the composition of any one of the canonical apocalypses. They are all helpful to the study of apocalyptics in the broader sense, and admonish us that the idealistic manner of portraying God's creation and government of the world is admirably adapted to serve the purposes of divine revelation. The older biblical apocalypses, and especially the Book of Daniel, seem to have created a kind of passion for this class of sacred writings, and, as is always the case, the successful and popular work is followed by imitations of varying character. The genuine coin is often followed by the counterfeit and spurious; not a few of the later apocryphal apocalypses are of this spurious stamp.

All these apocryphal writings are obviously later than the Book of Daniel. But some of them, or portions of several, are older than the Apocalypse of John. Their composite and pseudonymous character as a class is a fact to be duly noted. That John's Apocalypse is of the same composite and pseudonymous character ought not on any *a priori* ground to be either assumed or denied. The presumption might indeed be that this masterpiece would conform in this particular to all others of its kind. But such a question cannot be settled by presumptions. Appeal must be made to all relevant facts and to a sound and rational method of interpretation. Every plausible hypothesis is entitled to a fair hearing. All the favor asked for the expositions presented in this volume is that they be carefully read and judged without passion or prejudice.

INDEX

511